Keister's Corporation Accounting And Auditing: A Practical Treatise On Higher Accounting ......

David Armel Keister, Henry Clay White

KEISTER'S

CORPORATION ACCOUNTING AND AUDITING.

A PRACTICAL TREATISE

ON HIGHER ACCOUNTING.

DESIGNED FOR THE USE OF

ACCOUNTANTS, AUDITORS, BOOK-KEEPERS, FINANCIAL EXPERTS, BUSINESS MEN, INVESTORS, STOCKHOLDERS, COR- PORATION OFFICERS AND LAWYERS.

BY

D. A. KEISTER,

CONSULTING ACCOUNTANT, CORPORATION AUDITOR AND FINANCIAL AND INDUSTRIAL EXPERT.
CLEVELAND, NEW YORK AND CHICAGO.

WITH AN INTRODUCTION
BY

HON. HENRY C. WHITE,

LATE JUDGE OF THE PROBATE COURT AT CLEVELAND

FOURTEENTH EDITION

$4.00

CLEVELAND.
THE BURROWS BROTHERS COMPANY.
1912.

J. F. TAPLEY CO.
New York

INTRODUCTION.

A text book, to be valuable, must be written by one who has been a conscientious student of the subject treated, and who has, himself, had a long, varied and practical experience.

Mr. D. A. Keister, the author of this book, commenced the study and practice of the Science of Accounts in 1875, and has had practical experience in every subject mentioned in his book, and that with many of the largest wholesale, retail, manufacturing and financial establishments in the United States.

He had considerable experience in professional work while in tne employ of others; but since 1888 he has been engaged exclusively in that line; examining banks, railroads, building associations and general corporation auditing; settling estates, assignments and receiverships and preparing statements for courts; reviewing the work of defaulters, making special investigations of corporate accounts and property for banks, syndicates, trust companies and prospective investors.

The business of public accounting has long since been demonstrated to be a necessary profession. The profession of accountant has held an honorable place for many years; so many, in fact, that we find it upon a firm footing in England and Scotland two centuries ago. The auditing of accounts, public and private, was intrusted to men who made a specialty of the business.

In Great Britain, public accountants are authorized by, and practice under act of Parliament. A law recently passed by the Legislature of the State of New York has a similar import. It is a general practice in the United States and England, with companies and various important corporations to regularly employ public accountants to make examination of their affairs, and when publishing their periodical statements of financial standing and business progress, to append the signatures of such public officials. Such a practice not only puts the question of solvency and standing beyond doubt, but must strengthen and popularize their names in their respective fields of operation. The duty and service of the public accountant are by no means limited to the matter of searching out and reporting upon the possible shortages in the cash and the loss or gain in business, but the proper departmenting of accounts, the planning of books and formulæ, assisting and advising in the general organization and duties of office, so that proper safeguards and methods may be adopted to insure accuracy with dispatch, and proper classification of articles for obtaining results, is a part of the duty and service of the professional.

A well-devised system, showing at all times, with the least labor and greatest accuracy, the true condition of the business, is of paramount importance. Such a system enables those most interested to follow the minutest fluctuations of the business and successfully weather the fiercest financial storms, that cause the soundest institutions to tremble, and send many that have been fairly well managed, tottering down to irretrievable ruin.

Andrew Carnegie, the Iron King, has said in one of his able addresses:—"There is not a science or class of men on whom the business world is more dependent than the Science of Accounts and Accountants."

Bookkeepers, accountants or business men, occupying or aspiring to the highest positions in their profession, or to commercial supremacy, will find this volume, not a compilation, but to contain all the subjects of higher accounting and advanced business methods, treated in a thoroughly practical and masterly manner.

Having known the author for a long time, and had occasion to critically examine this volume, I unhesitatingly recommend him and his book as the highest authority on accounts.

HENRY C. WHITE,
Judge of the Probate Court
at Cleveland.

Nov. 10, 1896.

CONTENTS.

Street Railway Consolidation.

The stock of both companies to be redeemed at par, and new stock issued in its stead. The assets and liabilities of both companies to be assumed by the new corporation. Two entries are given to consolidate. Bonds are sold at par, premium and discount.

An Ice Company Incorporated.

An assessment is called to cover losses and to produce a Working Capital.

A Manufacturing Company Incorporated.

A Patent right is bought with stock. Capital Stock Reduced. Entries are given to Increase and Decrease the value of assets before declaring a dividend.

Reduction of the Capital Stock of a Bank.

To cover losses by speculation.

A Manufacturing Company Incorporated.

Capital Stock $80,000. There are eight stockholders, each to hold $10,000 paid up stock by paying $2,500 each. The balance of $60,000 representing nominal or fictitious value is disposed of with proper entries.

Stock Forfeited for Non-Payment.

Stock Forfeited. Stock and Installments Forfeited. These entries depend upon how the Capital Stock account has been treated.

Rubber Trust.

Formation of a Trust, or the consolidation of six large rubber companies. The new company purchases all the property, machinery, material, etc., at an appraised value, and issues in payment full paid stock of the consolidated company. The liabilities and accounts due the old companies are to be liquidated by themselves. Common Stock is issued for the assets taken by the Trust, and Preferred Stock is placed in the market for sale.

Complete entries are given for this operation.

Forfeiture of Stock.

Entries for the forfeiture of stock depends upon how the Capital Stock accounts have been kept.

Entries are given for the forfeiture of stock, the stockholder receiving credit for the installments paid, when the Capital Stock account has been credited for full authorized capital.

Instructions are given to open, conduct and close the following:

Classification of Accounts.

Capital Stock and Funded Debt.

Cost of Road and Equipment.

Superintendence and General Expenses. Engineering. Right of way. Real Estate and Buildings. Roadbed and Track. Overhead Construction. Rolling Stock. Miscellaneous Equipment. Power Plant. Cable and Carrying Sheaves. Repair Shops. Additions and Betterments.

Earnings.

Passengers. Express. Mail. Advertising. Interest. Rents, and Miscellaneous.

Operating Expenses.

Miscellaneous.

Salaries of General Officers and Clerks. Office Service. Stationery. Insurance. Legal. Injury to Persons and Property. Contingent. Franchise.

Transportation.

Car Service. Car Barn. Oil and Waste for Cars and Machinery. Supplies. Wrecking, Sanding, Sweeping and Cleaning of Conduits. Stable and Power House. Provender and Fuel.

Maintenance of Way and Structures.

Repairs and Renewals of Roadbed and Track. Repairs and Renewals of Overhead Wire. Repairs and renewals of Buildings and Wharves.

Maintenance of Rolling Stock and Power Equipment.

Repairs and Renewals of Cars and Vehicles. Repairs and Renewals of Cable Sheaves and Grip Dies. Repairs of Harness and Stable Equipment. Horse Shoeing. Renewals of Horses and Mules. Repairs of Electric Car Equipment-Motor Armature. Gears and Pinions. Trolleys and Miscellaneous. Repairs of Power Plant—Steam, Cable and Electric. Tools, Machinery and Miscellaneous.

Fixed Charges.

Interest. Rent. Taxes. Franchise Charges.

Assets.

Construction. Equipment. Real Estate and Buildings. Stocks and Bonds. Franchise. Other Investments. Cash. Bills Receivable. Accounts Receivable. Supplies. Sinking Fund. Sundries, etc.

Liabilities.

Capital Stock. Funded Debt. Interest Due and Accrued. Dividends Unpaid. Audited Vouchers Payable. Wages Payable. Accounts Payable. Bills Payable. Sundries. Loss and Gain (Deficit), etc.

2

KEISTER'S
CORPORATION ACCOUNTING
AND AUDITING.

CHAPTER ONE.

Expert Accounting.

There is no part of an accountant's duty that requires greater skill or more deliberate forethought than that involved in the management of a set of books during changes and settlements in Partnership. A clear and comprehensive knowledge of the science is imperative on account of the great variety of changes and varied conditions of things existing in business. There is usually but little trouble in arriving at a correct solution when the books have been kept by Double Entry, but when they have been kept by Single Entry, or in an irregular and unsystematic manner the case is far different.

One of the most important questions connected with a settlement between partners, is the determination of the Losses and Gains of the business.

When the Assets and Liabilities are taken at their nominal valuation, and the books have been kept by Double Entry, all that is required is to close the books, and the balances of the partner's accounts will show how they respectively stand with the firm. However, to effect an equitable adjustment between partners, a variety of circumstances may have to be taken into consideration.

Some Assets and Liabilities may be over due and some may be short due, while there are always some bad or doubtful accounts for which allowances must be made. The basis of all such settlements is of course the original article or contract between the partners.

Within the last ten years the conversion of private partnerships into Joint Stock Companies has become very general, the object being to extend their trade by the introduction of new capital which could not be obtained on the principles of the ordinary partnership.

In opening the books of a mercantile or partnership business we have only positive values to deal with, whilst in opening the books of Stock Companies, we are compelled to resort to values of another kind; viz:—positive, nominal and fictitious, and it is in the creation and disposition of these fictitious and nominal values that difficulties seem to arise.

A book-keeper whose knowledge and experience does not extend beyond the affairs of ordinary business certainly is not competent to conduct the accounts of a corporation.

I have found in my experience of fifteen years, that there are few book-keepers who can correctly adjust the affairs of a partnership and incorporate into a Joint Stock Company.

The adjustment of the varied conditions of things existing in business, requires on the part of the accountant, a level head, skill in accounts, master of practical mathematics, and a thorough knowledge of mercantile law, business customs and commercial ethics.

Having been called upon frequently to adjust the books kept by those whose knowledge and experience has not gone beyond that of an ordinary business, has led me to believe that there is a long felt and universal want of practical instruction in Stock Company accounting, and to supply this want these lessons have been prepared.

The transactions in these lessons are not imaginary, but they have all been met in my experience in adjusting and auditing the books of some of the most extensive, wholesale, retail and manufacturing establishments, in the United States. These transactions are difficult, and as they are presented with numerous conditions and propositions, it is guaranteed that any one mastering them need never fear any that may arise in business.

The introduction of each subject will be fully illustrated and explained, and when each lesson has been completed to the best of your ability, compare your work with the key shown on pages 486 to 499. This will enable you to find your mistakes, if any, and to give you a thorough understanding of every point, as this work is arranged for home study as well as a book of reference. Master this work and you will be competent to keep or audit any set of books.

Miscellaneous Journal Entries.

It is universally conceded by accountants that the most important and difficult part of book-keeping is in making the Journal Entries. When transactions are correctly journalized, mistakes should not occur in the Ledger, as posting is merely mechanical work, requiring, however, the greatest care and accuracy.

These miscellaneous entries will be found of great variety, and to contain all the principles or rules for journalizing any transaction that may occur in business.

Note. Journalize each transaction and perform all your work just as you would in practical book-keeping.   By these entries it is not meant that cash, merchandise, etc., are to be journalized in business.   This form is shown, to give you a thorough understanding of journalizing by making the fewest entries.   In practical business there would be a separate book kept for merchandise, cash, bills payable, etc.   Some systems require a great many books, but the principle of journalizing is always the same.

Rules for Journalizing.

The DEBITS and CREDITS arising out of every transaction must, in amount, be equal.

Proprietors' or Partners' Accounts.   Credit for all investments and gains.   Debit for all withdrawals and losses.

General Rule.   Debit whatever you receive, or costs value. Credit whatever you part with, or produces value.

Cash.   When is cash debited and credited?   Debit cash when you receive Coin, Currency, Bank Drafts, Certificates of Deposit, Checks or Sight Drafts in your favor.   Credit when you part with or pay any of these.

Personal Accounts.   When is a personal account debited?   When he gets into my debt or I get out of his debt, he is Dr. for the amount.

When is a personal account credited?   When he gets out of my debt or I get into his debt, he is Cr. for the amount.

Property.   When is a property account debited and credited?   When property becomes mine, it is Dr. for the cost or value, and when it costs anything afterwards, it is Dr. for the cost.   It is Cr. for what it produces, and for its value, or what is received for it when sold.

Notes and Drafts.   Whenever you draw on a person, either at sight or time, credit the person drawn on.   Whenever a person draws on you either at sight or time, Dr. the drawer.   Whenever you give your own note or accept a time draft Cr. Bills Payable.   Whenever you pay your own note or time draft Dr. Bills Payable.   Whenever you receive another person's note or time draft, Dr. Bills Receivable. Whenever you collect or otherwise dispose of another person's Note or time Draft. Cr. Bills Receivable.

NOTE—The names or titles, expressive of causes and effects which incur expenditure or produce value, become subject to the terms Dr. and Cr., because they owe us for the value we expend on them, and we owe them for the value they produce or give us.   By this simple and just method of viewing and treating the common affairs of business, a most complete and admirable balancing system of keeping accounts has been invented; one which constantly preserves an even balance between the Dr. and Cr. values, and presents to our sight and understanding all we may desire to know regarding our assets and liabilities and our losses and gains.

Time Draft.

$100.00   Cleveland, Ohio, Dec. 31, 1893.

At ten days' sight pay to R. H. Pond....................or order
One hundred ....Dollars
value received, and charge the same to account of

To P. J. Twiggs,   H. H. Smith,
           Cincinnati, Ohio.   1222 Euclid Ave.

PAYEE'S ENTRY.

R. H. Pond (the Payee) Dr's. Bills Receivable to H. H Smith, (the Drawer).

DRAWER'S ENTRY.

H. H. Smith (the Drawer) Dr's. R. H. Pond (the Payee) to P. J. Twiggs (the Drawee).

DRAWEE'S ENTRY.

P. J. Twiggs (the Drawee) Dr's. H. H. Smith (the Drawer) to Bills Payable.

Sight Draft.

$500.00   Cleveland, Ohio, Dec. 16, 1893.

At sight, pay J. D. Hammond...................................or order
Five hundred..Dollars
value received, and charge the same to account of
To H. B. Wright,   J. G. Hower.
           104, 5th Ave., Pittsburg.

PAYEE'S ENTRY.

J. D. Hammond (the Payee) Dr's. Cash to J. G. Hower (the Drawer).

DRAWER'S ENTRY.

J. G. Hower (the Drawer) Dr's. J. D. Hammond (the Payee) to H. B. Wright (the Drawee).

DRAWEE'S ENTRY.

H. B. Wright (the Drawee) Dr's. J. G. Hower (the Drawer) to Cash.

Interest and Discount. Debit when you pay interest. Credit when you receive interest.

Expense. Debit expense for all it costs to conduct business. The expense account is usually divided into different accounts, such as, Salaries, Insurance, Rent, etc. Credit expense for anything that might be sold or returned, not used.

Required, the Journal Entries for the following Transactions.

Ex. 1. Sold to J. H. Brown Merchandise amounting to $2560. Received in payment S. C. Robbin's Note with Interest accrued 62 days at 6%. Face of Note $1290. Balance on account 30 days net.

Ex. 2. Bought of J. M. Howard, Merchandise as per invoice $1050. Gave in Payment Jno. Smith's Note for $450 at 2½% discount. Draft at ten days sight on H. J. Harris for $200 and my Note at 60 days to balance. Paid Freight $8.90.

Ex. 3. T. J. Smith failed, as endorser on his Note for $550, I paid it with protest fee $2.00.

Ex. 4. Bought invoice of Merchandise from A. R. Boyd amounting to $1920. Paid him W. M. Britt's acceptance for $2500 short due 30 days, at its Present worth. Interest 6%. Received a check for $300 and had the balance placed to my credit.

Ex. 5. Bought 200 shares L. S. & M. S. R. R. Stock for $100 per share. Paid cash $15,000, gave my Note, 6 months with interest 6% for the balance.

Ex. 6. T. B. Wood draws on me at sight favor Union National Bank for $2000 with exchange ¼ of 1%. I accepted.

Ex. 7. Discounted my 30 day Note at State National Bank for $3000. Discount 8%. Proceeds placed to my credit.

Ex. 8. Sold for cash to H. T. Hand, my Draft at sight on A. K. Hudson for $1000 at ½ of 1% discount.

Ex. 9. Sold Slade & Potter invoice of Hardware $800. Received in payment my note to The Bingham Co. $500, with interest accrued 63 days 5% and for the balance, including interest on the Note their Sight Draft on J. E. French which he has accepted in my favor.

Ex. 10. Received from the Liverpool and London and Globe Insurance Co., their sight draft on the American Exchange National Bank for $1575.50. Our claim for loss on their policy No. 1748797.

Ex. 11. Received from the L. S. & M. S. R'y Co. their check for $400 for a 2% quarterly dividend on 200 shares of stock (par value $100).

Ex. 12.   I lost a $20 gold piece when on my way to the Bank to deposit.

Ex. 13.   Paid to T. C. Willard our Attorney at Law, his annual fee of $300.   Cash.

Ex. 14.   Received from S. W. Gaines, Administrator of my uncle's estate, the titles to the following named property :   An eight-story stone and brick office, building situated on the corner Superior Street and Public Square, valued at $450,000.   No Encumbrance. One two-story stone and frame residence situated and known as 1390 Euclid Ave., valued at $80,000 on which there is a mortgage in favor of the East End Saving Bank Co., for $20,000.   One hundred shares of the capital stock of the Cleveland Electric R. R. (par value $100) and cash $5000.

Ex. 15.   Bought a sight Draft on Drexel, Morgan & Co., N. Y. for $975, Exchange $1\frac{1}{4}\%$ and remitted to Stern Bros. to balance account.

Ex. 16.   Brown, Smith & Co. have assigned.   I receive from the assignee on their Note of $974.50 in my favor, 50c. on the dollar in cash to settle in full.

Ex. 17.   H. T. Pratt, Uniontown, Pa., has returned Merchandise as per invoice $170.   I paid freight and expressage, $5.

Ex. 18.   I have drawn a sight Draft on P J. Jones, for $5000 and sold it to Tom Piper at $\frac{1}{4}\%$ discount and received my own Note for $4500 and the balance in cash.

Ex. 19.   I owe S. Ewart & Co., Pittsburg Pa., for net proceeds of shipment and wish to remit.   Total sales $7000, Com. $3\frac{1}{2}\%$, exchange $1\frac{1}{2}\%$, premium on Bank exchange which I purchased for cash.

Ex. 20.   I am endorser on Power's Note of $1000.   Powers is able to pay but half of it.   I pay the balance in cash.

Ex. 21.   The First National Bank discounted my note at 90 days for $1500 at 6% placing the same to my credit.   I deposited with the bank, as security, three $1000 4% U. S. Bonds.

Ex. 22.   Bought Merchandise of Jno. Ressler as per bill $1000. Gave in payment my note at 30 days for $400, Sight Draft on C. B. Hildreth, for $300, and balance on account.

Ex. 23.   Received of Theo. Hohl, Springfield, Ohio, to balance account his check for $100.   Note for $100 at 60 days.   Interest 6% and E. R. Brewer's order on me for $50 for which Brewer has credited me.

Ex. 24.   I loaned $500 cash to Thos. Davis to be returned in 15 days.   He left with me a $1000 U. S. Coupon Bond, as collateral.

Ex. 25. Marshall & Co. have drawn on me at sight, for $300, in favor of Thomas & Beck. I refused to accept and returned the Merchandise bought of them.

Ex. 26. Keim & Harris have accepted my Sight Draft for $325 in favor of Roberts & Son to whom I remit.

Ex. 27. Commenced business with cash $3000. Real Estate $10,000, Merchandise $7500, Note for $1200 against J. Wilson with interest accrued $10.50, Note for $600 against A. Mason with interest accrued $7.20, B. F. Miller owes on account $125, J. P. Keller owes $750. Owe on note to Mack & Co., $675 with interest accrued $15.75. Owe Brown Bros. on account $5000 and to H. C. Patterson $125.

Ex. 28. Sold Dreyfus, Kohn & Co., New York, Merchandise amounting to $2148.60. Received in payment Dustin's Note at 4 months for $1000 with interest accrued to date for 2 months 15 days at 6%. Our own acceptance for $1000 at 60 days, 35 days past due including grace, on which we allowed interest at 10% per annum and the balance on account at 60 days.

Ex. 29. Bought for J. Wade 100 shares Brush Electric Stock at $150 (par $100) for which he paid me cash ¼ of 1% on par value.

Ex. 30. Kent finds that he made a mistake and posted a credit of $120 for F. P. Lewis, into Miller's account.

Ex. 31. Bought a house and lot from V. C. Taylor, paid cash $3500 and assumed a mortgage on the place for $1500 with $70 accrued interest and a claim of $600 held by James Young the builder. Required, the Journal Entries for yourself and V. C. Taylor.

Ex. 32. Black bought a farm of Brown, price $7800. Brown had mortgaged the farm for $5000. He has paid interest promptly and $1500 on the principal. Brown had twenty cows, three horses, one wagon, one carriage, with a Chattel Mortgage on them for $1000. Black buys the cows, horses, etc., allows Brown $200 for growing crops, assumes both mortgages and paid Brown $5500 in cash.

Ex. 33. H. H. Smith, owed me on account $250. F. M. Potter assumed the debt, paid $150 cash, balance charged to his account.

Ex. 34. Collected for Hower & Higbee, Cleveland, at ⅔% Com. their sight Draft on Braddock & King, of Mt. Pleasant, Pa., for $3000, and invested the proceeds at ¼% Com. in a Draft on Henry Clews & Co., New York, paying ½% premium for exchange. Face of Draft remitted Hower & Higbee, $..............? Com. for collecting $.........
......? Com. for investing $........... ...?

Ex. 35. Deposit in Mercantile National Bank for collection P. T. Barnum's Note for $1000 with interest at 10%; W. J. Johnston's

Acceptance for $300, a Certificate of Deposit from Garfield National Bank, N. Y., for $1000, collection fee ¼%, a sight exchange on U. S. National Bank, N. Y., $250, collection fee 1-10%. Our Sight Draft on W. H. Marker, Chicago, for $1000, and Perry's check on Manufacturers National Bank of Springfield, Ill., for $675.10, collection fee ⅛%.

Ex. 36. Sold Merchandise to J. P. King amounting to $369.84. Received in payment my Note favor F. May for $179.20 interest accrued thereon $4.09, and a Certificate of Deposit to balance account. $...............?

Ex. 37. Paid our Note due to-day at City Bank for $3000 by giving a new Note at 60 days for $2000, and check for the balance including interest on New Note at 7%.

Ex. 38. Bought goods at forced sale amounting to $2950 for cash, and sold them before any entry was made upon the books for $3247 cash.

Ex. 39. Bought ten City of Cleveland Bridge Repair Bonds of $1000, each at $1075, bearing interest at 4%. Paid cash.

Ex. 40. Sold Burrows & Bosworth 50 Doz. Knives at $5. Received in payment C. A. Case's Note for $279 with accrued interest $2. Paid the difference in cash.

Ex. 41. T. B. Hood failed and assigned for the benefit of creditors. We have agreed to accept 33⅓% on the dollar. Our claim, $3193.24 on which we received cash to settle, $...............? Balance lost $...............?

Ex. 42. Gould gave Vanderbilt a Draft at 20 days sight on Rockefeller for $15,000. When presented for acceptance, Rockefeller offered to cash it if Vanderbilt would allow discount on basis of 4%. Vanderbilt accepts, and Rockefeller pays cash. Required, Journal Entries for each party.

Ex. 43. Bought for cash ₐₜ 1¼% premium, a sight Exchange on Brown Bros. for $1829.68. Remitted same to Peck & Co. to pay our acceptance.

Ex. 44. Commenced business with Merchandise $3000, Cash $4000. Notes against sundry persons amounting to $1570. Account against H. B. Wright $950, Wm. Wood $406, Real Estate $2500. I owe on outstanding Notes $3900, an Account due R. Thomas $1200, Wm. Edwards $640.

Ex. 45. Slade & Potter, who have been doing business as partners, and wishing to preserve from their book-keeper a knowledge of the amount of capital possessed by each, have kept their separate

Stock Accounts in a Private Ledger, having in the Public or General Ledger a general Stock account representing the united capital of both partners. But as there exists no longer any reason for observing this privacy, they have decided to close up the General Stock account in the general Ledger, and open in its stead separate accounts with each partner. Balance of Stock account in general Ledger $20,000, Slade's account in Private Ledger showing a balance of $12,000 and Potter $8000. What Entry?

Ex. 46. Paid the watchman $5 for his prompt and daring work in extinguishing fire in warehouse.

Ex. 47. Received from Carter & Co. a Sight Draft on Phila. in settlement of invoice of the 18th inst., for $700 less 5% for cash 10 days.

Ex. 48. Paid Smith's Sight Draft on me for $509, favor State National Bank with Cash.

Ex. 49. Redeemed with cash my 6 month note, favor A. Jones for $500 and interest at 6 %. $...............?

Ex. 50. Collected for Marshall, Field & Co., Chicago, their Sight Draft on Hower & Higbee this city, for $3000. Collection fee ½%, proceeds to the credit of Marshall, Field & Co. $...............?

CHAPTER TWO.

Ex. 51. A. R. Duncan took out an open policy of Insurance May 1, '93 in the National Insurance Co. giving Demand Note for $1300 and Interest 6%. Premiums on Shipments amounted to $1175 during the season. Duncan settles with the Insurance Co. Nov. 4, '93, paying cash in full of all demands.

Ex. 52. McKinley bought Merchandise of Pattison amounting to $565.32, gave in payment Smith's note at 6 months for $200, 4 months 23 days accrued Interest at 7%, Forakers 30 day acceptance for $175 due in 27 days at its present worth, Interest 6%, and a sight draft on Grover Cleveland for balance.

Ex. 53. I have a certificate of Deposit on the Pacific National Bank, San Francisco, Face of Certificate $10,000. In New York this paper is at a discount of 1%. I exchange this Certificate for a sight Exchange on Western National Bank, Denver. The Market Value of this sight exchange is the same as the Market Value of the Certificate, but the exchange is at a discount of 1-10 of 1%.

Ex. 54. White bought Merchandise of Black for $1079, gave in payment Black's acceptance for $590 and paid the difference in cash. Black's Entry.

Ex. 55. James Hoke began keeping our books April 1, '93 at $60 per month. We discharged him for carelessness and negligence, October 1, '93. He has taken goods amounting to $50. Cash $190 on account. We charged him with a Ledger that he spoiled $18, charged him 7 days lost time at $2.25 and paid him cash to balance account. Show his Ledger account as it should stand with proper entries.

Ex. 56. Gould, Vanderbilt and Astor are partners, sharing L.&G. in proportion to Inv. Gould has in the business $20,000. Vanderbilt $10,000, and Astor $15,000. Vanderbilt doubts the ability of Rockefeller to pay his account, and offers Gould his interest in the account for ½ of the amount. Gould accepts, and gives Vanderbilt his check. Rockefeller's Bill is $300. Required the entry on the firm's books.

Ex. 57. Compromise with Rockefeller for 50c. on the dollar, take his note at 30 days Interest 6%, and receipt in full. Give entry on firm's books.

Ex. 58. J. H. Sommers owes me $1200. I offered a discount of 2½% for Cash. Sommers, not having the money, discounted his note at 90 days at 7%, the Note producing the sum required to discount my claim. Show Sommer's Journal.

Ex. 59. Baird owes Larimer $300. He pays ¼% premium for Bank Draft with cash and remits Larimer. Show Baird's entry.

Ex. 60. Morgan is admitted to our firm as a partner. He invests in cash $2500. Latta's Bond and Mortgage for $3000. 10 shares First National Bank Stock at $130 (Par $100). Horse and Wagon $500.

Ex. 61. Received from the Lockwood-Taylor Hardware Co., a Draft on New York to settle invoice of 1st inst. for $675.00, less 3 per cent for prompt payment in 10 days.

Ex. 62. Sold a bill of goods amounting to $205. Received in payment 50 bu. Potatoes at $1.60, 50 Doz. Eggs at 25c., 3 bbls, apples @ $3 and cash to balance.

Ex. 63. Bought Merchandise amounting to $347.50, 60 days time. Bought Sight Exchange for Cash, premium ¼ of 1% to discount the bill at 2%.

Ex. 64. Shipped Jones & Laughlin Steel Rails amounting to $11, 250, we to pay the freight. Received draft at 60 days sight on Carnagie & Co., for $3000 at present worth on basis of 8% int. Cash $5000. Sight Exchange on Cincinnati for $1300 at ¾ of 1% Discount and their note for three months that we may discount it at 6% and net enough to settle in full. Jones and Laughlin paid freight and sent us receipted freight bill amounting to $795.00.

Ex. 65. Wilson retires from the firm of Jones, Smith & Wilson receiving a check for ½ of his net capital, and a note for the balance at one year at 6%. Wilson's net capital is $15675.80. What entry in firm's books?

Ex. 66. Bought of the City Bank their bill at 60 days sight on Baring Bros., London, for 7200 Dollars, for Cash at 8% premium and remitted to Taylor & Co. My commission ¼% for investing.

Ex. 67. Bought of Henry Clews his bill at 60 days' sight on Rothschilds for 2000 Dollars. Premium 8%. Paid him in his note $500, balance in cash.

Ex. 68. Brown's note for $1,500 due to-day was renewed for same amount for 60 days. Received Int. in Cash at 6%.

Ex. 69.   Paid my note in favor of J. B. Fox, which has been held under protest since the 10th inst. for $8000;Int.$5.33, Protest Fee $1.72 by selling him the Fifth Ave. Block $4800.   Balance in cash.

Ex. 70.   Have allowed a claim of 3c. per lb. on 1000 lbs. wool, sold to the New England Mfg. Co.   Not up to standard.

Ex. 71.   J. B. Hanna having failed, made an assignment.   His acceptance in our favor has been protested.   We charge the amount of the draft and protest fee to C. H. Wood the drawer.   Paid protest fee $1.50, Draft $300.00.

Ex. 72.   Bought a block of five stories on Superior St. for $30,-000.   Paid Cash $25,000 and gave a bond and mortgage for the balance, int. 5%.

Ex. 73.   T. B. Pritchard buys F. S. Cramer's entire interest in the firm of Snyder, Hanis, Bassett & Co. for $15000 and pays cash Cramer's balance as shown by the firm's Ledger, is $11,326.50.   Entry in firm's books.

Ex. 74.   Bought a farm of V. C. Taylor for $9230.   Gave in payment a Bond and Mortgage on the farm at 3 years, Int. 5% for $4665.   Cash for balance.   Insured for $4,000 in Liverpool & London Insurance Co. for 3 years, paid $25 for title and $40 premium with cash.

Ex. 75.   Paid Taxes for 1893 on farm with cash $95.50.

Ex. 76.   Paid Wm. Downie $207.50 for painting my farm house and buildings by giving him a receipt in full for the balance of his account $215.75.

Ex. 77.   Commenced business, Cash $5000.   Bills Receivable $2500. Merchandise $7500.   Wm. Johnston owes $1000.   Business Block 100 Superior St. $75,000.   I owe Bills Payable $1500.   Brooks & Co. $3200.   The W. Bingham Co. $300.

Ex. 78.   Exchanged Notes with J. E. Hannon for our mutual accommodation, each at 30 days, $1000.

Ex. 79.   Exchanged notes with D. Kennedy for our mutual accommodation.   Each note at 30 days $1000.   I have discounted his note and received cash for net proceeds.   Discount $10.50.

Ex. 80.   F. K. Strong, who lately failed, paid me 50c. on the dollar for the note I hold against him due last month.   Received a new note endorsed by P. Black for $500.   Balance is lost.

Ex. 81.   Sold Merchandise to Jno. Thomas amounting to $3355. Received in payment my acceptance favor R. Hay due this day $2000. Cash $355 and an order at sight for the balance on G. J. Warden, which I deposit on account with Warden.

Ex. 82. Jno. Brown's note for $500 endorsed by E. S. Root remains unpaid since yesterday, have charged the same to Root's account. What entry?

Ex. 83. Found a $20 note on the counter and placed same in money drawer until claimed.

Ex. 84. Discounted William's Note of $3000 and int. at 5%, 4 mo. to run from Sept. 16, '93. Discounted Nov. 3, '93 at 6%. Proceeds placed to my credit.

Ex. 85. Requested B. K. Jamison & Co., Philadelphia, Pa., to invest the proceeds of collection against Jno. Wanamaker in sight exchange on New York and remit the same to H. B. Claflin & Co. Exchange on New York at Philadelphia at ½% prem Amt. $2,218.86.

Ex. 86. Bought a 60 day sight draft on U. S. National Bank, New York for $2096.24 and remitted same to E. A. Wright of Philadelphia to balance account. Face of draft $2096.24. Exchange at ¾%. Interest allowed for 63 days at 6%. Amount of check drawn to cover the purpose. The Exchange is at a Discount.

Ex. 87. I owe H. A. Miller $2354.40. Paid him with his own note for $2250. Interest accrued on same $3.75 and cash for the balance.

Ex. 88. Insured my property for $25,000 through the agency of G. H. Olmsted & Co. for 3 years at 80c. premium, placed as follows: $5000 in Atlas of England, $5000 in Liverpool and London and Globe of London, $5000 in Norwich Union of Philadelphia, $5000 in Northern of New York, and $5000 in Union of Philadelphia. Policies and survey $2.50. Paid the amount with cash.

Ex. 89. Discounted our note at 90 days at 6% and bought sight exchange on New York to settle our account with A. T. Stewart & Co. for $765.50, Exchange at ¼ of 1% premium. Deposited as collateral 50 shares Union National Bank Stock. (Par $100)

Ex. 90. Hower & Higbee are doing business as equal partners. Hower offers to sell his entire interest in the business to Higbee for $75,000 which Higbee accepts, giving his personal check for the amount. Hower's Stock account is $67,500. What entry on firm's books.?

Ex. 91. Bought Merchandise of Norris Bros. amounting to $675. Paid in part by their note dated Feb. 5, received Feb. 27, for $350. The Balance, including discount on note, is credited to account. Discount on note for 13 days is 76c.

Ex. 92. Sold to J. R. Zuck on account my draft at 30 days on H. R. Freed for $500.

Ex. 93. Bought Merchandise of J. S. Braddock amounting to $350: Paid in part by draft on J. S. McCaleb at 30 days sight for $175.32. Balance on account.

Ex. 94. Discounted in cash my acceptance of April 1, being D. W. John's draft for $400. Discount for 41 days allowed. $2.74.

Ex. 95. Sold to J. H. Vance, my draft on A. H. Strickler for $300. Received in part payment W. J. Hitchman's acceptance of Strickler's draft on him, and due Dec. 1, for $200. Cash for the Balance $100.

Ex. 96. Accepted M. E. Johnson's sight draft for $485.10, Ex. $\frac{1}{8}$ of 1% in favor City Bank, payable at the State National Bank.

Ex. 97. Bought for cash of the Wick Banking Co., at $\frac{3}{4}$% premium, a Bill of Exchange on Bank of N. America, N. Y., for $2000, and remitted the same to Lord & Taylor in payment of our acceptance now due. Premium at $\frac{3}{4}$% $15.00.

Ex. 98. Drawn for private account $100 cash.

Ex. 99. S. A. Boyd paid his account in full yesterday in cash, to-day it is discovered that one $20 note is counterfeit.

Ex. 100. One teamster while delivering goods, had a 'run off' and totally destroyed china and cut glass-ware which had been sold for $100 cash, also killed the horse valued at $200.

NOTE—The acceptance of a draft is an engagement on the part of the drawee to pay the same; and in accepting it he assumes an absolute liability, and sustains thereafter the same relation to the draft that the maker does to a note.

When a draft is accepted, the drawee calls it his **acceptance**, and credits his Bills Payable account for the amount of his acceptance, unless it be a **sight** draft, in which case, if payment be not made at the time of accepting, he credits the holder of the bill, for it is no longer negotiable, but must be disposed of between the acceptor and the holder. From this, it is seen that a sight draft can never become a Bill Payable, for as soon as presented it is due, and no overdue paper is entitled to the appellation or legal protection of a bill.

CHAPTER THREE.

Single Entry Changed to Double Entry.

It is surprising to know to what extent Single Entry book-keeping is practiced even in houses doing a large business, because business men themselves are ignorant of the superiority of Double Entry.

Transforming the Single Entry Ledger into a Double Entry one, though simple as the process may appear after it is explained, it will be found that many accountants are not aware that there is any way of changing the principle of keeping the books but by the laborious and tedious process of transferring all the accounts to a new Ledger—an operation that is seldom necessary unless the old Ledger is filled.

The process of changing a set of books from Single to Double Entry is very simple. The characteristic difference between Single Entry and Double Entry consists in the use and application of the terms Dr. and Cr. These, in Single Entry, being applied only to persons or their representatives, it follows that the Single Entry Ledger can contain none other than personal accounts. Before proceeding to change a set of books from Single to Double Entry, it is necessary first to ascertain the loss or gain in business.

General Rule for Ascertaining the Gain or Loss in Single Entry.

To the liabilities add the balance of the stock account, when a credit ; but when a debit add it to the assets ; the difference between the assets and liabilities, when thus increased by the balance of the stock account, is the net gain or net loss in business,—net gain when the former exceeds the latter; net loss when the latter exceeds the former.

A great many bookkeepers and business men contend that a Trial Balance cannot be taken from a Single Entry Ledger. Nothing can be more absurd, and here is the proof :—

Ex. 147.

Trial Balance.

	Ledger Footings.	
T. J. Smith (partner)...............................	$ 742|50	$ 8241|50
A. J. Cooper (partner).............................	1200|00	10000|00
J. A. Boltz.......	575|00	321|00
J. S. Braddock..............................	920|00	561|00
H. R. Freed................................	321|00	200|00
J. R. Zuck.................................	1100|00	900|00
R. E. Fulton..........................	300|00	.........|...
Snyder & Co.............................	120|00	.........|...
John Husband & Bro........................	500|00	1800|00
S. A. Clark..............................	1875|50	2500|00
E. R. Brewer.............................	174|00	500|00
O. C. Jones.	.........|...	150|00
Bal. of the Ledger............................	17345|50	.........|...
	$25173|50	$25173|50
Day Book footings, Page 1.........................	$ 4321|00	$ 8000|50
" " " " 2.....................	2031|00	7541|35
" " " " 3.....................	1050|00	4691|40
" " " " 4.....................	426|00	4940|25
Bal. of the Day Book...........................	17345|50	.........|....
	$25173|50	$25173|50

Remarks on the Trial Balance.

The proof of the correctness of the work in Single Entry books does not consist in *equal* debits and credits, but in *equal* balances of Day Book and Ledger. All the sums in the debit column of the Day Book being posted to the Dr. side of the Ledger and all the sums in the Cr. column being posted to the Cr. side of the Ledger, it is evident that the *difference* between the debits and credits of one book must be equal to that of the other. As none of the accounts upon the Ledger had been closed at the time of taking off this Trial Balance, we make use of the totals for the purpose of showing that the footings of the two books must agree. These footings will *not* agree, however, after any of the accounts in the Ledger have once been closed; but instead of taking the totals as we have done here, the same proof would have been obtained had we used the balances only, and in business this is the better way.

To Ascertain the Loss or Gain.

After proving the Ledger as in the above Trial Balance, we next ascertain the gain or loss as stated in the *General Rule*, by taking an inventory, which we find as follows:

Ex. 148.
Inventory.

Mdse. per Inventory	$12105 00	
First Nat. Bank Stock (12 shares)	1200 00	
Cash on hand	5221 50	
Bills Receivable, per Bill Book	6729 31	
Personal accounts (due us), per Ledger	1354 00	
Total Assets		$26609 81
Bills Payable, per Bill Book	$ 5730 00	
Personal accounts (we owe) per Ledger	2400 00	
T. J. Smith, bal. of his stock acct	7499 00	
A. J. Cooper, " " " "	8800 00	
Total Liabilities		24429 00
Net Gain		$2180 81
T. J. Smith's half is.............$1090.40		
A. J. Cooper's half is............. 1090.41		

Closing the Single Entry Ledger.

After taking off the Trial Balance and ascertaining the Gain or Loss, the next step is that of closing. To do this an entry is made in the Day Book, crediting the partners with their respective shares of the Net Gain, or debiting them with their shares of the Net Loss. These entries are then posted to the Partners' accounts in the Ledger; the accounts are then balanced, and balances brought down to new accounts; when this is done the Ledger is closed, since closing is nothing more nor less than the determination of the balances of the Partners', Proprietors or Stock accounts. As the remaining accounts are all Personal, they are subject to the same principles as in Double Entry. From the above it is seen that it is just as easy and certain to determine the Loss or Gain in Single as in Double Entry.

Process of Changing.

From the Inventory taken as above, you get the results and effects of the business in Single Entry. To change to Double Entry is only to Debit the Assets to the Liabilities. (Note.—The difference will be the Net Cap., hence the partners are each credited in this opening entry with their new balances.)

If the Old Single Entry Ledger is to be Used.

If the old Ledger is to be used, the opening entry should not under any circumstances be any different than if a new one is to be opened. To use the old Ledger it will be necessary to post only the new accounts to be opened, while all the Personal Accounts are all ready in Double Entry condition, and are marked on the Journal "posted," as in the opening Journal entry below from the above results.

Ex. 149.

Mdse. per Inventory...............................	$12105.00	
First Nat. Bank Stock (12 shares)................	1200.00	
Cash on hand......................................	5221.50	
Bills Receivable, per Bill Book...................	6729.31	
Accounts Receivable (Posted).....................	1354.00	
	$26609.81	
To Bills Payable (per Bill Book)..............		$ 5730.00
" Accounts Payable (Posted)...............		2400.00
" T. J. Smith (Net Cap.)....................		8589.40
" A. J. Cooper (Net Cap.)..................		9890.41
		$26609.81

If a new Ledger is to be opened, you will have to Debit and Credit the Personal Accounts separately, instead of taking them collectively. Should there be a great number of Personal Accounts to transfer, it is far better to make the entry as above, and transfer from the old Ledger direct to the new. After posting the above entry in old Ledger, and transferring the Personal Accounts to new Ledger, take a Trial Balance; if correct, you are ready for business; if not, you must check your work at once and find the error. The operation of changing from Single Entry to Double Entry is so simple, and has been so thoroughly illustrated and explained, that further treatment would be useless.

Ex. 150. The following Trial Balance was taken from the books of Brown, Bingham & Jones. Losses and Gains shared equally. Show a statement of the Assets and Liabilities and the Loss and Gain account, properly closed.

Trial Balance.

Brown, ⎫			$ 6000 00
Bingham, ⎬ Partners			13000 00
Jones, ⎭			12500 00
Mdse. (Invty. $7000.00)...........................	$12921 00		7350 00
Bills Payable....................................	3180 00		6180 00
Bills Receivable................................	7000 00		5000 00
Commission			1225 00
Real Estate ($15,000.00)........	15000 00		1575 00
Salary acct....................................	715 66		
Int. and Dis..................................	17 50		137 50
Insurance (Unexpired $25.00).....................	125 00		
First Nat. Bank Stock (Unsold $1476.00)......	1710 00		375 00
Furniture Fix. (Invty. $450.00).	575 00		
Expense acct. (Coal on hand $36.00)............	427 30		
Rent acct....................................	1575 00		
Cash	22260 55		14600 92
Q. Willson....................................	4300 00		2795 00
Bingham's private acct.......................	325 00		
Mdse. Co. No. 1 (Invty. $450.00)..............	1290 00		840 00
Adv. Co. No. 1 (Invty. $875.00)..................	1795 00		795 00
Adv. Co. No. 2 (Invty. $200.00).................	200 00		
P. D. Myer....................................	1000 00		1431 11
Carne's Consg't................................	57 10		
Loss and Gain................................	24 80		694 38
	$74498 91		$74498 91

Ex. 151. Day & Co. have been doing business as partners, and have kept their books by Single Entry. They wish to admit J. D. Watterson as a partner, and have their books kept by Double Entry. From their books and Inventory they find the following Assets and Liabilities: Mdse. per Inventory, $9241.00; Cash, $850.00; Real Estate, $3000.00; Bills Payable, $975.00; W. M. Day's credit, $5390.00; T. J. Simon's credit, $6400.00. They owe personal accounts, $4175.00. Persons owe them $6941.00. Store Fixtures, $571.00. What was the Gain or Loss? What is each partner's net capital? J. D. Watterson is admitted and invests $3000.00 cash, Mdse. $2000.00, Bills Receivable (guaranteed) $1500.00. Give a full solution for finding the Loss or Gain, admit the new partner and make the entry to open the books by Double Entry, and admit the partner by using one entry.

CHAPTER FOUR.

Partnership Law.

Mercantile View of a Firm.

Partners are collectively called a firm. Merchants and Lawyers
have different notions respecting the nature of a firm. Business men
and Accountants are apt to look upon a firm in the light in which Lawyers look upon a corporation, i. e., as a body distinct from the members
composing it, and having rights and obligations distinct from those of
its members. Hence, in keeping partnership accounts the *firm* is made
debtor to each partner, for what he brings into the common stock, and
each partner is made debtor to the *firm* for all that he takes out of that
stock. In the mercantile view, partners are never indebted to each
other in respect to partnership transactions; but are always either
debtors to, or creditors of the firm.

Owing to this impersonification of the firm, there is a tendency to
regard its rights and obligations as unaffected by the introduction of a
new partner, or by the death or retirement of an old one. Notwithstanding such changes among its members, the *firm* is considered as
continuing the same; and the rights and obligations of the old firm
are regarded as continuing in favor of, or against the new firm, as if
no changes had occurred. The partners are the agents and sureties of
the firm ; its agents for the transaction of its business; its sureties for
the liquidation of its liabilities so far as the assets of the firm are insufficient to meet them. The liabilities of the firm are not regarded as the
liabilities of the partners, except in case they cannot be met by the firm
and discharged out of its assets.

Legal View of a Firm.

Lawyers do not recognize a firm as distinct from the members
comprising it. In taking partnership accounts and in administering
partnership assets, courts have, to some extent, adopted the mercantile

view, and actions may now be brought by, or against partners in the name of their firms; but speaking generally, the firm as such has no legal recognition.   The law, ignoring the firm, looks to partners composing it; any change amongst them destroys the identity of the firm; what is called the property of the firm is their property, and what are called the debts and liabilities of the firm, are their debts and their liabilities.   In point of law, a partner may be the debtor or the creditor of his co-partners, but he cannot be either debtor or creditor of the firm of which he himself is a member.

A member of an ordinary partnership fills a double character; he is both a principal and an agent.   As a principal he is bound by what he does himself and by what his co-partners do, on behalf of the firm, provided they keep within the limits of their authority; as an agent he binds them by what he does for the firm, provided he keeps within the limits of his authority.   But a partner is not the surety of the firm. Every member of an ordinary partnership, however numerous the partners may be, is liable as a principal to have his private property seized for a partnership debt, whether the firm has assets to pay it or not, a od not only so, but the property of the firm is liable to be seized for the private debts of any of the partners comprising it.   This non-recognition of the firm, in the mercantile sense of the word, is one of the most marked differences between partnerships and incorporated companies.

Agreement to Share Profits.—The Essence of a Partnership.

The basis of all partnerships is an agreement to share the profits arising from some business or undertaking.

Usually, but not necessarily, partners have a joint capital or stock, by the employment of which the profits to be shared are expected to arise; and in ordinary partnerships, but not in companies, each partner usually takes an active part in the prosecution of the partnership business.   Nothing, perhaps, can be said to be absolutely essential to the existence of a partnership except a community of interest in profits resulting from an agreement to share them.   But, although this is so, the usual characteristics of an ordinary partnership are a community of interest in profits and losses, a community of interest in the capital to be employed, and a community of power in the management of the business engaged in.

Whether an agreement creates a partnership or not depends on the real intention of the parties to it.   If the agreement is not in writing the intention of the parties must be ascertained from their words and conduct. If the agreement is in writing, its true construction must be determined; but, even then, a written contract may be departed from and modified by a new verbal agreement between all the partners proved by conduct inconsistent with the written document.

Agreements to Share Profits Only.

Except in cases specially provided for by statute, an agreement to share profits, nothing being said about losses, amounts *prima facie* to an agreement to share losses also; for it is but fair that the chance of gain and of loss should be taken by the same persons; and it is natural to suppose that such was their intention, if they have said nothing to the contrary. It follows from this, that where no statute interferes, an agreement to share profits is *prima facie* an agreement for a partnership; and accordingly it has been held, that unless an intention to the contrary can be shown, persons engaged in any business or adventure and sharing the profits derived from it, are partners as regards that business or adventure.

Partnership Articles.

The rights and obligations of partners, are to a certain extent, regulated by special agreement, the true meaning of which is to be ascertained by the ordinary rules of construction.

In considering the effect, however, of partnership articles, the following are to be borne in mind:

In the first place, partnership articles are not intended to define, and are not construed as defining all the rights and obligations of the partners. A great deal is left to be understood. The rights and obligations of partners, so far as they are not expressly declared, are determined by general principles, which are always applicable when not clearly excluded.

The attainment of the objects which the partners have declared they had in view is always regarded as of the first importance. All the provisions of the articles are to be construed so as to advance and not defeat those objects; and however general the language of partnership articles may be, they will be construed with reference to the end designed, and, if necessary, receive a restrictive interpretation accordingly.

Any provision, however worded, will, if possible, be construed so as to defeat any attempt by one partner to avail himself of it for the purpose of defrauding his co-partner. Thus it is very common for partners to agree that half-yearly accounts shall be made out and signed, and not be afterwards disputed; notwithstanding such a clause, if one partner knowingly makes out a false account, and his co-partner signs it upon the faith that it is correct, he will not be bound by it.

Every power conferred by the articles on any individual partner, or any number of partners, is deemed to be conferred with a view to the benefit of the whole concern; and an abuse of such power, by an exercise of it, warranted perhaps by the words conferring it, but not by the truth and honor of the articles, will not be countenanced.

Any article, however expressed, is capable of being abandoned by the consent of all the partners; and this consent may be evidenced, not only by express words, but by conduct.

If it is proposed to make an alteration in the articles by an agreement which shall be binding on all parties, notice of the proposed change and of the time and place at which it is to be taken into consideration, must be given to all partners, and those who object to such changes will not be bound by the others.

If a partnership, originally entered into for a definite time, is continued after the expiration of that time, without any new agreement, the articles under which the partnership was first carried on continue, so far as they are applicable to a partnership at will, to regulate the rights and obligations of the partners.

Usual Clauses in Partnership Articles.

In framing articles of partnership, it should always be remembered that they are intended for the guidance of persons who are not lawyers; and that it is therefore unwise to insert only such provisions as are necessary to exclude the application of rules which apply when nothing to the contrary is said.

The articles should be so drawn as to be a code of directions, to which the partners may refer as a guide in all their transactions, and upon which they may settle among themselves differences which may arise without having recourse to Courts of Justice.

The Nature of the Business.

The nature of the business should always be stated. Upon it depends the extent to which each partner is to be regarded as the implied agent of the firm in his dealings with strangers, and upon it also in a great measure depends the power of a majority of partners to act in opposition to the wishes of the minority.

The Place of Business.

The place of business should always be stated; and if the place is held on lease which will expire during the partnership, provision should be made for the renewal of the lease, or for the acquisition of another place of business. Otherwise the business may come to a premature end.

The Time of the Commencement of a Partnership.

Articles of partnership, like other instruments, take effect from their date; and if they are executed on the day of their date, and contain no expression indicating when the partnership is to begin, it must be taken to commence on the day of the date of the articles, and parole evidence to show that this was not intended, is not admissible.

The Name or Style of the Firm.

This should always be expressed; and it should be declared that no partner shall enter into an engagement on behalf of the firm except in its name. Such an agreement is capable of being enforced; and it may be of use in determining, among the partners, whether a given transaction is to be regarded as a partnership transaction or not.

Duration of the Partnership.

If the time for which the partnership is to endure is not limited to a definite period, either expressly or by necessary implication, the partnership may be dissolved at the will of any partner. But it must not be forgotten that a partnership entered into for a definite time is dissolved by the death of any one of its members before that time has expired, and that it is therefore necessary to provide for these events in order to give effect to the agreement as to time.

The Capital and Property of the Firm.

The articles should always carefully specify what is and what is not to be considered partnership property; particularly where one partner is, or is to be, solely entitled to what is to be used for the common purposes of all.

If one partner is entitled to land which is to become partnership property; it is usual to have that land conveyed or assigned to trustees for the firm, this will prevent a private sale without notice.

The proportions in which the capital is to be contributed by the partners, and the proportions in which they are to be entitled to it when contributed, should be carefully expressed.

It by no means follows that the partners are to be entitled to the assets in the proportions in which they contribute to the capital. If no express declaration upon the subject is made, the *prima facie* inference is, that all the partners are entitled to share the assets (minus the capital) equally, although they may have contributed to the capital unequally.

The capital should be expressed to be so much money; and if one of the partners is to contribute lands or goods instead of money, such lands or goods should have a value set upon them, and their value in money should be considered as his contribution. If this be not done, the articles and accounts and the proportions in which profits and losses are to be shared will be less perspicuous and free from doubt than will otherwise be the case.

Interest, Allowance, Etc.

The allowance of interest on capital and on advances should be made the subject of special agreement. The interest should be made payable before the profits to be divided are ascertained, and the interest on advances should be made payable before interest on capital.

Money Withdrawn.

Most articles of partnership contain a clause authorizing each partner to draw out of the partnership funds a certain sum per month for his own private purposes. Such a clause should provide for the repayment with interest of whatever may be drawn out in excess of the sum mentioned.

Amount of Attention to be Given to the Affairs of the Firm.

The time and attention which the partners are to give to the affairs of the firm should be expressly mentioned; especially if one of them is to be at liberty to give less of his time and attention than the others.

Liability of Incoming Partner.

As the firm is not liable for what is done by its members before the partnership between them commences, so upon the very same principle a person who is admitted as a partner into an existing firm does not by his entry become liable to the creditors of the firm for anything done before he becomes a partner.

If an incoming partner chooses to make himself liable for the debts incurred by the firm prior to his admission therein, there is nothing to prevent his so doing.

Though an incoming partner is not liable for the debts of the firm prior to his admission, there are many cases in which the new partner and the new firm are held liable from their dealings with creditors for the obligations of the old firm.

An incoming partner who succeeds an outgoing partner by purchase or who joins with the survivors on the death of one partner, is liable only by agreement for the prior debts of the old firm, and such agreement can only be enforced by the old firm.

An account rendered by a partner is in its nature an admission, and the statement of an account by one partner binds the firm.

The admission of one partner with reference to a partnership transaction is evidence against the firm, but is not necessarily conclusive. An admission by one person who afterwards enters into partnership with others is no evidence against them, merely because they and he are partners when the evidence is sought to be used.

Admission by an active partner after dissolution, that debt has not been paid, binds the dormant partner.

If a creditor of one of several partners takes from his debtor a bill or note in the name of the firm for his debt, without the knowledge of the other partners, he cannot sue the firm on such note or bill.

A declaration by a partner, though made during the existence of a partnership, that a liability incurred by a third person, at his request, in the borrowing of a sum of money, was for the benefit of the firm, is not binding upon his co-partner. Had a note been given in the partnership name, the rule would have been different. Then the co-partner would have to show that the note was given for the individual debt of the partner who gave it.

Declaration or admission that a person is a partner is evidence against him that he is a partner, and that there is a partnership, and statements and correspondence in business matters are competent to charge the speaker or writer as a partner.

Consent of the Partners.

It is usual to insert in partnership articles a clause prohibiting any partner from doing certain things without previously obtaining the consent of the others; i. e., becoming surety, releasing debts, drawing, accepting or indorsing bills, otherwise than in the usual course of business.

Liability of Partners.

An agent who contracts for a known principal, is not liable to be himself sued on the contract into which he has avowedly entered only as agent, consequently, a partner who enters into a contract on behalf of his firm, is not liable on that contract except as one of the firm; in other words the contract is not binding on him separately, but only on him and his co-partners jointly.

It has often been said that in equity partnership debts are separate as well as joint; but this proposition is inaccurate and misleading. It is true that a creditor of a partnership can obtain payment of his debt out of the estate of a deceased partner, but the judgment which such a creditor obtains is quite different from that which a separate creditor is entitled to; and it is a mistake to say that the joint creditor of the firm is also in equity a separate creditor of the deceased partner.

If a creditor of a firm sues the surviving partners and receives judgment against them he cannot obtain payment of his demand out of the assets of a deceased member of the firm.

It has long been held that a creditor of the firm is himself entitled to obtain payment from the estate of the deceased, even although he may have taken as a security for his debt a bond or covenant binding the partners jointly.

If a creditor sues the surviving partners and obtains judgment against them, he will be therefore precluded from proceeding to enforce his original claim against the estate of the deceased partner, but if the creditor first seeks payment out of the estate of a deceased partner he is not precluded from afterwards suing the surviving partners.

By the common law of this country, every member of an ordinary partnership is liable to the utmost dollar of his property for the debts and engagements of the firm. The law, ignoring the firm as anything distinct from the persons composing it, treats the debts and engagements of the firm as the debts and engagements of the partners, and holds each partner liable for them accordingly.

The agency of each partner commencing with the partnership,

and not before, it follows that the firm is not liable for what may be done by any partner before he became a member thereof. So that if several persons agree to become partners, and to contribute each a certain quantity of money or goods, for the joint benefit of all, each one is solely responsible to those who may have supplied him with the money or goods agreed to be contributed by him; and the fact that the money or goods so supplied have been brought in by him as agreed, will not render the firm liable.

Dissolution.

A partnership which is incapable of being repudiated by any of its members, may be terminated by a variety of events. Disregarding mutual consent on the part of all the partners, and such events, if any, as by the partnership articles, may be specially made grounds of dissolution; the causes of dissolution of an ordinary partnership may be reduced to the following; viz :

1. The will of any partner.
2. The impossibillity of going on; in consequence of
Misconduct,
Insanity.
The hopelesss state of the partnership business.
3. The transfer of a partner's interest.
4. The occurrence of some event which renders the partnership illegal.
5. Death.
6. Insolvency.

Notice of Dissolution.

If a partnership is dissolved, or one of the known members retires from the firm, until the dissolution or retirement is duly published, the power of each to bind the others remains in full force, although as between the partners themselves a dissolution or a retirement is a revocation of the authority of each to act for the others. Thus, if a known partner retires, and no notice is given, he will be liable to be sued in respect of a promissory note made since his retirement by his late partner, even though the plaintiff had no dealings with the firm before the making of the note. And in determining which was first in point of time, viz., notice of the dissolution or the making of the note, effect must be given to the presumption that the instrument was made and issued on the day it bore date, unless some reason to the contrary can be shown.

A partner who retires and does not give sufficient notice, exposes himself to the risk of being sued for torts committed subsequent to his retirement by his late co-partners or their agents; and in the absence of proof of the true state of things he would be held liable for them.

If a dormant partner is known to certain individuals to have been a partner, he is to them no longer in the situation of a dormant partner, and must therefore give them notice of his retirement if he would free himself from liabilities in respect to the future transactions between them and his late partners.

Importance of Notifying Dissolution.

It is obvious, therefore, that on the dissolution of a firm or the retirement of a partner, it is of the greatest importance to give notice of the fact. Notice of dissolution or retirement should be published in a paper of regular issue for at least three weeks. Each and every creditor of the firm should also be notified.

If a partner retires and gives notice of his retirement by advertisement and letter, he will continue to incur liability if he is in any way held out as a partner. If a retiring partner's name is allowed to remain printed over their place of business, he will be liable notwithstanding the notice, for there is no evidence to show that he has retired.

Winding Up of Partnerships.

In order to wind up the affairs of a dissolved partnership, it is necessary first to pay its debts; secondly, to settle all questions of account between the partners; and thirdly, to divide the unexhausted assets, (if any) between the partners in proper proportions, or, if the assets are insufficient for these purposes, then to make up the deficiency by a proper contribution between the partners. This can be done by the partners themselves, or their representatives.

In Regard to the Creditors of the Firm.

Whether a partnership dissolution be general or partial, does not discharge any of the partners from liabilities incurred by them previous to the time of dissolution.

In order that a member of a firm, wholly or partially dissolved, may be freed from his liability to a person who was a creditor of the firm at the time of its dissolution, such creditor must either have been paid, or satisfied, or must have accepted some fresh obligation in lieu of that which existed when the firm was dissolved.

Except in a few special cases, a notice of dissolution or retirement is requisite to determine the responsibility of each partner in respect to such future acts of his late co-partners.

A notice of dissolution generally, as by advertisement, is not sufficient to affect an old customer, unless it can be brought to his knowledge.

After dissolution and notice, partners cease to be responsible for the future acts of each other, unless they continue to hold themselves out as partners, in which case the notice is of no avail.

In Regard to Partners Themselves.

Upon the dissolution of a partnership, and in the absence of any agreement to the contrary, it has been seen that each partner has a right to have the partnership assets applied in liquidation of the partnership debts, and to have the surplus assets divided.

The right of each partner is to insist on a sale of the partnership assets; there being in the absence of special circumstances, no right in any partner to have the value of his own or of any co-partner's share determined by valuation, or to have the partnership property, or any portion of it, divided in specie.

Each partner has a right to insist that nothing further shall be done, save with a view to wind up the concern.

For the purposes of winding up, the partnership is deemed to continue; the good faith and honorable conduct due from every partner to his co-partners during the continuance of the partnership, being equally due so long as its affairs remain unsettled; and that which was partnership property before, continuing to be so for the purpose of dissolution, as the rights of partners require.

To wind up the partnership affairs means, to get in its credits, convert its assets into money, pay its debts, and divide the residue which belongs as much to one of the late partners as to another; and if they cannot agree among themselves, recourse must be had to the Court, which will if necessary appoint a receiver, direct a sale of the assets and payment of the partnership debts, and restrain a partner from interfering with the proper winding up of the partnership.

CHAPTER FIVE.

Partnership.

A Partnership is an association of two or more persons who combine their capital, skill and labor, or all of them, for the purpose of conducting some lawful business, and for sharing in the profits or losses arising therefrom, according to the terms of their agreement.

Capital is the money, property, goods, etc., invested in the business.

Partners are distinguished as Active, Nominal, Silent and Special.

Active Partners are those who are actually known as Partners, and who share all the profits or losses in the business.

Note. Active Partners are called Ostensible Partners, whose names are made known and appear to the world as Partners, and who in reality are such and take all the benefits and risks.

Nominal Partners are those who have no real interest in the business, but who assume the responsibility of Partners by lending to the Partnership their names and credit.

Note. Nominal Partners appear and are held out to the world as Partners, but have no real interest in the firm's business.

Silent Partners are those whose names are concealed, and are not therefore known as Partners. They are, however, actual Partners, and conceal their names principally to avoid liability to the creditors of the firm. Should a Silent Partner take an active part in the business of the firm, such action would render him as liable as the other partners.

Note. "Kent's Commentaries" defines Silent Partners as Dormant Partners, whose names are not known or do not appear as Partners, but who, nevertheless, are silent partners, and partake of the profits, and thereby become partners, either absolutely or to all intents and purposes, or at all events in respect to third persons.

Special Partners are those who furnish a certain portion of the capital of the firm, and are liable only for that amount. If the extent of their liabilities, however, is not published and legally recorded, they may be held equally liable with the other partners.

Partnership Adjustment is a settlement of Partners' accounts, setting forth the net investments, liabilities assumed, withdrawals, losses or gains, and showing net capital or net insolvency at closing or settling the Partnership's interests. Partnership settlements are usually made when a new member is admitted to the firm, and when a dissolution takes place; also at regular intervals, according to the Articles of Co-partnership.

Articles of Co-partnership, or Partnership Contract, is a written instrument, setting forth the agreement between the Partners; specifying the amount of each Partner's Investment; the limitation of the Partnership; the proportion allowed to be withdrawn by each Partner; the proportion of profit or loss which each Partner shall bear, and such other particulars or stipulations as may be deemed expedient.

Note. It not infrequently happens that one Partner's experience or business knowledge is the only Investment which is required of him. Sometimes one or more of the Partners receive a regular salary in addition to their proportionate share of the profits, for keeping the books, or some other special duty. Oftentimes interest is allowed on each Partner's Investment, and interest charged on all sums withdrawn. Each and every detail, however, should be fully set forth in a carefully drawn Partnership Contract.

The Capital of a firm is the entire value of its Assets or Resources.

The Assets or Resources of a firm are its entire property, including all debts or obligations due to the firm.

The Liabilities of a firm embrace all the debts or obligations due by the firm to its creditors.

The Investment is the aggregate of the money or property jointly contributed by the partners.

The Net Investment is the difference between the total sum invested and the total withdrawals.

The Average Investment is an average sum in the continuous use of the firm when several investments, withdrawals, or both, have been made at different times.

The Insolvency of a firm is the total amount due the Creditors in excess of the firm's Assets or ability to pay.

The Net Gain is the excess of gains over the losses.

The Net Loss is the excess of losses over the gains.

The Net Capital of a firm is the excess of Assets over all Liabilities, except such as stand to the Partners' credit. The Adjustment of Accounts between partners involves often the nicest discrimination and the most complete knowledge of the bearings of different entries. The numerous difficulties existing in Partnership settlements are so complicated and irregular, that any attempt to supply *Rules* to meet every case would be preposterous. It is, however, possible to give such general principles and illustrations as will apply in most cases, but a thorough knowledge of the science of accounts, with good common sense to apply it, will be found an important requisite; yet with all the knowledge and experience that can be had, complications will arise that will tax your skill to the utmost.

Note. Remember that all partnership settlements are made according to the Original Agreement, and in making such settlements be sure to have a thorough understanding of the Agreement, master the principles herein given, and you will soon be master of any complications that may arise.

When the Loss or Gain is shared in proportion to each Partner's Investment. Principle. Divide the Profit or Loss by the sum of the Investments; this will give the per cent. of Profit or Loss that each Partner must bear. Multiply each Partner's Investment by the per cent. of Profit or Loss thus found, and the product will be his respective share of Profit or Loss.

What would be each Partner's share of Profit or Loss in the following accounts, if shared in proportion to amounts invested? Net Gain $3150.00.

Brown.	Cr.	Black.	Cr.	White.	Cr.
|| $3400.00		|| $2900.00		|| $4200.00

ILLUSTRATION.

$3400.00+$2900.00+$4200=$10,500.00, Total Investment.
$3150.00÷$10,500.00 (Net Gain) =30%.

30% gain $3400.00=$1020.00, First Partner's Share.
30% " $2900.00= 870.00, Second " "
30% " $4200.00= 1260.00, Third " "

$3,150.00 (Net Gain Proof.)

Ex. 152. Sharing the Gains or Losses in proportion to the investment. How much of the Gain would each receive from the following statement?

E. R. Brewer.	Theo. Hohl.	Loss and Gain.
|| $7500.00	|| $500.00	|| Net Gain, $5000.00
1500.00		
|| $9000.00	||	||

Ex. 153. When the Losses or Gains are to be divided in proportion to each Partner's Investment and Time. Principle. Multiply each investment for the time it was in use of the firm and divide the product by the time for which the Losses or Gains are adjusted.

If the profits are divided in proportion to the capital invested and the time it was employed, what would be each partner's average investment and share of the profits, from the following accounts. Net Gain, $4620.00.

C. W. Strickler.		S. K. Ebersole.	
March 1..$1500.00	Jan. 1......$6000.00 July 1..... 2900.00	July 1....$3000.00	Jan. 1......$6000.00 March 1.. 3000.00

ILLUSTRATION.

Jan. 1, 1892, C. W. Strickler invested $6000.00×2=$12000.00 for 1 mo.
Mar. 1, " " " withdrew 1500.00

            Balance..............$4500.00×4=$18000.00 for 1 mo.
July 1, 1892, C. W. Strickler invested.. 2900.00

          Amt. invested.....$7400.00×6= 44400.00

               12) $74400.00

      C. W. Strickler's average investment..... $6200.00

Jan. 1, 1892, S. K. Ebersole invested $6000.00×2=$12000.00 for 1 mo.
Mar. 1, " " " " 3000.00

           Amt............ $9000.00×4= 36000.00 for 1 mo.
July 1, 1892, S. K. Ebersole withdrew 3000.00

            $6000.00×6= 36000.00 for 1 mo.

              12) $84000.00

    S. K. Ebersole's average investment.. ... $7000.00

C. W. S. average investment, $6200.00+S. K. E. average investment $7000.00=$13200.00, Total Investment. $4620.00 (Net Gain) ÷$13200.00 (Net Investment)=35% profit.

    35% gain on $6200.00=$2170.00, Strickler's Profit.
      "   "   7000.00= 2450.00, Ebersole's   "

      $4620.00, Proof.

Ex. 154. The following partners dissolved at the end of the year with a net capital remaining of $2600.00. How should it be adjusted?

J. B. Hoke.		Wm. H. Ramsay.	
May 1...$1600.00	Jan. 1......$8000.00	May 1...$3200.00	Jan. 1....$8000.00
Sept. 1... 3500 00		Sept. 1... 3500.00	
Nov. 1... 900 00		Nov. 1... 700.00	

When the partners of a firm agree to invest certain proportion of the capital upon condition of receiving a fixed share of the profits, the Partner who fails to invest his proportion of the capital, virtually has the use of the difference between his required Investment and the sum actually placed to his credit. If a partner invests less than the sum required, he is charged interest on the deficiency, and if he invests more than the sum required, he is allowed interest on the excess.

To adjust the Partner's Accounts, when the proportion of Profit or Loss is fixed and Interest is allowed on the Excess and charged on the Deficit of each Partner's required Investment.

Principles. 1—Compute the interest on each Investment and Withdrawal from the time they were made to the date of settlement ; subtract the Debit interest from the Credit interest, and the difference will be the interest on each Partner's Net Investment.

2—Add together the Balances of interest thus found, and their sum will be the interest on the entire Net Capital. Find such a proportion of this interest as would be allowed each Partner—the same as if he made the required investment.

3—If the interest of any Partner's Net Average Investment exceeds the interest of his required Investment, the difference will be the Interest due to such Partner ; if less, the difference will be the Interest due from such Partner.

4—The excess of Investments over the Withdrawals, plus the Net Interest due such partner, or minus the Net Interest due by such Partner will be his Present Worth.

5—If the sum of the Withdrawals of one of the Partners be in excess of that of his Investments, such excess, plus the interest thereon, plus the interest on his required Investment, will be his net insolvency.

Note. If any Partner's total Debit interest be greater than his total Credit interest, the difference will be the interest of such Partner's net average indebtedness to the firm, which should be subtracted from the sum of the interest balances to the credit of the remaining Partners, to find the interest of the firm's net average capital. The interest of any Partner's net average indebtedness to the firm should be added to the interest of his required investment to find the total interest due from such Partner.

Ex. 155. The following Partner's Accounts were handed us Dec. 31, for adjustment. The Net Gain was $3600. The Co-partnership was entered into Jan. 1, '93 for one year under the following conditions: Markle was to invest $\frac{4}{9}$ of the capital and share $\frac{4}{9}$ of the gains. McClay was to invest $\frac{3}{9}$ of the capital and share $\frac{3}{9}$ of the gains. McCormick was to invest $\frac{2}{9}$ of the capital and share $\frac{2}{9}$ of the gains. Interest at the rate of 10% per annum was to be allowed each partner investing more than his proportion, and interest was to be charged each partner if he invest less than his proportion.

O. P. Markle.

April 23, '93,	Withdrew,	$1500	Jan. 1, '93,	Invested,	$16000
June 16, '93,	"	800	Mar. 18, '93,	"	2400
Aug. 17, '93,	"	900	Oct. 20, '93,	"	3000
	Total Withdrawn,	$3200		Total Investment,	$21400

Henry McClay.

July 28, '93,	Withdrew,	$600	Jan. 1, '93,	Invested,	$12000
Dec. 4, '93,	"	800	" 21, '93,	"	1800
			May 17, '93,	"	600
	Total Withdrawn,	$1400		Total Investment,	$14400

Wm. McCormick.

Mar. 30, '93,	Withdrew,	$6000	Jan. 1, '93,	Invested,	$6000
Sept. 5, '93,	"	4000	Aug. 3, '93,	"	600
	Total Withdrawn,	$10000		Total Investment,	$6600

ILLUSTRATION.

Jan. 1, '93,	$16000.00	interest for 1 year at 10%....	$1600.00	
Mar. 18, '93,	2400.00	" " 288 days at 10%,	192.00	
Oct. 20, '93,	3000.00	" " 72 " " 10%,	60.00	
	Interest on O. P. Markle's total investment,		——	$1852.00
Apr. 23, '93,	$1500	interest for 252 days at 10%......	$ 105.00	
June 16, '93,	800	" " 198 " " 10%......	44.00	
Aug. 17, '93,	900	" " 136 " " 10%......	34.00	
	Interest on amount withdrawn......................		——	$ 183.00
	Interest due O. P. Markle per his account........			$1669.00

Jan. 1, '93, $12000.00 interest for one year at 10%,	$1200.00	
" 21, '93, 1800.00 " " 344 days " 10%,	172.00	
May 17, '93, 600.00 " " 228 " " 10%,	38.00	
Interest on H. McClay's investment............	———	$1410.00
July 28, '93, $600 interest for 156 days at 10%.......	$ 26.00	
Dec. 4, '93, 800 " " 27 " " 10%.......	6.00	
Interest on amount withdrawn..................	———	$ 32.00
Net Interest due on McClay's investment per his account..		$1378.00
Jan. 1, '93, $6000 interest for one year at 10%......	$ 600.00	
Aug. 3, '93, 600 " " 150 days " 10%......	25.00	
Interest on McCormick's total investment.....	———	$ 625.00
Mar. 30, '93, $6000 interest for 276 days at 10%....	$ 460.00	
Sep. 5, '93, 4000 " " 117 " " 10%....	130.00	
Interest on amount withdrawn..................	———	$590.00
Net Interest due Wm. McCormick per his ac't.		$ 35.00

$1669.00+$1378.00+$35.00=3082. Net interest.
$3082.00÷9=$342.44 $\frac{4}{9}$=$\frac{1}{9}$ "
$342.44 $\frac{4}{9}$ x 4=$1369.78. O. P. Markle's $\frac{4}{9}$ Net interest.
$342.44 $\frac{4}{9}$ x 3=$1027.33. H. McClay's $\frac{3}{9}$ Net interest.
$342.44 $\frac{4}{9}$ x 2=$ 684.89. Wm. McCormick's $\frac{2}{9}$ Net interest.

$1669.00—$1369.78=$299.22, Interest due O. P. Markle.
$1378.00—$1027.33=$350.67, " " H. McClay.
$ 684.89—$ 35.00=$649.89, " from Wm. McCormick.

O. P. Markle invested..................	$21400.00	
Drew out..................................	3200.00	
Net Investment........................	$18200.00	
$\frac{4}{9}$ Net Gain........................	1600.00	
Net Interest per investment..........	$ 1369.78	
Net Int. drew from other partner...	$ 299.22	
Amt. due O. P. Markle Jan. 1, '94,	———	$21469.00

Henry McClay invested................	$14400.00	
Drew out..................................	1400.00	
Net Investment..........................	$13000.00	
$\frac{3}{9}$ Net Gain........................	1200.00	
Net Interest per investment........	1027.33	
Net Int. drew from other partner	350.67	
Am't due H. McClay Jan. 1, '94,	———	$15578.00

Wm. McCormick drew out.........$10000.00
" " invested 6600.00
          ——————
  Insolvency.......................$ 3400.00
Net Interest due partners........... 649.89
          ——————
          $ 4049.89
Less ⅔ Net Gain....................... 800.00
Wm. McCormick's insolvency, } —————— $3249.89
 January 1, '94................ }

Explanation. First compute the interest on the Investments and Withdrawals of each Partner, and find the total Net Interest to be $3082.00. Dividing this sum by 9 gives ⅑ of the Net Interest due the Partners in proportion to their Investments; and multiplying by 4, 3, and 2 respectively, gives the Net Interest due each Partner at their required proportions. Since O. P. Markle's proportion was $1369.78, while his Actual Net Interest was $1669.00, the difference, or $299.22, must be due him from one or both the other Partners. So, also, there is a difference of $350.67 due H. McClay. As but $35.00 interest is credited to Wm. McCormick, when, if he invested his proportion, there should be due him $684 89, it is evident he must owe the other Partners the difference between $35 00 and $684.89, or $649.89. Markle's Net Investment, added to his ⅓ gain and Net Interest, amounts to $21,469.00, the sum due him Jan. 1, '94. H. McClay's Net Interest and ⅓ Net Gain, added to his Net Investment, will amount to $15,578.00, or the sum due him Jan. 1, '94. Wm. McCormick, being insolvent, would have been $4049.89 were it not for his ⅔ Net Gain, or $800.00. Deducting his Net Gain, or $800.00, from $4049.89, we have $3249.89, the sum due the other Partners by Wm. McCormick Jan. 1, '94.

Hence the following Journal entry to adjust the interest:

Wm. McCormick.............. $649.89
  To O. P. Markle....... $299.22
  " H. McClay.........   350.67

Ex. 156. Webster, Clay & Calhoun formed a co-partnership Jan. 1, '93, to invest equally and share in Gains and Losses equally. They were to pay interest at 9% per annum if the investment be less than agreed, and were to receive interest if investment be in excess. Jan. 1, '94, Webster retired from the firm. What was the condition and interest of each partner? Net Gain, $6842.19. Partners' Accounts as follows:

Webster.

May 5, '93, Withdrew..... **$1200**	Jan. 1, '93, Invested....... **$8000**
Aug. 13, '93, " 1800	April 15, '93, " 6400
Nov. 16, '93, " 2400	May 20, '93, " 4000
	June 24. '93, " 1600

Clay.

Mar. 26, '93, Withdrew... **$3000**	Jan. 1, '93, Invested....... **$9000**
May 5, '93, " ... 8000	July 24, '93, " 9000
June 14, '93, " ... 5500	Oct. 12, '93, " 1600
Sept. 2nd, '93, " ... 4800	

Calhour.

April 27, '93, Withdrew.... **$2000**	Jan. 1, '93, Invested....... **$7500**
June 4, '93, " 3600	" 25, '93, " 6000
Aug. 2, '93, " 800	Feb. 14, '93, " 4000
	May 25, '93, " 2800

Give the full solution of this adjustment.

To Find the Net Gain or Net Loss.

Principle. Add the Partners' Investments to the other Liabilities and subtract their sum from the sum of the Resources, and the difference will be the Net Gain. Or subtract the sum of the Resources from the sum of the Partners' Investments and the other Liabilities, and the difference will be the Net Loss.

Ex. 157. A. G. Norris and James Ferguson entered into co-partnership. A. G. Norris invested $2200 and Jas. Ferguson invested $2800 ; at the end of the year the firm had cash $4625 ; Bills received $3500, Mdse. 3282. They owed Benton, Myers & Co. $1200 and Bills Payable $1827. What was the condition, Loss or Gain, and how much ?

Note. This principle will not be illustrated, as it is fully explained in the lesson of changing from Single to Double Entry.

To find the Net Capital of a firm at commencing, the Net Loss or Net Gain, the Assets and Liabilities being given, except the investments.

Principle. Deduct the sum of the Liabilities, omitting the Par.-ner's Investments from the sum of the Assets, and the difference will be the Present Worth. Deduct the Net Gain or add the Net Loss from the Present Worth, thus found and the result will be the Net Capital at commencing.

Should such Liabilities exceed the Assets deduct from their sum the sum of the Assets and the difference will be the Firm's Present Insolvency. From the Insolvency thus found deduct the Net Loss and the difference will be the Firm's Net Capital at commencing.

Ex. 158. Laird and Thomas entered into a co-partnership, to share gains or losses equally. At the Settlement their Assets were Mdse. $9320.00, Bills Received $1420.00, Cash $7240.00, Real Estate $11600.00. The Liabilities were due King & Co. $2720.00, Bills Payable $6200.00, due on Bond and Mortgage $2250.00, and a Net Gain $2410.00. Laird invested $\frac{5}{8}$ of the capital and Thomas $\frac{3}{8}$. How much did each invest?

ILLUSTRATION.

Resources.		Liabilities.	
Mdse...........................$9320.00		Bills Payable...............$6200.00	
Bills Rec'd.................. 1420.00		King & Co.........,...... 2720.00	
Cash 7240.00		Bond & Mort. Payable.. 2250.00	
Real Estate.................11600.00		Total Liabilities........11170.00	
Total Resources..........29580.00			
Total Liabilities..........11170.00			
Present Worth............18410.00		$\frac{5}{8}$ of $16000.00=$10000.00,	
Less Net Gain............. 2410.00		Laird's Investment.	
Net Cap'l at Commenc't,16000.00		$\frac{3}{8}$ of $16000.00=$6000.00, Thomas' Investment.	

Ex. 159. Smith and Randolph formed a co-partnership; Smith invested $\frac{5}{8}$ of the capital and Randolph $\frac{3}{8}$. How much did each partner invest according to the following. Assets: Mdse. $4700.00, Cash $1875.00, Real Estate $12500.00, Personal Accounts $2840.00, Bills Received $2400.00. Liabilities: Personal Accounts $4625, Bills Payable $3560, Mortgage Payable $8000.00, Interest Payable $72.00. Their Net Loss being $4342.

To Find the Insolvency at Commencing.

Principle. Subtract the sum of the Resources from the sum of the Liabilities, when the latter are greater than the former. To the difference thus found add the Net Gain or deduct from it the Net Loss, or should the sum of the Assets be greater than that of the Liabilities, subtract the latter from the former. Add to the difference thus found the Net Loss, or subtract from it the Net Gain. The result will be the Firm's Insolvency at commencing.

Ex. 160. Boltz and Schwartz are partners. At the beginning they were insolvent. At closing, their Resources were Mdse. $13800.00, Cash $4200.00, First National Bank Stock $2175. Liabilities: Brown

& Co. $8432.00, Husband & Bro. $4435.00, Mortgage Payable, $8050, Bills Payable $3500.00.   Net Gain $11758.00, shared equally.   Boltz' proportion of the insolvency was $\frac{5}{8}$ and Schwartz $\frac{3}{8}$.   What was each partner's insolvency at commencing.

ILLUSTRATION.

Resources.		Liabilities.	
Mdse.......................$13800.00		Brown & Co.............$ 8432.00	
Cash........................ 4200.00		Husband & Bro......... 4435.00	
1st Nat'l Bank Stock.. 2175.00		Mort. Pay.......... ..... 8050.00	
		Bills Pay................. 3500 00	
$20175.00			
			$24417.00
$16000.00 $\times$ $\frac{5}{8}$=$10000.00, Boltz' Insolvency.		Total Resources...... 20175.00	
$16000.00 $\times$ $\frac{3}{8}$ = $6000.00, Schwartz' Insolvency.		Net Gain...................	$ 4242.00 11758.00
		Insolv'y of firm at com. $16000.00	

PROOF.

Boltz' Ins. at com.$10000.00		Brown & Co........................$ 8432.00	
" half net gain 5879.00		Husband & Co.................... 4435 00	
		Mort. Pay........................ 8050.00	
B.'s Pres. Insolv..	$ 4121.00	Bills Pay......................... 3500.00	
S.'s Ins. at com....$ 6000.00			
" half net gain.. 5879.00			
S.'s Pres. Insolv...	$ 121.00		
Resources...........	20175.00		
	$24417.00		$24417.00

Ex. 161.   Knight, White & Wright are partners.   At commencing Knight was insolvent $\frac{4}{11}$, White $\frac{5}{11}$, and Wright $\frac{2}{11}$.   Losses and Gains shared equally.   What was the net insolvency of each at commencing, and the condition of each partner at closing, from the following statement?

Assets.		Liabilities.	
J. P. Barr................. $2369.00		Johns & Co............... $1614.77	
O. P. Shupe.............. 3140.00		W. A. Biddle........... 3164.37	
J. D. Brown.............. 435.00		O. D. Myer............... 3765.14	
Cash. 5160.00		J. L. Hndson........... 1211.62	
Bills Rec.................. 4432.71		Fox & Co................. 1240.72	
Int. Rec................... 178.45		Bills Payable........... 8469.11	
Real Estate.............. 2100.00		Loss and Gain (net)... 882.96	

CHAPTER SIX.

Ex. 162. Boyd & Lyon formed a co-partnership; the investments and withdrawals were as shown in the following accounts. At the end of the year, Boyd purchased Lyon's entire interest for spot cash. How much did he pay him? Net gain of $1860.00, shared equally.

Dr.	Boyd.	Cr.	Dr.	Lyon.	Cr.
$250.00		$3000.00			$2000.00
		1720.00			2200.00

Ex. 163: Dodge and Hodge are partners in business. Dodge invested $7000.00 for 4 months and $6000.00 for 8 months. Hodge invested $3000.00 for 2 months, $9000.00 for 3 months, and $8000.00 for 5 months. Losses and Gains shared in proportion to the average investment. Net Gain $7280.00. What was each partner's share of the gain?

Ex. 164.

J. P. Keller.

7—4—'93,	$10000.00	1—1—'93,	$14000.00

F. A. Plotner.

7—4—'93,	$8000.00	1—1—'93,	$14000.00

Wm. Todd.

7—4—'93,	$12000.00	1—1—'93,	$21000.00

What was the interest of each partner Jan. 1, 1894? If Keller was to invest $\frac{2}{7}$ of the capital, Plotner $\frac{3}{7}$, and Todd $\frac{2}{7}$? Losses or gains equally divided, and interest at 8% allowed on each side of the partners' accounts. Net Gain $12,000.

Ex. 165. Doe, Roe & Coe were partners in business, sharing losses and gains equally. Each partner was to pay $4.00 for every day absent. Doe lost 20 days, Roe lost 25 days, and Coe lost 30 days. How would you adjust the matter, if the partners agreed to settle between themselves, without making any entries upon the books?

Ex. 166. What was the Gain or Loss from the following statement?

Assets.		Liabilities.	
Mdse..........................	$7224.00	Bills Pay...................	$ 2800.00
Cash........	4324.00	H. R. Freed.............	8200.00
Bills Rec....................	1300.00	B. F. Biller.............	4500.00
J. H. Brown..............	8500.00	Stock (Investment)....	12000.00

Ex. 167. How would you adjust the following statement, if Losses and Gains are equally shared? Was there a net gain or a net loss? Is the statement correct? What was each partner's net capital after adjustment? What was the correct amount of sales?

M. T. Herrick.		Samuel Mather.	
$7381.00 ||	$13246.00	$5369.00 ||	$12863.00

Assets.		Liabilities.	
Cash..........................	$3125.25	Bills Pay...................	$2575.00
Mdse	4222.84	Int. Pay....................	172.49
Bills Rec....................	375.00	Accounts Pay............	310.71
Accounts Rec.............	1784.67	Mortgage Pay............	2000.00
Fur. and Fix.............	1596.00	Int. Pay....................	65.18
Real Estate................	4500.00		
Horse and Wagon........	520.00		

Merchandise.		Expense.	
Bo't, $6128.07 || Sales, $62324.33		Total, $2148.94 ||	

Ex. 168. What was each partner's insolvency at commencing and each one's net capital at closing? The statement at closing as follows:

Resources.		Liabilities.	
Bills Rec....................	$1644.00	Bills Pay...................	$2149.00
Cash.........................	2440.60	P. D. Myer................	3241.67
Accounts Rec............	4234.73	W. E. Kneale...	1340.33

Woodburn withdrew $260.00. Rush paid sundry expenses for the firm $375.00. Net Gain $2136.72.

Ex. 169. Suppose the total Liabilities of a firm, including the Partners' investments, to be $18794.16, and the total Resources, except the amount of cash on hand, $12414.20, and net gain of $1240.60. If all accounts were correct and the Cash Book and cash were in the safe, what balance of cash should the Cash Book show?

Ex. 170. Brown, Black, Green & Gray formed a co-partnership. Brown was to receive $\frac{1}{8}$ of the gains, Black $\frac{1}{4}$, Green $\frac{1}{6}$, and Gray $\frac{1}{8}$. The remainder of the gains to be placed to Reserve Fund. Each Partner was to invest $12000.00, on condition of receiving the above proportion of profits; but Brown invested but $10000.00, Black $9000.00. In consequence of the failure of Brown and Black to invest $12000.00, how should the gain be divided among all the partners? Net Gain $18240.00.

Ex. 171. M. E. Johnson and T. F. Beidler formed a co-partnership. Johnson invests $2000.00; Beidler invests $4000.00. Johnson to manage the business for $50.00 per month, which is to be paid by Beidler, as Beidler is not required to devote any time to the business. Seven % interest is to be allowed the partner investing more than the other, and Gains and Losses are to be equally shared. At the end of the first year the following abstract is taken from the books. Beidler wishes to retire from the firm and is willing to leave $3000.00 of his capital with Johnson on 6% interest for 6 months, the balance to be paid in cash. In settlement Johnson purchased from Beidler his share in the doubtful accounts at a discount of $66\frac{2}{3}$%. (10% of the Accts. Rec. considered doubtful.) What is Beidler's interest upon settlement? How much cash is due Beidler from Johnson? and what was Johnson's net income from the business? Johnson withdrew $850.00; average time $4\frac{1}{2}$ months. Beidler is charged with $760.00 (excluding salary of Johnson); average time 5 months and 20 days.

Assets.		Liabilities.	
Mdse	$6493.68	Bills Pay.	$2834.60
Bills Rec.	1921.60	Int. "	43.84
Int. Rec.	194.60	Accts. "	373.42
Cash	1096.40		
Accounts Rec.	2184.50		
Horse and Wagon, Etc.	370.00		
Fur. and Fix.	294.00		

Ex. 172. John, Harry, James and Samuel have been doing business as partners, John and Harry each receiving $\frac{5}{16}$ of the profits, James $\frac{1}{4}$, and Samuel $\frac{1}{8}$. James retired from the business. After closing the books for a settlement with James, his account showed a credit balance of $1960.00. The new firm give their Note to James for his interest. What entry?

You may ask, Why introduce an example so simple? Who so ignorant as not to be able to answer it correctly? Well, notwithstanding its extreme simplicity, the case is one which, after being under litigation for several years, engaging the attention of courts and learned counsel, and consuming a large amount of money in the payment of costs and fees, was submitted to the author on the supposition that some extremely difficult points were involved therein. What, spend several years, consume the time of court and counsel, to solve this problem? Yes. Well, but, you ask, what was the difficulty? As the transaction is here stated, what is there connected with it out of which a dispute could arise? Nothing. What was the nature of the difficulty? It was the division of James' capital among the remaining partners. John and Henry claimed that they should be credited each with $\frac{7}{18}$ of it, and Samuel with $\frac{1}{8}$ of it; Samuel, on the other hand, contended that each should be credited with $\frac{1}{3}$ of it. All the difficulty grew out of the idea that the capital of the new firm was the same as that of the old firm, not knowing that, in retiring, James had withdrawn his capital, leaving the remaining partners in exactly the same condition, as to capital, after, as they were before the dissolution. For, in retiring, James, on taking the firm's Note, withdrew his capital just as effectually as if they had paid him in cash. The Assets of the new firm, of course, were identical with those of the old firm, but its Liabilities were greater by the amount of the Note given to James, hence its capital was so much less than the old firm's. They were, therefore, contending about the division of a thing that did not exist, and, as it frequently happens, both parties were mistaken, though it is not to be presumed that their long contention had, in the slightest, improved their tempers, or better fitted them to perceive and admit the truth when properly presented. However, to do the parties justice, must say that when the question was once fairly explained to them, they accepted the solution with much better grace than is usual in such cases,—probably from the fact that each had the satisfaction of knowing that, although he was in error, his opponent was not right. I should not attempt to predict the fate of the bookkeeper that would allow his employers to go to law over such a trifling little thing; however I can imagine the wrath heaped upon his empty head.

CHAPTER SEVEN.

Stock Company or Corporation Accounting.

A corporation was described by Chief Justice Marshall as "an artificial being, invisible, intangible, and existing only in contemplation of law." A corporation has also been designated a legal entity, a creature of the law, a legal institution, a fictitious or political person. These and similar definitions have received the approval of many eminent authorities.

According to Kyd, a corporation is "a collection of many individuals united into one body, under a special denomination, having perpetual succession under an artificial form, and vested by the policy of the law with the capacity of acting in several respects as an individual, particularly of taking and granting property, of contracting obligations, of suing and being sued, of enjoying privileges and immunities in common, and of exercising a variety of political rights, more or less extensive according to the design of its institution, or the powers conferred upon it, either at the time of its creation or any subsequent period of its existence."

If this definition be correctly understood, it is not inconsistent with that given by Chief Justice Marshall, who treats the collection of individuals constituting the corporation as a united body, and personifies it, while he considers the individuals who together compose this body merely as component parts. Kyd, on the other hand, describes a corporation as a collection of many individuals authorized to act *as if they were one person*. It is apparent that both definitions describe the same thing regarded from different points of view.

The word "corporation" is but a collective name for the corporators or members who compose an incorporated association; and where it is said that a corporation is itself a person, or being, or creature, this must be understood in a figurative sense only. While a corporation may, from one point of view, be considered as an entity, without regard to the corporators who compose it, the fact remains self-evident that a corporation is not *in reality* a person or a thing distinct from its constituent parts.

The conception of a number of individuals as a corporate or col-' lective entity occurs in the earliest stages of human development, and is essential to many of the most ordinary processes of thought. Thus the existence of tribes, villages, communities, families,˙ clans, and nations implies a conception of these several bodies of individuals as entities having corporate rights and attributes.   An ordinary co-partnership or firm is constantly treated as a united or corporate body in the actual transactions of business, though it is not recognized in that light in the procedure of the courts of law.   So, in numberless other instances, associations which are not legally incorporated are consid-ered as personified entities acting as a unit and in one name,—such as political parties, societies, committees, courts, etc.

A legally constituted corporation is ordinarily treated at law, as well as in the transaction of ordinary business, as a distinct entity or person, without regard to its membership.   In most cases this is a just as well as convenient means of working out the rights of the real persons interested; however, it is essential to a clear understanding of many important branches of the law of corporations to bear in mind distinctly that the existence of a corporation independently of its share-holders is a fiction ; and that the rights and duties of an incorporated association are in reality the rights and duties of the persons who com-pose it, and not of an imaginary being.

Different Kinds of Corporations.—Aggregate and Sole.

The word "corporation" has been applied to various widely dissimilar classes of institutions.   Thus, certain corporations, called corporations *aggregate*, are composed of many members ; while others, called corporations *sole*, consist of a single person each.   The King, the Governor of a State, or any other public officer who is invested with any of the attributes of a corporation by reason of his official position, is in this respect a corporation sole.

Private and Public Corporations.

Corporations have also been divided into *public* corporations and *private* corporations.   The difference between these two classes of corporations is radical, and hence they are in many instances governed by widely different principles of law.   Private corporations are asso-ciations formed by the voluntary agreement of their members, such as manufacturing, railroad and banking companies.   Public corporations are merely government institutions, created by law, for the administration of the public affairs of the community. States, counties and municipalities are examples of public corporations.

Whether a corporation be public or private depends wholly upon its organization. Shares in a corporation may be held by a State in the same manner as by a private individual. The fact that a part, or even all, of the shares in a corporation are held by the State, does not necessarily render it a public corporation. A State may undoubtedly establish a bank as a government agency, subject to government control, thus giving it the characteristics of a public corporation, unless prohibited by the Constitution ; but if a corporation is formed by the State with transferable shares, for the purpose of conducting the banking business in the same manner as a private corporation, it must be classed as a private corporation in name as well as in fact.

Religious, Charitable and Civil Corporations.

Private corporations have been subdivided into *ecclesiastical* or religious corporations, *eleemosynary* or charitable corporations, and *civil* corporations.

Religious corporations are those which are formed for the advancement of religion, or the administration of church property for religious purposes. The distinguishing feature of charitable corporations is that they are formed for the administration of charitable trusts, and not for the profit of the incorporators themselves. The term "*civil* corporations" applies to all those incorporated associations which are formed for the temporal benefit of their members, such as railroad companies, manufacturing companies, banks, clubs, and other associations of a similar character.

The real nature of a corporation, in every case, depends upon the charter or articles of association under which it is formed, and must be determined by reference thereto ; whether the association should be termed a public, or private, or religious, or charitable, or civil corporation is simply a question regarding the meaning of those words.

Quasi Corporations.

Associations and government institutions possessing only a portion of the attributes which distinguish ordinary private or public corporations have sometimes been denominated *quasi* corporations.

Towns and other political divisions, school districts, boards of commissioners, overseers or trustees of the poor, etc., having authority to act and bring suit as united bodies without regard to their membership for the time being, are *quasi* corporations of a public character. Individual public officers having authority to sue, in their official capacities, upon contracts made with their predecessors in office, are examples of quasi corporations sole. Joint stock companies may be cited as quasi corporations of a private character. They are associations having some of the features of an ordinary common law partnership, and some of the features of a private corporation. Their constitution varies greatly, and they may be found of every possible variety, from an ordinary copartnership to a corporation in the strictest sense of the word. Their real organization and character must in each case be determined by the laws and articles of agreement under which they are formed; whether they are to be called co-partnerships, or joint stock companies, or corporations, is solely a question of definition.

The Formation of Joint Stock Companies or Corporations.

Preceding the organization of any Joint Stock Company, the objects, the utility, and the probabilities and possibilities of its success are discussed by those who originate the idea or devise the plan of the proposed company. Frequently a prospectus is issued, setting forth in detail the plan of the originators, thereby securing numerous subscribers to the capital stock. When the plans for the organization of a stock company are complete, the first step to be taken is to call a meeting of the projectors and intended stockholders, and proceed to draw a charter or articles of incorporation, which must contain—

The name of the corporation, which shall begin with the word "The" and end with the word "Company," unless the organization is not for profit. (This is not required by all states.)

The place where it is to be located, or where its principal business is to be transacted.

The purpose for which it is formed.

The amount of its capital stock, if it is to have capital stock, and the number of shares into which the stock is divided, etc.

The different States have their own laws regarding the formation of corporations, and should be thoroughly understood before attempting to incorporate into a stock company.

This charter or article of association, when drawn according to statute, is signed by the incorporators, and acknowledged before any person authorized to take acknowledgments. The official character of the officer before whom the acknowledgment of the articles of incorporation is made shall be certified to by the clerk of the court of the county in which the acknowledgment is taken.

The charter or articles of incorporation are then forwarded to the Secretary of State, who shall record the same, and a copy, duly certified by him, shall be *prima facie* evidence of the existence of such corporation.

Subscriptions to the capital stock are then made, and a certain percentage paid up, according to the laws of the different States.

Until the corporation has been fully and completely organized under the laws of the State, no attempt should be made to do business.

An Unlimited Liability Corporation is one in which the stockholders are individually liable for the debts of the company.

A Single or Limited Liability Corporation is one in which the stockholders are liable only for the amount unpaid on their shares.

A Double Liability Corporation is one in which the shareholders are liable for an amount equal to their subscriptions or shares. All U. S. National banks are corporations of double liability.

Note. The liability of shareholders and the rights of creditors is a branch of law that every one should thoroughly understand. The subject as it is treated in chapter 22, though brief, will be found invaluable to the investor.

Capital Stock, or *authorized capital*, is the par amount of capital authorized by the charter or articles of incorporation. The *paid-in capital* is the amount received from the stockholders on the shares for which they have subscribed.

Capital Stock Increased or Decreased. A corporation has no implied authority to alter the amount of its capital stock, when the charter has definitely fixed the capital at a certain sum. The shares of a corporation can neither be increased nor diminished in number, or in their nominal value, unless this be expressly authorized by the company's charter. It follows, therefore, that a corporation cannot buy its own stock, unless expressly authorized by its charter to do so, for such purchase would diminish the amount of the company's capital. There are exceptional cases, however, in which a corporation may become a purchaser or transferee of shares of its own stock, although its charter does not authorize a reduction of capital ; as, for example, where the shares are received in discharge of a debt which cannot be collected otherwise, or where the shares are received as a gift, and the company's real capital therefore remains undiminished. When a company does receive or become owner of its own stock, it is held as

Treasury Stock.

Treasury Stock is stock held by the Treasurer. and is considered an asset, to be sold as an opportunity may offer. Frequently a company is organized and the entire capital stock is subscribed and paid in, and that the whole capital is then invested in plant or machinery, leaving the company without funds to operate its business. In this case the stockholders. instead of increasing the capital stock, donate *pro rata* to the company a specified number of shares, to be put on the market and sold for Working Capital.

Working or Operating Capital. Many corporations set aside a certain amount of money for the purpose of conducting the business, which is kept in a working capital account.

Watered stock is stock issued above the authorized capital, which is sometimes distributed among the shareholders without payment. When the amount of the capital stock of a corporation is fixed by its character or articles of association no authority exists to alter the amount so fixed, or to issue additional shares. The agents of the corporation, and even the majority of the stockholders, would have no authority to create new shares after the limit fixed by the charter or articles of association of the company was reacted. The issue of certificates for any shares in excess of the amount so fixed would therefore be unauthorized, commonly called watered, for such certificates would involve a false representation to the world that the holder of the certificate was a shareholder in the company.

The Par or Nominal Value of Stock is the sum named in the certificate of stock. When stock sells for more than the original or par value, it is said to be above par, or at a premium ; when for less, it is below par, or at a discount.

Preferred Stock is stock taking preference of the ordinary stock of a corporation ; one on which a dividend is declared out of net earning, before any dividend can be declared on the common stock.

Preferred stock can be issued only when authorized by its charter, and is issued to obtain means to carry on the business; or in case of re-organization 'of railroads, etc., preferred stock is issued to prevent the sacrifice of the company's property.

Guaranteed Stock is entitled to its stipulated dividend before all other classes, whether it is earned in any one year or not, as its right to an annual dividend is carried over from year to year, thus rendering the shares especially valuable.

Clandestine Stock is stock issued secretly for the purpose of raising funds to cover losses or expenses unknown to the public.

The **Market Value** of stocks and bonds is what they will sell for in open market. The market value of bonds depends upon the certainty of their payment at maturity, and the interest they bear compared with the current rate of interest in the money market. The value of stocks depends upon the dividends they pay, etc.

A **Dividend** is a division of the profits among the stockholders of a corporation. Dividends are declared annually, semi-annually, or quarterly.

A **Cash Dividend** is a dividend paid in cash.

An **Installment Dividend** is applied on the stockholders' unpaid subscriptions. It is equivalent to paying the dividend in cash and then collecting the installment.

A **Stock Dividend** is a dividend paid by issuing to the stockholders new stock, or, in the absence of a profit, it may be additional stock, to be paid out of the capital or the future profits of the company. Stock is watered if dividends are so paid.

A **Fictitious Dividend.** If the business of a company has been conducted without profit, the directors will often inflate the value of stock in trade, plant or other asset of the company, or charge large items of expense to property accounts to create a net gain. When this is done, as is too often the case, a false or fictitious profit is shown, from which a fictitious dividend is declared, although it is dishonest and unlawful.

It frequently happens that companies do not make a profit, from unusual causes. When this is the case, a dividend can be declared from the surplus fund which has been set aside for such contingencies. A dividend from the surplus fund is not classed as a fictitious dividend.

Franchise is a special privilege granted to certain parties or corporations, by the municipal, State or general government. A street railroad is granted the privilege of laying tracks and operating street cars on certain streets, etc. Their right is a franchise.

An **Assessment** is a levy or tax at a certain per cent; is collected from the stockholders to make up losses, etc.

An **Installment** is a call upon the unpaid stock which subscribers are required to pay at a specified time.

A **Trust** is an organization for the control of several corporations under one management by the devise of a transfer by the stockholders in each corporation of a majority of the stock to a central committee or board of trustees, who issue in return to such stockholders certificates showing in effect that, although they have parted with their stock they are still entitled to dividends.

A **Syndicate** is an association of persons or corporations formed for the purpose of promoting some particular enterprise, or discharge some trust.

Gross Earnings are the total receipts of a company.

Net Earnings or Net Profits are what remain after deducting all expenses.

Bonds are written or printed obligations of individuals, corporations, cities, States or nations, to pay a specified sum of money at a specified time. Bonds usually bear interest at a fixed rate, payable annually, semi-annually or quarterly. Bonds issued by a State or nation usually have no other security than the confidence of the people, while those issued by individuals or corporations, for loans, are secured by mortgages upon their property.

Bonds are known according to their priority of lien, the class or characteristics of the property upon which they are secured, such as First Mortgage, Second Mortgage, etc., Consols, Income, Sinking Fund, etc.

Registered Bonds are bonds that are payable to the order of the holder or owner; consequently cannot be negotiated unless assignment be duly acknowledged.

Coupon Bonds are those having interest coupons or tickets attached, which specify the amount of interest due each year, half year or quarter. They are detached and presented for payment when the interest is due.

Bonds also derive their name from the rate of interest they bear, or from the dates at which they are payable, or from both, such as 5-twenties of '62.

Hypothecating Stocks and Bonds is depositing them as collateral security for borrowed money, etc.

A Mortgage is a conditional deed conveying the real or personal property to the creditor as fully, and in precisely the same way, as if it were sold to him outright. It is given as security for the payment of a debt, etc.

Collaterals are **Securities,** Bonds, Stocks, Notes, etc., which are pledged, or placed in the hands of the lender as security for the performance of covenants or the payment of money, in addition to the principal security.

Surplus Fund, or Reserve Fund, is a certain portion of the annual profits of a company, set aside for the purpose of creating a fund to meet reverse in profits, or unforseen emergencies, etc. No well regulated corporation will declare a dividend equal to the net profits.

Bonus is a premium or commission given for a charter, or for some special privilege granted to a corporation. It may be paid in cash or in stock of the company.

Rebate is a discount from the nominal value or price. Stocks are sometimes sold or issued at a certain per. cent. rebate on the nominal or par value.

The immense amount of property now embarked in Banking, Insurance, Manufacturing, Railroad and Mercantile Corporations, gives an importance to this subject scarcely inferior to any other at the present time. Thousands of corporations are being incorporated every year throughout the United States, and to-day more than three-quarters of the entire wealth of the nation is controlled by corporations.

The importance of a proper regulation of corporations by the State is receiving the attention of our Legislators. The manner in which three-quarters of the nation's resources is managed is a matter of most vital concern to every inhabitant of the country. The solidarity of interests is such that all must be affected thereby. A humane, discreet, and honest administration of this enormous property will contribute very perceptibly to the prosperity of our country, while a dishonest, wasteful, and soulless management of corporate interests must exercise a baleful influence upon our entire economic life, and upon those other higher spheres of national life to which it should minister. It is not merely the fact that more than three-quarters of the resources of the country now belong to corporations which should exact serious thought, it is the drift of things which is of the most importance. The corporate principle is daily extending. What is to be the outcome of this? Let us have corporation laws to protect the investing public by requiring periodical examinations of their accounts and financial affairs, by competent accountants. Let us have a National Association of Experts to meet the requirements of such laws, and give our profession the prominence it is justly entitled to.

CHAPTER EIGHT.

The Books Used in Stock Company Accounting.

The general account books of a corporation are similar to those used by firms and individuals. There are, however, a number of auxiliary books necessary in a corporation that are not required in the ordinary partnerships. These auxiliary books are: the Minute Book, Subscription Book, Installment Book, Installment Scrip Book, Certificate of Stock Book, Transfer Book, Stock Ledger, and Dividend Book.

The forms given for these auxiliary books will be found to answer every requirement, although most corporations have forms adapted to their own business. Very frequently, however, the accounting of large companies is on the poorest principles. Stock company books should be arranged and kept by the best methods and accountants that it is possible to procure. The managing officers should know the true condition of their books in every detail, at all times, and should be ready at an hour's notice to render a statement to the Directors and Stockholders. Such a system depends upon the ability of the accountant.

Minute Book.

The Minute Book is a journal or record of the proceedings of the Board of Directors and stockholders of the corporation. It is generally kept by the Secretary or Cashier, and is made up mostly of the resolutions passed, the business transacted, and the names of the members present.

It is not customary or necessary to take down the remarks or opinions expressed by the members. When matters of this kind are introduced in this book, it is done for the purpose of giving the reader a better view of the existing circumstances. It is usual, however, to record the more important resolutions which were not passed, especially such as were defeated by a recorded vote of ayes and nays. Very often the minutes of a meeting consist of nothing beyond the date, names of the members present, and the signature of the Secretary.

Subscription Book.

This Book contains the names and addresses of the subscribers to the Capital Stock, and the number of shares subscribed for by each subscriber.

CLEVELAND, O., January 1st, 1894.

We, the undersigned subscribers to the Charter and By-Laws of the Union Rolling Mill Co., do hereby subscribe for the amount of the Capital Stock of the above-named company set opposite to our respective names in this Subscription Book.

Date.		Names.	Number of Shares.	Address.
1894 January	1	O. D. Myer,	One Hundred shares,	40 Euclid Ave.
		J. B. Higbee,	One Hundred shares,	1220 Euclid Ave.
		H. B. Hunt,	Two Hundred shares,	20 Hickox St.
		A. K. Hudson,	Fifty shares,	980 Doan St.
		H. A. Dixon,	Four Hundred shares,	Buffalo, N. Y.
		T. C. Willard,	Two Hundred shares,	Soc. for Savings Bld.
		D. W. Johns,	One Hundred shares,	Pittsburg, Pa.

In witness to the foregoing subscriptions, and to the signatures, we, the undersigned, do hereby subscribe our names in the city of Cleveland, State of Ohio, January 1st, 1894.   R. H. BOYD, President.

N. C. BOSWORTH, Secretary.

Note.—Subscriptions are binding from the time they are made, although the contract by which stock subscribers become members of a corporation does not go into effect until all conditions precedent have been complied with and the corporation is created. The contract of the subscribers is not a contract with the corporation, but a contract between themselves. It has been held that a mutual contract to become shareholders in a corporation to be formed thereafter is binding, even at common law.

Installment Book.

This Book is made out from the Subscription Book.

From this Book the totals of Installments paid in are carried to the General Cash Book, and from this Book the individual stockholders or subscribers to the capital stock are credited for the payments, in the accounts in the Stock Ledger.

The Installment Lists are made out just before an Installment becomes due.

Installment List No. 1.

Subscription to the Capital Stock of the Union Rolling Mill Co. First Installment 10% due January 10, 1894.

When Due.		Names.	No. of Shares.	Amount of Installment		Interest.	Amount Received.	L. F.	When Paid.
Jan.	10	O. D. Myer	100	$1000	00		$1000 00		Jan. 10, 1894
"	10	J. B. Higbee	100	1000	00		1000 00		Jan. 10, 1894
"	10	H. B. Hunt	200	2000	00		2000 00		Jan. 10, 1894
"	10	A. K. Hudson	50	500	00		500 00		Jan. 10, 1894
"	10	H. A. Dixon	400	4000	00	$15 50	4015 50		Jan. 20, 1894
"	10	T. C. Willard	200	2000	00		2000 00		Jan. 10, 1894
"	10	D. W. Johns	100	1000	00		1000 00		Jan. 10, 1894
				$11500	00	$15 50	$11515 50		

MEMORANDA:

January 10th, entered in Cash Book $7500.00
January 20th,   "   "   "   4015.50
                                    ————————
                                    $11515.50

Installment Scrip Book.

This Book is filled up with stubs and receipts which are given to the stockholders when money is paid on their subscriptions. When the stock is all paid in, these receipts are surrendered to the company and Certificates of Stock issued.

Form of Installment Scrip Book.

Installment Scrip No. I. Cleveland, O., Jan. 10, '94. 100 Shares. 1st Installment 10 per cent. $1000.00 Received the scrip O. D. Myer.	INSTALLMENT SCRIP.	$1000.00. 100 Shares. THE UNION ROLLING MILL COMPANY. Received from...........O. D. Myer.........the sum of ....One Thousand................ ....Dollars, the same being Ten Per Cent. and the First Installment on One Hundred Shares of the Capital Stock of THE UNION ROLLING MILL COMPANY. Said shares are reserved and set apart for him or his assigns on condition of the fulfillment of the terms of subscription. In witness whereof, we hereunto subscribe our names this tenth day of January, 1894. N. C. Bosworth, Sec'y. R. H. Boyd, Prest.

Certificate of Stock Book.

This is a Book of blank certificates and stubs, usually a work of the engraver's art. These certificates are issued to the stockholders in exchange for the Installment Scrip, when the full subscription to the capital stock has been paid. On the back of these certificates a blank form is printed for transferring.

Form of Stock Certificate.

No. 67.	INCORPORATED UNDER THE LAWS OF OHIO.
No of Shares, **10.**	**No. 67.** ✳✳ **Shares 10.**
To whom issued.	**The Kneale & Gibbons Printing Co.**
Seth Scott.	**OAPITAL STOOK, $50,000 00.**
Dated *May 3rd*, 1894.	This Certifies that......*Seth Scott*.........is the owner of
	...................*Ten*...........Shares of the Capital Stock of
From whom trans-	*The Kneale & Gibbons Printing Co.*. transferable only on
ferred.	the Books of the Corporation in person or by Attorney
	on surrender of this Certificate.
Received Certificate	In Witness Whereof, the duly authorized officers
No.	of the Corporation have hereunto subscribed their
	names and caused the corporate Seal to be affixed
Issued Certificate	at *Cleveland, O.*, this *Third* day of *May*, A.D. 1894.
No.	*Wm. Low*, Prest. *John Smith*, Sec'y.

Note.—When the Stock is sold or transferred the old certificate is returned and a new one is issued.

Transfer Book.

This is a Book of printed forms and blanks, to be filled up on occasion of a stockholder transferring any part of the shares standing on the Stock Ledger in his name. Each certificate authorizes the Secretary, Cashier, President or Agent, to transfer a certain number of shares from the account of the signer to that of some other party. Transfers are also made by Powers of Attorney, which Powers of Attorney are left with the company and are usually attached to the stub. From this book transfers are posted into the Stock Ledger, but the transfers do not in any way affect the general books.

NOTE.—The by-laws of corporations should provide that the shares shall be transferable only by entry upon the books of the company. If stock is transferred without an entry upon the company's books, it would be impossible to know who are entitled to vote at meetings, to whom dividends can be paid, and who are liable, as stockholders, to the company and to creditors.

Form of Transfer Book.

s.r. Cleveland, O. Jan. 10, '94. O. D. MYER to C. A. PARSONS 50 Shares of $100.00 each.	$5000 00		CERTIFICATE OF TRANSFER OF STOCK.	50 Shares. Cleveland, O., Jan. 10, 1894. *For Value Received*, I hereby assign and transfer to C. A. PARSONS, all of my right, title and interest in *Fifty* Shares of the Capital Stock of The Union Rolling Mill Company. Standing in my name on the books of said Company.
No. Certificate.				
Cancelled.	Issued.			*Witness,*
5	12 & 13			A. J. Elias. O. D. Myer.

Dividend Receipt Book.

In this Book is kept the record of each dividend, the shares held by each stockholder, and the amount of dividend thereon, with the signature of the stockholder as a receipt for his dividend, unless it be a large corporation, as in case of railroads. When there are a great number of stockholders, they are paid by voucher.

Form of Dividend Receipt Book.

DIVIDEND No. 1, OF 8 PER CENT., DECLARED JANUARY 31, 1894.

Name of Stockholder.	No. of Shares.	Amount of Dividend.		Date of Payment.		Signatures.
O. D. Myer,	100	$ 800	00	Feb.	1	O. D. Myer.
J. B. Higbee,	100	800	00	"	3	J. B. Higbee.
H. B. Hunt,	200	1600	00	"	5	H. B. Hunt.

Note.—After a Dividend has been declared, and the stockholders so notified, it becomes a positive Liability.

Stock Ledger.

The Stock Ledger is auxiliary to the General Ledger. It is devoted to and occupied entirely by the accounts of the stockholders, for their respective shares of stock in the company.

The entries in this book are derived in the first place from the Installment Lists, and after from the Transfer Book, which serves as Journal to this Ledger, as it shows the names of the parties to be charged and those to be credited for the shares sold or transferred.

In ordering the Stock Ledger, have it contain a few Ledger ruled pages in the fore part, upon one of which open an account with Capital Stock. Debit Capital Stock with all the Installments paid ; then, as you have credited the stockholders from the Installment Book, it will keep this Ledger in balance, and will also show the actual paid in capital.

Form of Stock Ledger.

Dr.   Cr.

Date.	Certificates.	No. Shares	Par Value.	Date.	Certificates	Install-ments.	No. Shares	Par Value
Apr. 1	Renewed by No. 20	25		Jan. 9	No. 1,		100	
" 1	Transf'd to R. Doe	75		Apr. 1	No. 20,		25	

Note.—When a stockholder actually transfers all or any portion of his stock, the original certificate must be returned to the company. Paste the old certificate to the stub from which it was first detached, stamping the old certificate across the face, "Cancelled April 1, 1894," noting on the stub to whom the transfer was made, and issue a new certificate for the shares so transferred. Should only part of the shares named in the old certificate be transferred, issue a new certificate to the original owner for the number he retains, noting on the old stub, " Renewed by No. 20," and on the stub of the new issue, "For No. 1, Cancelled." Then debit his account in the Stock Ledger as above.

To Convert a Private Partnership Into a Joint Stock Company.

Ex. 186. S. W. Burrows and N. C. Bosworth have been conducting a Retail Hardware business as partners. To secure more capital and add other lines of goods, it has been proposed to incorporate into a Joint Stock Company, from the following statement of Assets and Liabilities. By this statement it is readily shown that the net capital of the firm is $15,355.50, but they have decided to form a stock company with a capital of $35,000.00, appropriating for themselves 125 shares each, par value $100.00, or $25,000.00, for their interest and established trade or good will of the old firm, 50 shares to be subscribed by other parties and paid in cash ; the remaining 50 shares to be held as Treasury Stock for future sales.

Assets.		Liabilities.	
Cash....	$7425.91	Bills Pay	$5700.00
Mdse	8998.75	Reserve Fund	551.50
Bills Rec	2500.00	Accts. Pay. (give names)	1000.00
Fur. and Fix	50.00	N. C. Bosworth	9204.88
Accts Rec. (give names)	3632.34	S. W. Burrows	6150.62
	$22607.00		$22607.00

First Entries.

Close the old books by the following Journal entries:

The Burrows-Bosworth Hardware Company, $22607.00

To Cash	$7425.91
" Mdse	8998.75
" Bills Rec	2500.00
" Accts. Rec. (give names)	3632.34
" Fur. and Fix	50.00

The above entry balances all the resource accounts in the old books, and opens an account in the old Ledger with the new company, which is called The Burrows-Bosworth Hardware Company, thereby showing that the resources of the old firm have been transferred to the company.

Bills Pay	$5700.00
Reserve Fund	551.50
Accts. Pay. (give names)	1000.00
N. C. Bosworth	9204.88
S. W. Burrows	6150.62
To The Burrows-Bosworth Hardware Co	$22607.00

This entry closes all the Liability accounts and the partners' accounts, showing they have been transferred to the new company. It also closes the account of The Burrows-Bosworth Hardware Co.

The Subscription Book having been opened, the following subscriptions to the capital stock are made: S. W. Burrows 125 shares, N. C. Bosworth 125 shares, F. M. Slade 25 shares, H. H. Smith 10 shares, and F. M. Potter 15 shares.

The entry for opening the stock company books is as follows:

Cash	$7425 91
Bills Rec	2500.00
Mdse	8998.75
Fur. and Fix	50.00
Accts. Rec	3632.34
Franchise	2393.00
Treasury Stock	5000.00
Subscription	5000.00
To Capital Stock	$35000.00

This entry gets the capital stock account on the Ledger, together with all the assets as transferred from the old firm.

Many accountants claim that the capital stock account should be credited for the *paid-up* capital only. I claim that the capital stock account should have credit for the full authorized capital. The capital stock account in the Stock Ledger shows the amount paid in.

By referring to the statement of assets, it will be found to amount to $22,607.00, the total real value out of which the corporation was formed with a capital stock of $35,000.00. The amount of the assets will be found to be $2393.00 less than the amount subscribed by Messrs. Burrows and Bosworth; now in order to get the full authorized capital on the books it is necessary to make up the deficit on the debit side by using the Franchise account. Some accountants object to using fictitious accounts to get the real accounts upon the books. It would be very gratifying indeed to know how to open the books of some corporations without their use. It matters little how many fictitious accounts you may use in order to get the real accounts or full authorized capital on the books, as they in no way affect the Losses or Gains, neither are they Assets to collect or Liabilities to be paid.

Treasury Stock account is charged for 50 shares held for sale at some future time. When the Treasury Stock is sold, say for Cash, the Journal or Cash entry would be :—

Cash............................. $5000.00
　　　To Treasury Stock............... $5000.00

This entry would close the Treasury Stock account.

Subscription account is charged for the shares subscribed by Slade, Smith and Potter. When their subscriptions are paid the Journal or Cash entry will be :—

Cash............................. $5000.00
　　　To Subscription.................... $5000.00

This entry will close the Subscription account.

Next in order will be to get the approved Liabilities of the old firm upon the books of the company. This is done by using another fictitious account, as in the following entry.

Contingencies.................. $6700.00
　　　To Bills Payable...................... $5700.00
　　　" Accts. " 1000.00

By using "Contingencies" as an account to get the Liabilities on the company's books is the same as the Franchise account. Any other name would serve, however. It will be seen that the Partners' accounts and Reserve Fund do not belong to this entry. The Partners will be represented in the Stock Ledger, while the Reserve Fund was closed into the Partners' accounts on the old books.

The above entries will open the books for the new company, after which, and in all cases, they are conducted like any other books, except at closing, which is fully explained a little further ahead.

Many accountants do and feel justified in opening an account with each subscriber or stockholder. They argue that they are really debtors to the company as soon as they subscribe for stock. This is quite true, but the fact still remains that they are liable to lawful action should they refuse or neglect to pay for the stock subscribed. I fail to see how a claim for delinquency can any more readily be substantiated by having them charged upon the Ledger. Then why not save the labor?

Many corporations are formed wherein the incorporators contribute a plant, a patent, a piece of land, or something else, which forms the basis of the company. They, in consideration of this contribution, generally divide the voting shares among themselves, who never expect to pay in a dollar, but create Treasury Stock to produce the money for working or operating capital. It would not be an easy matter to open an account with the subscribers or stockholders in cases of this kind. However, should the company be compelled to call an assessment on the stock to meet expenses, etc., a Journal entry, *Stockholders* To *Assessment No.* 1, would then be in order.

If a company is formed and all the stock subscribed for, and positively will be paid in cash, then the following entry may be used :

Stockholders Dr. To Capital Stock.

This entry may be made upon the ground that the incorporators have taken all the stock at its par value, and are therefore debtors. But let us suppose, as is often the case, that it is found after some months' operating that—say after 75% of the subscriptions have been paid in—no more money was needed ; here you would have an account with each subscriber owing a balance. If the company should deem it unnecessary to call further installments, it positively would be incorrect in principle and effect for the stockholders to be represented as debtors to the company. However, under such conditions I should close their accounts, "*Contingencies* To *Stockholders*," and if the company should find it necessary to call another installment after having closed the stockholders' accounts, open an account, "*Stockholders* To *Contingencies.*" This entry will open the "*Stockholders*'" account, to be closed when the assessment is paid. Again, suppose that stock is subscribed with the full understanding that they are to pay full par value, and then find that 60% will be sufficient to conduct the business; in this case they do certainly receive dividends on the full face value of each share held by them. The same holds good if stock is bought at a discount; and no greater claim than the face or par value, if bought at a premium or above par. Under the above conditions, the entry would be—

" Contingencies To Capital Stock."

If the subscribers pay by installments, or otherwise, debit cash and credit "contingencies." When all is paid in, the contingency account will close; but if 60% is sufficient, then carry the balance of the contingency account as a Resource, until closed by further installments in the future. The following method may be preferred :—

Certificates of Stock To Capital Stock.

When cash is received from the subscribers, debit cash and credit certificates of stock. Should 60% be sufficient, as in the preceding statement, make the entry—

Contingencies To Certificates of Stock.

It would not be improper to carry the balance of the certificate of stock account, should that balance actually represent unsold stock.

At the close of the year an inventory has been taken and a net gain of $10,000.00 has been realized. Now comes the closing of the corporation books.

All the accounts producing profit or loss are closed into the Loss and Gain account, the same as in any set of books, and the net gain is $10,000.00. The first entry would be :—

Loss and Gain........................ $10,000.00
　　　To Surplus............................... $10,000.00

This entry will close the Loss and Gain account by opening an account with Surplus, which is credited. Some bookkeepers prefer to carry the balance of "Loss and Gain," instead of " Surplus," contending that Loss and Gain is easier to understand, and that many get it into their heads that Surplus represents actual cash. We will, however, close the Loss and Gain account into Surplus, throughout this work; it is more scientific. The balance of this account must be carried as a liability; but it must not operate for or against the gains of any subsequent period.

To Declare a Dividend.

The Loss and Gain account showing a net gain of $10,000.00, which has been closed into Surplus, is now ready for a Dividend to be declared. As stated before, no well regulated company will declare a

Dividend for the full amount of Gain or Surplus. In determining **this** question, there are several important points to be considered. First, how much cash is there in the treasury? What necessary improvements, building or machinery, etc., should be provided? What liabilities are due and must be paid? What are the available assets? These points should be heavily weighed by the Directors before declaring a Dividend. They may depend upon early maturities, and with propriety borrow money to pay Dividends. It may be that a large amount of money has been received from the sale of stock, with which the liabilities can be discharged, and declare a Dividend also. Even though a Dividend could be declared for the full Surplus, and have plenty of cash remaining, it is not wise to do so. A Surplus Fund should be allowed to accumulate, from which withdrawals can be made in case of an off year, or a period without profit.

Let it be remembered that the Capital Stock is $35,000.00, Net Gain $10,000.00, and a Dividend declared on the Capital Stock of 10%. What entry?

Surplus...................................... $3500.00
        To Dividend No. 1, 1894................... $3500.00

Debit "Surplus" and credit Dividend No. 1, 1894. This is a positive liability as soon as declared. As the stockholders receive their Dividends, take their receipts in the Dividend Receipt Book. The Dividend account remains open until all Dividends are paid. An account must be opened with each Dividend declared, numbering it in regular order and the year as above. Do not make one Dividend account answer for all Dividends; it will be confusing. The Surplus account now has a credit balance of $6500.00; this credit must stand as a liability, and should the company lose $3000.00 the next year, they could then declare a Dividend of 10%.

Stock Ledger.

A full explanation of the Stock Ledger having been given in the introduction, it is deemed unnecessary to give any further instructions, only to say that if you open the books by debiting Stockholders and crediting Capital Stock account for installments due, or debit Cash for installments paid and credit Capital Stock account for the same from the Cash Book, direct to the general Ledger, then you must change the order of the Capital Stock account in the Stock Ledger by charging that account with the full par value of the shares issued, and credit each stockholder for the same. The Stock Ledger will then show the amount of stock issued, while the Capital Stock account in the general Ledger will show how much has been paid in.

This is incorrect. As stated before, let your opening entry give Capital Stock credit for full authorized capital, and let the Stock Ledger show amount of capital actually paid in.

Ex. 187.   W. E. Kneale and L. N. Gibbons formed a co-partnership January 1, 1893, investing and withdrawing as follows:—

W. E. Kneale.	L. N. Gibbons.
April 15, $3500 ‖ Jan. 1, $8500	July 20, $2000 ‖ Jan. 1, $10600

The firm was dissolved Jan. 1, 1894.   Assets and Liabilities as follows :—

Assets.	Liabilities.
Cash.............................$8000.00	Bills Pay., averag. due 6-21-94, $4230.00
Bills Rec., averag. due 5-21-94, 7500.00	
Personal Accounts................. 5800.00	

What is L. N. Gibbons to receive at dissolution, he sharing one-third of the gains and losses ; interest allowed on all sums invested, and charged on all sums withdrawn by the partners ; the notes both for and against the firm being taken at their present worth ; 5 % allowed for bad or doubtful debts on the Personal accounts? Give full solution and entry to adjust the interest between the partners.

Ex. 188.   What is a Partnership ?

Ex. 189.   How are Partnerships distinguished?   Define each.

Ex. 190.   What is an Article of Co-partnership, and what should it contain?

Ex. 191.   What are Assets and Liabilities?   What does the difference represent ?

Ex. 192.   What is an Investment ?

Ex. 193.   When is a firm Solvent ?

Ex. 194.   When is a firm Insolvent ?

Ex. 195.   How do you find each Partner's share of Profit or Loss, when the Loss or Gain is shared in proportion to each Partner's Investment ?

Ex. 196.   How do you find each Partner's average Investment and share of the Profits, when the Losses and Gains are to be divided in proportion to each Partner's Investment and Time ?

Ex. 197.   How do you adjust the Partners' accounts when the proportion of Profit or Loss is fixed and Interest is allowed on the Excess and charged on the Deficit of each Partner's required Investment ?

Ex. 198.   How do you find the Net Capital of a firm at commencing, the Net Loss or Net Gain, the Assets and Liabilities being given, except the Investments ?

Ex. 199.   How do you find the Insolvency at commencing?

CHAPTER NINE.

The Books of a Mercantile Firm Changed to Joint Stock Company.

The Mdse., Personal Accounts, etc., due the firm taken in payment for stock. What are the Journal entries under the following conditions?

Ex. 200.

J. D. Ramsay, P. J. Leonard, W. W. Boynton, and J. C. Hale have been conducting business as partners, and have this day been incorporated into a Joint Stock Company, with a capital stock of $30,000.00, consisting of 300 shares, par value $100 each. The incorporators subscribe for stock in proportion to their interest in the old firm. J. D. Ramsay subscribes for 75 shares, P. J. Leonard 60 shares, W. W. Boynton 50 shares, and J. C. Hale 40 shares, leaving 75 shares unsubscribed. The old firm has no liabilities, and the incorporators pay for their stock with the assets of the old firm.

To open the books of the company, make the following entry :—

Subscription. $22500.00
Treasury Stock.............. 7500.00
To Capital Stock................. $30000.00

Debit Subscription account for amount of stock subscribed, Debit Treasury Stock for amount held in the treasury for subsequent sales, and Credit Capital Stock account for full authorized capital. As the new company accept the assets of the old firm in payment for their subscription, Debit the Assets and Credit Subscription.

Cash ....$ 6500.00
Mdse............................ 13000.00
Bills Rec. 3000.00
To Subscription.. .... $22500.00

This operation places the assets on the company's books; also closes the Subscription account. You may ask why it would not do as well to debit the assets in the first entry, instead of subscription. Practically it would amount to the same thing, but it is thought best to have entries on the Journal correspond with subscriptions in the

Subscription Book. Again, in the formation of some companies there are no assets; hence the Subscription account.

Suppose J. A. McCurdy buys 50 shares of stock and pays cash $2500.00 and his note 60 days for $2500.00; what entry?

Cash	$2500.00	
Bills Rec.	2500.00	
To Treasury Stock		$5000.00

Since this stock was held as Treasury Stock, we Credit it for all sales.

Explanations for Journal and Cash Book Entries.

In all entries made upon the Journal or Cash Book, make a complete and full explanation of transactions, though it may require ten pages to do it. Very often controversies arise, and when transactions are thoroughly explained they are easier to adjust.

Ex. 201. **A Commercial Business is Incorporated into a Joint Stock Company, with a Capital of $60,000.00.** They have $30,000 in Assets, but no Liabilities. The incorporators divide the majority of stock among themselves. What are the Journal entries? Assets as follows :—

Machinery	$10000.00
Real Estate	15000.00
Accts. Rec.	5000.00
	$30000.00

First entry should be :—

Franchise	$30000.00	
Machinery	10000.00	
Real Estate	15000.00	
Accts. Rec.	5000.00	
To Capital Stock		$60000.00

Franchise is used instead of Subscription. When the subscriptions are paid make this entry: *Cash Dr. To Contingencies.* Then Credit the stockholders in the Stock Ledger for same. When the subscription is known it can be used to open the books. Yet it is not really necessary to use the Subscription account; any other term would answer as well; but when subscriptions are made and can be used, as in the preceding examples, it is deemed best to do so, because the Journal entry will then agree with the Subscription and Minute Books.

Suppose the Assets of the company to be a steam engine, $30000, the opening entry could be :—

Machinery.................... $60000.00
    To Capital Stock............... $60000.00

There is no objection to the above entry. The machinery cost $30000.00, but it is entered up at its nominal value of $60000.00. It is not a speculative resource, therefore it matters not what value is placed upon it. It would also be proper to use this entry :—

Franchise..................... $30000.00
Machinery 30000.00
    To Capital Stock................. $60000.00

Which is practically the same as the first entry given.

It may happen that the stock is all taken and paid up, and the company still not have funds enough to operate. Each stockholder donates to the company a certain number of shares, to the amount of say $10000.00, for the purpose of raising more funds. In this case Debit Treasury Stock and Credit Working Capital. Should any of the donated shares be sold, Debit Cash and Credit Treasury Stock. The stockholders will surrender their original certificates of stock and receive new ones, less the number of shares donated, and be Debited in the Stock Ledger also for the number of shares donated.

Suppose some of the Treasury Stock is sold at a discount, what entry ?

Cash $1000.00
Working Capital.............   1000.00
    To Treasury Stock............... $2000.000

In this entry stock has been sold at a discount of 50%. We debit Cash $1000 and Working Capital $1000, and credit Treasury Stock $2000. Many bookkeepers would feel justified in debiting Loss and Gain instead of Working Capital. It must be remembered that the company did not, practically or otherwise, lose $1000. It is not this sort of Loss and Gain that makes up the dividend of a corporation. If they had bought this stock at par, then sold at a discount or premium, the case would be somewhat different. Companies are not allowed to deal in their own stock.

Reserved Fund

Is a fund set aside for any special purpose, and should always represent *actual* cash. This cash should be taken from the general cash, and have a separate bank account, with extra Check and Bank Book. To create a Reserved Fund, make this entry: *Reserved Fund*

To Cash (with full history). This entry takes the cash from the general cash account and places it in the Reserved Fund.

To buy a plant, machinery or anything out of the Reserved Fund first take the amount required out of the Reserved Fund and place it into the common or general cash, as follows : *Cash* (posted from C. B.) *To Reserve Fund.* To buy the plant—say warehouse and lot $5000— entry would be :—

> *Real Estate To Cash* (full history, etc.)

Suppose a dividend is to be paid out of the Reserved Fund, then :

> *Surplus To Dividend No. 3,* 1894 (full history).

Then :—

> *Cash* (C. B.) *To Reserved Fund* (history).

Then :—

> *Dividend No.* 3, 1894, *To Cash* (posted from C. B.)

The above cash entries might be omitted from the Journal, as they can be as fully explained in the Cash Book. Numerous advantages are to be gained by giving a complete description of all such transactions, which should be made upon the Journal.

CHAPTER TEN.

Partnership Books Changed to Joint Stock Co.

The partnership of Beck, Carr & Co. was incorporated into a Joint Stock Company, with a capital stock of $200,000.00, consisting of 2000 shares, par value $100. Beck, Carr and French are to take stock at par for their net interest in the partnership, and the remainder of the stock is to be subscribed by other parties, whose subscriptions are to be paid in quarterly installments of 25%. What are the first steps to be taken by the firm? If the old books are to be used, what entry is required? If new books are to be opened, what entry? Also, what books are to be used in addition to the regular account books?

Answers. The first steps to be taken by the firm will be to instruct the bookkeeper to close the books, divide the Losses and Gains according to Articles of Agreement, and bring down the balances of all Assets and Liabilities. They should then advertise the dissolution, hold the proper preliminary meetings, and procure a Charter of Incorporation. The books used in addition to the regular account books are : the Subscription Book, Installment Book, Installment Scrip Book, Certificate of Stock Book, Transfer Book, and Stock Ledger. The bookkeeper having closed the books as instructed, we will assume the Assets and Liabilities as follows :—

Assets.		Liabilities.	
Cash	$15,000.00	Accts. Pay.	$32,800.00
Mdse	25,000.00	Bills Pay	25,000.00
Bills Rec	10,500.00	Beck	20,000.00
Accts. Rec	17,300.00	Carr.	20,000.00
Real Estate	40,000.00	French	10,000.00
	$107,800.00		$107,800.00

If the old books are to be used the following entry will open them:

Beck	$20,000.00	
Carr	20,000.00	
French	10,000.00	
Treasury Stock	150,000.00	
To Capital Stock		$200,000.00

This entry takes the partners' accounts out of the General Ledger and opens the Treasury Stock account, also the full authorized capital. The partners will then be Credited in the Stock Ledger from Certificate of Stock Book for their respective shares of stock. All the other accounts remain in the General Ledger in exactly the same condition as for the old firm.

When any of the Treasury Stock is sold for cash, Debit Cash and Credit Treasury Stock. If subscribed, to be paid for in installments, as per the above agreement, Debit Subscription and Credit Treasury Stock. When the installments are paid, Debit Cash and Credit Subscription.

If a New Set of Books is to be Opened,

The first entry in the old books should be :—

The Beck-Carr Mfg. Co	$107,800.00	
To Cash		$15,000.00
" Mdse		25,000.00
" Bills Rec		10,500.00
" Accts. Rec		17,300.00
" Real Estate		40,000.00

This entry will close all the resource accounts in the old books, showing they have been transferred to the new company.

Accts. Pay	$32,800.00	
Bills Pay	25,000.00	
Beck	20,000.00	
Carr	20,000.00	
French	10,000.00	
To The Beck-Carr Mfg. Co.		$107,800.00

This entry will close all the liability accounts in the old books; also, close the account of the B.-C. Mfg. Co., showing that all the liabilities have been transferred to the new company.

Entries Required to Open the Books of the New Company.

The Beck-Carr Mfg. Co. was incorporated, as stated, for $200,000, the old firm to take stock at par for their interest. Beck subscribed for 200 shares, Carr 200 shares, French 100 shares, Brown 100 shares, Willson 200 shares, Johnson 200 shares, and Lane 200 shares ; the balance held as Treasury stock.

Subscription	$120,000.00	
Treasury Stock	80,000.00	
To Capital Stock		$200,000.00

As Beck, Carr and French have paid their subscriptions, Credit them in Stock Ledger for their respective amounts.

In order to get the Assets and Liabilities on the new books, also to show that Beck, Carr and French have paid their subscriptions, make the following entry :—

Cash	$15,000.00	
Mdse	25,000.00	
Bills Rec	10,500.00	
Accts. Rec	17,300.00	
Real Estate	40,000.00	
To Accts. Pay		$32,800.00
" Bills Pay		25,000.00
" Subscription		50,000.00

This entry places all the Assets and Liabilities on the company's books ; also credit the Subscription account for amount of Beck, Carr and French's subscriptions, which have been paid with the effects of the old firm.

The first installment of 25% on the stock subscribed by Brown, Willson, Johnson and Lane has been called and paid.   What entry?

Cash $17,500.00

    To Subscription...................... $17,500.00

A net gain of $20,000 has been made, and the Directors have declared a Dividend of 10% on the Capital Stock issued, and created a Surplus Fund for the balance of the net gain.   What entry?

Loss and Gain.................. $20,000.00

    To Surplus Fund...................... $20,000.00

Then :—

Surplus Fund.................... $12,000.00

    To Dividend No. 1, 1894........... $12,000.00

Suppose the Dividend is paid in stock to Beck, Carr and French and to the other subscribers whose stock is not yet paid up, the Dividend to be credited on their next installment ; what entry?

Dividend No. 1, 1894........ $12,000.00

    To Treasury Stock.......... .... $5000.00
    " Subscription......................   7000.00

The amount of stock issued is 1200 shares.   New stock is issued to Beck, Carr and French out of the Treasury Stock, while the Dividend to the other stockholders is credited on their subscription or next installment.   This creates, or rather leaves, a Surplus Fund of $8000.   If the Dividend should be declared on the authorized capital, it is readily shown that the Treasury stock is entitled to a Dividend. This should not be, as Treasury stock is not paid up stock, therefore cannot earn Dividends.   Dividends should be declared on the paid-in capital, or on the stock issued.   In this case the stock is not fully paid as issued, but will be, hence they are entitled to Dividends on the stock subscribed by them.   If the company should buy its own stock, or in any way become possessed of it for value, then Treasury stock should be entitled to the Dividend thereon, until it should be placed in the Loss and Gain account or otherwise disposed of.

Ex. 203.   **A Joint Stock Company is Incorporated to Conduct a Manufacturing Business.**   The corporate name is **The Keystone Iron Company.**   The capital stock is $1,000,000, 10,000 shares, par value $100.   Twenty per cent. of the subscription is to be paid in cash, and 20% is to be paid every sixty days thereafter until paid up. The business is to commence on receipt of the first installment.   The following subscriptions were made by the incorporators : P. D. Briggs

1000 shares P. M. Arthur 1000 shares, G. A. Boyer 1000 shares, Wm. Chisholm 1000 shares, Geo. Warmington 1000 shares, L. A. Cobb 1000 shares, M. T. Herrick 1000 shares ; the remaining 3000 shares held by the Treasurer.   The first entry on the books should be :—

Subscription	$700,000.00	
Treasury Stock	300,000.00	
To Capital Stock		$1,000,000.00

I claim the above is the only correct way to open the books as incorporated. When the subscriptions are paid in full or by installments, credit the Subscription account and debit Cash. If any of the Treasury stock is sold, credit it as heretofore.

It frequently happens that a bookkeeper cannot have his own way, but must obey the instructions of his superior, i. e., they want the Capital Stock account credited only for installments paid. All the various methods practiced by accountants will be fully explained and illustrated, leaving the student to adopt his own method, based upon sound reasoning. Suppose the subscriptions to be as stated above, and 20% paid in cash, the Capital Stock account to be credited only as installments are paid; also, that the Treasury stock be opened; what entry ?

√ Cash	$140,000.00	
Treasury Stock	300,000.00	
To Capital Stock		$440,000.00

Check. The √ (check mark) should be used when a cash entry appears in the Journal or a Journal entry in the Cash Book. The check mark is to indicate that the item debit or credit has been posted.

If this entry is made in the cash book it will produce a credit to capital stock which has already been posted through the Journal, hence the use of the check mark. When entries of this kind are used they sometimes cause serious complications, therefore, they are not recommended only when absolutely necessary.

All transactions affecting the stock or opening entries should have their origin and full history upon the Journal.

If it is preferred, the entry can be made in the Cash Book thus :—

Dr. Cash	Cash Cr.

To Capital Stock....$440,000.00
  For 4400 shares at $100 of the Keystone Iron Co. on which an installment of 20 per cent. has been paid, etc.
	By Treasury Stock..$300,000.00
	  For unpaid stock, etc.

Again; if it is preferred, the $140,000 cash may be entered in the Cash Book, and the $300,000 Treasury stock may be entered from the journal. It is readily seen that the first entry is the plainest, shortest and best to use.

A net profit at the close of the year is $250,000. They declared an installment Dividend of 20% instead of a Cash Installment due, and to pass the balance of net gain to the Surplus Fund. What entries:

                Loss and Gain................. $250,000.00
                        To Surplus Fund.................... $250,000

Then :—

                Surplus Fund................. $200,000.00
                        To Dividend No. 2, 1894......... $200,000.00

Thus leaving a Surplus Fund of $50,000. After the following entries have been made, credit each stockholder in the Stock Ledger for his respective amount , and give to each an Installment Receipt.

                Dividend No. 2, 1894...... $200,000.00
                        To Subscription..................... $200,000.00

To Whom Dividends are Payable.—The strictly *legal* right to require payment of a dividend is in those persons who were shareholders on the books of the company at the time the dividend was declared; but the right of equitable assignees will be protected by the courts. The agents of a corporation are justified in paying dividends to the shareholders on the company's books, unless notified of the rights of equitable assignees.

Profits must be divided ratably among all the shareholders; *when a dividend is declared, a specific sum should be made payable on each share.* A shareholder is entitled to share in all profits divided by the company after he becomes a member. No discrimination can be made against a shareholder who received his shares from the company after the dividend had been earned; for the price of the shares would have included a proportionate part of the accumulated profits.

A shareholder in a corporation has no *legal* claim to profits earned by the company until after a dividend has been declared by the proper agents; nor can he compel the directors to declare a dividend unless they withhold profits which they have no discretionary power to retain for further investment. A suit to enforce the declaration of a dividend must be brought in equity, and all the conditions precedent to the right of maintaining an ordinary shareholders' bill must be complied with. However, after a dividend has been declared payable to all shareholders, each shareholder is entitled to recover his distributive share in an action of assumpsit against the corporation.

CHAPTER ELEVEN.

A Mining Machine Company.

Ex. 204. J. H. Brown has invented a Mining Machine of great value, which he has Patented, and has interested several capitalists, who incorporate a Joint Stock Company for the purpose of manufacturing the Machine. Brown agrees to take 100 shares for his Patent Right. The Capital Stock is $200,000, 2000 shares, par value $100. The incorporators subscribe for as many shares as they like. What entry ?

Brown's Patent Right.................. $200,000.00

For the amount of the nominal value of J. H. Brown's Patent Mining Machine, transferred to The U. S. Mining Machine Co. by J. H. Brown, by deed of assignment dated Jan. 1, 1894, recorded this Journal, p. 10. (Copy Deed in full in this entry.)

To Capital Stock............................. $10,000.00

For the amount of 100 shares of the nominal par value $100, of the Capital Stock of The U. S. Mining Machine Co., organized upon the basis of 2000 shares, par value $100, $200,000. Said 100 shares have been issued to J. H. Brown for his Patent Mining Machine, deeded to the company by him, with all rights, titles and claims belonging to him.

To Capital Stock............................. $140,000.00

For the amount of 1400 shares, of the nominal par value $100, of the capital stock of The U. S. Mining Machine Co., divided among the incorporators as follows :—

B. C. Hurst, 400 shares.

I. L. Hudson, 400 shares.

J. E. Hannon, 400 shares.

A. M. Thomas, 100 shares.

F. L. Dyke, 100 shares.

To Working Capital.......................... $50,000.00

For the amount of 500 shares, of the nominal par value $100, of the capital stock of The U. S. Mining Machine Co., set apart for working capital or operating purposes.

The following entry will also open the books:=

Brown's Patent Right..............	$10,000.00	
Franchise.............................	190,000.00	
To Capital Stock.............................		$150,000.00
" Working Capital..........................		50,000.00

Still another entry may be used :—

Subscription....	$140,000.00	
Brown's Patent........................	10,000.00	
Treasury Stock.......................	50,000.00	
To Capital Stock.............................		$200,000.00

In the preceding entries, "Brown's Patent Right" is charged in the first case $200,000, being the nominal value given ; while in the second and third entries it is charged $10,000, the apparent cost. The company can, however, without violation, value it as it may choose; but it must not be understood by this that a company can place nominal and fictitious values on the Speculative Resources, Positive Liabilities or Expense accounts, but in opening the books a nominal value may be given to such properties as Mine, Plant, Franchise, Steamer, Machinery, Land, etc., either to increase or decrease. As stated above, nominal and fictitious values cannot be given to Speculative Resources or Positive Liabilities, because they would *affect* the Loss and Gain. The *Law* requires that Dividends must be paid from the profits of the business. To make profits by inflating values is unlawful in reality. The last entry given should be used under conditions of this kind. It is the simplest, because when the subscriptions are all paid the subscription account will close, and when the Treasury stock is all sold, that account will close, leaving the books opened without any fictitious accounts, which should be done when it is possible to do so, that those not versed in accounts may understand them ; but when the conditions require fictitious entries, use as many as need be to get real values upon the books.

A Lumber Company.

Ex. 205. J. L. Woods is the owner of a Lumber and Planing Mill Business, the Ground and Buildings of which are valued at $100,000 ; Machinery, Tools, Etc., $79,000, and the Lumber $93,500. He proposes to Jenks, Gray, Bell and Cartright to organize a Joint Stock Company with a Capital Stock of $1,000,000, 10000 shares, par value $100, under the following conditions : J. L. Woods is to receive 1000 shares for the ground and buildings, 790 shares for the machinery and tools, and 935 shares for the lumber, all full paid stock.   Jenks subscribed for 1500 shares, Gray 1500 shares, Bell 1500 shares, and Cartright 775 shares, 1000 shares to be held in the treasury for future sales, and 200 shares to be given each incorporator for extra services rendered in organizing the company, they to pay 10% of the nominal par value of the shares thus given, for which they are to receive full paid stock.   They are then to donate to the company 100 shares each, to be put on the market and sold, the proceeds to be used as operating capital.   What are the entries?

Subscription	$800,000.00	
Treasury Stock	100,000.00	
Cash	10,000.00	
Bonus	90,000.00	
To Capital Stock		$1,000,000.00

The incorporators have subscribed for 8000 shares, or $800,000, 1000 shares held as Treasury Stock; then they each receive 200 shares by the payment of 10% for organizing the company.   Debit the Cash received, also Bonus $90,000, which has been paid in stock, and Credit Capital Stock for full authorized capital, $1,000,000.

Then :—

Real Estate	$100,000.00	
Machinery, etc	79,000.00	
Lumber	93,500.00	
To Subscription		$272,500.00

This entry brings the property, as listed, upon the books, to the credit of subscription, being the value of said property for which J. L. Woods receives his stock; therefore it closes the amount of *his* subscription.   When the other subscribers pay their subscriptions, the Subscription account will close.   Credit them in the Stock Ledger for their respective shares.

Now they donate to the company 100 shares each.

Treasury Stock	$50,000.00	
To Working Capital		$50,000.00

When the stockholders donate the stock to the company Debit each stockholder in the Stock Ledger for the shares donated, and Credit Treasury Stock in the Stock Ledger for the same.

The following is another form that may be used to open the books :—

Franchise	$717,500.00	
Real Estate	100,000.00	
Machinery	79,000.00	
Lumber	93,500.00	
Cash	10,000.00	
To Capital Stock		$1,000,000.00

When the subscribers pay their subscriptions, Debit Cash and Credit Contingencies, etc. The first entry is the plainest; therefore I would recommend it.

The books having been opened as illustrated in the first entry, we will suppose now that the company sold 100 shares of the Treasury stock at par for cash. What entry?

Cash............................. $10,000.00
    To Treasury Stock.......... .... $10,000.00

One hundred shares sold at 5% discount for cash. What entry?

Cash............................. $9,500.00
Working Capital.................   500.00
    To Treasury Stock................... $10,000.00

One hundred shares sold at 5% premium for cash. What entry?

Cash............................. $10,500.00
    To Treasury Stock................... $10,000.00
    " Working Capital.................   500.00

Here we have sold stock at par, at a premium and at a discount, Treasury Stock account receiving credit for full face value every time. Had this been the original capital stock, it would have been credited for full face or par value also. A company handles its own stock, in its own books, only at the par value. Stock sold above and below par is an apparent gain and loss. This is true, but it is not this class of Loss and Gain that should affect the legitimate gains of the business.

Working capital, when created as shown in the Third Journal Entry, represents a fictitious Liability, and is therefore a gain. This account must not be closed when dividends are declared. It should remain a permanent credit until the company winds up its affairs, and then it should be closed into Loss and Gain, because the proceeds which were received for the stock that gave credit to this account produced this gain. The Loss or Gain on the sale of Treasury stock belonging to Working Capital is to be carried to the Working Capital account.

The Working Capital account must be debited or credited, as the case requires, when Treasury Stock belonging to it is sold at a loss or gain.

Review.

Ex. 206. Describe a corporation.

Ex. 207. How many kinds of corporations are there?

Ex. 208. Define a Public, Private, Civil and Quasi Corporation.

Ex. 209. How are Private Corporations formed in your State?

Ex. 210.   What is a Limited Liability Company?

Ex. 211.   What is a Single Liability Company?

Ex. 212.   What is a Double Liability Company?

Ex. 213.   What is Authorized Capital Stock?

Ex. 214.   What is Treasury Stock, and how is it created?

Ex. 215.   What is Working Capital?

Ex. 216.   What is Watered Stock?

Ex. 217.   When is Stock at par, premium and discount?

Ex. 218.   What is Preferred Stock?

Ex. 219.   What is Guaranteed Stock?

Ex. 220.   What is Clandestine Stock?

Ex. 221.   What is the Market Value of Stocks and Bonds?

Ex. 222.   What is a Dividend?

Ex. 223.   What is a Cash Dividend?

Ex. 224.   What is an Installment Dividend?

Ex. 225.   What is a Stock Dividend?

Ex. 226.   What is a Fictitious Dividend, and how is it created?

Ex. 227.   What is a Franchise?

Ex. 228.   What is an Assessment?

Ex. 229.   What is an Installment?

Ex. 230.   What is a Trust?

Ex. 231.   What is a Syndicate?

Ex. 232.   What is a Bond?   How many kinds are there, and how do they get their names?

Ex. 233.   What is a Mortgage?

Ex. 234.   What do you understand by Collateral Securities?

Ex. 235.   What is a Surplus or Reserved Fund?

Ex. 236.   What is a Bonus and what is a Rebate?

Ex. 237.   What is a Minute Book, and how should it be kept?

Ex. 238.   What is a Subscription Book?   Illustrate one with subscriptions.

Ex. 239.   What is an Installment Book?   Show one filled out.

Ex. 240.   What is an Installment Scrip Book?   Illustrate one.

Ex. 241.   What is a certificate of Stock?   Give a form of one.

Ex. 242.   What is a Transfer Book?   Give a form of one.

Ex. 243.   What is a Dividend Receipt Book?   Show a form.

Ex. 244.   What is a Stock Ledger?   Give a form you would like best.

Ex. 245.   Post and Kirkwood have been conducting a stove manufacturing business as partners.   Dec. 31, 1893, they close their books and find the following statement of Assets and Liabilities:—

Assets.		Liabilities.	
Plant and Machinery,	$40,000.00	Accts. Payable........	$10,400.00
Pig Iron.................	10,000.00	Bills Payable..........	5,000.00
Patterns.................	5,700.00	C. A. Post.............	50,000.00
Cash....................	16,400.00	C. J. Kirkwood.......	44,300.00
Accts. Rec.............	32,941.00		
Bills Rec...............	4,659.00		
	$109,700.00		$109,700.00

Jan. 1st, 1894, they incorporate into a Joint Stock Company, with a capital stock of $150,000, 1500 shares, par value $100. C. A. Post is to receive 550 full paid shares for his interest in the old firm, and C. J. Kirkwood is to receive 500 shares for his interest. B. F. Whitman subscribes for 50 shares, T. F. Beidler 50 shares, G. A. Rudd 10 shares, V. Meakin 10 shares. The balance held as Treasury stock.

Ex. 246. B. F. Whitman pays his subscription in cash, T. F. Beidler pays his in pig iron, G. A. Rudd gives a 60-day note, V. Meakin deeds a piece of ground. What are the opening entries?

Ex. 247. One hundred shares of the Treasury stock were sold for ten $1000 U. S. Bonds, at par. What entry?

Ex. 248. A net gain of $17,500 was made during the year, and a Dividend of 10% declared, the balance to remain in surplus. What are the entries?

Ex. 249. A commercial business is incorporated into a Joint Stock Company, with a capital stock of $60,000, 600 shares, par value $100. They have Assets as follows and no liabilities. The incorporators divide the majority of stock among themselves. What Journal Entry to open the books?

Ex. 250. Suppose the Assets of the company to be plant and machinery valued at $40,000, what entry would you use?

Ex. 251. Each of six stockholders donated 50 shares to the company, to be sold for operating purposes. What entry?

Ex. 252. One hundred shares of this stock were sold for cash. What entry?

Ex. 253. Fifty shares of this stock were sold for $90 per share, for Mdse. What entry?

Ex. 254. Fifty shares of this stock were sold for $115 per share, for cash. What entry?

Ex. 255. The net gain was $6000. What entry?

Ex. 256. A dividend of 6% was declared, and $2400 placed to surplus. What entry?

Ex. 257. The Dividend was paid, $1800 in cash and $1800 in stock. What entry?

CHAPTER TWELVE.

An Oil Company.

Ex. 258. Samuel Warden is the owner of a piece of land on which he has found oil. Geo. Boyd, Amos Trout, Jos. Steele, A. Ruff, and M. Rumbaugh agree to pay him $25,000 to donate the land for the purpose of incorporating a Joint Stock Company. Warden is to receive full paid stock for his full right and title in the land. The other incorporators are to subscribe for same amount of stock donated to Warden, and are to pay 25% cash down and the balance of their subscriptions in equal installments every 60 days. Capital Stock $200,000, 2000 shares, par value $100. The remaining shares to be sold for operating purposes. What entry?

Plant account...............	$200,000.00	
To Capital Stock...................		$150,000.00
" Working Capital..............		50,000.00

Or this entry :—

Subscription...................	$125,000.00	
Land Account..............	25,000.00	
Treasury Stock.............	50,000.00	
To Capital Stock...................		$150,000.00
" Working Capital		50,000.00

The Subscription account is debited for the subscriptions of Boyd, Trout, Steele, Ruff, and Rumbaugh. Warden having paid for his stock by donating the land, Debit Land account for the appraised value, Debit Treasury stock for amount of stock held by the Treasurer, and Credit Capital Stock and Working Capital. If the first installment of 25% has been paid, this entry can be used :—

Subscription....................	$93,750.00	
Treasury Stock..............	50,000.00	
Cash.............................	31,250.00	
Land Account...............	25,000.00	
To Capital Stock...................		$150,000.00
" Working Capital..............		50,000.00

Any other name could be given the Plant or Land account, which should have a full and complete history. The history for Subscription should contain the number of shares subscribed for, and by whom. The Treasury Stock account should state the number of shares, and how created. An explanation for the Plant account should be about as follows: For the appraised value of 30 acres of land, situated in Venango county, State of Pennsylvania, donated to the Excelsior Oil Co. by Samuel Warden, with all his rights, titles, claims and privileges, as per Deed dated January 1st, 1894; said Excelsior Oil Co. incorporated with a capital stock of $200,000, consisting of 2000 shares, par value $100 each. Also copy the Deed. To save space here the history of all transactions has been omitted; but on your books make them full and clear; omit nothing of importance to save writing.

A Retail Grocery Company.

Ex. 259. A Joint Stock Company is incorporated to conduct a Retail Grocery business, with a Capital Stock of $65,000, 650 shares, par value $100. Four hundred shares of stock are taken by the incorporators, they to pay $10 per share. The remaining 250 shares are reserved for Working capital. Real Estate is bought and paid for partly in cash and partly in stock. Money is borrowed to pay Dividends. Dividends are declared and paid in stock. What entries?

Subscription.....................	$40,000.00	
Treasury Stock...............	25,000.00	
To Capital Stock....................		$40,000.00
" Working Capital...............		25,000.00

Or:—

Franchise.......................	$65,000.00	
To Capital Stock....................		$40,000.00
" Working Capital...............		25,000.00

The incorporators have received $40,000 worth of stock, even though they should never be required to pay more than the first installment of 10%. The Capital Stock, however, is nominally paid up to the extent of $40,000.

What entry for the installment of 10%?

A. Adams, his 10% on 100 shares........	$1000.00
H. R. Groff, his 10% on 100 shares......	1000.00
T. Davis, " 10% " 100 "	1000.00
H. C. Wheeler, his 10% on 100 shares...	1000.00
To Installment No. 1.............................	$4000.00

When the subscribers pay their 10%, credit their accounts, and then issue to them their stock. Number the installments of assessments in regular order, and carry the Installment account as a liability.

· If the books are opened as shown in the last entry, the stockholders individually charged and *Capital Stock* credited, after which no more installments are required, the stockholders would be holding stock representing $40,000, while the *Capital Stock* would only be credited with $4000, the amount paid in. If shares are delivered when the first installment is paid, the Capital Stock is nominally paid up to the nominal par value of the certificates of stock issued.

The company buys Real Estate, and pays for same partly in cash and partly in stock. Buys from V. C. Taylor a three-story brick block on Superior Street, corner of Public Square, for $15,000, pays him $7500 in cash and issues him 75 shares full paid stock for the balance of $7500, What entry?

Real Estate............................ $15000.00
    To Cash.................................... $7500.00
    " Treasury Stock....................... 7500.00

Money Borrowed to Pay Dividends.

A net gain of $6000 has been realized, and a Dividend of $4000 has been declared. There being no cash in the treasury, money is borrowed to pay the Dividend. What entries, if they discount their note at the bank?

Loss and Gain......................... $6000.00
    To Surplus............................... $6000.00
Then :—
Surplus......... .... $4000.00
    To Dividend No. 1, 1894.............. $4000.00
Then :—
Cash..................................... $4000.00
Discount............................... 20.00
    To Bills Payable........................ $4020.00
      Note at 30 days favor the Union National Bank, to
      pay first Dividend, 1894, by order of Directors, etc.
Then :—
Dividend No. 1, 1894.............. $4000.00
    To Cash................. .... $4000.00

To Pay Dividends With Stock.

If all the original Capital Stock has been issued, and the company should issue stock to pay Dividends, it would be " *Watering*." But Treasury stock may be sold, and the proceeds used to pay Dividends, provided the business has made a profit, as Dividends can only be paid out of profits, as stated before.

If the Dividend be paid with stock, the entry will be:—

        Working Capital..................... $4000.00
            To Dividend No. 2, 1894.............. $4000.00

Then:—

        Dividend No. 2, 1894............... $4000.00
            To Capital Stock........................ $4000.00

The above would be the entry if the stock was watered. If paid out of the Treasury Stock, the entry would be:—

        Working Capital..................... $4000.00
            To Dividend No. 2, 1894.............. $4000.00

Then:—

        Dividend No. 2, 1894............... $4000.00
            To Treasury Stock...................... $4000.00

The last two entries differ somewhat from those made in previous Dividends. The reason is this: The Treasury Stock is held for Working Capital; but if it is sold to pay Dividends, Working Capital does not receive the benefit, hence it is reduced and the Surplus is retained by the company. At some future time the company can replace the credit to Working Capital by *Debiting Surplus Fund* and *Crediting Working Capital*.

A Limited Manufacturing Company.

Ex. 260. **Anderson, Holden, Burton, Blee and Fulton form a Limited Partnership Company. The opening entries are made independently of the Subscription and Installment Books. Capital Stock $100,000, 1000 shares, par value $100.** Anderson takes 200 shares and pays Cash=$20,000; Holden takes 200 shares= $20,000, and pays $10,000 Cash and a Warehouse which he deeds to the company for $10,000; Burton takes 200 shares=$20,000, and pays $10,000 Cash and Mdse. for $10,000; Blee takes 200 shares= $20,000, and pays Cash; Fulton takes 200 shares=$20,000, pays Cash $10,000 and gives his Note for $10,000 at 30 days. What entry to open the books?

Cash... $70,000.00
For amount received from Anderson... $20,000
   "   "   "   " Holden...... 10,000
   "   "   "   " Burton....... 10,000
   "   "   "   " Blee........... 20,000
   "   "   "   " Fulton....... 10,000

Real Estate...................................... 10,000.00
As per Deed given by Holden for Warehouse
on River Street, etc., in payment for stock.

Mdse... 10,000.00
Per Inventory, received from Burton in pay-
ment for stock, etc.

Bills Receivable............................... 10,000.00
Note at 30 days from Fulton in payment for
stock, etc.

       To Capital Stock............................... $100,000.00

Issue them their certificates of stock, and credit them in the Stock Ledger accordingly.

Holden sells 100 shares of his stock to Baldwin for $10,000 Cash, and the remaining 100 shares to the company, one-half of which is paid in Cash, the balance with the company's Note at 6 months. What entry?

     Treasury Stock................. $10000.00
         To Cash.................................... $5000.00
        " Bills Payable......................... 5000.00

The transaction between Holden and Baldwin does not enter upon the books of the company, only that Holden is debited in the Stock Ledger and Baldwin is credited. The Treasury Stock account is credited also in the Stock Ledger.

The net gain for the year is $15,000. The Board of Directors declare a Dividend of 10% and create a Reserve Fund of $5000. What entry?

     Loss and Gain.................... $15,000.00
         To Surplus............................. $10,000.00
        " Reserve Fund.................... 5,000.00

Then :—

     Surplus Fund.................... $10,000.00
         To Dividend No. 4, 1894............ $10,000.00

In the above Dividend No. 4, Treasury Stock is entitled to a Dividend on 100 shares, or $10,000, which at 10%=$1000. This $1000 is a gain and belongs to the company. To take it out of the Dividend

No. 4 and place it on the books for future distribution, the following entry is made :—

Dividend No. 4, 1894............... $1000.00

    To Surplus Fund........................ $1000.00

If Treasury Stock is credited for the Dividends, as is done by many bookkeepers, would it not be fair for the person who should buy the Treasury stock to receive its Dividends? Why should the purchaser receive Dividends on his stock as soon as he buys it? The established custom is to declare Dividends on the amount of stock issued. Say the Capital Stock is $100,000, and $50,000 paid in or stock issued, and the net gain $10,000. On the Capital Stock this would pay 10%, but on the paid up capital it would pay 20% Dividends; therefore Dividends should be declared on the paid-in capital, because the $50,000 produced the gain, instead of $100,000 being required to do it.

Treasury Stock should be credited by Inventory for the value of the unsold stock.

There are a great many points regarding Dividends, Stock account, etc., which should be determined by the Board of Directors, leaving the accountant to do as they direct, whether it be in accordance with good accounting and correct principles, or not. You will be expected to obey. Be careful ; do not be made a scape-goat or a tool. Sacrifice your position rather than your honor and reputation by doctoring the accounts and carrying out the unlawful cussedness of a lot of knaves. Many corporations are formed and innocent stockholders fleeced by unscrupulous organizers, who then lay the blame on the ignorance of the bookkeeper. Be master of the situation ; know your duty and do it, regardless of the consequences. In the end you will succeed.

CHAPTER THIRTEEN.

A Printing and Publishing Company.

Ex. 261. Credit and Stock Dividend Declared under Special Conditions. Gibbons, Bayne, Kneale, Hatch and Caldwell formed a Limited Partnership Company for the purpose of conducting a Printing and Publishing Business. The Capital Stock is $75,000, 750 shares, par value $100. Gibbons subscribed for 100 shares, Bayne 100 shares, Kneale 200 shares, Hatch 150 shares, and Caldwell 100 shares. They were to pay for their stock in Machinery, Type, Paper, etc., of the old partnership. At the end of the year there was a net gain of $16,500. The company declared a dividend for full amount of the net gain, payable in stock as far as it would go, and credited each stockholder for his respective share of the excess. What are the Journal Entries?

Subscription	$65,000.00	
Treasury Stock	10,000.00	
To Capital Stock		$75,000.00

Then :—

Machinery	$45,000.00	
Type, etc.	15,000.00	
Paper	5,000.00	
To Subscription		$65,000.00

Or the first entry could be :—

Machinery	$45,000.00	
Type	15,000.00	
Paper	5,000.00	
Treasury Stock	10,000.00	
To Capital Stock		$75,000.00

Entry to declare Dividend :—

Loss and Gain	$16,500.00	
To Surplus		$16,500.00

Then :—

Surplus	$16,500.00	
To Dividend No. 1, 1894		$16,500.00

Then :—

Dividend No. 1, 1894......... $16,500.00

To Treasury Stock...................	$10,000.00
" Gibbons...........................	1,000 00
" Bayne	1,000.00
" Kneale............................	2,000.00
". Hatch........................	1,500.00
" Caldwell	1,000.00

This entry issues the Treasury Stock in part payment of the Dividend, and credits the stockholders in their personal accounts for their respective shares of the balance of the net gain. Then issue to them their stock and credit them in Stock Ledger. Each stockholder's proportion of the Treasury Stock is equal to $15\frac{5}{13}\%$ on $65,000 Capital Stock. The balance of the net gain is $6500, or 10% on $65,000 ; $15\frac{5}{13}\%$ of $10,000 Treasury Stock results in uneven amounts. The stock is divided as nearly as possible, but none issued for less than one-fourth shares, while the stockholders arrange among themselves for the amounts over the value of one-fourth of a share.

A Mining Company.

Ex. 262. **The Westmoreland Coal Co. was incorporated in Pittsburgh, Pa., Jan. 1, 1888, with a Capital Stock of $1,200,000, 12,000 shares, par value $100 each.** All the shares were subscribed and paid for in Cash ; entries shown. Stock sold for Cash ; mines and plants bought for Cash. Capital Stock reduced under various conditions. Common Stock changed to Preferred Stock. Preferred Stock issued. Dividends declared on Preferred Stock and Common Stock. Stock watered, and entries to inflate values, etc.

The whole amount of Stock being subscribed and paid in Cash, the first entry would be in—

CASH BOOK.

To Capital Stock...... $1,200,00.00	
(Full history.)	

Or enter in the Journal :—

Subscription.............. $1,200,000.00
    To Capital Stock.................. $1,200,000.00

Then as the subscriptions are paid enter in the Cash Book :—

Cash Dr. To *Subscriptions.*

The company then bought of the H. C. Frick Coke Co. two
Mines and Plants—the Hecla Mine at Mt. Pleasant, Pa., with Land,
Buildings, Machinery, etc., for $550,000, and the Broadford Mines at
Broadford, Pa., with Plant complete, for $600,000,—paying for them in
cash.   What entry ?

        Hecla Mines................. $550,000.00
          (Full history and Deed.)
        Broadford Mines.............   600,000.00
            To Cash.............................. $1,150,000.00

At the end of the year the net gain was $162,000, and a Div-
idend of 10% was declared.   What entry?

        Loss and Gain................. $162,000.00
            To Surplus........................... $162,000.00
Then :—

        Surplus........................ $120,000.00
            To Dividend No. 1, 1888........... $120,000.00

This leaves a Net Surplus of $42,000.   The market value of the
stock rose very high, and it was voted by the stockholders to water
the stock and distribute *pro rata* among themselves $600,000 of full
paid stock, and increase the value of the two mines and plants.   What
entry ?

        Hecla Mine.................... $300,000.00
        For 3000 shares at $100, issued
        to stockholders. See Minute
        Book, p. 140.
        Broadford Mine...............   300,000.00
          (History.)
            To Capital Stock.................... $600,000.00

This operation and declaration of the stockholders increases the
capital stock of the company by watering, which can be done only by
law ; nevertheless, it is of frequent occurrence.   However, when this
entry is made, issue and deliver the stock to the stockholders *pro rata*,
and post the same to Stock Ledger.   Instead of inflating the value of
the mines, the entry could have been *Franchise*, *Contingencies*, or any
account that represents no value.

Now, suppose that, instead of a net gain, the company had lost
say $200,000, and in consequence the stockholders decide to reduce
the capital stock to $900,000, and to pass the difference between the
$200,000 net loss and the $300,000 reduced stock to the credit of
Surplus.

What are the entries in the General Books and Stock Books for the above transactions?

In the General Books the entry to reduce Capital Stock would be:

Capital Stock.................. $300,000.00

To Loss and Gain.................... $200,000.00

" Surplus.......................... 100,000.00

(Full history.)

The Capital Stock having been reduced, the old certificates of stock must be taken up, and new certificates issued to the stockholders for the stock still owned by each. Debit each stockholder in the Stock Ledger for the shares surrendered.

If the Capital Stock is reduced and the shareholders are to receive the par value in cash, the entry would be:—

Capital Stock To Cash.

Suppose there is Treasury Stock unsubscribed amounting to $50,000, and it is desired to reduce the Capital Stock for the amount of the Treasury Stock, the entry would be:—

Capital Stock To Treasury Stock.

Again, suppose that the Capital Stock is to be reduced, and the stockholders are paid a part in cash, what would be the entry when the certificates are surrendered?

Capital Stock

To Cash

" Loss and Gain

After reducing the Capital Stock as shown above, the company find at the end of another year that practically they have not gained anything or lost anything, and to provide more Working capital they decide to issue $250,000 of Preferred Stock. The conditions are that the Preferred Stock shall receive an annual Dividend of 6% of the profits of the company before any Dividend shall be declared on the Common Stock. After declaring the Dividend of 6% on the Preferred, should there remain a sufficient gain to declare a Dividend on the Common Stock and Preferred Stock of 3% or more, then such Dividend should be declared; but should the gain be less than 3% it should remain to the credit of Surplus or Reserve Fund until another Preferred Dividend is made. Should the profits not equal a 6% Dividend, the same should be declared on the Preferred Stock as far as possible, or rather at as high a rate as possible. The above resolutions are in accordance with law. Preferred Stock receives Dividends first ; then, if anything remains, another Dividend is declared for the balance of the gain on all the stock, Preferred and Common. As decided by the stockholders, $250,000 Preferred Stock was placed in the market. What entry?

      Franchise....................... $250,000.00
          To Preferred Capital Stock........ $250,000.00

Or if this stock was subscribed and paid for in cash, then :—

      Cash... .... $250,000.00
          To Preferred Capital Stock........ $250,000.00

In the Stock Ledger *Debit Preferred Capital Stock* and *Credit* the *Stockholders* for the same, showing clearly that it is Preferred Stock. If a stockholder has Preferred and Common Stock, open up an account in Stock Ledger with him for each stock separately.

To declare a Dividend on the Preferred Stock, the Journal entry would be :—

    Surplus To *Preferred Stock Dividend No.* 1, 1894, etc.

To declare a General Dividend on Preferred and Common Stock, the entry would be :—

    Surplus
        To *Preferred Stock Dividend No.* 1, 1894.
        " *Dividend No.* 1, 1894.

NOTE.—The Stock Certificates for Preferred Stock would be so marked. Preferred Stock is to be preferred to Common Stock, but Guaranteed Stock is the most valuable, because a certain Dividend or Interest is guaranteed by the company, while on Preferred and Common if there is any gain you get, if there is no gain you get nothing.

CHAPTER FOURTEEN.

A Limited Wholesale Grocery Company.

Ex. 263. **Wm. Edwards has been conducting a Wholesale Grocery, and has this day formed a Limited Partnership Company, with a Capital Stock of $250,000, 2500 shares, par value $100. The corporate name is The Wm. Edwards Grocery Company, Limited,**

Wm. Edwards subscribed for 1500 shares.........				$150,000.00
J. D. Boyd	"	"	500 "	50,000.00
H. A. Jones	"	"	100 "	10,000.00
C. J. Thomas	"	"	200 "	20,000.00
S. S. West	"	"	200 "	20,000.00

The Assets and Liabilities of Wm. Edwards, as shown by his books and inventory, are as follows :—

ASSETS.

Cash	$51,500.00
Mdse. (Inventory)......................	132,000.00
Bills Rec...............................	30,000.00
Accts. Rec.............................	41,500.00
Store Fixtures.........................	2,100.00
Total.................................	$257,100.00

LIABILITIES.

Accounts Payable......................	$25,000.00
Bills Payable..........................	40,000.00
Total.................................	$65,000.00

First entry to open the books:—

Subscription.................. $250,000.00	
To Capital Stock.....................	$250,000.00

Wm. Edwards pays for his stock out of the assets of his former business as follows: Mdse. $100,000, store fixtures $2100, Bills Receivable (which he guarantees) $30,000, and Cash $17,900. What entry?

Mdse......................... $100,000.00	
Store Fixtures.............. 2,100.00	
Bills Rec.................... 30,000.00	
Cash........................ 17,900.00	
To Subscription.....................	$150,000.00

The other subscribers pay for their stock as follows: J. D. Boyd, 500 shares Union National Bank stock, par value $100, $50,000; H. A. Jones deeds a four-story brick block on Water Street, $10,000; C. J. Thomas gives his Note in favor of the company at four months, $20,000; S. S. West pays cash, $20,000. What entry?

Union National Bank Stock.. $50,000.00
Real Estate...... .... 10,000.00
Bills Receivable.................. 20,000.00
Cash................................ 20,000.00
    To Subscription....................... $100,000.00

Had all the stock been paid for at the time of incorporating, the following entry would be correct also:—

Mdse............................. $100,000.00
Store Fixtures.................. 2,100.00
Bills Receivable................. 50,000.00
Cash....... .... 37,900.00
Union Nat'l Bank Stock..... 50,000.00
Real Estate...................... 10,000.00
    To Capital Stock....................... $250,000.00

The new company have purchased from Mr. Edwards the balance of merchandise belonging to him, on account, which amounts to $32,000. It is also agreed that the new company shall collect all accounts, and credit Wm. Edwards, and that they shall also pay all personal accounts and Bills Payable, and charge Wm. Edwards for the same.

Journal entry to buy the stock of Mdse. belonging to Wm. Edwards:—

Mdse.. .... $32,000.00
    To Wm. Edwards..................... $32,000.00
        (Full history.)

When any of the personal accounts or Bills Payable of the old house of Wm. Edwards are paid by the new company, enter the same in the books of Wm. Edwards, and at the same time *Debit Wm. Edwards* and *Credit Cash* in the books of the company. When any of the personal accounts or Bills Receivable of the old firm are collected by the company, enter the same in the books of the old firm, and at the same time *Debit Cash* and *Credit Wm. Edwards* in the books of the company.

A Manufacturing Company.

Ex. 264. Single Entry Stock Books Changed to Double Entry and a Stock Dividend Declared.

The Cleveland Manufacturing Co., Limited, was organized Jan. 1st, 1893, with a Capital Stock of $25,000, 250 shares, par value $100. The Capital Stock paid up is $20,000, and is held by the following named parties: C. C. Dewstoe, 50 shares, $5000; S. W. Burrows, 45 shares, $4500; L. M. Southern, 54½ shares, $5450; W. H. Van Tine, 50½ shares, $5050. Fifty shares are held as Treasury Stock.

Jan. 1st, 1894, the company decided to open a new set of books, to be kept by Double Entry, close the old Single Entry books, and declare a Stock Dividend equal to the unsold Treasury Stock, and issue the same to the stockholders in proportion to the stock held by each.

Statement of Assets and Liabilities Taken Dec. 31, 1893.

ASSETS.

Merchandise (per Inventory)	$5339.40	
Cash	3100.45	
Bills Receivable	2500.00	
First Nat'l Bank Stock (20 shares)	2000.00	
Machinery and Tools (per Inventory)	10000.00	
Furniture and Fixtures (per Inventory)	590.00	
Real Estate (per Inventory)	5900.00	
Horse and Wagon (per Inventory)	500.00	
Treasury Stock	5000.00	
Accounts Receivable	11592.76	
Total Assets		$46522.61

LIABILITIES.

Capital Stock	$25000.00	
Bills Payable	8341.37	
Accounts Payable	5621.75	
Total Liabilities		$38963.12
Difference is a Net Gain		$7559.49

The above statement determines the net gain for the year.

The following Journal Entry is made to open the books by Double Entry:—

Merchandise $5339.40
Cash... 3100.45
Bills Receivable............................... 2500.00
First National Bank Stock................. 2000.00
Machinery and Tools........................ 10000.00
Furniture and Fixtures..................... 590.00
Real Estate............................ ...... 5900.00
Horse and Wagon........................... 500.00
Treasury Stock.............................. 5000.00
Accounts Receivable....................... 11592.76
  To Capital Stock................................. $25000.00
  " Bills Payable.................................. 8341.37
  " Accounts Payable............................ 5621.75
  " Loss and Gain................................. 7559.49

To declare a Dividend payable in Treasury Stock and pass the balance of the net gain to Reserve Fund, what entry?

Loss and Gain......................... $7559.49
  To Surplus.................................... $7559.49

Then :—

Surplus.................................. $7559.49
  To Reserve Fund........................ $2559.49
  " Dividend No. 1, 1894.............. 5000.00

To declare a Dividend equal to the Treasury Stock, which is $5000, on $25,000 capital, or a Dividend of 25% :—

C. C. Dewstoe, 50 shares, or $5000, 25% Dividend..... $1250.00
S. W. Burrows, 45 " " $4500, 25% " 1125.00
L. M. Southern, 54½ shares, or $5450, 25% Dividend, 1362.50
W. H. Van Tine, 50½ " " $5050, 25% " 1262.50
                             $5000.00

Since the shares of stock are $100 each, it is impossible to issue them to the stockholders for the full proportion of their respective shares. The stock is issued for half shares, however, in order to get as near the full amount as possible.

C. C. Dewstoe's proportion is $1250, and he receives 12½ shares.

S. W. Burrows' proportion is $1125, and he receives 11 shares, balance $25.00.

L. M. Southern's proportion is $1362.50, and he receives 13½ shares, balance $12.50.

W. H. Van Tine's proportion is $1262.50, and he receives 12½ shares, balance $12.50.

To issue the new certificates as above, it will be readily seen that Burrows, Southern and Van Tine have a credit combined amounting to $50, or one-half share, being too small an amount to issue to any one of them ; hence it is agreed that the stock be issued as above proportioned, the half share to remain as Treasury Stock until some future time. What entry when the stock is issued?

Dividend No. 1, 1894............... $4950.00
    To Treasury Stock...................... $4950.00

Now, it is agreed by the stockholders that S. W. Burrows shall receive the half share of Treasury Stock. What entry ?

Dividend No. 1, 1894............ .... $50.00
    To Treasury Stock......................... $50.00

In the Stock Ledger *Debit Treasury Stock* and *Credit* the *Stockholders* for the new certificates.

In adjusting the Dividend as above, it will be noticed that Burrows' interest in the half share is $25, Southern's interest is $12.50, and Van Tine's interest is $12.50. It is issued to Burrows as agreed, but is not paid for, and no more entries are necessary on the books. How shall he pay for it ? Burrows' interest in the half share is $25 ; hence he pays the others for their interest, and takes the stock.

Note. This is a very puzzling entry and should be thoroughly understood. Considerable trouble has arisen out of this very problem, simply because it was not disposed of correctly by the bookkeeper. Many similar entries occur that baffle the skill of the accountant ; but we fail to see why it should be so, for this reason : Until this half share of Treasury Stock is issued the Dividend remains unpaid for that amount, and as soon as the half share is issued the Dividend is fully paid as declared, and is simply a matter of settlement between the stockholders for their share of it. If the company issued the stock each one's share calls for, it would be necessary to issue in denominations of one-eighth. Stock is seldom or never issued for less than one-half share, though it is sometimes issued in one-fourth shares.

No. 265. A Joint Stock Company is incorporated to conduct a general store, with a Capital Stock of $80,000, 800 shares, par value $100. Six hundred shares are taken by the incorporators, they to pay $10 per share. The remaining 200 shares are held for Working Capital. The incorporators pay $10 per share and receive full paid stock. What entry or entries?

Ex. 266.   They bought a block corner Ontario and Huron streets, for which they paid cash $2000 and stock $10,000 (100 shares).   What entry?

Ex. 267.   A net gain of $5000 was realized for the year.   What entry?

Ex. 268.   A Dividend of 5% was declared.   What entry?

Ex. 269.   A Surplus of $1000 was created.   What entry?

Ex. 270.   A mortgage of $4000 was placed on the above property to raise money to pay the Dividend.   What entry?

Ex. 271.   John D. Carbaugh has invented a corn planter of great value, which he has patented.   A Stock Company was incorporated to manufacture it, with a Capital Stock of $200,000, 2000 shares, par value $100.   Carbaugh is to receive 250 shares full paid stock for his Patent Right, which he deeds to the company.   The incorporators subscribe as follows: C. W. Strickler, 100 shares; C. S. Overholt, 400 shares; J. H. Clark, 150 shares; R. E. Fulton, 100 shares; Jas. Neil, 500.   The remaining shares are set apart as Working Capital. Give two entries to open the books, with full explanations.

NOTE.—**The Power of the States to Regulate Particular Classes of Business.**   The extent to which a State can by legislation regulate the business and affairs of an association, whether it be incorporated or not, necessarily depends largely upon the nature of the business in which the association is engaged.   Legislative powers extend over all matters of public interest; but where the public are not interested, private rights cannot be interfered with.   If a particular kind of business or employment is of such a character or of such magnitude that the public are directly interested in its proper management, it falls within the legislative duties of the government to regulate the same.   And under these circumstances the Legislature cannot be ousted from its proper sphere of action by the fact that a number of individuals have agreed to form a co-partnership or corporation for the purpose of carrying on the business in question.   Thus the public are obviously interested in a very high degree in the proper management and operation of railroad and insurance companies; and hence the Legislature may make rules and regulations for the proper management and operation of railroad and insurance business, etc., whether conducted by corporations or not.   The power of legislative interference is much more limited in case of companies formed for the purpose of carrying on employments in which the public are less directly concerned, such as manufacturing, mining, or buying and selling.   The constitutionality of the legislation generally depends upon the answer to the question: Was the legislation designed to accomplish some object of public interest?

CHAPTER FIFTEEN.

Street Railroad Consolidation.

Ex. 272. The East Cleveland Railway Co. and the South Side Street Railway Co. have consolidated under the following conditions: The new company is to be called The Cleveland Electric Railway Co., with a Capital Stock of $2,500,000, consisting of 25,000 shares, par value $100. The old stock of both companies to be redeemed at par and new stock issued in its stead. The Assets and Liabilities of both companies to be assumed by the new corporation. Eighteen thousand shares are taken by the old stockholders and 7000 shares held by the Treasurer to be sold for Operating Capital. What are the entries?

Statement and Condition of The East Cleveland Ry. Co.

ASSETS.

Construction..	$500,000.00
Motors, Cars and Trucks........................	350,000.00
Power House...	275,000.00
Car Barns..	24,000.00
Office Furniture......................................	1,500.00
Cash..	42,000.00
Franchise..	425,000.00
Total Assets..................................	$1,617,500.00

LIABILITIES.

Capital Stock..	$1,000,000.00
First Mortgage Bonds............................	310,000.00
Accts. Payable..	17,500.00
Second Mortgage Bonds.........................	175,000.00
Surplus...	100,000.00
Interest due on First Mortgage Bonds......	8,000.00
" " Second " "	7,000.00
Total Liabilities............................	$1,617,500.00

Statement and Condition of The South Side Street Ry. Co.

ASSETS.

Cash..	$ 32,500.00
Franchise	300,000.00
Office Furniture....................................	975.00
U. S. 6% Bonds....................................	30,000.00
Iuterest due on U. S. 6's........................	900.00
Power House...	200,000.00
Construction	502,625.00
Motors and Cars....................................	275,000.00
Car Barns...	18 000.00
Total Assets.......................................	$1,360,000.00

LIABILITIES.

Capital Stock.......................................	$800,000.00
Bills Payable..	35,000.00
Surplus..	50,000.00
Accounts Payable..................................	12,500.00
First Mortgage Bonds...........................	200,000.00
Interest due on same.............................	5,000.00
Second Mortgage Bonds........................	250,000.00
Interest due on same.............................	7,500.00
Total Liabilities..............................	$1,360,000.00

What entries should be made in the books of The East Cleveland Railway Company to close them up?

First entry :—

The Cleveland Electric Ry. Co..... $1,617,500.00

To Construction.....................................	$500,000.00
" Motors, Cars, etc.............................	350,000.00
" Power House....................................	275,000.00
" Car Barns.......................................	24,000.00
" Office Furniture...............................	1,500.00
" Cash..	42,000.00
" Franchise.......................................	425,000.00

With full history, showing that the Assets have been transferred to the new company

Second entry :—

Capital Stock..............	$1,000,000.00
First Mortgage Bonds........	310,000.00
Accts. Payable............	17,500.00
Second Mortgage Bonds.....	175,000.00
Surplus	100,000.00
Int. due on 1st M. Bonds....	8,000.00
" " 2d " "	7,000.00

To The Cleveland Electric Ry. Co. $1,617,500.00

With full history, showing that the Liabilities have been transferred to the new company. The above entries will close all accounts in the books of the East Cleveland Ry. Co.; also close the account with the new company.

What entries are required to close the books of the South Side Street Ry. Co.? The entries required to close the books of this company would be the same as for the East Cleveland Co., showing that the Assets and Liabilities have been transferred to the new company.

Now that the books and accounts of both companies are closed, what entry is necessary to open the books of the new consolidated?

Journal Entry.

Construction.....................	$1,002,625.00
Motors	625,000.00
Power Houses..................	475,000.00
Barns............................	42,000.00
Furniture and Fixtures.....	2,475.00
Cash............................	74,500.00
U. S. Bonds, 6's..............	30,000.00
Interest on U. S. Bonds.....	900.00
Franchise	725,000.00
Treasury Stock..............	700,000.00

To Capital Stock..........................	$1,800,000.00
" First Mortgage Bonds................	510,000.00
" Accts. Payable.........................	30,000.00
" Second Mortgage Bonds.............	425,000.00
" Surplus.................................	150,000.00
" Int. due on First Mort. Bonds......	13,000.00
" " " Second " "	14,500.00
" Bills Payable...........................	35,000.00
" Working Capital......................	700,000.00

The above entry would open the books by combining the Assets and Liabilities of the two companies. The following entry is recommended, as it gives the Assets and Liabilities separately :—

Construction, E. C. Ry.	$500,000.00
" S. S. St. Ry.	502,625.00
Motors and Cars, E. C. Ry. Co.	350,000.00
" " S. S. St. Ry.	275,000.00
Power House, E. C. Ry. Co.	275,000.00
" · S. S. St. Ry.	200,000.00
Barns, E. C. Ry. Co.	24,000.00
" S. S. St. Ry.	18,000.00
Furniture and Fixtures, E. C. Ry. Co.	1,500.00
" " S. S. St. Ry.	975.00
Cash, E. C. Ry. Co.	42,000.00
" S. S. St. Ry.	32,500.00
U. S. Bonds, 6's, S. S. S . Ry.	30,000.00
Interest on U. S. Bonds, 6's, S. S. St. Ry.	900.00
Franchise, S. S. St. Ry.	300,000.00
" E. C. Ry. Co.	425,000.00
Treasury Stock	700,000.00

To First Mortgage Bonds, E. C. Ry. Co.	$310,000.00
" " " " S. S. St. Ry.	200,000.00
" Accounts Payable, E. C. Ry. Co.	17,500.00
" " " S. S. St. Ry.	12,500.00
" Second Mortgage Bonds, E. C. Ry. Co.	175,000.00
" " " " S. S. St. Ry.	250,000.00
" Surplus, E. C. Ry. Co.	100,000.00
" " S. S. St. Ry.	50,000.00
" Interest on First Mort. Bonds, E. C. Ry. Co.	8,000.00
" " " " " S. S. St. Ry.	5,000.00
" " Second " " E. C. Ry. Co.	7,000.00
" " " " " S. S. St. Ry.	7,500.00
" Bills Payable, S. S. St. Ry.	35,000.00
" Capital Stock	1,800,000.00
" Working Capital	700,000.00

If desired, the Franchise account can be omitted and the amount therein added to Construction, Motors, etc. In many cities street railroads are required to pay for the privilege of the streets ; then an account must be kept with Franchise for what it has cost. If the Franchise is granted say for 25 years, at a certain amount, then before declaring the annual Dividend $\frac{1}{4}$ of this cost should be written off, to arrive at accurate results.

Suppose the company desires to extend its lines and add other improvements which will cost $500,000. To raise this amount the stockholders decide to issue Bonds ; also, to take up the bonds of the old companies. To do this it will be necessary to issue $1,500,000 in First Mortgage Bonds. The old First and Second Mortgage Bonds are redeemed and new ones issued, the balance to be placed on the market and sold, as follows :—

$200,000 bonds sold at par. What entry?

Cash.............................. $200,000.00
      To First Mortgage Bonds........ $200,000.00

$200,000 Bonds sold at 10% discount. What entry?

Cash.............................. $180,000.00
Loss and Gain................   20,000.00
      To First Mortgage Bonds......... $200,000.00

The balance, $100,000, sold at a premium of 10%. What entry?

Cash.............................. $110,000.00
      To First Mortgage Bonds......... $100,000.00
      " Loss and Gain...................   10,000.00

What entry when the old Bonds are redeemed?

First Mort. Bonds E. C. Ry. Co.... $310,000.00
    "   "   " S. S. St. Ry......   200,000.00
Second Mort. Bonds E. C. Ry. Co...   175,000.00
    "   "   " S. S. St. Ry ...   250,000.00
      To First Mortgage Bonds............... $935,000.00

When the Interest is paid on the Bonds, *Debit Interest* and *Credit Cash.*

When a corporation issues Bonds, they are secured by mortgages. No entry is made of such Mortgage, as it is already covered in the Bond account, and is also shown in the Minute Book. When entering the first sale of Bonds, copy in the entry the Mortgage given. Bonds are not a Liability until they are sold ; hence they should have no account upon the books until they are sold. Bonds are not a Liability while in the hands of brokers or agents. Should they report sales, then the Bonds must be accounted for.

CHAPTER SIXTEEN.

An Ice Company.

Ex. 273.   The Buckeye Ice Company of Cleveland, O., wishing to cover losses amounting to $40,000, and to produce an Operating Capital of $35,000, calls an Assessment of 25 per cent. on its Capital Stock of $300,000.   Assessment $75,000, payable in cash.

Assume the assessment to be paid.   What entry ?

        Cash............................... $75,000.00
                To Loss and Gain..................... $40,000.00
                " Working Capital.................. 35,000.00

Suppose that at the end of the year $30,000 of the $35,000 Working Capital had been lost, and a second assessment of 10% was levied to procure more Working Capital.   What entries ?

        Working Capital............... $30,000.00
                To Loss and Gain..................... $30,000.00
                (For loss of past year, etc.)

(Entry when the assessment is paid.)

        Cash............................... $30,000.00
                To Working Capital................. $30,000.00

Suppose the company pays $25,000 for an Ice Machine for manufacturing ice ; what entry ?

        Working Capital............... $25,000.00
                To Cash................................ $25,000.00
        For amount withdrawn from Working Capital and used to purchase machinery.

Since the company gave no value for the cash received from the assessments, and the Working Capital has been used for other purposes, Loss and Gain must receive credit ; therefore, when the books are closed we make the following entry :—

        Machinery $25,000.00
                To Loss and Gain..................... $25,000.00

Some bookkeepers would credit Loss and Gain when cash was received.   It really is a gain, as nothing was given for it ; but it must be remembered that this cash was for Working Capital, as the Capital account was thereby increased.   In the end, however, it must go to Loss and Gain.

A Manufacturing Company.

Ex. 274. The Reed Fly Screen Manufacturing Company was incorporated January 1st, 1893, with a Capital Stock of $100,000, 1000 shares, par value $100. Eight hundred shares were issued to Reed in part payment for his Patent Right for the State of Ohio; 200 shares were subscribed and paid in cash. All stock was fully paid.

The Patent Right was paid for as follow:—

800 Shares fully paid Stock, $100.........	$80,000.00
Cash........................	5,000.00

The books were opened by the following entry:—

Patent Right..................	$80,000.00
Cash............................	20,000.00
To Capital Stock....................	$100,000.00

From the Cash Book was posted:—

Patent Right......................	$5,000.00
To Cash.	$5,000.00

January 1st, 1894, it was deemed advisable that the Capital Stock be reduced to $50,000, making a reduction of $50,000. What entry?

Capital Stock..................... $50,000.00
For 50 per cent. of Capital Stock,
or from $100 to $50 per share; 1000
shares @ $50=$50,000 reduction.

　　To Patent Right....................... $42,500.00
　　For 50 per cent. reduction of its cost, etc.

　　To Loss and Gain.................... 7,500.00
　　For 50 per cent. reduction of 150 shares
　　sold for cash and held by the Treas-
　　urer, which is now reduced 50 per cent.
　　and is evidently a gain. The cash re-
　　ceived from the sale of the remaining
　　shares was deducted in the credit to
　　Patent Right.

After reducing the Capital Stock as above, the stockholders will surrender their stock certificates and be Debited for same in Stock Ledger. Then issue to them new certificates for the remaining shares held by each. If you Debit them in the Stock Ledger for entire amount of certificates, then you must Credit them again for the new certificates.

To Increase or Reduce the Value of Assets Before Declaring a Dividend.

Ex. 275. **The Plant and Quarry of the Berkshire Marble Co. of Boston, have fairly increased in value $20,000, owing to the discovery of limestone on another part of their land.** What entry is necessary on the books?

The correct way would be to make a new Inventory of the Plant, for the new valuation. When closing the books credit the account by Inventory, and close it into Loss and Gain, bringing the Inventory down for new account. If it is desired, however, the entry could be made thus :—

Plant............................ $20,000.00

To Loss and Gain.................... $20,000.00

If this entry is used, then the Inventory must include the increased value.

Suppose the Plant has decreased in value since the last dividend was declared, say $10,000, owing to heavy operating and reduced prices ; what entry would you make?

Inventory the Plant for $10,000 less than the last, and close into Loss and Gain ; or—

Loss and Gain.................... $10,000.00

To Plant $10,000.00

The company owns 300 shares of The N. Y. & N. E. Ry. Co. stock, par value $100, which has decreased from 125 to 115, a decrease of 10 points per share. What entry should be made in the books before declaring a Dividend, to show the actual condition of the company?

Loss and Gain (old acct.)........ $3000.00

To Loss and Gain (new acct.)...... $3000.00

Note. Post the debit entry ; then close the books. After the books have been closed, post the credit entry. This entry first shows a Loss on this stock, which has been declared as a Loss, for this Dividend. Now, if this stock had been sold at the time it would have been an actual Loss ; but the credit to Loss and Gain new account holds it as a Gain until the next Dividend, or until the stock is sold. Many corporations inflate the value of their assets instead of writing off the depreciation. National Banks are compelled by law to correctly value their assets, and we trust that all corporations will be required to do likewise at an early date.

CHAPTER SEVENTEEN.

Reduction of the Capital Stock of a Bank.

Ex. 276. The Buckeye Banking Company of Lima, Ohio, have lost \$230,000 Speculating in Oil. The Capital Stock is \$500,000. At a meeting of the Stockholders an entire new Board of Directors was elected. It was decided to reduce the Capital Stock to \$250,000, and the Directors were instructed to confine the business to the regular lines of Banking.

What are the entries to be made?

Capital Stock.................... \$250,000.00
For \$250,000 reduction of Stock,
as per Minute Book, p. 31, annual meeting of Stockholders,
etc.

  To Loss and Gain..................... \$230,000.00
  For loss as shown in the annual state-
  ment.
  To Cash................................ 20,000.00
  Returned to stockholders upon surren-
  der of 50 per cent. of their stock.

If cash is not paid at the time of reduction, then credit stockholders, and as payments of cash are made to them debit them and credit Cash. When they have all been paid Stockholders' account will close. It is not meant by this that each stockholder will be credited, but that an *account* with Stockholders be opened.

All the old stock certificates must be taken up and canceled and new stock issued. Debit the Stockholders in Stock Ledger for certificates returned and credit them for the new ones issued.

The bank whose Directors and officers, from the President downwards, are prone to indulgence in stock speculations, and who seem to be currently more taken up with the occupation of studying the vibrations and revolutions of the Stock Exchange, than with the business of banking—the business which is nominally their sole profession,—cannot be considered an institution that is managed with due prudence and safety. Defalcations are liable to be the outcome of such a situation. The bank which is managed without a due regard for the laws of banking, and with an open disregard of the principles of strict

honor and honesty, equity and fairness, is surely in a bad way, and
also particularly open to losses from the irregularities of employes
who are demoralized by their surroundings—who live under the influence of bad example.

A Manufacturing Company.

Ex. 277. A manufacturing company has been organized with a
Capital Stock of $80,000. There are eight stockholders, each holding
$10,000 of *paid up* stock. The amount of cash actually paid in is
$16,000, and machinery $4000, making a total of $20,000, the balance
of $60,000 representing nominal or fictitious value, with nothing to
offset it. Each stockholder stands credited on the books of the company with his investment of $2500, some having paid cash, others
having put in machinery, etc., to cover same amount. What are the
proper entries to make that the books may show $10,000 stock held
by each stockholder, and a credit to Capital Stock of $80,000? This
is a very simple operation, but it has puzzled many readers of "*The
Bookkeeper*," having appeared in its columns in November, 1893.
The solutions given by the readers are amusing, to say the least.
Before making the entries, let us understand the conditions, which are
as follows: The company was incorporated for $80,000, eight stock-
holders taking $10,000 each, receiving their stock by paying $2500
for it, the balance of $7500 being allowed to each as a Bonus for
organizing the company, probably, hence their stock is paid up. The
only entry necessary to open the books would be:—

> Cash.................................. $16,000.00
> Machinery 4,000.00
> Bonus............................... 60,000.00
>
>   To Capital Stock......................$80,000.00

Instead of Bonus, you may charge Franchise, or any other account
of fictitious value.

Then credit each stockholder in the Stock Ledger for the shares,
and debit Capital Stock.

Should the stockholders ever be called upon to pay this balance
of $7500, then debit Cash and credit Bonus. If they are not called
upon, carry Bonus as a fictitious asset, which can do no harm.

Some of the entries and explanations given in answer to the
above in "*The Bookkeeper*" would fill a page in an 18-inch Journal,
and then not be correct. It is evident that the solutions and entries
are from those without Joint Stock Company experience, or who have
been through some of our so-called Business Colleges.

Stock Forfeited for Non-Payment.

Ex. 278.   Some companies incorporate in their Charter that subscribers who fail to pay their Installments when called upon shall forfeit their stock to the company, and that they shall be held liable for the discount or be paid the premium, if sold for more or less than the par of the unpaid balance.

Many companies also provide that, if any Installments are due and unpaid, the Installments already paid shall be forfeited, as well as the stock, without legal action.   When stock is subscribed under such provisions, no legal action is necessary, because it is a part of the contract.   A company can dispose of forfeited stock in any manner it may see fit.

Suppose J. R. Ressler subscribes for 20 shares of stock in a company at $50, and has paid two 12½ per cent. Installments.   Failing to pay the other Installments, he surrenders or forfeits his stock to the company.   The Installments paid are to be credited to him.   The Capital Stock was all subscribed.   Capital Stock was credited for full authorized capital, and stock certificates issued in full to each subscriber upon the payment of the first installment.   Under these conditions what entry would you make to receive the stock from Ressler?

Treasury Stock......................... $1000.00

To J R. Ressler........................... $250.00
" Subscription........... .... 750.00

Ressler is credited for the Installments paid on his subscription. Subscription account is credited because, when Ressler paid his Installments, Subscription was credited, and now that he has forfeited his stock, the balance of his subscription is thereby canceled.   Treasury Stock is debited, as it is held by the Treasurer for sale.

Suppose Ressler had forfeited both Stock and Installments, what would be the entry?

Treasury Stock......................... $1000.00

To Loss and Gain........................ $250.00
" Subscription........................... 750.00

Loss and Gain is credited for the amount of Installments paid by Ressler.   It is his loss and the company's gain.   However, it is not this class of Loss and Gain that a company should seek

J. B. Roberts subscribes for 20 shares of stock in a company at $50, and has paid four 12½ per cent. Installments.   Failing to pay the other Installments, he forfeits the Stock and Installments paid.

9

When the books were opened the Capital Stock account received credit only for the Installments paid. What entry when Roberts forfeits his Stock and Installments?

Capital Stock............................ $500.00

    To Loss and Gain......................... $500.00

Debit Capital Stock, because the amount paid in has been reduced. If a Treasury Stock account had been kept and Capital Stock had credit for full authorized capital, you would then debit Treasury Stock.

Suppose that the books were opened with the full authorized Capital credited, and Roberts, instead of forfeiting his Stock and Installments, sells it to Tarbell for cash ; that is, Tarbell pays Roberts $500, the amount of his Installments, and the Stock is transferred to Tarbell, who pays the balance in cash ; what entry?

Cash $500.00

    To Subscription.......................... $500.00

Tarbell paying the balance of Roberts' subscription in cash is the same as though Roberts had paid it himself Debit Roberts in the Stock Ledger for the Stock returned, and credit Tarbell for the amount taken by him.

Suppose, again, that Roberts forfeits his stock under the above conditions, and it is credited for Installments paid, and the stock is sold to Tarbell for $800 cash ; what entry?

Treasury Stock........................ $1000.00

    To Subscription...... .... $500.00

    " To Roberts............................ 500.00

Roberts is credited for Installments paid. Subscription is credited because the stock has been returned and is no longer subscribed for.

What entry when Tarbell buys the stock for $800 cash?

Cash $800.00

Roberts.................................... 200.00

    To Treasury Stock...................... $1000.00

Roberts is charged for the $200 loss on the sale of his stock.

CHAPTER EIGHTEEN.

Rubber Trust.

Ex. 279. The National Rubber Trust was incorporated in New York, January 1st, 1890, by the consolidation of The Ohio Rubber Co. of Cleveland, The New England Rubber Co. of Boston, The Goodrich Rubber Co. of Akron, The Keystone Rubber Co. of Philadelphia, The Metropolitan Rubber Co. of New York, and the Goodyear Rubber Co. of Providence. The Capital Stock is $10,-000,000, 100,000 shares, par value $100 ; 40,000 shares, or $4,000,000, Preferred Stock ; 60,000 shares, or $6,000,000, Common Stock.

The new company is to purchase all the property, machinery, material, etc., at an appraised value, and issue in payment full paid stock of the consolidated company. The liabilities and accounts due the·old companies are to be liquidated by themselves. The total appraised value of the old companies is $6,000,000, as shown in the statement below, for which Common Stock was issued. The Preferred Stock was placed in the market for sale.

Plant, Machinery, etc.		Real Estate.	Cash.	Furnit're and Fixtures.	Horses and Wagons.	Material.	Total.
Ohio Rubber Co.	$ 543,035	$61,240	$30,000	$3,500	$1,500	$60,725	$ 700,000
N. Eng. Rubber Co.	767,735	150,000	25,725	4,100	2,200	100,240	1,050,000
Goodrich Rubber Co.	750,000	141,000	40,100	2,700	1,950	196,350	1,132,100
Keystone Rubber Co.	777,771	152,000	31,205	3,224	1,800	74,000	1,040,000
Metropo.'n Rubber Co.	695,350	169,000	60,000	3,600	2,700	69,950	1,000,000
Goodyear Rubber Co.	721,800	174,500	75,500	3,700	2,400	100,600	1,079,900
	$4,255,691	$847,740	$262,530	$20,224	$12,550	601,265	$6,000,000

From the above statement and conditions what entries would you make to open the books of the Company, Trust or Combine?

Subscription............... $6,000,000.00
Treasury Stock.......... 4,000,000,00
    To Capital Stock.................. $6,000,000.00
    " Preferred Capital Stock..... 4,000,000.00

Issue the stock to the stockholders, and credit each of them in the Stock Ledger. The stockholders in the Ohio company will receive 7000 shares, New England company 10,500 shares, Goodrich company 11,321 shares, Keystone 10,400 shares, Metropolitan 10,000 shares, and the Goodyear company 10,799 shares. In large corporations, where there are a great number of stockholders and shares are constantly changing hands, a "Transfer Clerk" is employed for that purpose only.

What entry is made to place the assets of the new company on the books?

Plant and Machinery,	Ohio Co.		$543,035.00
"	"	New England Co.	767,735.00
"	"	Goodrich "	750,000.00
"	"	Keystone "	777,771.00
"	"	Metropolitan "	695,350.00
"	"	Goodyear "	721,800.00

$4,255,691.00

Real Estate, Ohio Co.		61,240.00
" New England Co.		150,000.00
" Goodrich "		141,000.00
" Keystone "		152,000.00
" Metropolitan "		169,000.00
" Goodyear "		174,500.00

847,740.00

Cash, Ohio Co.		30,000.00
" New England Co.		25,725.00
" Goodrich "		40,100.00
" Keystone "		31,205.00
" Metropolitan "		60,000.00
" Goodyear "		75,500.00

262,530.00

Furniture and Fixtures,	Ohio Co.		3,500.00
"	"	New England Co.	4,100 00
"	"	Goodrich "	2,700.00
"	"	Keystone "	3,224.00
"	"	Metropolitan "	3,000.00
"	"	Goodyear "	3,700.00

20,224.00

Horse and Wagon, etc.,	Ohio Co.		1,500.00
"	"	New England Co.	2,200.00
"	"	Goodrich "	1,950.00
"	"	Keystone "	1,800.00
"	"	Metropolitan "	2,700.00
"	"	Goodyear "	2,400.00

12,550.00

Material, etc.,	Ohio Co.		60,725.00
"	"	New England Co.	100,240.00
"	"	Goodrich "	196,350.00
"	"	Keystone "	74,000.00
"	"	Metropolitan "	69,950.00
"	"	Goodyear "	100,000.00

601,265.00

To Subscription.................................... $6,000,000.00

In making an entry like the above, where property, etc., have changed hands, and where titles are to be made for the same, copy all Deeds, Mortgages, Contracts or Leases in full with each entry upon the Journal. This, of course, will consume a considerable amount of space and labor; but if accurately and properly done, much litigation may be saved in the future. Spare no time, space or labor when a full, clear record is necessary.

The above Journal entry would open the books of the new company, showing the appraised value of the assets from each of the old companies.

As to how the books of the new company are to be kept, much depends upon the general management. If each plant is to keep its own books, make its own collections, and pay its own bills, then the main office will charge each plant for the value of the assets in its possession, and proceed as heretofore. When the books are closed at the end of the year, each plant will be debited for the net gain or credited for the net loss, in the books in the main office. But if all the accounts are to be paid from the main office, the only work of keeping accounts by the different plants will be that of the customers, and when collections are made they are deposited and a draft sent to the main office for the full amount daily. Each plant will also have a bank account for expenses only, the money being received from the main office and paid by check and voucher. All the invoices are to be properly checked and vouched for, and recorded, but not in Double Entry form. The invoices are then sent to the main office, where they are entered to the credit of the proper parties and paid from the main office. The record of invoices kept by the different plants must agree with the accounts kept in the main office. A daily abstract of sales is sent to the main office. These reports are recorded and must agree with the final balance sheet which is sent promptly on the last day of each month. There is also a weekly recapitulation of receipts, expenditures, sales, etc., showing check and voucher number for payments, summary of sales, etc., which shall be proven in the main office at the end of the month, when all paid checks and vouchers are sent to headquarters.

If the books are kept in the main office, as just described, it is easily seen that the closing of the books would be done and the result unknown to the different plants; but as each plant is charged with the material at commencing, the bookkeeper could determine the Loss or Gain of his plant, because the vouchers and invoices will show the expense of operating and the additional material purchased, although not charged to material account.

In the books at the main office each plant would be charged with all money sent it, all material, etc., purchased, and credited for all proceeds. The proper keeping of a set of books of a company doing so much business is simply a practical management of system and details, which should be the plainest, requiring the least amount of work, and showing the entire condition of the company at all times.

It will be noticed that the *unsubscribed* stock is Preferred Stock, the old stockholders taking the Common Stock in payment for their shares in the old companies. This will give the new company better opportunity to sell stock, and produce a larger capital, because Preferred Stock is easier to dispose of than Common Stock. Usually when all the Common Stock is taken by the incorporators, the company is capitalized for an amount that will pay say one and one-half shares of the new stock for one of the old, thereby receiving a benefit of increased stock.

Suppose the net gain for the year is $1,500,000, what entries should be made?

> Loss and Gain............. $1,500,000.00
>
> To Surplus........................... $1,500,000.00

The company declares a Dividend of 5% on the Preferred Stock and a general Dividend of 10% on the Preferred and Common Stock, and to pass $300,000 to Reserve Fund. What entry?

> Surplus............................... $1,500,000.00
>
> To Preferred Stock Dividend No. 1, 1891... $ 200,000.00
> " Dividend No. 1, 1891....................... 1,000,000.00
> " Reserve Fund............................ ..... 300,000.00

Enter the Dividends in the Dividend Book and pay them with vouchers, *Debiting Dividend account* and *Crediting Cash.*

Stock and Installments Forfeited.

Ex. 280. John Hardy subscribed for 10 shares of the Capital Stock of a Company at $100 per share and paid two 10 % installments.

Failing to pay the third installment, he forfeited his stock to the company and had credit for the installments paid. What entry, if Capital Stock received credit for full authorized capital?

Ex. 281. What entry if Stock and Installments were both forfeited?

Ex. 282. If the Capital Stock account was credited for Installments only, what entry?

A Brewing Company.

Ex. 283. The Cleveland Brewing Company was incorporated February 1, 1893, with a Capital Stock of $75,000, 750 shares par value $100. The entire stock was subscribed by ten different persons who paid cash in full.

Ex. 284. Show a Subscription Book properly filled out with names and subscriptions as you may choose, and give the opening entries.

Ex. 285. A net gain of $8000 was realized the first year. Declare a 5 per cent. dividend, pass the balance to surplus, give all entries to close, and show the Dividend Book properly filled, etc.

CHAPTER NINETEEN.

National Banks.

Formation of National Banking Associations.

Associations for carrying on the business of banking may be formed by any number of natural persons, not less in any case than five. They shall enter into articles of association, which shall specify in general terms the object for which the association is formed, and may contain any other provisions, not inconsistent with law, which the association may see fit to adopt for the regulation of its business and the conduct of its affairs. These articles shall be signed by the persons uniting to form the association, and a copy of them shall be forwarded to the Comptroller of the Currency, to be filed and preserved in his office.

Requisites of Organization Certificate.

The persons uniting to form such an association shall, under their hands, make an organization certificate, which shall specifically state:

First. The name assumed by such an association; which name shall be subject to the approval of the Comptroller of the Currency.

Second. The place where its operations of discount and deposit are to be carried on, designating the State, Territory or District, and the particular county and city, town or village.

Third. The amount of Capital Stock and the number of shares into which the same is to be divided.

Fourth. The names and places of residence of the shareholders, and the number of shares held by each of them.

Fifth. The fact that the certificate is made to enable such persons to avail themselves of these advantages.

How Certificate Shall be Acknowledged and Filed.

The organization certificate shall be acknowledged before a Judge of some court of record, or Notary Public, and shall be, together with the acknowledgment thereof, authenticated by the seal of such court, or Notary, and transmitted to the Comptroller of the Currency, who shall record and carefully preserve the same in his office.

Corporate Powers of Associations.

Upon duly making and filing articles of association and an organization certificate, the association shall become, as from the date of the execution of its organization certificate, a body corporate, and as such, and in the name designated in the organization certificate, it shall have power—

First.   To adopt and use a corporate seal.

Second.   To have succession for the period of twenty years from its organization, unless it is sooner dissolved according to the provisions of its articles of association, or by the act of its shareholders owning two-thirds of its stock, or unless its franchise becomes forfeited by some violation of law.

Third.   To make contracts.

Fourth.   To sue and to be sued, complain and defend, in any court of law and equity, as fully as natural persons.

Fifth.   To elect or appoint Directors, and by its Board of Directors to appoint a President, Vice President, Cashier, and other officers, define their duties, require bonds of them and fix the penalty thereof, dismiss such officers or any of them at pleasure, and appoint others to fill their places.

Sixth.   To prescribe, by its Board of Directors, by-laws not inconsistent with law, regulating the manner in which its stock shall be transferred, its Directors elected or appointed, its officers appointed, its property transferred, its general business conducted, and the privilege; granted to it by law exercised and enjoyed.

Seventh.   To exercise, by its Board of Directors, or duly authorized officers or agents, subject to law, all such incidental powers as shall be necessary to carry on the business of banking ; by discounting and negotiating promissory notes, drafts, bills of exchange, and other evidences of debt ; by receiving deposits ; by buying and selling exchange, coin, and bullion ; by loaning money on personal security ; and by obtaining, issuing, and circulating notes according to the provisions of law.

But no association shall transact any business, except such as is incidental and necessarily preliminary to its organization, until it has been authorized by the Comptroller of the Currency to commence the business of banking.

Power to Hold Property.

A national banking association may purchase, hold, and convey real estate for the following purposes, and for no others :—

First.   Such as shall be necessary for its immediate accommodation in the transaction of its business.

Second.   Such as shall be mortgaged to it in good faith by way of security for debts previously contracted.

Third.   Such as shall be conveyed to it in satisfaction of debts previously contracted in the course of its dealings.

Fourth.   Such as it shall purchase at sales under judgments, decrees, or mortgages held by the association, or shall purchase to secure debts due to it.

But no association shall hold the possession of any real estate under mortgage, or the title and possession of any real estate purchased to secure any debts due to it, for a longer period than five years.

Requisite Amount of Capital.

No association shall be organized with a less capital than one hundred thousand dollars; except that banks with a capital of not less than fifty thousand dollars may, with the approval of the Secretary of the Treasury, be organized in any place the population of which does not exceed six thousand inhabitants.   No association shall be organized in a city the population of which exceeds fifty thousand persons with a less capital than two hundred thousand dollars.

Shares of Stock and Transfers.

The capital stock of each association shall be divided into shares of $100 each, and be deemed personal property, and transferable on the books of the association in such manner as may be prescribed in the by-laws or articles of association.   Every person becoming a shareholder by such transfer shall, in proportion to his shares, succeed to all the rights and liabilities of the prior holder of such shares ; and no change shall be made in the articles of association by which the rights, remedies or security of the existing creditors of the association shall be impaired.

How Payment of the Capital Stock Must be Made and Proved.

At least 50 per centum of the capital stock of every association shall be paid in before it shall be authorized to commence business, and the remainder of the capital stock of such association shall be paid in installments of at least 10 per centum each, on the whole amount of capital, as frequently as one installment at the end of each succeeding month from the time it shall be authorized by the Comptroller of the Currency to commence business, and the payment of each installment shall be certified to the Comptroller, under oath, by the President or Cashier of the association.

Proceedings if Shareholders Fail to Pay Installments.

Whenever any shareholder, or his assignee, fails to pay any installment on the stock when the same is required by the preceding section to be paid, the directors of such association may sell the stock of such delinquent shareholder at public auction, having given three weeks' previous notice thereof in a newspaper published and of general circulation in the city or county where the association is located, or if no newspaper is published in said county or city, then in a newspaper published nearest thereto, to any person who will pay the highest price therefor, to be not less than the amount then due thereon, with the expenses of advertising and sale ; and the excess, if any, shall be paid to the delinquent shareholder. If no bidder can be found who will pay for such stock the amount due thereon to the association, and the cost of advertisement and sale, the amount previously paid shall be forfeited to the association, and such stock shall be sold as the directors may order, within six months of the time of such forfeiture, and if not sold it shall be cancelled and deducted from the capital stock of the association. If any such cancellation and reduction shall reduce the capital of the association below the minimum of capital required by law, the capital stock shall, within thirty days from the date of such cancellation, be increased to the required amount ; in default of which a receiver may be appointed, to close up the business of the association.

Increase of Capital Stock.

Any association may, by its articles of association, provide for an increase of its capital from time to time, as may be deemed expedient. But the maximum of such increase to be provided in the articles of association shall be determined by the Comptroller of the Currency, and no increase of capital shall be valid until the whole amount of such increase is paid in, and notice thereof has been transmitted to the Comptroller of the Currency, and his certificate obtained specifying the amount of such increase of capital stock, with his approval thereof, and that it has been duly paid in as part of the capital of such association.

Reduction of Capital Stock.

Any association may, by the vote of shareholders owning two-thirds of its capital stock, reduce its capital to any sum not below the amount required by law; but no such reduction shall be allowable which will reduce the capital of the association below the amount required for its outstanding circulation, nor shall any such reduction be made until the amount of the proposed reduction has been reported to the Comptroller of the Currency, and his approval thereof obtained.

Right of Shareholders to Vote.

In all elections of Directors, and in deciding all questions at meetings of shareholders, each shareholder shall be entitled to one vote on each share of stock held by him. Shareholders may vote by proxies duly authorized in writing; but no officer, clerk, teller, or bookkeeper of such association shall act as proxy; and no shareholder whose liability is past due and unpaid shall be allowed to vote.

Election of Directors.

The affairs of each association shall be managed by not less than five Directors, who shall be elected by the shareholders at a meeting to be held at any time before the association is authorized by the Comptroller of the Currency to commence the business of banking, and afterward at meetings to be held on such day in January of each year as is specified therefor in the articles of association. The Directors shall hold office for one year, and until their successors are elected and have qualified.

Oath Required From Directors.

Each Director, when appointed or elected, shall take an oath that he will, so far as the duty devolves on him, diligently and honestly administer the affairs of such association.

Individual Liability of Shareholders.

The shareholders of every national banking association shall be held individually responsible, equally and ratably, and not one for another, for all contracts, debts, and engagements of such association, to the extent of the amount of stock therein, at the par value thereof, in addition to the amount invested in such shares; except that shareholders of any banking association now existing under State laws, having not less than five millions of dollars of capital actually paid in, and a surplus of 20 per centum on hand, both to be determined by the

Comptroller of the Currency, shall be liable only to the amount invested in their shares, and such surplus of 20 per centum shall be kept undiminished and be in addition to the surplus provided for by law; and if at any time there is a deficiency in such surplus of 20 per centum, such association shall not pay any dividends to its shareholders until the deficiency is made good; and in case of such deficiency the Comptroller of the Currency may compel the association to close its business and wind up its affairs.

Executors, Trustees, Etc., Not Personally Liable.

Persons holding stock as executors, administrators, guardians, or trustees shall not be personally subject to any liabilities as stockholders; but the estates and funds in their hands shall be liable in like manner and to the same extent as the testator, intestate, ward or person interested in such trust funds would be if living and competent to act and hold the stock in his own name.

Deposit of Bonds Required Before Issue of Circulating Notes.

Every association, after having complied with all the provisions of law, preliminary to the commencement of the banking business, and before it shall be authorized to commence banking business under the law, shall transfer and deliver to the Treasurer of the United States any United States registered bonds, bearing interest, to an amount not less than $30,000.00 and not less than one third of the capital stock paid in. Such bonds shall be received by the Treasurer upon deposit, and shall be by him safely kept in his office, until they shall be otherwise disposed of, in pursuance of the provisions of law.

Increase or Reduction of Deposit to Correspond With Capital.

The deposit of bonds made by each association shall be increased as its capital may be paid up or increased, so that every association shall at all times have on deposit with the Treasurer registered United States bonds to the amount of at least one-third of its capital stock actually paid in. And any association which may desire to reduce its capital, or to close up its business and dissolve its organization, may take up its bonds upon returning to the Comptroller its circulating notes in the proportion required, or may take up any excess of bonds beyond one-third of its capital stock, and upon which no circulating notes have been delivered.

Comptroller to Determine if Associations May Commence Business.

Whenever a certificate is transmitted to the Comptroller of the Currency, as provided, and the association transmitting the same notifies the Comptroller that at least 50 per centum of the capital stock has been duly paid in, and that such association has complied with all the provisions of law required to be complied with before an association shall be organized to commence the business of banking, the Comptroller shall examine into the' condition of such association, ascertain especially the amount of money paid in on account of its capital, the name and place of residence of each of its Directors, and the amount of the capital stock of which each is the owner in good faith, and generally whether such association has complied with all the provisions of law required to entitle it to engage in the business of banking; and shall cause to be made and attested by the oaths of a majority of its Directors, and by the President or Cashier of the association, a statement of all the facts necessary to enable the Comptroller to determine whether the association is lawfully entitled to commence the business of banking.

Certificate of Authority to Commence Banking to be Issued.

If, after a careful examination of the facts so reported, and of any other facts which may come to the knowledge of the Comptroller, whether by means of a special commission appointed by him for the purpose of inquiring into the condition of such association, or otherwise, it appears that such association is lawfully entitled to commence the business of banking, the Comptroller shall give to such association a certificate, under his hand and official seal, that such association has complied with all provisions required to be complied with before commencing the business of banking, and that such association is authorized to commence such business. But the Comptroller may withhold from an association his certificate authorizing the commencement of business, whenever he has reason to suppose that the shareholders have formed the same for any other than the legitimate objects contemplated by the law.

Place of Business.

The usual business of each national banking association shall be transacted at an office or banking house located in the place specified in its organization certificate.

Dividends.

The Directors of any association may, semi-annually, declare a dividend of so much of the net profits of the association as they shall judge expedient; but each association shall, before the declaration of a dividend, carry one-tenth part of its net profits of the preceding half year to its surplus fund, until the same shall amount to 20 per centum of its capital stock:

Associations Not to Loan or Purchase Their Own Stock.

No association shall make any loan or discount on the security of the shares of its own capital stock, nor be the purchaser or holder of any such shares, unless such security or purchase shall be necessary to prevent loss upon a debt previously contracted in good faith; and stock so purchased or acquired shall, within six months of the time of its purchase, be sold or disposed of at public or private sale; or, in default thereof, a receiver may be appointed to close up the business of the association.

Prohibition Upon Withdrawal of Capital.

No association, or member thereof, shall, during the time it shall continue its banking operations, withdraw, or permit to be withdrawn, either in the form of dividends or otherwise, any portion of its capital. If losses have at any time been sustained by any such association, equal to or exceeding its undivided profits then on hand, no dividend shall be made; and no dividend shall ever be made by any association, while it continues its banking operations, to an amount greater than its net profits then on hand, deducting therefrom its losses and bad debts. All debts due to any association, on which interest is past due and unpaid for a period of six months, unless the same are well secured and in process of collection, shall be considered bad debts within the meaning of this section. But nothing in this section shall prevent the reduction of the capital stock of the association.

Enforcing Payment of Deficiency in Capital Stock.

Every association which shall have failed to pay up its capital stock, as required by law, and every association whose capital stock shall have become impaired by losses or otherwise, shall, within three months after receiving notice thereof from the Comptroller of the Currency, pay the deficiency in the capital stock by assessment upon the shareholders pro rata for the amount of capital stock held by each; and the Treasurer of the United States shall withhold the interest upon all bonds held by him in trust for any such association, upon notification from the Comptroller of the Currency, until otherwise notified by him. If any such association shall fail to pay up its capital stock, and shall refuse to go into liquidation, as provided by law, for three months after receiving notice from the Comptroller, a receiver may be appointed to close up the business of the association. It is also provided that if any shareholder of such bank shall neglect or refuse, after three months' notice, to pay the assessment, as provided in this section, it shall be the duty of the Board of Directors to cause a sufficient amount of the capital stock of such shareholder or shareholders to be sold at public auction (after thirty days' notice shall be given by posting such notice of sale in the office of the bank, and by publishing such notice in a newspaper of the city or town in which the bank is located, or in a newspaper published nearest thereto), to make good the deficiency, and the balance, if any, shall be returned to such delinquent shareholder or shareholders.

Embezzlement—Penalty.

Every President, Director, Cashier, Teller, Clerk, or agent of any association, who embezzles, abstracts, or willfully misapplies any of the moneys, funds, or credits of the association ; or who, without authority from the Directors, issues or puts in circulation any of the notes of the association ; or who, without such authority, issues or puts forth any certificate of deposit, draws any order or bill of exchange, makes any acceptance, assigns any note, bond, draft, bill of exchange, mortgage, judgment, or decree ; or who makes any false entry in any book, report, or statement of the association, with intent, in either case, to injure or defraud the association or any other company, body politic or corporate, or any individual person, or to deceive any officer of the association, or any agent appointed to examine the affairs of any such association ; and every person who, with like intent, aids or abets any officer, clerk or agent in any violation of this section, shall be deemed guilty of a misdemeanor, and shall be imprisoned not less than five years or more than ten.

List of Shareholders, Etc., to be Kept.

The President and Cashier of every national banking association shall cause to be kept at all times a full and correct list of the names and residences of all the shareholders in the association, and the number of shares held by each, in the office where its business is transacted. Such list shall be subject to the inspection of all the shareholders and creditors of the association and the officers authorized to assess taxes under State authority, during business hours of each day in which business may be legally transacted.   A copy of such list, on the first Monday in July of each year, verified by the oath of such President or Cashier, shall be transmitted to the Comptroller of the Currency.

Voluntary Dissolution of Associations.

Any association may go into liquidation and be closed by a vote of its shareholders owning two-thirds of its stock.

Individual Liability of Shareholders in Case of Liquidation; How Enforced.

When any national banking association shall have gone into liquidation, the individual liability of the shareholders may be enforced by any creditor of the association, by bill in equity, in the nature of a creditor's bill, brought by such creditor on behalf of himself and any other creditors of the association, against the shareholders thereof, in any court of the United States having original jurisdiction in equity for the district in which such association may have been located or established.

Notice of Intent to Dissolve.

Whenever a vote is taken to go into liquidation, it shall be the duty of the Board of Directors to cause notice of this fact to be certified, under the seal of the association, by its President or Cashier, to the Comptroller of the Currency, and publication thereof to be made for a period of two months in a newspaper published in the city or town in which the association is located, or nearest thereto, that the association is closing up its affairs, and notifying the holders of its notes and other creditors to present the notes and other claims against the association for payment.

Deposit of Lawful Money to Redeem Outstanding Circulation.

Within six months after the date of the vote to go into liquidation, the association shall deposit with the Treasurer of the United States lawful money of the United States sufficient to redeem all its outstanding circulation.   The Treasurer shall execute duplicate receipts for money thus deposited, and deliver one to the association and the other to the Comptroller of the Currency, stating the amount received by him, and the purpose for which it had been received, and the money shall be paid into the Treasury of the United States, and placed to the credit of such association upon redemption account.

10

To Withdraw Circulation and Take Up Bonds Deposited.

Any association desiring to withdraw its circulating notes, in whole or in part, may, upon the deposit of lawful money with the Treasurer of the United States in sums not less than $9000.00, take up the bonds which said association has on deposit with the Treasurer for the security of such circulating notes, which bonds shall be assigned to the bank in the manner specified, and the outstanding notes of said association, to an amount equal to the legal tender notes deposited, shall be redeemed at the Treasury of the United States, and destroyed as now provided by law. Provided, that the amount of bonds on deposit for circulation shall not be reduced below $50,000.00.

Exemption as to an Association Consolidating With Another.

An association which is in good faith winding up its business for the purpose of consolidating with another association shall not be required to deposit lawful money for its outstanding circulation; but its assets and liabilities shall be reported by the association with which it is in process of consolidation.

Examination by Special Agent.

On receiving notice that any national banking association has failed to redeem any of its circulating notes, the Comptroller of the Currency, with the concurrence of the Secretary of the Treasury, may appoint a special agent, of whose appointment immediate notice shall be given to such association, who shall immediately proceed to ascertain whether it has refused to pay its circulating notes in the lawful money of the United States, when demanded, and shall report to the Comptroller the fact so ascertained. If, from such protest and the report so made, the Comptroller is satisfied that such association has refused to pay its circulating notes, and is in default, he shall, within thirty days after he has received notice of such failure, declare the bonds deposited by such association forfeited to the United States, and they shall thereupon be so forfeited.

Continuing Business After Default.

After a default on the part of the association to pay any of its circulating notes has been ascertained by the Comptroller, and notice (of forfeiture of the bonds) thereof has been given by him to the association, it shall not be lawful for the association suffering the same to pay out any of its notes, discount any notes or bills, or otherwise prosecute the business of banking, except to receive and safely keep money belonging to it, and to deliver special deposits.

Notice to Holders; Cancellation of Bonds; Redemption at Treasury.

Immediately upon declaring the bonds of an association forfeited for non-payment of its notes, the Comptroller shall give notice, in such manner as the Secretary of the Treasury shall, by general rules or otherwise, direct, to the holders of the circulating notes of such association, to present them for payment to the Treasury of the United States, and the same shall be paid as presented in lawful money of the United States; whereupon the Comptroller may, in his discretion, cancel an amount of bonds pledged by such association equal at current market rates, not exceeding par, to the notes paid.

Appointment of Receivers.

On becoming satisfied that any association has refused to pay its circulating notes as herein mentioned, and is in default, the Comptroller of the Currency may forthwith appoint a receiver, and require of him such bonds and security as he deems proper. Such receiver, under the direction of the Comptroller, shall take possession of the books, records, and assets of every description of such association, collect all debts, dues, and claims belonging to it, and, upon the order of a court of record of competent jurisdiction, may sell or compound all bad or doubtful debts, and, on a like order, may sell all the real and personal property of such association, on such terms as the court shall direct, and may, if necessary to pay the debts of such association, enforce the individual liability of the stockholders. Such receiver shall pay over all money so made to the Treasury of the United States, subject to the order of the Comptroller, and also make report to the Comptroller of all his acts and proceedings.

Votes for Agent on Shares of Deceased Owners—How Given.

In selecting an agent, administrators or executors of deceased shareholders may act and sign as the decedent might have done if living, and guardians may so act and sign for their ward or wards.

Notice to Present Claims.

The Comptroller shall, upon appointing a receiver, cause notice to be given, by advertisement in such newspapers as he may direct, for three consecutive months, calling on all persons who may have claims against such association to present the same, and to make legal proof thereof.

Dividends.

From time to time, after full provision has been first made for refunding to the United States any deficiency in rede.ming the notes of such association, the Comptroller shall make a ratable dividend of the money so paid over to him by such receiver on all such claims as may have been proved to his satisfaction or adjudicated in a court of competent jurisdiction, and, as the proceeds of the assets of such association are paid over to him, shall make further dividends on all claims previously proved or adjudieated; and the remainder of the proceeds, if any, shall be paid over to the shareholders of such association, or their legal representatives, in proportion to the stock by them respectively held.

Injunction Upon Receivership.

Whenever an association against which proceedings have been instituted, on account of any alleged refusal to redeem its circulating notes as aforesaid, denies having failed to do so, it may, at any time within ten days after it has been notified of the appointment of an agent, apply to the nearest Circuit, or District, or Territorial Court of the United States, to enjoin further proceedings in the premises; and such court, after citing the Comptroller of the Currency to show cause why further proceedings should not be enjoined, and after the decision of the court or finding of a jury that such association has not refused to redeem its circulating notes, when legally presented, in the lawful money of the United States, shall make an order enjoining the Comptroller, and any receiver acting under his direction, from all further proceedings on account of such alleged refusal.

Fees and Expenses.

All fees for protesting the notes issued by any national banking association shall be paid by the person procuring the protest to be made, and such association shall be liable therefor; but no part of the bonds deposited by such association shall be applied to the payment of such fees. All expenses of any preliminary or other examinations into the condition of any association shall be paid by such association. All expenses of any receivership shall be paid out of the assets of such association before distribution of the proceeds thereof.

Receiver May be Appointed When National Banks Violate any Provision of Law, or Neglects for Thirty Days to Pay a Judgment. or Becomes Insolvent.

Whenever any national banking association shall be dissolved, and its rights, privileges and franchises declared forfeited, or whenever any creditor of any national banking association shall have obtained a judgment against it in any court of record, and made application, accompanied by a certificate from the clerk of the court stating that such judgment has been rendered and has remained unpaid for the space of thirty days, or whenever the Comptroller shall become satisfied of the insolvency of a national banking association, he may, after due examination of its affairs, in either case, appoint a receiver, who shall proceed to close up such association, and enforce the personal liability of the shareholders.

Appointment of Occasional Examiners.

The Comptroller of the Currency, with the approval of the Secretary of the Treasury, shall, as often as he deems necessary or proper, appoint a suitable person or persons to make an examination of the affairs of every banking association, who shall have power to make a thorough examination into all the affairs of the association, and, in doing so, to examine any of the officers and agents thereof on oath ; and shall make a full and detailed report of the condition of the association to the Comptroller.

All persons appointed to be examiners of national banks not located in the redemption cities, or in any one of the States of Oregon, California, and Nevada, or in the Territories, shall receive compensation for such examination as follows :   For examining national banks having a capital less than $100,000, $20 ; those having a capital of $100,000 and less than $300,000, $25 ; those having a capital of $300,-000 and less than $400,000, $35 ; those having a capital of $400,000 and less than $500,000, $40 ; those having a capital of $500,000 and less than $600,000, $50 ; those having a capital of $600,000 and over, $75 ; which amounts shall be assessed by the Comptroller of the Currency upon, and paid by, the associations so examined, and shall be in lieu of the compensation and mileage heretofore allowed for making said examinations ; and persons appointed to make examination of national banks in the cities, or in any of the States of Oregon, California, Nevada, or in the Territories, shall receive such compensation as may be fixed by the Secretary of the Treasury upon the recommendation of the Comptroller of the Currency, and the same shall be assessed and paid in the manner hereinbefore provided.

Limit of Visitorial Powers.

No association shall be subject to any visitorial powers other than those authorized by law, or vested in the courts of justice.

Transfers—When Void.

All transfers of the notes, bonds, bills of exchange, or other evidences of debt owing to any national banking association, or of deposits to its credit; all assignments of mortgages, sureties on real estate, or of judgments or decrees in its favor; all deposits of money, bullion, or other valuable thing for its use or for the use of any of its shareholders or creditors; and all payments of money to either, made after the commission of an act of insolvency, or in contemplation thereof, made with a view to prevent the application of its assets in the manner prescribed, or with the view to the preference of one creditor to another, except in payment of its circulating notes, shall be utterly null and void; and no attachment, injunction, or execution shall be issued against such association or its property before final judgment in any suit, action, or proceeding in any State, county, or municipal court.

Use of the Title "National."

All banks not organized and transacting business under the national currency laws, and all persons or corporations doing the business of bankers, brokers, or savings institutions, except savings banks authorized by Congress to use the word "national" as a part of their corporate name, are prohibited from using the word "national" as a portion of the name or title of such bank, corporation, firm, or partnership; and any violation of this prohibition shall subject the party chargeable therewith to a penalty of $50 for each day during which it is committed or repeated.

Bank Bookkeeping.

The opening entries for the books of National Banks are always founded on actual values, and are therefore very simple. The number and forms of books used in a bank depend upon the volume of business, the cashier's preference as to a system of accounting, and the knowledge and ability of the head bookkeeper. The details of a banking business are uniform and simple; the main difference in different institutions is from the extent rather than from the character of the business. The difference lies in the classification of labor, rather than in the character of the entries or the avenues of profit.

Ex. 284. The Union National Bank of Cleveland was incorporated with a Capital Stock of $1,000,000, 10,000 shares, par value $100.

Stockholders.

S. M. Strong,	1000 shares,	$100..............		$100,000.00
S. T. Everett,	1000 "	$100.............................		100,000.00
E. H. Bourne,	1000 "	$100.............................		100,000.00
Lee McBride,	1000 "	$100.............................		100,000.00
M. A. Hanna,	1000 "	$100.............................		100,000.00
J. C. Weideman,	1000 "	$100.............................		100,000.00
S. W. Sessions,	1000 "	$100.......................-......		100,000.00
W. C. Scofield,	1000 "	$100.............................		100,000.00
J. C. Card,	1000 "	$100.............................		100,000.00
J. D. Watterson,	1000 "	$100.....		100,000.00

10,000 shares, $100............................$1,000,000.00

What entry to open the books?

    Subscription............... $1,000,000.00
        To Capital Stock.................... $1,000,000.00

The subscribers paid the first installment of 50%, as required by law. What entry?

    Cash............................. $500,000.00
        To Subscription............... .... $500,000.00

As the subscribers pay their subscriptions, credit them in Stock Ledger and debit Capital Stock, as in other corporations.

National Banks are required to pay in at least 50% of the Capital Stock before commencing business, and the remainder shall be paid in installments of at least 10% each on the whole capital, as frequently as one installment at the end of each succeeding month from the time it shall be authorized to commence business. Therefore, the first entry can be omitted, crediting Capital Stock as the installments are paid.

Bank bookkeeping is so simple, and the law governing National Banks is so fully set forth, that further illustrations would be useless· Any person who has kept mercantile books can readily adapt himself to the forms used in banks.

A Mining Company.

Ex. 285.　John J. Hunter is the owner of 300 acres of coal land in the famous Connellsville coke region, and has organized a Joint Stock Company known as the Pennsylvania Coal and Coke Co., for mining coal and manufacturing coke. The Capital Stock is $1,000,000, 10,000 shares, par value $100. Hunter deeds the land to the company and receives 3000 shares full paid stock. The remaining shares were all subscribed and paid in cash. What entry?

Ex. 286.　The net gain for the year was $110,000. What entry?

Ex. 287.　A Dividend of 8% was declared, and the balance of the net gain was left as surplus. What entry?

Ex. 288.　The 8% Dividend created a rise in the market value of the stock, and it was voted by the shareholders to water the stock and distribute *pro rata* among themselves $500,000 full paid stock, and increase the value of the land, mines, etc. What entry?

Ex. 289.　At the end of the second year the net loss was $100,-000, and in consequence the Capital Stock was reduced to wipe out the loss. Capital was reduced $250,000. What entry?

Ex. 290.　What disposition is made of the difference between the $250,000 reduction and the loss of $100,000?

Ex. 291.　What is done with the certificates?

Ex. 292.　What entries are made in the Stock Ledger?

Ex. 293.　What entry if the capital is reduced and the stock-holders receive par value in cash?

Ex. 294.　If there is Treasury Stock unsubscribed amounting to $250,000, and it is desired to reduce the Capital Stock for the amount of the Treasury Stock, what entry?

Ex. 295.　At the end of the third year there was practically nothing lost or gained, and the company, to raise more money, issue $250,000 Preferred Stock. What entry?

Ex. 296.　If this stock is subscribed and paid in cash, what entry?

Ex. 297.　What entries in Stock Ledger?

Ex. 298.　What entry to declare a Dividend on Preferred Stock?

Ex. 299.　What entry to declare a general Dividend on both Common and Preferred Stock?

CHAPTER TWENTY.

Bonds Issued by a Corporation.

The power to execute and issue bonds belongs to all public and private corporations, and for this they hold a common seal. When in a bond the name of the payee is left blank, the lawful holder may sign his name as such. The United States Supreme Court decided that, in general, coupon bonds issued by corporations, drawn payable to bearer, and apparently intended to pass from hand to hand, are to be regarded and treated as negotiable instruments. Coupon bonds of the ordinary kind, payable to bearer, pass by delivery ; and purchasing of them, in good faith, is unaffected by want of title in the vender. The burden of proof on a question of faith lies on the party who assails such possession. In some States, detached coupons are transferable by delivery, and the holder may sue in his own name ; in other States, the courts have decided that coupons disconnected from the bond with which they were issued are *not* negotiable without a legislative enactment to that effect. Coupons of bonds issued by public officers are valid when signed by a printed *fac simile* of the maker's autograph adopted for that purpose, even if such signing is not expressly authorized by statute. As a rule, coupons bear interest from the time of a demand of payment after their maturity. A railroad company issuing bonds by authority of Legislature, and stipulating to pay a higher rate of interest than the legal one, must continue to pay that higher rate if the bonds are not paid when they become due. Bonds that have been executed and placed for sale in the hands of an agent or broker do not, while yet on sale, constitute *property* subject to seizure, under an attachment against such corporation.

There is a wide difference between bonds issued by a governmental organization and an individual promissory note. The governmental bonds are commercial securities, and are similar to currency. Payment made in negotiable bonds for property bought by a city is the same as if currency had been used in the transaction, if the terms and circumstances of the contract imply that intention ; and such manner of payment implies that the vender intended no reservation of lien or privilege to secure the bonds at maturity.

Ex. 300. The city of Cleveland desires to issue bonds for building and repairing bridges, amounting at par to $100,000, drawing interest at the rate of 5% per annum, payable semi-annually, redeemable at the pleasure of said corporation after seven years, and payable 15 years from the date of said bonds.

The corporation binds itself to raise semi-annually a Sinking Fund bearing 5% per annum for accumulation to meet the payment of the bonds within 15 years.

The most important thing to be done in bond operations is to calculate the Sinking Fund; but as this does not require to be done until the end of six months after issue, we will consider the calculation in its natural order.

(1) Those bonds sold at date of issue may be sold at par, or at a premium, or at a discount.

(2) Those bonds sold in the first half year may be sold as above, "with interest."

(3) We will suppose $60,000 of these bonds to have been sold the first six months, viz., $30,000 at 102, yielding for face value $30,000 and $600 for premium, but at the date of issue (i. e., without accrued interest); also, $20,000 of bonds sold at par after date of issue, with interest amounting to $200; and $10,000 bonds at 98, yielding for face $10,000, for interest $400, and having discount $200. These represent the results of the first six months.

(4) We will suppose on the first day of the second half year, a day when there will be no accrued interest on the bonds, that $20,000 of bonds are sold at par, yielding, of course, $20,000, and that lastly in the same half year $10,000 of bonds are sold at 101, yielding $10,000 for face, $100 for premiums, and $100 for interest accrued.

The Sinking Fund on $60,000 issued during first half of year will, as will be shown, be $1366.66. The Sinking Fund on $90,000, issued on both half years, as will be shown, will be $2083.39. We will suppose that the Sinking Fund set aside at the end of first six months for investment yields during second six months $30 interest, and that the accumulations of Sinking Fund and investment produce for interest during third half year $80.

(5) We will suppose that no more bonds are sold.

The above conditions present the whole of the problem.

The annuity table following will enable us to calculate the Sinking Fund.

Annuity Table.	
Time in half years.	Present value of $1, payable at end of every half year. Interest payable half yearly at 5 per ct. per annum.
1	.9756
2	1.9274
3	2.8560
4	3.7620
5	4.6458
6	5.5081
7	6.3494
8	7.1701
9	7.9709
10	8.7521
11	9.5142
12	10.2578
13	10.9832
14	11.6909
15	12.3814
16	13.0550
17	13.7122
18	14.3534
19	14.9789
20	15.5892
21	16.1845
22	16.7654
23	17.3321
24	17.8850
25	18.4244
26	18.9506
27	19.4640
28	19.9649
29	20.4535
30	20.9303

This table serves a three-fold purpose: (1) If we wish to purchase an annuity of $1, payable at the end of every half year, with money at 5%, it shows we shall have to pay $20.9303. (2) If we owe a debt of $20.9303, and are allowed to pay $1 at the end of every half year for 15 years, with money at 5%, we discharge both principal and interest. For if six months' interest on $20.9303, or 0.5232, be added to the $20.9303, and then the half-yearly payment of $1 be taken from the same, the debt is reduced to $20.4535, the amount opposite No. 29 in the table. Proceeding in this way for the 30 half years, the debt of $20.9303 will have been entirely paid by $30, the difference between $30 and $20.9303 being the interest paid. (3) In 2 the interest due the first half year was 0.5232, and $1 was paid, first to cover the interest, and the balance to be applied on account of principal. This balance is 0.4768, and is called the Sinking Fund. This Sinking Fund is set aside at the end of the first half year (0.4768), and theoretically invested immediately in securities producing 5% per annum, and at the end of the second half year there is added to it six months' interest (0.0119) and the Sinking Fund (0.4768), obtaining as a result 0.9654. This 0.9654 is again supposed to be invested, and at the end of the third half year six months' interest on 0.9654, together with the 0.4768, the Sinking Fund, is added to the 0.9654, producing at the end of the third half year $1.4663.

The accumulations of the Sinking Fund are offsets to the original debt, and the difference between these and the original debt shows the amount of debt unprovided for.

At the end of six months the Sinking Fund was 0.4768, showing the debt unprovided for, the difference between $20.9303 and 0.4768, or $20.4535.

At the end of 12 months the accumulations of the Sinking Fund are 0.9654, showing the debt unprovided for, the difference between 20.9303 and 0.9654, or $19.9649.

At the end of 18 months the accumulations of the Sinking Fund are 1.4663, showing the debt unprovided for, the difference between

20.9303 and 1.4663, or $19.4640. The portion of the debt unprovided for will be seen by referring to the table opposite 29, 28 and 27.

The Sinking Fund is a bookkeeping contrivance, by means of which we can easily tell how much has been provided toward payment of the debt, and it is an offset to the debt, so as to show, by taking the difference between the debt and the Sinking Fund account, the amount of the debt unprovided for. If we multiply all the present worths of the table by, say, 1000, we shall obtain a table similar to the one we have, except payment per six months will be $1000 instead of $1. But we require for loans issued during first six months $60,000. So we want to know what number multiplied into 20.9303 produces $60,000. The number sought is 60,000 divided by 20.9303, or $2866.66. The payment of $2866.66 every half year for 30 half years will pay off the debt of $60,000, and the Sinking Fund is the difference between $2866.66 and $1500, or $1366.66, the $1500 being six months' interest on $60,000.

In the second half year there must be a change in the amount of the Sinking Fund, as there is an additional issue of $30,000. The amount payable half yearly to pay off a debt of $30,000 in $14\frac{1}{2}$ years equals 30,000 divided by 20.4535 (see table), or $1466.73. Of this amount $750 is six months' interest on $30,000, and the remainder, $716.73, the Sinking Fund for $30,000. The total Sinking Fund at the end of 12 months is the sum of these two Sinking Funds, or $2083.39, and the total semi-annual interest payable at the same time the sum of the interests, or $2250.

The bookkeeping part of it is very simple, and will be illustrated by indicating the results in the Ledgers, without reference to the books of original entry. We will consider first the General Ledger and afterwards the Investment Ledger for Sinking Fund investments.

(1) Debit cash $30,000 for face of bonds sold, and credit Bond account with same.

(2) Debit cash $600 for premium on $20,000 bonds sold, and credit Profit and Loss account.

(3) Debit Cash $20,000 for face of bonds sold, and credit Bond account.

(4) Debit Cash $200 for accrued interest on bonds ($20,000) sold, paid by purchaser, and credit Interest account.

(5) Debit Cash $10,000 for face of bonds sold, and credit Bond account.

(6) Credit Cash with $200 for discount on $10,000 bonds sold, and debit Profit and Loss.

(7) Debit Cash with $400 accrued interest, paid by purchaser of $10,000 bonds, and credit Interest.

(8) Credit Cash with Sinking Fund set aside for investment, $1366.66, and debit Sinking Fund with same.

(9) Credit Cash for $1500 for interest paid bondholders, and debit Interest account.

This is the end of the first half year. It will be observed that the only two accounts touching the income are the Interest account and the Loss and Gain account, and, so far as this bond business is concerned, they only contain interest and premiums and discounts. If the money raised by the bonds was put into plant or anything subject to depreciation, it would be necessary to—

(10) Debit Profit and Loss with Sinking Fund, $1366.66, and credit Depreciation account with same. If there is any objection, from the circumstances of the case, credit Reserve account instead of Depreciation.

Posting for the second half year is as follows:—

(11) Debit Cash $20,000 for face of bonds, and credit Bond account.

(12) Debit Cash $10,000 for face of bonds, and credit Bond account.

(13) Debit Cash $100 for premium, and credit Loss and Gain.

(14) Debit Cash $100 for interest accrued, and credit Interest account.

(15) Credit Cash $2250 for interest paid bondholders, and debit Interest account.

(16) Credit Cash $34.17 for interest on Sinking Fund, and debit Sinking Fund for same.

(17) Credit Cash for new Sinking Fund $2083.39, and debit Sinking Fund for same.

We will now suppose the investments of the Sinking Fund have produced $30 interest.

(18) Debit Cash $30, interest from Sinking Fund investment, and credit Interest.

(19) Debit Loss and Gain for addition to Sinking Fund, $2117.56, and credit Depreciation with same.

Posting for the third half year is as follows:—

(20) Credit Cash $2250 for bond interest to bond'iolders, and debit Interest.

(21) Credit Cash $87.11 for six months' interest at 5% on $3484.22 accumulation of Sinking Fund, and debit Sinking Fund with same.

(22) Credit Cash with Sinking Fund, $2083.39, and debit Sinking Fund.

(23) Debit Cash with $80, the supposed amount realized from Sinking Fund for interest, and credit Interest account for same.

(24) Debit Loss and Gain for addition to Sinking Fund for last six months, $2370.40, and credit Depreciation with same.

We proceed in this same manner from time to time, but it is thought enough has been illustrated to give a clear understanding of these accounts; therefore, we will now proceed to the Investment Ledger. The following are the entries:—

The Appropriation account of the Sinking Fund is merely the balance account, i. e., the account to put the accounts in equilibrium.

(1) Debit Sinking Fund account with $1366.66, Sinking Fund set apart for investment, and credit Appropriation account with same.

(2) Debit Investment account (A) with money invested in (A) $1300, and credit Sinking Fund.

(3) Debit Sinking Fund with additions to Sinking Fund, $2117.56, and credit Appropriation account.

(4) Debit Investment account (B) with investments made, $2150, and credit Sinking Fund account.

(5) Debit Sinking Fund account with interest accrued on investment, $30, and credit Appropriation account when the interest is received.

(6) Debit Appropriation account with $30 on handing over to general business $30 earned by investment, and credit Sinking Fund with same.

CASH.

(1)		$30,000.00	(6)		$ 200.00
(2)		600.00	(8)		1366.66
(3)		20,000.00	(9)		1500.00
(4)		200.00			
(5)		10,000.00			$3066.66
(7)		400.00	(15)		2250.00
			(16)		34.17
		$61,200.00	(17)		2083.39
(11)		20,000.00			
(12)		10,000.00			$7434.22
(13)		100.00	(20)		2250.00
(14)		100.00	(21)		87.11
(18)		30.00	(22)		2083.39
		$91,430.00			$11854.72
(23)		80.00			

SINKING FUND.

(8)	$1366.66		
(16)	34.17		
(17)	2083.39		
	$3484.22		
(21)	87.11		
(22)	2283.39		

INTEREST.

(9)	$1500.00	(4)	$200.00
(15)	2250.00	(7)	400.00
	$3750.00		$600.00
(20)	2250.00	(14)	100.00
		(18)	30.00
		(23)	80.00

LOSS AND GAIN.

(6)	$ 200.00	(2)	$600.00
(10)	1366.66	(13)	100.00
(19)	2117.56		

BOND ACCOUNT.

		(1)	$30,000.00
		(3)	20,000.00
		(5)	10,000.00
		(11)	20,000.00
		(14)	10,000.00

DEPRECIATION ACCOUNT.

		(10)	$1366.66
		(19)	2117.56

SINKING FUND ACCOUNT.

(1)	$1366.66	(2)	$1300.00
(3)	2117.56	(4)	2150.00
(5)	30.00	(6)	30.00

APPROPRIATION ACCOUNT OF SINKING FUND.

(6)	$30.00		(1)	$1366.66
			(3)	2117.56
			(5)	30.00

INVESTMENT ACCOUNT (A).

(2)	$1300.00

INVESTMENT ACCOUNT (B).

(4)	$2150.00

By proceeding on the lines here indicated from time to time, I believe you will have no difficulty in understanding the subject and pursuing it to the end.

To Find the Rate Per Cent. of Investment.

Principle.—Divide the Rate Per Cent. of Increase by the Market Value and the Quotient will be the Rate Per Cent. of Investment.

Ex. 301. If 6% bonds are purchased at 106 and 5% bonds at 90, which investment would yield the larger income?

Operation.—$6 \div 1.06 = 5\frac{35}{53}\%$. $5 \div 90 = 5\frac{5}{9}\%$. $5\frac{35}{53}\% - 5\frac{5}{9}\% = \frac{50}{477}\%$. $\frac{50}{477}\% \times 100 = 10\frac{230}{477}$. Six per cent. bonds are $10\frac{230}{477}$c. on the $100 better.

Ex. 302. I purchased railroad bonds at 40% below par, and thus realized 10% on the price of the bonds when the annual interest on same was paid. Also, purchased State securities bearing the same rate of interest 20% below par, and received annually on the latter $2400. What did I pay for the State securities?

Operation.—$10\% \times .60 = 6\%$ rate of income. $2400 \div .06 = \$40,000$. $\$40,000 \times .80 = \$32,000$, cost of State securities.

Ex. 303. What would be the rate per cent. of income on the cost of each if U. S. 10–40's be purchased at 108, U. S. 4¼'s of '86 at 106, and U. S. 4's of '91 at 105, if the semi-annual interest received on the 10–40's be $250, and the quarterly interest of 4's of '86 $112.50, and the quarterly on the 4's of '91 $200? How much must be paid for each at the above quotations?

Operation.—$5 \div 1.08 = 4\frac{7}{27}\%$; $4\frac{1}{2} \div 1.06 = 4\frac{4}{17}\%$; $4 \div 1.05 = 3\frac{17}{21}\%$: $\$250 \times 2 = \$500$ annual interest ; $\$500 \div .05 = \$10,000$; par $\$10,000 \times 1.08 = \$10,800$, cost of 10–40's.

$\$112.50 \times 4 = \$450$ annual interest ; $\$450 \div .045 = \$10,000$ par ; $\$10,000 \times 1.06 = \$10,600$, cost of $4\frac{1}{2}$'s.

$\$200 \times 4 = \$800$ annual interest ; $\$800 \div .04 = \$20,000$ par ; $\$20,000 \times 105$, $\$21,000$ paid for 4's.

The great amount of stocks and bonds which are in the market, and are likely to remain there during many years to come, renders a general knowledge of the principles which govern the accumulation of interest and the net rate per cent. of investment a subject of great public and private importance, and it is believed that a thorough understanding of the subject, as given in this lesson, will enable anyone to provide for the various funds in bond issues, and to accurately calculate the rate per cent. of profit on investments under all conditions.

11

United States of America,

STATE OF OHIO

$ 1000.

NO

CITY OF CLEVELAND

BRIDGE REPAIR BOND.

THE CITY OF CLEVELAND hereby acknowledges itself bound and indebted to J. K. Bole, or bearer, in the sum of ONE THOUSAND DOLLARS, which sum it promises to pay at the American Exchange National Bank, in the City of New York, on the first day of October, A. D. 1897, with interest thereon at the rate of FIVE per cent per annum, payable semi-annually, on the first day of April and October in each year, on presentation and surrender of the annexed coupons as they severally become due.

This Bond is one of a series of bonds aggregating $100,000, numbered from 1938 to 2053, issued for a loan to pay the cost and expense of constructing or repairing bridges situated within the corporate limits of the city, under authority of an act of the General Assembly of the State of Ohio, entitled "An act to authorize cities of the second grade of the first class to issue bonds for the purpose of erection or repair of certain bridges therein," passed May 4, 1891, and ordinance No. 2528 of said City of Cleveland.

It is hereby Certified that all the proceedings for the issuance of this bond have been had in due form as required by law. The Faith and Credit of the City of Cleveland are pledged for the payment of the principal and interest at maturity.

In Testimony Whereof the City of Cleveland has caused this bond to be executed, its corporate seal to be hereto affixed, and these presents to be signed by its Mayor and City Auditor this first day of September A. D. 1892.

SEAL

_____ City Auditor.

_____ Mayor.

$25 The City of Cleveland will pay the bearer at the American Exchange Nat. Bank in the City of New York on the first day of April, 1895. Twenty-five Dollars, interest due on Bridge Repair Bond.
W. W. Armstrong, Treas

$25 The City of Cleveland will pay the bearer at the American Exchange Nat. Bank in the City of New York on the first day of October, '94. Twenty-five dollars, interest due on Bridge Repair Bond.
W. W. Armstrong, Treas

$25 The City of Cleveland will pay the bearer at the American Exchange Nat. Bank in the City of New York on the first day of April, 1894. Twenty-five Dollars, interest due on Bridge Repair Bond.
W. W. Armstrong, Treas

$25 The City of Cleveland will pay the bearer at the American Exchange Nat. Bank in the City of New York on the first day of October, '93. Twenty-five Dollars, interest due on Bridge Repair Bond.
W. W. Armstrong, Treas

$25 The City of Cleveland will pay the bearer at the American Exchange Nat. Bank in the City of New York on the first day of April, 1893. Twenty-five dollars, interest due on Bridge Repair Bond.
W. W. Armstrong, Treas

$25 The City of Cleveland will pay the bearer at the American Exchange Nat. Bank in the City of New York on the first day of October, '92. Twenty-five Dollars, interest due on Bridge Repair Bond.
W. W. Armstrong, Treas

CHAPTER TWENTY-ONE.

Partnership Adjustment, Consolidation, Stock Company Incorporated, Branch Houses, Etc.

Ex. 304. G. A. Baker, T. C. Pratt, and A. M. Thomas have been conducting a retail hardware business as partners, under the firm name of Baker, Pratt & Co. August 21, 1893, A. M. Thomas notifies the other partners that he will retire. Baker and Pratt will then consolidate with Jones, Taylor & Co., whose store will be conducted as a branch.

The following is the Trial Balance of Baker, Pratt & Co., Aug. 21, '93, and is given for adjustment under the following conditions: In the articles of co-partnership the new firm is to be allowed on all balances due on personal accounts a discount of 5%, and a discount of 2% on all notes due the firm. The accounts have all been averaged and their maturities given as shown in the Trial Balance. Interest is to be computed on all items due either to or by the firm. Points shown: Balance due Thomas, entries to consolidate, entries to incorporate, entries to conduct branch houses, etc.

Trial Balance of Baker, Pratt & Co., Aug. 21, 1893.

(Due Date.)		Debit		Account	Credit		(Due Date.)	
Sept.	1	$ 2,700	00	G. A. Baker,	$ 5,600	00	Mar.	1
April	1	2,000	00	T. C. Pratt,	8,000	00	Feb.	1
June	1	1,500	00	A. M. Thomas,	5,000	00	May	1
		7,505	00	Cash,				
				Discount and Interest,	395	00		
		25,000	00	Mdse. Inventory $8,000,	26,000	00		
		185	00	Loss and Gain,				
Dec.	21	12,500	00	Bills Receivable,				
		1,275	00	Expense,				
				Bills Payable,	10,750	00	Nov.	27
June	12	2,500	00	D. Kennedy,	1,290	00	Oct.	19
April	17	2,600	00	V. Mekin,	3,700	00	May	22
Feb.	21	1,650	00	C. A. Case,	3,500	00	"	17
July	15	6,250	00	J. R. McBride,	5,300	00	Nov.	21
Dec.	16	5,650	00	W. S. Rehm,	2,680	00	Sept.	13
Aug.	17	4,750	00	S. S. West,	3,850	00	June	24
		$76,065	00		$76,065	00		

Note.—First adjust the interest on the partners' accounts, then determine the amount of interest to be allowed to or by the firm on the notes that are not due at the date of settlement; then ascertain amount of interest in favor of or against the firm on all personal debits or credits, by computing the interest in all cases from the date of settlement to the date of maturity of the item, whether it be earlier or later than the date of settlement.

After finding whether the balance is in favor of the old or new firm, and making the entry to adjust the accounts regarding the losses on notes and personal accounts due the firm, we are prepared to determine the partners' balances for settlement Aug. 21.

The first step is to find the interest due to or from the members of the firm, as shown below :—

Interest to Pratt's credit on $8000 invested 201 days........... $268.00
    "   "   debit on $2000 withdrawn 142 days........ 47.33

    Leaving a balance to Pratt's credit.......................... $220.67

Interest to Baker's credit on $5600 invested 173 days........... $161.47
    "   "   " $2700 withdrawn 11 days........ 4.95

    Making the total to Baker's credit................. .... $166.42

Note.—The amount withdrawn by Baker does not average due until after the date of settlement; therefore, he is entitled to a credit for the interest thereon.

Interest to Thomas' credit on $5000 invested 112 days........... $93.33
    "   "   debit on $1500 withdrawn 81 days.......... 20.25

    Leaving a balance to Thomas' credit........................ $73.08

To adjust the interest between the partners, make the following entry :—

        A. M. Thomas.............................. $80.31
           To G. A. Baker............................. $13.03
           " T. C. Pratt 67.28

The amount of Thomas' debit is the difference between his credit of interest and one-third of the total credit of interest. The next step is to determine the amount of

Interest in Favor of the Firm.

On Bills Payable,		$10,750 for	98 days	....		$175.58
" C. A. Case,	Dr.,	1,650 "	181 "	....		49.78
" V. Meakin,	"	2,600 "	126 "	....		54.00
" S. S. West,	"	4,750 "	4 "	....		3.17
" W. S. Rehm,	Cr.,	2,680 "	23 "	....		10.27
" J. R. McBride,	Dr.,	6,250 "	37 "	....	$38.54	
" J. R. McBride,	Cr.,	5,300 "	92 "	....	81.27	119.81
" D. Kennedy,	Dr.,	2,500 "	70 "	....	$29.17	.
" D. Kennedy,	Cr.,	1,290 "	59 "	....	12.68	41.85
Total.....................						$454.46

Interest Against the Firm.

On Bills Receivable,		$12,500 for 122 days	....	$254.17
" W. S. Rehm,	Dr.,	5,650 " 117 "	....	110.17
" S. S. West,	Cr.,	3,850 " 58 "	....	37.22
" C. A. Case,	"	3,500 " 96 "	....	56.00
" V. Meakin,	"	3,700 " 91 "	....	56.12

Total..	$513.68
Deduct amount in favor of the firm.....................	454.46
Balance of interest against the firm.....................	$59.22

Hence the following Journal entry :—

Interest (old account).................... $59.22

To Interest (new account)............... $59.22

Note.—The credit of this entry is not to be posted until after the debit has been first posted and the old account closed up.

Next determine the discounts allowed to the new firm on the Bills Receivable, and balances of the personal accounts as per contract and as shown below :—

Balance due from S. S. West...........................	$	900.00
" " " W. S. Rehm.......................		2,970.00
" " " J. R. McBride		950.00
" " " D. Kennedy.......................		1,210.00

5% off this sum.............................	$ 6,030.00	is	$301.50
2% off Bills Receivable	12,500.00	is	250.00
Total deduction for bad or doubtful debts............			$551.50

Next open an account with Contingencies, which is to be credited with the amount of this discount, that is made to reduce the above accounts to a cash valuation, and make the following Journal entry :—

Loss and Gain........................ $551.50

To Contingencies......................... $551.50

Note.—The Contingency account is in no sense a debt or obligation of the firm; it is merely an offset against the nominal value of the assets, with a view of reducing them to their estimated cash valuation.

The accounts may now be closed and the balances brought forward, when the Ledger will show the following balances :—

DEBIT BALANCES.		CREDIT BALANCES.	
Cash	$7,505.00	Bills Pay	$10,750.00
Mdse	8,000.00	V. Meakin	1,100.00
Bills Rec	12,500.00	C. A. Case	1,850.00
W. S. Rehm	2,970.00	Contingencies	551.50
S. S. West	900.00	Discount and Int	59.22
D. Kennedy	1,210.00	T. C. Pratt	8,508.71
J. R. McBride	950.00	G. A. Baker	5,354.46
	$34,035.00	A. M. Thomas	5,861.11
			$34,035.00

The balance due A. M. Thomas is $5861.11, which is paid to him in cash, leaving the Assets and Liabilities of the new firm as follows:

ASSETS.		LIABILITIES.	
Cash	$ 1,643.89	Bills Payable	$10,750.00
Mdse	8,000.00	V. Meakin	1,100.00
Bills Rec	12,500.00	C. A. Case	1,850.00
W. S. Rehm	2,970.00	Contingencies	551.50
S. S. West	900.00	Discount and Int	59.22
D. Kennedy	1,210.00	E. C. Pratt	8,508.71
J. R. McBride	950.00	G. A. Baker	5,354.46
	$28,173 89		$28,173.89

Baker and Pratt consolidate with Jones, Taylor & Co., to incorporate into a Joint Stock Company, with a Capital Stock of $50,000, consisting of 500 shares, par value $100 each:

The Assets and Liabilities of Jones, Taylor & Co. are as follows:

ASSETS.		LIABILITIES.	
Mdse	$ 6,540.00	Bills Payable	$ 6,000.00
Cash	6,000.00	Accts. Payable	7,540.00
Bills Receivable	1,500.00	T. A. Jones	5,000.00
Accts. Receivable	5,500.00	D. R. Taylor	5,000.00
Real Estate	8,000.00	Wm. Britt	4,000.00
	$27,540.00		$27,540.00

G. A. Baker subscribes for 100 shares, T. C. Pratt 65 shares, T. A. Jones 65 shares, D. R. Taylor 65 shares, Wm Britt 55 shares, I. R. McKay 50 shares, J. C. Trask 50 shares; the remaining 50 shares held as Treasury stock. Baker, Pratt, Jones, Taylor and Britt are to receive full paid stock for their subscriptions, which are paid out of the effects of the old firms. McKay and Trask pay their subscriptions with cash. What entry to consolidate, and open the books for the corporation?

Cash	$17,643.89
Mdse	14,540.00
Bills Receivable	14,000.00
Real Estate	8,000.00
Accounts Receivable	11,530.00
Treasury Stock	5,000.00
Franchise	6,526.11

To Bills Payable		$16,750.00
" Accounts Payable		10,490.00
" Capital Stock		50,000.00

The above entry combines the Assets and Liabilities of both firms, and opens the books for the new company with full authorized capital, Treasury Stock, etc. The books of the old firms should be closed as shown in the Eighth Lesson, page 63.

Branch Houses.

There are two methods of conducting the accounts with branch houses. The method to be adopted should depend largely upon the number of branches and the extent of the business.

First. If the branches are to buy their own goods, collect and pay their own accounts, then they must be debited for the Assets and credited for the Liabilities belonging to their respective plants.

We will suppose the corporate name of this company is the City Hardware Company, and that the old plant of Jones, Taylor & Co. shall be known as the East End branch. If this method is adopted, the East End branch would be debited and credited as follows:—

East End	$19,540.00

To Mdse	$6,540.00
" Cash	6,000.00
" Bills Receivable	1,500.00
" Accounts Receivable	5,500.00

Then :—

Bills Payable..........................	$6,000.00	
Accounts Payable......................	7,540.00	
To East End..........................		$13,540.00

The entries made on the books of the branch would, of course, be just the opposite from these, crediting the parent house for the Assets received, and debiting the parent house for the Liabilities assumed.

The above are the only entries required on the books at the main office until the end of the year. Then, if the branch has made a profit, the entry on their books would be :—

Loss and Gain To Parent House.

On the books of the parent house the entry would be :—

East End To Loss and Gain.

If the branch has been operated at a loss, the entry on their books would be :—

Parent House To Loss and Gain.

On the books of the parent house the entry would be :—

Loss and Gain To East End.

If the parent house furnishes merchandise, cash, etc., during the year, the branches would be debited, and if the branches furnish merchandise or turn over cash to the parent house, they are credited. Some houses charge these goods at *cost* price, and others charge them at a profit.

Second. If the parent house is to buy all goods, pay all accounts, etc., then the branches will be charged only for the amount of goods in their possession when the books were opened, and for all goods sent to them thereafter. The account with the parent house would be the only liability account kept, which would represent their capital.

The branches would keep the accounts with their own customers, make their own collections, and turn the money in to the parent house. At the end of the year the proceedings for closing the books are the same as in any other business,—finally debiting the parent house for the net loss, or crediting the parent house for the net gain.

The first method is the better one, and should be adopted.

The methods of conducting the accounts with branch houses are very simple, and it is thought that further explanation would be useless.

A Manufacturing Company.

Ex. 305. **Single Entry Stock Books changed to Double Entry and a Stock Dividend declared.**

The Ohio Iron Company, Limited, was organized Jan. 1st, 1893, with a Capital Stock of $150,000, 1500 shares, par value $100. The Capital Stock paid up is $140,000, and is held by the following named parties: J. C. Keim, 300 shares; C. C. Harris, 400 shares; P. C. Jones, 400 shares; J. A. Springer, 200 shares; H. A. Burgess, 100 shares; and 100 shares held as Treasury Stock.

Jan. 1, 1894, the company took an inventory, and decided to open the books and have them kept by Double Entry.

The following is a statement of the company's Assets and Liab'ties: Mill and Furnace, $75,000; Pig Iron, $20,000; Account. Payable, $41,000; Bills Receivable, $17,450; Machinery and Patterns, $31,000; Bills Payable, $10,000; Capital Stock, $150,000; Accounts Receivable, $77,550.

Ex. 306.   What is the gain or loss?

Ex. 307.   What entry to open the new books by Double Entry?

Ex. 308.   Declare a Dividend equal to the amount of Treasury Stock, and issue the same to the shareholders in proportion to the amount of stock held by each, and pass the balance of the net gain to Reserve Fund.

CHAPTER TWENTY-TWO.

Corporation Law.

Illegal Incorporation.

Ex. 309. A corporation cannot be formed legally unless authorized by the Legislature. The Legislature of a State has no power to constitute a person a member of a private corporation without his consent, nor can the Legislature compel a subscriber for shares in a proposed corporation to accept shares in a different corporation from that for which the subscription was made. It is also a settled fact that a State cannot alter the contract between the shareholders by legislative enactment.

Shareholders in a corporation cannot by their ratification render legal the illegality of forming a corporation without complying with the statutory prerequisites.

If a charter or general incorporation law prescribes certain formalities to be complied with by the persons wishing to form a corporation under it, the due performance of the formalities must be complied with. No authority to form a corporation from a charter or law of nature can be obtained until they have been complied with.

A subscription to the capital stock of a company about to be formed under a charter or general law does not constitute the subscriber a shareholder until all conditions precedent to the legal incorporation of the company have been fulfilled.

Construction of Charters.

The charter of a corporation serves a two-fold purpose: It operates as a law conferring upon the corporators the right of franchise to act in a corporate capacity; and, furthermore, it contains the terms of the fundamental agreement between the corporators themselves. Corporations are usually formed by the adoption of articles of association and the subscription of capital, in pursuance of general incorporation laws. The articles of association of a company thus organized, taken in connection with the laws under which the organization takes place, form the constitution of the association and answer the same purposes as a special charter. They contain the terms of the agreement of association between the shareholders, and indicate the character and extent of the business in which the company shall engage. Authority to enter into a contract which is in violation of an express prohibition of the charter of a corporation, or a general rule of law, can never be implied.

A corporation has implied authority, in the absence of a prohibition in its charter, to acquire and hold any property, whether real or personal, which may be required in carrying on the business for which the company was formed. A corporation may acquire and hold whatever property may be reasonably useful and convenient in attaining its legitimate ends. A corporation may dispose of any or all of its property (unless expressly restrained by law), in the same manner as an individual.

Corporations, like co-partnerships, transact their business and are known to the world under particular names. A corporation may sue and be sued as an entity, under the name by which it is known in its charter.

Alteration of Charter.

The charter of a private corporation cannot be altered without the consent of the Legislature, nor without the consent of every member of the corporation. That such consent cannot be implied, seems self-evident. A grant, by the Legislature, of permission to act in a corporate capacity for a specified purpose, does not *impliedly* authorize the grantees to assume corporate powers for any other purpose. Nor do the stockholders of a corporation, when they unite to do business under a particular charter, *impliedly* agree to become parties to a different charter.

Corporations cannot effect a consolidation without the unanimous consent of the members of each company, and such consent cannot be inferred as an implied condition of their charter or articles of association.

Charters of incorporation are frequently granted subject to a reservation of power in the Legislature " to repeal, alter, or suspend " them at pleasure. A charter thus granted may be repealed or modified by the Legislature at any time, against the will of every member of the company.

By-Laws.

It is implied in the charter of every private corporation formed for the pecuniary profit of its members, that the majority shall have power to make reasonable rules and regulations, or by-laws, for the better government of the company. The validity of by-laws prescribed by the majority depends upon the implied agreement of all the shareholders, in forming the company, and therefore any by-law properly enacted by the majority is as binding upon the members of the company as a provision contained in the charter itself. By-laws regulating the manner of holding meetings and electing officers, and of transferring stock, are proper. By-laws may also be made to regulate the directors and other agents of the company in managing the company's business. The majority may prescribe how many directors shall constitute a quorum, providing the charter contains nothing to the contrary.

The charter of a corporation is its fundamental law; it prescribes the main objects for which the company was formed. By-laws which are calculated to assist in carrying into effect the purposes of the company are valid; but every by-law which is contrary to the charter, either in its main purposes or in its special provisions, is void and unauthorized.

Capital Stock.

The undertaking of the members of a corporation to contribute the amount of capital agreed upon is frequently, by its implied terms, subject to conditions precedent, which cannot be dispensed with except by mutual consent. Thus, the members of a corporation cannot be required to pay assessments upon their shares until the company is authorized by law to begin its business. Until that time the company can have no use for its capital.

If the capital of a corporation is fixed by its charter at a certain amount, the company has no authority by law to begin the prosecution of its enterprise until the whole amount of the capital has been subscribed, and therefore a shareholder cannot be compelled to contribute his proportion of the capital before that time. When the capital stock and number of shares are fixed by the act of incorporation, or by any vote or by-law passed conformably to the act of incorporation, *no assessment* can be lawfully made on the share of any subscriber until the whole number of shares has been taken. Under an act of incorporation providing that the capital of a company shall not exceed a certain amount, and shall be determined from time to time by the board of directors, no assessments can be laid upon a subscriber until the amount of the capital has been fixed.

A vote of the directors that the subscription books be closed on a certain day in effect fixes the company's capital at the amount then subscribed. If the time during which subscriptions may be received is limited by the charter, the amount of the company's capital becomes fixed through lapse of the time prescribed.

Shareholders are liable to pay calls upon their subscriptions to meet the expenses in preliminary preparations, before the whole amount of its capital has been subscribed.

If a company is authorized by the terms of its charter to begin operations after a certain amount of capital has been subscribed, this necessarily implies that the stockholders may from that time be required to pay the amount they have agreed to contribute for that purpose.

If a corporation is authorized by its charter to increase the amount of its capital stock, and an increase is voted, a subscriber for new shares will be liable to pay calls without regard to the amount of the new shares which have been taken.

A corporation cannot, without statutory authority, become an incorporator by subscribing for shares in a new company ; nor can it do this indirectly through persons acting as its agents or tools. The right of forming a corporation is conferred by the incorporation laws only upon persons acting individually, and not upon associations.

A corporation has no implied authority to alter the amount of its capital stock, when the charter has definitely fixed the capital at a certain amount. The shares of a company can neither be increased nor decreased in number, or in their nominal value, unless this be expressly authorized by the company's charter.

·A corporation cannot purchase its own shares, unless expressly authorized by its charter to do so, for such purchase would diminish the amount of the company's capital.

There are exceptional cases in which a corporation may become a purchaser or transferee of shares in its own stock, although its charter does not authorize a reduction of capital ; as, for example, when the shares are received for a debt which cannot be collected otherwise, or when the shares are received as a gift, and the company's real capital therefore remains undiminished. A corporation can buy its own stock out of its net gains, which would not reduce its capital.

Directors of a corporation have no right, under any circumstances, to purchase shares in the company with the company's own money, for the purpose of controlling the election of officers.

Shares that may be owned by the company in the company's name or in the name of the trustee, cannot be voted on by either the trustee or the company's officers.

If the capital of a corporation is increased by the issue of new shares after an amendment of the company's charter, it is plain that creditors whose claims arose before the increase of capital have no special equities against the holders of the new shares, and cannot compel them to contribute more capital than was legally due to the corporation itself.

Where the amount of the capital stock of a corporation is fixed by its charter or articles of association, no authority exists to alter the amount so fixed, or to issue additional shares. The issue of certificates for any shares in excess of the amount so fixed would be unauthorized, for such certificates would involve a false representation to the world that the holder of the certificate was a share holder in the company. It is "Watered Stock."

Franchise.

The word "franchise" is generally used to designate a right or privilege conferred by law. When the legislature grants a charter of incorporation it confers upon the grantees of the charter the right or privilege of forming a corporate association and of acting within certain limits in a corporate capacity; this right or privilege is called the corporate franchise.

In speaking of the value of franchises, care must be taken to distinguish between the different meanings of the word "value." One meaning of the word is *price*, or the amount for which a thing can be sold. In this sense franchises have clearly no value whatever, because, by their nature, they are not transferable. They cannot be sold, or leased, or mortgaged, nor can they be taken in execution; on the other hand, franchises clearly have a value, if the word "value" is used to signify the advantage derived from their posession or in other words their *utility*.

Prospectus.

The agents of a corporation are subject to the general rule of the common law, that a person is liable for the direct consequences of a false and fraudulent representation whereby another is misled. It has often been decided that directors are liable for fraudulent representations as to the financial condition of the company, whereby others are induced to give credit to the company, or to purchase its obligations or shares of its stock. If directors issue reports or prospectuses intended for general circulation and to advertise and give credit to the company with the public, they are responsible for the natural consequences of their action in this respect: and therefore, if the reports or prospectuses are false, and were made fraudulently, any person into whose hands they come in the ordinary course of events, and who is misled thereby, has his action against the directors; it is not necessary that the misrepresentation be made by the directors directly to the parties misled.

To maintain an action for false representations, it is necessary to show that the representations were false, because directors cannot be held liable for false representations, unless they were made with knowledge of their falsity or carelessness.

Subscriptions for Shares.

Subscriptions for shares are binding from the time they are made, although the contract by which stock subscribers become members of a corporation does not go into effect until all conditions precedent have been complied with, and the corporation created.

There is an important difference between sales of shares and subscriptions. When a person agrees to take or to purchase shares, the intention is to buy the certificates representing the shares, as salable securities. The purchaser does not become a shareholder until he has received the certificates; on the other hand, the effect of an ordinary subscription is to constitute the subscriber a shareholder immediately, with the right to vote at meetings, and share in dividends, and subject to a liability to contribute the amount of the shares when assessed.

If a person's name is placed upon the subscription books of a corporation without his authority or consent, the subscription will not bind him. Subscriptions cannot be released when once made.

An offer to become a shareholder in a corporation to be formed thereafter may be revoked at any time before acceptance, whether the offer accompany a contract to take shares or not. But a mutual agreement to become shareholders, or to subscribe for shares, is binding between the parties as a contract, and cannot be revoked.

An offer or contract to become a shareholder in a corporation, or to subscribe for shares thereafter, does not become binding or create a liability until all the conditions precedent, upon which the offer or contract was made, have been performed. No liability is incurred unless the corporation which is organized is the specific corporation which was contemplated at the time of the agreement.

After a corporation has been formed, and shares are subscribed in excess of the amount allowed by the charter, the additional subscriptions do not alter the contract among the existing members; the subscriptions made after the full amount has been subscribed are void, and the subscribers do not become members of the corporation.

A person subscribing for shares as agent for another, but without authority, does not become a shareholder in place of the principal whose name he subscribed.

If the charter under which a corporation is formed provides that persons wishing to become members of the company shall subscribe for shares upon stock books, this evidently contemplates that the contract between the shareholders shall be made in writing, and according to the forms provided, and hence an oral agreement will not under any circumstances be sufficient to constitute the contractor a shareholder. This, however, has no application to a contract to purchase shares and to become a shareholder in a corporation after it has been fully organized.

The contract of membership in a corporation is not terminable at the will of either of the parties to it, as in case of any ordinary contract of partnership; a shareholder in a corporation has no power to dissolve his connection with the company of which he is a member; nor can the agents of a corporation consent, on behalf of the company, to the withdrawal of any stockholder.

A shareholder in a corporation can escape from the obligations of his contract only by one of the following methods: (1) by a transfer of his shares, and an acceptance of the transfer on the part of the corporation, thus effecting a complete novation; (2) by a forfeiture and sale under authority expressly conferred upon the company by its charter; (3) dissolution of the company; (4) by act of the majority in winding up the business of the company and surrendering its charter; (5) by act of the shareholder, where permission to withdraw is expressly conferred by the charter; (6) by unanimous consent of the members of the company, under legislative authority.

Directors.

Any person of sound mind, who is capable of acting as agent for another, may be elected director or trustee of a corporation, unless some special qualification is prescribed by the charter or by-laws of the company.

The directors of a corporation are generally required to be shareholders by express provision of the company's charter.

The directors of a corporation should be men of practical business experience and judgment, and should be selected by the majority by reason of their peculiar fitness to manage the corporate affairs.

A board of directors has no authority to make a material and permanent alteration of the business or constitution of the company, even though the alteration be within the company's chartered powers. Such an alteration can be effected only by authority of the stockholders at a general meeting. Directors of a corporation have no authority to wind up the company, or to sell any property which is necessary in order to carry on its business. Directors cannot depart from the company's chartered purposes.

Directors have no right, under any circumstances, to use their official positions for their own benefit, or the benefit of anyone except the corporation itself.

Directors of a corporation have no authority to represent it in transactions with another corporation in which they are shareholders, if their interest in the latter company might induce them to favor it at the expense of the company whose interests have been intrusted to their care. A director or agent may deal with the corporation if the latter is represented by other agents.

If directors of a corporation knowingly issue unauthorized and void certificates of shares, or invalid transferable obligations of the company, they are liable to any purchaser or subsequent transferee of the certificates or obligations who takes them relying on their apparent validity. The company may likewise be liable, under these circumstances, in an action for damages, on account of the deceit practiced by its agents.

Meetings.

The majority are authorized to act for the corporation of which they constitute a part only when called together in a proper manner. The object of requiring the majority to express their will by vote at a meeting is to enable all the shareholders to consult and deliberate together. Every shareholder is entitled to be present at such meeting, and to have a reasonable hearing. For this reason, it is essential that all the stockholders be properly notified of a meeting before it is held. If notice to any one was omitted, those present at the meeting have no authority to act for the whole body of members, and the transactions at the meeting will not be binding as corporate acts.

But if the charter or by-laws of a company fix the time and place at which regular meetings shall be held, this is itself sufficient notice to all the stockholders, and no further notice is necessary.

, A meeting of the stockholders is not binding upon the company unless it was called by some person having authority, or unless all the members entitled to vote are present. The charter or by-law should state explicitly to whom authority should be given to call meetings.

The notice of a meeting of the shareholders of a company must

12

fix the exact time and place of the meeting, and in certain cases, must state the nature of the business to be transacted.

A distinction has been made between regular and special meetings. Regular meetings are held at stated times, according to the charter or by-laws of the company, while special meetings are called at irregular or unusual times, at the option of the officer having authority to make the call. A notice calling a special or extraordinary meeting must state particularly what the purpose of calling the meeting is; and no business can be transacted at the meeting except in relation to the matters specified.

The right to vote at the meetings of a corporation belongs *only* to its members or stockholders.

The members of a company must vote personally, and cannot vote by proxy unless the right to vote by proxy is expressly conferred by the company's charter or by-laws.

The general rule is, that the directors of a corporation have no implied authority to act singly; they can act only as a board, unless especially authorized to act individually. Notice of the meetings of directors of a corporation must be given in the same manner as notice of the meetings of shareholders.

Transfer of Shares.

A transfer of shares in a corporation means the substitution of a new shareholder in place of the outgoing shareholder in the company, and an assumption by the new holder of all the rights and obligations which attached to the transferring shareholder by reason of his ownership of the shares. This involves a novation of the contract of membership. The transferor ceases to be a shareholder in the company; he is thus discharged from all further liability to contribute capital, unless the contrary be expressly provided in the company's charter. A transferor of shares loses all right to share in the company's profits and to participate in the management of its affairs.

The transferee becomes a shareholder in the place of the retiring member, and impliedly assumes all the obligations which rested upon the former holder as member of the company, and is liable for calls to the same extent as the former holder.

It is usual to provide in the articles of association or by-laws of a corporation that no transfer of shares shall be allowed until all unpaid calls shall have been satisfied.

The general rule is, that, as between a company and its shareholders, a transferor is discharged from all liability on account of calls made after the execution of the transfer, and that the obligation to pay these calls falls upon the transferee ; but a transferee of shares cannot be held liable upon a call made before he became a shareholder in the company.

A corporation is *never* obliged to treat shares as paid up until they have in *fact* been paid up.

If shares are transferred after a call has been made, but before it has been paid, the transferor remains liable to the corporation. Should the transferor subsequently pay the call, the company would be obliged to credit the shares with the amount paid, whoever may have become the holder of the shares. But if the call should remain unsatisfied and the shares not be paid up, the company would be entitled to make a new call upon the subsequent holder.

If a corporation should issue certificates declaring the shares to be paid up, a *bona fide* purchaser would be entitled to become a shareholder, free from further liability, whether the shares were in fact paid up or not.

The right of a transferee of shares to dividends declared after the transfer was executed, but payable out of profits earned before that time, must be considered separately, as against the company and as against the transferor.

The general rule is, that, as between a corporation and its shareholders, those persons are entitled to dividends who are shareholders at the time the dividends are declared, irrespective of the time at which they were earned.

A provision in the charter of a corporation authorizing the board of directors " to regulate " transfers, does not give them the power to restrain transfers at their discretion, or to prescribe to whom they shall be made ; it merely enables them to prescribe reasonable formalities to be observed in executing transfers.

After a corporation has become insolvent, it is the duty of the company to wind up its business, call in the outstanding capital, and satisfy creditors. After a company has failed, every shareholder may claim that every other shareholder who was a party to the speculation and shared in the chances of success shall bear a proportionate part of the loss ; and a transfer of shares to an insolvent, or any other person unable to perform the obligations which rested upon the transferor, is unauthorized and will not hold.

The right of a shareholder to transfer his shares necessarily ceases upon dissolution of the corporation ; for after a dissolution the contract of membership is at an end.

The incorporating statutes, or by-laws, of corporations having transferable shares in almost every instance provide that the shares shall be transferable only on the books of the company, and that a new certificate shall be issued to the transferee upon surrender of the outstanding certificates.

It would be practically impossible to know who are entitled to vote at meetings, to whom dividends can be paid, and who are liable, as shareholders, to the company and to the creditors, if a transfer should be executed without an entry of the transfer upon the company's books.

Shares are generally bought and sold, like tangible property, by delivery of the certificates issued by the company to the holder. These certificates indicate on their face to what extent the shares have been paid up.

If shares are sold by delivery of the certificates, it is reasonable to suppose that they are sold in the condition in which they appear to be at the time of the sale. If the certificates show that the shares have been paid up only partially, it is a fair implication that they are sold as partly paid up shares, and that the purchaser, and not the seller, is to be responsible for the amount remaining unpaid. It would seem to be immaterial in this respect whether a call was made before the sale or not.

In determining the right to dividends as between the vendor and purchaser of shares, it is a well settled rule of construction that the vendor retains the right to all dividends declared before the sale, and the vendee is entitled to all declared thereafter, unless otherwise agreed upon by the parties. This is the rule, whether the dividend be payable before or after the sale, and whether the sale be private, or on the stock exchange, or in the open market.

The fact that shares are held or transferred by a person as executor is notice that there is a will open to inspection upon the public records, and the company and persons taking a transfer of the shares are bound, at their peril, to take notice of the contents of the will.

It is the duty of a corporation which has issued a negotiable certificate for shares, and whose shares are transferable upon the books, not to permit a transfer to be executed upon the books, or to issue a new certificate, until the outstanding certificate has been surrendered. Both the company and the transferee would be chargeable with notice of the rights of the holder of the outstanding certificate, and if the latter was equitably entitled to the shares, he would have a right to set the transfer aside. If the company should recognize the transfer as valid, and refuse to accord to the holder of the certificate his legal rights, it would become liable to make good his damages; and if it should issue a new certificate to the transferee, it would become liable upon both the outstanding certificates to innocent purchasers for value.

Preferred Shares.

Shares which confer upon the holder special privileges or benefits that do not belong to the other members of the corporation are called Preferred Shares. The precise nature of the privileges or benefits thus conferred depends upon the terms of the resolution under which the shares are issued, and the form of the certificate delivered to the holders.

Thus, it is often provided that the holders of the preferred shares shall have priority in the distribution of profits, and shall receive annual dividends at a specified rate before the other shareholders receive anything; the payment of these dividends is sometimes expressly guaranteed. The agreement of a company to pay to preferred shareholders certain annual dividends is always subject to an implied condition that the payments shall be made only out of net profits which are legally applicable to the payment of dividends.

If a corporation has agreed or guaranteed that the holders of preferred shares shall be paid dividends at a certain rate per annum, and the profits at the time are insufficient to enable the company to perform its agreement, the arrears must be made up out of the profits subsequently earned, and no dividends can be paid to the holders of the common stock until the preferred shareholders have been fully paid.

Ordinarily, preferred shareholders have no preference in the distribution of the company's capital when the business is wound up. A right of this kind cannot be presumed from the fact that a preference has been given in the payment of dividends; but, under an express agreement, a preferred shareholder may be entitled to withdraw the amount of his shares before the other stockholders can take anything.

Forfeiture of Stock.

The members of a corporation may be compelled to contribute their respective shares of the capital stock by an action at law brought in the name of the corporation; and, at common law, this is the only remedy which can be resorted to. A corporation has no lien upon the shares of its members to secure the payment of assessments, unless it be expressly conferred by provision of the charter, by general statute, or by special agreement between the parties. Nor can the shares of a member be declared forfeited and sold by the agents of the company for non-payment of assessments, except by virtue of an express grant of authority. Even the holders of a majority of shares in a company have no authority to bind the minority through a by-law providing for a forfeiture and sale of the shares of those members who failed to contribute their proportion of the capital ; there must be an express *grant* of authority.

In many instances, however, it has been provided in charters and general incorporation laws that the shares of a stockholder may be declared forfeited and sold for non-payment of assessments.

A valid forfeiture can take place only by action of the legally appointed agents of the company having the requisite authority under the charter.

A forfeiture and sale of the shares of a stockholder wholly dissolves the delinquent member's connection with the company. He is not entitled thereafter to any of the privileges of membership, and ought not to be compelled to bear any of the burdens which are incidental to that position.

The liability of a shareholder ceases at the time when the forfeiture is complete and his connection with the company has been severed.

If the charter provides that the shares of a delinquent member shall be declared forfeited and be sold to pay the unpaid calls, the holder's connection with the company would not ordinarily be deemed severed and the forfeiture complete until after a sale has taken place and a new party become invested with the shares. Hence, the owner would be entitled to pay the calls and discharge the default at any time before the shares were actually sold ; but after a sale has taken place it would be impossible to reinstate the owner in his rights, and, therefore, no right of redemption could exist.

A forfeiture for the purpose of escaping liability to creditors is void.

Dividends.

The ultimate object for which every ordinary business corporation is formed is the pecuniary profit of its individual members. Any net increase of the capital of an institution of this kind is a gain upon the united investment of its shareholders, and may be distributed amongst them as profits, each shareholder being entitled to his proportionate dividend or share.

It is a fundamental rule, that dividends can be paid only out of the profits or the net increase of the capital of a company, and cannot be drawn upon the capital contributed by the shareholders for the purpose of carrying on the company's business.

The right to declare a dividend depends upon the state of the company's finances at the time when the dividend is declared. The question usually is, whether or not there would remain a net increase upon the original investment, after deducting from the assets of the company all present debts and making provision for future or contingent claims. It is immaterial at what time the increase was earned.

A company may be largely indebted and yet be entitled to pay dividends to its shareholders before the indebtedness has been paid; and it is even proper to borrow money for the purpose of paying a dividend, provided a surplus would remain after deducting the amount of the company's capital and indebtedness from the fair value of the assets which it owns.

If the capital of a banking, manufacturing, railroad, telegraph, insurance or other similar company is invested in machinery, land or fixtures used in carrying on its business, the machinery, land and fixtures may be valued at their original cost, provided they be kept up in their original condition.

Any depreciation of the value of the company's property resulting from the uncertainty of the speculation in which the company has embarked, or from a failure to carry on business profitably by reason of the state of trade, or similar causes, may be disregarded; but any depreciation caused by design, accident, or wear and tear in using the property, should be made up out of the earnings before any dividend is declared.

The capital of a mining company is not designed to be used like that of a banking or manufacturing company, in carrying on business permanently. The working of a mine necessarily causes it to become exhausted and to depreciate in value, and this depreciation cannot be repaired.

A mining company has no right to draw upon its capital by borrowing money, or by selling a portion of its property, in order to declare a dividend. It can only use the net proceeds of working the mine for this purpose, and clearly no dividend can be declared without considering the rights of creditors and providing for future liabilities.

Money obtained by a company upon the sale of forfeited stock, or as compensation for property taken under the power of eminent domain, or as interest or penalty on account of the failure of a contractor to complete his work, cannot be treated as profits.

A dividend properly declared by the directors of a company cannot subsequently be revoked. Stockholders have a legal claim against the company for the payment of the amount of the dividend. It is a positive liability as soon as declared.

The strictly *legal* right to require payment of a dividend is in those persons who were shareholders on the books of the company at the time when the dividend was declared, but the rights of equitable assignees will be protected by the courts.

A corporation which has earned a surplus may, in many instances, retain the money for the purpose of making improvements, or for the payment of debts, instead of dividing it among the shareholders.

The actual capital of the company is thus increased, while the nominal or share capital remains unchanged; consequently, the value of its shares will be increased. If the charter of a company authorizes it to increase the amount of its capital stock by the issue of new shares, this may be done either by receiving new stock subscriptions or by selling paid up shares at par for cash. The only essential is, that each share be represented at its par value by real capital.

If there is stock unsubscribed, it may be issued in payment of dividends ; the above is the method when the capital is all subscribed. Dividends payable in cash do not apply to dividends payable in stock.

Negotiable Instruments.

Corporations have authority to execute negotiable promissory notes, whenever the use of commercial paper is appropriate as a means of accomplishing their chartered purposes.

Corporations have an implied right to draw and accept drafts and bills of exchange, and to execute other classes of commercial securities. A corporation has implied authority to endorse negotiable paper for any authorized purpose, and the power of endorsement may be exercised both for the purpose of transferring the legal title from the corporation, and for the purpose of guaranteeing payment to the transferee.

A corporation cannot lend its credit without a consideration, or sign its name to negotiable paper for the accommodation of others.

A law forbidding certain corporations from issuing negotiable paper as a circulating medium, or from dealing in commercial paper, does not affect the implied right of issuing and receiving negotiable paper in ordinary trading transactions, or for any purpose incidental to the legitimate business for which the corporation was formed.

The agents of a corporation can be enjoined, at the suit of a shareholder, from issuing negotiable instruments in the name of the corporation for any unauthorized purpose; for if passed into the hands of a *bona fide* purchaser, may become binding.

Liability of Shareholders and Rights of Creditors.

Creditors of a corporation have the same rights as creditors of an individual to enforce their claims against the property of their debtor. They may subject any legal or equitable assets belonging to the corporation to the payment of their claims.

Under the common law, the members of a corporation are not individually liable to any extent for its debts, unless there is an express provision in the company's charter creating a liability. The obligation assumed by a shareholder to contribute the amount of his shares as capital for the common benefit, is regarded as assets belonging to the association as an entity. Creditors can obtain the benefit of this obligation only after having established their claims by judgment against the corporation.

The courts of law recognize a corporation only as an entity, without regard to its membership; the real relation between creditors of a corporation and the shareholders composing it is ignored. Obligations of the corporation are recognized only as obligations of the corporate entity, and only property of which the legal title is in the corporate name can be subjected to the payment of the corporate debts. Under the common law, the dissolution of a corporation destroys all legal remedy of its creditors.

A corporation cannot indirectly deprive its creditors of the security to which they are justly entitled, by executing certificates of indebtedness, or a mortgage on its property, to persons from whom it has not received a valuable consideration in return. The holders of the securities so issued would not be entitled to share with the *bona fide* creditors in the distribution of the company's assets. If, however, securities so issued are of a negotiable character, and have passed into the hands of *bona fide* purchasers, the latter would be accorded the same rights as other creditors to share in the corporate assets.

Creditors of a corporation are entitled to an injunction to restrain any threatened waste or diversion of the corporate assets which would result in the destruction of their security, and *thereby cause them irreparable loss.*

In considering the right of a creditor of a corporation to restrain a misapplication of the company's assets, it is therefore necessary to bear in mind—

   1.   A creditor cannot complain of any dealing with the corporate assets unless it be in excess of the wide powers of management retained by the corporation.

   2.   The ordinary remedy of a creditor is by obtaining judgment and execution against the corporation, and, if necessary, by creditors' bill.

   3.   A creditor who has not established his claim by a judgment against the company cannot enjoin any dealing with the company's assets, or obtain the appointment of a receiver, unless it be clear that he would suffer irreparable injury if left to pursue his ordinary remedy.

   In the absence of a statutory prohibition, a corporation has the same power of making preferences amongst its creditors, in the distribution of its assets, as an individual.

   An assignment of all the assets of a corporation to the trustee to pay certain creditors in full, leaving the others unpaid, will be sustained both at law and in equity.

   A corporation is under no implied obligation to its creditors to continue to carry on business.

   Creditors of a corporation are not parties to the charter contract, nor have they any interest in the franchise.

   The charter of a corporation may be altered at any time, without the consent of the company's creditors; an alteration may properly be regarded as a *recission* of the first charter, and the formation of a new company under a different constitution out of the old company. The creditors of a corporation have no better right to complain of a change of the charter of the company, than the creditors of a partnership to complain of an alteration of the articles between the partners.

   The liability assumed by the stockholders in a corporation to contribute the amount of their shares as capital, is usually subject to certain expressed or complied conditions precedent, such as the subscription of a certain aggregate amount of capital and the making of regular calls or assessments; but after these conditions have been complied with and the liability has matured, it is treated as a legal debt due the corporation.

   Debts due a corporation are equitable assets, and may be reached by creditors through the aid of a court of chancery, if the legal assets which can be reached by execution prove insufficient.

   One of the objects of fixing the capital of a corporation, by its charter, at a definite amount, is to provide a fund to pay the company's legal obligations, and secure those who may give it credit.   A corporation has, therefore, no legal right to begin its business operations and incur debts until the amount of capital fixed by its charter has been subscribed.

If the charter or laws under which a corporation was organized provide that the company may issue or sell its shares as fully paid up, on payment of less than their par amount into the company's treasury, creditors would have no equitable right to insist on having the shares paid up at par.

If the agents of a corporation wrongfully issue certificates representing paid-up shares to a person whose shares are not paid up, the false representations will not bind the company, and the holder of the shares will remain liable. However, if certificates for paid-up shares, issued by the regular agents of a company in the ordinary form, have been transferred to an innocent purchaser, the company will be bound by the statement in the certificates, that the shares were fully paid up. A purchaser having notice that the shares were not paid up would not be protected.

The shareholders in a corporation cannot, by an agreement with the company's agents, or by a resolution adopted by themselves, cancel their shares and release themselves from liability to contribute the amount unpaid on their shares in discharge of the company's existing debts. Such cancellation and release would have no effect upon the rights of existing creditors, unless they were parties to the arrangement; and in the event of the insolvency of the company, the discharged shareholders would be liable to contribute the amount unpaid on their shares.

Foreign Corporations.

The term "foreign corporation" is applied to any corporation outside of the jurisdiction of the State by which it was chartered.

It is a general rule of the common law, that corporations chartered by foreign States may carry on business and extend their operations so long as they do not depart from the charters under which they were originally formed. The rule of law is said to exist by the comity among States.

Consolidation.

Authority is frequently given to corporations, either by special charter or by general law, "to consolidate" with other corporations. The meaning to be attached to the word "consolidate" when thus applied, and the important legal consequences following from a consolidation, have as yet been only partly determined by the courts.

There is no doubt that the general effect of a consolidation is the formation of one corporation by the shareholders of several corporations, and the dissolution of the latter as originally constituted. But the important questions remain: What is the constitution of the united corporation, and what franchises belong to it? What are its assets, and what are its rights and liabilities with respect to the debtors and creditors of the original companies?

Corporations cannot be consolidated without the consent of the shareholders of both companies. This consent cannot be implied. A consolidation would involve the formation of a new company by the shareholders, under a new constitution. A clause in the charter of a corporation providing that the company may be consolidated with other companies, enters into the fundamental contract between the shareholders, and under a provision of this character a consolidation may be effected by vote of the majority on behalf of the whole association.

Two corporations may be united—

1. By dissolving both companies and destroying their legal identity, and creating a new corporation out of the members of the old.

2. By dissolving one of the companies and destroying its legal identity, while preserving the other company and issuing shares in that company. In this case the legal identity of the company remains unchanged.

3. By preserving the legal identity of both companies. This may be done by issuing shares in one company to the shareholders in the other company in exchange for their shares, thus making the one company the holder of all the shares in the other company; or by regarding the united shareholders of both companies as shareholders in each corporation, both corporations, however, acting under similar charters and under the same management.

A private corporation formed by the consolidation of several companies differs in no respect from other corporations in its nature and constitution. It is a voluntary association of individuals, to whom the State has granted authority to act in a corporate capacity, within certain limits.

The constitution of a corporation formed by consolidation is generally composed of several separate instruments.

The franchises of the united company are always derived from the act authorizing the consolidation. Sometimes the same act describes the enterprise of the new company in terms, and thus provides a complete constitution; but more commonly it refers to the charters of the old companies, and, unless the contrary be expressly provided, it seems that the purpose and enterprise of the new company would be to carry on the business of both of the original companies.

After the consolidation of a corporation with another company, the liability of the consolidated company is substituted in place of the liability of each of the original companies to its creditors, at least to the extent of the assets received. The consolidated company takes the assets of the original companies burdened with the obligations which these companies owe to their creditors, but not with greater obligations.

Dissolution.

An ordinary business corporation may cease to do business and wind up its affairs whenever a majority of the shareholders deem this to be advisable; but the franchises conferred upon the shareholders by the State are not extinguished by the mere cessation of business thus brought about. The company still continues to be a corporation in the eyes of the law, and may sue and be sued in that capacity; and it is possible that a corporation which has voluntarily ceased to do business and sold out its property, may in certain cases reorganize and begin its business anew, if this appears desirable to a majority of the shareholders.

A corporation can be dissolved, and its existence *wholly* terminated by extinguishment of the corporate franchise conferred by the State upon the body of corporators; for so long as this franchise exists the company continues to be a corporation in legal contemplation, and may sue and be sued in that capacity. The dissolution of a corporation and the extinction of its franchises may occur in either of the following ways :—

First. By expiration of the charter.

Secondly. By failure of an essential part of the corporate organization, provided it cannot be restored.

Thirdly. By dissolution and surrender of the franchises with the consent of the State.

Fourthly. By legislative enactment, if no constitutional provision be violated.

Fifthly. By forfeiture of the franchises and judgment of dissolution obtained in a proper judicial proceeding.

If a corporation was chartered to exist during a limited period of time, or until a certain day, its existence will cease upon the expiration of the time or the occurrence of the day prescribed by the charter.

The *lawful* existence of a corporation cannot be continued, even by unanimous consent of its members, after their franchise of acting in a corporate capacity has expired.

It is clear that, by the use of apt words in the charter or statute under which a corporation is formed, its franchises may be so limited that they shall expire upon the happening of any prescribed event or contingency. A distinction must, however, be made between words limiting the existence of a corporation until the happening of a prescribed event, and a provision making the happening of an event a cause for declaring a forfeiture of the charter as upon condition subsequent. In the former case the charter will expire of itself by its own limitation, but in the latter case a judicial determination of the ground of forfeiture is required before the corporation becomes dissolved. If the charter of a railroad company contains a proviso that unless the company shall begin and complete its road within a certain period of time "its corporate existence and powers shall cease," the corporation will lose its franchises without a judgment of forfeiture, if it does not build the road within the prescribed time.

The insolvency of a corporation and an assignment of all 'of its property for the benefit of creditors, or the appointment of a receiver, will not extinguish the franchises with which the company has been invested by its charter, or put an end to its corporate existence. The legal existence of a corporation can be cut short only through a forfeiture of its franchises, declared at the suit of the State granting them, or a surrender by act of the shareholders.

The dissolution of a corporation, at common law, not only means that the company has lost its franchises and can no longer *act* in a corporate capacity, but it implies that the corporation has wholly ceased to exist, in legal contemplation, and will not be recognized as a corporate body for any purpose.

Suits brought by or against a corporation are abated by its dissolution; and a judgment purporting to be rendered against a corporation which is not in existence is a nullity.

It is frequently said that debts due to or from a corporation become extinguished by its dissolution; but this is not strictly accurate. The obligation of the debt remains, although the remedy in the name of the corporation be lost,—not by any implied condition in the contract creating the debt, but from necessity, because there is no person existing in legal contemplation in whose favor or against whom the debt can be enforced.

Winding Up.

Ordinary trading corporations are formed solely for the pecuniary benefit of their shareholders.   It is therefore no more than reasonable that the majority of an association of this description should have a discretionary power to give up the joint speculation, and wind up the company's business, whenever they deem this step to be in the interest of the whole association.   •

The law is settled accordingly; and it may be stated as a rule, that it is an implied condition in the charter of every corporation formed solely for the pecuniary profit of its shareholders, such as an ordinary trading or manufacturing corporation, that its business may be wound up whenever the majority may, without the consent of the minority, sell the whole of the company's property, close up the business, distribute the assets, and surrender the charter to the State.

Upon winding up the business of a corporation, the proceeds of a sale of its assets, after paying off creditors, must be distributed among the shareholders in cash.

In order to obviate the inconvenient consequences ensuing from the dissolution of a corporation at common law, statutes have been passed in many of the States providing for the winding up of dissolved companies, and the distribution of their assets according to the equitable rights of those interested.   Thus, in some States it is enacted that after the dissolution of a corporation for any cause, the company shall continue to be a body corporate during a term of years, for the purpose of prosecuting and defending suits and settling up its affairs, but not for the purpose of carrying on its regular business.   In other States, trustees or receivers are appointed, whose duty it is to collect the assets of the company and liquidate its debts.

After a corporation has been dissolved, or has lost its franchise or right to continue its operations, it may be reorganized or revived pursuant to authority newly conferred by the State.

Stock—Its Ownership and Transfer.

The issuing of stock certificates, and their cancellation when they have become void through transfer of the shares they represented, is a business demanding the exercise of the extremest caution and care. The Form of Transfer Book shown in the Eighth Lesson, page 61, will be found as good as you can adopt.

In issuing certificates of stock the utmost care must be taken to fill them out correctly in every particular.   Write the names of persons to whom they are issued fully, and never indulge in initials in place of the first Christian names, or in the use of pet household or nick-names—for instance, Molly for Mary, Emma for Emeline, Harry for Henry, etc. It is not a good plan, either, to insert the shareholder's place of residence in the body of the certificates. Certificates live long ; residences are often changed.

In issuing stock certificates to trustees, administrators, or executors, some description of the trust or the names of the parties or estate for whom they are acting should be inserted in the certificate.

No certificate should read in this way: " Robert Burns, trustee, is the owner of 100 shares in the company "; it should read : " Robert Burns, trustee under the will of Dr. P. Thayer," etc.

In delivering to the new holder certificates of shares, it is always very desirable that they should be passed over direct to the owner, or his duly authorized representative, and take a receipt for the same on the stub of the Stock Certificate Book. When they are transmitted, let it be by express, and affix the receipt obtained from him to the stub. It is not safe to send stocks and bonds through the mails, even though they may be registered.

In cancelling the old—the retired—certificates, it is well to draw across their face emphatic ink lines or a rubber stamp printing the date of cancellation, and then cut from them a portion of their signatures. These retired certificates should be pasted to their original stubs, showing that they are void, and the page upon the Transfer Book recording it. In spoiling the signature on stocks do not cut it entirely out, but cut clearly into it, allowing it to show that it was original.

In transferring the stock the transfer officer must first of all have the old certificate surrendered into his hands. Then be positive that the person who presents it for transfer and who claims to be the stockholder named in the certificate is the *bona fide* owner.

The simple fact that he may have possession of a certificate does not warrant the transfer officer in making a transfer without an identification of the holder, for in case it should afterwards prove that the certificate had been stolen by the bearer, the company making the transfer, without taking precautions to require an identification, would have reason to regret its careless action.

The certificate holder may, perhaps, only represent the stockholder through a power of attorney executed by the real owner of the certificate, and may refer the transfer clerk to signatures on its dividend book as a verification of his identity, or the identity of the signatures on his power of attorney. They may be identical, and they may be forged, too.   Insist upon a positive identification.

In transferring certificates, in many cases, the transfer clerks feel great uncertainty whether they are doing just the right thing or are taking risks which they ought not to take, for the variety of forms of ownership of stock result in many questions which have to be settled when transfers are made.   Let us look at some of these questions :—

First.   The powers of attorney which are so common an accompaniment to the certificate.

Be sure, if at all possible, that the power is not a forgery.   A company in Philadelphia not long ago was victimized by a plausible scoundrel, who presented himself to the secretary holding in his hands a certificate of stock which he had stolen, accompanied by a power of attorney, which he had forged, signatures of witnesses and all, and requested a transfer, which was unsuspectingly made by one of the most experienced secretaries.

It is not safe to accept a power of attorney or probate certificates and similar instruments if they are old.   I have known of instances where transfers have been made under documents of this sort which had become valueless by various kinds of natural deaths.   Powers of recent date are more desirable, and in some cases indispensable.

Let us consider the duties and responsibilities which are to be met with in making transfers of stock to guardians, executors, administrators and others representing the deceased owner.   It is from errors or negligence in such transfers that trouble has generally come.

In transferring shares standing in the name of a trustee, be very careful that he does not leave the channels to which he may have been confined by the instrument which gives him his authority.   See that he makes no transfer not in harmony with the common law or statute law governing action of trustee, etc.

An administrator is an official appointed by the Probate Court, and it is in the regular line of his duties to transfer any shares belonging to the estate which he is settling.   The transfer clerk should demand of the administrator the probate certificate of his appointment; the date should be recent, to guard against authority that might have been revoked.   Letters of administration are always sufficient evidence of an administrator's authority to make transfers.

Executors stand in nearly the same position.   It is only necessary to see the probate certificate of the executor's appointment.   An executor always has the right to sell and transfer property to pay debts of the estate in his charge.   If there are any doubts as to the

13

necessity of transfers, the company should consult the will or be otherwise properly informed as to the circumstances.

In transferring for guardians, the corporation should have good proof that the parties representing themselves as guardians are really so, and having probate proof of that fact, persons dealing with them in good faith will be protected.

Should an executor show the probate certificate, and the original certificate of stock be surrendered, and a transfer is made with parties with whom you are well acquainted, and it should be discovered that a will had been made of later date, the transfer made under authority of the first would be void, and if there is much difference in the two wills the situation would be an embarrassing one.

It is not safe to allow stock to remain in the name of the dead stockholder in the hands of executors and administrators, because they are drawing dividends, and the heirs not wishing to transfer. There are various reasons why it is not well to move along in this careless and indefinite way, and if transfers of this sort are delayed complications are apt to arise.

Suppose an executor has a certificate of stock for 100 shares, and in making settlement for the estate sells 50 of these shares, the transfer should be made to their purchaser for the number bought and issue a certificate to the executor for the remaining shares. I have known an executor to make a transfer of this kind and ask to have the remaining shares issued in the name of the deceased holder, the same as the original surrendered. It is not good practice to re-issue stock in the names of dead men.

Companies are frequently requested to reissue or transfer stock when the persons owning shares lose or mislay them or they are destroyed by fire. Stock should not be reissued or transferred under these circumstances unless the parties will furnish the company with a satisfactory bond guaranteeing them from any loss which may come from the presentation of the original certificate.

Shareholders should notify the company in which they are owners, of any change in their names. They should go to the company in person, or by attorney, with their certificate in hand, and make a transfer of their stock to the new name they have adopted. Such cases are very frequent, especially among women holding shares of stock in their maiden names and taking new names by marriage. Transfers of this sort should be made in this way : The old certificate was written Susan Crane ; in transferring Susan Crane should sign " Susan Crane-Thomas, formerly Susan Crane." The transfer should be made to herself, Susan Crane-Thomas.

It is clearly established that a married woman making a transfer of stock standing in her maiden name should add the statement, "formerly Miss ——"; and in transferring stock for married women the approval of the husband must be obtained.

In transferring certificates of stock much trouble, time and money can be saved by bearing these points in mind. Too great care cannot be taken.

Gas Company Consolidation.

Ex. 310.　Jan. 1, 1894, The Cleveland Gas Company, The West Side Gas Company and The Citizens' Gas Company consolidated, with a Capital Stock of $2,500,000. The corporate name is The City Gas Company. The new company is to purchase the plants, etc., of the old companies at an appraised value, and issue one and one-fourth shares of full paid stock in the new company for each share in the old companies. The liabilities and accounts due the old companies are to be liquidated by themselves. The total appraised value of the old companies is $1,900,000, as shown in the following statement, for which Common Stock is issued. The balance of $600,000 Preferred Stock was placed in the market for sale.

	Plants.	Real Estate.	Fur. & Fix.	Coal.	Tar.	Materi-al, etc.	Cash.	Total.
Cleveland Gas Co.........	$550,000	$17,500	$1,125	$20,000	$9,500	$1,900	$114,000	$714,025.00
West Side Gas Co.......	400,000	14,600	1,071	16,000	7,000	1,721	100,000	540,392.00
Citizens' Gas Co..........	500,000	17,000	995	17,500	8,100	1,650	100,338	645,583.00
	$1,450,000	$49,100	$3,191	$53,500	$24,600	$5,271	$314,338	$1,900,000.00

A.　What entry to close the books of each of the old companies?

B.　What entry to open the books of the consolidated company?

CHAPTER TWENTY-THREE.

AUDITOR AND AUDITING.

Ex. 311. Auditor is derived from the Latin *Audire*, to hear; it is the name given to an official appointed by competent authority for the purpose of examining, on behalf of the government, courts of law, corporations, associations or individuals, the accounts of persons to whom have been lawfully entrusted the receipt and disbursement of money or other property. The government may appoint such officials by virtue of Acts of Congress passed April 3, 1817 and Feb. 24, 1819. In general practice an Auditor is an officer of the court assigned to state items of debit and credit between parties in suits when accounts are in question, and exhibit balances. Auditors may be appointed by courts either of law or equity, at common law in actions of accounts, and in many states by special statute in other actions. They have authority to take testimony, to examine books and other vouchers, and in some states to examine witnesses under oath. Their report must embrace a special account, giving items allowed and disallowed, and the exceptions, if any, taken by either party, to their decisions.

An Auditor's report is final as to facts in some jurisdictions, unless vitiated by fraud or gross error, but is subject to examination as to points of law contained in it. Elsewhere it is *prima facie* jury evidence, and rebuttal testimony may be introduced to prove incorrectness; in still other states it has no effect until sanctioned by the court.

Corporation Auditors.

It is customary with many corporations for the Directors or Stockholders to elect or appoint a person or persons to examine and audit the accounts and financial affairs of the Company; and sometimes a Finance Committee is appointed to approve and order paid all bills, and to examine and attest the correctness of the books and balance sheet before declaring a dividend.

Many large corporations, like Railroads, Manufacturing, Mining and Insurance Companies, employ an Auditor permanently to make regular periodic audits and examinations of the accounts of the different accounting officers and agents at their various plants and offices.

Too often some society young gentleman or others having influential friends are appointed as Auditors through some reason other than merit.   It requires comparatively but very little knowledge of accounts to keep ordinary books, and so far as relates to the simple work of checking the books, and of comparing the disbursements with the vouchers they have no difficulty; but in the higher work of accounting and auditing, they are totally unfamiliar and incompetent. It requires much study and practice to achieve the title of Accountant, and but few bookkeepers ever attain to that high degree.

Business men should demand a certificate of competency from some reliable Bureau of Audit or Institute of Accounts, of bookkeepers, accountants and auditors, before they are intrusted with the responsibilities of these positions.

Value of an Audit.

The real value of a thorough and systematic audit of the accounts and financial affairs of firms and corporations is not adequately appreciated, but the very severe lessons the investing public have learned through the failures in the last few years is certainly causing them to pay more attention to the importance of periodical audits and examinations by the professional Accountant and Auditor.

Such a practice not only puts the question of solvency and standing beyond doubt, but must strengthen and popularize their names in their respective fields of operation, and protect shareholders and the investing public from fraudulent operations by an unscrupulous Board of Directors.

In England there is a law known as "The Companies Act 1862," and when a company has been incorporated by special Act of Parliament, or if registered under this Act, the law requires of them an annual audit by a Chartered Accountant.

The National Bank Act of the United States is a similar law, requiring all National Banks to be examined by Bank Examiners who are appointed by the Comptroller of the Currency, to whom they report the condition of the banks examined.

Every State in the Union should enact Corporation Laws similar to the National Bank Act of the United States and the Companies Act of England, requiring all Private Corporations enjoying a Charter from the State to have their accounts and financial affairs investigated and audited at least once a year by a Professional Accountant and Auditor.

The silence of the law on many points concerning corporations, particularly on the matter of requiring a strict investigation of their financial affairs, often results in serious and unjust regulations in their management, and in loss to their stockholders and to the investing public.

The numerous failures and wholesale robberies unearthed in many of our large Railroads and Financial Institutions within the last few years, resulting in the appointment of Receivers and Assignees, is a subject that is receiving the profoundest thought of State Legislatures.

Duties and Qualifications of Auditors.

An Auditor should be the critical examiner of the work of the bookkeepers and financial officers, the representative of the stockholders, and the supervisor of the Board of Directors should they neglect their duties, perform fraudulent operations, or purposely prepare incorrect statements or accounts to be presented to the Firm or Stockholders of the company.

An Auditor should be a thoroughly scientific accountant, with an established character, and a will of iron ; he should have a thorough knowledge of the National and State Banking Laws, and of the Statutes of the State relating to the Department of Public Accounts, Finance, Assessments, and of the duties and responsibilities of State and County Treasurers, Auditors, Commissioners, etc. He should be a man of uncompromising integrity, know his duty, and do it without fear or favor.

The duties of an Auditor are not only numerous and responsible, but frequently intricate, and at times very disagreeable. Sometimes differences arise between the Auditor and the Directors as to the manner in which the Statements and Accounts should be stated, or as to other matters connected with his office. As the Auditor is the Stockholders' representative, his principal duty is to guard their interest, although the Directors may accuse him of interfering with what they may consider their own particular duties and rights; he should not allow himself to be influenced by their arguments, when he is confident his ideas would, if carried out, be a benefit to all concerned.

Directors are usually men of ability, integrity and honor, and when such is the case an Auditor will find his duties easy and pleasant to perform. Every facility will be afforded him, questions will be promptly and correctly answered, he will have ready access to all books, securities and documents; any suggestions he may offer to systematize their method of accounting will be adopted, if proven to be advantageous.

If Bookkeepers or Directors have neglected their duties, performed fraudulent operations, or have purposely prepared false statements and accounts to submit to the Proprietors or Stockholders, the Auditor will then find every possible obstacle thrown in his way to prevent his discovering and exposing their deceptions. When such is the case the Auditor has a very responsible, difficult and unpleasant task before him. However, he should not allow himself to become "rattled," tired out, or hurried into certifying accounts until he has required all questions to be answered, and each doubtful item explained to his entire satisfaction. If Directors or Bookkeepers refuse to answer or explain, the Auditor would, if he be firm, refuse to give his certificate, which would place the directors or bookkeepers in an embarassing position, if they should attempt to appear before the Stockholders or Proprietors without it.

System of Bookkeeping.

An Auditor should be able not only to audit and verify the books and accounts of a company, but also, if he find the books are carelessly kept, or if the system upon which they are conducted is cumbersome, or such as to require unnecessary labor or time, he should be able to suggest a better method, the adoption of which might not only save expense, time and labor, but also ensure greater accuracy.

The books of many companies are very loosely and unsystematically kept by low grade, careless and incompetent bookkeepers, whereas, if competent, careful help were to be employed, a great deal of unnecessary work might be concentrated into fewer books, or perhaps even be dispensed with altogether.

The Directors are the Managers of the Company on behalf of the Stockholders, to whom they are responsible, and it is important that, in *his* anxiety to do his duty towards the Stockholders, the Auditor should be careful not to interfere in the management of the Company by insisting on the adoption of any of his propositions as to the system of Bookkeeping or other matters. He should endeavor to introduce his improvements by friendly, courteous suggestions, and by putting them forward gradually.

Principles of an Audit.

It is thought by a great many that an audit is simply to check the amounts posted from the books of original entry to the Ledger, prove the additions in the Cash Book, check the balances from the Ledger to the Balance Sheet, and compare payments with receipts, etc. In order to correct this absurd idea, I would say that, to enable an Auditor to certify as to the accuracy of the Books and Accounts examined, and to make an audit effectual he should seek to detect and guard against errors of three kinds, namely: 1, Errors of Principle; 2, Errors of Omission; 3, Errors of Fraud.

By "Errors of Principle" is meant such as are apt to be made by those not proficient in the science of accounts.

By "Errors of Omission" is meant those items which have accidentally been omitted either on the Debit or Credit side.

By "Errors of Fraud" is meant those entries intentionally made to defraud and embezzle.

The Professional Accountant and Auditor is the servant of the Public, and just what the Public wants so will he be willing to give.

If a complete audit of the accounts of a Firm or Corporation is called for, then the Auditor will examine critically each item to detect all errors, as I have just described. But if it is desired to know what the earnings of the Company have been and no more, he will merely supply this information. If in addition it is desired to know whether the working capital is sufficient or otherwise, he would equally furnish this information if asked to do so. When an Auditor is called upon to make a special examination upon some particular point, it is not reasonable to suppose that he will examine or certify to anything but the point in question.

If a Partnership business is to be converted into a Joint Stock Company, and the prospective Stockholders should desire to know of the Auditor whether or not the proposed capital of the company is sufficient or not, he should prepare: first, a statement of the net average annual earnings for a series of years; second, whether or not the net assets to be taken constitute in themselves sufficient working capital to run the business without borrowing; and third, if in his opinion the value of the good will or bonus, if any, is based upon correct calculation. This would give the investors an idea of the worth and soundness of the undertaking, and would constitute the duties of the Auditor in regard to this point.

List of the Books and Documents.

The Auditor, before entering upon the duties of his first audit of a Firm's or Company's accounts, would find it greatly to his advantage to secure a complete list of all the books kept, both Financial and Statistical, with all Financial Statements, Balance Sheets, Vouchers, and everything connected therewith.

He should also obtain a copy of the original prospectus, if the company be a new one, also a copy of the Charter, Articles of Agreement and By-Laws. A careful examination of these books and documents, together with what explanations he may deem advisable to ask of the officers and bookkeeper regarding the nature of the business, and the system of conducting their accounts, will better prepare him to proceed with his audit.

Capital Stock Account.

In auditing the accounts of a Corporation, the Auditor should give the Capital Stock Account his first attention, to see that the Capital is neither more nor less than authorized by the Charter and Articles of Association. He should also ascertain if the Capital is made up of Common Stock or whether it contains Preferred or Guaranteed Shares.

The opening entries should be critically examined. If there is Treasury Stock, Working or Operating Capital, he should note its character and how produced.

The Minute Book, Subscription Book and Stock Ledger should be examined to ascertain the actions of the Directors and Stockholders, also to see how, upon what conditions and by whom, the subscriptions to the Capital Stock have been made, the amount paid thereon, and if there are any delinquents or forfeitures. The amount of the subscriptions paid should be compared with the Installment Book and the Installment Scrip Book. If the Company be a new one, the Certificates of Stock issued should be compared with the Installment Scrip Book.

If property is purchased the Auditor should see that the titles have been properly recorded, and that all costs and payments have been properly entered. He should also ascertain if all mortgages, Bonds, etc., were duly recorded, and registered according to law.

Preliminary Expenses.

There are almost always numerous preliminary expenses incurred in organizing Stock Companies. In dealing with this account the

Auditor should critically examine each item. The following may be properly charged to the Preliminary Expense Account, and any others in addition which have been properly expended for the formation and establishment of the Company, viz.: the expense for preparing the Articles of Association, the fee to secure the Charter, Printing, Prospectus, Plans, Account Books, and Brokerage paid to those for selling Stock, etc.

Writing Off Preliminary Expenses.

The expenses incurred in the formation of a Company are usually brought together under the Preliminary Expense Account as just stated, and as it would be unfair towards the business of the first year to charge the whole amount to Loss and Gain, it is customary to write off a proportion, say one-fourth each year for the first four years, at the end of which time the account would thus be extinguished.

Having satisfied himself that the Capital Stock and all the opening entries are correct, the Auditor may then give his attention to the

Cash Book.

The items on the credit side of the Cash Book should be checked with the vouchers or receipts; these vouchers should be critically examined. If cash is paid on account, or to balance an account, the account should be examined to ascertain if the balance is correct ; this may prove to agree, yet the account may be a fictitious one. The credits of the account should be checked with the original invoices, which invoices should be marked O.K. by the Buyer and Receiving Clerk. If not satisfied with this, the Auditor should refer to the Order Book and Correspondence.

When money is paid to take up Notes, the signatures on the notes should be partially destroyed, then filed away as a receipt in addition to the check, if paid by check. Every well managed concern should pay all accounts by check and voucher. The statement or invoice should be pasted to the voucher, and when the checks are returned from the bank, they should be attached thereto also. The checks and vouchers should bear the same number, and when they are so kept, a great amount of labor can be saved the Auditor, and will also enable the officers to examine them with very little trouble.

The vouchers should consist of actual receipts, and the Auditor should require the receipts to be produced.

When satisfied that the expenditures have been properly made, and the cash accounted for, the Auditor must then ascertain if the charges have been made against the proper accounts. It is important to know that all items have been charged to the proper accounts, because if posted to the wrong account the books may not necessarily be out of balance, but it would eventually affect the Assets in the Annual Statement.

The balance of cash in the Bank can easily be compared with the account on the stubs in the Check Book; these balances very seldom agree, as checks drawn may not have been presented for payment. From the Banker's balance deduct the amount of outstanding checks, and the amounts should then agree.

Vouchers, Documents, etc., Carefully Arranged.

The officers of the Company can render the Auditor a great deal of assistance by having all Vouchers and Documents previously arranged in numerical order. By so doing considerable time can be saved, and if any should be found missing, duplicates could be obtained before beginning the Audit. I have long made it a practice not to accept any vouchers, papers, etc., for examination, which are not properly arranged.

Purchase Book.

It is merely mechanical work to audit this book, yet there are points that should have the closest attention, as "Errors of Fraud" are frequently practiced by bookkeepers or others, increasing the credits of some accounts in order that they may pocket the money, and charge it to the account thus increased. Sometimes fictitious accounts are opened for the same purpose.

The amounts in this book can be verified by the original Invoices, Order Book, Letter Book, etc.

Sales Book.

In Mercantile and Manufacturing companies the principal source of profit is derived from Sales, which may be classed under two heads: 1, Cash Sales; 2, Credit Sales.

All **Cash Sales** should be entered at once in the Cash Book, from whence the entries are examined, which process is so simple that further comment is unnecessary.

Credit Sales should receive the Auditor's most careful attention, as it is from this source that bad and doubtful debts arise.

It is also a simple operation to examine the entries in this book, and it is expecting a great deal to ask an Auditor to examine every item, but if "Errors of Fraud" are sought, every amount must then be examined.   I have detected many false entries made in the Sales Book in this way.   Say there would be a charge to a good paying customer of $550, this amount would be changed and posted $450; when the remittance of $550 is received, the customer would be credited $450 which would balance his account; the check or draft would be placed in the cash, and $100 in currency put in the bookkeeper's pocket, thus keeping the cash in balance.

If the Auditor is suspicious of any accounts in this book, after comparing it with the Ledger, the original order should be referred to, also the salesman's ticket.   If there is a difference that leads to further suspicions, the Auditor should write the customer for a duplicate of the bill and receipt; these amounts can be verified with the credits; if there is a difference it can be learned from the Banker if such check was deposited on or about such date, thus making it an easy matter to detect.   It would be difficult for operations of this kind to be practiced when there are a number of bookkeepers, cashiers, etc., yet the cunning knave is always alert.   If the Auditor be capable he will detect and bring the guilty one to justice.

Accounts and Bills Receivable.

The Auditor should go carefully through the list of the Bills Receivable to ascertain whether they have been discounted or are on hand, and if on hand and overdue, whether or not they have been paid, and no credit given.   If any have been discounted, they should be carefully listed, for the Company is liable should they not be paid when due.

Regarding the Accounts Receivable, he should notice what time they were to run; if overdue, why they have not been collected.   It is very important that due provision be made periodically for bad and doubtful accounts, otherwise there will appear among the assets accounts that can never be collected.   Too many concerns carry their customers accounts as good, and make no provision for bad and doubtful ones, thereby continue to pay good dividends, whereas, if a sufficient amount should be written off for expected loss, no dividends could be paid at all.   It is practically impossible for any business to be carried on without bad debts being occasionally incurred.   An Auditor cannot be expected to be acquainted with, or even to ascertain the financial condition, of those indebted to the Company, but it is a part of his duty to prevent the Company taking credit for full amount of all accounts.

The Auditor should require a list of all those who are indebted to the Company at the date the books were closed.   This list should be classified under three heads, namely: good, doubtful and bad. The amount due from the good ones may be considered worth full value, while the doubtful ones should be regarded as worth 50 to 80 per cent. of face value; the balance 50 or 20 per cent. which is considered doubtful, together with the total of those considered bad, should be treated as shown in Lesson 16, Page 108.

Should there be accrued interest on any of the Bills Receivable or Personal Accounts, Loss and Gain should have credit therefor as shown in Lesson 21, Pages 145 and 146.

Accounts and Bills Payable.

The Auditor should be very critical in examining the Accounts and Bills Payable, to see if there are any outstanding Accounts or Notes that have not been credited, and whether or not the Company owes the Accounts and Bills Payable as shown by the books. If there is accrued interest on the Accounts and Bills Payable, the Auditor should adjust the same as shown in Lesson 21, Pages 145 and 146. Entries of this character, however, pertain to the duties of the bookkeeper, but it is the duty of the Auditor to adjust such matters in his audit if they have been omitted by the bookkeeper.

General Expenses.

Items of General Expense which are not of sufficient importance to require separate Ledger Accounts, are usually included in one General Expense Account. The Auditor should, however, for his own information, examine the principle items, as it may contain some unauthorized payments.

Salary Account.

Under this account is kept the remuneration of the officers, bookkeepers and others on the regular office force. Very often an attempt is made, especially with new companies, to omit certain charges to this account until after the dividend has been declared, thus making a better showing. This is done upon the ground that they have not been paid, that the exact amounts are not known, or have not been agreed upon. This the Auditor should positively refuse to allow, and should defer the audit until the amounts have been ascertained, or a satisfactory estimate has been made and charged.

Wages.

The wages paid to workmen, mechanics, and others whose remuneration depends upon the quantity of work done, should be kept separately. In all well regulated establishments, the wages are charged to the particular department to which they belong. Wages, and other costs to manufacture, should be included in the cost price of the article manufactured. The Auditor should see that all wages paid are charged to the proper accounts, else the expense to operate or cost to manufacture will not be accurate.

Commission.

Frequently Traveling Salesmen and other Agents are paid entirely by a commission, or are allowed a commission in addition to their regular salaries, on the amount of business done for the Company. When commission is paid, the amount so allowed should be stated separately and the Auditor should be satisfied that there are no commissions paid or unpaid which are not charged. Neither should he allow commission to be deducted from the sales. Money is often advanced to traveling men or agents to be deducted from commissions expected to be earned. The Auditor will find it a tedious task to ascertain how much of the amounts advanced should be charged. The sales, etc., will have to be carefully examined to determine the amount earned, which amount should then be charged. The balance should be carried as an Asset for the unearned portion of the commission, which should stand in the agent's name.

Rent, Taxes, etc.

Under this heading should be included the rent of offices, grounds, and buildings in which the business of the Company is transacted. When a portion of the premises of which the Company is the lessee is sub-let, the Auditor should see that there are no credits for rents which might have been paid in advance. Only such portion of these payments as are earned should be credited.

Agents' Accounts.

The Auditor should be particular that commission and all other charges which will be allowed to Agents are deducted from their balances and charged, so that the difference only, which is the amount the Company should ultimately receive, is taken credit for among the Assets. Accounts which are considered bad or doubtful should be treated as previously stated.

Branch Houses.

It is impossible for the Auditor to make such a thorough investigation of the affairs of a Company's Branches as it is his duty to do. When all the records of the business are kept in the main office, he should critically examine the returns from the branches, and ascertain if they are properly consolidated with the books in the main office. To make an audit effectual, the Auditor should be sent to the Branches to examine everything in detail.   If, however, the managers of the Branches certify that the figures are correct, the Auditor should present his report to the Stockholders subject to such certificates.

Merchandise Returned and Rebates.

The Auditor should not allow Rebates or Goods Returned to or by the Company to be charged to the Merchandise account.   To show the true amounts of purchases and sales a Merchandise Returned and Rebate account should be kept, and all Merchandise Returned and Rebates should be entered therein.   When the books are closed, the Debit side of this account should be deducted from the aggregate Credit of Merchandise, and the Credit amount deducted from the aggregate Debit of Merchandise.   The Merchandise Account will then be closed in the regular way.

The Auditor should also see that all shipping cases, freights, cartage, or any other accounts affecting Merchandise are closed into Merchandise account, in order to determine accurately the gain or loss thereon.

Repairs (Errors of Principle.)

The Auditor should critically examine each entry for Repairs, etc. to see whether or not any " Errors of Principle " have been made. Unless a Company is in a prosperous condition, there is a great tendency to add to the amount standing on the books by charging Repairs, etc., to Property Accounts.   This the Auditor should positively refuse to allow, unless it is desired to show the Loss or Gain on such property, in which case it should be charged for all additional costs, and credited for all rents, sales, or whatever it may produce.

If Real Estate, Machinery, etc., are owned by a Company for the prosecution of their enterprise, the accounts representing the expenditure thereon should be closed, and no additions allowed, except for additional buildings, ground, and machinery necessitated by increased business.

Should the Auditor find the buildings of a Factory to be charged, say, with Taxes $300, Repairs, etc. $3000, this would be an "Error of Principle," as property was debited when an account showing Loss and Gain should have been charged, consequently the property is made to show a false value of $3300, and the business a false gain of $3300. There are exceptional cases, however, in which an Auditor would be justified in carrying a portion of Repairs as an Asset, as for example, if the sum expended for Repairs be very heavy in any one year, he may charge one-half, one-third or one-fourth to Loss and Gain, provided however, that other repairs would not be needed for the next two, three or four years, the balance being placed to a separate account and carried as an Asset.

Stocks and Bonds.

If a Company holds Stocks and Bonds as an investment, the Auditor should see whether they are as represented on the books, are on hand, or whether they have been pledged or hypothecated. The accounts with Stocks and Bonds should show the number of the shares or bonds, the numbers of the Certificates, and the amounts. In case of Stocks, the amount paid upon those of each Company should be stated, and any liability to further calls. A Company should not hold shares of other Companies, which are not fully paid and non-assessable. The Auditor should inform the Stockholders of any liability attached to Stock, which is held for investment.

When a Company holds shares in other Companies as an investment, the accrued interest can only be estimated, as the rate of dividend which will be declared cannot of course be known. The Auditor should not allow the rate to be too high; calculation can easily be made for the interest, from the investments in Bonds and Mortgages, as the rates are fixed.

If a Company has loaned or borrowed money, secured by Mortgages and Bonds, the Auditor should examine them carefully to ascertain if they have been properly entered and recorded according to law. These accounts should represent the actual sums advanced.

Securities.

The Auditor must be careful to see that the Securities held by the Company for advances made are accompanied by the necessary Bonds and Mortgages. He should also see that the unpaid coupons are attached to all bonds payable to bearer. In order that this may be done in a businesslike and methodical manner, the Auditor should have prepared for him a list of all securities, with full particulars of each, with their value as taken credit for. All the Securities should be stated separately, as the same class may have been deposited with the Company by more than one borrower.

The Auditor should have all the securities in his possession together with the keys to the safety vault, so that documents which he has inspected as being held against a loan cannot be reproduced to him as the security deposited for other loans. If the Company sustains a loss on any of its investments in Bonds, Mortgages, or any class of securities, the amount should be distinctly stated, and not be concealed by being included in any item of expenditure.

Premiums, Transportation, Etc.

The principle source of income of all companies transacting Insurance business, whether Life, Accident, Fire or Marine, is the premiums they receive for undertaking the risk of insurance. In auditing the accounts of an Insurance Company, the Auditor must be careful to see that only those premiums are credited which fall due in the period under audit. Premiums paid in advance falling due after the date of closing the books should not be taken credit for, but should be carried as a Liability.

The principle loss of Insurance Companies consists of the "claims" under its policies, and in dealing with this item the Auditor must be careful to ascertain that all the unsettled claims have been entered in the "Register of Claims." Instances have occurred of Managers concealing letters announcing heavy losses until after the books have been closed. The Auditor will find it a difficult matter to discover frauds of this nature.

All "claims admitted" which have not been paid at the time the books are closed must be carried as a liability.

The revenues of Railroads, Steamships and other similar companies consist mainly of receipts for transportation of passengers and freight. Banks derive theirs principally from discounting commercial paper, while Gas and Water Companies from the rates they charge for the consumption of their respective products. These demand no special instructions for the guidance of the Auditor. He must, however, be careful to ascertain that no amounts are taken credit for which have not been properly earned, and that when it is necessary to make an estimate, it must be done on a reasonable and conservative basis.

Depreciation of Plant, Machinery, Patent Right, etc.

The Auditor should recommend a proper amount to be written off for depreciation of Plant, Machinery, Leasehold, Patent Right, Goodwill, etc. This should be a percentage on the cost. The rate should be low or high as it is to be seldom or frequently repaired or replaced. The balance should be carried as an asset to represent its true value.

The rent, cost of maintaining plant, machinery and the salaries of officers and workmen, frequently pull so heavily on the revenue of a new Company that the Directors defer charging Loss and Gain for depreciation; which is probably the only way a dividend could be paid. If the Directors do not write off a depreciation the Auditor should so notify the Stockholders.

The expenditures of a new enterprise are usually as heavy in its early years as they are when the business has become established, and it is in the early years of a Company's existence the Auditor has the greatest difficulty to persuade the Directors to charge Loss and Gain an amount sufficient to provide for the depreciation of the period under audit.

Increase or Decrease the Value of Property, Stocks and Bonds.

To increase or decrease the value of Property, Stocks and Bonds, proceed as in Lesson 16, Page 108. The same rule applies when the books have been closed with an over or under valuation of Stocks and Bonds.

Dividends.

It is the duty of the Auditor to see that no inflated statements are made for the purpose of aiding Dividends. The Auditor should vigorously oppose a Dividend which has not been legitimately earned. Should the Directors persist in doing so, the Auditor should state clearly to the Stockholders that the dividend would be fictitious and illegal. Fictitious dividends are of frequent occurrence, and are declared to deceive the public as to the Company's prosperity, and thus inflate their stock.

Market and Intrinsic Value of Stocks and Bonds.

In handling accounts involving Stocks and Bonds, the Auditor should remember that there is generally quite a difference between their Market Value and Intrinsic Value. The Market Value of the Stock is generally determined by comparing the dividend of the Stock with the current rate of interest in the money market. The Market Value of good dividend paying stock is above its real or intrinsic value, while the market value of low dividend paying stock is often below its real or intrinsic value.

Position of the Auditor.

One of the most unpleasant situations in which an Auditor can be placed is when he is compelled to notify the Stockholders that the Company is not in a prosperous condition, and that the books are inaccurate, etc. Should he find the books to be carelessly and inaccurately kept, and false statements prepared for the Stockholders, then he must positively refuse to give his certificate.

Usually an Auditor has very little trouble to induce the Directors to write off a sufficient amount for depreciation when the Company is prosperous, but when a period of depression in trade arrives, the Directors will, without any intention of acting dishonorably, present a statement showing a profit equal to those of former years, while in reality it is considerably less. To the inexperienced this may seem impossible, but it is of frequent occurrence nevertheless.

If the Directors refuse to amend the accounts, it is difficult for the Auditor to decide what course to pursue. Under these circumstances he should prepare for the Stockholders a full report of the accounts, setting forth clearly therein the points at issue between the Directors and himself, and sign the accounts subject to such report.

Surplus.

Surplus is a certain portion of the annual profits of a Company, set aside for the purpose of creating a fund to meet reverse in profits, or unseen emergencies, etc. No well regulated corporation will declare a dividend equal to the net gain. National Banks are required to create a Surplus Fund. See Lesson 8, pages 66 and 67, and Lesson 19, page 125.

Reserve Fund.

A Reserve Fund is a sum set aside for some special purpose, and should always represent actual cash. The cash should be taken from the General Cash as shown in Lesson 9, pages 71 and 72. The Auditor should recommend that a Surplus and Reserve Fund be created, though it be started in a small way.

Inventory.

The Auditor should critically examine the Inventory of Merchandise, Real Estate, Machinery, Plant, Store and Office Fixtures, etc., to ascertain whether or not the values have been inflated. A certain percentage should be written off for depreciation. Each Inventory should be compared with those of former years.

A great many concerns Invoice their stock of Merchandise at cost price, while others take it at the market value. The only correct way is to Invoice stock at cost price; there can be no profit until sold. If invoice is taken to sell out, it would be proper to take it at Market Value.

Defalcations.

Conscientious Bookkeepers and Directors will rather court than object to criticism, investigation or verification, as it confirms their work, increases confidence, and places them at ease with the Proprietors or Stockholders, while the defaulter will usually be uneasy, ill-natured, and claim that he never makes mistakes, etc. Extensive defalcations are generally committed by persons who thoroughly understand the books and the business, who so cleverly cover them up as to tax the skill of the Auditor to the utmost. But the Auditor will critically examine every transaction in detail; every erasure, alteration or inter-line should be carefully examined, for every dash, dot or character may have a meaning. The Auditor should not leave them until their mean-ing has been made satisfactory. He should ascertain the amount of business done each year, what it cost, and what the Loss or Gain was. He should compare one year's business with another; if any variations in the results, they should be noted; and when there is a marked dif-ference he should ascertain the cause, whether by the withdrawal of capital, depression in trade, change of management, depreciation of values, etc. If the output has maintained its average with no greater expense, and no cause can be assigned for the discrepancy, then it is safe to say that fraud has been committed somewhere. The Auditor should then seek to obtain positive evidence of defalcation, by testing the accuracy, cause and effect of every transaction from the original entry, to its proper place in the Ledger, see that all transactions are properly entered in the book of original entry from the orders, invoices, receipts, checks, freight bills, correspondence, etc. Check every posting. Examine every item posted to the different expense accounts. Find the total amount of cash received and disbursed. Check the bank account with check book and examine all checks to ascertain if the amounts and signatures are correct. Find the total purchases and sales, independent of cross entries. Verify the footings of all books of original entry. Verify the footings of every account in the Ledger, whether ruled up and closed or remaining open. Examine closely all entries in the Cash Book, and verify the payments with the vouchers. See that the Inventory is correctly valued, and verify the footings. Satisfy yourself as to the cause of every erasure, alteration, interline, etc., tracing it back to its original entry. Take off a Trial Balance as the Ledger shows.

The Auditor should make a full and comprehensive note as he proceeds, of every error, omission, alteration, interline or other irregular work requiring explanation, and give the dates and pages for ready reference. When the Auditor has completed his task of auditing and examining the books of an Individual, Firm or Corporation, he should then prepare a

Financial Statement,

The items of which should be so clearly stated that any person of ordinary intelligence could understand them without a knowledge of the science of accounts. This statement should be divided into two parts, the one showing the Assets and Liabilities, the other the Losses and Gains.

In stating the Assets and Liabilities, the *total* amounts of the personal accounts due to or by the Company can be stated as Accounts Receivable and Accounts Payable respectively; all the other accounts should be set forth under their proper headings, that they cannot be mistaken for realizable and marketable securities.

In preparing the statement of Losses and Gains, the debit side should show upon what accounts and property all losses have been sustained, while the credits should show the gains.

The most unsatisfactory item which can be found in a Financial Statement is that representing a Net Loss.

If the books show a net loss, the Auditor should state it so clearly and in such a manner that the amount could not possibly be supposed to represent an asset.

BANK EXAMINATIONS.

Bank Examinations can be made in various ways and under different circumstances. In National Banks there are generally one or two examinations each year by the United States Bank Examiner, who examines the institutions to the best of his ability, and according to rules laid down by the Comptroller of the Currency, to whom his reports are made. These reports are seldom, if ever, seen by the bank officers, and unless the Examiner chooses to inform them that everything is right they are none the wiser. In State Banks, examinations are made by State Bank Examiners under State laws, but these reports are filed with the Banking Department of each State, and of course the officers of banks do not have access to them.

There seems to be a misconception in the mind of the public regarding the duties of National and State Bank Examiners, and when a bank fails many people blame them for not doing their duty. It should be clearly understood that bank examiners are not detectives. They cannot go over all the transactions of a bank for any length of time, and if a defalcation can be concealed from the officers or directors for a series of years, it can hardly be expected that a Bank Examiner, in the course of an examination made once or twice a year, will unearth it. It is true that it is their business to look after such things, still they cannot be expected to do impossibilities.

The officers and directors of a bank are responsible if anything goes wrong, and the blame must rest upon them.

There is no rule for examinations that will make men honest, but bank officers should strive by all means in their power to throw such safeguards around employes that they will be better able to resist the temptation to do a wrong act. The first requisite of a careful bank examination is, that the party to be examined should not be informed beforehand. If the least chance be given for a man to prepare for an examination, he can generally do so in such a way that the best of systems will be defeated. If the Directors purpose sending experts to examine a bank, the officers should know nothing whatever about it until the Examiners put in an appearance with their authority. Under no circumstances should the department to be examined be notified until the examiners are ready to take charge of the books and money. I offer the following instructions for examination of the different departments.

Receiving-Teller's Department.

1st. Count all cash and see that it agrees with the amount called for by Receiving-Teller's proof.

2d. Look back and list all checks drawn in other banks received on deposit during the day, and if a Clearance-House Bank, look back all checks intended for the Clearing-House, and see that they are properly listed and the amounts correctly transferred to the Clearance House sheet.

3d. Examine carefully items called city and foreign office, and see that nothing is being held which is not collectable the next day or which is not in shape to be charged to the different correspondents of the bank.

4th.   List all Checks on your bank received on deposit during the day and see that they, together with the Checks in other banks, city and foreign office, and cash equal the total amount of deposits received, which should also be carefully listed and tickets footed.

In looking back Checks drawn on other banks, great care should be exercised to see that none are fictitious and that all are properly accounted for as coming through some department of the bank.

Paying-Tellers' Department.

1st.   Count all cash and see that it agrees with the amounts called for by the Paying-Tellers' Proof.

2nd.   Carefully list all Checks that have been paid by the Paying Teller that day, and see that the total equals the amount called for by his books.

3rd.   Scrutinize all charges made by him to the other Tellers, all cash items, so called, receipts for currency shipped, Clearance House transactions, and any Entry from his desk that is out of the usual course of business.

4th.   See what tickets, if any, are held in his cash, and make careful report of such.

5th.   See that the total amount of cash on hand, with the amount of Checks paid by him during the day and the amounts charged to the other Tellers or different departments of the bank, equals the total amount of his cash at the close of business on the previous day.

Third Tellers' Department.

1st.   Count the cash.

2nd.   Carefully check all charges made to out-of-town correspondence from the foreign office of the previous day, proving the same.

3rd.   Carefully check city office of the previous day and see that everything has been collected which is called for by the proof of that day.

4th.   Carefully call back all mail received on the day of examination and see that proper Entries have been made for same, and if a Clearance House Bank, carefully prove the additions to the Clearance House Sheet.

5th.   Scrutinize all Items appearing on his books as coming from any department in the bank and check back to their source.

6th.   See that nothing has been charged to him by the other Tellers or charged by him to them which has not been properly Entered.

Great care should be used to see that all Checks handled by him are *bona fide*, and that there are no Checks in his department taken from mail that have not been credited.

Examine all Notes left for collection, past due Items of all descriptions, and anything on the desk of irregular order.

Discount Department.

1st. List Bills discounted or compare with discount tickler and prove same with general Ledger.

2nd. Any Bills discounted that are away for acceptance, collection, etc., must be proven by letter, care to be used to see that all have been actually sent, as some may have been ordered back, prepaid, etc.

3rd. Report all collateral Loans not covered by required margin.

4th. Report all past-due paper.

5th. If special deposits are held on discount desk carefully compare same with list and see that proper receipts have been taken for any delivered.

6th. Carefully list and report any securities which are not held as special deposits or collateral to Loans.

7th. Report any and all collateral that you are unable to find quotations for.

8th. Select certain calculations made by the Discount Clerk during a period of three or four months before the examination and see if correct.

Individual Bookkeeper.

1st. Check the Credits in the Depositors accounts with the amounts received by the Receiving Teller.

2nd. If Notes have been discounted, or Notes and Drafts have been collected for Depositors, check these Credits, with the Discount and Collection Register.

3rd. Check all charged in the Depositors accounts with the amounts paid by the Paying Teller.

4th. Check the Depositors balances, with same in general Ledger.

General Bookkeeper.

1st. Take a proof of the general Ledgers.

2nd. Count and prove all Bonds, Stocks and Mortgages on hand called for by the Ledger. If any be away verify by correspondence.

3rd. Examine United States Treasurer's duplicate receipt of bond to secure circulation and United States deposits.

4th.   Write Reserve Agent and all correspondents to advise you at your private address the balance due the bank at close of business on date of examination.   Upon receipt of same careful comparisons should be made.

5th.   Examine current expenses, taxes paid and premium account and see that no irregular Entries have been made.

6th.   Examine the various earnings accounts and see that there are no improper Entries.

7th.   Prove the account with the United States Treasurer by his letters of advice.

8th.   Prove the circulation received from Washington.

9th.   Certificates of Deposit should be proven from the Certificate book and register.

10th.   Carefully **verify** certified accounts.

11th.   Carefully prove the individual Deposits.

12th.   List and prove Cashier's Check outstanding, etc., etc.,

To follow the instructions and suggestions given in this lesson, it is confidently believed that the experienced Accountant will have but little difficulty in adapting himself to any forms and be thoroughly competent to audit the books of any individual, firm or corporation.

To Cover Losses and Produce a Working Capital.

Ex. 312.   The Ohio Paint Mfg. Co. wishing to cover a $25,000 Loss and produce a Working Capital of $25,000 called an assessment of 20 per cent. on its Capital Stock of $250,000.   The assessment $50,000 was paid in Cash, what Entry?

Ex. 313.   If $25,000 were lost at the end of the next year and an assessment of 10 per cent. was called to procure more Working Capital, what Entry?

Ex. 314.   What Entry when the assessment is paid.

To Increase or Decrease the Value of Assets before Declaring a Dividend.

Ex. 315.   If the property of a company fairly increases in value say $10,000, what Entry is necessary, or how would you get the new value on the books?

Ex. 316.   If the property decreases what disposition should be made of it?

Ex. 317.   If the market value of Stock in your possession is reduced $25 per share, what Entry should be made before declaring a Dividend?

CHAPTER TWENTY-FOUR.

Miscellaneous Points and Short Methods.

Names Applied to Property and Accounts. In bookkeeping each kind of Property and Service is known by a distinct name: this is done that each may show the loss or gain thereon.

Merchandise is used to represent all kinds of goods. In certain lines of trade, an account is kept with each kind of goods, as Coal, Lumber, Iron, Cotton, Wheat, Sugar, etc. The Debit side of the Merchandise account shows the amount of goods purchased, or the cost, while the credit side shows the amount of goods sold, or what it has produced.

To find the Loss or Gain on Merchandise, the account should be closed by adding the amount of goods on hand to the credit side, the balance is then ascertained. If it be on the credit side, it shows the gross gain; if the balance be on the debit side, it shows the gross loss. The Loss or Gain thus found is carried to the Loss and Gain account: to the debit side if it is a loss, to the credit side if it is a gain. The account is then footed and will be found to balance. The Inventory is then brought down to new account, as it is the amount of Merchandise on hand.

Cash is the name given to all Coin, Currency, Bank Drafts, Certificates of Deposit, etc. The debit side of the cash account shows the amount of cash received, and the credit side the amount of cash paid out. The balance, which is always on the debit side, should equal the amount of cash on hand.

Stock or Proprietor's Accounts, are kept with the partners to show the investments and withdrawals. These accounts are credited with the investments and net gain, and debited with the withdrawals and net loss. A Partner's Stock Account should not be made the receptacle of small items, but should remain open, showing only the investments and withdrawals, also the net Gain or net Loss.

Partner's Private Account. A Private Account should be kept with each partner, which should be credited with salary and debited with merchandise or cash withdrawn. When the books are closed at the end of the year, the balance of the Private account is closed into the Stock account.

The Stock account is the last account closed, because, if the business has a net gain the capital has been increased; therefore the proprietor should be credited for the increase. If there has been a net loss, the capital has been reduced, therefore the proprietor should be debited for the reduction.

Real Estate. Each kind of property should have its own account, as Forest Hill Farm, The Cuyahoga Building, etc. The debit side of this account should show the actual cost, and the credit side the sales or what it has produced, as rents, etc. Insurance, taxes, repairs, and other similar expenses should *not* be charged to the property, but to expense. If extensive improvements are made, however, the account should be debited with same, to show the actual cost only. The only items that should be charged to property are those which increase the value of it. Insurance, taxes, etc., are necessary expenses to keep the property up, but they do not increase its value.

All property accounts are closed the same as the Mdse. account.

Stocks. Shares of Stock in corporations should be called by their respective names, as First National Bank Stock, Penn'a R. R. Stock, etc. These accounts are debited for the cost and credited for the sales and dividends. If there are any shares unsold when the books are closed, the account should be closed by Inventory, then into Loss and Gain.

Bonds. Investments in Bonds should be kept by their respective names, as U. S. 4's, City of Cleveland Bridge Repair Bonds, etc. These accounts are conducted and closed the same as accounts with Stocks.

Bills Payable is the name given to written promises to pay, and by which an account is kept with all Notes and Acceptances given by the firm or corporation. The account is credited when a note is given or a time draft accepted. When you pay or otherwise redeem your notes and acceptances, the account is debited with same. The credit side of the account shows the amount of notes or acceptances issued, and the debit side the amount of those paid. The account is closed "To Balance" always. This balance shows the amount of your notes and acceptances still unpaid and held by others.

Bills Receivable is the name given to Notes, Time Drafts, Acceptances, etc., which you hold against others. This account is debited for all notes and time drafts received, and is credited when you collect or otherwise dispose of them. It is a Real Account, and is always closed "By Balance." This balance shows the amount of notes, etc., still in your possession unpaid.

Bank Account. If a Bank account is kept, it is debited with all deposits and credited for all withdrawals or checks issued. The balance will always be on the debit side, unless the account is overdrawn. It is useless and unnecessary to keep a bank account in the Ledger; it can be kept just as accurately on the stub of the check book and save a great deal of labor. If a combined Cash Journal is used, the entries on the stubs can be entered therein, but if a large number of checks are issued, it is better to use the Check Book as book of original entry.

A Mortgage is a conditional deed conveying the real or personal property to the Creditor as fully, and in precisely the same way, as if it were sold to him outright. It is given as security for the payment of a debt, etc.

Mortgages Receivable is a name given the Mortgages received to secure a debt, loan, etc. An account is kept with Mortgages Receivable precisely the same as Bills Receivable.

Mortgages Payable is a name given the mortgages issued to secure a debt, loan, etc. An account is kept with Mortgages Payable precisely the same as Bills Payable.

Personal Accounts are those kept with persons. They are debited for the amount they get into our debt, and for the amount we get out of their debt. They are credited for the amount they get out of our debt, and for the amount we get into theirs. Personal Accounts are closed "To or By Balance."

Expense Account is an account kept for all items paid for conducting the business; it is considered a loss, though we may have received benefit in many ways by means of that loss.

Sub-division of Expense Accounts. As it is a matter of gratification to the business man to have a more explicit and comprehensive statement of the expenses at the end of the year, it becomes necessary for him to classify his expenses by opening accounts for the different items of outlay. When the expense is subdivided, any unusual increase of a certain kind will attract attention at once. When the expenses are sub-divided, miscellaneous items not belonging to any one of the special accounts are charged to the Miscellaneous Expense Account. The expenses in a large business are usually sub-divided as follows:

Interest and Discount is simply a term used for the use of money. When we pay for the use of money, we debit *Interest* for the use of the money which we receive and credit *Cash* for the cash we give for use of that money. When we are paid for the use of money which we have given we debit *Cash* for the cash received and credit *Interest* for the use of the money we give. The account closes into Loss and Gain.

Accrued Interest is interest due to or by the firm or corporation on past due Personal accounts, Bills Receivable, Bills Payable, Bonds, etc. Accrued Interest is computed when the books are closed, to show the true condition of affairs.

Interest Receivable account is kept to show amount of interest accrued in our favor, which is not shown on the books, for which amount the account is debited. It is credited when the interest is paid.

Interest Payable account is kept to show amount of interest accrued against us, which is not shown on the books, for which amount the account is credited. It is debited when we pay the interest. To determine the exact worth of the business when the books are closed, it is necessary to ascertain the amount of Interest Receivable and Payable, but it is a difficult matter to keep the accounts straight, because when the interest is paid it is difficult to determine what portion to enter to Interest Receivable or Payable. Again, interest that may be charged may never be paid. The only practical way to handle accrued interest is to make the entry thus: '' Interest Old Account " to '' Interest New Account " as shown in Lesson 21, page 147.

Store, Office and Shop Expense. This account is kept to show the various items of expense connected with each department, as Postage, Janitor, etc. These accounts close into Loss and Gain.

Salary Account is an account kept to show the amount paid for the year to Bookkeepers, Clerks, Managers, etc. It is debited for the amount allowed or paid employes for services. There are no credits to this account unless some salaries have not been earned, but have been charged at the time the books are closed. The account is closed into Loss and Gain.

Light and Fuel account is an expense account kept to show the amount paid for lighting, heating, etc. It is debited for what it costs and credited for what may be sold, and for the amount unused when the books are closed. It closes into Loss and Gain.

Rent and Taxes are expenses, and an account is kept to show the cost per year on property, etc. It is debited for the amount of all rent and taxes paid, and credited for any unexpired rent or taxes which may have been paid in advance. It is closed into Loss and Gain.

Collection and Exchange are items of expense, and an account is kept that it may show the cost to collect accounts, notes, drafts, etc. It is debited for all cash paid for collecting drafts, notes and accounts, and for exchange on bank drafts, etc. It is credited for rebates, if any, and closed into Loss and Gain.

Commission and Brokerage are other items belonging to expense, and an account is kept to show the Loss or Gain in this particular branch. It is conducted and closed precisely the same as the Interest and Discount account. When the books are closed there is frequently commission due on shipments partly sold, for which an account sales has not been rendered. This is a gain which is not, but should be, shown in the books the same as Accrued Interest in Lesson 21, p. 147.

Freight, Express and Custom-House Charges are not practically items of expense, but it is the usual custom to close this account into Loss and Gain. This account is kept that we may know the amount paid for receiving and shipping goods. It is debited for freights, cartage, expressage, etc., and credited for rebates or overcharges, if any. This account should always be closed into the Merchandise account when the books are closed. The reason for this is, that it is an additional cost, also that Merchandise gets credit therefor by a certain percentage being added to the invoice price. In case of fire the amount of this account should be added to the loss, etc.

Advertising. In some branches of trade this is a very large account. It is kept, of course, to show the annual cost to advertise the business. It is debited for all cash paid for advertising, and credited for any unexpired contracts when the books are closed. It closes into Loss and Gain.

Litigation. This is a very extensive account, especially with Railroad and Insurance Companies. The account is debited for all cash paid for Law and Court Fees. Usually there are no credits. It closes into Loss and Gain.

Traveling Expense. This is an extensive account with large wholesale houses and manufacturers who employ commercial travelers. The account is debited for all money paid for traveling expenses, baggage, etc. It closes into Loss and Gain.

Suspended List. This is an account which is kept to show the amount of all doubtful accounts. All accounts which are not considered bad, but doubtful, should be closed into this account, giving name, amount of each and Ledger page. This account is debited for all accounts considered doubtful, and credited for all payments subsequently made. When any accounts are paid which have been closed into the

Suspended list they should be re-opened, then credited for the payments: this will show the customers who will pay in *time*. If any of the accounts in the Suspended List cannot be collected, they should then be charged to Loss and Gain and credit Suspended List for the amount.

A Furniture and Fixtures account is kept by most all business houses, that they may know the amount invested therein, or what is required to conduct the business. The account is debited for the amount on hand at the beginning, and for all that is purchased thereafter, and is credited for the sales, if any. When the books are closed a certain percentage should be written off for depreciation in wear and tear; the account is then closed "By Inventory" the same as the Merchandise and other property accounts.

Insurance. An account is kept with insurance to show the amount of premiums paid for insuring goods and property against loss by fire, water, etc. The account is debited for all cash paid on premiums, and when the books are closed this account should be credited for the unexpired premiums, and is then closed into Loss and Gain. Some business houses do not inventory unexpired premiums, taxes, etc., but call the whole amount a loss at once. In case of loss, and as soon as the insurance has been adjusted and the claims acknowledged, the Insurance Companies should be charged with the amount of the claims, and credit merchandise, property, or whatever the loss consisted of.

Machinery Account, in some branches of trade, is an extensive one, and is debited for the amount on hand at the commencing, and for the amount of new machinery purchased thereafter. This account should not be charged for repairs or for machinery replaced, but should be charged to Repair account, which account is closed into Loss and Gain. Any additional machinery required by reason of increased trade should, however, be charged to the Machinery account. When the books are closed, a certain percentage should be written off for depreciation in wear and tear. It would then be closed "By Inventory," which would represent the actual value. This inventory balance, of course, is then brought down to new account. Repairs on machinery, etc., do not add to its value, therefore they should not be charged to represent value.

A Horse and Wagon Account is kept by those having their own teams. It is conducted precisely the same as the machinery account.

A Pattern and Patent Account is necessary in some lines of business. No special instructions are necessary, as the account is conducted precisely the same as the Machinery account.

A Material Account is kept by many manufacturers, as articles are often manufactured in excess of the demand; storage is then secured, and goods are then shipped to various markets and kept on sale. In such cases the regular Merchandise Account should not receive credit for such shipments; only as sales are made from such storage branches is the Merchandise Account to receive credit. A special book should be provided for the purpose, and the details of such shipments should be systematically kept, and as rapidly as sales of such goods are made and entered upon the Sales Ledger, this book should be made to correspond, so that when an Inventory is taken, every article is easily accounted for. When the books are kept in this way, they will show actual Assets and Liabilities.

The Construction and Equipment Account of Railroads is usually divided into the following accounts: Depots, Road Buildings, Lands, Surveying, Grading, Bridging, Tunneling, Locomotives, Cars, Coaches, Telegraph, Fencing, Incidentals, etc. These accounts are conducted the same as other property accounts, and should have a certain percentage written off each year for depreciation. See Lesson 25.

The Operating Expenses of railroads are subdivided as follows: Stations, Shops, Trains, Engines, Cars, Coaches, Track, Buildings, Oil and Waste, Fuel, Incidentals, etc. These accounts are conducted the same as other expense accounts, and should be closed into Loss and Gain.

Loss and Gain Account is the receptacle of all Losses and Gains, and like all other secondary accounts, it is a branch of the Stock account, the others being tributary to this. Hence, in closing the Ledger, it is necessary first to close all the other secondary accounts into this, after which this must be closed into the Stock or Partner's accounts; if a corporation, it closes into Surplus if there is a gain. As the account is debited for all losses and credited for all gains, it follows that if the balance is on the debit side it shows the net loss in business, but if the balance is on the credit side it shows the net gain.

Arrangement of Accounts in the Ledger. When but one Ledger is used, the bookkeeper will find it a great convenience to have the customers' accounts in the fore part; next to these should be the creditors' accounts, reserving the back part of the Ledger for the miscellaneous accounts. This arrangement of accounts will be more fully appreciated if read in conjunction with the classification of accounts in condensed Trial Balances.

A Merchandise Discount Account should be kept by all who take and give cash discounts on the goods they buy or sell, that the Merchandise account may show the true gain on the goods handled. This account should be debited for all discounts allowed by the firm or company, and credited for all discounts taken by them The account should then be closed into the Merchandise account, (same as Merchandise Returned and Rebate account as shown in Lesson 23, p. 189,) the total debit being deducted from the aggregate of the Merchandise Credit, and the total credit deducted from the aggregate of the Merchandise Debit ; the reason for this is plain, yet it has never been presented in any other work on the subject of accounts. For an illustration we will say, a merchant sells a bill of goods amounting to $500 on 60 days time, or will allow a cash discount of 5 per cent 10 days. 3 per cent 30 days or net 60 days ; this is practically three different prices—$500 if paid in 60 days, $485 if paid in 30 days, and $475 if paid in 10 days. Of course the Merchandise account will be credited with $500, and if either of the discounts should be taken, the Merchandise account receives credit for $15 or $25 more than will be received for it, therefore this account should be kept separately, that the total discounts taken by the customers can be ascertained, which should be deducted from the total sales, while the total discounts taken by the firm is deducted from the total purchases, to show the *actual* purchases and sales.

To Inventory Discounted Goods. The price fixed should be the price before the discount was taken off.

To Find the Inventory Without Invoicing. First find the average per cent of gross gain for a period of four or five years, which we will assume to be 25 per cent ; then assume the total purchases to be $10,000, and the total sales $8 000, as per the Merchandise account. To find the cost of the goods which sold for $8000, allowing 25 per cent gross gain, divide the amount of sales ($8000) by 100 per cent, plus the rate per cent of gain, and the quotient will be the cost of the goods sold, or $6,400 ($8000÷125 per cent = $6400). The cost of the sales deducted from the cost gives the amount of merchandise on hand ($10,000—$6,400=$3,600, Inventory). In some lines of business it is a very tedious task to take an inventory, therefore many large concerns close their books by this method every alternate year.   In case of loss by fire it is necessary, sometimes, to determine the amount of merchandise from the books by this method, which is the most accurate that can be adopted.

To Find the Loss and Gain. There are two methods of determining the Loss or Gain in business. First, by classifying the Assets and Liabilities, and taking the differences of their aggregate; in partnership the partners' net investments are classed as liabilities Second, by classifying the Losses and Gains, and taking the difference of their aggregate.   The first method can be used under all circumstances when the assets and liabilities can be obtained, but no item of Loss or Gain can be included. The second method can be used only when the books have been properly kept by Double Entry.   Refer to Lesson 4, pages 27 to 31.   The various items of Loss and Gain are in reality represented in the Assets and Liabilities, for a gain is the result of a Resource received, without giving property therefore, hence it is on hand to increase the list, and thereby affecting the gains; while a loss is the result of a Resource disposed of, without receiving property value therefore, hence it is absent from the list, and thus the amount of resources is decreased and the loss increased correspondingly.

Cash Sales.   In a manufacturing business there are usually but few cash sales; sometimes cash is received with the order, which is entered in the Cash Book to the credit of the purchaser, and when the goods are shipped they are then charged.   Some business houses merely enter the cash and credit merchandise.   It is a good plan to credit the purchaser for the payment for future reference; of course this would add to the work of the bookkeeper, but if there are many of such customers, then a special book should be kept in alphabetical order, giving the prices, discounts, etc. In a retail business each salesman makes a cash ticket showing the amount of cash received, the amount of the sale, with the number of the cash boy and his own number.   This ticket, with the goods, is sent to the Wrapper or Parcel Clerk, who stamps the date and his own number thereon, and compares the amount of the sales with the price of the goods; the ticket and cash is then sent to the cashier, who assorts them to make up his cash for the day, each salesman's tickets being listed separately to ascertain the amount of each one's sales.   If each salesman has a special department, their sales tickets will show the amount of the department sales.

Credit or Charge Sales.   Jobbers and manufacturers usually have a Credit Man, whose duty is to ascertain the financial standing of those who ask credit ; this is done by personal investigation, and by special reports through the Mercantile Agencies.   If he is satisfied to trust the customer, he will O. K. the order and send it to the warehouse.   In case of a retail establishment where credit is asked, the salesman writes the name and address of the customer, with full particulars of the sale.   In case the customer be a new one, the salesman will ask for references; this report is then sent to the credit man; if he allows the credit the ticket and goods are then sent to the Parcel Clerk, who checks and stamps it if found correct. It is then sent to the delivery department, where it is again checked and stamped; it is then sent to the charge department, where it is billed and entered into the Sales Ledger.

By Express C. O. D. If many shipments are made by Express C. O. D., the accounts should be kept with the Express Companies instead of the customers. The Express Companies are responsible, and must return the goods or the money, and by keeping the accounts with them it does away with keeping numerous small accounts.

By Freight C. O. D. Goods shipped by Freight C. O. D. should not be sent direct to the customer, but should be sent to a Bank or Banker, to whom should be sent the Bill of Lading and a Sight Draft on the customer; at the same time send the customer an Invoice, informing him to which Bank you have shipped his goods. He will then go to the Bank and pay the draft. The Banker will then give him the Bill of Lading, and an order to get the goods from the Railroad Company. This is a very convenient way to ship goods, as freight rates are so much less than express; although the railroad company assumes no extra responsibility, the point of safety is, that the goods are shipped in the name of the Banker, and the customer cannot get them until he pays the Draft.

Entering Invoices. It will be found very convenient to keep all the invoices in a file alphabetically arranged, until the end of the month, then credit them up in one total amount to the respective creditors. Some bookkeepers credit the invoices as soon as they are received, but this makes too much work. After the invoices have been credited, they should be fastened together and filed away. They can be checked as readily in this way as if credited separately.

Entries in Special Columns. In making entries in a Journal or Cash Book having special columns, the name of the account should be omitted, because the amount being placed in the special column, signifies the account to which it belongs. When the line is thus left blank make a check ($\sqrt{}$) mark to prevent making another entry on same line.

Explanation of Entries. Every original entry should have a full, clear explanation; much trouble can be saved by so doing. The bookkeeper should remember that although he may fully understand his own entries, others may not, and may misconstrue them. Time and book space should not be spared when a full, clear and plain explanation is required.

" To and By."   These are prefixes having no essential value, and should be omitted in Journal and Cash Book Entries and in the Ledger. They serve a good purpose for the beginner, but the progressive accountant has no use for them.

Charge Bookkeepers.   In many large houses where they have a great many customers, they require a number of Charge Bookkeepers, whose duty it is to keep the customers' accounts only.   Such accounts are sub-divided alphabetically, and distributed in about equal proportions among the bookkeepers, each having his own Ledger.   If there were two charge bookkeepers, one would have a Ledger containing all accounts from A to L inclusive, the other would have a Ledger for all accounts from M to Z inclusive.

Credit Bookkeeper.   Business houses whose purchases are heavy and the bills numerous, employ a Credit Bookkeeper whose duty it is to keep the Credit or Purchase Ledger in which the accounts of the company's creditors appear.

Admitting a New Partner.   There are several ways of admitting new partners, but the following are the most common: 1, Some are admitted by making a specified cash investment, for a certain interest in the gains and losses. 2, By paying to the partners a specified sum for a share of their respective interests. 3, By paying to the partners a stated price for half, quarter or third interest of the gains and losses. 4, By paying to the firm a specified sum for a certain interest in the entire stock, and a certain share of the gains and losses.   In the first case, where a cash investment was made for a certain interest in the gains and losses, the investor would be credited for the amount of his investment, and cash would be debited.   Second, the old partners should be debited for their interest sold, and the new partner credited for his investment.   Third, when a bonus of cash is paid to the partners for a certain interest in the gains and losses, no entry should be made in the books for the cash received unless it should be invested in the firm.   The partners sold only an interest in their respective proportion of the gains and losses, therefore the only thing necessary to be done is to divide the amount received between the old partners, or invest it to their respective credits in proportion to the interest sold, and then to draw new articles of co-partnership specifying each partner's interest.   Fourth, when a specified amount is paid for an interest in a certain part of the whole capital of a firm, the amount paid should be divided between the old partners in proportion to the net capital of each; the old partners should then be debited for their respective proportion of the amount sold, and credit the purchaser for his interest bought.

Retiring Partner. When a partner retires from the firm it is necessary to take stock, and close the books to ascertain the amount due each. The entries to be made for a retiring partner are very simple, and should not be confused, as in Example 172, page 45.

Renewing Notes. When the maker of a Note is not able to pay it at maturity, the holder will allow him to renew it by giving a new Note for such a sum as will, when discounted, net the amount due on the old note, or a new Note is drawn for same amount as the old one, and the maker pays cash for the discount. When a Note is renewed no entry is necessary on the books, except on the Bills Receivable Book to mark it renewed and enter the new Note.

Depreciation. Each year a certain percentage should be written off all property, for depreciation in wear and tear. To arrive at accurate results this must be done. See Lesson 30.

Insolvency. An individual, firm or corporation is *insolvent* when the Liabilities exceed the Resources. The difference between the sum total of the Resources and the sum total of the Liabilities is the *net insolvency*, which difference will appear on the *debit* side of the Stock Account.

Accommodation Paper. An Accommodation Note is one for which the acceptor or maker has received no consideration, but has lent his name and credit to accommodate the drawer, payee or holder. Of course he is bound to all other parties precisely as if there were a good consideration, for otherwise it would not be an effectual loan of credit. But he is not bound to the party whom he thus accommodates; on the contrary, that party is bound to take up the paper, or to provide the accommodation acceptor, or maker, or endorser, with funds for doing it, or to indemnify him for taking it up. And if, before the bill or note is due, the party accommodated provides the party lending his credit with the necessary funds, he cannot recall them; and if he becomes bankrupt, they remain the property of the accommodation acceptor, or maker, who, if sued on the bill or note, can charge the party accommodated with the expense of defending the suit, even if the defense were unsuccessful, if he had any reasonable ground of defense, because the defense was for the benefit of the party accommodated, inasmuch as he must repay the accommodation party if he pays the bill or note. The maker of an accommodation bill or note should charge the party accommodated and credit his Bills Payable account, because he is liable to pay it if it falls in the hands of a third person.

Foreign and Inland Bills of Exchange. Bills of Exchange may be Foreign Bills, or Inland Bills. Foreign Bills are those which are drawn or payable in a foreign country; and for this purpose each of our States is *foreign* to the others.   Inland Bills are drawn and payable at home.   Every bill is, on its face, an inland bill, unless it purports to be a foreign bill.   If foreign on its face, evidence is admissible to show that it was drawn at home.   If a bill be drawn and accepted here, but afterwards actually signed by the drawer abroad, it is a foreign bill.   If a foreign bill be not accepted, or be not paid at maturity, it should at once be protested by a notary public.   Inland bills are generally, and promissory notes frequently, protested ; but this is not generally required by the law.   The holder of a foreign bill, after protest for non-payment, or for non-acceptance, may sue the drawer and indorser, and recover the face of the bill, and in addition thereto his damages, which damages, on protest, are generally adjusted in this country by various statutes, which give greater damages as the distance is greater, and an established usage would supply the place of statutes if they were wanting.

Indorsement.   An Indorsement is anything written on the back of a Note or Bill which pertains to the payment thereof.   When endorsing Checks, Bills or Notes, write your name on the back in the same way as it is written on the face.   If your name is not spelled correctly you should also misspell it in your indorsement, then write it correctly.

There are six forms of Indorsement: 1, Indorsement in Blank; 2, Indorsement in Full; 3, Qualified Indorsement; 4, Conditional Indorsement; 5, Restrictive Indorsement; 6, Indorsment with Protest Waived.

1.   *An Indorsement in Blank* is one in which the indorser writes his name only, without any remarks, as John Brown.

2.   *An Indorsement in full* is one in which the indorser limits the payment of the Note or Check to some particular person by writing across the back on the left end of the instrument, *Pay to the order of John Doe* and then signing his name.

If a Note or Check should be lost or stolen which is indorsed in blank, the finder or thief could collect it, but if it be indorsed in full it requires the name of the payee, therefore it is much safer.

3.   *A Qualified Indorsement* is one that releases the indorser from all responsibility, as *pay to the order of John Doe, without recourse to me, Jno. Williams* ; or *without Recourse, Jno. Williams* ; or *pay to the order of John Doe, Jno Williams, Agent.*

4.   *A Conditional Indorsement* is one that names some special condition that must be complied with before the payment can be made

to the holder.   Thus, *pay to John Doe when he shall have completed the boat he is now building for me, Jno. Brown*

5.   *A Restrictive Indorsement*, is one which limits the payment to some particular person and stops the further transfer of the Note, Bill or Check, as *pay to John Doe only, Jno. Brown.*

6.   *An Indorsement with Protest Waived* is one in which the indorser waives Protest, thus remaining responsible to the holder of the Note, without receiving notice of Protest, if the maker fails to pay it, thus: *Protest Waived, John Brown.*

Pay Roll Help.   In large mining and manufacturing companies where a great many men are employed, the Pay Roll Book is a very interesting one, because, if it is properly arranged it can be used as a book of original entry.   In addition to having the pay roll contain special columns, the accountant will find a rate and wage table of great value, for instance, in case of a mining company where different rates are paid for mining coal, a rate sheet should be made for each rate, covering the largest number of wagons mined by any one man.   In making up the Pay Roll the use of these rate sheets will not only save time, but mistakes are less apt to be made, when so many calculations are necessary.   Any firstclass stationer can furnish a wage table for day labor.

Payments on Discounted Notes.   When payments are received on Notes which have been discounted and still in the bank, the money should be taken to the bank, and the amount endorsed thereon.   No entry is necessary on the books, except to make a memorandum of such payments in the Bills Receivable Book.

Checking Payments.   In large houses where goods are sold on different terms, payments on account are usually intended to cover certain bills, when the remittance is received it is advisable to turn to the account in the Ledger and check the items covered in such settlement: one advantage of this is that the unchecked items at any time will show the balance due on an account.   In checking payments, the amounts charged should be marked by letters, as *a. b. c.* etc; the same letter should be used for the credits.   When all the letters of the alphabet have been used to check items in an account, begin at *a* again Numbers should not be used, they are misleading.

Footings Carried Forward.   When forwarding accounts to new pages in same Ledger, or to a new Ledger, during the year, the total debit and credit footings should be carried forward, instead of the balances between the debit and credit sides.   This is especially necessary with merchandise and similar property accounts in order that the total cost and sales may be shown by the account.

To Open a New Ledger. When the books are closed at the end of the business year, and new ones are to be opened. then only the balances and inventories are to be transferred, except the Bills Receivable and Bills Payable accounts which should be continued.

To Check filled Pages. When a Ledger page is filled and closed up or balanced, so that no more entries can be made on it, make a check mark at the top immediately over the centre of the name to indicate that it is *dead*. To check all dead pages in this way will save a great deal of time, when taking a Trial Balance as it can be passed quickly without examination.

To Establish a Factory. It is often desired to establish a Factory or Mill in connection with the regular business and have the accounts kept in the general books.

When this is done, open an account with the Factory or Mill and debit it for the cost of construction and equipment, and for all goods delivered, money paid and obligations assumed on account of it, and credit it for all goods and money received from it.

The Duty of a Bookkeeper on taking Charge of a Set of Books. The first duty of a Bookkeeper in taking a set of books from another bookkeeper to keep is to take a Trial Balance to ascertain whether or not the books balance. If they do not, the proprietors should be informed of the condition, and that they must be made to balance before proceeding. The firm should direct that the error be sought, or force a balance by entering the "out of balance" amount in Loss or Gain, or to make a statement of the Assets and Liabilities and open a new set of books. 2. Study carefully the method by which the books have been kept. 3. Examine the index to the Ledger and find out what other than personal accounts have been kept, so that you may know into what accounts expense has been divided. 4. See what auxiliary books are used. 5. See whether Ledger accounts are kept with the banks in which deposits are made. 6. See that the cash on hand agrees with the balance shown by the books. 7. Have the bank book written up, and should there be any discrepancy, see whether the unpaid checks would make up the difference: if they do not, the error must be found by comparing the various deposits, and checks issued. 8. See that the Bills Receivable on hand agree with the Bill Book and the Ledger Account of Bills Receivable. 9. Give notice to payers of the near maturity of Bills Receivable. 10. Notice whether any Bills Payable are due or will mature in a few days, and report to the firm.

11. See that all collaterals are on hand as shown by the books. **12.** If the method of keeping the books, as kept by the preceding book-keeper is such as requires unnecessary work and unscientific, formulate your own plans and report to the firm of your desires in a courteous way, bearing in mind that business men are often opposed to changing the methods which they have long been accustomed to, unless the advantages are made very clear to them. 13. If the books have been kept by Single Entry, prepare a statement of Assets and Liabilities, then change the books to Double Entry.

The Duty of a Bookkeeper leaving Charge of a Set of Books. For a bookkeeper to preserve his reputation for competency, honesty, honorable dealing and duty to the firm, he should on leaving a set of books, write them up to date and submit a Trial Balance. Have the Bank book balanced and show that the cash on hand agrees with the balance as shown by the books, and show that the Bills Receivable, Bonds, etc. on hand agree with their accounts, etc.

Comparative Statements. Many bookkeepers could greatly increase their salaries if they would study their employer's interests, and render in service double the value for which they receive compensation. One of the best ways a bookkeeper can increase the value of his services to his employer is to render a daily, monthly and yearly comparative statement of the business. The following is a good form for

Statement of Daily Sales :

JANUARY.

Department	1						2					
	1892		1893		1894		1892		1893		1894	
Dry Goods	325	00	476	50	591	00						
Groceries	400	00	395	00	450	00						
Hardware	250	00	320	00	375	00						
Total Sales for the day	975	00	1191	50	1416	00						

The following monthly, quarterly and yearly, Comparative Statement will be appreciated by all business men, as it can be made with as many columns as desired and, to run for 5 or 10 years. The records to be entered therein can easily be obtained at the end of the month, when it should be written up and submitted to the General Manager.

MONTHLY, QUARTERLY AND YEARLY COMPARATIVE STATEMENT.

M'th	Yr	Total Purchas's	Total Sales.	Credit Sales.	Cash Sales.	Average Daily Sales.	Cash Received	Cash Paid.	Expense	Bills Receiv'b'l on Hand	Bills Payable.	Accounts Receiv'b'l	Accounts Payable
Jan.	'94												
Feb.	"												
Mar.	"												
1st Qu	"												
Apr.	"												
May	"												
June	"												
2d Qu	"												
July	"												
Aug.	"												
Sep.	"												
3d Qu	"												
Oct.	"												
Nov.	"												
Dec.	"												
Year	"												

Each quarter is footed separately, and to find the total amounts for the year, add together the quarterly totals, or omit the quarterly totals and foot the entire column. This statement can be ruled to contain department sales, etc.

The Clearing House System.

This is one of the modern shorthand processes in banking which few students of finance outside of banking circles seem clearly to understand. There is nothing intricate or mystifying in this quick method of making bank settlements. The circle of banks associated in any settling arrangement of this class simply agrees to make a conjunction through representatives, messengers and settling clerks, and at the place of meeting effect those exchanges which in ante-clearing House days were made by the slow and wearisome methods of the old fashioned familiar type. This old method demanded that every bank having claims upon the other banks should send out messengers to collect the same over the counters, and that all banks having payments to make to other banks should by their representatives make special trips to the creditor banks to cancel the obligations. There was much weary traveling for the messengers, a great amount of paying and receiving by the Tellers, and much incidental work from exposure of funds, all of which has, to a very great extent, been done away with by the institution of Clearing Houses.

The following is the form of settling clerk's statement; for convenience all banks belonging to the Clearing House are numbered. The figures to the extreme left are their numbers and against the numbers are their names. The arrangement of the order of their numbers and names is in accordance with the age of the institution.

Settling Clerk's Statement.

No.	BANKS.	1st Debit.	Additions.	Total Debit	Bank's Cr.	No.
1	U. S. National	5471 20	400 00	5871 20	3210 20	1
2	Am. Ex. National	374 00	6124 00	6498 00	7142 00	2
3	First "	10791 50	945 00	11736 50	8050 00	3
4	Garfield "	6541 00	1128 00	7669 00	9172 00	4
5	Traders "	9000 00	294 00	9294 00	7245 00	5
	Footings	32177 70	8891 00	41068 70	34819 20	
				Balance	6249 50	Gain
					41068 70	

The "First Debit" column of figures represents the amounts of cash, checks, etc., which the bank holds, and has made up before the early morning receipts, against the banks against which the sums are set. "Additions" are the later receipts of demands against these same banks; "Total Debit" the sum of "First Debit" and "Additions," these three columns are made up at the bank before starting for the Clearing House.

The fourth column of "Bank's Credit" records the sums which each of the other banks brought into the clearing *against* the U. S. National and its total is of course the aggregate of the demand of each of its clearing neighbors. The difference between the foot of these two columns is the gain or loss which has been the outcome of the morning's settlement. In this case I have given a small sheet where the morning's clearing gain is $6,249.50: that is, all the banks of the Clearing House brought in and delivered to the U. S. National, Checks against itself amounting to $6,249.50 less than the Checks on the other banks which the U. S. National took to clearing and delivered to them, and the U. S. National is, therefore, entitle to a cash payment from the Clearing House of that amount.

As the Clearing House session begins promptly at 10 o'clock it is necessary for a settling clerk to be at the bank some time before that hour in order to properly prepare his statement, although it is mainly made up at the bank. The preparation of this sheet is conducted differently in banks, but an ordinary method is to make the first debit entries from the record on the Teller's book where the Checks have been listed against each bank and footed as a part of the previous day's work. These checks have also been assorted and perhaps listed on the "Exchange Slip." Then comes the Checks received in the morning's mail or by early deposit, and of these a supplementary entry is made against each bank and on the slips, and the amount of the additions in each case is carried into the second column and a total extended into the third column of the sheet, and a final footing made. The checks on each bank are then pinned up with the proper Exchange Slip; the footings of the slips compared with the entry on the sheet, and the packages put in numerical order for delivery at the Clearance-House.

EXCHANGE SLIP NO. 3.

First National

FROM

No. 1 U. S. Nat. Bank

July 23d, 1894.

		10	000	00
			791	50
		10	791	50
			945	00
		11	736	50

The next thing to do is to make out the check tickets which are to be delivered to the other banks with the packages.

Check Ticket.

```
+-------------------------------------------------+
|                   NO. 3.                        |
|            First National Bank                  |
|                    FROM                         |
|          No. 1 U. S. National Bank.             |
|                                                 |
|   11.736      Dollars,      50      Cents        |
+-------------------------------------------------+
```

This morning preparation for the clearing is one of the busiest periods of the day, both the Tellers and their Clerks and probably assistants from other departments put in the best work they are capable of; there is never any time to spare, and the bank whose clerks never have to run in order to reach the Clearing House in time to avoid a fine is a marvel of good management.   Each bank sends to clearing a settling clerk in charge of its sheet and to receive packages, and a messenger to carry and deliver its packages.

When the settling clerk enters the Clearing House and passes to his place he delivers at the Manager's desk a Credit Ticket showing the total amount he has brought in from which the Manager's clerk makes a credit entry to his account.

```
+---+-----------------------------------------------------+
| C |  NO. I.      NEW YORK CLEARING HOUSE.                |
| R |                                                      |
| E |                              July 23d, 1894.         |
| D |  CREDIT                                              |
| I |       UNITED STATES NATIONAL BANK     $41,068.70    |
| T |                                                      |
|   |                      BROWN, Settling Clerk.          |
+---+-----------------------------------------------------+
```

The Settling Clerks take their places in order on the inside of a long counter each with his own Messenger standing over against him on the outside of the counter.

The Manager strikes the bell at 10 o'clock and off starts the whole line of Messengers along the counter keeping their relative positions and order and delivering a package and check ticket or a blank to each Settling Clerk as they pass before him.

The work of the Settling Clerk is to list down in his fourth column the amount of each package as handed in by the Messengers filing before him.

In three or four minutes his fifty or so packages are all in and he can make a footing and strike a balance as is shown on the sheet above. The next thing to do is to make out the balance ticket showing the figures as they are on the sheet.

BALANCE TICKET	**NO. I.** **NEW YORK CLEARING HOUSE..**
	DR. U. S. National Bank, Amount Received, $34,819.20
	CR. U. S. National Bank, Amount Brought, 41,068.70
	Balance $................. , due Clearing House.
	Balance due the U. S. Nat'l Bank........................$6,249.50.
	BROWN, *Settling Clerk.*

This is to be handed to the clerk at the Manager's desk, but before doing so the Settling Clerk will assort the check tickets which have been put by the different Messengers into a receptacle on his desk, and by them check off the hurried entries which he made from the packages themselves. When satisfied that his work is right he sends up his balance ticket and from these tickets the Manager's Clerk completes his sheet and makes the final footings which prove all the work.

The bank's Settling Clerks have from 10 o'clock to 10.30 to make their settlement.

It generally takes from five to ten minutes for the Manager's Clerk to make his settlement, and if his sheet proves, the work of the morning is ended and the clerks may go home. If an error is shown to be in some of the sheets they must be gone over again, the clerk having the error must send up a corrected balance ticket, and is fined $2 for every fifteen minutes after 10.30 that it takes to find the error.

The banks which have lost at the clearing must pay the amount of their several losses to the Clearing House before 12.15 o'clock. In the large cities they must pay funds such as are proper to be held as reserve by the banks.

These funds are all received by the Clearing House Manager and his clerks, counted, and made up in proper form to be paid out at 1.30 o'clock to those banks which gained at that morning's clearing. Of course the losses and the gains will in their totals exactly balance each other, and the Clearing House after handling its millions through the day, closes at two o'clock without a penny in the till.

In paying and receiving these losses and gains considerable work and risk in the way of actual transfer of cash is saved by the use of Clearing House orders, which may be said to pass as cash between the settling banks, and which are received and debited or credited as such by the Clearing House Manager. Such a vast amount of exchange business and complicated clerical work is transacted in a very short time at the daily morning settlement of the Clearing House, that it is very important that the representatives of the banks, two from each who do the work in question should be careful, accurate and capable of performing considerable clerical labor. They must give their undivided attention to their business and should not indulge in idle talk or unbusiness-like behavior, as the slightest error on the part of one clerk may prolong indefinitely the entire settlement.

In view of these facts Clearance Houses have inserted in their by-laws very strict rules, imposing fines for tardiness, errors, etc.

The New York Clearing House since the day of its establishment thirty-four years ago, until the 1st of July this year cleared upwards of $1,150.000.000.000.00. Nothing but the science of astronomy, with its prodigious figures and incalculable distances, suggests the enormity of this amount; these figures represent to a considerable extent, the amount of exchanges effected by this country in that time. They also suggest to what an enormous extent the business of this country is done, not by gold or silver dollars, or by bank Notes, but by that informal, in one sense irresponsible currency which we call bank Checks, and this also indicates to what an enormous extent the business of the country rests upon honor and confidence, since a bank check is nothing more than an order to somebody to pay somebody else some money.

The operations of this institution in a single year are colossal enough; in 1892 they reached the enormous total of $36,279.905.235.39 and this sum of more than thirty-six billions of dollars represents liquidations that were effected in plain English, by swopping checks and then canceling them, so that by this operation it was necessary to pay in actual cash a little less than $2,000.000.000. The enormity of the daily business is suggested by the figures of one day's transactions, which reached the sum of $229,461,342.72, and of this magnificent sum all but about $4,000,000 represented a liquidation brought about by the exchange of bank checks. Upon one occasion there were cleared more than $60,000,000, and the balance that had to be paid into the Clearing House was only one cent. This, of course, is simply a later day refinement of the earlier processes of trade whereby the cobbler exchanged a pair of shoes for a bushel of meal. But the enormity as well as the extremity to which this refinement is carried is strikingly suggested by one operation which recently took place in the Clearing House when one of the New York banks had clearances amounting to nearly $1,250,000 and yet it had to pay only seventy-six cents in cash into the Clearing House.

The power of this unique and irresponsible institution, irresponsible in the sense that it is not governed by any statutory regulations, is suggested by two incidents which have occurred within recent years:

In the spring of 1884 there was a time of suspicion in the financial world. Rumors of ominous portent were afloat, it was said that one or two great banking houses were in difficulties, and the money market which is as sensitive to rumor as a lake to the gentle zephyr began to show signs of panic. At last the crash came. The Metropolitan Bank, one of the greatest financial institutions of New York, announced that it was unable to meet its obligations. Wall Street was wild with excitement. There is no more awful spectacle than that which is seen upon the streets near the New York Stock Exchange when the time of panic has come. Men seem to be no longer human beings, but maddened brutes, and such a spectacle was witnessed upon that day. Nobody knew who was safe. Everybody knew that when one bank like the Metropolitan fails others go down like the row of blocks which children in their play upset.

In an instant almost the Clearing House was notified. Messengers were sent hurrying to notify the different members of the Association to come at once to the hall where the members meet. There gathered within an hour a company of men whose action could extend this panic so that the whole country would become involved, or on the other hand they might be able to crush it out upon the spot. They represented hundreds of millions of dollars; they controlled the greater number of the banks in New York. Some of them were men of supreme ability. All of them had such expressions upon their countenances as indicated the consciousness of tremendous responsibility.

One of these men, Geo. S. Coe, a man who at the outbreak of the civil war had done those things which gave the government a loan of $50,000,000 in gold when it was in desperate extremity, arose and said that if the Metropolitan Bank could show any assets sufficient to meet ultimately its liabilities, he was in favor of taking them and letting the Clearing House become responsible for the obligation. They asked for these assets and when they were shown it was found that they were not sufficient to save the bank.

"But we can save other banks that are threatened, and thus stop this panic" said one of the members.

It so happened that some banks have securities, which in ordinary times were regarded as sound enough, but which in time of panic would be difficult to turn into money.   The Clearing House voted to say to all threatened banks that if they would turn over their securities to the Clearing House, then the Clearing House would issue its certificates for the obligations of those banks, and each bank in the Association would receive these certificates in place of cash for the settlement of balances.   That was all that was needed.   The Metropolitan Bank had to go under, but when Wall Street and the financial world in fact knew that the Association Banks of New York stood behind some of its weaker members, then it was known that the danger was over.   The panic was thus ended, and when confidence was restored it was easy for these weaker banks to market their securities, and in that way redeem the certificates which the Clearing House had issued.

The general community did not know at the time, although bankers knew it, that it was the action of the New York Clearing House which prevented a panic that might have been as disastrous as that of 1857 or 1873.

Nearly four years ago the financial world was stunned by a report that the great banking house of Baring Bros. had suspended payment. A crisis was imminent, also during the stringency of 1893 this mighty institution saw that the time had come to make use of its enormous power.   On both occasions the board met, took the securities of the tottering banks and issued Clearing House certificates to pay balances, thus this mighty engine with its colossal power was able to stay panic and prevent wreckage.

It has been felt by some financiers that this mighty power could be used to bring about colossal misfortune on which the bankers would reap their profits.   And that is true, but before it could be thus used the majority of the bankers composing the Association would have to change their natures and become cold-blooded villains.

Indexing and Folioing.   Before beginning to post, take your index and write the Ledger pages of all accounts to which you are about to post.   When all the accounts are thus folioed you can lay the index aside, and proceed without reference to it, which will save a great deal of time.   As the items are posted they should be checked.

When new accounts are to be opened in the Ledger, first turn to the index and write the name and the page number before writing in the Ledger.   By making this a regular practice it will prevent opening a duplicate account and save much trouble to find an account, if you should fail to index it.

Posting Guide.   The following cut represents a blotter to be used while posting to prevent posting to the wrong side of the account.

In posting from any book of original entry, make it a special point to post all the debits at one time and all the credits at another, instead of each debit and credit item alternately.   By posting one side of the book at a time, it is an easy matter to keep in mind to which side of the Ledger you are to post, thus saving many mistakes which are made otherwise.   There is no excuse for posting to the wrong side of an account if this method is used, together with the *Posting Blotter*, one side of which is marked DR., the other CR.   When posting to the *debit* side, lay the blotter with the corner covering the credit side.   When posting to the *credit* side turn the blotter over and cover the debit side.   If this blotter is once used it will never be abandoned.

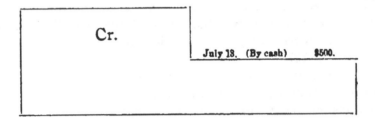

Dollars Posted as Cents; or Cents as Dollars.   If the difference in the Trial Balance be a sum consisting of dollars and cents which, when added together, make 99, omit the cents, add 1 to the dollars, and the sum will be found posted as dollars when it should have been posted as cents, or *vice versa*.   Thus: \$73.26.   73+26=99; omit the cents and add 1 to the dollars gives \$74.   \$74 will be found posted as 74 cents, or 74 cents as \$74.

Correcting Errors.   Never erase a wrong entry, or figures, all corrections should be made by ruling a light line through the error and writing the correct amount above.

Reverse Posting is a modern feature in the science of accounts for testing the accuracy of the postings.   The plan employed by many consists in putting a small colored ticket in the page to which an item has been posted.   A Reverse Posting Book is also used, which is ruled with debit and credit money columns.   With this book and the colored slips, the bookkeeper proceeds to post, and as he posts an item into the Ledger, he places therein one of these colored posting slips, debit or credit as the case may be.   These slips are entered where the posting was made, leaving the ends projecting so as to be easily seen, using red slips for *credits* and yellow for *debits*.

When each book has been posted, he takes the Reverse Posting Book and posts into it the items just posted into the Ledger. The postings to the Test Book are then footed, and compared with the footing of the Journal or other book just posted, and if the two footings agree, he concludes that the posting has been correctly performed. The amounts posted to the Test Book are taken from the Ledger as indicated by the posting slips. If the footings of the books of original entry correspond with the footings of the Reverse Posting Book, the Ledger is considered to be in balance, and a Trial Balance unnecessary until the end of the fiscal year, when the books are closed. In using this method each book of original entry must be proven separately. My objections to this plan are the recopying of amounts, the liability to omit a slip after a post has been made, and the possibility of the slips sliding down between the pages out of sight, or getting lost in other ways. I have experienced all of these difficulties, and think that a better method is to dispense with the slips, and as soon as an item of debit or credit is posted, it is also entered in the Reverse Posting Book, the footing of which should agree with the footings of the books of original entry.

Proof Posting and Ledger Proof System. This system of proof posting is the most accurate that has ever been devised. Although it is not infallible, it will detect errors in footing, balances, transpositions, amounts carried forward, omissions, etc. An error in posting can be located at once to the page and account without reference to the Ledger. It can be adopted at any time, in any set of books without changing the system of bookkeeping, without additional books or labor.

The secret of the system is in reducing the amount posted to a single number less than (11) eleven. This is done by casting out the elevens, or by dividing the amount by eleven, and taking the remainder as the reduced or check number. A simpler way to produce the check number is to add the figures in the odd places and subtract from this sum the sum of the figures in the even places, always beginning at the right. If the remainder should exceed ten it must again be reduced, as no check number can be greater than 10. For instance, to reduce $15.19, we add the figures in the odd or first, third, fifth and seventh places, beginning at the right; $9+5=14$, from which we subtract the sum of the figures in the even or second, fourth and sixth places. $1+1=2$; $14—2=12$. This being greater than 10 must again be reduced by subtracting the sum of figures in the even places from

the sum of the figures in the odd places, or 2—1=1, the check number. If you will divide 1,519 by 11 you will find the remainder to be
1, which is the number reduced or the check number. If the sum of
the figures in the odd places be less than the sum in the even places,
then it will be impossible to subtract. But when such is the case, you
must add to the sum of the figures in the odd places, 11 or any multi-
ple of 11 or 22, 33, 44, etc. It matters not how much is added, it will
produce the right check number. To reduce $19,191.91, we must add
33 to the figures in the odd places, thus, 33+1+1+1+1=37, from
which we subtract 9+9+9=27. 37—27=10, the check number. It
matters not how large or how small the number, it can be reduced to
a single number less than eleven. If the number should be one (1), of
course the check number would be 1, because it is the only figure,
and being in the odd place there is nothing to take from it. If the
amount should be 100, it is readily seen that the check number would
also be 1. If the amount should be 1,000, we see that there are no
figures in the odd places, but must add 11 and subtract 1, leaving 10,
the check number. With but a little practice you can reduce any number in an instant.

After practicing the reduction of various numbers, you will find
it can be adopted to prove addition, subtraction, etc. To prove addition, find the check number for each amount, and write it at a convenient place that they can be footed. Then reduce the footing of the
column to its check number, and see if it agrees with the check number taken from the footing of the check numbers. If they do not agree,
the footing is wrong, or you have produced a wrong check number.

```
    56,721—        5
     1,215—        5
   192,374—        6
    12,176—       10
  _____    _____
   262,486=4     26=4
```

To prove subtraction the principle is the same. Suppose $5,728.94
to be the amount of the debit side of an account, and $2,929.38 to be
the amount of the credit side, you will subtract the amounts as usual;
but in addition to that you write the check numbers for both amounts
and subtract them as follows:

```
    $5,728.94—        3
     2,929.38—        8
  _____      _____
    $2,799.56=6       6
```

In this case we find the check number of the balance to be 6; and in subtracting the check numbers we see that 8 cannot be taken from 3, therefore we add 11, which equals 14—8 gives 6, the proof number.

Having used the check numbers in proving addition and subtraction, we will now apply it to the prevention and detection of errors in posting.

Suppose the following to be a column in the Journal, and to prove the posting, we will first folio all the accounts. This is done that further reference to the Index is done away with.

Amount.	L. F.	Ck.	Debits.
134.59	341	6	D. E. Hammond.
880 00	571	0	J. C. Brown.
90.00	239	2	Boyd Brothers & Company.
162.71	642	2	The Howard Company.
455.00	390	4	J. D. Smith & Company.
869.99	421	0	Miller, Horne & Company.
238.25	349	10	Baker, Pratt & Company.
100.00	578	1	Williams & Joy.
1,000.00	296	10	D. R. Edwards.
150.00	151	7	C. P. Parker.
9=$4,080.54		9	

Assuming the following to be the Ledger:

LEDGER.

DR.		CR.	DR.		CR.
341	D. E. Hammond.		421	Miller, Horne & Co.	
6	$134.59		0	$869.99	
571	J. C. Brown.		349	Baker, Pratt & Co.	
0	880.00		10	238.25	
239	Boyd Bros. & Co.		578	Williams & Joy.	
2	90.00		1	100.00	
642	The Howard Co.		296	D. P. Edwards.	
2	162.71		10	1,000.00	
390	J. D. Smith & Co.		151	C. P. Parker.	
4	455.00		7	150.00	

We will turn to page 341 therein and charge D. E. Hammond $134.59; and, as soon as the amount is posted, find the check number and write it at any convenient place on the same line. Then turn to the Journal or other book from which you are posting, and enter the check number in such a way that they can be easily footed. When you have new books made, have a special column for the check numbers. It must be remembered that the check number must ALWAYS be produced from the amount as it is posted, and not as it stands in the book of original entry. The check numbers should be so written in the Ledger that they can be easily footed to prove the footings.

As we post $134.59 we find the check number to be 6, and to J. C. Brown's account, on page 571, we post $880.00 and produce the check number 0. Whenever the check number is 0, it must be entered the same as though it were a number. If you should neglect to write the check number when it is 0, the amount to be posted might be omitted.

After posting all the items from the Journal, we then prove the work by reducing the sum of the column and the sum of the check numbers, which we find to be 9. When the check numbers are entered in the Journal, Cash Book, etc., we do not stop to see if the amounts there produce the same check numbers as they are produced from the Ledger; but if we find that the columns do not produce the same check, we start at the top of the column and prove the check number for each amount as it should be posted. If you find a wrong check number, you can refer to the account in the Ledger and find an error in posting, or that you have produced the wrong check number. Take the first amount and suppose it should have been posted to Hammond's account, page 341, as $143.59 instead of $134.59. Then we would have the check number 4. This of course would not agree in the proof, but upon examination we would find at once that we have a check number 4 which should have been 6. By this means an error can be located to the page and account without referring to the Ledger.

When carrying totals forward the check numbers must also be carried up.

The check number must be used for every item that is posted, and in taking a Trial Balance, if the debit and credit totals are taken, then you must prove the footings of the accounts by the check numbers and carry them to the Trial Balance Book. This is done that each page of the Trial Balance Book can be proven separately. If only the debit and credit balances are taken in the Trial Balance, the balances must be proven as illustrated, by subtraction, always carrying the check number for the balances to the Trial Balance Book.

If the system is used at all times, it will prove its great value; but, if items are posted, and footings are made without it, you need not expect good results.

Ruling up Accounts.   When an account is balanced, it should be ruled up and closed.   If one side of the account should contain more items than the other, the closing lines for both sides of the account should be made on the same line; while the blank lines intervening should be ruled out by drawing a distinct line from the closing lines to the line containing the last item.   This will prevent posting an item to an account which has been closed.

How to Take a Trial Balance.   Before taking a Trial Balance go through the Ledgers and carefully foot each account with a sharp-pointed pencil, and write the footings directly under the last item, placing units under units, tens under tens, etc.

All acccounts that are found to balance should be ruled up as directed.

Some accountants take a Trial Balance by using the total debit and credit footings, while others use only the debit and credit balances. By using only the debit and credit footings, a great amount of labor will be saved, which would be required to figure the differences.   The advantages in using the debit and credit balances, are that the Trial Balance will be easier to foot, and that it will also show the balance of each account, which is required by many business men.   In point of saving labor, the first method is favored.   When the amounts have been transferred to the Trial Balance, and before the footings are made, the whole work should be checked as some errors might have been made which would not only necessitate checking, but would cause considerable trouble in changing footings.

Errors in Trial Balances.   Seeking errors in Trial Balances is the most disagreeable part of a bookkeeper's work.   He may perform his work with the greatest care, yet errors will be made that are very perplexing and difficult to find.   There are numerous methods for locating errors in Trial Balances and to prove each side of the Ledger separately, all of which render valuable assistance; but there are times when they will not work, the only salvation being to check the books. The following is one of the best methods for proving the Ledger that that can be adopted.   Assuming this to be the

TRIAL BALANCE

Stock Account......................	....	...	5,000	00
Cash.	.... $9,832	00	7,234	21
Merchandise	 15,671	00	13,327	00
Bills Pay.	....		250	00
Banks and Co	 1,725	50	....	...
Expense..	50	70	....	...
J. D. Brown............................	 1,534	94	230	50
H. A. Fuller............................	672	41	1,519	24
S. W. Burrows........................	150	00	75	00
A. E. Schmidt........................	....	80	733	10
E. F. Mielly............................	300	00	1,575	50
Does not balance by $7.20; Schmidt's debit of 80 cts. should be $80.00; making a difference of	$29,937	35	..........$29,944	55
	.79	20		
Fuller's credit should be $1,591.24 instead of $1,-519.24; the difference is.........	....	...	72	00
	$30,016	55	$30,016	55

In which two errors have purposely been made; one on the debit and one on the credit side. These are made to fully illustrate the method of detecting existing errors, and to ascertain the exact amount each side is wrong.

The Ledger is increased by posting to it from the auxiliary books, and is diminished by ruling up accounts to close or to bring down balances.

In footing the above Trial Balance we find that it is out $7.20. It frequently happens that an error like this would occur by omitting to post an item of this amount, or that one-half the amount might have been posted to the wrong side, and in many cases the error can be found very quickly by seeking these amounts.

Without stopping to find this amount, the proof will be applied to ascertain on which side of the Ledger the errors exist, and determine how much each side must foot.

Amount of the previous Trial Balance.........$	0,000.00	$ 0.000.00
Amounts posted from the Journal...............	3,950.34	3,950.34
"　　　"　　　" Sales Book and to Cr. of Mdse................	10,000.00	10,000.00
"　　　"　　　" Cash Book to accounts,	9,832.00	7,234.21
"　　　"　　　to Cash account................	7,234.21	9,832.00
Trial Balance should foot (unless some accounts are closed................................$	31,016.55	$31,016.55
Deduct the amount of accounts which have been closed	1,000.00	1,000.00
Trial Balance must foot...................$	30,016.55	$30,016.55

In order to prove the Ledger by this system, it will be seen that a record of all the accounts which have been closed or ruled up must be kept.

It has been shown that the Trial Balance must foot $30,016.55, but we find the debit side to be $29,937.35, and the credit side $29,944.55. Therefore, we find the debit side is

$30,016.55	$30,016.55
29,937.35	29,944.55
$79.20 short.　And the credit side	$72.00 short.

We now know what amount is to be added to each side of the Trial Balance.

Take the error of $79.20, which is divisable by 9. We conclude that it is an error of transposition or transplacement.

Deduct from imaginary ciphers..................	$00.00
The cents of the error.............................	79.20
Leaves	.80

Which being changed to dollars, we know that $80 has been taken as 80 cents. By referring to the Trial Balance we find that the only 80 in the debit column occurs in Schmidt's account; and turning to the Ledger we find that his debit is $80. After making this correction the total footing will agree with the proof.

The credit side is found to be $72.00 less than the proof. Applying the same rules, we find that it is an error of transposition, as it is divisable by 9. 72 divided by 9＝8. Now follow down the credit column and find which figure in the dollar column is 8 more than the figure (on the same line) in the tens of dollars column, and we find that H. A. Fuller has a credit of $1,519.24; the figure 9 in the dollar column being 8 more than the figure 1 in the tens of dollars column, and by referring to his account in the Ledger, we find his credit to be $1,591.24. When this correction is made, both sides of the Trial Balance will be equal and agree with the proof. Should the $72.00 be in excess of the proof, you would find which figure in the dollar column is 8 less than the figure (on same line) in the tens of dollars column. If this system is applied, it will be found in most cases to produce the exact amount of the Trial Balance, and to find the error at once. .

Combination Check Journal. The cuts illustrating this method are photo-engraved from an original page of my Combination Check Journal. For lack of space the page has been divided; the first represents the Debit, and the second the Credit side. The page is ruled short to show the foot lines.

(See pages 234 and 235.)

A careful study of the arrangement of this book will prove its great value; first, the two cuts represent an original page, the division between the Debit and Credit sides being the explanation column in the center. The Debit and Credit Ledger titles are together, next to these are the Ledger folio columns, and nearest to these are the columns mostly used for posting. This brings the Ledger Titles, folios, and amounts all together, and is a great convenience in posting.

The columns for Debtors' accounts Debited and Credited are used for all amounts charged or credited to the customers. It is not meant by this that the sales are to be Journalized, but the column for Debtors' accounts Debited is to be used with the Credit Sales column.

The amount of the Credit Sales for each day is taken from the Sales Book and entered in these columns for record only. The difference between the Debtors' columns will show the amount due the firm.

The Creditors' accounts Cr. and Dr. are used the same, except all the Creditors' paid are charged in the Creditors' Debit column, and all purchases, etc., entered in the Creditors' credit column; the difference between these columns shows the amount of the firm's indebtedness.

All the columns are to be posted in total at the end of the month, except Expense, Customers' Debit and the Credit Sales column, unless a charge affecting the Debtors should occur other than Credit Sales. It will be seen that there is but one column for Expense: this is used for all the accounts as classified in the record above. When an entry is made belonging to any of these accounts it is to be numbered, this number to correspond with that in the record, and is to be written in the C. R. column at the extreme left.   The only extra work required in keeping the Expense accounts in this way is, that all the items in the column on each page must be separated, and the total of each number entered in its proper place in the Classified Record.   The amounts for these accounts on each page should be entered in the Record above the base line in red ink, as shown in No. 3, Rent $150. This is done so the *total* up to date, including the amounts on the last page, can be written on the base line in black; these totals must agree with the total footing of the Expense column.   At the end of the month the totals as shown in the Classified Record are posted to the Ledger.

All the other columns which do not contain items to personal accounts are posted in totals at the end of the month.   The total amount of the Credit Sales column must agree with the total footing of the Sales Book.

Your attention is also called to the numbers at the head of the columns: these numbers correspond with those in the " Condensed Statement," and are used as a guide in carrying the totals at the end of the month, to make the statement.

The few items given will suffice to illustrate the value of the classified Record, etc.   We will assume this to be the last page for the month, and carry the totals of each column to the Record.   First, we find the sales for the day to be $5500; these are entered in their proper columns, with only a check mark on the line, as they are not to be posted, and as the columns signify to what they belong.   A check mark is used to prevent another entry on same line.   Next is a credit to Harris & Co., for mdse. bought, at 60 days; as Harris & Co. are creditors, the amount is entered in the Creditors' Credit column, from which it is posted.   The Third entry is for Rent paid by Check No. 7491; as Rent is No. 3 in the Record, the number is written in the C. R. column.   The Fourth entry is Cash Received from D. W. Boyd on account; this is entered to his credit in the Debitors' Credit column. In the last entry Morrow & Co. have been paid $2000 on account; this of course is charged to them in the Creditors' Debit column.

The first line at the bottom is for the footings for the page, the next for the amounts brought forward, and the last for the total to be carried forward.   This is necessary, in order to get the footings for each as required in the Record.   If you wish to keep the amounts of the special columns, it will be necessary to enter them the same as those in the Expense column by using red ink, except in the Condensed Statement, where the totals to date only are used.

Combination Check Journal

Upper form

DR.	L.F.	No.	EXPENSES.	L.F.	CR.
		1	Labor,		
		2	Salaries,		
		3	Rent, Lighting, etc.		
		4	Taxes,		
		5	Insurance,		
		6	Fuel,		
		7	Furniture & Fixtures,		
		8	Cartage & Drayage,		
			Carried Forward,		

DR.	L.F.	No.	EXPENSES.	L.F.	CR.
		9	Frt & Ex. Charges		
		10	Stationery,		
		11	Shipping Cases, etc.		
		12	Machinery,		
		13	Litigation,		
		14	Postage,		
		15	Sundry Expense,		
		16	Commission,		
			Carried Forward,		

DR.	L.F.	No.	EXPENSES.	L.F.	CR.
		17	Samples, &c.		
		18	Traveling Exp.		
		19	Advertising,		
		20			
		21			
		22			
		23			
		24			
			Total Expenses,		

Lower form

CLEVELAND, O. ....August 30 — 94.....

Debits

C R	EXPENSE Dr.	Disc't and Interest Given.	MDSE. RETURNED TO US.	MDSE. BOUGHT.	CASH RECEIVED.	Debtors Accounts Debited.	Creditors Accounts Debited.	SUNDRIED. Dr.	CK L.F.	Debits	EXPLANATIONS

Combination Check Journal.

CONDENSED STATEMENT.

DR.	L.F.	No.		No.	L.F.	CR.
51¢		25	Discount & Int.	34		
10 00		26	Mdse. Returned,	37		
1044 50		27	Cash,	33		21 50 00
1802 60		28	Mdse.,	35		55 00 00
			Cash Sales,	36		

No.		DR.	CR.
29	Mdse. Inventory, Dr.	55 00 00	1300 00
31	Cash,	1500 00	8 341 50
	Furniture, Fixt. & Machy.	4000 00	4000 00
	" " Balance		1000 00
32	Stationery,	7 53 00 0	400 00
	Accounts & Bills Rec. Dr.	2000 00	2 944 50
30	" " Balance	553 00 0	553 00 0
	Total,		2 391 50
	Accounts & Bills Payable		
	Net Cash		

Credits

	L.F.	CK	Debtors Accounts Credited.	SUNDRIES. Cr.	Creditors Accounts Cr.	CASH PAID.	Disc't and Interest Taken.	Expense. Cr.	CREDIT SALES.	CASH SALES.	Mdse. RETURNED BY US.
									55 00 00		
Latest Ind Co.	350 6		150 00 0		7 53 00 0	1500					
CK 4749											
L. H. Boyd	9714					2000 00			55 00 00		
CK 7630			150 00 0	2219225	753 00 0	2150 00			55 00 00		
			1 50 00 0	2219225	753 00 0	4150 00					

The total amount of the Expense column is $1270: this will be found to agree with the various expense items as entered in the Record. The Discount column No. 25 amounts to $5.14; this is carried to the Record in the second illustration to No. 25. The column for Mdse. Returned to us amounts to $10.00, and is carried to No. 26. Mdse. Bought is No. 28, and amounts to $18021.61. The totals of all the other columns are carried to the Record according to numbers, which brings the total debits and credits of each on the same line.

To some the use of this system may seem cumbersome, and require a great deal of extra labor, but such is not the case. It is true that it requires some extra work and great care, but it saves so much in other ways that everything is in favor of it, while upon each page the exact condition of the business is shown.

If the accounts in the Ledger are classified, or if there are three Ledgers used, one for the customers or Sales Ledger, one for the creditors or Purchase Ledger, and one for the miscellaneous accounts, the use of this book will prove the accuracy of each separately, by a

Classification of Accounts in Condensed Trial Balance.

The accounts of the Ledgers are naturally divided into four classes, viz., 1, Stock, Proprietors' or Partners' Accounts; 2, General Miscellaneous Accounts; 3, Debtors' Accounts; 4, Creditors' Accounts.

Stock, proprietors' or partners' accounts and general accounts. as mdse., bills payable, bills receivable, cash, expense, etc., being limited in number, the difficulty of detecting errors in trial balances arises from the great number of individual accounts. This difficulty is greatly reduced by dividing the trial balance into the above four classes, containing in totals all entries which have been posted to the Ledger. These condensed accounts are opened with the totals of the corresponding balances at the end of the preceding month, or at the beginning of the year, and the entries are made in bulk after posting at the end of each month, directly from the footings of the Combination Check Journal, Sales Book, etc. They are debited for the totals of the debit entries, and credited for the totals of the credit entries, which have been posted from the books of original entry into the four classes of accounts.

The totals of mdse. sold or returned, cash paid out, bills payable issued, etc., to individual accounts, must appear on the debit side, while the totals of mdse. bought or returned, cash received, bills receivable received, etc., from individual accounts, are entered on the credit side of the condensed debtors' or creditors' account, and therefore on the opposite side of the condensed general account.

The balances with which to open these new accounts are readily obtained by taking the trial balance for the previous month and dividing it as follows:

TRIAL BALANCE.

Gen'l Dr. Balances,		Stock or Partners' Balances,	$75,000
	$50,000	Gen'l Cr. Balances,	30,000
Debtor's Balances,	65,000	Creditors' Balances,	10,000
	$115,000		**$115,000**

Whenever a creditors' account should result in a debit balance, or a debtor's account give a credit balance, these balances must be deducted from the total of the creditors' or debtors' balances to arrive at the net balances of all creditors' or debtors' accounts. The following is the form of the **Condensed Trial Balance**:

STOCK OR PARTNERS' ACCOUNT.

Withdrawals, etc.	Balance, etc.

GENERAL ACCOUNT.

Dr. Balance,	Cr. Balance,
Mdse. Bought,	Mdse. Sold,
Cash Rec'd,	Cash Paid,
Bills Rec. Rec'd,	Bills Pay. Issued,
Mdse. Ret'd to us, etc.	Mdse. Ret'd by us, etc.

CREDITORS' ACCOUNT.

Mdse. Ret'd to	Balance,
Bills Pay. Issued,	Mdse. Bought,
Cash Paid, etc.	Etc.

DEBTORS' ACCOUNT.

Balance,	Cash Rec'd,
Mdse. Sold,	Bills Rec. Rec'd,
Etc.	Mdse. Ret'd from, etc.

If there should be any errors in the Trial Balance, proceed at once to prove each Ledger separately, by using the above condensed form. It is readily seen that the balances of the Debit Ledger must agree with the difference between the Debtors' debit and credit columns in the Check Journal, with the balances brought forward from the previous month; the balances of the Credit Ledger must agree with the Creditors' debit and credit columns in the Check Journal, with the balances brought forward from the previous month; while the Miscellaneous Ledger must agree with the footings in the Classified Record, Special and Sundry Columns, and such items as might have been posted to this Ledger. Therefore, if an error should appear in the Trial Balance, each book can be proven separately. It proves the correctness of the entries into any of the four classes of accounts. It enables the bookkeeper to locate the error to the different classes of accounts, and also to ascertain if the error is on the debit or credit side.

The Combination Check Journal, Condensed Trial Balance, and the Proof Posting and Ledger Proof System used together, is the best and most accurate system the world has ever seen.

The Invoice Sales Book. This is the greatest labor-saving system that has ever been devised for retailers who render itemized bills at the end of the month.

The following cuts are photo-engraved from originals, and are given to fully illustrate the system. By referring to the first cut, we find an invoice attached to a stub; upon this stub the charges are made direct from the sales-ticket, and at some convenient time during the month, the bills are made from the stubs, and are ready for the customers at any time.

These books can be made to contain full page bills, also to have two, three and four to the page. This can be arranged however, to meet the requirements of the business; if various sizes are required they can be made on loose sheets, punched and placed in a patent binder, as needed; when the bills have all been detached at the end of the month the stubs can be removed and bound permanently, making a book of each month. If only one size is used, they should be made up in books and bound with about 250 sheets, and paged; when the bills have been detached, the covers can be cut off even with the stubs, which will require less space. To use this book, an index is required, and when an account is started upon the stub it is to be indexed therein at once. The Ledger page is also written on the stub and bill, so that at the end of the month, with the Journal and Cash Book posted, and all tickets charged, you are ready to prepare the bills for the mail, by footing the stubs and bills, the totals of which must agree.

THE S. W. BURROWS COMPANY,
HOT WATER AND STEAM HEATING.
VENTILATING AND PLUMBING.
1891 EUCLID AVENUE   CLEVELAND, OHIO   Mar. 31, '94

Sold to Henry A. Eger

#1303 Euclid Ave.

		PLUMBING	HEATING
Mar. 1	Hot Water Contract		195000
	Plumbing		75000
	Gas Fitting		17300
13	Labor extra Bath Tub	14300	
	" Gas Fitting		135

248

THE S. W. BURROWS COMPANY.
HOT WATER AND STEAM HEATING.
VENTILATING AND PLUMBING.
1891 EUCLID AVENUE   CLEVELAND, OHIO   Mar. 31, '94

Sold to J. N. Topliff

#1331 Euclid Ave.

		PLUMBING	HEATING
Mar. 15	Plumbing Contract		160000
	Heating		175000
17	Labor extra Gas Pipes	750	

The use of this system will save nearly 75 per cent of the work required by others. It matters not how many items are purchased during the month, they can all be found upon one or possibly two stubs instead of having to look over many pages of the old forms, and instead of having to post the amount of each purchase, the total of each account is posted, under the date of the last day of the month, thus, errors in posting are reduced to a minimum.

Should the stub be too small for the month, it can be footed in short and the amount carried to a new one; on the old stub should be written "carried to page—" and on the new stub "from page—" thus leaving reference to all items without referring to the index. After the stubs and bills are all footed, the bills are then detached, and as the Ledger pages have been written upon all the stubs and bills (if the customer has a Ledger account) you can refer to the account in the Ledger to add the balance if any, or deduct any credits that may have been made without having to refer to the index.

After the bills have been mailed, the footings of the stubs are posted to their respective accounts, and the totals are carried from page to page, the total for the month being posted to *credit* of merchandise.

The original size of the first cut was 15½ inches wide by 16 inches long, containing three bills to the page, though the size and number of bills to each may be varied according to the requirements of the business.

If an itemized ticket is sent with all goods, and a duplicate kept on file, then the pages of the book can be greatly reduced in size. The stub would then be used only for the date and amount, while the bill takes the form of a statement. The tickets are filed according to date for reference, etc.

A careful examination of this system will prove its great worth as a labor saver and ready reference, but a still greater saving of labor will be found in the following illustration.

The stub used in this form is blank about 1½ inches wide, and is used only for binding.

The charges are made at once upon the bill, and must be written with the best copying ink; at the end of the month the bills are footed, and then copied into an impression book, from which they are posted. The Ledger pages should be written upon all bills before copying, so it will not be necessary to folio the impression book, and that reference to the Ledger to add balances, etc., can be made without referring to the index. The total footing of the impression book is then posted to *Credit* of Mdse. Great care must be exercised in making these bills,

The Burrows-Bosworth Hardware Co.
HARDWARE, STOVES, FURNACES, PAINTS, OILS, ETC.
PLUMBING AND TINNING.
1222 AND 1224 EUCLID AVENUE.

L.B. 491

Cleveland, Ohio, *May 31. 94*

Sold to *J. A. Hamilton*
1390 Euclid Ave.

TELEPHONE 1311.

May	1	Plumbing Contract	900	00
		Heating "	455	00
		Tinning "	175	50
	3	10 Gals. Linseed Oil	6	40
		480# White Lead	32	00
		2 Paint Brushes	3	50
	7	1 Refrigerator	50	00
		10# 4d Wire Nails		40
	10	1 G. C. Lawn Mower	10	00
		1 Lawn Rake		75
	11	2 Tubs	3	50
	14	1 Hoe		75
		100 ft Lawn Hose	15	00
	17	1 doz Brooms	3	00
	31	1 Garland Range	50	00
			$ 1705	80

as a great many of them must be copied a month after being written. The writing should be plain, without shading, but firm, and with the best copying ink that can be obtained.

Rendering Statements—Wholesale. In a wholesale business where the accounts are long and numerous, the work required to make the statements is a very tedious task. With many business houses it is impossible to get their statements out before the 8th and 10th of the month, and while this work is being done the trial balance is delayed, and the work for the new month accumulating. All this delay and over-work can be prevented by using the system herein illustrated and explained. I have used it with a set of books consisting of four Ledgers, containing 6500 active accounts, and was never later than the 2d day of the month mailing statements. There is no change in the system of bookkeeping, and no extra books required. The same form of statement is used, except that they are made with a stub at the top, as shown in the inset form. They are made in length to suit the requirements of the accounts, and are printed upon loose sheets, perforated and punched, so they can be easily placed in, or removed from, a suitable binder. If the Ledgers are large the statements should be made into forms covering about 200 pages of the Ledger; this will make them more convenient to handle. It is an easy matter to arrange the statements in the binders to correspond with the accounts in the Ledger, and if any new accounts are opened, or started after the statements have been arranged and folioed, the binder can be opened and the new ones added in their proper order. If a suitable binder cannot be procured, use large brass fasteners; they will answer as well, and are much cheaper. About the 10th of the month, or as soon as convenient, you can begin to make the statements; once or twice a week after posting the sales, you can go through the Ledger and make statements for all accounts up to date, and by keeping all the work up, at the end of the month the statements can all be ready for the mail by the first or second, regardless of the length or number of accounts. After rendering a statement, write the balance in pencil in the Ledger, and check it at some convenient place. If any are omitted, they will be easily detected. If this system is once used, it is safe to say it will never be abandoned.

The Voucher System of Bookkeeping. A great deal of interest has been manifested of late in what is called "The Voucher System" of bookkeeping. Although it is practically new, it has been thoroughly tested, and is used by many of the largest firms and corporations in the country. The system is intended to do away with the necessity of keeping accounts with creditors, and is used only where the accounts are promptly settled. It is better adapted to some kinds of business than to others, but it is generally recognized as an accurate, satisfactory system, that can be used in almost any kind of business. Some objections have been brought against it, prominent among them are that more time is consumed by its use than by the ordinary system, and that much trouble is had because so many of the vouchers sent out from the office are never returned. In answer to these objections can say, from experience, that all things being equal, the voucher system will save time and labor. As to the return of vouchers, this has been overcome by having the check and voucher printed upon the same sheet, thus insuring their return through the banks, or by printing in bold type at the bottom of the voucher these words—**Please date, receipt, and return this voucher by first mail.''**

VOUCHER No. 1.

To Gray, Jenks & Co.

City.

THE CHAS. A. WOOD CO.

MANUFACTURERS OF

SASH, DOORS, BLINDS.

And dealers in BUILDERS' SUPPLIES.

CLEVELAND, O.

DATE	DESCRIPTION	AMOUNT
SEP. 10		$1 000 00

Correct,

Theo. N. Burtnett.
BOOKKEEPER.

Approved by

C. A. Wood.

$ 1000.00   Received of THE CHAS. A. WOOD CO.

ONE THOUSAND - - - - - - - - Dollars,

in settlement of account as above.

GRAY, JENKS & CO.

per Mitchell.

Date Sept. 11, 1894.

CASH.

Voucher No. 1

THE CHAS. A. WOOD CO.
CLEVELAND, O.

To Gray, Jenks & Co.

$ 1000.00

Paid Sept. 11,'94. *Ck No* 7131

CHARGED TO

Lumber	$1 000	00
Mdse		
Mch. and Equipment		
Real Estate		
General Expense		
Factory Expense		
Fuel		
Hardware		
Paints, Oils and Glass		
Cartage		
Horse and Wagon		
Insurance and Tax		
Glue and Sand Paper		
Labor		
Tools		
Salary, Com. and Trav. Ex		
Office		
Total	$1000	00

The ordinary books used in double-entry bookkeeping are all that are required, except a " Voucher Record," a form of which is given, with entries for illustration. The system can be commenced at the beginning of any month, but it is preferable to commence its use with the beginning of the fiscal year.

When invoices are received for material, they are first checked by the receiving clerk, the prices are then guaranteed by the buyer, who then turns them over to the bookkeeper, who will see that the extensions and footings are correct. If any errors are found, he should make the corrections upon the invoice in ink, being very careful to add to or deduct from the total, as the case may be. Cash and Trade discounts should also be deducted from the total. When the invoices are thus prepared, the bookkeeper or voucher clerk should then attach the invoice to a voucher, either with paper fasteners or mucilage. The vouchers are then entered in the Record in numerical order as shown in the following form, which is used by The Chas. A. Wood Co. of this city, one of the largest manufacturing companies in the country.

When a great many bills are received from one house and settlements made monthly, they can be entered in total at the end of the month, but if they bear different terms of credit they should be entered' accordingly.

A careful examination of the Voucher Record and the entries made therein will enable any one to thoroughly understand and use it.

When the vouchers are entered they should be folded in such a manner as to leave the printed outside square and neat. If payment is to be made at once, they should be given to the cashier, who would draw a check for the amount, and instead of any other explanation on the stub, simply write " On account Voucher No. —." If payment is to be made at some future date for the advantage of a cash discount or for other reasons, the voucher should be filed away in a box marked "Vouchers unpaid."

When all the vouchers have been entered, both paid and unpaid, at the end of the month, add all the columns in the Record, and be sure that the total of all the special columns equal the "Total amount" column. Then open an account in the Ledger for each account represented by a special column, and post the total of each for the month to the debit side, then post the amount of the "Total amount" column to the credit of "Accounts payable." When posting from the Cash Book the total of the Voucher column on the credit side is posted to the debit of "Accounts payable." This account is necessary to keep the books in Double Entry form, as there are no accounts kept with creditors. The difference between the debit and credit side of this account will always represent the amount of the indebtedness exclusive of Bills and Mortgages Payable; this difference must always correspond with the total of the unpaid vouchers on file.

The "Sundries" column at the extreme right will be found very convenient, as accounts are apt to arise for which no column is provided upon the Record. Each item in the Sundries column must be posted to the Ledger. When items are entered in this column, the amounts must be included in the Total amount column.

The "Personal Account" column at the left is used only for contra accounts, or where a voucher is paid by contra account instead of cash. Each item in this account must be posted to the contra account in the Ledger, and the total amount of the column posted to the debit of "Accounts Payable."

The first entry upon the Record as shown by the Cash Voucher is to Gray, Jenks & Co. for lumber. The bookkeeper, Theo. N. Burtnett, has certified that the extensions and footings are correct. C. A. Wood has approved it for payment, and Gray, Jenks & Co. have receipted it.

On the opposite side of the Voucher it is numbered, dated, showing the total amount, the number of the check by which it was paid, and the account to which it is charged, etc.

Many large concerns who use the Voucher system require all Journal entries to be made first by the proper official upon a Journal Voucher; they are then turned over to the bookkeeper for entry, in numerical order. This requires some extra labor on the part of the Voucher Clerk, but it is a check against fictitious entries.

The entries upon the Record are practically Journal entries in double entry form, and are so plain and self-explanatory that further explanation is thought unnecessary.

In using the Voucher System, the greatest care and attention to details in every particular is of the utmost importance; any carelessness or neglect on the part of those using it will cause more trouble than in that of the old systems. But if it is kept with care and accuracy, it will give perfect satisfaction to all concerned.

FRAUDULENT BOOKKEEPING.

It was my intention to omit this subject in this work, fearing that it might teach bookkeepers something of which they are ignorant, and impel them to do just what it is intended to prevent.

The fact is, however, that a man who is dishonest can always conceive methods of his own for committing fraud without instruction, and a necessity therefore arises for employers and auditors to be informed of such conceptions, and be provided with the means of preventing and detecting their execution.

A favorite opinion with those who have nothing but a theoretical knowledge of bookkeeping is, that a Trial Balance proves the correctness of the Ledger, and the accuracy of every detail and posting before reaching the Ledger: nothing can be more absurd.

The only benefit to be derived from frauds in accounts arises from a desire to absorb the **Cash** ; therefore it follows that if cash is taken, it can be detected by examining the cash account only.   When cash is received or paid out, it must be accounted for, and if the difference between the debit and credit side does not correspond with the amount of cash on hand, the discrepancy will show at once, but in most cases the defaulter will be particularly careful to make his original entries correctly.   To the inexperienced it may seem strange, but it is true, nevertheless, that fully three-fourths of such thefts can be found by examining the footings. You may wonder how the entries can be made correctly and fraud be committed.   You may argue that a bookkeeper would not dare to make fraudulent entries because the discrepancy would appear in the Trial Balance, but he can easily cover his tracks by changing the footings in the cash book, and then make a corresponding error in the footings of the Journal or Sales Book. Of course he cannot make the error to any personal accounts, as it would lead to detection, but merchandise, expense, or some similar large account, will have to suffer, which would keep the books in balance.   You will nearly always find double mistakes and forced balances intentional; they seldom occur by accident.   If you fail to discover anything by this method, then examine the **original Ledger Entries and Ledger balances.**   If the bookkeeper or cashier fails to credit a customer on the cash book when payment is made, they conceal the delinquency by placing the credit directly upon the Ledger, or it may not be entered or posted anywhere at all, but foots both sides of the account alike and rules it up.   Of course this necessitates a counter-balancing error in another place or places to keep the books in balance, and Merchandise is generally the account to be favored with the increase.   To detect such entries it will be necessary to verify the footings of every account in the Ledger, whether ruled up and closed or remaining open.   The Merchandise account may have been doctored in the Sales Book, Invoice Book, Journal, or any book or account that has connection with the Merchandise account.   This method of swindling is more liable to accidental detection than any other, and is not of very frequent occurrence, and, unless you are quite certain that fraud is being practic d, I would not recommend a search requiring so much labor.

Transposition of figures is another easy plan to defraud, and one that is more frequent than the preceding. · Of course the magnitude of the transposition depends on the extent of the business, and can be practiced upon small as well as large amounts, as often as the defaulter may be in need of cash.

Entries of this kind will require a corresponding transposition in some representative account, in order to keep the books in balance.

It frequently happens that figures are transposed accidentally, but when it so happens the error must be discovered and corrected. There is no excuse for a contra error of this kind, and when one is found it will bear the closest investigation. Frauds of this kind are usually practiced in this way: if the bookkeeper or cashier should receive a payment of.................. ....\$2866.00

and credits it on the Cash Book as................... 2686.00

There is a difference of............................... \$ 180.00

Or he may enter an expenditure.......................\$2532.00
When the amount really paid was.................... 2352.00

Leaving a difference of...............................\$ 180.00

Again, suppose in footing a page of the Cash Book, the debit side Foots...\$16441.00
But is carried forward.............................. ... 14641.00

Here is a difference of......................... ....\$ 1800.00

Or the credit side is carried forward...............\$16441.00
When it foots only 14641.00

Leaving as before.....................................\$ 1800.00

To detect errors of this kind, it is necessary to examine the Cash Book with both eyes wide open. It is surprising how often you may look right at an error of this kind and yet fail to detect it, as the figures look and sound as if they were correct. In cases of this kind the original entry can be made *wrong*, while the *correct* amount may be posted. The discrepancy is then balanced or counterbalanced in the "Merchandise" or some similar account, and then what is to prevent the cashier or bookkeeper from putting the surplus in his pocket?

Not long since I was called upon to adjust a partnership dissolution. I soon discovered that there was a discrepancy in the cash of $10,000. The matter was reported to the Firm at once, and it is needless to say that they were dumbfounded; however, they ordered a complete audit of their books. Not a single fraudulent entry had been made to conceal the discrepancy. The cashier, upon receiving heavy remittances during the day, would withhold entering a number of the larger checks, but he would deposit them to make the balance he should have had. When other large remittances would be received, the old checks would be entered up, and neglect to enter the new ones, etc. In case a note had been discounted in bank, the proceeds would appear on the note-book, and on the margin of his check book, but would not be entered on the cash book for several days. By manipulating the cash in this way he was able to keep such a balance exhibited as would create no suspicion. Fraud of this kind can be prevented by requiring the cashier to render daily an itemized statement of his cash balance—how much in coin, currency, in bank, on memoranda, on the Petty Cash Book, etc., etc. These statements should be rendered in detail on printed and dated blanks, and should be kept for future reference. Any delayed entries or false exhibits can be detected at once.

Petty Cash Book. These books have become quite an institution in houses doing any cash business, but if business men knew what opportunities they afford for dishonesty they would soon be discarded. On one side all sales for cash are entered, and on the other are entered all small items of expense, as freight, gas, etc. At the end of the month the totals are entered on the large Cash Book to be posted to their respective accounts in the Ledger.

These books are dangerous to keep, as items of expense can be entered twice—once in the Petty Cash Book and once in the Large Cash Book. A freight bill can be charged once by itself, and then charged again by including it with others, as follows:

By Freight paid C. & P. R'y.............................$62.50
By Freight paid on Pig Iron............................. 50.00

The first charge may contain the freight on the Pig Iron, or you might find it entered in the large Cash Book also.

Petty Cash books are not necessarily kept in double entry form, therefore incorrect additions are of frequent occurrence, and as the errors are not revealed in a Trial Balance, no counteracting entries are required.

Entering Invoices. Fictitious accounts are frequently opened by defaulters.   The account is credited for any amount desired and money is drawn and charged against it.   In other cases where the accounts of some creditors are quite large, the amount for the month is increased to suit the requirements of the defaulter, and when the settlements are made, they get their portion of it and charge the whole amount to the creditors.

These frauds can be practiced only where the Cashier or Bookkeeper is allowed plenty of rope.

Sales Book.   The Sales Book is also a good mark for a defaulter. Fraudulent entries are frequently made in this way.   Say there would be a charge to a good paying customer of $1550, this amount would be changed and appear in the Sales Book $1150; when the remittance of $1550 is received, the customer would be credited $1150, which would balance his account, the check or draft would be placed in the cash and the Bookkeeper would take $400 change, thus keeping his cash in balance: See lesson 23, page 185-186.

Discounted Notes.   If a Company is in the habit of giving Notes, the Bills Payable account should have the most careful attention, as the Bookkeeper or Cashier may have a habit of charging Cash with a Note occasionally, which never existed.   The Cash-Book may be examined every day, and an entry "By Bills Pay" may not be detected; if similar entries are of frequent occurrence, it might naturally be taken for granted that this note is one of the many given, whereas if the Bill-Book were to be examined it might be discovered that there were none due on this day, and that the amount so charged is a fraud.

If a Firm or Company is in the habit of borrowing money from banks, you should get from them occasionally a list of such Notes as they hold unpaid, then test the correctness of the Bills Payable account, the balance of which should agree with the amount of unpaid Notes as shown on the Bill-Book.   When paid, all Notes should be kept, numbered and filed away as vouchers, the signatures of which should be partially destroyed; if Notes are not properly cared for when paid, the dates can easily be changed and discounted again, for the benefit of the defaulter; such frauds are of frequent occurrence.

Pay Rolls.   Manufacturers and large dealers who employ a great many workmen do not pretend to keep personal accounts with them in their Ledger, but each one's time is entered on the Pay Roll, and the total charged to manufacturing, merchandise or other account.

One of the largest frauds ever committed in this city was by the

Pay Roll Clerk of one of the largest manufacturing companies in the country; sometimes fictitious names would be entered, and he would draw the money; not being detected in this, as he had complete charge as Timekeeper and Paymaster, the total footings were stuffed from $1,500 to $3,000 dollars per month. Frauds of this kind can be prevented by requiring each person to sign the Pay Roll as he gets his money, and by examining the calculations, footings, etc.

Bookkeepers Personal Accounts should be critically examined; frauds are frequently practiced by them drawing cash, charging it to themselves, but deliberately posting the item to merchandise or expense. It might also be well to investigate the Bookkeeper's style of living, and see if it corresponds with the salary he is getting.

The best way to prevent fraud is, to have a self-proving system of books, devised to suit the nature of business. Then do not give the Cashier or Bookkeeper "full swing," but require of them a daily statement of the business, and last but not least have special periodical audits by a Professional Accountant and Auditor.

Other illustrations of fraud could be given, but those herein mentioned are of most frequent occurrence, and it is thought that further instructions would be useless.

Discounts. Bookkeepers and others who frequently have occasion to make comparisons of discounts for the purpose of ascertaining their relative values will find the following table of great value.

10	and	5 off	$=14\frac{1}{2}$	per cent off.			45, 10	and	5 off	$=52\frac{23}{40}$	per cent off.	
15	"	5 "	$=19\frac{1}{4}$	"	"	"	50	"	5 "	$=52\frac{1}{2}$	"	"	"
20	"	5 "	$=24$	"	"	"	50	"	10 "	$=55$	"	"	"
20	"	10 "	$=28$	"	"	"	50, 10	"	5 "	$=57\frac{1}{4}$	"	"	"
25	"	5 "	$=28\frac{3}{4}$	"	"	"	55	"	5 "	$=57\frac{1}{4}$	"	"	"
25	"	10 "	$=32\frac{1}{2}$	"	"	"	55	"	10 "	$=59\frac{1}{2}$	"	"	"
25, 10	"	2 "	$=33\frac{3}{4}$	"	"	"	55, 10	"	5 "	$=61\frac{3}{4}$	"	"	"
30	"	5 "	$=33\frac{1}{2}$	"	"	"	60	"	5 "	$=62$	"	"	"
30	"	10 "	$=37$	"	"	"	60	"	10 "	$=64$	"	"	"
30, 10	"	5 "	$=40\frac{3}{10}$	"	"	"	60, 10	"	5 "	$=65\frac{4}{5}$	"	"	"
35	"	5 "	$=38\frac{1}{4}$	"	"	"	65	"	5 "	$=66\frac{3}{4}$	"	"	"
35	"	10 "	$=41\frac{1}{2}$	"	"	"	65	"	10 "	$=68\frac{1}{2}$	"	"	"
35, 10	"	5 "	$=44\frac{17}{20}$	"	"	"	65, 10	"	5 "	$=70\frac{3}{10}$	"	"	"
40	"	5 "	$=43$	"	"	"	70	"	5 "	$=71\frac{1}{2}$	"	"	"
40	"	10 "	$=46$	"	"	"	70	"	10 "	$=73$	"	"	"
40, 10	"	5 "	$=48\frac{7}{10}$	"	"	"	70, 10	"	5 "	$=74\frac{7}{20}$	"	"	"
45	"	5 "	$=47\frac{3}{4}$	"	"	"	75	"	5 "	$=76\frac{1}{4}$	"	"	"
45	"	10 "	$=50\frac{1}{2}$	"	"	"	75	"	10 "	$=77\frac{1}{2}$	"	"	"
							75, 10	"	5 "	$=78\frac{5}{8}$	"	"	"

Table for Marking Goods bought by the dozen.

To make	12	per cent	remove the	point one	place to	the left	and	subtract	1/15	itself.
"	16⅔	"	"	"	"	"	"	"	1/36	"
"	20	"	"	"	"	"				
"	25	"	"	"	"	"		add	1/24	"
"	26	"	"	"	"	"		"	1/20	"
"	28	"	"	"	"	"		"	1/15	"
"	30	"	"	"	"	"		"	1/12	"
"	32	"	"	"	"	"		"	1/10	"
"	33⅓	"	"	"	"	"		"	1/9	"
"	35	"	"	"	"	"		"	1/8	"
"	40	"	"	"	"	"		"	1/6	"
"	44	"	"	"	"	"		"	1/5	"
"	50	"	"	"	"	"		"	1/4	"
"	60	"	"	"	"	"		"	1/3	"
"	80	"	"	"	"	"		"	1/2	"

The result obtained by the above table is the cost of 1/12 dozen.

To find the Cost when the Price is per Hundred. Multiply the price per hundred by the quantity, and point off *two* more decimal places than are found in both factors.

To find Cost when the Price is per 1000. Multiply the price per 1000 by the quantity, and point off *three* more decimal places than are found in both factors.

To find Cost when the Price is per Ton of 2000 lbs. Multiply the weight by one-half the price per ton of 2000 lbs., and point off *three* more decimal places than are contained in both factors.

All aliquot parts of 100 are rates per cent, and can be applied with great advantage in commercial calculations. Those who desire to become proficient in commercial contractions will find the following table very convenient—

TABLE OF ALIQUOT PARTS.

Aliquot Parts of	1 Per Cent	100 or $1.00.	1000	1 foot or Dozen.	Sterling Money. £	Sterling Money. S.	1 Ten of 2000 lbs.
					S. D.	D.	
One thirty-second is	.0003125	3⅛	31¼	⅜ of 1 in.	0. 7½	⅜	62½
One-sixteenth is......	.000625	6¼	62½	¾ of 1 in.	1. 3	¾	125
One-eight is...........	.00125	12½	125	1½	2. 6	1½	250
One-fourth is..........	.0025	25	250	3	5. 0	3	500
Three-eighths is......	.00375	37½	375	4½	7. 6	4½	750
One-half is.....	.005	50	500	6	10. 0	6	1000
Five-eighths is.........	.00625	62½	625	7½	12. 6	7½	1250
Three-fourths is......	.0075	75	750	9	15. 0	9	1500
Seven-eighths is......	.00875	87½	875	10½	17. 6	10½	1750
One-twelfth is.........	.000833⅓	8⅓	83⅓	1	1. 8	1	166⅔
One-fifth is............	.0020	20	200		2. 0	2.8	400
One-sixth (2/12) is......	.001666⅔	16⅔	166⅔	2	3. 4	2	333⅓
One-third (4/12) is......	.00333⅓	33⅓	333⅓	4	6. 8	4	666⅔
Five-twelfths is.......	.004166⅔	41⅔	416⅔	5	8. 4	5	833⅓
Seven-twelfths is......	.005833⅓	58⅓	583⅓	7	11. 8	7	1166⅔
Two-thirds (8/12) is.....	.0066⅔	66⅔	666⅔	8	13. 4	8	1333⅓
Five-sixths (10/12) is.....	.00833⅓	83⅓	833⅓	10	16. 8	10	1666⅔
Eleven-twelfths is.....	.00916⅔	91⅔	916⅔	11	18. 4	11	1833⅓
One-fortieth is........	.052	2½	25	⅜ of 1 in.	0. 6	⅜	50

Interest. There is no other branch of commercial calculations which requires greater accuracy and speed than computations in Interest

Interest is usually computed on the basis of 360 days to the year. This custom, though not strictly accurate, is almost universally adopted throughout the United States because of its convenience. A month is considered the twelfth part of a year, and as consisting of thirty days; and interest for any number of days less than a month is estimated by the proportion which such number of days shall bear to thirty.

The U. S. Government and foreign nations record 365 days to the year, and each day is considered $\frac{1}{365}$ of a year. All government securities, therefore, are computed on the accurate basis. On the accurate plan a day is called $\frac{1}{365}$ of a year, the difference between the Interest obtained by both methods will be $\frac{1}{360}$ or $\frac{1}{72}$ itself.

Sixty days Six per cent Interest Method. This method of computing Interest for short terms is an accurate and speedy one. The Interest on any sum for 60 days at 6 per cent can be found by drawing a perpendicular line two places to the left of the decimal point of the principal. The result will be the Interest in dollars and cents.

What is the Interest on $1575.24 for 60 days at 6 per cent? By pointing off two places to the left we have $15 | 75. Interest. To find the Interest for any number of days more or less than 60, first find the Interest for 60 days, then take as many times the Interest for 60 days as the given days are times 60 days; or such a part of the Interest for 60 days as the given days are the part of 60 days.

What is the Interest on $9428.72 for 93 days at 6 per cent?

$94	28.72=Interest for 60 days.
47	14.3 =　　"　　"　30　"
4	71.4 =　　"　　"　3　"
	"　　"
$146	14.4　　　　"　　"　93 days.

The following table is based on the Interest of the given principal at 6 per cent for 60 days. As in 360 days the principal will earn 6 per cent, in 60 days or $\frac{1}{6}$ of a year it must earn 1 per cent or $\frac{1}{100}$ of the principal, which is found by removing the decimal point two places to the left. Hence, in any principal containing dollars only, the Interest at 6 per cent for 60 days will be as many cents as there are dollars in that principal. Therefore, to find the Interest at 6 per cent for parts of 60 days proceed as in the following—

TABLE.

For 59 days' int. subtract		$\frac{1}{60}$.	For 30 days' int. divide by		2.
" 58 " " "		$\frac{1}{30}$.	" 24 " " multiply by the dec.		.4
" 57 " " "		$\frac{1}{20}$.	" 20 " " divide by		3.
" 55 " " "		$\frac{1}{12}$.	" 18 " " multiply by the dec.		.3
" 54 " " multiply by the dec.		.9	" 15 " " divide by		4.
" 50 " " subtract		$\frac{1}{6}$.	" 12 " " multiply by the dec.		.2
" 48 " " multiply by the dec.		.8	" 10 " " divide by		6.
" 45 ' " subtract		$\frac{1}{4}$.	" 6 " " "		10.
" 42 " " multiply by the dec.		.7	" 3 " " "		20.
" 40 " " subtract		$\frac{1}{3}$.	" 2 " " "		30.
" 36 " " multiply by the dec.		.6	" 1 " " "		60.

NOTE.—To find the Interest for any number of days not mentioned in the table, the student should combine one or more of the parts of 60 days, worked by the methods shown therein.

To find the Interest at any Rate per cent. First find the Interest at 6 per cent, and then take such proportion of the obtained Interest as the given rate is more or less than 6 per cent.

To find the Interest at 7 per cent, add $\frac{1}{6}$ of the Interest to itself.
"   "   8 " $\frac{1}{3}$ "   "   "
"   "   9 " $\frac{1}{2}$ "   "   "
"   "   10 " $\frac{2}{3}$ "   "   "
"   "   12 "   multiply "   " by 2
"   "   5 "   subtract $\frac{1}{6}$ of the Interest from itself.
"   "   4 "   " $\frac{1}{3}$ "   "   "   "
"   "   3 "   " $\frac{1}{2}$ "   "   "   "
"   "   2 "   " $\frac{2}{3}$ "   "   "   "
"   "   1 "   divide the Interest by 6.

VALUABLE INTEREST RULES.
BASIS, COMMERCIAL YEAR OF 360 DAYS, OR 30 DAYS PER MONTH.

4 *per cent.*—Multiply the principal by the required number of days, divide by 9 and point off three places.

5 *per cent.*—Multiply by the number of days, and divide by 72, and point off two places.

6 *per cent.*—Multiply by the number of days, divide by 6, and point off three places.

8 *per cent.* Multiply by the number of days, divide by 45, and point off two places.

9 *per cent.*—Multiply by the number of days, divide by 4, and point off three places.

10 *per cent.*—Multiply by the number of days, and divide by 36, and point off two places.

12 *per cent.*—Multiply by the number of days, divide by 3, and point off three places.

15 *per cent.*—Multiply by the number of days, and divide by 24, and point off two places.

18 *per cent.*—Multiply by the number of days, divide by 2, and point off three places.

20 *per cent.*—Multiply by the number of days, divide by 18, and point off two places.

NOTE.—The Interest in each case will be dollars and cents.

Thousand days 36 per cent Interest Method.   This is the quickest and most accurate Interest method known.   The principle of it is that any sum at Interest for 1000 days at 36 per cent, the Interest will equal the principal, figuring the year at 360 days; or $36\frac{1}{2}$ per cent counting 365 days to a year; therefore, the Interest for 100 days, 10 days or 1 day is readily found by removing the decimal point 1, 2 or 3 places to the left.   For example, the Interest on

$5761.39 for 1000 days at 36 per cent is $5761.39
    "   "   100   "   "   "   576.13
    "   "   10   "   "   "   57.61
    "   "   1   "   "   "   5.76

To find the Interest for any number of days.   Say for 99 days, first find the Interest for 100 days then subtract the Interest for 1 day.   To find the Interest for 75 days, first find the Interest 10 days, and multiply by 7, then multiply the Interest for 1 day by 5 and add it to the Interest for 70 days, etc; this will in every case give the Interest at 36 per cent for 360 days to the year, or $36\frac{1}{2}$ per cent for 365 days to the year.

To find Interest at any rate per cent.   Proceed as follows:

To find Interest at 1 per cent, divide the principal at 36 per cent by 36
  "   "   2   "   "   "   "   36   "   18
  "   "   3   "   "   "   "   36   "   12
  "   "   4   "   "   "   "   36   "   9
  "   " $4\frac{1}{2}$ "   "   "   "   36   "   8
  "   "   6   "   "   "   "   36   "   · 6
  "   "   9   "   "   "   "   36   "   4
  "   "   12   "   "   "   "   36   "   3
  "   "   5. first find the Interest at 6 per cent than subtract $\frac{1}{6}$ itself.
  "   "   7   "   "   "   6   "   " add $\frac{1}{6}$ "
  "   "   8   "   "   "   6   "   " " $\frac{1}{3}$ "

For example, what is the Interest on $9759.99 for 999 days at $4\frac{1}{2}$ per cent?

18

$9759.99 at 36 per cent for 1000 days is $9759.99
"   "   "   "   1 day is   9.75

$9759.99 at 36 per cent for 999 days is $9750.24
$9750.24÷8=$1218.78 Interest at 4¼ per cent.

With a little practice this method can be used with greater speed and accuracy than any other method known.

Averaging Accounts, is the process of finding the average time, for the payment of the balance of an account containing both debits and credits, without loss of Interest or Discount to either Debtor or Creditor.

The *Product Method* is very simple but requires too many separate calculations.   The *Interest Method* is to be preferred, because any rate of Interest can be used which is most convenient; and as any amount for 1000 days at 36 per cent shows its own Interest (as explained above), this method applied to averaging will be found the quickest and most accurate.

Investing.   The *first* element of a good investment is that the *principal* shall be perfectly secure; that it shall not be diminished through depreciation of values, nor loss through want of sound security. The *second* element is that the principle can be readily obtained if it is wanted; security must be "convertible:" that is, easily realized. An investment, however secure which ties up money irrevocably for years, is not a first-class one.   The other *and secondary* elements of a good investment refer to the *Interest* or *return*.   The *first* object is to have this paid promptly, and if not promptly paid, readily collected without much or any expense or trouble.   The *second* object is to have the Interest as large as possible.   I would have you particularly observe that I have mentioned these four elements of a good investment in the order of their importance.   Very frequently, in fact always, the temptation is to reverse the order, and to allow a large Interest, especially if the promise is to pay promptly when due, to overbalance the considerations about the security of the principal.   This is by far the most frequent cause of loss.   Every one may rest assured that it is a sound ordinary rule that where an Interest above the legal rate is offered whether by an individual or a company, it means that the investor will incur some risk with his principal.

Sound business men agree that a good investment should repay the investor compound Interest at 6 per cent, this being the legal rate of Interest in most states, and if promptly collected and re-invested will yield the return mentioned.

This correct principle is constantly overlooked in practice even by those who know it best, by regarding this as too small a gain; persons through miscalculations, do not receive so much.

The mistakes which are most frequent in calculating the probable or actual value of an investment, result from not considering all the bearings of this simple measure of value.   I will illustrate this subject by some plain examples.

Suppose unimproved land is bought amounting to $12,000 and after holding it eight years, it is sold for $21,000.   Inasmuch as $12,000 at compound Interest for eight years=$19,126.18, it would appear to have been a fine investment.   But meanwhile unavoidable expenses have been incurred for fencing, taxes, surveying, commission on sale, etc., which average 2 per cent a year, or $240.00.   Therefore from the gross proceeds you must subtract:

$240 at compound Interest for 7 years=$360.86
240   "   "   "   6   "   = 340.32
240   "   "   "   5   "   = 321.17
240   "   "   "   4   "   = 302.98
240   "   "   "   3   "   = 285.84
240   "   "   "   2   "   = 269.66
240 simple   "   "   1   "   = 254.40
240 cash   240.00
                                               ―――――――
                                               $2375.23

Selling price, $21,000
Expenses,   2,375.23
                 ―――――――
$18624.77 Net on investment.

Then $19,126.18 compound Interest on $12,000 for 8 years minus
   18624.77 the net proceeds
   ―――――――
   $501.41 loss.

In other words, you have actually lost over $500 on what you might have made by an easy 6 per cent operation.   The temptation of large annual percentage frequently leads to the same result.   The percentage is in fact paid from the principal, although it does not appear so on the face of the transaction.

Let us suppose an investment of $2000 in Gas Stock, which pay at the end of the first year, 15 per cent; the second year, 12 per cent; the third year, 9 per cent, at the end of which time the company sell out to another company at a fair valuation, say two-thirds of the first cost.

The returns have been large, has it been a good investment?

Compound Interest of $2000, for 3 years at 6 per cent=$2382.02
   15 per cent of $2000, at compound Interest 2 years=$337.08
   12   "   "   " Interest for 1 year   = 180.00
   9 per cent cash,   254.40
   ⅔ of cost   1333.34

                                  $2104.82

                Difference, $277.20

Here the actual loss compared with a 6 per cent investment is $277.20 or nearly $100 a year. Yet there are many persons who continue making investments of this kind, and seeing they receive a handsome Interest on their money, and the aggregate foots up more than the principal, imagine they are improving on the 6 per cent plan.

Stock Exchange. Works on history and political economy are singularly deficient in the treatment of Stock Exchange business, and in fact completely ignore its important relations to the financial mechanism. Literary publications rarely enter into the consideration of this topic, which is foreign to the thoughts and classical education of most authors. Financial Journals address their articles to the relatively narrow circle which is familiar with stock-markets and financial affairs. It therefore happens that the Stock Exchange, which is a most potent factor in the financial world and one which powerfully affects wide interests, is imperfectly understood. Doubtless there are many persons who regard the Stock Exchange merely as a noisy congregation of brokers who gamble in the securities of governments and joint stock companies, under the guise of legitimate business. Deeper insight into the functions, practices and characters of the Stock Exchanges in the three great cities of New York, London and Paris may induce a broader and happier conception of their dignity and utility.

Those who teach political economy in our schools or write treatises on it for publication, are seldom familiar with the operations of Stock Exchanges. It follows that in discussing and wrangling over the question of the evils or advantages of an adverse "balance of trade" between nations, they are likely to consult chiefly the statistics of imports and exports of commodities, merchandise and specie without trying to trace the more elusive but very palpable movement of financial securities.

During the first eight months of 1888, to illustrate, the balance of trade, commercially was $92,000,000 against the United States, but during that time we exported only about $22,000,000 in specie, leaving $70,000,000 unaccounted for. We should have been compelled to ship this $72,000,000 in specie to settle the international account, had not foreign capital purchased liberally of our railroad bonds and stocks. The balance of trade is nominally always against England, but instead of losing wealth, as the figures might suggest, that country is constantly growing richer by returns on investments. Unless the ebb and flow of securities between great financial centres be studied and traced, the figures of international trade balances may be misconstrued or, indeed, wholly misunderstood. Political economy has at best hardly established itself on the safe basis of an incontrovertible science, and it cannot afford to omit the facts and figures of Stock Exchanges in making up its conclusions as to balances of trade, interest on capital, and the production and distribution of wealth.

A Stock Exchange is an organization of persons, and a place of meeting for the business of buying and selling such stocks as have been recognized or listed for such dealing. English usage limits the term stocks to government stock, annuities, etc., while the term shares denotes the stock of railroads, banks, etc. In American usage a great variety of bonds and shares are all included under stocks, and are subject to Stock Exchange transactions when they have been placed on the Exchange list or "listed." Bonds representing national, state, county, and city engagements to pay debts, and the bonds or shares of railroads, banks, mining, manufacturing, telegraph, telephone, insurance and other companies are dealt in as stock, if they are important enough to be listed. Two kinds of sales of stocks are made, that of the Exchange in a regular way and for *bona fide* sale ; and that of the street outside, called jobbing, and generally speculative for mere betting on what prices will be. The form for the first is by a call of the list of the stocks. This is made twice a day, and these two calls mark what are known as the first board and the second board. The government, state, and railroad bonds are called in a room specially allotted to that purpose. But in practice the sales are made outside these formal calls, brokers crying out what and how many shares they offer, and at what price, or what they want to buy, and at what price. These cries appear to make indescribable confusion to the unaccustomed ear, yet are readily distinguished and understood by those engaged, and transactions closed and noted accurately. Persons are appointed for the purposes to take record of these sales, and furnish a report which is sent in all directions for public information, or to officers where buying and selling of stocks is privately conducted. The record is made with free use of abbreviations: in the case of bonds, C means coupon, R registered and O B delivery at the opening of the books of transfer.   P R 400: 125: S. 60, means 400 shares of Pennsylvania Railroad stock at $125, to be delivered at the seller's option any time within 60 days; but if rendered 'B 60' the option is with the buyer.

Stock is bought and sold not only outright, with payment in full, but also without intent to deliver, on what is called a margin, the object being to speculate in its future value.   The buyer puts down 10 per cent of the par value of the stock, and awaits the turn of the market.   If this is downward, the buyer's broker either sells if the fall goes so low as to be under the buyer's margin, or calls for more margin.   If it is upward, the buyer sells at a favorable time, and pockets the amount realized by the rise, also recovering his 10 per cent.   The brokers commission for buying or selling stocks is ⅛ of 1 per cent to all persons not members of the Exchange, called also the brokers board.   Members pay $2 per hundred shares.   To contract to deliver stock at a future day, expecting meanwhile to buy at a reduced price, is called selling "short" and those who do this and thus desire a fall of values, and try presumably to secure fall or shrinkage by efforts to depress or squeeze smaller holders are called "bears."   Those are termed "bulls" who have bought for a rise of price and wish to toss prices upward: they are said to be "long" of the stock.   To sell a "put" is to agree to buy a certain number of shares of a particular stock at a certain price, within a stated time, provided the buyer of the put and seller of the stock is prepared to deliver it at the time and price named.   To sell a "call" is to agree to deliver in the same way.   The parties agree on the cost of these "stock privileges" as they are called, according to the time involved, the condition of the market, etc, etc.

The New York Stock Exchange was organized in 1817.   It has now a membership of 1100, and a handsome building on Broad and New streets, with a great hall for doing business and vaults for storing securities, said to be the best ever constructed.   The present value of membership is $25,000, but as much as $34,000 has been paid. Memberships now can only be obtained by purchase from retiring members, as the Exchange has none for sale.

The rules of the Stock Exchange are very strict; a high standard of integrity is maintained, and all disputes are settled by a committee of arbitration.

Speculating—Gambling.   During the past century panics have recurred in cycles of about ten years, and many superficial observers attribute them wholly to unhealthy Speculating or Gambling, and condemn Stock Exchanges as breeding places of disaster.   Speculating has a bad name and it may be worth while to see what it really implies or describes. Evidences of public debt, and the shares and bonds of incorporated companies are easily transferred, and actively dealt in on the Exchanges and frequently are footballs for Speculation, especially before their values are well established. Risk and uncertainty are the two qualities essential to speculative transactions, and just so fast and so far as they are eliminated, just so fast and so far they cease to invite speculation. All must alike deplore the frequent instances where haste to get rich in speculative markets has involved innocent persons in loss and ruin, or tempted men to betray their trusts. While panics have injured the pride and purse of individuals, and for the moment prostrated the energies of the industrial world, they have not arrested the progress of material civilization, but, indeed, seem, in a measure, to be merely an outgrowth from it. The extension of the credit system, which is one of the refinements of modern commerce, and the introduction of labor-saving machinery which rapidly displaces labor and deranges values, are two of the potent causes of commercial crisis. The subdivision of the title of ownership of such great engines of progress as manufacturing, mining, shipping, banking, trading, telegraph, telephone, cable, water and gas companies, is indispensible to their organization and operation. The fortune of no individual would be ample to set these forces into motion on a gigantic scale.

The Stock Exchanges of the world offer a standing reward to men of talent and integrity everywhere, to discover new opportunities and to suggest untried experiments for the employment of capital, with a prospect of more than an investor's rate of interest.

Not long ago steam was applied to locomotion by land and sea and electricity to the transmission of thought and speech. Their introduction was an experiment; they were at first a speculation, and not an investment. Speculation is truly the handmaid of enterprise, and the two are so closely associated that one cannot be curtailed without crippling the other.

The person who buys more shares than his capital will permit him to pay for, is derisively called a "speculator."

But does this act essentially differ from the practices of what, by common consent, are called legitimate commercial undertakings? The merchant buys in advance of his immediate wants and in excess of them and his capital. But the critic here says "on the Stock Exchange speculators go so far as to sell what they do not possess," or, in Stock Exchange parlance, they "go short." But how about a contractor who agrees to build a house before he owns a plank, or brick, or nail; or who agrees to build a railroad before he buys a cross-tie, a rail or a shovel? How about the manufacturer who sells his sheeting and his steel rails before the cotton is grown or the ore extracted from the mine? Even China sells its products to us ahead of their production. The fact is, that the element of speculation constantly comes more prominently into the plans of the whole world. Those who produce or buy what they need only from day to day, jog along as did the canal boats and stage coaches of our ancestors. The great manufacturers and merchants of to-day must cast the horoscope of coming conditions and read its prophecy aright or be overcome by more prescient rivals. They must anticipate and discount the future, and become speculators in the highest acceptation of the word. When speculating becomes gambling it is time then to call a halt. Every instance in which money has been made by this gambling method, is made the most of and talked about from one to another, but when money is lost by it, there is very little said about it. So the general impression one gets from the ordinary conversation, leads one to think that the chances in speculation are at least even, but such is not the case. The "lambs" are constantly being "shorn," and unless you are in a position to positively know all the ins and outs of the markets, have plenty of money, and can devote time and attention to it, you had better let the entire subject severely alone.

The So-called Bucket Shops. The Stock and all other Exchanges of this country have a parasite in the so-called "bucket shop" which covers the land with a speculative gambling mildew. It has discredited the legitimate business of regularly constituted exchanges in the eyes of people, especially in the smaller communities, who form their ideas of real market-places from the character of these gambling houses.

No doubt many an innocent critic inveighs against Exchanges and their members, because he imagines the "Bucket-shop" is a section of the Exchange, and a miniature brokerage office. This parasite is indigenous to the United States, and happily its ravages abroad are relatively light.

A broker, it matters not whether in stocks, grain, cotton, real estate, insurance or shipping, is an agent. His interest and that of his principal are identical. In a Stock Exchange, for example, he meets other brokers, and through the collision of orders and opinions, arising from operations of speculators and investors, news and events, sympathy with the dealings in other Exchanges, etc., a series of prices is established.   These quotations go to the "bucket shop" keeper, who exhibits them to his speculative visitors.   In effect he says to them: "The markets in the various Exchanges are in progress; they will fluctuate.   If you wish to wager that they will go up, name the amount of money you will bet on this, and I will take it, limiting your possible loss to that sum.   If you wish to do the reverse, I am likewise willing.   Put up the stakes with me, and give me a commission on the bet, and we will await the result."   Here his interest is diametrically opposed to that of the "customer," and if he should happen to be a man of easy morals, the quotations and information furnished might be qualified to suit the case.

Betting on what the price of a stock will be when the persons making the bet do nothing except to guess what others through their negotiations will make it, is as unadulterated gambling as betting on which horse will win a race.   When a client buys a stock through a broker, thinking that it will advance, as when he buys a cargo of flour because he thinks the wheat crop is short and that it will go higher, he takes his position commercially in the market, contributing by the act of his purchase to bring about the very result expected.   He relieves somebody of the stock or the flour.   When, however, he as a third person, merely puts up his money on what other persons, solely and without his intervention in the article dealt in, will do, he is as far outside the pale of commerce as if he bets on the throw of dice. The Exchanges have tried to suppress "bucket shops" by appeals to law and legislation, but by some strange obliquity of mental vision, those who alone can give relief do not seem to see the vicious nature of this financial pest.   There is hardly a town in the land but what has or has had a shop of this description.   They are financial nomads, changing their firm names and habitat to suit their pecuniary exigencies.   They belong to no association, are accountable to no authority, and the sums they owe confiding customers are generally too small to justify an appeal to law; besides, many patrons would not like to advertise their dealings.

There are thousands of these "Bucket-shops" in the country, and many of them are in small towns where there is no legitimate speculative or investment business in stocks, and where no legitimate broker could bring quotations and thrive.

"A Bucket-shop" business is a poor counterfeit of real Stock Exchange business, and it ought to be suppressed, as it is not conducted on legitimate commercial principles.

Another form of gambling is that which consists in receiving property without rendering a just equivalent. Gambling for stakes is a system of polite robbery, genteel murder, and fashionable suicide.

It is well known that many men who stand high in society, are engaged in this vice. It is well known that many buildings which rear their fronts proudly, in our large cities have been erected or purhased with money thus obtained. It is well known that the stock of goods in many a store is the product of this very crime. But does this fact change the nature of gambling? Not at all. Respectable men cannot make it a respectable vocation; gold has no transforming influence over it, silver cannot cover its hideousness; music cannot drown its wails of woe. If you would waste a fortune, become a gambler. If you would in the shortest time scatter the earnings of years, resort to the gay saloon, and engage in games of chance, and drink in the dear delights of the gambler's purgatory.

The gambler inevitably becomes a ruined man. He may win for a time, he may fill his purse with his ill-gotten gain, but the unseen hand will sweep them away, and leave him penniless. Men begin to gamble with a very different opinion. They want wealth, and deem the game of chance the best method of securing it. They set sail upon the sea of guilt with the idea of becoming rich without labor or toil. But how sadly does experience controvert this sentiment. Gambling, instead of being the royal road to fortune, proves to be the path to sure poverty. Instead of being the flower-blooming way to affluence, it is found to be the thorn-planted road to crime and disgrace; some live and die, all surrounded with the wealth thus gotten, but these are the exceptions to the general principle, and form no argument in favor of such crimes.

Gambling is a system of falsehood, truth is one of the loveliest of the virtues. The man of truth is an estimable character. Truthfulness consists, not simply, in always avoiding direct falsehood, but in an upright, consistent course of action. Gambling is entirely opposed to truth. In itself, it is a lie, its promises are hollow and deceptive, its pleasures false and fleeting. It is carried on by falsehood; from the very nature of the case, the gambler cannot be a man of truth.

Gambling is a system of wholesale theft. I know that it is not what is usually denominated theft, but though called by another name, it is no less really that crime. Many trusted bookkeepers and cashiers are regular patrons of the gambler's den. Usually luck is against them, they lose all, win it back they must; but out of money, they appropriate their employers' money, but it is lost, and the once trusted and highly respected man is a ruined, disgraced defaulter.

Fly from the gambler's house as from the door of death. Fly from the gambler himself. He will strive to ruin you, poison is in his heart and falsehood on his tongue. He seeks your ruin, and he will succeed if you allow yourself to be tempted.

Intemperance.—Poverty in itself is not a crime. No disgrace belongs to the man, who by reverses in business, is led down from affluence to destitution. The poorest man who walks this earth of sorrow, or who toils in vain to clothe and feed his children, can stand in the presence of the man of millions with no consciousness of inferiority. But when poverty is the result of crime, it becomes at once sinful and disgraceful ; when it is the result of gambling, drinking or lying, it covers its victim with a robe of shame. Under any circumstances it is exceedingly unpleasant and inconvenient to be *very* poor, and by most men poverty is dreaded as one of the worst evils. Poverty is as sure to follow a course of intemperance, as light and heat to follow the rising of the sun.

The old proverb that "the drunkard shall come to poverty" is too true, and wherever we behold drunkeness, we also gaze upon squalid misery. Go into any community and you will find affluence to be the result of sobriety, and destitution the sure attendant of dissipation.

So universal is this fact, that we expect a man to ruin himself, squander his poverty, become idle and worthless, when he commences a course of intemperance. You can predict with almost unerring certainty, that a few years will make him a pauper or a criminal, and leave him in a mad-house or prison, the result of his crimes.

The wretched beings, who often reel along our streets, the miserable creatures, who hide in cellars, bar-rooms and taverns, were once as respectable as those who now walk the earth, with proud step and lofty look. But forgetting that "the drunkard shall come to want," they took the social glass and drank its contents. The pledge was disregarded, and the warnings of friends unheeded. Step by step, they descended from respectability and affluence to wretchedness and woe. Property was wasted, and character sacrificed, self-respect took its flight, and those who were once the enterprising, industrious, hopeful men of our country, are now reeling, staggering inhabitants of dens and dives of infamy.

CHAPTER TWENTY-FIVE.

Railway Accounting.

Revenue.

The revenue of a railway is derived from the following sources: Freight, Passenger, Express, Mails and Miscellaneous.

Freight Earnings.

The business of the freight department is very complicated, and to have a proper control over it requires the most minute and constant watchfulness. From the moment freight is received by the company up to the time of its delivery to the consignee, the most incessant supervision is required.

An analysis of the freight traffic discloses the almost infinite variety of the articles transported. The expenses attending the transportation of the different classes and grades of freight, vary greatly. The transportation of coal, lumber, coke, and similar freights requires much less expensive appliances than that of general merchandise. So far as clerical work, blanks and accounts are concerned, it costs as much, or more, to transport a package weighing ten pounds, as a car of live stock.

The details that must be observed in handling merchandise are very great. When received at the freight station it is checked, and a receipt given. Each class of freight must be grouped, weighed, and entered upon the check or receiving book. If the freight is in bad order, its condition must be carefully noted. Every item is methodically checked when loaded in the car for shipment, and when it goes forward to its destination, it must be accompanied by a way-bill or manifest, giving every particular description, such as, where billed from, where billed to, date, number of car, number of manifest, the weight, an exact description of the articles, the local charges and advances if any, that have been made upon it. A letter press copy of this way-bill must be taken, and a duplicate of it forwarded to the general office. The bill is then entered upon the station books and at the close of the month, the agent is required to report its date, footings and destination separately, grouping it in its proper place with other bills to the same station during the month.

The conductor of the train that takes the freight must also take the way-bill. He should make a record of it for transmission to the general office. When the freight arrives at its destination, it is checked from the car, item by item, and any shortages, or evidences of its being in bad order, are carefully noted upon the bill. Upon its delivery the charges are collected and the consignee's receipt taken.

There are many kinds or classes of freight for which the company is not held responsible for its condition or quantity.

When the freight is received at its destination the agent must make the same records and reports that are required from the forwarding agent. The receiving agent returns the original way-bill with his reports at the end of the month, instead of returning a duplicate.

The earnings from freight should be entered upon the books in the month in which it is billed, without reference to the date of its arrival at destination or the time of the collection of the charges.

Sometimes the quantity of freight forwarded is not known until after it reaches its destination. This is frequently the case with coal, coke, ore, grain in bulk, and similar heavy freights. When such is the case, and the quantity cannot be ascertained by a certain day in the following month, then the freights should be carried forward into the returns for the succeeding month.

Passenger Earnings.

The expense of conducting the passenger business is not nearly so great as that of the freight, so far as accounts and clerical labor are concerned, while the work at the stations is much simpler.

The tickets provided for sale to the different points are printed, numbered and arranged in numerical order. When a ticket is called for, it is taken from the case, stamped and delivered to the passenger upon payment of the proper amount. The difference between the commencing number and closing number (of which a record is kept), is of course the number sold. The number of tickets sold multiplied by the rate gives the amount received for tickets sold to the point printed on the ticket; these amounts are then entered upon the books and blank reports. To undertake to describe the extent and variety of tickets in detail, and the special records and reports that must be kept of those sold would require a volume in itself.

The amount of passenger fares collected by agents and conductors should be credited to passenger earnings in the month in which it is collected. For this purpose an account may be opened say with " Foreign Coupon Ticket Collections;" this account should be charged with the tickets collected, in the month in which they are collected; then, when the report of the tickets sold has been received from the company selling them, said company should be charged and " Foreign Coupon Ticket Collections " credited.

Express Business.

The express business upon railroads is now most generally conducted by corporations organized for that particular purpose. At the smaller stations it is a very common practice for the agent of the railroad company to act as agent for the express company, although the business and responsibility of the one has no connection with the other.

Express companies pay the railroad companies for the use of their offices and cars, the transportation of their messengers and other valuable considerations upon the extent of the business done. Express companies should be charged monthly and Express Earnings credited, regardless of the time payments are made.

Railroad companies do not, as a general thing, require detailed reports from the express companies' agents for the purpose of arriving at the amount that should be paid.

The express companies are required to render weekly statements, thus greatly reducing the expenses of both companies. To prevent deception, the railway company should at all times have the privilege of examining the books and accounts of the express companies. The railway company should also have the right to require sworn statements of the business done by the express companies.

From this it will be seen that the collection of the revenue derived from the express business is very simple.

Transportation of Mails.

The collection from the Post Office Department for the transportation of the mails is also very simple, as the amounts are contracted for and settlements made quarterly. The Government should be charged in equal amounts monthly for the transmission of the mails and the Mail Earnings credited.

The Post Office Department usually designates postmasters along the railway, from whom the railway companies are required to collect the balance due them. The particulars of these collections are reported to the Auditor of the Treasury of the P. O. Department.

These reports are verified, and the amount the railway company has collected is deducted from the total amount due it, and the balance is paid by draft on the U. S. Treasury.

Miscellaneous Earnings.

The principal items of Miscellaneous Earnings are rents switching, storage, extra baggage, dockage, demurrage car-hire received over amount paid, and receipts from other petty and irregular sources. Miscellaneous Earnings are generally credited in the month in which they are collected, and from the items mentioned, it will be seen that they are collected partly through the hands of the agents and partly through the office of the Local Treasurer.

Extra baggage is reported by agents in the month in which the receipts for same are collected. Collections for switching, storage, dockage, etc., are credited to Miscellaneous Earnings in the month in which they are reported by the agents. Rents received are credited in the month in which the bills are passed to the Auditor for entry. The above rules are for the purpose of simplifying the accounts, they are of no particular consequence, and may be changed if desired.

The amount due other companies for the use of their cars should be charged to Miscellaneous Earnings and credited to the companies furnishing the same, in the month in which the cars are used. The amount due from other companies for cars used by them should be charged and earnings credited in the month in which the report of the service is received. If the amount due to other companies, during any month should exceed the amount due from them, the difference should be entered upon the books as an expense account.

As soon as the ticket, freight and other accounts have been examined and corrected by the different sub-departments having charge of such accounts, the results are certified to the Local Treasurer, to be by him credited to Earnings. The Local Treasurer must keep an account with each agent, conductor, and railway company. At the end of the month the agents render a balance sheet to the Local Treasurer; these balance sheets are compared with the returns received from the different sub-departments as stated above. If there are any errors, the balance sheets are made to conform with the returns from the department, and the agent notified.

Agents and others who collect the earnings of the road, are required to remit daily their entire collections (except change) as directed by the Local Treasurer.

The exact amount of earnings of the different classes is determined by the Local Treasurer, from the returns received from the different sub-departments, and not from the remittances of agents, therefore, separate remittances of the cash collected from the different sources are not necessary, and no statement is required, other than the remittance containing the total collections.

It has been shown that the earnings from the transportation of express and mails are paid directly into the Treasury, and the process of collection simple and direct, while the collection of and accounting for the earnings from freights, passenger and miscellaneous sources is somewhat complicated and difficult.

The books should be closed, the accounts balanced and audited monthly. The freight accounts are examined and audited by the Auditor of Freight Accounts. All freight reports are made to him. The passenger or ticket accounts are examined and audited in the general ticket department.

Conductors are required to send all tickets collected by them to the Auditor of Ticket Account , whose duty it is to examine into and verify the correctness of all returns from the general ticket office to the Local Treasurer.

Regarding the local finances of a railway it may be said that no officers except those in charge of the treasury department should be authorized personally to collect or handle the revenues of the company. No officer should be authorized or justified in putting himself in a position where well established checks and safeguards do not exist in sufficient force and method to enable him at any time to demonstrate the uprightness of his actions and the perfect correctness of his accounting before the most exacting tribunal.

Disbursments.

Construction.

This is one of the most important in railroad accounts, and should be used only to describe the first or original cost of structures, track, works and additions that add increased value to the property, the said structures or works being in the nature of accessions to the property of the company and not intended to replace something of a similar nature, worn out or destroyed at the same place or vicinity.

The cost of a thing once having been charged to construction, it must thereafter be kept in an equally good condition at the expense of the operating or current working expenses of the road.

The items chargeable to Construction, are right of way, franchises, increased facilities, grounds, and expenses connected therewith, engineering, expenses in negotiating Stocks and Bonds, discount suffered in the sale of Securities, interest on Bonds during Construction, interest and exchange, and all labor and material used upon the construction of road bed, buildings, etc.

The cost of new side tracks, less the cost of side tracks taken up, the cost of bridges, culverts, and viaducts where none before existed, the cost of additional buildings, including the machinery and appurtenances, the cost of additional telegraph lines and facilities, the cost of additions or improvements in the fixtures relating to track, the value of steel rails over iron rails, when iron is replaced with steel, the difference in value between iron laid of a heavier grade than that which it replaces, the cost of transportation of material and men for constructions, the cost of track repairs rendered necessary in consequence of its not having been constructed in a first-class manner originally, the balance of accrued interest and expenses on bonds, the cost of improving depot grounds, extending platforms, enlarging stock yards, the furniture, fixtures, tools and machinery necessary to equip a new building or structure and all additions or improvements of a substantial and permanent character to things already in use, should be charged to Construction.

When the Company's Stocks and Bonds are sold at a discount, the proceeds to be applied to construction and equipment, the construction or equipment account should be charged with such discount.

If the company purchase its own securities at a discount, this account should receive credit for the profits derived therefrom.

19

Interests that may have accrued at the time of purchase or sale of the company's securities should be charged or credited as the case may be to Bond Interest.

When new lines or extensions and the sidings incidental thereto are opened up, the following accounts should be kept that the actual cost in detail may be ascertained, preceding the accounts with the name of the new line or extension; Right of Way and Franchises, Engineering, Discount on sale of Securities, Interest on Bonds during Construction, Interest and Exchange, Cleaning and Grubbing, Grading Surfacing Track and Ditching, Track-laying, Ballasting, Iron and Steel Rails, Ties, Masonry, Culverts, Bridges, Miscellaneous Track Material. Tools and Machinery, Stationery, Buildings, Fences, Telegraph, Office and Station Furniture, Engine and Car service in Construction, Transportation of Men and Material, Equipment and Miscellaneous Expenses. When any part of the work is of an extraordinary character, a separate or special account should be kept with it, as tunnels, cuts, etc.

New Equipment.

This account embraces the cost of all additions to the rolling stock of the company. The equipment accounts are in their nature similar to those of Construction.

This account is charged with the cost of improvements added to the equipment.

When a new locomotive or car is constructed in the company's shops a separate account or order should be kept with each, to ascertain the actual cost, the cost of furniture, fixtures, tools, material, special expense, superintendence, fuel, in fact everything needed for the locomotive or car, for actual service, should be included in the cost. To the cost thus found, ten per cent. should be added to cover cost of transportation of material, wear and tear of tools and machinery, interest, light, etc.

When a locomotive or car burns up, or is destroyed, is lost or worn out, the one taking its place must be charged to operating expenses.

When rolling stock has once been charged to equipment, it must thereafter be kept in an equally good condition, all repairs or renewals being charged to the operating or current expense accounts.

Improvements.

This heading is intended to embrace the disbursements having for their object the betterment of the original property of the company, where a portion of the charges for the accounts to be opened under it belong to operating expenses, and a portion to construction. For instance: If a shingle roof on a Passenger Station be replaced with a slate roof, this would be improving the property, and the amount the slate roof cost in excess of the original cost of the shingle roof would be a proper charge to Construction.

The value of an improvement, without reference to the relative cost, would also be charged to Construction.

All disbursements for work of this character should be charged under the head of "Improvements," but great caution should be excercised to prevent any unjust or questionable charges being made.

Improvement accounts should be so concise and clear that the Treasurer may know just the kind of work done, without further inquiry. For instance: a Wood Bridge is to be replaced with an Iron one, the account should be "Improvement," replacing No. 10 Wood Bridge between Cleveland and Lorain, Cleveland Division, with Iron Bridge.

Road accountants should make a special monthly report to the Treasurer, of all accounts that come under the head of Improvements. This report should give an accurate description of the structure or thing being replaced or improved, and the original cost of the thing replaced. If the original cost is not known, or cannot be ascertained, the estimated cost should be given. This report should contain such other information as will enable the Treasurer to accurately determine the difference between the original or first cost and the cost or value of the improvement when completed.

The proportion of the improvement belonging to operating expenses as entered up by road accountants, should be charged to the different divisions by the Treasurer, to the accounts to which the improvements naturally belong. Until each improvement is completed, the total expended upon it should be charged by him to operating expenses.

Rebuilding.

In regard to the class of accounts that come under the head of rebuilding, it may be stated that when the cost of repairs or renewals is likely to exceed one-half the original cost, then, and not otherwise, an account should be opened under the head of "Rebuilding."

This account is intended to include the cost of renewing structures, that they may be practically the same when reconstructed, as when they were first built, and charged to Construction. For instance: if a freight-house should burn down, or from wear and tear require practically to be rebuilt, the cost of same should be charged upon the distribution books and accounts under "Rebuilding."

This same rule applies, generally to any bridge, building or structure that may be rebuilt.

An account should be opened whenever a building or stationary structure of any kind is rebuilt, giving the name, location and division, as "Rebuilding Kay's Water Station, Cleveland Division."

Road accountants must not charge the analogous operating account, for the cost of rebuilding anything, when a separate account has been opened for "Rebuilding."

Open an account with every particular engine, car or new equipment that is to be substantially rebuilt to replace rolling stock or machinery destroyed or worn out, as "Rebuilding Engine 640."

The cost of rebuilding equipment should include the cost of furniture and fixtures appertaining to the same.

The Treasurer should keep a special record of all structures rebuilt. When completed he should charge the proper accounts to the different divisions.

Bond Interest.

An account is kept with Bond Interest and is to be charged with the total amount of the interest on the mortgage bonds. If there is accrued interest on the bonds when they are sold, the account should be credited for the amount. Bond Interest should be entered on the books each month as it accrues. The estimate is made at the commencement of the fiscal year, for six months in advance, on the basis of the bonded debt. One sixth of the interest thus found for the half-year should be entered up monthly; any differences that may occur in consequence of bonds being withdrawn and cancelled, or new bonds issued during the half-year, should be considered in the charge for the sixth month. The amount of interest thus charged should be credited to "Accrued Bond Interest."

The actual interest paid by the company each month, should be charged each month to the account of "Accrued Bond Interest." The amount of interest thus charged should correspond with the cancelled coupons in the coupon register, and the vouchers for interest on the registered bonds outstanding.

Premium on Gold Coupons.

This account is supplementary to Bond Interest, and should appear with it under the liabilities of "Accrued Bond Interest." It embraces the premium paid on the interest due on coupon and registered gold bonds.

The amount of premium should be estimated and charged each month the same as directed for Bond Interest. The entry for the sixth month should be made to harmonize exactly with the charges for the premium actually paid for the half-year.

Interest and Exchange.

This account is to be charged with the interest paid on the floating debt, the amount paid for foreign or domestic exchange, the premium paid for the company's own bonds, and for the discount or loss suffered in the sale of securities owned by the company, except the securities issued by the company. The account should be credited for the interest received from securities and money loaned.

When the account is closed with a credit balance, the amount of such credit should be deducted in the statements from "Bond Interest." When the balance is on the debit side, the amount should appear in the reports as a charge to Income.

Rental of Leased Lines.

This account represents the rental of lines leased or rented by the Company, in which it has not a controlling proprietary interest. It should be charged each month, with the rental accruing for such month, using a separate account for each line or company. The account does not embrace any portion of the current working or incidental expenses of leased or rented lines. The Company does not pay, nor is it responsible for the interest on the bonded debt of the leased lines.

Dividends on Stock.

An account should be opened for the dividend on each class of stock, as "Dividend No. 1—1896 on Preferred Stock," etc., the same as directed on pages 93, 94 and 116.

Office and Station Furniture.

An account must be opened for each division of the road for which expense is incurred for office and station furniture. Charge to this account the cost of all furniture, renewals and repairs, for use at stations, or in any of the offices of the company.

When the expense is not chargeable to any particular division, then a special account should be opened for such disbursements as, "Office & Station Furniture, Common." The proportion of this common expense is charged to the different divisions on the basis that the gross earnings of the different divisions bear to the gross earnings of the whole road.

The more important articles coming under this head are, awnings, axes, baggage trucks, brushes, brooms, counters, chairs, carpets, curtains, copying presses, clocks, desks, freight trucks, gas fixtures, inkstands, lamps, lanterns, letter boxes, sofas, stoves, tables, ticket cases, ticket stamps, telegraph instruments, wheelbarrows, waste baskets, water coolers, pails, warehouse trucks, saws, shovels, etc. This account must not be confused with Office and Station expenses.

Office and Station Expenses.

A separate account must be opened for each division incurring office and station expenses, and must not be confused with the office and station furniture. When the expense is on account of the whole road, a separate account should be opened and charged same as directed for Office and Station Furniture.

The more important items chargeable to this account are, horses, care of horses, harness, wagons, horse feed, cleaning offices, mail bags, printing time tables, printing notices and orders, postage, packing cases, repairs of wagons and harness, shoeing horses, lamps, hose, matches, marking pot, wrapping paper, twine, towels, soap, scrub brushes, nails, files, flags, chalk, water tanks, sponges, printing freight and passenger tariffs, etc., etc.

Furniture and Fixtures for Cars.

This account should be charged with the cost of repairs and renewals of furniture and fixtures in the passenger, baggage, express, mail, officers business and way cars. The furniture and expenses peculiar to offices in connection with officers' and business cars should be charged to their respective operating accounts for such disbursements.

The total amount entered under the head of Furniture and Fixtures for cars is apportioned and charged to the different divisions, on the basis that the mileage of the classes of cars on each division bears to the total mileage of such cars on the whole road. The material used should be charged to the account when it is sent out from the shops and store-houses.

Items belonging to this account are, axes, ashpans, water cans, wash basins, water coolers, ventilator sticks, tallow and waste buckets, switch ropes, switch chains, soap, wrenches, cuspidors, shovels, scoops, signs, stoves, stove fixtures, lamps, mail car lamps, oil cans, pokers, matting, matches, saws, sledges, hammers, hatchets, jack screws, keys, curtains, coal boxes, dippers, check boxes, dusters, flags, frogs, chisels, chairs, chair cushions, car cushions, bell cord and hangers, bullseye lamps, etc., etc.

Superintendence.

This account is charged with the salaries of the executive officers, general managers, heads of the principal departments and the superintendents of the several divisions. The salaries of the division superintendents should be charged to the division upon which they are engaged.

When a Superintendent has charge of more than one division, his salary should be apportioned between such divisions on the basis of the gross earnings of each to the whole. The salaries of the other officers coming under this head should be charged under an account as, " Superintendence Common," and the several divisions charged with their proportion on the basis of the gross earnings of such divisions to the gross earnings of the whole road.

When the expense is common, but for some particular branch of the services, such as the General Freight Agent, the expense should be allotted to the different divisions on the basis of the freight earnings of the different divisions to the freight earnings of the whole road, and the account should be charged on the distribution sheets as "Superintendence for Freight Common."

Agents and Clerks.

This account embraces the salaries of local and general agents, located at all points on the road. It also includes the salaries of train dispatchers, train masters, cashiers, assistants, clerks, telegraph operators, messenger boys, station baggagemasters (not baggagemen) check clerks, etc., at general and division offices and stations.

An account should be opened for the different divisions for which expense has been incurred under this head, charging such divisions with their proportion of wages of agents and clerks.

When the expense is common, but for some particular branch of the service, say for passanger business, the expense should be divided between the different divisions on the basis of the passenger earnings of the different divisions to the passenger earnings of the whole road.

When the wages are chargeable in common to the whole road, open an account as, say, "Agents and Clerks Common," and the amount thus charged should be divided between the different divisions, on the basis of the total earnings of the different divisions to the gross earnings of the whole road.

Foreign Agents.

This account is intended for the salaries and expenses of that branch of the services, having for its object the soliciting of business.

It is charged with the salaries and expenses, except the rent paid, of freight and ticket agencies treated at points off the line of the road. It is also charged for the salaries and traveling expenses of the General Passenger Agent and attaches of his office, and for the wages and expenses of traveling agents or solicitors of the company.

The proportion of this account chargeable to the different divisions is figured on the basis that the gross earnings of the different divisions bear to the gross earnings of the whole road, except when the disbursement is on account of some particular branch of the services, in which case it should be apportioned on the basis of the earnings of such branch.

Engineers, Firemen and Wipers.

This account is to be charged with the running time of locomotive engineers, firemen, and for the wages of wipers and dispatchers, at round houses and engine houses.

Should the engineers and firemen be employed in the shops, their time for such labor should be charged in the distribution of labor books the same as the time of others engaged in similar work.

The proportion of the account to be allotted to the several divisions is based on the percentage that the mileage of locomotives on the several divisions bears to the total mileage of locomotives on the whole road.

Conductors, Baggagemen and Brakemen.

This account is kept for the wages of conductors, baggagemen, and brakemen on passenger and freight trains. The wages of such persons, when employes are engaged exclusively on fuel and gravel trains, are charged to Fuel, Track Repairs, etc., as the case may be.

When conductors, baggagemen and brakemen run in common upon two or more divisions, the several divisions over which they run should be charged on the basis that the number of miles run on such divisions bears to the total miles run by them.

Laborers and Switchmen.

This account includes the time of laborers engaged at the shops in handling material and in performing other general work of a cheap and unskilled character, not properly chargeable to other accounts, such as common laborers about depots, coopers, delivery men, flagmen at crossings, freight house foremen, freight callers, inspectors, messengers, policemen, porters, station baggagemen (not baggage masters), scalesmen, switchmen in yards, telegraph repairmen, warehousemen, yardmasters, etc.

The account is also charged for such labor as tearing down buildings, placing derailed cars and locomotives on track, handling freight disturbed by wrecks or lost from cars, pumping water, supplying engines with fuel and improving station and shop grounds.

When the wages of laborers and switchmen are chargeable in common to the whole road, the amount thus charged should be apportioned to the different divisions, on the basis of the total earnings of the different divisions to the gross earnings of the whole road.

Track Repairs.

Each division of the road should have an account with track repairs, and should be charged with the wages of roadmasters, track foreman, track men, track watchmen, flagmen, conductors, brakemen and other men connected with gravel trains, men employed in gravel pits, including the tools used by them.

This account is also charged with the cost of keeping tunnels in order, the cost of loading and unloading iron, steel and ties, ditching and ballasting track, the cost of ditching and clearing and removing ice and snow, cutting weeds, brush and grass, and the expenses of track scales. New ties, iron and steel rails, and all other track material should be charged directly to this account at the time it is distributed

Ties are charged to the division for which they were purchased as fast as they are inspected and delivered. When new iron and steel rails are purchased, they are charged by the Purchasing Agent at the time the bills are credited for payment, "New Iron and Steel Rails on Hand." As fast as they are distributed for use on the line, the different divisions should be charged.

Track repairs should be charged with the value of the iron to be laid less the value of the old iron to be taken up, estimating ten per cent loss in weight. When steel is used to replace iron rails, the difference between the value of new iron and steel is properly chargeable to Construction. The value of the old material taken up should be charged to "Track Material on Hand," and the total value of the iron or steel laid down is credited to "New Iron and Steel Rails on Hand "

All material and labor expended upon the construction of new side tracks, or the taking up of old side tracks, should be charged to Track Repairs; at the end of the fiscal year the actual number of feet laid is ascertained, also the exact number of feet taken up, the balance of the account is adjusted by charging it to new construction and crediting track repairs, or vice versa, as the case required.

Side Tracks.

At the end of each fiscal year, the superintendents of the several divisions are required to report the number of feet of side tracks laid during the year, specifying for each siding its section and location; the quantity and kind of rails, and the rate and cost for each; the quantity, rate and cost for common and switch ties, bolts, spikes, splices, angle bars, fish plate, joints, frogs, switches and fixtures, the cost of labor, and the total cost of each side track.

Track Inventory.

An inventory of track material and tools is taken on the last day of the fiscal year, under the direction of the division superintendents.

The inventory must embrace an accurate record of all old and new track material on hand, not actually in use, except iron and steel rails. It is taken by the different section foremen and others, and is consolidated for the division in the offices of the different division superintendents. The consolidated inventory for each division, with the detailed section inventories from which it is made, must be forwarded to the Purchasing Agent without price or cost.

Fence, Gate and Crossing Repairs.

All material embraced under the head of this account is charged up at the time the material is distributed from the different storehouses and shops of the company. This account is charged with the expenses of keeping viaducts and overhead bridges in repair, the cost of railways running under the track, in fact, all expenses incurred for crossings for the convenience and safety of the public, not necessary to the actual existence and operation of the track. The cost of keeping in repair the cattle guards, hedges, trees, stock yards, snow fences, signs at crossings, etc., is charged to this account.

Fence Material Inventory.

A separate inventory should be taken of the material belonging to the department of fences, gates and crossings. The inventory is to be taken under the direction of the division superintendents, upon the same principle as that governing the track inventory, etc.

Repairs of Bridges and Culverts.

This account is charged with the expenditures for repairing bridges and culverts, except the cost of rails, ties, spikes, bolts, chairs and splices used upon the track, which are properly chargeable to track repairs.

This account is also charged with the wages of bridge watchmen, the disbursements on account of houses for watchmen, and the expense of keeping the same in repair, the supplies used in the watch houses, the wages of men engaged upon pile-drivers, the cost of filling trestle bridges or similar structures, and the wages of men from other branches of the service, for the time worked upon this class of structures.

When an important bridge or culvert is rebuilt, wholly or in part, a separate account should be opened with it, as, "Rebuilding Tinkers Creek Bridge, Cleveland Division."

The following are the different classes of structures coming under the head of this account, with the characteristics peculiar to each, viz:

Stone Arch Culvert.—Arch, bench walls, excavation for foundation on hard pan, piles or timber, foundation, filling, paving, spandel-walls and wings.

Open Culvert.—Covering, plank, stone or timber sides.

Iron Bridge.—Substructure. — Excavations for foundation on hard pan, stone piles or timber, foundation, pier, wall plate, superstructure for Iron Bridge, bottom chord, floor beams, lateral rods and pins, posts, painting, suspension bars, stringers, top chord.

Wood Bridge.—(Howe Truss and combination.) — Substructure.—Bolsters, caps, foundation, mud-sills, piles, posts, sills, sway-brace bolts and washers, wall plates. Superstructure.—Angle blocks, bottom chord, chord bolts and washers, clamps and keys, floor beams, lateral blocks and braces, top chord, truss rods, tie plates, stringers, vertical braces, vibration braces.

Wood Bridge.—(Trestle or Pile.)—Caps, mud-sills, piles, posts, sills, stringers, stringer bolts and washers, sway braces, sway-brace bolts and washers.

Water Station and Fuel Shed Repairs.

The principal items of expense in connection with water stations are: House for pumping engine, house for watchmen, hose, labor expended in repairing, pumping engines, pumps, pump fixtures, penstocks, buckets, stoves, tanks, tubs, windmills, wells, waterhouses, etc.

The following are the principal items coming under the head of fuel sheds: Fuel houses, coal bins, coal buckets, cranes, derricks, labor platforms, scoops, chutes, sieves, wood or coal yards, wood racks, wheel barrows, etc.

Every item charged under the heading of this account must specify the location and name of the structure upon which the expense was incurred.

When any structure, coming under this account, is rebuilt, a separate account must be opened for it.

When offices proper are used in connection with these buildings, the furniture and fixtures for such should be charged as directed for offices.

"Freight and Passenger Station Repairs."

Each division of the line should keep an account for repairs of freight and passenger stations, and charge it with all work done, material furnished, or money expended on same. When a structure is rebuilt, a special account should be opened with it.

The class of structures coming under the head of this account, are:

Baggage rooms or houses, eating houses, express houses, elevators, freight offices, freight houses, general office, merchandise and ore docks, offices of superintendents and assistants, platforms for freight and passengers, waiting rooms, residences, stables, ticket offices, telegraph offices, ware-houses, etc., etc.

Shop and Engine House Repairs.

All charges to this account must specify the exact location and the name of the structure for which disbursement is made. Whenever a structure coming under this account is re-built a separate account must be opened for it.

The principal structures coming under this account are as follows: Blacksmith shops, boiler shops, bridge builders' shops, car shops, car repair sheds, cooper shops, oil houses, paint shops, pattern rooms, round houses, rail mills, store houses and platforms, shop offices, scrap houses, shop fences, shop grounds and yards, tin shops, tool rooms, turn tables, etc.

Repairs put upon turn tables come under this head, but the cost of putting up, or repairing any machinery that may be used in any of the buildings named is not properly chargeable to this account.

Engine and Tender Repairs.

This account is charged with all labor and material expended in keeping the engines and tenders in as good condition as when originally constructed. Whenever reference is made to engines or locomotives it must be understood to embrace the tenders as well. When an engine is rebuilt wholly or in great part, an account should be opened with it, as, "Rebuilding Engine No. 625." This account is also charged with the fuel consumed by the blacksmiths and others while at work upon the engines.

The proportion of expenses of the different divisions of the road for keeping engines in repair is arrived at in the office of the Local Treasurer, and is based upon the mileage of locomotives: i. e. the charge to each division for repairs bears the same proportion to the cost for the whole road that the mileage of locomotives on each division bears to the mileage of the whole road.

Tools and Machinery Repairs.

This account is charged with the cost of repairing and renewing the tools and machinery used in shops, engine rooms, engine houses,

.ses, rail mills, foundries, etc. It includes all expenditures .r plows, steam pumps in shops and engine houses, machinery .ixtures peculiar to steam shovels, pile drivers, wrecking cars, etc., .o the oil and waste used in lubricating and the cost of waste used in cleaning machinery, and the labor on same, except stationary engineers.

The total cost for keeping tools and machinery in repair is charged to the several divisions on the same basis as that of engine and tender repairs.

Passenger and Baggage Car Repairs.

This account is charged with all items of labor and material used in connection with the repairs of passenger, baggage, mail, express, officers and business cars, including air-brakes and fixtures, air and steam heating apparatus, labor, lubricating, cleaning, also the tools used by car repairers, lubricators, lighting, cleaning, etc., except "furniture and fixtures" otherwise specified.

If a car is rebuilt, wholly or in great part, a separate account must be opened for it, as, "Rebuilding Baggage Car No. 40."

The expense of repairing passenger and baggage cars is apportioned to the different divisions of the road, on the basis that the mileage of the cars on such divisions bears to the total mileage of the cars in question on the whole line; that is to say, the charge to each division for repairs of passenger, baggage, express, mail, officers, and business cars bears the same proportion to the cost for the whole road, that the mileage of such cars on each division bears to the total mileage made by such cars on the whole line.

Freight Car Repairs.

This account includes all classes of freight and common cars, such as box, boarding, caboose, way, coal ditching, flat, gravel, milk, ore, refrigerator, stock, dump and hand cars, also wrecking and pile-driving cars, but not the machinery belonging to the same.

The general class of items chargeable to this account are the same as given for passenger and baggage cars. The cost of tools used in repairing this class of cars, also the cost of links and pins should be charged to this account.

If the tools furnished car repairers are used by them in common on passenger and freight cars, the cost should be charged to these accounts on the basis that each class of cars bears to the total number of cars on the whole road.

If a car is rebuilt, a separate account should be opened for "Rebuilding Box Car No. 1050." If a number of cars are rebuilt at the same time, and material and labor are being expended in common upon them, open an account with the lot, as "Rebuilding stock 250-251, 259."

If the company rebuild cars belonging to another company, a separate account should be opened for it.

The proportion to be allotted to each division for keeping freight cars in repair, is based on the proportion which the mileage of freight cars on each division bears to the total mileage of freight cars on the whole road.

Foreign Car Repairs.

All labor expended and material used on foreign cars should be charged the same in all respects as are the cars belonging to the company.

A detailed statement of all labor expended and material used on cars belonging to other companies is sent to the Car Accountant on the first of each month for the preceding month, so that the superintendent may be able to act intelligently in disposing of the charges.

Upon receipt of this statement, the superintendent of the Car Department will make bills against the different companies, whenever it is proper to do so, usually adding 15 per cent.

The cost of repairs upon new cars or engines, belonging to other companies, in transit over the company's lines, should be paid by the station agent, and the amount added to the way-bill, as advanced charges.

Fuel.

All fuel should be charged at the time the accounts are credited for payment, a separate account being kept for coal and wood.

Coal.

This account is charged with the first cost of the coal, including the amount paid for transportation over other lines, the cost of loading and unloading, and the wages of watchmen, inspectors and others employed in connection with it, not otherwise provided for.

All fuel purchased for use by the blacksmiths, tinsmiths, boiler makers and other mechanics at the shops, should be charged the same as other material, to the shop to which it is forwarded.

Wood.

...a...unt is charged with the first cost of the wood, including ...aid for transportation over other lines, the cost of loading the...g, and the wages of watchmen, inspectors, wood train a...pense of preventing and putting out fires, and all other ...connected with this branch, not otherwise provided for.

Fuel Inventory.

...t ...e end of each half-year an accurate inventory is taken of all ...and belonging to the company, a separate inventory being ...ire... for wood and coal. These inventories should show the ...nti... and quality of sawed and unsawed, hard and soft wood, hard ...d soft coal, slack, etc., at each point on the line.

The total amount charged to "Coal" and "Wood" respectively ...made to harmonize exactly with the inventories, the difference between the inventories and balances on the books being charged or credited, as the case requires, to the different expense accounts for fuel, on the basis of the relative amounts already charged to such accounts at the time the inventories are taken.

In like manner the balance standing on the books under the head of material, track material, iron and steel rails, etc., is made to harmonize accurately with the amount of the several inventories specified, any difference there may be, being charged or credited, as the case requires, to the different accounts affected, on the basis of the relative amount charged to the several operating accounts using the particular kind of material embraced in the inventory at the time the inventories are taken.

Fuel Used by Locomotives.

Charge this account with all fuel consumed by locomotives in active service. The fuel used upon engines while in the shop for repairs, should be charged as a part of the cost of the repairs.

The fuel used by locomotives is charged to the divisions on which it was used.

Fuel and Lights Used in Cars.

This account is charged with the cost of oil, kerosene, gasoline, wicking, candles, etc., used for lighting all classes of cars. The cost for lights is charged at the time the material is sent out, to stations and elsewhere, from the storehouses having such material in charge.

It is charged with the fuel used in heating all classes of cars, and the wages of those employed in this connection.

The total amount charged to this account is apportioned to the different divisions of the road, on the basis that the mileage of passenger, baggage, mail, express, business and caboose cars on the different divisions bears to the total mileage of such cars on the whole road.

Fuel and Lights Used in Shops and Stations.

This account is to be charged with the cost of oil, gasoline, kerosene, gas, electric lights, wicking and fuel used in lighting and heating shops, stations, offices and buildings, also the amount consumed for signals, switches and tracks.

The cost of lighting and heating material is charged at the time it is sent out, a separate account being kept with each division.

The fuel used at water stations and fuel sheds; also the fuel and lights used by stationary engines, wrecking cars, pile drivers and steam shovels should be charged to this account.

When the cost is not properly chargeable to any particular division, then a special account should be opened, as " Fuel and Lights used at Stations and Shops, Common." The proportion of this common expense is charged to the different divisions on the basis that the gross earnings of the different divisions bear to the gross earnings of the whole road.

Oil, Waste and Tallow Used by Locomotives.

The oil, waste and tallow used to light and lubricate locomotives, (not the cost of labor) should be charged to this account. The oil and waste used in repairing engines in shops is not to be charged to this account, but it is charged the same as other material.

The proportion of the amount chargeable to the different divisions is based on the mileage of locomotives, the same as repairs of engines and tenders.

Oil, Waste and Tallow Used on Cars.

The oil, waste and tallow (not the cost of labor) used in lubricating all classes of cars, is charged to this account. The material to be used for this purpose should be charged at the time it is distributed from the shops or storehouses.

. The proportion of this account belonging to the different divisions is apportioned on the basis that the mileage of cars on the different divisions bears to the total mileage of cars on the whole road.

Advertising.

This account is charged with the cost of advertising the road in books, newspapers, railway guides, magazines, hand bills, folders, maps, etc., including the cost of frames, glass, fixtures, bulletin boards and distribution.

The account is apportioned to the different divisions on the basis that the passenger earnings of the different divisions bear to the total passenger earnings of the whole road.

Insurance.

This account is charged with the cost of insuring the property of the company, or the property intrusted to the company, the expense of collecting insurance, etc.

When the insurance does not belong to any particular division, but chargeable to some particular branch of the service, the account should be kept as, "Insurance Common," and allotted to the different divisions on the basis of the earnings of the different divisions, from the department interested, to the earnings of the whole road from such departments.

Rents.

Charge to this account the rent of offices, buildings and grounds, but not the expense of keeping them in repair.

Each division should have its own account for Rents, but when the expense is in common for the whole road, or some particular department, it should be treated precisely the same as for "Superintendence."

Taxes.

All taxes assessed and paid on the real estate, personal property and earnings of the company for national, state, county and municipal purposes and for sinking funds of county bonds, etc., not otherwise provided for, are chargeable to this account.

When the tax belongs in common to the whole road, or to certain divisions, it should be apportioned to the different divisions on the basis of the relative gross earnings of such division.

Car Hire Paid Over Amount Received.

This account is charged with the amount paid for the use of cars belonging to other companies, on the different divisions, over and above the amount received by the company for the use of its cars by foreign roads.

If the amount charged for any month, for the use of the company's cars used by other roads, exceeds the amount credited to other companies for the use of their cars, the balance should be included in " Miscellaneous Earnings "

Stationery, Printed Blanks and Tickets.

This account is charged with all stationery, printed blanks and tickets used by the company. The proportion of this account is chargeable to the different divisions on the basis that the total earnings of the different divisions bear to the aggregate earnings of the whole road.

The stationery and printed blanks are in charge of the Stationery Clerk, and the tickets under the control of the General Passenger Agent. At the close of the fiscal year, a special inventory is taken by the Stationery Clerk upon forms furnished him.

Loss and Damage.

This account is charged with the cost of freight, baggage lost and damaged, the amount paid for property destroyed by fire or otherwise, for live stock killed or injured, attorneys' fees, court expenses, wages and expenses of adjusters, and others specially employed in connection with this branch of the service. These items should be charged to the divisions upon which the expense was incurred, if it is known; when it is not known, the amount becomes common to the whole road.

When the expense is common to the whole road, it is apportioned to the different divisions on the basis of the gross earnings of the different divisions to the aggregate earnings of the whole road.

When the expense is common to the whole road, but chargeable to some particular branch of the service , it is allotted to the different divisions on the basis of the earnings of the different divisions from the departments interested, to the earnings of the whole road from such departments.

Injury to Persons.

This account is charged with disbursements on account of persons killed or injured. It includes court costs, fees and expenses of attorneys, doctors, coroners, undertakers' fees, board bills, hotel expense, the wages of those specially employed in connection with this department. also the time of employees detailed as witnesses.

Each division of the road should keep an account with Injury to Persons, but when this cannot be done, the expense becomes common to the whole road, it is then apportioned to the different divisions on the basis of the gross earnings of the different divisions to the total earnings of the whole road.

Teaming Freight, Baggage and Mails.

To this account is charged the amounts paid for delivery, transferring and hauling freight with trucks and wagons, the wages of the men employed, the cost of the teams, trucks and wagons and the expenses incident thereto, when employed for this service only. It also includes the cost of transferring baggage, mails, etc.

Each division should have its own account unless the expense does not belong to any particular division, it is then treated as directed for "Loss and Damage," under similar circumstances.

Material.

The charges to this account are made at the time the accounts of purchase are entered by the Auditor for payment, and should embrace all material on hand at the several shops and storehouses. All bills should be audited for payment in the month in which the material is received. Each shop or storehouse should be charged on the books at the time the bill is audited for payment, provided it has been received and receipted for by the clerk in charge.

All charges for freight on material over other lines, should be charged as part of the cost of such material.

When material is given out, it is charged by the clerks at the shops and storehouses to the accounts upon which it is used, at invoice prices.

An accurate account of all material received, manufactured and disbursed, is kept by the clerks at shops and storehouses.

Old Material and Scrap.

This account is charged with all material which may accumulate or reach the different shops and storehouses. The accounts from which it is received should be credited. When this class of material is forwarded to another shop, it must be invoiced and charged to that shop, the same as new material; or if it is used for any purpose it must be charged to the account upon which it is used, the same as if it were new.

Old Rails.

When old rails and scrap are sent to rolling mills or otherwise disposed of, from shops and storehouses after having been taken as "Old Material," they must be accounted for.

Iron and Steel Rail Inventory.

On the last day of each fiscal year, a separate inventory should be taken for old and new iron and steel rails on hand, giving the linear part and weight of each class. The instructions in reference to track material and tools describe exactly the form to be observed in regard to the inventory of Iron and Steel Rails.

Various Persons.

This account represents the charges against individuals and corporations, except railroads, transportation companies and local traffic accounts.

Accounts of this character are entered on a special Register in the Auditor's office, each bill being credited to the account or accounts entitled to it.

Miscellaneous Expense.

This account is charged with all general legal services and expenses, including fees and expenses incidental to suits in courts, the fees of the Trustees of the mortgage bonds, the expenses incident to the meetings of stockholders and directors, the expenses for the detection and punishment of crimes against the company and the traveling expenses of officers (when not otherwise provided for) and other miscellaneous, necessary and proper expenses.

The expenses connected with this account should be charged to the division to which they actually belong.

When not chargeable to any particular division, an account should be kept with "Miscellaneous Expenses Common;" and each division charged with its proportion on the basis of the gross earnings of the different divisions to the gross earnings of the whole road.

The salaries of the heads of shops, foremen, clerks, storekeepers, superintendents of bridges and buildings, should be equitably apportioned and charged to the several accounts or works in progress, the basis being the amount of time devoted to each, no charge being allowed to any labor expense account.

CHAPTER TWENTY-SIX.

Electric Light Accounting.

There are very few electric light companies, who keep their accounts in such shape that they may know the unit cost of supplying electric current.

In this lesson we shall endeavor to illustrate a system, whereby the actual cost of Arc and Incandescent lighting and Motor Power may be ascertained.

To devise a system of accounts specially adapted to Electric Light Stations, one should have a thorough knowledge of the construction, operation and management, while the construction is mechanical, and is not within the scope of this work, we will have to pass it, and direct our attention to the forms used in operation and management.

The items of expense necessary to operate a large station are very numerous, and unless the practical operations are well systematized and the working force well disciplined, it will be difficult to arrive at accurate results, even with a well devised system of accounts.

In starting a new plant, considerable time will be required to organize and systematize the working forces as well as in the preparation of the books and records.

After a company has been formed, or, if an old company is to be re-organized, the first point to be considered is the organization of its officers, and employees. This organization depends, however, upon the size of the plant, and the local conditions. The system herein illustrated is intended for a large plant, therefore, variations can easily be made, to meet the requirements of small or medium sized plants.

For the benefit of those unfamiliar with the organization, operation and management of an Electric Light plant, we will first direct our attention to the plan of organization, forms of reports and record books, thereby gaining a better understanding of the accounts to be used.

A careful examination of the following diagram will give a sufficient knowledge of organization, without further explanation.

Organization of an Electric Light Plant.

Stockholders.
Directors.

President.

Counsel

Gen'l Mgr.

Secretary.

Treasurer.

Auditor.

Asst.
Mgr.

Purchasing
Agent

Canvassers.

Collect'r.

General Superintendent.

Chief
Book-keeper.

Cashier.

Assistant
Book-keeper.

Asst. Supt.

Supt. of Construction.

Electrician.

Chief
Engineer.

Dynamo
Engineer.

Trimmers.

Storekeeper
and Clerks.

Inspectors. — Day. — Arc. / Incandescent. / Motor.

— Night. — Arc. / Incandescent. / Motor.

Electrical
Instruments
Testing
Mchy.

Installation
Inspector.

Insulator.

Foreman.
Cables
and
Conduits. — Linemen. — Arc. / Incandescent. / Motor.

Asst. Engr.

Steam Fitter.

Coal Heavers.

Firemen.

Oilers.

Asst. Engr.

Repairers.

Oilers.

Cleaners.

Foremen.
Overhead
Construc-
tion. — Groundmen.

Carpenters. — Helpers.

Masons.

Trucks.

After the company has been formed, and the working force thoroughly organized, then the details of the management or operation should be systematized. In referring to the management or operation, we mean that relating to reports and records only.

The forms herein given are all practical, and while they may not be perfect in every case, they will be found very useful in connection with the general books, to arrive at the unit costs for supplying current.

The kilowatt is the unit necessary for electricians, but for the convenience of the officials, some less technical unit should be used. The Incandescent-lamp-hour and the Arc-lamp-hour are practical terms, easily understood, and easily converted to or from Kilowatts.

The Arc-hour unit is a necessity, where Arc-lamps of different Candle Power (c. p.) are used, as the expenses are about the same for the various sizes, excepting fuel and carbons.

The lamp-hour is a convenient unit, from the fact that many companies sell current upon that basis.

As soon as the company is ready to supply current, they should seek to obtain customers, all of whom should make application upon a blank form, furnished by the company. When the following form is used, and the conditions are complied with, it becomes a contract. Many companies use a special form for contract, but it is not recommended, because it appears too much like an ironclad legal document, and in this way lose a great many customers, that might otherwise be secured.

It frequently happens that customers will require an increase in their supply of current. When such is the case, they should sign an "Increase Application." The increase application blanks should be printed upon paper of a different color than the original. The original application should not be destroyed, but remain on file and the increase application attached to it.

The form of contract is an important matter, but if this form of application is used, it will meet all requirements.

No.----------

Application.

Cleveland,----------

Forest City Electric Light and Power Co.

The undersigned requests you to place on the premises, No.----------Street, in such position as designated by----------Electric Lights or----------as follows:

Incandescents.				Motors.			Arcs.	Nights per Week.	To Burn.		Period of Contract.
				H. P.	H. P.	Fan.			From	To	From
10 C.P.	16 C.P.	20 C.P.	32 C.P.						........M.	........M.	To

To be supplied with electric current daily as stated above, for which----------agree to pay monthly at the rate of----------cents per night for arc-lamps, and----------cents per month per incandescent lamp, and----------cents per----------hour for current supplied through meter, or----------per month for motor power. It is understood and agreed that you are to furnish all apparatus, fixtures, and material for arc-lights, and make all connections from your main circuits to the building, also connections to circuits for incandescent lighting or motors.

It is further agreed and understood that all fixtures for incandescent lighting are to be furnished by----------, and that the wiring will be done upon the latest improved methods, and is to be done by----------, and for which----------agree to pay at the rate of----------per lamp. This application is subject to the conditions printed on the back, and of which they are to be considered a part.

Accepted----------   Signed----------

Forest City Electric Light and Power Co.

Per----------   Per----------

All Agreements or promises outside of the terms of this contract are unauthorized.

The following should be printed upon the back of the application:

Application No............

Cleveland, O..............................189......

Name...

Address...

Contract begins...

Expires...

Work order No................Issued........................

Conditions.

1st.   That.........will carefully protect all lamps and other equipments, and be responsible for the safety of those within our buildings.

2nd.   ....will not allow any person access to lamps, equipment, etc., except the employees of your company, who show Company Badge.

3rd.   That.........will pay all expense for changing or altering lamps or other equipments made at..................request.

4th.   That the whole amount of this contract shall become due and payable, if payment be not made, as herein agreed.

5th.   That all claims for non-service, shall be made in writing to the company, within ten days of the time, when such non-service occurred.

6th.   That.........will notify the company, in writing, to continue or discontinue the service of current at the expiration of this contract. Failing to give such written notice, within.........days, then it shall be understood and agreed, that this contract has been renewed for the same time, and at the same prices as heretofore.

7th.   That any failure on the part of the Forest City Electric Light and Power Co. to furnish current shall not render said Company liable for damages beyond a pro rata deduction from its bills for the actual loss of time.

8th.   That.........hereby release the Forest City Electric Light and Power Co. from all claims on account of damage by fire, when the wiring, placing of lamps and other equipments within the building is done in compliance with the requirements of city ordinances or the Board of Fire Underwriters; and

9th.   That.........will grant the Forest City Electric Light and Power Company all necessary privileges for i troducing and maintaining said lamps and other equipments and wires; the placing of the lamps and equipments and furnishing lights by you is the consideration for ....agreement herein.

Contract Record.

All applications that have been accepted by the company, are entered in the Contract Record, a form of which is given below. A careful examination of the form, will show its usefulness, as columns are provided for the proper distribution of equipment, which can be easily recapitulated to show the amount of apparatus of all kinds connected for service. This cost should include everything from the outside line to, and into the building, including transformers and arc-lamps.

In the early years of electric lighting, all wiring of buildings and the installation of all apparatus was done by the lighting companies, but the wonderful development in the electrical field, in recent years has produced many electrical engineers and contractors by whom most of the wiring and installation is now done, leaving the company to furnish only the street-service connection, current and perhaps arc-lamps and transformers, however, the contract record is designed to meet all requirements. The accounts to be charged with the cost of wiring installation, etc., are treated hereafter, under the subject of "Installation."

The first form may be used as the left, and the second the right hand page. If the customers are numerous, it can be ruled as a single page.

Work Orders.

A written order should be issued by the proper person for all work requiring labor and material. These orders should be written upon a printed form, on which an account of labor and material should be accurately kept, in order that all expenditures may be charged to the proper accounts. Each order should be numbered, and all reference to that job should be made by the order number printed thereon.

The form of work order following that of the contract record, is simple and can be used for all departments. Some managers use different blanks of different color, for different departments, but it will be found better to use a single standard for all purposes.

When a great many orders are used, rubber stamps can be used to good advantage, by having them made to fit the blank space between the printed lines, covering all necessary points for the more important divisions for which orders are issued.

The form of work-order shown should be printed upon good paper, perforated, numbered and bound into books of about 200 each. A convenient size for the order is 5″ x 6″, and the stub 4″ x 5″.

Work Order.

Order No.---Date -------	The Forest City Electric Light & Power Co.
To ---------------------	
Work -------------------	Work Order No.------Date------------------
	To.-------------------------------
	Proceed at once to execute the following instructions and keep an accurate account of all material and labor on the back of this order, and use the above order number for all storeroom orders and time tickets.
	(The details of the order are written here or printed with rubber stamps.)
Work completed and returned by----------189--	Completed--------189-- Signed------Foreman.

Stockkeeper's Requisition.

The stockkeeper should have a blank form, upon which to notify the Purchasing Agent of the need of supplies. The form required is simple, and will not be illustrated.

Purchasing Agent's Stock Order.

The Purchasing Agent should use a blank form, printed with copying ink, in ordering material and supplies. A special impression book should be kept in which all orders should be copied, and when the goods have been received, a record of it should be made on the letter press copy. This form is simple and need not be shown.

(Left-hand page.)

Contract Record.

Name of Customer.	Number and Street.	Number of Contract.	Date of Contract.	Term of Contract.	Contract Begins.	Contract Expires.	Rate.

(Right-hand page.)

The Forest City Electric Light and Power Co.

Installation.			Work Order Number.	Incandescent Lamps.						Motors.				Arc Lamps.										Circuit Number.
Cost of Material.	Cost of Labor.	Total Cost.		.... C. P.	.... C. P.	.... C. P.	.... C. P.	.... C. P.	.... C. P.	Number.	H. P. Each.	Volts.	Maximum Amperes.	1 Night. o'clock.	1 Night. o'clock.	6 Nights. All Day.	6 Nights. All Night.	6 Nights. o'clock.	6 Nights. o'clock.	7 Nights. All Day.	7 Nights. All Night.	7 Nights. o'clock.	7 Nights. o'clock.	

NOTE.—Convenient size for double page 10" x 14"; single 12" x 24".

Stockkeeper's Receipt for Material.

When supplies have been received by the Stockkeeper, he should notify the Purchasing Agent, by using a special blank. This will enable him to check up invoices, orders, etc. The form is a simple one and needs no further explanation.

Foreman's Order for Material.

All material required by workmen must be obtained from the stockkeeper, upon a written order from the Foreman. These orders are then filed by the Stockkeeper as receipts.

In order that all material may be charged to the proper person or account, the "work-order" number must always be given. The General Manager's or Superintendent's approval is necessary only when large quantities or valuable material is required. The following form will answer every purpose:

Foreman's Requisition.   No.............

The Forest City Electric Light and Power Co.

..................................Stock Keeper.

Deliver to the bearer for use on Work Order No....................

Date................   ....Foreman.

Line Foreman's Report.

This report is to be made by the line foreman, and should be accurate. These reports should be made daily if more than one day is required to complete the job, they should then be attached to the work order and returned to the office. From these reports and work-order the accurate cost of that particular work can be ascertained.

Line Foreman's Report.
The Forest City Electric Light and Power Co.

Work Order No......

Date......

Employees.

No...... Foreman...... hrs. @......
...... Men "......
...... Men "......
...... Men "......
...... Men "......
...... Men "......
...... Men "......
...... Trucks "......

Employees.

No...... Foreman...... hrs. @......
...... Climbers "......
...... Groundmen "......
...... Trucks "......

Street Location.

From.	To.	Side.

Cross-arms put on.

2 Pin	4 Pin	6 Pin	8 Pin	10 Pin	12 Pin	14 Pin

New Circuit Number.
Attached to Circuit Number.

No. Holes Dug.	No. Poles Erected Removed.	Height Above Ground.

No. Feet Wire Strung Removed.	B. & S. Gauge.	Type of Installation.

Remarks.
....
....
....
....

Pole No...... on ...... side of ...... street,
Locate pins and wires on above diagram.

......Foreman.

Cable Foreman's Report.

The cable foreman's report is used by the foreman on cable or underground line work, in the same manner as that used by the line foreman for pole lines.

Cable Foreman's Report.

The Forest City Electric Light & Power Co.

Date....................　　　　　　　Work Order No...........

Location on what street or avenue.	Side of street.	No. feet cable drawn in or out.	B. and S. gauge.	Type of installation.	Cable circuit number.	Number joints made.	Name of insulator.	Name of plumber.

Diagram of Manhole.

Show on this diagram location of all cables drawn in or out.

	Men Employed.	Amount.	Remarks.
	No.		
	......Foreman.........hrs. at......		
	......Men............ " "		
	......Men............ " "		
	.... Men.............. " "		
	......Insulators........ " "		
	......Plumbers......... " "		
	......Inspectors........ " "		
	......Trucks........... " "		...............Foreman

Time Ticket.

The Forest City Electric Light and Power Co.

This Ticket must be in Office before 9 A. M.

Name ....

Occupation..........................　　　Work Order No..............

Make but One Entry on this Ticket.

Location of Job.	Regular Hours.	Extra Hours.	Rate.	Amount.

Approved...Foreman.

Time Tickets.

Each employee should fill out a time ticket for each day, and return it to the office, where they are copied into a time.book or pay-roll. Each ticket must be approved by the foreman.

While it may be somewhat bothersome, it will be found useful, to have workmen return a time ticket for "construction work" and another for "operation."

Space has been provided in the blank to locate the different jobs, the work order numbers and the number of hours, this places the responsibility for the man's time, and locates the expense.

The amount of fuel, water, oil, waste, etc., used, should be reported daily by the chief engineer. The items are few, the form simple and need not be shown.

The forms illustrated will be found sufficient to accurately determine the cost of construction and operation. Many other records are necessary, but as they do not bear directly upon the accounts, forms will not be given, it is sufficient to enumerate a few of them. A Pole Register is used, in which is shown the location and number of each pole. A Line Register is used, to show the location of circuits on poles, with a diagram of all attachments to every pole where the location or direction of wires has been changed. The Arc-circuit Register shows location and make-up of the circuit. A Transformer Register is used, to show the name of the customer cut in on it, the location, number of lamps wired, and the capacity. A Lamp-renewal Record is kept to show the number and value of the lamps renewed each month. A Conduit Record is kept to show the location, size and length of ducts, etc. A Record of Subsidiary Pipe connections is kept to show location, size, bends, boxes, etc. There is also an Output Register, for Constant-potential Circuits, and an Output Register, for arc-circuits, Meter book, etc., etc.

Before entering into a description of the general books, it is thought advisable to give the analysis and general classification of the accounts.

The following classification is submitted as embracing all the important features necessary to keep an accurate account of the different departments of the business.

The classification is treated under the following heads, viz.: Resources, Liabilities, Operating Expense, Income from Operation, Loss and Gain. These headings are subdivided and the matter that is properly chargeable to the different accounts is fully designated and explained.

Classification of Electric Light Accounts.

Resources.

Construction Accounts.
- Land.
- Station and Buildings.
- Motive Power.
- Arc Apparatus.
- Incandescent Apparatus.
- Power Apparatus.
- Pole-lines.
- Installations.
- Conduits.
- Cables.

Representative Accounts.
- Customers.
- Open Accounts Receivable.
- Bills Receivable.
- Investments.
- Sinking Fund.
- Store.
- Cash.
- Suspense.
- Insurance Advanced.
- Franchise and Patents.

Liabilities.
- Bills Payable.
- Open Accounts Payable.
- Wages Payable.
- Taxes Payable.
- Rents Payable.
- Interest Coupon Account Payable.
- Audited Vouchers Payable.
- Bonds Payable (Mortgage Account).
- Dividend Payable.
- Capital Stock.
- Surplus.

Manufacturing.
- Fuel.
- Water for boilers, water rent or tax
- Oil and Waste.
- Labor (on manufacturing).
- Repairs to Motive Power.
- Repairs to Electrical Apparatus.
- Sundries (Man'f'g).

Operating Expense.	Distribution.	Maintenance of Pole-lines. Maintenance of Conduits and Cables. Maintenance of Installations. Maintenance of Motors, Transformers, and Arc-lamps. Incandescent-lamp Renewals. Arc-globes. Carbons. Labor (on distribution). Sundries (on distribution).
	General Expense.	Maintenance of Real Estate and Buildings. Rents, Due and Accrued. Taxes, Due and Accrued. Insurance, Due and Accrued. Interest, Ordinary. Legal Expenses. Salaries, Office and Official. Labor (general expense). Sundries (general expense.)
	Income from Operation.	Power, Stationary Motors. Power for Street Railways. Arc-lighting, Street. Arc-lighting, Commercial. Incandescent Lighting, Street. Incandescent Lighting, Commercial. Incandescent Lighting, Residence. Rent of Meters. Rent of Motors. Miscellaneous Income.
	Loss and Gain Accounts.	Interest, Due and Accrued (Coupon Acct). Rebate. Depreciation (Machinery and Franchise). Loss and Gain. Dividends declared.

Resources.

The construction accounts as shown in the classification, are Land, Station and Buildings, Motive Power, Arc-Apparatus, Incandescent Apparatus, Power Apparatus, Pole-lines, Installations, Conduits, and Cables, and should be conducted as follows:

Land.—This account is charged with the cost of all land, waterways, dams, etc., owned by the company. The cost of all improvements of a permanent nature, belonging to this account must also be charged to it. If the improvement is an important one, an account should be kept with it to ascertain the exact cost, then when the books are closed, it should be closed into land account.

Stations and Buildings.—Charge this account with the cost of all buildings, stocks, etc., also the cost of permanent improvements. If desired, an account can be kept with the improvements, and at the end of the year, or when completed, it should be charged to station and building account.

Motive Power—The items chargeable to this account are engines, steam-boilers, pumps, piping, gearing, pulleys, shafting, water-wheels and all their appurtenances, including the first lot of belting up to the dynamo pulley; all permanent tools for the use of the department are also chargeable to it. The improvements made should be charged as in the land and building accounts.

Arc Apparatus.—The full cost of all arc--lighting, dynamos, connections, controllers, regulators, instruments, and switch boards belonging to the arc-lighting system, must be charged to arc-apparatus. Permanent improvements or increased facilities are chargeable as shown in the above accounts. When it becomes necessary to replace or repair arc-apparatus, it must be charged to "Repairs to Electrical Apparatus."

Incandescent Apparatus.—The full cost of all apparatus pertaining to incandescent lighting is chargeable to this account, such as, incandescent-lighting, dynamos, connections, transformers, exciters, regulating apparatus, switch boards and appliances, and meters for incandescent lighting; it is better, however, to keep a special account for meters. Improvements are charged as in Arc-Apparatus.

Power Apparatus.—This account is charged with the full cost of all apparatus used to furnish electric power, the items are, generators, dynamos, connections, regulators, switchboards, rheostats and exciters, used to generate electric current for power only. Improvements for this account are charged as above stated.

Pole-Lines.—This account is chargeable with the full cost of poles set, all lines of overhead wires, cross-arms, braces, and all apparatus outside the station, used on pole-lines, such as arc cut-out switches, junction and feeder boxes, lightning arresters, and connections to, but not including arc-lamps and transformers. The line, fixtures and first lamps used for incandescent street lighting, are also charged to this account.

Installations.—Charge to this account the cost of the installations of incandescent lamps, arc-lamps, motors and all other apparatus used by the customer, but owned by the company. Incandescent installation includes all material used on the customer's premises, belonging to the company. Arc installations include only the lamp and its attachments, and if the cost of hanging is not paid by the customer, it should be charged to "Expense," because Arc-lamps for commercial purposes are used somewhat temporarily, therefore, the cost of putting up is an expense, moreover the material used is seldom of any account after removal.

Conduits.—This account is chargeable with the full cost of constructing underground conduits for electrical conductors, including the cost of all subsidiary or service connections, to buildings and street lamp-posts, this also includes labor, material, unpaving and repaving, but does not include wires, cables or conductors.

Cables.—Charge to this account the cost of all subsidiary or service connections to buildings and street lamps, also the cost of all underground conductors of every kind.

Representative Accounts.

The representative accounts as shown in the classification are, customers, open accounts receivable, bills receivable, investments, sinking fund, store, cash, suspense, insurance advanced, franchise and patents.

Customers.—Customers are charged at the end of the month with the total amount of current, power or light used, according to their contracts. They are credited with all cash payments, rebates and allowances.

An account is kept in the general ledger with "Customers" and is charged with the total monthly earnings from the customers' ledger, and is credited with total monthly payments, rebates and allowances; the balance shows the amounts due from customers, and must agree with the total of the delinquent accounts on the customer's ledger.

Open Accounts Receivable.—These accounts are kept with persons who buy supplies or other items not connected with the operating department. Persons using light or power must not be entered under this head.

Bills Receivable.—This account is treated as described on page 201.

Investments.—If the surplus funds are invested in stocks or bonds, the accounts should be conducted as described on pages 190 and 201.

Sinking Fund.—This is a certain sum set aside to provide for the payment of bonds, or other obligations maturing at some future time. The money thus placed is treated as an asset, and usually draws interest. This account should be treated as shown in lesson 20.

Store.—If the plant be a large one, it should have a regular supply department. The Storekeeper should also be a good Book-keeper. All material or supplies received should be charged, and the value of all used should be credited, at the same time charging the different departments using the same. Where a great deal of material and supplies are used, a well arranged storehouse will pay the expense of its keeping in the saving of supplies. It makes it possible to render more accurate reports, and the balance as shown by the storekeeper's books will represent very nearly the amount of supplies on hand.

If the plant be a small one, it will not be necessary to employ a regular storekeeper, as the man in charge, the chief engineer or dynamo-man can be empowered to give out supplies.

The keeping of this account will be more fully treated with explanation of the Voucher Record and Abstract of Operating Expense.

Cash.—This account should be treated as shown on page 200.

Suspense Accounts.—These accounts are treated as shown in Suspended List, page 204.

Insurance Advanced.—This account should be conducted as shown on page 205.

If it is desired to dispose of the premium in monthly installments for the purpose of making accurate monthly reports, proceed as directed in "Insurance Due and Accrued."

Franchise and Patents.—This account is chargeable with the cost of franchises or privileges, and for patent rights, whether purchased outright or for a term of years. If franchises are paid for in the form of an annual tax, or if patents or royalties are paid, they should not be charged to this account.

At the end of the year, or when the books are closed, a certain percentage should be written off for depreciation as shown on pages 190, 211—and in lesson 30.

Liabilities.

The liability accounts as shown in the classification are, bills payable, open accounts payable, wages payable, taxes payable, rents payable, interest coupon account payable, audited vouchers payable, bonds payable, dividends payable, capital stock and surplus, and should be conducted as follows:

Bills Payable.—This account is conducted as shown on page 201.

Open Accounts Payable.—These are accounts kept with creditors; they are credited with the amount of audited vouchers, and charged with payments, the same as other personal accounts.

These accounts are kept only when the company does not settle for each invoice.   If these accounts are not numerous, they can all be kept under one account, viz., ''Miscellaneous Accounts Payable.''

Wages Payable.—If wages are paid periodically, there will be no use for this account until the end of the year.   If there are any wages unpaid, when the books are closed, the account must be credited with the amount.   When paid, it is charged.   If monthly reports are made, this account should be credited with the amount of unpaid wages, as a liability.

Taxes Payable.—When the books are closed at the end of the year, this account must be credited with the total amount of taxes due and accrued.   It is charged when payments are made.

If taxes are payable in advance, some companies carry the amount advanced as an asset, the same as ''Insurance Advanced,'' while others charge the total amount of these accounts to Loss and Gain. To be accurate, the amount advanced should be carried as an asset.

Rents Payable.—This account should be conducted the same as Taxes Payable.

Interest Coupon Account.—This account is credited with the amount of interest due and accrued on the company's bonds.   It is charged when payments are made.   When the books are closed, this account should show the amount of interest payable, although it may not be due.

Audited Vouchers Payable.—This account is credited with the amounts of all invoices audited and approved.

The keeping of this account depends upon how the material is handled.   If the material is kept in a storehouse by a storekeeper, then the audited vouchers are charged to the " Store," and credited to the account "Audited Vouchers," provided, however, an account is not kept with the creditor.

If the Store or Stock account is not kept, the total amount of the vouchers is to be credited as above, at the same time charging the accounts to which the items belong on the "Abstract Book."

Bonds Payable.—(Mortgage Account.) This account should be treated as shown on pages 105, 135 to 145.

NOTE.—When bonds are sold at a discount, or premium, the difference may be charged or credited to the account for which purpose the bonds were issued. When bonds are issued for property, franchises, patents, rights of way, etc., the value must be charged to the account for which they were issued.

Dividends Payable.—When a dividend is declared it becomes a positive liability. The account is credited for the amount declared and charged when payments are made. The balance shows the amount of unpaid dividends. See pages 66, 67, 75, 77, 130, 192, etc.

Capital Stock.—This account should be conducted as shown on pages 57 to 150.

Surplus.—This account should be conducted as shown on pages 66 and 67.

Operating Expenses.

The operating expenses of Electric Light plants are divided into three classes, viz., Manufacturing, Distribution and General Expense. The accounts in these departments must be charged with the entire cost of conducting the business, and keeping the plant and machinery in good repair. At the end of the year, or when the books are closed, these accounts are closed into the operating expense account.

Manufacturing.

The manufacturing accounts as shown in the classificatian are, fuel, water, oil and waste, labor (on manufacturing) repairs to motive power, repairs to electrical apparatus, sundries, (manufacturing) and are chargeable as follows:

Manufacturing.—This account is charged with all disbursements for operating and maintaining the plant, machinery, repairs to and labor on any part of the apparatus inside the station, and used for the production of the current ready for distribution at the switchboards. This includes boilers and engines through the shafting, belting, dynamo and attachments, up to and including the switchboards and their attachments. The account is charged with every expenditure made for getting the current ready in the station, and delivering it to the lines ready for distribution. As the items to this account are numerous, it has been subdivided as above .

Fuel.—This account is charged with the cost of all fuel used for motive power. The cost should be the actual cost in the bin; this will include carting, unloading, housing, freights, dock or yard charges, etc.

Water.—(for boilers, etc.) Charge this account with the cost of all water for motive power.

Oil and Waste.—This account is charged with all oil, grease, waste, wiping towels, etc., used for cleaning machinery. If there are any packing cases, freight, express or other charges, they must be added to the original cost.

Labor on Manufacturing.—To this account is charged the wages of engineers, firemen, coalheavers and oilers for steam engines, engineers, oilers and tenders for dynamos, watchmen, gatemen and other laborers on water-power, the work done in the station by the electricians, switchboard-men, helpers and others about the station, and one-half of the general superintendent's salary.

Repairs to Motive Power.—All repairs to steam boilers, flues, engines, pumps, piping, heaters and all other steam apparatus, water-wheels, gears, shafting, pulleys, bearings and belting up to the dynamo pulley, are charged to this account. The items to this account are somewhat numerous, and when the office force is sufficient, I think it advisable to divide it as follows: Repairs to Boilers, Repairs to Engines, Repairs to Shafting and Belting, Repairs to Water-wheels.

The construction and plant accounts should be charged with the first belting, and packing for pumps and engines. All repairs thereafter are chargeable to Repairs to Motive Power, while renewals must be charged "Sundries" (Manufacturing.)

Repairs to Electrical Apparatus.—This account is charged with all repairs to electrical apparatus inside the station, used to manufacture and prepare the current ready for distribution, this includes repairs to connections and conductors from dynamos to switchboards, repairs to dynamos and all appurtenances, as armatures, regulators (not rheostats) pulleys, connections, controllers and switches, switchboards and all attachments, as rheostats, connection bars, lightning arresters, potential-indicators, current-indicators, automatic and fuse cut-outs, switches. ˒

Sundries (for manufacturing.)—To this account is charged all items that do not belong to any of the above divisions of the manufacturing department, such as new belting to replace old, packing for pumps and engines, dynamo brushes, piston-rods, etc., only items of *renewals* but not *repairs* are charged to this account.

Distribution.

Distribution in electric lighting means the distributing of electrical current from the switch boards in the station, through the lines to the customer or to the installations in the streets and buildings. This account is charged with the cost of maintaining the lines and all apparatus outside the station. This account is subdivided as shown in the classification into the following: Maintenance of pole-lines, maintenance of conduits and cables, maintenance of installations, maintenance of motors, transformers, and arc lamps, incandescent-lamp renewals, arc-globes, carbons, labor (on distribution) and sundries (on distribution.) At the end of the year these accounts are to be closed into the distribution account. They are chargeable as follows:

Maintenance of Pole-Lines.—This account is charged with all repairs to the overhead construction, renewals and the maintenance of the same. These repairs include poles, wire, hoods and hanger-boards of arc-lamps, junction-boxes, taps from the lines to transformers, arc-lamps, and to house circuits, fuses, outside and inside lightning arresters, outside arc-circuit switches, primary switches and all attachments and appurtenances belonging thereto. This account ends at the main switch in the building of the customer.

Maintenance of Conduits and Cables.—The items chargeable to this account are the repairs to and maintenance of an underground system of pipes or conduits holding the cables, including all main, distributing and sub-siding ducts, repairs to cables and all underground conductors; also including all main cables, distributing cables and taps and cables to buildings up to and including the primary switch, or cut-out placed directly at the entrance to the consumer's premises.

Maintenance of Installation.—Charge this account with the cost of repairs to and maintenance of all installations. These repairs include the changing of the location of incandescent lamps, wiring, apparatus, and connections from the line or main switch to the lamps, replacing cut-outs, fuses, moulding, repairing wiring to fixtures, and all other attachments in buildings, or connected with the circuit inside of buildings, replacing arc-lamps for city use.

Maintenance of Motors, Transformers and Arc Lamps.—This account is charged with all repairs to motors belonging to the company, when not properly chargeable to the user, repairs to transformers, repairs to and cleaning arc lamps. To have satisfactory results, the arc-lamps must be kept in good repair and adjustment.

Incandescent Lamp Renewals.—This account is charged with cost of all incandescent lamps used to replace those destroyed or burned out, this cost should include charges for packing, delivering, etc. The account is credited with all lamps sold, in order to ascertain the gain or loss. The first lamps used for new installations, must not be charged to this account, they are charged to construction or to the customer.

Arc-Globes.—This account is charged with the cost of all globes used on arc-lamps; this cost must include charges for packing, delivery, etc.

Carbons.—This account is chargeable with the cost of carbons for use in arc-lighting; this cost must also include all charges for packing delivery, freight, express, etc.

Labor (on distribution).—This account is charged with all wages and salaries paid for maintaining and operating, the distribution of the electrical current, such as wages of trimmers, line-men (not on construction), helpers, inspectors, ground-men, meter-men, insulators and plumbers on underground cables, and any part of the electricians' time that may be devoted to this department.

Sundries (on distribution.—This account is chargeable with all items not coming under some one of the subdivisions of this department, such as tools used in distribution not charged to "Expense," use of cables, stable rent, horse-hire, rents for privileges on poles, on pole lines, in underground conduits, etc.

General Expenses.

The general expense as shown in the classification, is subdivided as follows, maintenance of real estate and buildings, rents due and accrued, taxes due and accrued, insurance due and accrued, interest (ordinary), legal expense, salaries (office and general), labor, (general expense), sundries (general expense), and are closed at the end of the year into general expense.

Maintenance of Real Estate and Buildings—Repairs to buildings, grounds, smoke-stacks, dams for water power, race-ways, tail-races and all other items belonging to the real estate and buildings must be charged to this account.

Rents Due and Accrued.—If monthly reports are made, this account will be a necessity, in order to arrive at accurate results. When it is kept it is charged with the monthly amounts due for all rentals (excepting water and telephone), whether paid or not.

Taxes Due and Accrued.—When this account is kept, it is for the same purpose as Rents Due and Accrued. It is charged with the monthly amounts due for taxes of all kinds, on real estate, machinery, franchises, conduits, cables, plant, pole-line, etc. Water tax is chargeable to Manufacturing as it is used in that department.

Insurance Due and Accrued.—This account is charged with the monthly amount of all the insurance on the whole plant and buildings. This account is treated the same as those mentioned above.

Interest. Ordinary.—To this account is charged the interest paid on borrowed money, used in the ordinary course of business. If interest is received from deposits or loans it may be credited to this account.

Interest on bonds, mortgages or other securities, issued by the company must not be confused with this account.

Legal Expenses.—All expenses of a legal nature, such as, fees paid to attorneys for collecting accounts, the retainer and salary of counsel, and attorney's fees connected with any litigation by the company, are charged to this account.

Salaries, (Office and Official).—This account is charged with all salaries of clerks, accountants, collectors, cashiers, canvassers, directors, managers and general officers.

Labor (general expense).—The items chargeable to this account are the wages of storekeeper, and helpers, watchmen and the cost of all other labor not belonging to other accounts.

Sundries (general expense).—This account is chargeable with all unusual expenditures that cannot be classified under any of the foregoing accounts, such as office expenses, books, stationery, traveling expenses, telephone rental, fuel, lights, telegrams and all other expenses incurred in running the office.

Income From Operation.

Every item of income derived from operating the plant must be included in this account. Income from any other source than operation must not be confused with this account. Miscellaneous items will be treated in a separate "Miscellaneous Income" account.

As it is desirous to know the amount of income derived from each department of the business, the account is subdivided into the following: power stationary motors, power for street railways, arc-lighting, street, arc-lighting commercial, incandescent lighting, street, incandescent lighting, commercial, incandescent lighting, residence, rent of meters, rent of motors, miscellaneous income. The use of the income accounts will be treated under the subject of customers' ledgers and abstract book.

Power, Stationary Motors.—This account is credited with the income from current furnished for running stationary electric motors for power purposes in factories, shops, stores, etc. The rental of motors is cared for in another account.

Power for Street Railways.—The income from current furnished street railways is credited to this account. The basis of the calculation is made sometimes by the car per day, as per car-mile run, by the electrical horse-power hour, or by the kilowatt-hour.

Arc Lighting, Street.—The income from the rental of arc-lamps or current furnished to the city, including lights used in public streets, parks, etc., is credited to this account.

Arc Lighting, Commercial.—This account is credited with the income from rental of arc lamps used by business houses, factories, etc.

Incandescent Lighting, Street.—The income from rental of incandescent lamps or current furnished for lighting the public streets, parks, alleys, etc., as credited to this account.

Incandescent Lighting, Commercial.—The income from rental of incandescent lamps or current furnished to stores, shops, factories, etc., is credited to this account.

Incandescent Lighting, Residence.—Credit this account with the income from incandescent lamps rented, or current furnished for lighting private residences.

Rent of Meters.—Credit this account with the income from rent of meters for measuring the amount of current used.

Rent of Motors.—The income from the rental of motors for stationary power purposes in stores, shops, factories, etc., is credited to this account.

Miscellaneous Income.—This account is credited with the income from sources other than operation. There are very few entries to be made to this account.

Loss and Gain.

The accounts into which Loss and Gain are sub-divided are, interest due and accrued, coupon account, rebate and depreciation, (machinery and franchise.)

Loss and Gain.—This account should be treated as shown on pages 206 and 207.

Interest, Due and Accrued, Coupon Account.—This is treated the same as Rent, Taxes and Insurance Due and Accrued.

Rebate.—Charge to this account all rebates or allowances on customers' bills. The total amount of this account should be credited to "Customers" in the General Ledger, at the end of the month; it must not be confused with rebates or discount on supplies, merchandise returned, and rebates on merchandise should be treated as shown on pages 189 and 206.

Depreciation of Machinery and Franchise.—This account should be charged with the amount deducted from the value of plant machinery, etc., as shown on pages 192 and 211.

Customers' Ledgers.

On the following inset, two forms of Customers' ledgers are shown, one for customers on a contract basis, the other for customers on a Meter basis. When a company furnishes current by both methods, a ledger should be kept for each, and when there are a great many customers using arc and incandescent lights it will be found

advantageous to keep a separate book for each department. The forms shown are greatly reduced in size, and placed on one sheet for want of space.

Customers' Contract Ledger.—A glance at the form of this book will reveal its usefulness. One writing of the customer's name is all that is required for a year.

This ledger is opened by writing the customers' names and addresses in alphabetical order. The contract number, date of expiration, installation, and rate should then be entered. In the first balance column is entered the balance due from Old Ledger, the total amount due of this column must agree with the balance of customer's account in the General Ledger.

In order to make the charges for month, the number of lamps must first be entered. The charges for the month are then entered in the column provided for that purpose. The total amount of the charges for the month is posted to the debit of customer's account in the General Ledger. The footing of this column represents the amount of business for that month in this department. In the credit column is entered all payments and in the rebate column is entered all discounts and allowances, posted from the Cash-Book.

The totals of the Amount Paid and Rebate columns are credited to Customer's Account in General Ledger. These totals will also prove the cash posting. Each month is self-proving.

To ascertain the Amount Due at the end of the month, (which balance must agree with the balance due Customers Account in General Ledger) to the balance due from previous month, add the charges for current month, from this, deduct the amount paid and rebate and enter the balance in the balance due column. The accuracy of this work is proven by taking the totals of each column for the month, the same as for each customer, i. e., the total balance due at the beginning and the total charges for the month must equal the total credits and the balance at the end of the month.

Customers' Meter Ledger.—The form of this Ledger is quite similar to the Contract Ledger; the only essential difference is the column provided for Meter-readings and calculations, with columns for the different sizes of incandescent lamps connected. The "Rate per Hour" means per watt-hour, per ampere-hour, or any like unit that may be desired. Columns have also been provided for meter number, and factor or multiplier.

The previous and present meter-readings are entered in the columns provided. The difference is found by subtracting the previous reading from the present. The charges, credits and balance due are treated, and the work proven as described in Contract Ledger. The total charges and credits being posted to Customer's Account in General Ledger.

If the bills are entered monthly, and payments made in full, it would require but one line per month, but if bills are rendered weekly, or semi-monthly, and payments made on account, more space will be required.

Cash Book.—The form of the cash-book is very simple, and so well understood that forms need not be shown. The only difference is that a column should be provided on the debit side in which is entered the payments by customers, also a column for rebate on customers' accounts: While Rebate is merely a Journal entry, it is much more convenient to enter it on the same book and at the same time as the cash payments. The individual customers are credited separately with the rebate on their accounts, while the footing of the rebate column is credited to the "Customers Account" in the General Ledger and "Rebate" charged.

On the credit side there should be a column for the Voucher Number, also one for "Audited Vouchers."

When payments are made on Audited Vouchers they are entered on the credit side of Cash Book in column of Audited Vouchers. At the end of the month the total footing of the "Audited Vouchers" column is entered in the General Ledger to the debit of that account. The balance of the Audited Vouchers account will show the amount owing to the creditors, except that shown in open accounts. Payments to persons having open accounts are entered separately upon the Ledger.

From what has been given, it is readily seen that the Voucher System is to be used, thus doing away with keeping a great many individual accounts. In some cases, however, it may be necessary to keep open accounts with some, where there is trading back and forth.

When the Cash Book has been provided with the special columns as stated above, the Voucher Record which takes the place of the Journal is of next importance. While the Voucher Record is practically a Journal, it can hardly be called by that name.

Voucher Record.—The Voucher System saves a great deal of time and labor, and is very accurate. Although the system is fully ex-. plained on pages 242 to 246 it is thought advisable to illustrate the Voucher Record, as intended on above accounts.

The following form has been used by the writer, with entire satisfaction. When the accounts are classified and subdivided, this form can be used in many kinds of business with but few alterations.

When invoices are received for material, they are first checked and prices and extensions are guaranteed by the proper persons. If any errors are found, the corrections should be made upon the invoice with ink, being very careful to add to or deduct from the total as the case may be. Cash and Trade discounts should also be deducted from the total. When the invoices are thus prepared they are then attached to a voucher, a form of which is given on page 243. The voucher and attached invoices then go to the proper person for approval and signature.

The items of the invoices are then distributed to the accounts to which they belong, in the distribution on the back of the voucher.

The Voucher is then numbered, and entered in the Record, each item being entered into its own column as shown on the back. The total amount of the voucher is then credited to "Audited Vouchers," or to the person's account if one is to be kept. The name of the creditor must be written in the space provided, and the amount entered in the "Open Accounts" column. Thereafter the voucher will be known by its number.

When a voucher is paid, for which an account has been opened, it is charged to the Cash Book in the "Open Accounts" column. The balance of this account shows the indebtedness to sundry creditors. When a voucher is paid, which has been credited to "Audited Vouchers," it must be charged on the Cash Book to "Audited Vouchers." The Balance of this account shows the amount of vouchers unpaid. The balance of the Open Accounts Payable and the Audited Vouchers Account, shows the indebtedness of the company, except Bonds and Mortgages.

A voucher is made for all pay-rolls and other labor payments, and must be treated as invoices. The items are distributed as for any other account.

If a cash payment is made on account, and not in full settlement of the invoice, a receipt should be taken and attached to the original voucher, at the same time charging the person for the payment.

If a cash payment is made on account of an "Audited Voucher" the amount paid should be charged to Audited Vouchers, then deduct the amount paid from the original amount, or it will probably save trouble if the account be transferred to the Ledger as an "Open Account Payable."

At the end of the month, after the vouchers have all been entered in the "Record," the columns should all be footed and proven. The total footings of all the columns in the division of General Expense, should be entered in the column "Total General Expense," the same with Distribution, Manufacturing, etc. The sum of all the debit footings thus found should equal the sum of the footings of the "Open Accounts," and "Audited Vouchers."

The total of all the columns in the division of Distribution, Manufacturing, etc., are then posted to the debit of their respective accounts in the General Ledger. The footings of the "Open Accounts" and "Audited Vouchers" columns are posted to the credit of their respective accounts, thus keeping the books in balance, while the posting is reduced to a minimum.

Sometimes an error will occur, or it may be desired to transfer an item from one account to another; when such is the case, credit the account in the Sundries Column and charge the proper account in the column to which it belongs. A Voucher should be made for all such entries, with full explanations.

Store Account.—If the material is kept in a store-room by a store-keeper, then it will be necessary to charge the "Store Account" from the invoices on the Voucher Record instead of charging the items to the various accounts. When the material is distributed from the Store it is then charged to the various accounts, and Store Account credited, though not for each item, as the total for each day may be used, thereby saving a great many entries.

The balance of the "Store Account" at the end of the month shows the amount in value of the supplies on hand. This balance will not agree exactly with that of an inventory, but will be accurate enough for practical purposes, if the account and material are carefully handled.

Mon

Monthly Statement of Operating Receipts and Expenses.

From the Voucher Record and Customer's Ledgers, the operating receipts and expenses can easily be taken and entered monthly on a sheet like that shown on page 216.

This form can be ruled upon a large sheet of paper, and made to run for five or six years. It will only be necessary to change the headings of the columns, any number of which may be used, as follows:

Arc Lighting.		Incandescent Lighting.			Rents of		Power.		Miscellaneous Income.	Total Income.
Street.	Commercial	Street.	Commercial	Residence.	Motors.	Motors.	Stationary Motors.	Street Railways.		

Construction.	Manufacturing.	Distribution.	General Expense.	Due from Customers.	Accounts Payable.	Audited Vouchers Payable.

In addition to the above statement, there should be issued monthly a summary of operations, showing the itemized expenses for each division as shown by the Voucher Record, the lamp-hours, lamps, material, fuel oil, etc., used, proportion of expenses, labor, etc. This information can easily be obtained from engineers' and foremen's reports.

CHAPTER TWENTY-SEVEN.

Street Railway Accounting.

Street railways having been organized so long, and the income being strictly cash, the accounting is very simple when properly systematized; however, neglect in properly organizing or conducting this department will be as fatal to the financial success of the road, as would neglect in the operating department.

In order to properly conduct this department, an efficient clerical force is necessary, and the work should be done in accordance with proper rules and regulations, combining and condensing the items as much as possible.

Street Railway Accounting is very similar to that given for Electric Lighting. A few general headings are used, which are subdivided into as many accounts as may be desired.

The Voucher System should be adopted, using the same form of Voucher Record as given for Electric Lighting, excepting the change of headings and subdivisions.

A careful examination of the following classification will enable one to arrange a Voucher Record without any difficulty, however, the general headings and subdivisions will be fully explained.

Cost of Road and Equipment.

Superintendence and General Expense.—This account is charged with the salaries and personal expenses of general officers, their assistants, clerks, stationery, furniture, fuel and all other office supplies.

Engineering.—To this account is charged the wages of engineers, draughtsmen, and assistants, with the office, stationery and other expenses.

Right of Way.—The cost of obtaining franchises, the salaries and expenses of agents in securing consents, and all payments for right of way are chargeable to this account.

Classification of Street Railway Accounts.

History, Capital Stock and Funded Debt.

Cost of Road Bed & Equipment.
- Superintendence and General Expense.
- Engineering.
- Right of Way.
- Real Estate and Buildings.
- Road Bed and Track.
- Overhead Construction.
- Rolling Stock.
- Miscellaneous Equipment.
- Power Plant.
- Cable and Carrying Sheaves.
- Repair Shops.
- Additions and Betterments.

Operating Expenses.

Miscellaneous
- Salaries of General Officers and Clerks.
- Office Service and Supplies.
- Insurance.
- Legal.
- Injury to Persons and Property.
- Contingent.
- Franchise Account.

Transportation.
- Car Service.
- Car Barn.
- Oil and Waste { For Cars. For Power House.
- Supplies.
- Wrecking, Sanding, Sweeping and Cleaning Conduits.
- Stable and Power House.
- Provender and Fuel.

Maintenance of Way and Structures.
- Repairs and Renewals of Road Bed and Track.
- Repairs and Renewals of Overhead Wire.
- Repairs and Renewals of Buildings, Docks, and Wharves.

Maintenance of Rolling Stock and Power Equipment.
- Repairs and Renewals of Cars and Vehickles.
- Repairs and Renewals of Cable Sheaves and Grip Dies.
- Repairs of Harness and Stable Equipment.
- Horse Shoeing.
- Renewals of Horses and Mules.
- Repairs of Electric Car Equipment. { Motor Armature. Gears and Pinions. Trolleys. Miscellaneous.
- Repairs of Power Plant { Steam. Cable. Electric.
- Tools and Machinery.
- Miscellaneous.

Classification of Street Railway Accounts.—Continued.

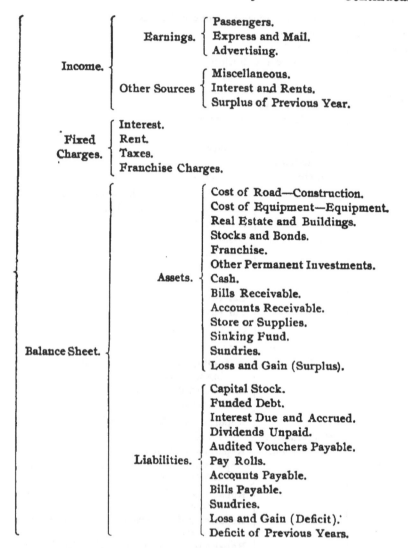

Real Estate and Buidings.—This account is charged with the cost of all real estate and buildings used exclusively for railroad purposes, including all necessary furniture and fixtures.

Any property owned by the company, not used for railroad purposes, should be kept in a separate account as an investment.

Road Bed and Track.—This account is chargeable with the cost of the foundation, material and labor laying track, paving, wiring, etc.

Overhead Construction.—The items chargeable to this account are, poles, wire, insulating devices, and the cost of placing the same.

Rolling Stock.—Charge this account with the cost of cars, trucks, grips, motors, wiring, trolley, switches, furnishings, etc.

Miscellaneous Equipment.—Charge this account with the cost of wagons, sweepers, snowplows, with grip or electrical equipment, and other vehicles.

Power Plant.—This account is charged with the cost of engines, boilers, generators, pit machinery, cable winding drums, tension devices, cranes, pumps, shafting, switchboards, belting, piping, foundations, and all labor placing same, also with heating and lighting appliances.

Cable and Carrying Sheaves.—The cost of wire ropes with carrying and terminal sheaves and the labor placing same ready for operation, are charged to this account.

Repair Shops.—This account is charged with the cost of all iron and wood working machinery, tools and power, if it is independent of the power plant, also the expense of placing the machinery, etc.

Additions and Betterments.—Charge this account with such expenditures as actually increase the construction and equipment, also such expenses for renewals or repairs as exceed what is necessary to make good any depreciation of road and equipment.

Income.

Earnings.

Income from Passengers.—This account is credited with the cash receipts for fare and sale of tickets.

Income from Mail and Express.—Receipts for transporting freight, express and mail are credited to this account.

Income from Advertising.—Credit this account for receipts for advertising in cars, buildings, and on tickets.

Miscellaneous Income.

Credit this account with the receipts from the sale of manure, old material and worn out animals. If desired the receipts from these sources may be credited to the account, to which the new material purchased to replace the old is charged.

Interest and Rents.—This account is credited with the interest received on securities or loans, also rents for buildings, grounds, leased lines or tracks, and power furnished other companies.

Surplus of Previous Years.—The net income, less the payments made therefrom, on the business of the previous years, is credited to this account.

Operating Expenses.

Salaries of Officers and Clerks.—The salaries of the general officers, heads of departments, division superintendents, their assistants and clerks, should be charged to this account.

Office Service and Supplies.—The items chargeable to this account are, books, stationery, blanks, tickets, circulars, advertising, wages of porters, messengers, and expense of heating and lighting the general offices.

Insurance.—This account is charged with the cost of insurance on the property used for Railroad purposes, the cost of guarantee against accidental bodily injuries, or death of employees, passengers and the public, and the cost of conducting employees' mutual aid association.

If preferred, the cost of guarantee may be charged to Guarantee Account, or Injuries to Persons and Property.

Legal.—This account is charged with the salaries, fees, and expenses of attorneys for all legal purposes.

This account may be subdivided if preferred.

Injuries to Persons and Property.—Charge this account with payments made for damages to, or destruction of property (not belonging to the company) for persons killed or injured, wages to disabled employees, medical attendance and other expenses, (except legal).

Removal of Snow and Ice.—This account is charged with the cost of labor, salt and other expense for removing snow and ice from tracks, walks, etc.

Contingent.—Any miscellaneous expenses or rents incurred exclusively in the operation of the road, for which other provision is not made, should be charged to this account.

Franchise Account.—Charge this account with the cost of repaving streets, over and above the repairs, which are chargeable to maintenance of way.

Transportation.

Car Service.—This account is charged with the wages paid conductors, motorneers, gripmen, inspectors, starters and others employed on or about the cars while in service.

Car Barn.—The items chargeable to this account are, the wages of barn foremen, shifters, cleaners, inspectors, tools for same, and the cost of heating and lighting barns and sheds.

Oil and Waste.—Charge this account with the cost of all oil, grease, tallow and waste used in lubricating cars, motors, engines, shafting, winding drums, pumps in powerhouse, generators, and on the rope and carrying pulleys.

Supplies.—The items chargeable to this account are, flags, lanterns, portable registers, switch stocks, conductors punches, and all other items not chargeable to repairs.

Wrecking, Sanding, Sweeping and Cleaning Conduit.—This account is charged with sweeping track, cleaning conduit, and sanding, also the cost of removing obstructions and wrecks, replacing derailed cars, and cost of labor required.

Stable and Power House.—The wages of engineers, foremen, electricians, and all others employed in and about the stable or powerhouse are charged to this account.

Provender and Fuel.—This account is charged with the cost of feed, and the labor preparing same for use, the cost of bedding, medicine and veterinary services, also the cost of fuel used in power houses, including freight charges, water rents, and cost of pumping. Usually this account is sub-divided.

Maintenance of Way and Structures.

Repairs and Renewals of Road Bed and Track. This account is charged with the cost of rails, ties, paving blocks, sand, the wages paid roadmaster, foreman and laborers, in maintaining, repairing and placing new material for track, joints, switches, bonds, and supplementary wire, and tracks in buildings.

Repairs and Renewals of Overhead Construction. —The items chargeable to this account are, repairs and renewals of poles, wires and all insulating appliances.

Repairs and Renewals of Buildings, Docks and Wharves.— Charge this account with the cost of all material, and expense of distributing same, and all labor repairing buildings, stations, offices, car and repair shops, stables, scales, pits, turntables, cranes, wharves, powerhouse and other buildings used for railroad purposes.

Repairs and Renewals of Cars, Sweepers, Snowplows and Other Vehicles.—The items chargeable to this account are the cost of new cars purchased to make good any depreciation, the cost of material and labor in repairing, renewing, or rebuilding cars, trucks, grips, scrapers, wheels, axles, brakes, sand boxes, springs, pilots, journal boxes, etc.

Repairs and Renewals of Cables, Dies and Sheaves.—The cost of cables, splicing and placing the same in line, the cost of lining and renewing, carrying pulleys and terminal sheaves, are chargeable to this account.

Repairs of Harness and Stable Equipment.—This account is charged with the cost of material and labor in repairing harness, etc. Any new harness or stable equipment purchased to make good any depreciation, is also charged to this account.

Horse Shoeing.—Charge this account with the cost of all material and labor for shoeing horses and mules.

Renewals of Horses and Mules.—This account should be charged only with the cost of horses and mules purchased to replace those worn out.

Repairs of Electric Car Equipment.

Motor Armatures and Fields.—This account is charged with the cost of new armatures and fields purchased to make good any depreciation, also the cost of material and the labor of removing, repairing, replacing and making all connections, etc.

Gears and Pinions.—Charge this account with the cost of new gears and pinions necessary to replace those discarded, also the cost of renewals, repairs and the labor removing and replacing same.

Trolleys.—New trolley wheels and poles used to replace those worn out or destroyed, and the cost of repairs, renewals and labor on same must be charged to this account.

Miscellaneous.—The items chargeable to this account are repairs and renewals of all auxiliary electric appliances, such as lightning arresters, switches, rheostats, brushes, fuses, pans, brush holders, and repairs of motors and fields not mentioned above. Strictly speaking, brushes and fuses are not repairs, and may be charged to supplies under the transportation expenses.

Repairs of Power Plant.

Steam Plant.—The cost of repairs to engines, pumps, boilers, steam pipe, belting and shafting, should be charged to this account.

Cable Plant.—This account is charged with the cost of repairs and renewals to winding drums, gears and tension apparatus.

Electric Plant.—This account is charged with the cost of renewals and repairs to generators, and their parts, with labor of removing and replacing; also renewals of switchboard equipment, and all connections.

Tools and Machinery.—Charge to this account the cost of repairs and renewals of car and repair shop equipment.

Miscellaneous.—All expenses for maintenance of equipment not otherwise provided for, are charged to this account.

Fixed Charges.

Interest.—Payments made on account of funded or floating debt are charged to this account.

Rents.—The rental paid for leased lines, power houses, buildings, stables, sheds, etc., for railroad purposes, must be charged to this account.

Taxes.—Charge to this account the taxes paid on property used in operating the road, on earnings, and capital stock.

Franchise Charges.—This account is charged with payments made to city on gross earnings, in consideration of franchise.

Assets and Liabilities.—The sub-divisions of these accounts are self-explanatory, and will need no further attention.

Having properly analyzed the accounts, the bookkeeping becomes a very simple matter. Three principle books only are required, the Voucher Record, Ledger and Cash Book. The common form of the Ledger will suffice, and needs no explanation. The Voucher Record, as stated before, is identically the same as used in Electric Lighting, with headings changed. The Cash Book is similar to that used in Electric Lighting, however, a form is shown, a careful examination of which will reveal its usefulness without further explanations.

Receipts.

Name of Conductor.	L.F.	Tickets.	Fares	Total.	Central Ave. Line.	Cedar Ave. Line.	Euclid Ave. Line.	Wade Park Av. Line.	Office.	Miscellaneous.	Total.

Disbursements.

	L. F.	Check No.	A. V. No.	Sundries.	Audited Vouchers.	Miscellaneous.	Total.		

The number of auxiliary books, report blanks, etc., will depend upon the size of the road, and the extent and number of departments into which the business is divided.

When supplies are received, they may be charged to the various operating accounts, to which they belong. At the end of the month, an inventory is taken of the supplies on hand, and deducted from the various accounts, the difference will show the amount of expenditure for such accounts. This will show what supplies are on hand, and leave the accounts charged with the amounts used.

If the road is large, build and repair their own cars, then the material should be kept by a Stockkeeper with a complete set of books. For a complete analysis of material, or store account, you are referred to the lesson on Electric Light Accounting.

Forms of reports of Operating Receipts, Expenditures, Financial and Comparative statements could have been shown in this lesson, but they have been omitted, and will be found in the lesson on Expert Examinations of Street Railways.

CHAPTER TWENTY-EIGHT.

Estate Accounting.

Estate Accounting is a subject of great importance, and one that should be thoroughly understood. It is not the purpose of this lesson to describe a system or give forms of the books used in keeping such accounts, but merely to point out the legal principles relating to accounts, as they should be understood by Executors, Administrators and Guardians, whose duty it is to administer property according to the will of a testator, or by order of the court.

The Disposal of Property by Will.

This gives rise to the subject of Estate Accounting, consequently the formation of Wills should receive attention first.

It is a very difficult matter to make an unobjectionable will. There are some blank forms for wills printed, but there are but few cases in which they can be applied, as wills are made under a great variety of circumstances. One may be called upon to make his own will, or for a friend or neighbor, under circumstances that would not permit delay, and it may be properly drawn where the author has a knowledge of the legal principles, but in every instance a competent lawyer, experienced in this branch of law, should be consulted whenever it is possible so to do.

Any person of full age and of sound mind and memory, and not under any restraint, having any property, personal or real, or any interest therein, may give and bequeath the same to any person by last will and testament lawfully executed. In some of our States minors may bequeath personal property; and a frequent limitation of the age for such bequests, is eighteen years for males, and sixteen years for females.

The testator should say distinctly, in the beginning of the instrument, "that it is his last will," while the law gives effect to a last will always, it is well and usual to say "hereby revoking all former wills," provided, however, other wills have been made.

Every last will and testament should be in writing, and signed at the end thereof, by the party making the same, or by some other person in his presence and by his express directions, and should be attested and subscribed in the presence of such party, by two or more competent witnesses, who saw the testator subscribe, or heard him acknowledge the same. The witnessing part is of very great importance. The requirements in the different States are not precisely alike; but they all are intended to secure such attestation as will leave the fact of the execution of the will, and its publication as such, beyond doubt. A testator should sign, seal and declare it to be his last will and testament in the presence of two or more disinterested persons as witnesses, and should then, each in the presence of the testator and of the other witnesses, sign his name as witness.

Each should see the execution which he says he witnesses; and the signing by the witnesses should all be seen by the testator when possible. If the testator is too feeble to write his name, let him make his mark, which is usually the cross.

It is important that witnesses should be selected with great care, as their evidence is first to be taken if a question should arise regarding the testators sanity. Married women, minors and any person competent to transact ordinary business may be witnesses, but no person should be witness who is a legatee, or an executor, or otherwise interested in the will, when a legatee is the only witness by which a will can be proven, the devise or bequest to him is rendered void, thus leading to unintended results.

In the body of the will, the testator should express his wishes as clearly and accurately as possible.

The word "bequeath" applies properly to personal estate, only, the word "devise" to real estate only, therefore, it is safe to begin "I give, bequeath and devise my estate and property as follows: that is to say," then proceeds to say what shall be done with each piece of property, or sum of money.

A testator should always name his executors; but the will is perfectly good without any executor being named, for the court will appoint an "administrator" with the will annexed.

Codicils.

A codicil is a small additional will, it is a testamentary disposition, not revoking the former will, but varying it in some way, or making changes. There can be but one will, and that the last; yet there may be any number of codicils, all valid.

Revocation of Wills.

A will shall be revoked by the testator tearing, cancelling, obliterating, or destroying the same, with the intention of revoking it, by the testator himself, or by some person in his presence, or by his direction; or by some other will or codicil, in writing, executed according to law.

A will is revoked by the operation of law, if the testator afterwards marry and have a child. If, after this a testator intends that his will shall take effect, he should expressly confirm it, or better still, make a new will. If a testator leaves anything to his wife, and intends that she should have it instead of dower, or of the additional rights which recent statutes in some of the States have given her, he should say so. Then she will not have both, but may choose between the provisions of the law and that of the will, taking whichever she prefers, and leaving the other.

Executors and Administrators.

An executor is a person named in the will of a deceased person, to settle his or her estate. There may be one or more, male or female. An administrator is one appointed by the court to settle the estate of a deceased person. If the deceased left a will, but did not appoint an executor, or the apppointed executor refuses to act, resigns, or dies, or for any reason fails to act, an administrator is appointed by the court, "with the will annexed." The wife of a deceased husband or the husband of a deceased wife, generally has the right to be appointed administrator, after them the next of kin in the order of relationship. But the courts have some discretion in the matter.

In this country, the judicial officer, or judge who has the charge of the settlement of estates, proof of wills, and of proceedings under them, is generally called the Judge of Probate. But in some states he is called Surrogate, Registrar of Wills or of Probate, Judge of the Orphan's Court, etc. The Judge of Probate is usually a county officer, and his jurisdiction is limited to his county.

An executor derives his authority from the will, and his duties begin at the death ot the testator.

An Administrator derives his authority from the Court, while the title of an Administrator does not exist until the grant of administration, it goes back to the death of the deceased; but then only in order to protect the estate and not for any other purpose. The duties of an administrator are substantially the same as those of an executor; excepting that he must distribute and dispose of the estate as the law requires, as he has no will to direct him, unless he is an administrator with the will annexed.

While the property of a testator must be distributed and disposed of as directed in the will or by the court, the law must in all cases be complied with. Many persons are appointed to act as executors or administrators who have little or no knowledge of the law governing their duties and actions, but in all cases, and at all times the court will instruct and direct upon all matters, and its orders must be carried out

For an executor or administrator to properly conduct and close up an estate, they should make a complete study of all laws governing such matters of the State in which the estate is located. This is a broad, deep subject and should be thoroughly understood, as one is apt to be called upon at any time to serve in this capacity.

While the following instructions are based upon Ohio Laws, they would be found to differ very little if based upon the laws of other States.

When an estate consists of real estate only, it is not so difficult to conduct and close up, as when it consists of real and personal property, that is, when the testator was a joint or sole owner in a mercantile or manufacturing business.

The writer's entire time during the last three months of 1895, was devoted to auditing the books and preparing an account for the Probate Court, for the executor of an estate in this city, which consisted of real estate $125,000, and a house furnishing installment store $40,000, that had been conducted by the executor for three years. The audit and report was made preparatory to closing up the estate. While the name cannot be given, the items will be used to give the principles a practical application, and to make the instructions clear.

Every executor or administrator shall, within three months after his appointment, make and return upon oath, into court, a true inventory of all the goods, chattels, moneys, rights and credits of the deceased, which are, by law, to be administered, and which shall have come to his possession or knowledge.

If the court at the time of granting letters of administration or letters testamentary, shall think fit, it may also order the executor or administrator to also include in the inventory an appraisement of all the real estate of the deceased.

The estate and effects comprised in the inventory shall be appraised by three suitable, disinterested persons, who shall be appointed by the court, and sworn to a faithful discharge of their trust.

A notice of the time and place of making such inventory and appraisement shall be served by the executor or administrator not less than five days previous thereto, on the widow, legatees, and next of kin. At the appointed time, the appraisers shall, in the presence of such of the legatees, or creditors of the testator, as shall attend, proceed to estimate and appraise the property and estate; and each article or item shall be set down separately, with the value thereof, in dollars and cents, in plain figures.

The inventory shall contain a particular statement of all bonds, mortgages, notes, and all other securities for the payment of money, belonging to the deceased, which are known to such executor or administrator, specifying the name of the debtor in each security, the date, the sum originally payable, the indorsements thereon, if any, with their dates, and the sum which, in the judgment of the appraisers can be collected on each claim.

The inventory shall also contain a statement of all other debts and accounts belonging to the deceased, which are known to such executor or administrator, specifying the name of the debtor, the date, the balance or thing due, and the value or sum which can be collected thereon, in the judgment of the appraisers.

The inventory shall also contain an account of all money belonging to the deceased, which shall have come to the hands of the executor or administrator; and if there be none, the fact shall be so stated in said inventory.

The appraisers shall also set off and allow to the widow, and children under the age of fifteen years, if there be any, or if there be no widow, then to such children, sufficient provisions or other property to support them for twelve months from the death of the decedent; and if the widow or children have, since the death of the deceased, and previous to such allowance, consumed for their support any portion of the estate, the appraisers shall take the same into consideration in determining the amount of the allowance.

When there is not sufficient personal property, or property of a suitable kind, to set off to the widow or children, the appraisers shall certify what sum or further sum, in money, is necessary for the support of such widow or children.

The appraisers shall not include in the inventory, the provisions, property or money, set off and allowed by them, to the widow or children, but the same shall be stated in a separate schedule, signed by them, and returned, with the inventory, to the court, by the executor or administrator.

Upon the completion of the inventory, it shall be signed by the appraisers, and a copy thereof shall be retained by the executor or ad-ministrator, and he shall return the original to the Probate Court.

If any executor or administrator shall neglect or refuse to return such inventory within three months after his appointment, the Probate Court shall issue an order requiring such executor or administrator to return an inventory according to law, or to show cause before the court why an attachment should not be issued against him.

Whenever personal property, or assets of any kind, not mentioned in any inventory that shall have been made, shall come to the knowledge or possession of an executor or administrator, he shall cause the same to be appraised in manner aforesaid, and an inventory thereof to be returned, within two months after its discovery. The making and return of such inventory may be enforced in the same manner as in the case of the first inventory.

The executor or administrator shall, as far as he is able, collect the assets of the estate, within one year after the date of the adminis-tration bond.

If, from the situation of the assets belonging to the estate, more than eighteen months, from the date of the administration bond, is re-quired for their collection, the court may, upon motion, and being satisfied thereof by the affidavit of the executor or administrator extend the time for that purpose.

Every executor or administrator shall, within eighteen months after his appointment, render his account of his administration upon oath, and he shall in a like manner render such further accounts of his administration, every twelve months thereafter, and also at such other times as may be required by the court, until the estate shall be wholly settled, and he may be examined upon oath on any matter relating to his accounts and the payments therein mentioned, and also touching any property or effects of the deceased, which have come to his hands.

The time allowed by the court to collect the assets of the estate, shall not operate as an allowance of further time to file the accounts.

If any executor or administrator shall fail to render his acccounts as directed, he may be compelled to do so, as in case of failing to file an inventory.

In rendering such account, every executor or administrator shall produce vouchers for all debts and legacies paid, and for all funeral charges and just and necessary expenses, which vouchers shall be filed with their amounts, and they, together with the account, shall be depos-ited and remain in the Probate Court.

No executor or administrator shall be accountable for any debts inventoried as due to the deceased, if it shall appear to the court that they remain uncollected without his fault.

Many other points relative to the sale of real and personal property, distributing of proceeds, proceedings by creditors against heirs and devisees proceedings when estate is insolvent, etc., might be given, but it is thought that sufficient has been stated to guide the accountant in conducting estate accounts, however, a careful study of the statutes of your State, should be made.

After the law has been complied with, it is an easy matter to conduct the accounts of an estate, yet, many points arise that require the nicest discrimination.

While the law requires an inventory to be taken within three months after an executor or administrator has been appointed, it should be taken at the earliest possible moment, as the inventory is intended to be as at the death of the testator. When an estate consists of real estate only, a delayed inventory may not cause much trouble or inconvenience, but when a part of the estate consists of a business house with a large stock of goods, and the business is to be continued, it will become more difficult the longer it runs.

When the business of a testator is to be continued by an executor or administrator, I would advise in all cases to open a new set of books according to the inventory taken by the appraisers. Although the appraisers have nothing to do with the testators liabilities, the executor or administrator should ascertain the items and amounts as completely and accurately as possible. The books should be devised to meet the special requirements of the business, and be kept by Double Entry.

The books should be so arranged and kept that the true condition of the business might be shown at all times. This point is of the greatest importance to executors and administrators, because the law holds them personally responsible for the liabilities under certain provisions.

If other assets should come into the hands of the executor or administrator, properly belonging to the inventory, or if other liabilities should be ascertained after the books have been opened, they should be entered at once, with proper explanations.

The yearly allowance and annuities to the widow and children must be entered as liabilities, they are not payable, however, until after the payment of debts.

The system of accounting used by the executor for the estate above referred to, was devised by the writer, and consisted chiefly of the Combination Check Journal, as shown on page 232, with special columns for the important items of the business and real property. The accounts were so conducted that a true and accurate condition of the business was shown at all times. It was well that the accounts were so kept, as the heirs brought suit to have the executor removed, on the grounds of withholding assets, appropriating funds to his own use, etc , the suit was won by the executor, however, but the result might have been different, had the books been kept otherwise, and not to the strict letter of the law.

Within eighteen months after an executor or administrator has been appointed, he must file an account of his administration, also every twelve months thereafter, until a final account is rendered, with these accounts all vouchers for expenditures must also be filed. To comply with this requirement, a voucher check should be used, for the payment of all accounts and bills, except for small items of expense, where a voucher cannot be had.

For these the executor or administrator should make a voucher weekly or monthly.

In rendering an account for an estate of this kind, two accounts should be made, one for the business and one for the estate proper.

The account for the estate should show receipts and expenditures itemized, with vouchers numbered, while the business account should show the accounts as taken from the Ledger, showing the voucher numbers for each account, that is, say the Rent Account is $2,000, the amount would be covered by Vouchers 1127 to 1139, etc.

Should you ever be called upon to act as an executor or administrator, or to keep the accounts of an estate, study carefully the laws of your State, and if an attorney is not employed, go to the court for instructions and information.

Guardians and Trustees.

Guardians of all descriptions are treated by courts as trustees; and in almost all cases they are required to give security for the faithful discharge of their duty, unless the guardian be appointed by will, and the testator has exercised the power given him by statute, of requiring that the guardian shall not be called upon to give bonds. But, even in this case, such testamentary provision is wholly personal; and if the individual dies, refuses the appointment, resigns it, or is removed from it, and a substitute is appointed by court, this substitute must give bonds.

In this country, the guardian is held to have only a naked authority, not coupled with an interest. His possession of the property of his ward is not such as gives him a personal interest, being only for the purpose of agency. But for the benefit of his ward he has a very general power over it. He manages and disposes of the personal property at his discretion, although it is safer for him to obtain the power of the court for any important measure. He may lease the real estate, if appointed by will or court; he cannot, however, sell the real estate without leave of the proper court. Nor should he convert the personal estate into real without such leave.

As trustee, a guardian is held to a strictly honest discharge of his duty, and cannot act in relation to the subject of his trust for his own personal benefit in any contract whatever. He must neither make nor suffer any waste of the inheritance, and is held very strictly to a careful management of all personal property. He is responsible not only for any misuse of the ward's money or stock, but for letting it lie idle; and if he does so without sufficient cause, he must allow the ward interest or compound interest in his account. The general duties of every guardian of any minor are:

First. To make and file, within three months after his appointment, a full inventory, verified by oath, of the real and personal estate of his ward, with the value of the same, and the value of the yearly rent of the real estate; and failing so to do for thirty days after he shall have been notified of the expiration of the time, by the probate judge, said probate judge shall remove him and appoint a successor.

Second. To manage the estate for the best interest of his ward.

Third. To render, on oath, to the proper court, an account of the receipts and expenditures of such guardian, verified by vouchers, once in every two years, or oftener, upon the order of the court.

Fourth. At the expiration of his trust, fully to account for and pay over to the proper person all of the estate 'of his ward remaining in his hands.

Fifth. To pay all just debts due from such ward, out of the estate in his hands, and collect all debts due such ward, and, in case of doubtful debts, to compound the same, and to appear for and defend all suits against such ward.

Sixth. When any ward has no father, or having a father who is unable or fails to educate such ward, it is the duty of his guardian to provide for him such education as the amount of his estate may justify.

Seventh. To loan or invest the money of his ward within a reasonable time after he receives it, in notes or bonds secured by first mortgage on real estate of at least double the value of the loan or investment.   Or investments may be made in bonds of the United States, or any state on which default has never been made in the payment of interest, or in county or municipal bonds, issued in conformity to law; or with the consent and approbation of the Probate Court, investments may be made in productive real estate, the title to which shall be taken in the name of the guardian as such.

Eighth.   To obey and perform all orders and judgments of the proper courts touching the guardianship.   Guardians' and trustees' accounts are conducted upon the same general principles of law, as estates, and as this has been fully explained, further instruction is unnecessary, suffice it to say that the statutes of the state, relative to guardianship should be carefully studied.

Assignees—Trustees.

An assignee is a person to whom an assignment is made by an insolvent debtor, to administer his affairs for the benefit of his creditors.

A trustee is a person whom the court has appointed or whom the creditors have elected to hold or manage property for the benefit of another.

When any person, partnership, association, or corporation, shall make an assignment of any property, money, rights, or credits in trust for the benefit of creditors, it shall be the duty of said assignee, within ten days after the delivery of the assignment, and before disposing of any property so assigned, to appear before the court, and give a bond for the faithful performance of his duties according to law.

The statutes are not so definite in their provisions in the matter of designating who may or may not be assignees or trustees for the benefit of creditors, as they are as to guardians, administrators, or executors.   But they do provide that the court must remove an assignee who does not give proper bond within ten days, and appoint a trustee in his place.

As soon as the assignee shall have given bond, the court must appoint three suitable, disinterested persons as appraisers of the property and assets of the assignor.

If the assignee fails to give bond, then such appraisers must be appointed for the same purpose, as soon as the trustee shall be appointed, and shall have given bond.

The assignee or trustee must, within thirty days after giving bond, unless the court shall allow a longer time, make and file in the court an inventory, verified by his oath, of all the property, money, rights and credits of the assignor included in the assignment, which shall have come to his possession or knowledge, together with an appraisement thereof by the appraisers under their oath.

At the time of filing the inventory, the assignee or trustee must also file a schedule of all the debts and liabilities of the assignor within his knowledge. This schedule must be verified by the oath of the assignee or trustee, and must contain the post office address of each creditor, as far as the same can be given.

The assignee or trustee shall proceed at once, to convert all the assets received by him, into money, and to sell the real and personal property assigned, including stocks, bonds, etc., upon such terms as the court may order.

Whenever the court shall be satisfied that it would be for the advantage of the creditors of the assignor, the court may order the business to be carried on by the assignee.

At the expiration of eight months from the appointment and qualification of the assignee or trustee, and as often thereafter as the court may order an account shall be filed with said court, by the assignee or trustee, containing a full exhibit of all his doings as such, together with the amount of all claims remaining uncollected and the amount, which in his opinion may thereafter be collected.

Whenever, on settlement, the account shall show a balance remaining in the hands of the assignee or trustee, subject to distribution among the general creditors, a dividend shall be declared by the Probate Judge, payable out of such balance, equally among all the creditors entitled, in proportion to the amount of their respective claims against the assignor.

An assignee or trustee should direct that the books be opened to conform with the inventory of the appraisers, and shall have them conducted upon the principles of double entry. The system of accounting should depend upon the nature and extent of the business.

When the books have been properly opened and conducted, it is an easy matter to render a partial or final account. There is no prescribed form of such accounts, but they should be made in as simple a manner as possible, and the simpler and plainer it is, the better it is, if it be accurate and complete.

Every assignee and trustee should have a thorough knowledge of the law. He should not transact any important business without the advice and consent of the court, to whom he is responsible.

There are so many points in which the assignee and trustee are held personally liable, that I would advise a written order from the court, for all important matters. Trouble might be saved also, by seeing that such orders are entered upon the Journal.

Receivers.

A receiver, in Law, is a person appointed by a Probate, Common Pleas, Circuit or Supreme Court Judge to take charge of property, when that property is held in trust or otherwise by some person or party, and there is danger of the property being removed, wasted, or squandered, or where the interests of third persons in the property, whether present, future, or contingent, are likely to be seriously injured.

The receiver should be an indifferent person between the parties, and usually has the power to do everything in and about the property which it does not seem proper to the court that either one of the parties should do. But he can exercise only such powers as are expressly given to him by order of the court appointing him.

The appointment of a receiver is an equitable remedy, and its object is prevention, rather than redress of injuries; the appointment is always a matter of discretion for the court. This remedy has become so frequent and important that the subject is now governed by statutes in nearly every state; but the courts still cling to the old principles of the courts of equity in relation to the appointment and conduct of receivers.

The general rules governing the appointment of a receiver are, first, that the power is to be exercised with great circumspection ; second, the court must be satisfied, generally by affidavit, that the claimant has title to the property, and that a receiver is necessary to preserve the property; third, fraud or imminent danger; if the court should not interfere, must be clearly shown ; and unless the danger is urgent, the court will not appoint a receiver unless notice of the application be given to the defendant in action.

On an application for a receiver, the court will closely scrutinize the conduct of the applicant, and unless it be perfectly blameless and beyond reproach, no receiver will be appointed.

The receiver is an officer of the court, and, before taking charge of the property, he must generally execute and file with the court a bond for faithful performance of his duties ; until the bond is approved by the court, he cannot assume control over the property.

Being an officer of the court, he cannot sue or be sued, unless leave for such action is first obtained from the court.

The effect of the appointment of a receiver is to take the possession of the property out of the hands of the parties to the suit ; but their right or title to the property is in no way affected by such appointment; his duty is to manage and to preserve the property under the control and with the advice of the court.

Receivers are frequently appointed when the legal holders are incapacitated from taking care of the property, e. g., infants and lunatics, when rights of other parties might be endangered; in cases where disputes arise between buyer and seller, and most generally in cases of insolvent firms and corporations.

When an application is filed for the appointment of a receiver, such application shall contain a statement of the reasons which induce the applicants to apply for such action, and these shall be annexed thereto.

1st.   A full, just and true inventory of all the estate, both real and personal, in law and equity, of the corporation, and of all the books, vouchers and securities relating thereto.

2d.   A full, just and true account of the Capital Stock, if any, of the corporation, specifying the names of the stockholders, their residence, the number of shares belonging to each, the amount paid in upon such shares respectively, and the amount still due thereon.

3rd.   A statement of all the incumbrances on the property of the corporation, and of all engagements entered into by it, which have not been fully satisfied or cancelled, specifying the place of residence of each creditor, and of every person to whom such engagements were made, the sum owing to each creditor, the nature of each debt or demand, and the true cause and consideration of such indebtedness.

To every such petition there shall also be annexed an affadivit of the applicants, that the facts stated in the application, and the accounts, inventories, and statements contained therein or annexed thereto, are just and true, so far as they know, or have the means of knowing.

Upon such petition, accounts, inventories, and affidavits being filed, an order is entered requiring all persons interested in the corporation to show cause, if they have any, why the appointment should not be made.   If it appear to the court that the corporation is insolvent, or that a dissolution thereof will be beneficial to the stockholders, and not injurious to the public interest, or that the objects of the corporation have wholly failed, etc., a judgment shall be entered dissolving the corporation, and appointing one or more receivers, of its estate and effects, for the purpose of winding up its affairs, or to operate its business until settlement of its financial difficulties.

A director, trustee, or other officer of the corporation or any of its stockholders, may be appointed a receiver. Such receiver shall be vested with all the estate, real and personal, of the corporation, from the time of filing his bond. He shall be trustee of such estate for the benefit of the creditors and stockholders.

If there be any sum remaining due upon any share of stock subscribed in the corporation, the receiver shall immediately proceed and recover the same, unless the person so indebted is wholly insolvent, and for that purpose may commence and prosecute an action for the recovery of such sum, without the consent of any creditor of the corporation.

As soon as a receiver has been appointed and his bond filed. he should give notice thereof by publication.

After the first publication of the notice of the appointment of a receiver, every person having possession of any property belonging to the corporation, and every person indebted thereto, must account and answer to the receiver for the amount of such debt, and for the value of such property.

The receiver shall call a general meeting of the creditors of the corporation, within four months from the time of his appointment, at which all accounts and demands for and against the corporation, and all its open and subsisting contracts, shall be ascertained and adjusted.

The receiver may, from time to time, make dividends of the money in his hands, among the creditors of the corporation, until they are paid in full; provided, however, he may have the funds; but no dividend shall be made to the stockholders until after the final dividend to creditors.

The receiver shall be subject to the direction and control of the court as to the time of making dividends, both to the creditors and stockholders of the company, and as to the time of winding up the corporation, and rendering his final accounts.

When required by the court, a receiver shall render a full and accurate account of all his proceedings to the court, on oath. In some states this account is referred to a referee or master commissioner for examination.

Before such account is rendered the receiver shall give notice by publication, specifying the time and place at which such account wi'l be rendered.

The referee to whom such account is referred, shall hear and ex-ːmine the proofs, vouchers and documents offered for or against the same, and shall report thereon fully to the court; and when the report is made, the court shall hear all concerned therein, and shall allow or disallow the account, and may decree the same to be final and con-clusive upon all the creditors of the corporation, upon all persons who have claims against it, and upon all the stockholders of the corporation.

It has been shown, that, with an application for the appointment of a receiver, a complete inventory of the corporation's effects must be filed, therefore when the receiver enters upon his administration, his first duty should be to make the books conform with the inventory, which should be kept stricty upon the principles of double entry.

When the books for a receivership have been properly opened and conducted, it will be found an easy matter to render a partial or final account therefrom.

Every important act of a receiver should be by and with the con-sent of the court. He should have all his orders in writing, also see that they have been entered upon the Court Journal.

It is not the purpose of these instructions to illustrate a system of accounting. The system to be adopted, depends upon the one in use, and the nature and extent of the business.

The ordinary principles of double entry are applicable to this as well as to any other branch of business, and if the instructions herein given should lead to further study on the subject, from the statutes of your own state, the purpose sought will have been accomplished.

CHAPTER TWENTY-NINE.

Building Association Accounting.

The plans and methods used in the management of Building and Loan Associations are numerous, and any attempt at the formation of a system of accounting undertaking to provide for all varying requirements, must fall short of success. The working of these institutions offers a broad field to the student of economics, and to the practical accountant.

Building Associations, since their introduction into the United States nearly sixty years ago, have appeared in several distinct forms, with so many modifications that an attempt to refer to all of them would be confusing, therefore, we will treat only those known to be the best.

Building or Savings and Loan Associations are corporations, and are now recognized generally as an important factor in the social economy of the country.

Shares of Stock.

Every member of an association is a stockholder, becoming such by subscribing for a certain number of shares. This subscription binds him legally to pay into the common fund, in regular installments, the amount represented by all of the shares for which he subscribed. The number of shares one member may hold is usually fixed by the constitution, or by-laws, and in some states the number is fixed by law.

In some instances the number of shares that may be held is not fixed, but only a specified number may be voted. This is done for the purpose of preventing a few heavy shareholders from obtaining and holding control of the association.

A stockholder in a building association pays only one dollar when he buys a share of stock, (except under certain circumstances) thereafter one dollar per month or week called *Dues* is paid, until the small sums thus paid, increased by the dividends to which he is entitled, equals par value of his shares.　When the par value is reached, the stock has matured, and the stockholder surrenders his shares to the association, and receives his money.　If he has had a loan equal to the value of his stock, the loan is cancelled when it matures.

Increase of Capital Stock.

The Capital Stock of an association is fixed originally in the articles of incorporation, the same as other corporations, but in most states associations have authority by their charters to increase their capital stock within the statutory limits and requirements.

The stock should be increased only when all the shares have been taken by *bona fide* subscriptions, because the increase involves additional expenses.　It is impossible to lay down uniform rules for increasing the capital.　All depends upon the nature of the association, the rules adopted by it, and the statutory requirements under which it is operated.　Associations increasing their stock should do so only under competent legal advice, and in strict accordance with law.

A provision in the charter of a terminating association for increasing the capital stock is unnecessary, as the term is generally understood, which will be shown hereafter

Shares are Transferable.

Shares of stock in building associations, like other corporations, are transferable by assignment and delivery, a method of which should be well defined in the constitution or by-laws.　A transfer of stock cannot be made, if it should in any way interfere with the corporate rights of the association.　If there are any arrears upon stock, it cannot be transferred until all arrears are paid, but when there are no arrears, and the holder of the stock has complied with all requirements the association is obliged to make transfers.　When transfers are made, a transfer fee is·charged to the person to whom the transfer is made.　This is an equivalent to the admission fee charged to new members.

Payment of Dues or Stock.

As stated above, payments on stock are made in small amounts weekly or monthly, called *Dues*, and when the stock is paid-up, it has reached its par, or expected value.　There is a vast difference between the expected and actual value of association stock, especially during the first years of a share-holder's membership.

, When a person subscribes for a share of stock of the par value of $500.00, he simply agrees to pay into the association a certain amount in regular weekly or monthly installments, until the accumulated payments, together with the accrued dividends thereon, shall amount to the par or full value of the share.   Therefore, it is plainly shown that the actual value of a share at any time is determined solely by the amount paid in and accumulated to date, and not by its face value.

Paid-Up Stock.

Each stockholder shares equitably in the profits made by an association, and when a dividend is declared it is credited to him.   Sometimes the dividends are drawn out, but to accomplish the purpose for which associations are formed, they should be left to the credit of the shareholders.   Therefore, as soon as the total amount of dues and dividends to the credit of any stockholder equals the full amount of his shares, the shares are paid-up or have matured.

Stock matures, or is paid-up at once, if the subscriber is simply seeking a safe and profitable investment, by paying the full value of his stock in one payment at the beginning.   This is frequently the case but as most of the members are wage-earners, and have become members of the association to accumulate by small savings, they most generally withdraw when their stock matures, either in cash, or the cancellation of a loan.   If desirable the owner of paid-up shares may leave his money with the association as an investment, and receive therefor a "Certificate of Paid-up Stock."   Unless restricted by the constitution, paid-up stock is entitled to dividends the same as running stock.

In a terminating association, shares must be paid off as they mature, this custom is still followed to a great extent in other associations. Unless required to do so, it is a question worth considering as to whether the funds should be withdrawn when the stock matures. The association may be able to use the money to good advantage, and may be seriously crippled by its withdrawal.   This is particularly true in the case of a serial association, where all the stock of each series matures at the same time.   To meet the payments which will then become due will necessitate the accumulation of a large amount of money.   When shares are maturing in small numbers from time to time, as in the permanent or perpetual associations, the accumulation of funds to meet them is not of so much consequence, as the addition of new members will supply the funds.

Building associations are conducted upon different plans, and in order to get a clear understanding of the manner in which the stock is issued, the various schemes will be reviewed.

Terminating Plan.

The first associations were conducted upon the terminating plan, and were useful, but they have given way largely to more popular plans. The scheme known as the Terminating Plan, contained three serious defects, which it was very desirable to obviate, namely, the dissolution of the association when the stock matured ; the large amount of back dues, which a new stockholder was obliged to pay, who took stock after the association had been running for some time, lastly the making of forced loans, that is, compelling the shareholder to become a borrower, whether he wanted to be or not.

In a terminating association all the stock was issued as of one date, as the associations are organized on the presumption that all the stock will be subscribed at the first meetings. but this is seldom done. The result is, that shares sold after the first meetings must be sold at such prices as to make them equal in value to those first issued. To accomplish this a sum must be charged equal to the amount paid in in installments by the subscriber to the original shares. Should the regular dues on shares be one dollar per week, a person subscribing for a share after the association has been running, say five weeks, must pay five dollars for the share. For every week the association has been running the subscriber would have to pay an additional dollar. Again, if the subscription is not made until after profits have been declared, the subscriber must pay such additional amount on his shares as will correspond with the earnings of the original shares up to that time. An association organized upon this plan is more difficult to enter each year, and is not well adapted to meet the conditions of the class of people who are most likely to be benefited by such associations.

From the foregoing it will be seen that all the shares of a terminating association are at all times of equal value, and when the total amount of dues paid in, and accrued dividends equal the face value of all the shares, the association terminates, and must wind up its affairs. Those who have borrowed money on their shares, have the mortgages cancelled as the debt has been paid, and those who have not borrowed receive the full value of their shares.

To overcome the defects in the terminating plan, the

Serial Plan

was developed.   Under this scheme, the stock is issued in series, at the beginning of each fiscal year, half yearly, quarterly and sometimes even oftener, as first series, second series, etc.

The development of the serial plan obviated two of the defects in the terminating plan.   It permitted the association to become perpetual, and it furnished a new series of stock so often that one taking stock at any time in the current series was not compelled to pay a large amount of back dues in order to place him in the same position that he would have been, had he taken his shares at the beginning. The serial plan also obviates the third defect, except in rare cases.   It permits of the accession of new share holders who become such for the express purpose of becoming borrowers.   When a terminating association had become two or more years old, the amount of back dues they were required to pay on their stock, in order to become stockholders, so they might become borrowers, was a very serious obstacle ; while under the serial plan, the amount was not large at any time.

At the end of the first term the assets of the association are divided by the total number of shares in the first series, this gives the value of the shares in the first series.   The second series is then issued and rated at par value.   The shares in the second issue run in the same manner as those of the first, and at the end of the second term, the sum total of the income of the term is divided by the total number of shares in both series, thus ascertaining the equitable withdrawal value of shares in each series.   The third series is then issued, and so on to the end.

It is readily seen that under this plan the older the series the greater the value of the shares.   The serial associations are more numerous at the present time than any other form.

The Perpetual or Permanent Plan.

Building associations became so popular, and developed so rapidly, that a demand arose for some other form of association, better adapted and more practical than either the terminating or serial plan. This demand resulted in the perpetual or permanent plan.   Under this plan associations are granted perpetual charters, as the amount of their capital stock is fixed at a certain sum.   This plan is no more entitled to be called a "permanent plan" than the serial plan, as both make the existence of the association perpetual.

As soon as a portion of the stock has been subscribed, the association is allowed to begin operations, and as soon as it is in operation new members are allowed to enter at any time, on an equality with the original subscribers, the stock of each member dating from the time of his entry.

Members may withdraw at any time, under this plan, by complying with the rules of the association, receiving their equitable share of the assets. It has been proven by experience that it is possible to work out the plans for the calculation of dividends, premiums, interest etc., and to arrange all the other details of the operations of an association, in such manner that it may be able to treat each share equitably upon its own merits, without interfering with the interests of any other share in any way.

Since this plan has been introduced, associations in large numbers have sprung up all over the country. While many improvements are still expected, it is likely that this plan will become the general form which building associations will eventually adopt.

The National Plan.

A building association is a money-*saving* institution, and is not, and in no speculative sense can be, a money-making institution for some of its members at the expense of others. It is in its very nature a mutual, co-operative society, and its affairs are managed by its own members for their own mutual interests. It deals only with its members. All that comes into it comes from members, and all that goes out of it goes to members. There are no outside producers and there are no outside beneficiaries. This being the nature of Building Associations it is apparent that they should be local in their organization and operation. In order that all members may have a personal knowledge of all the association's affairs, and may participate in its management, it is essential that the members have a personal knowledge of one another.

There may be some form of National Industrial, commercial or financial co-operation, but in the very nature of the institution itself, I doubt if there can be such a thing as a National Building Association. However, statistics show that about 5 per cent. of all associations are national. They are not mutual in their character, they are not mutual in their management, for some members profit at the expense of others; officers perpetuate themselves in office, and fix their own salaries. Stockholders do not, and cannot participate in its management, and are not advised of the transactions of the concern.

It is well known that it is possible for a national to have a superior method of operation to that of a local, and the reverse may be true. We must look beyond this for the distinguishing features, and we find these all reduced to one single, simple proposition; the success of a building and loan association depending, as it does, almost entirely upon the quality of its management, does the question of locality cut any figure?

A well-conducted national is certainly to be preferred to a badly managed local, and a well-conducted local has a decided preference over the badly managed national. We can go a little further and safely say, that everything being equal, the local is entitled to a greater consideration because of the advantage it enjoys of local self-government. There is generally an active interest taken in the management of the locals by nearly every shareholder.

The officers are constantly put upon their best metal in the performance of their duties, knowing that if derelict the next election means retirement. The loans are made with great caution and publicity, so that collusion and excessive loans are rare indeed. Should an officer approve and pass a bad loan, he will surely be called to account by some shareholder. In the Nationals the loans do not have this guardianship, except, perhaps, where there are local boards in active and effective operation, and even then there is danger of favoritism and partiality. The whole business of the Nationals must be done through agencies more or less unreliable, involving a larger percentage of expense than the locals. Office rent, advertising, salaries, commissions, appraisers' fees, attorneys' expenses, etc., all contribute to the disadvantage of the national over the local institution. Someone must stand this expense, and if profits are not proportionately greater, the shareholders are the burden bearers.

We regard the frequent changes in management amongst the locals as most decidedly in their favor, for it ensures the very best kind of service. The shareholders in the Nationals, do not have guaranteed them an intelligent voting prerogative, which frequently causes the retention of selfish and incapable men. The men seeking their proxies are the very ones concerned in keeping themselves in office under definite salaries. Right here it is to be observed that an officer desiring to perpetuate himself in a salaried position is constantly under a temptation to put the very best aspect of an association' condition before the shareholders, and to hold back the discouraging features. It is human nature to do this, and can be continued from year to year until scarcely anything but a shell is left of the concern.

The locals have an important and most decided preference over the Nationals in that they can know something of the personality of the borrowers. This is vital, and does not always receive that consideration which it deserves. They also are able to avoid loaning on raw property and are better acquainted with conditions that should govern every loan. We are not oblivious to the fact that such a state of things is possible with the Nationals but the chances are fewer for their prevailing. Economy in management is a most decided factor in determining the worthiness of a building and loan association. So, also, is the honesty and capability of its officers. With remotely situated associations it is extremely difficult and sometimes quite impossible to ascertain regarding their standing. Investors should move cautiously before extending their patronage where satisfactory answers cannot be given to their investigations.

Loans.

The funds of an association are loaned only to its stockholders. Every stockholder has the right to become a borrower, upon giving the required security, to an amount equal to the matured value of the shares owned by him. Although all stockholders have the right to become borrowers, it is not reasonable to suppose that all will want to borrow at the same time, but it does frequently occur that there will not be sufficient money to meet the demands of all who wish to borrow. When such is the case, to whom shall the loans be *made*.

That all may have a fair opportunity of securing this privilege, the rules of many associations and the statutes in a number of states require that at stated times the officers shall offer the money on hand, when it reaches a certain sum, for sale to the stockholders.

These requirements should specify the time and place at which the money will be offered for loan, and stockholders notified.

When there is competition for the use of the money, the officers will announce the number of shares or the amount to be loaned. Bids are then received. These bids are merely offers to pay certain premiums in regular weekly or monthly installments.

The highest bidder is the buyer provided, however, the security offered is satisfactory. If the security offered is not satisfactory, the loan goes to the next highest bidder, or the shares are put up and sold again.

This is the most equitable, popular and satisfactory method of deciding to whom a loan shall be made. However, the association should discourage the bidding of large premiums.

Premiums.

A premium is, and should be understood to be a bonus which a borrowing member agrees to pay for the privilege of having money advanced to him. Premiums for loans should not enter into any association for the sake of profits, but simply as a mode to decide who shall have the money. As the purpose of associations is to loan money to its members, it does not seem right, that a bonus should be paid to obtain it, but that the applications should be paid in the order in which they are filed. Some associations have adopted this system with great success.

When the plan of the association requires a uniform rate of interest, and the premium bid is understood to be a *bonus* to be paid at the time, the amount of that bonus will be controlled by the condition of the money market. If the demand for money is greater than the supply, the bonus will be accordingly, but if the supply exceeds the demand, no premiums should be bid.

There is great divergence upon the subject of the kind of premium bid and how paid in building associations, and it would be confusing to undertake to explain all of them, therefore, only a few general principles will be pointed out.

The unit in all loans, is the matured or par value of a share. The language of a borrower, when stating how much money he wants to borrow, describes it by saying "one share," if the shares are $200.00 each, he calls for a $200.00 loan, "five shares" for a $1000.00 loan, etc. If the loan is less than par of the share, it is a definite fractional part, one fourth or half of that sum.

The premium bid is simply so much a share, this is readily understood and easily computed. If the premium bid is a dollar per share, and the number of shares he is borrowing is ten, the total premium is $10.00, and the total amount of money he will receive will be $2000.00, less the premium, or $1990.00. Although he receives but $1990.00, he pays interest on $2000.00, and gives security for that sum.

Security.

As soon as a member has been awarded a loan, he must submit his security, if acceptable the money will be paid him.

The following are the securities required by associations:

1.　A bond conditioned upon the payment of the loan and the interest thereon, according to the provisions of the plan of the association.

2.　Assignment to the association, of the shares borrowed upon as collateral security for the payment of the loan.

3.　A first-mortgage upon unincumbered real estate, upon the same conditions as the bond and collateral.

4.　National, State, County, and Municipal bonds may also be given as collateral.

5.　In lieu of the mortgage, other shares of stock of the association may be pledged, provided their withdrawal value, added to the withdrawal value of the shares borrowed upon, shall exceed the amount of the loan and interest thereon, for six months.

This gives absolute security, as the association has the money with which to make good the loan in case of default.

A loan secured by a pledge of shares is a Stock Loan, and when secured by a mortgage, a Mortgage Loan.

If a borrower from any cause fails to keep up his dues and interest and becomes six months in arrears, the whole loan matures at once, and the association may begin an action to foreclose upon the securities.

The withdrawal value of the shares borrowed upon, at the time of commencing the action, must be applied upon the debt, and the stock cancelled, and the decree taken for the balance. Thereafter the procedure will be controlled by the courts.

Sale of Securities—Disposition of Proceeds.

When associations are compelled to foreclose a mortgage, or forfeited securities, they are bound to dispose of the property on the most advantageous terms. This is necessary for the protection of both the association and borrower. The proceeds received from the sale of securities must be applied as follows : 1st.—To the payments of dues. 2nd.—To payment of interest. 3rd.—To payment of premiums. 4th.—To payment of fines. 5th.—To payment of costs. If any balance remains it must be paid to the owner, and his receipt taken in full.

Fines for Non-Payment of Dues, etc.

The success of an association depends upon the regular payment of dues by its members, and in order to have these payments made promptly, the constitution and by-laws of every association require that they be made at a certain time, and fix penalties for default.

The general custom is to impose a fine, not exceeding ten per cent. for each month in arrears, for every dollar of dues or interest which a shareholder shall refuse, or neglect to pay at the time it is due.

When a member is in arrears for dues, the directors should ascertain the cause. If the member is a borrower, and his delinquency is due to misfortune, his case should be inquired into thoroughly, and the fine remitted, provided, however, the misfortune was not the fault of the member. Such care of overburdened members, will only add to the popularity of an association. Of course this does not apply to members who are careless and negligent.

Forfeitures.

When fines are not sufficient to compel members to keep up their payments, the association has the right to declare their stock forfeited, and to take possession of it, subject to the provision of the constitution. The constitution and by-laws should define very clearly the causes for which stock may be declared forfeited, and the method by which the forfeiture shall take place.

A stockholder who forfeits his stock relieves himself of further obligations in the way of dues, and consequently his membership.

Right of Withdrawal.

Shareholders in building associations have a right to withdraw the money invested, provided, however, the stock is free, by this is meant the stock of an investor and not that of a borrower.

This is a very important matter and requires the solution of two distinct questions. 1. What percentage of the profits should a withdrawing member receive? 2. Shall the withdrawal value be determined and fixed by the articles of association, or shall it be discretionary with the board of directors? For mutual protection of its members, the right must be exercised under proper restrictions. The constitution of every association should prescribe in detail the method of withdrawal. Usually any shareholder owning free shares may withdraw from the association, upon filing a written notice with the secretary, and at the next meeting of the board of directors they direct orders to be drawn upon the treasurer to pay such shareholder, according to the priority in the filing of such notices.

It must be remembered that every share of stock outstanding has two values upon the books of the association, viz., the "Holding Value" and the "Withdrawal Value." The holding value is made up of all the dues that have been paid in, plus all the profits that have been added in the distribution of profits. The withdrawal value is the sum which the association will pay to the shareholders who *withdraw* before their stock has reached its maturity. In determining the holding value of a withdrawing shareholder's stock, it is not customary to allow all the profits which have been added to his stock.

The association should retain some portion of it, not merely as a matter of profit to the association, but to cover any loss that may have occurred since the last distribution of profits, a portion of which the withdrawing shareholder should stand　The share of the profits returned, deducted from the holding value, will give the withdrawal value.

Distribution of Profits—Holding Value of Shares. Annual Series— Monthly Dues $1

The greatest care and accuracy should ·be exercised in the calculation and distribution of profits. Many associations have become greatly embarrassed on account of carelessness or incompetency in this connection. As this is the most important and difficult part of association accounting, the methods of calculation will be illustrated. Although there are several reliable interest and maturity tables published, accountants should be able to make the calculations without reference to them.

The gross profits of an association are made up of premuims, fines, interest, entrance and transfer fees, and the profits left by withdrawing shareholders. The principle item of profit is interest. The dues paid represent capital and cannot be reckoned as profits.

Our first illustration will be at the close of the fiscal year for an association which issues annual series only, with dues $1 per month. Before the distribution of profits is made, all the expenses of conducting the business should always be paid in full up to the time the distribution is made. For the purpose of illustration, let us assume the association has issued during the year, twelve hundred shares of stock; that two hundred of these shares have been withdrawn, and at the end of the fiscal year only one thousand shares are outstanding. There has been paid during the year, twelve dollars in dues upon each of these shares, making the total amount upon all the shares twelve thousand dollars.

If there are any arrears and fines on these shares, the amount should be treated as an asset, because the amount is due the association, and will be collected. The assets will then consist of cash, loans, (for which securities are held) dues, delinquent interest and fines accrued on same.

While the sum of the items just mentioned will constitute the assets on hand, there is another item that must not be lost sight of when the profits are to be distributed, that is, the interest on the loans for the last month of the fiscal year, which will not be paid until the first meeting of the new fiscal year. To ascertain the exact profits of the year, the interest accrued during the last month of the old fiscal year must be counted among the assets. The interest on the loans for the last month of the fiscal year, added to the above assets, gives the total assets for the purpose of distribution. The net profits of the year's business, is found by deducting the twelve thousand dollars liability for dues paid, (which constitutes the capital of the association) from the total assets. The net profit divided by the number of shares outstanding (one thousand) will give the sum that should be added to each share as a dividend, or divide the net profits by the total amount of capital, which is twelve thousand dollars, and this will give the percentage to be added to each dollar of the capital as a dividend.

The percentage method must be used if there are several series outstanding.

It will be noticed that in making this calculation, there were no liabilities other than the capital. When a distribution of profits is made, the only item of liability outside of capital, should be for borrowed money, and if the association has such a liability, it must be treated in making the statement to find the net profit for distribution.

The dividend added to the dues paid ($12.00) during the year, constitutes the holding value of each share of stock at the beginning of the next fiscal year, and the sum of such "Holding Value" of all the shares outstanding will constitute the capital of the association at the beginning of the next year.

The distribution of profits in an association issuing a yearly series at the end of its third fiscal year, will next be illustrated. There will be three series of stock outstanding the holding value of each share of the first and second series being determined at the last distribution of profits. Taking the holding value of one share in the first series and multiplying it by the total number of shares outstanding in that series at the end of the third fiscal year, gives the total holding value of the first series. A similar operation in reference to the outstanding shares in the second series, will give the total holding value of that series. Add the amounts thus found to find the total holding value of the first and second series, which constituted the total capital of the association at the beginning of the third fiscal year, upon which monthly interest has been received during the year.

It has been shown that upon each of the shares outstanding at the close of the third year there has been paid twelve dollars of dues. There has also been paid twelve dollars of dues on each share outstanding in the third series. These dues are not only a liability, but they have been added to the capital, and are entitled to share in the profits, and must be treated in this double aspect.

It is a very simple matter to treat them as a liability in making up the statement of assets and liabilities. The total number of shares outstanding in all three series, multiplied by twelve, will give the sum total as a liability, also as capital. By adding their sum total to the holding value of the first and second series as above found, we have the total liability of the association on account of capital. Should there be any other liabilities of any kind, they should be added to this total for the purpose of making the statement of assets and liabilities. The total assets are then ascertained, the items of which have been explained. These assets must also contain the interest which becomes due and payable at the first meeting in the next year.

By this method the interest will be as many dollars as there are shares borrowed upon. From the total assets, deduct the total liabilities, and the remainder is the net sum of the profits for the year, from which a dividend is declared.

Each dollar of the capital represented by the first and second series of stock is entitled to the same dividend, because it has been invested the whole year.

The dues paid during the third fiscal year have not been invested during the whole year, but have been paid from month to month, and invested from time to time, such being the case, it will be necessary to find what sum invested for a year would be their equivalent. For an illustration, we will first take the dues paid upon a single share, which is twelve dollars. The first dollar paid at the beginning of the year has been invested twelve months; the second dollar eleven months; the third, ten months, and so on to the twelfth dollar which has been invested one month.

The sum of the months is 12, 11, 10, 9, 8, 7, 6, 5, 4, 3, 2 and 1=78. If one dollar be paid and invested at the beginning of each month, it is equivalent to one dollar invested for seventy-eight months, and one dollar invested for seventy-eight months is equal to $6.50 invested for one month. The total number of shares outstanding in all the series multiplied by $6.50, will give the sum which if invested for the whole year, would produce the same income that the total dues will produce when received in monthly installments, and invested from time to time. This equated sum, added to the total value of the first and second series, will give the total sum by which to divide the net profits. The quotient will be the rate per cent. of dividend to be declared upon each dollar of the capital invested during the year.

To the "Holding Value" of a share in the first series, at the beginning of the third fiscal year, add the dividend on the dues paid during the year as equated above, and the dues themselves, and we shall have the holding value or capital value of the share at the beginning of the fourth fiscal year. The value of one share, multiplied by the number of shares in the first series, will give the total holding value of the first series.

A similar operation in reference to a share in the second series, will produce the holding value of second series, at the beginning of the fourth fiscal year.

For the third series, multiply $6.50 by the rate per cent of dividend, and add the $12.00 dues paid. The sum, thus found, will be the holding value of a share in the third series at the beginning of the fourth fiscal year. Multiplying the value of one share in the third series, by the total number of shares in the third series, will give the total value of this series.

If the calculations have been correct, the total value of the three series, will equal the total amount of the assets. If they do not agree, some errors have been made, which should be found and corrected at once.

This method of calculation can be applied for any number of series outstanding. The same operations are to be performed for each series, except the last, which have been described with reference to the first and second series as above. The operation regarding the dues paid during the year upon all series including the last series, is also the same as above.

The same method of calculation is used when stock is issued in semi-annual or quarterly series. The only variation will be in equaling the monthly payments, which will be for the shorter term instead of for one year. As stated elsewhere in this work, no company or association should declare a dividend for the full profits, a certain amount should be set aside for unforseen emergencies or unexpected loss.

Semi-Annual Dividend—Weekly Dues 50c. and $1.00.

The method explained in the foregoing covered stock issued in annual series, with *Monthly* Dues $1.00 per share. The next illustration will be for declaring Semi-annual Dividends, with *Weekly* Dues 50 cents, and $1.00 per share.

For the First Semi-annual Dividend we will assume that Mr. C. E. Cady has one $500 share of stock on which he has paid $1.00 per week dues for six months or twenty-six weeks. What would be his portion of a 6% semi-annual dividend?

Solution.—The sum of $1.00 paid weekly for a term of six months or twenty-six weeks is equal to an average credit of $13.50 for the term. A 6% semi-annual dividend on $13.50 is, 81 cents.

For the second and all subsequent dividends, we will assume that Mr. John Grabbe has three $500 shares (weekly dues $1 per share) and that he has paid $375. What would be his portion of a 7% dividend?

Solution.—From $375 the total amount paid, subtract the amount he has paid since the last dividend which is $3.00 per week for twenty-six weeks or $78.00. $375.00—$78.00=$297, 7% of the difference is $20.79, or dividend upon $297.00. The sum of $3.00 paid weekly for a term of six months, or twenty-six weeks is equal to an average credit of $40.50 for the term.

A 7 per cent. semi-annual dividend on $40.50 is $2.83. The dividend on $297 is $20.97 + $2.83 the dividend on the weekly payments since the last settlement = $23.80, the amount of dividend due on $375.

The average credits for the term as shown in the above solutions, are found by adding the number of weeks each $1.00 has been paid in. The sum of the weeks thus found, divided by the number of weeks in the term, gives the average amount of credit for the term. That is if $1.00 be paid at the beginning of the week and paid weekly for a term of twenty-six weeks, the first dollar would be on interest twenty-six weeks, the second dollar twenty-five weeks, the third dollar twenty-four weeks, and so on down to one. The total is 351 weeks. The credits on the payments are together equal to a credit on $1.00 for 351 weeks. One dollar for 351 weeks, is equal to as many dollars for twenty-six weeks, as twenty-six is contained times in 351 weeks, which is 13½ times or $13.50.

To illustrate computations of this kind:

Table No. 1.—Equated Credits on One Share at $1.00 Each

has been prepared, to show the equated payments of $1.00 per week, paid at the beginning of each week, for one to twenty-six weeks. By referring to the table you will observe two rulings at the foot of each column. The amount directly under the single line, is the number of weeks the payments bear interest. The number of weeks thus shown divided by twenty- six, the number of weeks in the term, will give the equated credit, which is shown directly under the double lines.

If the calculations are to be made, this table will be found very useful. It is also given to teach the method of calculation. However it need not be used in practice, as

Table No. 2.—Equated Credits $1.00 Per Share,

will save these calculations. This table is made from Table No. 1, and shows the average or equated credits for $1.00 per share, paid at the beginning of each week, for one to twenty-six weeks and for one to twenty shares, both inclusive.

For an illustration, let us suppose that W. E. Bardwell has five shares and has paid $1.00 per share, for seventeen weeks, what would be the average credit of his payments?

By referring to table No. 2, we find under five shares and opposite seventeen weeks $29.43, which is the average credit for the term. The average credit multiplied by the rate per cent. dividend will give the amount of the dividend.

It will be noticed that table No. 1, shows only the average of one share or $1.00, while table No. 2, shows the average for one to twenty shares. The average for any number of shares found by multiplying the number of weeks in table No. 1, by the number of shares, this product is then divided by twenty-six, the number of weeks in the term.

Table No. 3.—Equated Credits 50 Cents Per Share.

This table shows the equated credits for 50 cents per share per week, paid at the beginning of the week. These averages are found by multiplying the number of weeks in table No. 1, by the amount of the weekly payment, this product is then divided by twenty-six, the number of weeks in the term, the same as for payments of $1.00 per share.

These averages multiplied by the rate of dividend, will give the amount of dividend due the shareholder.

Table No. 4—Equated Credits $1.00 Per Share.

This table shows the equated credits for $1.00 per share, paid at the expiration of each week for 1 to 26 weeks. It will be readily seen that if the payments are made at the expiration of the week, instead of the beginning, the last payment will be made at the end of the term, and will not be on interest, consequently one week in the term of 26 weeks will be lost. This table is made from one similar to No. 1. From this one it will be an easy matter to make an equated table, if payments are made at the expiration of the week.

If the weekly payments are 25 cents, 75 cents or any other rate per share, an equated table could very easily be prepared by the above methods.

These average tables are very useful and will save a great deal of labor, but we will go a step further, and say that all the tables mentioned can be dispensed with by using the

Dividend Table No 5.

This table shows the dividend at 6 per cent. on the average credit for any number of weeks from 1 to 26, and for any number of shares from 1 to 20 at $1.00 per share, paid weekly at the beginning of each week.

For an illustration, let us suppose that a dividend of 6 per cent. has been declared, what would be your dividend on 5 shares, paid regularly for 23 weeks?

By referring to Table No. 5, under the column of 5 shares and opposite 23 weeks, we find $3.18, which is the dividend. Since the dividend table has been prepared from the average table, a table for any rate per cent. can easily be arranged, as in No. 5, by simply multiplying the average credits by the required rate.

If dividend tables are prepared, then the other tables need not be used, because the amounts shown in the dividend tables mean the dividend for the number of weeks, and shares as indicated, at 50 cents or $1.00 per share, payable at the beginning or expiration of the week, as the case may be.

A careful study of these calculations and tables will be of much interest, and save a great deal of time and labor.

Building Association Accounting.

The system of accounts adopted by Building Associations should be as simple as possible to secure accuracy. This, of course, cannot be accomplished unless double entry is used.

The forms of the books used are very simple, and need not be illustrated; however, the important books will be explained and a few specimen entries given, to make the subject perfectly clear.

It would involve a great amount of labor and expense to keep a ledger account with every member of an association, such as would show the exact amount of dues paid by him, and the dividends on his shares.

. The same information can be obtained otherwise with equal accuracy, and much less labor and expense. The main set of books will show the value of one share in each series, while every share of stock in the same series, has precisely the same value; therefore, an auxiliary set of stock-books showing the series in which, and the number of shares in a series, held by each member, will give all the necessary information, with which to find the value of the shares of each member. Simply multiplying the value of one share by the number of shares in the series held by the member will give the desired information.

The main set of books consists of a dues, interest and fines book, cash-received book, journal day-book, ledger and transfer book. The auxiliary books consist of a stock journal day-book, stock ledger, with an index giving the address of each member; stock trial-balance book, security record, index and trial-balance book for mail ledger, inventory book, and book containing by-laws, to be subscribed by members on joining the association.

The Dues, Interest and Fines Book.—The entries in this book are made as the money is paid in.

The Cash Received Book.—The entries in this book are made from the dues, interest and fines book, and from memoranda made by the secretary of other payments received, which do not properly belong in that book.

The dues column shows the amount of dues received, the interest column the amount of interest received, the fines column the amount of fines received, the entrance fee column the amount of entrance fees received, and is needed only when new shares have been issued to a member; the total column gives the total receipts, and is the sum of the entries in all of the other columns.

If the cash-received book is posted direct to the ledger, the " Dues " account will be credited with the monthly total of the "dues" column. " Interest " account is credited with the monthly total of the "interest" column; "Fines" account is credited with the monthly total of the " fines " column; "Entrance Fees" account is credited with the monthly total of the "entrance fee" column. "Loans" account is credited with monthly total of the loans repaid.

Members are credited with the excess of their payments over the amount due for dues, interest and fines. The money is turned over to the Treasurer, whose account is charged with the sum total of the credits enumerated. If the plan of the association is such as to require the payment of premiums, then a " Premium " column will have to be provided. Under the gross plan, the premiums are paid by being deducted from the face of the loan.

The Stock Journal Day-Book.—The entries are made in this book when shares are issued. It shows only the number of the certificates, the series and number of shares. The sum received appears in the cash-received book.

The Stock Ledger.—The entries in this book are taken from the stock journal day-book, and show the aggregate shares issued and redeemed in each series. The form of this ledger is necessarily different from the individual accounts in the stock ledger, because the information desired is entirely different.

Table No. 1.—Equated Credits of One Share at $1.00 Each. From 1 to 26 Weeks.

1	2	3	4	5	6	7	8	9	10	11	12	13	14	15	16	17	18	19	20	21	22	23	24	25	26
1	1	1	1	1	1	1	1	1	1	1	1	1	1	1	1	1	1	1	1	1	1	1	1	1	1
	2	2	2	2	2	2	2	2	2	2	2	2	2	2	2	2	2	2	2	2	2	2	2	2	2
		3	3	3	3	3	3	3	3	3	3	3	3	3	3	3	3	3	3	3	3	3	3	3	3
			4	4	4	4	4	4	4	4	4	4	4	4	4	4	4	4	4	4	4	4	4	4	4
				5	5	5	5	5	5	5	5	5	5	5	5	5	5	5	5	5	5	5	5	5	5
					6	6	6	6	6	6	6	6	6	6	6	6	6	6	6	6	6	6	6	6	6
						7	7	7	7	7	7	7	7	7	7	7	7	7	7	7	7	7	7	7	7
							8	8	8	8	8	8	8	8	8	8	8	8	8	8	8	8	8	8	8
								9	9	9	9	9	9	9	9	9	9	9	9	9	9	9	9	9	9
									10	10	10	10	10	10	10	10	10	10	10	10	10	10	10	10	10
										11	11	11	11	11	11	11	11	11	11	11	11	11	11	11	11
											12	12	12	12	12	12	12	12	12	12	12	12	12	12	12
												13	13	13	13	13	13	13	13	13	13	13	13	13	13
													14	14	14	14	14	14	14	14	14	14	14	14	14
														15	15	15	15	15	15	15	15	15	15	15	15
															16	16	16	16	16	16	16	16	16	16	16
																17	17	17	17	17	17	17	17	17	17
																	18	18	18	18	18	18	18	18	18
																		19	19	19	19	19	19	19	19
																			20	20	20	20	20	20	20
																				21	21	21	21	21	21
																					22	22	22	22	22
																						23	23	23	23
																							24	24	24
																								25	25
																									26
1	**3**	**6**	**10**	**15**	**21**	**28**	**36**	**45**	**55**	**66**	**78**	**91**	**105**	**120**	**136**	**153**	**171**	**190**	**210**	**231**	**253**	**276**	**300**	**325**	**351**
.04	.12	.23	.39	.58	.81	1.08	1.39	1.73	2.12	2.54	3.00	3.50	4.04	4.62	5.23	5.89	6.58	7.31	8.08	8.89	9.73	10.62	11.54	12.50	13.50

Table No. 2.—Equated Credits $1.00 per Share, paid at the beginning of each Week.

Number of Shares. Weeks	1	2	3	4	5	6	7	8	9	10	11	12	13	14	15	16	17	18	19	20
1	.04	.08	.12	.15	.19	.23	.27	.31	.35	.39	.42	.46	.50	.54	.58	.62	.66	.69	.73	.77
2	.12	.23	.34	.46	.57	.69	.80	.92	1.03	1.15	1.26	1.38	1.49	1.61	1.72	1.84	1.96	2.07	2.18	2.30
3	.23	.46	.69	.92	1.15	1.38	1.61	1.84	2.07	2.30	2.53	2.76	2.99	3.22	3.45	3.68	3.91	4.14	4.37	4.60
4	.39	.77	1.15	1.54	1.92	2.31	2.69	3.08	3.46	3.85	4.23	4.62	5.00	5.38	5.77	6.16	6.54	6.93	7.31	7.70
5	.58	1.15	1.72	2.30	2.87	3.45	4.02	4.60	5.17	5.75	6.32	6.90	7.47	8.05	8.62	9.20	9.77	10.35	10.92	11.50
6	.81	1.61	2.41	3.22	4.02	4.83	5.63	6.44	7.24	8.05	8.85	9.66	10.46	11.27	12.07	12.88	13.68	14.49	15.29	16.10
7	1.08	2.15	3.22	4.30	5.37	6.45	7.52	8.60	9.67	10.75	11.82	12.90	13.97	15.05	16.12	17.20	18.27	19.35	20.42	21.50
8	1.39	2.77	4.15	5.54	6.92	8.31	9.69	11.08	12.46	13.85	15.23	16.62	18.00	19.39	20.77	22.16	23.54	24.93	26.31	27.70
9	1.73	3.46	5.19	6.92	8.65	10.38	12.11	13.84	15.57	17.30	19.03	20.76	22.49	24.22	25.95	27.68	29.41	31.14	32.87	34.60
10	2.12	4.23	6.34	8.46	10.57	12.69	14.80	16.92	19.03	21.15	23.26	25.38	27.49	29.61	31.72	33.84	35.95	38.07	40.18	42.30
11	2.54	5.06	7.62	10.15	12.69	15.23	17.77	20.31	22.84	25.38	27.92	30.46	33.00	35.54	38.08	40.62	43.16	45.70	48.23	50.77
12	3.00	6.00	9.00	12.00	15.00	18.00	21.00	24.00	27.00	30.00	33.00	36.00	39.00	42.00	45.00	48.00	51.00	54.00	57.00	60.00
13	3.50	7.00	10.50	14.00	17.50	21.00	24.50	28.00	31.50	35.00	38.50	42.00	45.50	49.00	52.50	56.00	59.50	63.00	66.50	70.00
14	4.04	8.07	12.11	16.15	20.18	24.22	28.26	32.30	36.33	40.37	44.40	48.44	52.48	56.52	60.56	64.60	68.63	72.67	76.71	80.75
15	4.62	9.23	13.84	18.46	23.07	27.68	32.30	36.92	41.53	46.15	50.76	55.38	59.99	64.61	69.22	73.84	78.45	83.07	87.68	92.30
16	5.23	10.46	15.69	20.92	26.15	31.38	36.61	41.84	47.07	52.30	57.53	62.76	67.99	73.22	78.45	83.68	88.91	94.14	99.37	104.60
17	5.89	11.77	17.66	23.54	29.43	35.32	41.20	47.09	52.97	58.86	64.75	70.64	76.52	82.40	88.28	94.17	100.06	105.93	111.82	117.70
18	6.58	13.15	19.72	26.30	32.87	39.45	46.02	52.60	59.17	65.75	72.32	78.90	85.47	92.05	98.62	105.20	111.77	118.35	124.92	131.50
19	7.31	14.61	21.92	29.23	36.54	43.85	51.16	58.47	65.77	73.08	80.39	87.70	95.01	102.32	109.63	116.94	124.25	131.56	138.86	146.17
20	8.08	16.15	24.22	32.30	40.37	48.45	56.52	64.60	72.67	80.75	88.82	96.90	104.97	113.05	121.12	129.20	137.27	145.35	153.42	161.50
21	8.89	17.77	26.65	35.54	44.42	53.31	62.19	71.08	79.96	88.85	97.73	106.62	115.50	124.39	133.27	142.16	151.04	159.93	168.81	177.70
22	9.73	19.46	29.19	38.92	48.65	58.38	68.11	77.84	87.57	97.30	107.03	116.76	126.49	136.22	145.95	155.68	165.41	175.14	184.87	194.60
23	10.62	21.23	31.84	42.46	53.07	63.69	74.30	84.92	95.53	106.15	116.76	127.38	137.99	148.61	159.22	169.84	180.45	191.07	201.68	212.30
24	11.54	23.07	34.61	46.15	57.69	69.23	80.77	92.31	103.85	115.38	126.92	138.46	150.00	161.54	173.08	184.62	196.16	207.70	219.24	230.77
25	12.50	25.00	37.50	50.00	62.50	75.00	87.50	100.00	112.50	125.00	137.50	150.00	162.50	175.00	187.50	200.00	212.50	225.00	237.50	250.00
26	13.50	27.00	40.50	54.00	67.50	81.00	94.50	108.00	121.50	135.00	148.50	162.00	175.50	189.00	202.50	216.00	229.50	243.00	256.50	270.00

Table No. 3.—Equated Credits, 50 Cents per Share, Paid at the Beginning of each Week.

Number of Shares.	1	2	3	4	5	6	7	8	9	10	11	12	13	14	15	16	17	18	19	20
Weeks—1	.019	.04	.06	.08	.10	.12	.14	.15	.17	.19	.21	.23	.25	.27	.29	.31	.33	.35	.37	.39
2	.057	.12	.18	.23	.28	.34	.40	.46	.51	.57	.63	.69	.75	.80	.86	.92	.98	1.03	1.09	1.14
3	.115	.23	.35	.46	.58	.69	.81	.92	1.04	1.15	1.27	1.38	1.49	1.61	1.73	1.84	1.96	2.07	2.19	2.30
4	.19	.39	.58	.77	.96	1.15	1.34	1.54	1.73	1.92	2.11	2.31	2.50	2.69	2.88	3.08	3.27	3.46	3.65	3.85
5	.288	.58	.87	1.15	1.44	1.72	2.01	2.30	2.58	2.87	3.16	3.45	3.73	4.02	4.31	4.60	4.89	5.17	5.46	5.75
6	.404	.81	1.21	1.61	2.01	2.41	2.81	3.22	3.62	4.02	4.42	4.83	5.23	5.63	6.03	6.44	6.84	7.24	7.65	8.05
7	.538	1.08	1.62	2.15	2.69	3.22	3.76	4.30	4.84	5.37	5.91	6.45	6.99	7.52	8.06	8.60	9.14	9.67	10.21	10.75
8	.69	1.39	2.08	2.77	3.46	4.15	4.84	5.54	6.23	6.92	7.61	8.31	9.00	9.69	10.38	11.08	11.77	12.46	13.15	13.85
9	.865	1.73	2.60	3.46	4.33	5.19	6.06	6.92	7.79	8.65	9.52	10.38	11.25	12.11	12.98	13.84	14.71	15.57	16.44	17.30
10	1.06	2.12	3.18	4.23	5.29	6.34	7.40	8.46	9.52	10.57	11.63	12.69	13.75	14.80	15.86	16.92	17.98	19.03	20.09	21.15
11	1.27	2.54	3.81	5.08	6.35	7.62	8.89	10.15	11.42	12.69	13.96	15.23	16.50	17.77	19.04	20.31	21.58	22.84	24.11	25.38
12	1.50	3.00	4.50	6.00	7.50	9.00	10.50	12.00	13.50	15.00	16.50	18.00	19.50	21.00	22.50	24.00	25.50	27.00	28.50	30.00
13	1.75	3.50	5.25	7.00	8.75	10.50	12.25	14.00	15.75	17.50	19.25	21.00	22.75	24.50	26.25	28.00	29.75	31.50	33.25	35.00
14	2.02	4.04	6.06	8.07	10.09	12.11	14.13	16.15	18.17	20.18	22.20	24.22	26.24	28.26	30.28	32.30	34.32	36.33	38.35	40.37
15	2.31	4.62	6.93	9.23	11.54	13.84	16.15	18.46	20.75	23.07	25.38	27.69	30.00	32.30	34.61	36.92	39.23	41.53	43.84	46.15
16	2.62	5.23	7.85	10.46	13.08	15.69	18.31	20.92	23.54	26.15	28.77	31.38	34.00	36.61	39.23	41.84	44.46	47.07	49.69	52.30
17	2.94	5.89	8.83	11.77	14.71	17.66	20.60	23.54	26.48	29.43	32.37	35.32	38.26	41.20	44.14	47.09	50.03	52.97	55.91	58.86
18	3.29	6.58	9.87	13.15	16.44	19.72	23.01	26.30	29.59	32.87	36.16	39.45	42.74	46.02	49.31	52.60	55.89	59.17	62.46	65.75
19	3.65	7.31	10.96	14.61	18.26	21.92	25.57	29.23	32.88	36.54	40.19	43.85	47.50	51.16	54.81	58.47	62.12	65.77	69.42	73.08
20	4.04	8.07	12.11	16.15	20.19	24.22	28.26	32.30	36.34	40.37	44.41	48.45	52.49	56.52	60.56	64.60	68.64	72.67	76.71	80.75
21	4.44	8.89	13.33	17.77	22.21	26.65	31.09	35.54	39.98	44.42	48.86	53.31	57.75	62.19	66.63	71.08	75.52	79.96	84.40	88.85
22	4.87	9.73	14.60	19.46	24.33	29.19	34.06	38.92	43.79	48.65	53.52	58.38	63.25	68.11	72.97	77.84	82.71	87.57	92.44	97.30
23	5.31	10.62	15.93	21.24	26.55	31.84	37.15	42.46	47.77	53.07	58.38	63.69	69.00	74.30	79.61	84.92	90.23	95.54	100.84	106.15
24	5.77	11.54	17.31	23.07	28.84	34.61	40.38	46.15	51.92	57.69	63.46	69.23	75.00	80.77	86.54	92.31	98.08	103.85	109.62	115.39
25	6.25	12.50	18.75	25.00	31.25	37.50	43.75	50.00	56.25	62.50	68.75	75.00	81.25	87.50	93.75	100.00	106.25	112.50	118.75	125.00
26	6.75	13.50	20.25	27.00	33.75	40.50	47.25	54.00	60.75	67.50	74.25	81.00	87.75	94.50	101.25	108.00	114.75	121.50	128.25	135.00

Number of Shares.	1	2	3	4	5	6	7	8	9	10	11	12	13	14	15	16	17	18	19	20
Weeks — 1																				
2	.04	.08	.12	.15	.19	.23	.27	.31	.35	.39	.42	.46	.50	.54	.58	.62	.66	.69	.73	.77
3	.12	.23	.34	.46	.57	.69	.80	.92	1.03	1.15	1.26	1.38	1.49	1.61	1.72	1.84	1.95	2.07	2.18	2.30
4	.23	.46	.69	.92	1.15	1.38	1.61	1.84	2.07	2.30	2.53	2.76	2.99	3.22	3.45	3.68	3.91	4.14	4.37	4.60
5	.39	.77	1.15	1.54	1.92	2.31	2.69	3.08	3.46	3.85	4.23	4.62	5.00	5.39	5.77	6.16	6.54	6.93	7.31	7.70
6	.58	1.15	1.72	2.30	2.87	3.45	4.02	4.60	5.17	5.75	6.32	6.90	7.47	8.05	8.62	9.20	9.77	10.35	10.92	11.50
7	.81	1.61	2.41	3.22	4.02	4.83	5.63	6.44	7.24	8.05	8.85	9.66	10.46	11.27	12.07	12.88	13.68	14.49	15.29	16.10
8	1.08	2.15	3.22	4.30	5.37	6.45	7.52	8.60	9.67	10.75	11.82	12.90	13.97	15.05	16.12	17.20	18.27	19.35	20.42	21.50
9	1.39	2.77	4.15	5.54	6.92	8.31	9.69	11.08	12.46	13.85	15.23	16.62	18.00	19.39	20.77	22.16	23.54	24.93	26.31	27.70
10	1.73	3.46	5.19	6.92	8.65	10.38	12.11	13.84	15.57	17.30	19.03	20.76	22.49	24.22	25.96	27.68	29.41	31.14	32.87	34.60
11	2.12	4.23	6.34	8.46	10.57	12.69	14.80	16.92	19.03	21.15	23.26	25.38	27.49	29.61	31.72	33.84	35.95	38.07	40.18	42.30
12	2.54	5.08	7.62	10.15	12.69	15.23	17.77	20.31	22.84	25.38	27.92	30.46	33.00	35.54	38.06	40.62	43.16	45.70	48.23	50.77
13	3.00	6.00	9.00	12.00	15.00	18.00	21.00	24.00	27.00	30.00	33.00	36.00	39.00	42.00	45.00	48.00	51.00	54.00	57.00	60.00
14	3.50	7.00	10.50	14.00	17.50	21.00	24.50	28.00	31.50	35.00	38.50	42.00	45.50	49.00	52.50	56.00	59.50	63.00	66.50	70.00
15	4.04	8.07	12.11	16.15	20.18	24.22	28.26	32.30	36.33	40.37	44.40	48.44	52.48	56.52	60.56	64.60	68.63	72.67	76.71	80.75
16	4.62	9.23	13.84	18.46	23.07	27.69	32.30	36.92	41.53	46.15	50.76	55.38	59.99	64.61	69.22	73.84	78.45	83.07	87.68	92.30
17	5.23	10.46	15.69	20.92	26.15	31.38	36.61	41.84	47.07	52.30	57.53	62.76	67.99	73.22	78.45	83.68	88.91	94.14	99.37	104.60
18	5.89	11.77	17.66	23.54	29.43	35.32	41.20	47.09	52.97	58.86	64.75	70.64	76.52	82.40	88.28	94.17	100.05	105.93	111.82	117.70
19	6.58	13.15	19.72	26.30	32.87	39.45	46.02	52.60	59.17	65.75	72.32	78.90	85.47	92.05	98.62	105.20	111.77	118.35	124.92	131.50
20	7.31	14.61	21.92	29.23	36.54	43.85	51.16	58.47	65.77	73.08	80.39	87.70	95.01	102.32	109.63	116.94	124.25	131.56	138.86	146.17
21	8.08	16.15	24.22	32.30	40.57	48.46	56.52	64.60	72.67	80.75	88.82	96.90	104.97	113.05	121.12	129.20	137.27	145.35	153.42	161.50
22	8.89	17.77	26.66	35.54	44.42	53.31	62.19	71.08	79.96	88.85	97.73	106.62	115.50	124.39	133.27	142.16	151.04	159.93	168.81	177.70
23	9.73	19.46	29.19	38.92	48.65	58.38	68.11	77.84	87.57	97.30	107.03	116.76	126.49	136.22	145.95	155.68	165.41	175.14	184.87	194.60
24	10.62	21.23	31.84	42.46	53.07	63.69	74.30	84.92	95.53	106.15	116.76	127.38	137.99	148.61	159.22	169.84	180.45	191.07	201.68	212.30
25	11.54	23.07	34.61	46.15	57.69	69.23	80.77	92.31	103.85	115.39	126.92	138.46	150.00	161.54	173.08	184.62	196.16	207.70	219.24	230.77
26	12.50	25.00	37.50	50.00	62.50	75.00	87.50	100.00	112.50	125.00	137.50	150.00	162.50	175.00	187.50	200.00	212.50	225.00	237.50	250.00

6 Per Cent. Dividend Table No. 5.

Weeks	Number of Shares																			
	1	2	3	4	5	6	7	8	9	10	11	12	13	14	15	16	17	18	19	20
1			.01	.01	.01	.01	.02	.02	.02	.02	.03	.03	.03	.03	.03	.04	.04	.04	.04	.05
2	.01	.01	.02	.03	.03	.04	.05	.06	.06	.07	.08	.08	.09	.10	.10	.11	.12	.12	.13	.14
3	.01	.03	.04	.06	.07	.08	.10	.11	.12	.14	.15	.17	.18	.19	.21	.22	.23	.25	.26	.28
4	.02	.05	.07	.09	.12	.14	.16	.18	.21	.23	.25	.28	.30	.32	.35	.37	.39	.42	.44	.46
5	.03	.07	.10	.14	.17	.21	.24	.28	.31	.34	.38	.41	.45	.48	.52	.55	.58	.62	.65	.69
6	.05	.10	.14	.19	.24	.29	.34	.39	.43	.48	.53	.58	.63	.69	.72	.77	.82	.87	.92	.97
7	.06	.13	.19	.26	.32	.39	.45	.52	.58	.64	.71	.77	.84	.90	.97	1.03	1.10	1.16	1.23	1.29
8	.08	.17	.25	.33	.41	.49	.58	.66	.75	.83	.91	1.00	1.08	1.16	1.25	1.33	1.41	1.50	1.58	1.66
9	.10	.21	.31	.42	.52	.62	.73	.83	.93	1.04	1.14	1.24	1.35	1.45	1.56	1.66	1.76	1.87	1.97	2.08
10	.13	.25	.38	.51	.63	.76	.89	1.01	1.14	1.27	1.39	1.52	1.66	1.78	1.90	2.03	2.16	2.28	2.41	2.54
11	.15	.30	.46	.61	.76	.91	1.07	1.21	1.37	1.52	1.67	1.83	1.98	2.13	2.28	2.43	2.59	2.74	2.89	3.04
12	.18	.36	.54	.72	.90	1.08	1.26	1.44	1.62	1.80	1.98	2.16	2.34	2.52	2.70	2.88	3.06	3.24	3.42	3.60
13	.21	.42	.63	.84	1.05	1.26	1.47	1.68	1.89	2.10	2.31	2.52	2.73	2.94	3.15	3.36	3.57	3.78	3.99	4.20
14	.24	.48	.73	.97	1.21	1.45	1.70	1.94	2.19	2.42	2.65	2.90	3.15	3.39	3.64	3.88	4.12	4.37	4.60	4.84
15	.28	.55	.83	1.11	1.38	1.66	1.94	2.22	2.49	2.77	3.04	3.32	3.60	3.88	4.15	4.44	4.71	4.98	5.26	5.54
16	.31	.63	.94	1.25	1.57	1.88	2.20	2.51	2.82	3.14	3.45	3.76	4.08	4.39	4.71	5.02	5.33	5.69	5.96	6.28
17	.35	.71	1.06	1.41	1.77	2.12	2.47	2.82	3.18	3.53	3.89	4.24	4.59	4.94	5.29	5.64	6.00	6.36	6.71	7.06
18	.39	.79	1.18	1.58	1.97	2.37	2.76	3.16	3.55	3.95	4.34	4.73	5.13	5.52	5.92	6.31	6.71	7.10	7.50	7.89
19	.44	.88	1.31	1.75	2.19	2.63	3.07	3.50	3.95	4.38	4.82	5.26	5.70	6.14	6.58	7.01	7.45	7.90	8.33	8.76
20	.48	.97	1.45	1.94	2.42	2.91	3.39	3.88	4.36	4.84	5.34	5.81	6.30	6.78	7.27	7.75	8.24	8.72	9.20	9.69
21	.53	1.06	1.60	2.13	2.66	3.20	3.73	4.26	4.80	5.33	5.86	6.40	6.93	7.46	7.99	8.53	9.06	9.60	10.13	10.66
22	.58	1.17	1.75	2.33	2.92	3.50	4.09	4.67	5.25	5.84	6.42	7.00	7.59	8.18	8.76	9.34	9.92	10.50	11.09	11.68
23	.64	1.27	1.91	2.55	3.18	3.82	4.46	5.10	5.73	6.37	7.00	7.64	8.28	8.92	9.55	10.20	10.83	11.46	12.10	12.74
24	.69	1.38	2.08	2.77	3.46	4.15	4.85	5.54	6.23	6.92	7.61	8.30	9.00	9.70	10.39	11.08	11.76	12.46	13.15	13.84
25	.75	1.50	2.25	3.00	3.75	4.50	5.25	6.00	6.73	7.50	8.25	9.00	9.75	10.50	11.25	12.00	12.75	13.50	14.25	15.00
26	.81	1.62	2.43	3.24	4.05	4.86	5.67	6.43	7.29	8.10	8.91	9.72	10.53	11.34	12.15	12.96	13.77	14.58	15.39	16.20

The (Individual) Stock Ledger.—In this ledger is kept the accounts with the members to show how many shares of stock they have, how many have been borrowed on and how many have been pledged. The credit side shows how many shares have been acquired and the debit side how many have been withdrawn. The items are posted to this book from the Stock Journal Day-Book.

The remainder of the books are of simple form and need no explanations.

Most stationers carry a full line of blank books for Building Associations, but if the association is a large one, the books should be devised to meet all special requirements.

Specimen Entries.

At the first meeting of the association there was received Dues on 1000 shares, and Entrance Fees on same, $250 (dues $1 00 per share.) Entry would be,—

Cash or Treasurer.................... $ 1,250 00
  To Dues............................ $ 1,000 00
  To Entrance Fees.................... 250 00

Orders were drawn upon the Treasurer for incorporating as follows: T. H. Hogsett for attorney fees $50. Advertising Association notices $5. Incorporation fee $25.00.

Expense.............................. $ 80.00
  To Cash or Treasurer............... $ 80 00

Order drawn favor The National Safe and Lock Co., for Safe $250 Favor Brown & Co., for Office Furniture, Carpets, etc., $100.

Furniture and Fixtures............ $ 350 00
  To Treasurer.......................... $ 350 00

Received at second meeting Dues $10,000 and Entrance Fees $2,500.

Treasurer.......................... $12,500 00
  To Dues $10,000 00
  To Entrance Fees.................... 2,500 00

Loaned J. A. Jones on his bond and mortgage of city property, 10 shares at $5 per share premium. Shares $500 each.

Order drawn on Treasurer favor J. A. Jones for the amount less the premium.

Loans .... $ 5,000 00
  To Premium................. .... $ 50 00
  To Treasurer 4,950 00

E. H. Beach has withdrawn 5 shares series No. 1, on which he has paid dues to and including July meeting.

Capital Stock.. $	271	00
(1st series 5 shares @ $54.20.)		
Dues...	40	00
(8 months at $5.00)		
Interest...	8	20
(8 months on 5 shares.)		
To Loss and Gain....................................	3	40
(Profits retained on 1st series.)		
To Treasurer..	315	80
(Order favor E. H. Beach.)		

When stock is withdrawn debit Capital Stock account with the holding value of the shares at the last annual meeting, debit Dues account with the dues paid thereon during the current year, and credit Loss and Gain with the profits retained as in the above entry.

T. H. Hogsett, the Attorney for the Association, has paid over to the Treasurer the proceeds of the foreclosure of J. R. Stone. The decree of foreclosure cancels 10 shares 2d, series of stock, pledged by J. R. Stone, to secure loan, and applies the withdrawal value on Feb. 1st, 1896, of said shares thereon. Withdrawal value on Feb. 1st, 1896, of 2d series,

10 shares at...................... $35.34=.......... $	353	40
Less arrears of Dues......$70.00		
Less fines on arrears of		
Dues...................... $24.86	94	86
The withdrawal value of said shares as applied $	258	54
Capital Stock..	256	10
(2d series, 10 shares at $25.61.)		
Dues...	20	00
(2 mo. paid in current year on 10 shares of Stock at $20.)		
Treasurer..	1,853	92
(Amount paid him by Attorney)		
To Loans..	2,000	00
(10 shares loan to J. R. Stone foreclosed.)		
To Interest...	78	70
(On Loan and on Judgment.)		
Fines, etc...	49	72
(On arrears of Dues as above....... $24.86)		
(On arrears of Interest............... 24.86)		
To Loss and Gain....................................	1	60
(Profits retained on cancelled Stock 2d series, 10 shares at 16c.)		

The Attorney for the association reports the completion of the foreclosure of the mortgage to the Association made by C. H. Nichols, and that on May 5th, 1896, he bid off on behalf of the association the mortgaged property at $1,900, and that a judgment for deficiency of $200 has been entered in favor of the association against C. H. Nichols. The decree of foreclosure cancels 10 shares 3d series stock, pledged by C. H. Nichols, to secure the loan and applies the withdrawal value on Jan. 30th, 1896, of said shares thereon.

Withdrawal value Jan. 30th, 1896, of 3d series,
10 shares at..................... $24.50=.........	$	245	00
Less arrears of dues.......$60.00			
Less fines on arrears..... $25.00		85	00
Withdrawal value of said shares as applied.....	$	160	00

The Attorney's bill of costs and expenses of the foreclosure is audited and ordered paid, amounting to $150.

Capital Stock...................................	$	160	00
(3rd series 10 shares at $16.)			
Dues..		20	00
(Paid in current year.)			
Real Estate......................................		1,900	00
(Property bid off by Attorney.)			
Judgments Receivable........................		200	00
(For deficiency.)			
To Loans...		2,000	00
(10 shares loan to C. H. N. foreclosed.)			
Interest...		78	50
(On Loan and Judgment.)			
To Fines..		50	00
(On arrears of Dues............ $25.)			
(On arrears of Int.............. 25.)			
To Loss and Gain.............................		1	50
(Profits retained.)			
To Treasurer....................................		150	00
(Order from T. H. Hogsett for Atty's bill as audited.)			

Other entries of a similar nature might be given, but it is thought these will suffice for a clear understanding.

CHAPTER THIRTY.

Depreciation.

Depreciation is the actual loss upon assets which are diminishing in value, or it is an estimated sum charged against gross revenue; which amount is considered sufficient to replace the capital used up or reduced by wear and tear.

The loss or gain of an undertaking for any period is not simply the difference between the receipts and expenditures during that period, nor the current value of plant always the amount which has been paid for or expended upon it.

Importance of Depreciation.

In ascertaining the cost of production or manufacturing cost, one of the most interesting questions, as well as one of more or less controversy, is that pertaining to the charge for depreciation.

The method of providing for this charge and the amount of the same is the ever fruitful source of differences, which, when settled, affect the net results or profits of the period's transactions.

A manufacturer produces goods for sale; production is the result of consumption. The value and amount of such consumption represents the gross cost of the article manufactured. The difference between the value of the material consumed and the value or quality of the article manufactured is the loss or gain of the manufacturer. The importance, therefore, of knowing the actual value of that which is consumed, or the actual gross cost is readily seen to be indispensable to a successful manufacturing business.

Work and Wear.

The raw material, labor, rent charges, with fuel expenditure, can be accurately ascertained, but in the manipulation of them, work has to be performed; and as work means wear, the value of the wearing must be first ascertained before the cost of the product can be determined. In this consumption of raw material, labor, designing, fuel, machinery and buildings, an essential difference exists between the different items.

Raw material, labor and fuel are absolutely consumed within the time occupied in production; while machinery and buildings are consumed over a lapse of years. From year to year neither the exact value of the quantity consumed nor the exact value of the quantity remaining is known—but an estimate of the residual value remaining after its useful existence and the value of the usefulness of the machinery or buildings is spread over the number of years of its determined life.

Leases for a definite number of years afford a very appropriate illustration of the rule of basing the depreciation rate upon the life of the object. This is very simple, but when we come to the

Wear and Tear of Machinery,

we enter a difficult field, wherein one is dependent for the necessary technical knowledge of these assets upon the opinion of those who, not unfrequently, are opposed to a proper provision being made for such reduction.

A brief resume of the causes for such depreciation will be of use in determining the amount of the deduction.

1. Improvements which reduce the value in use of the present machine.

2. Introduction of new machinery combining two or more operators.

3. Reduced cost of labor and materials.

4. Wear and tear.

5. Exhaustion other than wear and tear.

6. Temporary causes.

Depreciation of the same kind of machinery depends upon the character of the business or class of trade engaged in, and the exigencies and nature of the particular business will determine whether the rate of depreciation be more or less.

In many kinds of business it may be found advisable, for the purpose of estimating depreciation, to divide the objects into classes, for although the general result of the business operations during a given time may be normal, yet by dealing separately with the depreciation of each class of appurtenances it may be found that some of the departments show abnormal results. A general rate of depreciation may lead to neglect what may comparatively be more profitable operations ; or to push a department of the business which, if it bore its full proportion of depreciation, would yield less than the average rate of profit.

This separation of departments is the more desirable as the same method of allocation will obviously not apply to *loose* plant and tools, and to plant and tools which are fixed.

Methods of Calculation.

Many different views prevail as to the best way of dealing with these questions, and owing to trades and processes of manufacture varying widely, it is impossible to lay down invariable rules. Questions as to the particular practice to be followed in any individual case must, to a large extent, be left to the judgment of those most intimately acquainted with the surroundings of the business.

The question of maintenance is very closely associated with that of depreciation. There might be said to be four factors which enter into the determination of any rule for arriving at the deterioration which has taken place.

1st. The cost of an article, whether it be a building, machinery or other asset. This may be either the cost price or, in case of the transfer of an established business, the estimated value of the object.

2nd. Its estimated tenure of life, regard being had to its functions and the conditions under which they are performed.

3rd. The extent and value of the renovation or restoration received by it from time to time.

4th. Its residual value, either as scrap or as an implement which, though possibly applicable to other uses, is no longer fit for its original purpose.

Whatever rule is determined upon, it is important that it should be consistently adhered to for a term of years, so that its accuracy may be fairly tested ; in order to avoid the accounts of particular years being treated abnormally, which in the case of corporations, whose shares are constantly changing hands, would lead to much injustice being done to individual proprietors.

If the various machines are divided into several classes, the question arises as to the rate of depreciation and on which account. The residual value of the machines may be based upon the following methods.

1st. That which expires by "Life," leaving no residual value, should be divided by the given number of years upon its original cost.

2nd. That which leaves a residue of value under any circumstances should be depreciated upon its diminishing amount.

The result of depreciating a machine (which has a residue value) upon its original cost, would produce an incorrect balance sheet, which if depreciated on the diminishing balance, the existence of the property would be continuously represented at the diminishing amount until reduced to its ultimate value at the hand of the auctioneer or dealer in second-hand machinery or as old iron. It must be borne in mind that as a machine grows older the charge for repairs increases and as we wish to equalize the total charges to revenue over the "life" of a machine the charges for repairs will be small at the beginning and increase in amount as the machine grows old in years. Therefore if the charge for repairs and the increasing charge for depreciation were made, the first cost of the machinery the later years of its "life" would be burdened without giving it credit for its better work at the beginning of its career. The depreciation being made on the diminishing value, the charges to revenue are equally divided over the whole life of the machine.

The following illustration will explain the effect on original cost and the varying burden of repairs.

						YEARS.					
On original cost............	1	2	3	4	5	6	7	8	9	10	11
Depreciation...............	6	6	6	6	6	6	6	6	6	6	6— 66
Repairs....................	1	2	3	4	5	6	7	8	9	10	11— 66
Total annual charge.........	7	8	9	10	11	12	13	14	15	16	17—130

						YEARS.					
On diminishing value........	1	2	3	4	5	6	7	8	9	10	11
Depreciation...............	11	10	9	8	7	6	5	4	3	2	1— 66
Repairs....................	1	2	3	4	5	6	7	8	9	10	11— 66
	12	12	12	12	12	12	12	12	12	12	12—132

A machine costing $1000. Life determined, say ten years. Depreciation ten per cent.

					YEARS.					
On original cost...........	1	2	3	4	5	6	7	8	9	10
Depreciation.........	10	10	10	10	10	10	10	10	10	10 —100
Repairs...............	1	2	3	4	5	6	7	8	9	10 — 55
Total annual charge...	11	12	13	14	15	16	17	18	19	20 —155

					YEARS.					
On diminishing value.......	1	2	3	4	5	6	7	8	9	10
Depreciation...........	10	9	8.10	7.29	6.56	5.90	5.31	4.78	4.30	3.87—65.11
Repairs................	1	2	3	4	5	6	7	8	9	10— 55
Total annual charge....	11	11	11.10	11.29	11.56	11.90	12.31	12.78	13.30	13.7 —120.11

This $120.11 with the residual value of $34.89 makes up the total charges of $155. Depreciation on the original cost is therefore a writing off of the actual capital without leaving the residual value.

Ratio of Diminution.

Calculating the depreciation of ten per cent. off leases having ten years to run—patents having a fixed life—or any other property which becomes absolutely extinguished in a determined number of years.

On Original Cost.

1st Year ....$1,000.	10 per cent.	$900 Ledger Balance.	
2nd " .... 1,000.	10 " "	800 " "	
3rd " .... 1,000.	10 " "	700 " "	
4th " .... 1,000.	10 " "	600 " "	

On property that has always a residue value, the principle being written off on the diminishing value:

On Diminishing Value.

1st Year ....$1,000.	10 per cent. dep.	$900 Ledger Balance.	
2nd " .... 900.	10 " " "	810 " "	
3rd " .... 810.	10 " " "	729 " "	
4th " .... 729.	10 " " "	656 " "	

	Original Cost.	Diminishing Values.
Reduction at end of 5th year on	50 per cent.	40 per cent.
" " " " 6th " "	60 " "	47 " "
" " " " 7th " "	70 " "	52 " "
" " " " 8th " "	80 " "	57 " "
" " " " 9th " "	90 " "	62 " "
" " " " 10th " "	100 " "	66 " "

or as follows:

	Original Cost.	Diminishing Values.
Residual value at end of 5th year on	50 per cent.	60 per cent.
" " " " " 6th " "	40 " "	55 " "
" " " " " 7th " "	30 " "	48 " "
" " " " " 8th " "	20 " "	43 " "
" " " " " 9th " "	10 " "	38 " "
" " " " " 10th " "	Life Ended.	34 " "

A new machine does not wear out as soon as an old one, and by depreciating on the diminishing value the total charges to revenue are equitably distributed over the life of the machine.

Thus we see that the ratio of diminution of realizable value is greater in the earlier than in the later years of the life of the machinery. This being true, I think the principle upon which depreciation of machinery should be valued, is to assess the residual value and then ascertain what rate of discount upon the diminishing value will serve to reach that residual value.

We must bear in mind that as soon as the original cost is reduced so as to represent the residual or break up value, further depreciation is unnecessary. But in this connection we must remember that with any system of depreciation the value of machinery as carried in the books of a manufacturer is never realized whenever the assets are sold, either at auction or private sale. With railway, gas, and steamship companies the depreciation partakes more of a renewal account, since the actual maintenance is only included in the revenue account.

There are items to which no general rule of writing off is applicable. Such are the cost of good-will, patents, trade marks, copyright designs, etc., for although, as in the case of patents, the life of the asset is clearly defined, the incidental advantages derived from the possession, for a term of years, of a valuable monopoly do not necessarily cease upon the expiration of the term of the patent. On the contrary, the value of the good-will may increase although the term of the patent is expiring. The obvious rule, therefore, is that in the balance-sheet such items should appear at their cost value, and need not be written down unless their realizable value as integral parts of a going concern falls below their cost value. Any estimated increment may be accounted for by the creation of a special fund, but until such estimated increased value is realized, it should not be considered as an element of profit.

Shareholders' Rights.

Preferred shareholders have a prior right to share in the profits, and that to a greater extent than the ordinary shareholders, but in case of liquidation of the company, both common and preferred shareholders participate equally in the division of the assets. Thus the interests of these two classes are conflicting, dividends to preferred stockholders being dependent upon the profits of the particular year only, preferred stockholders benefiting by no charge being made for depreciation. Providing the company retains sufficient assets to carry on its productive business, common stockholders derive an advantage correspondently greater as the provision made for depreciation increases; so that matters of accounting are best left in the hands of the company itself for determination, seeing that their capital, being the surplus of assets over liabilities, is a matter of paramount importance to both of them. If the working expenses exceed the correct gains, then no dividend may be declared, while on the other hand a company has the power to devote the surplus of income over expenditures, should it so decide. No obligation is imposed by law or statutes, whereby a reserve fund out of revenue is created to recoup the wasting nature of capital, so that profits may be the balance remaining after the payment of all charges, including depreciation. The principle of limited liability implies that the capital should be preserved intact for the safety of the creditors, in consideration of the counter balancing disadvantage that he, the creditor, has only a limited fund to look to for payment of his account.

Preferred shareholders stand, to some extent, on the same footing as creditors in relation to the common stockholders, seeing that should a diminution of capital take place, and a dividend be paid the common stockholder, the actual capital is being distributed in violation of the terms of its issue. Therefore, in case of shrinkage of capital, the correct procedure would be to write down the capital by reducing the nominal value of the shares, and the auditor should see that every item of expenditure fairly chargeable against the year's income, shall be brought into the revenue account for the year.

CHAPTER THIRTY-ONE.

Railway Auditing.

Instructions to Traveling Auditors—Their Duties—Reports of Each Examination—Defaulting Agents—Remittance and Freight Collections.

The revenue of railway companies is derived from five principle sources, viz: Freight, passenger, express, mails and miscellaneous. The revenue from freight, passenger and miscellaneous sources is collected almost entirely by the company's agents along the line, therefore, the first and most important duty of an auditor is to look after the funds of the company, collected by and passing through the hands of agents.

Agents are instructed how they shall keep their accounts, and all their books and blanks are furnished from the stationery supply store. Notwithstanding these detailed instructions, one of the most important duties an auditor has to perform is to exercise a constant and intelligent supervision over the manner of keeping accounts, carefully instructing the agents whenever they are wrong or in default.

The nature of the duties to be performed are delicate and very responsible, therefore, it is important that your intercourse with agents and others should always be frank, but governed by the utmost courtesy and tact. It is also your duty to see that the instructions for keeping the accounts are fully obeyed, but you must do so in a courteous and gentlemanly manner.

In making examinations and rendering reports of agents' accounts, you must be just and impartial, you must hold your judgment unbiased by either courtesies or want of deference shown you, in your official capacity, or personal intercourse with agents.

You must not allow personal resentments to govern your actions or change your statements.

Reports of all examinations of agents' accounts are made upon a blank provided by the Auditing Department, and usually embraces the following instructions: What is the name of the agent? When was he appointed agent? What was his business and where did he reside previous to his appointment as agent? Does he do the telegraphing? Has he a clerk? Does he keep his accounts systematically and neatly? Does he make charges for telegraph, post office and other foreign collections? Did you investigate to ascertain if there were any collections for switching, storage, loading, unloading, extra baggage, 'or from any other special sources of revenue? Did you find all such collections duly entered and properly accounted for in the cash book? Is the cash book kept in accordance with the prescribed instructions? Are all receipts and disbursements of cash entered upon the cash book at the proper time?

Did you check the cash book with the freight received and receipt book? Did the agent claim any unusual or unauthorized credits, if so, what were they? Did his cash account balance? Did the books show that the balance of cash on hand had all been collected since the last remittance? Does the agent remit, each day, the total amount of cash collected? What was the total amount of uncollected freight bills on hand? Did you check the uncollected freight bills to ascertain if the freight was actually on hand? Do you think the agent is energetic in his efforts to keep the amount of uncollected freight bills as small as possible? Does he notify consignees of the arrival of freight? Does the agent make a habit of delivering freight without collecting charges? Does the agent make a true statement of the uncollected freight bills? Did you find receipts for all advanced charges paid out? Was a statement of advanced charges sent to the Freight Auditor? Has the agent been cautioned about paying advanced charges on freight received for shipment? Is every way-bill copied into the Freight Received book immediately upon receipt of it?

Does the agent require the consignee, or the party holding his order, to receipt in the receipt book for each consignment at the time of its delivery? Do the footings of the freight received book and the receipt book agree with the freight report at the end of each month? Does the agent check the freight with way-bills, immediately upon their receipt, to ascertain shortage, condition, etc.? Is the abstract book written up weekly or monthly? Did you examine all his tickets, according to special instructions? Did you count all the tickets in his hands? Did you compare the tickets with the list furnished by the ticket department? Does the agent keep a complete record of tickets received, sold and on hand? Does the agent take a complete inventory of his tickets every month? When agent receives corrected sheets does he make his books to conform with them immediately? Does he properly account for overcharges in Overcharge Book and balance sheet? Are all the books and accounts kept in proper form? Does the agent make a trial balance to ascertain the exact condition of his accounts before making final remittance for the month? Did you locate all errors, and make corrections so the accounts can be accurately balanced? Does the agent indulge in any irregular or unauthorized practices? Are all his bondsmen still living? Are his securities perfectly responsible?

Make a list of the agent's remittances in addition to those received from the department. Give a general report of the station. In this report you should give such facts as you may deem necessary to give the department a full and complete knowledge of the agent's character and record.

In the Auditing Department a "Record Book of the Examination of Agents" should be kept, in which is entered in detail the reports of the examinations.

On the first day of each month, a report is rendered to the department, naming the stations, (in alphabetical order) examined during the preceding month, giving the date examined, etc.

All your communications, statements and reports, should be made in writing, and an impression copy taken for purposes of record. All your communications should be free from harsh or discourteous language. Express yourself clearly, but without giving unnecessary offense.

Special reports must be made at once in the following cases, viz., of defalcations, of agents known to have been defaulters previous to their employment by this company. If agents are found to be using the company's money, through ignorance, misapprehension, or otherwise. Dishonest practices in connection with their duties as agent of the company. Of agents who neglect or refuse to keep their cash and other accounts as instructed.

Any agent, cashier, or other employee, or official, who handles the company's funds, who is known to gamble, or to have any vice disreputable in its character, or of a nature likely to lead him to disregard the faithful obligation due the company, must be reported at once.

Defalcations must be reported, in cipher, immediately upon discovery, then every possible effort must instantly be put forth to secure a return of the stolen money; should you fail in this, then you must visit the agent's bondsmen, if his securities are individuals. If he is bonded in a Guarantee Company, the company must be notified forthwith. Every effort must be made to have the defalcation made good, without the delay incident to a vain and senseless recourse to the law.

Railway companies will never consent to withdraw or compromise their claims upon the bondsmen, in case of defalcation. You should urge a speedy and peaceful settlement upon the part of the bondsmen, stating, that although the company especially deprecates recourse to the law, nevertheless every effort that its boundless resources places within its control will be expended, if necessary, in enforcing its just claim.

If a defaulting agent fails to make good his defalcation, and his securities do not at once make good the amount, it is the auditor's duty, in the absence of special instructions to the contrary, to have the defaulter placed under arrest, and held to bail, to see that the bail is adequate, and when necessary employ an attorney.

In rendering an account for a defaulting agent, state the amount of the defalcation separately, as "Deficit in Cash Account." To this account you should secure the signature of the defaulter, as proof of its nature and accuracy. In cases of this kind, the agent's signature cannot always be obtained, neither is it absolutely necessary, but it will prove without unnecessary delay or demonstration, what the company is justly entitled to prove.

A defaulting agent must have credit for the total amount of wages due him, but the Division Superintendent and Pay Master must be notified of the amount allowed, directing that it be turned over to the Treasurer on the defaulter's account.

A defaulting agent should not be notified of his discharge while a settlement is pending. You should not discuss the dismissal of an agent in his presence, for the prospect of continuing in the service of the company, will act as a powerful incentive to induce him to put forth every effort to make good the deficiency in his cash account. If a discrepancy has been discovered, you should state all the facts in favor of the agent.

When an agent is found to be a defaulter, you should take charge of the cash affairs of the station, and remain in charge until a new agent is appointed, or until you receive instructions how to act.

When an agent claims relief from reputed losses from the destruction of offices by fire, or the breaking open of money drawers, ticket cases, etc; such claim must be examined into with the utmost care and caution. If you find that the agent has been careless and negligent, and has disregarded the established rules of the company, no relief should be afforded him.

Some men are appointed agents, who lack experience, and who need thorough and repeated instruction, therefore, you must bear in mind that one of your principal duties is to be their instructor. The progress of new agents must be carefully watched. If there are any discrepancies or delinquencies, you should note whether they have occurred through inexperience, or been occasioned by carelessness, indifference, dishonesty or otherwise.

You should study carefully the character and ability of an agent, and if you become convinced that he cannot, or will not, arrive at such a degree of efficiency as the position may require, you should make a comprehensive report of the matter to the department, for reference to the proper officer.

Agents are Required to Remit Daily.

This is the general rule governing the remitting of money, it must be enforced literally, as no one is authorized at any time, or under any circumstances to deviate from it. An agent is not permitted under any circumstances to withhold any part of his cash collections from his daily remittance, no matter how small the sum may be.

Each day, especially on the last day of the month, agents are required and expected to remit the exact amount collected, or the cash balance on hand. The working fund will be sufficient to transact the business of the station. Remittances may be made in even dollars, but never, in any case, to fall short of the total amount collected. If the daily collection or cash balance amounts to $93.72, he may remit $94.00, carrying the over remittance forward on his cash book, and repaying himself out of the collections for the succeeding day.

Conductors' reports of collections to the general ticket office, should correspond exactly with the amount remitted.

Conductors are required to remit to the Local Treasurer, or bank, as directed, the exact amount of each round trip, immediately upon their arrival at their destination.

Conductors must make a separate remittance for each trip, if the outbound trip is in one month, and the return trip is in another month.

The agent's balance sheet for the previous month, on file in the department, should be examined by you, on or about the tenth of each month to ascertain if the amount of uncollected freight on hand at the close of the month, and the amount of the remittances at the close of the month compare with the rest of the month. When the closing remittances for the month are out of proportion with the rest of the month, or the list of uncollected freight is disproportionately large, the agent should be investigated, as these are, generally, among the first indications of misappropriation.

When an agent's remittances are generally for even amounts, without stating the exact amount of collections, it is reasonable to suspect that he is not faithfully observing the rule governing remittances.

You should examine the records in the department to see if the last remittances for the month, as claimed by the agent, have been promptly received   If these remittances are not promptly received by the department, it would seem to indicate that they were not sent on the day claimed, and an investigation might elicit the fact that the business of the succeeding month was made to contribute the money required to balance the account current.

The working fund at every agency should be carefully examined, to see that it is no greater than is absolutely necessary to supply sufficient small change needed in the sale of tickets, etc., as no agent is allowed to increase his working fund without permission.   The working fund is furnished the agent, so as to render it unnecessary that he should retain in his hands any portion of the daily cash collections.

If the list of uncollected freight on hand at the end of the month, is made up of coal, lumber, or other large bills evidently not received at, or very near the end of the month, the agent should be instructed to make his collections as expeditiously as possible.

The report of freight received after the close of the month should correspond with the amount of credit taken for such freight.   When necessary, you should compare the dates of the uncollected with the dates of the duplicates on file in the Freight Auditor's Department.

If the balance sheet should contain any irregular notations or forced entries, you should write the agent, asking why such notations are necessary, and demand a full and satisfactory explanation.

Whenever special orders are given, or explanations required, you should keep the matter in mind, and see that they are carried out. Orders issued without careful reference afterwards, to see if they have been obeyed, will have a demoralizing effect.

About the twenty-fifth of each month, you should again examine the balance sheets, for the purpose of arriving at a general idea of each agent's manner of doing business, to see how the corrected balance sheet compares with the original, and to see if the corrections indicate that the balance was "forced" by the agent; if so, make a note of the fact, and write him. Compare the face of the balance sheet with the footing of the list of uncollected freight.

Freight bills are universally recognized as cash, therefore all charges for freight should be collected on delivery of the same. It is an established rule of every company, that the charges of freight be paid upon delivery. This rule is not deviated from, unless it is to meet competition. At competing points agents are expected to use great discretion and tact, in securing and holding business, nevertheless, an agent will be held responsible for any, and all losses, arising from his having delivered freight, before securing payment of all charges on the same.

In order to detect any irregularities, or wrong doing, on the part of agents, by which the company's interests may suffer, you will have to be ever on the alert, as a cunning knave will find some means to deceive.

Even though the agent whose accounts you are examining, is your friend, in whom you have the most implicit confidence, you must carefully guard against any relaxation of vigilance.

Manner of Checking Agent's Accounts When Out of Balance, etc.

In railway accounts, weeks are understood to close on the 7th, 14th, 21st, and last day of the month.

All books and blanks must be ordered from the stationary supply store, on the usual form of requisition.

All books, blanks, and accounts of the company must be written up in ink, and must be signed by the agent, personally.

Station agents should be given the following instructions, in order that the station accounts may be kept intelligently, and show an accurate and complete record of the cash business, and be reliable for reference in settling claims, which may be held against the company.

When freight is unloaded from cars, it must be checked with waybills. The check marks on the way-bill will show the number of packages checked out.

If freight is "over" or "short," it must be noted on the way-bill, and must be copied on the "freight received book," and "receipt book."

All errors of classification, extension, or rates, must be corrected, and the way-bill entered at once on the freight received book.

The amount of each consignment should be carried separately into the consignment column in the freight received book, so it can be readily checked with the cash book, in case of a discrepancy existing in the freight accounts.

The total footings of the way-bills, as they appear, must be entered in total of the way-bill column, for the purpose of checking the freight received book with the monthly abstracts of way-bills received.

The total of way-bill columns must agree with the total of consignment column. The total of the freight received book, at the end of the month, must agree with the total of the monthly freight report, which shows the aggregate amount of freight received from each station, and the total of the whole.

Way-bills must be entered in the account of the month in which they are dated and billed, even though they may not be received until after the close of the month. Way-bills are never carried forward to the subsequent month. When a new month's account is started, in the freight received book, a number of blank pages should be left, on which to enter the bills dated in the previous month, yet to arrive.

The "Freight Received and Receipt Book" is but one book in which the freight is entered when it is received, and when it is delivered it is receipted for in this book, hence the name, but for short it is called "Freight Received Book." This book should in all cases show the date of the delivery of freight.

As soon as the way-bills have been entered on the freight received book, expense bills must be made from the same, directly from the way-bill. As a check against errors of omission or otherwise, the amount of each expense bill should be compared with the amount of consignment shown on the freight received book.

Expense bills must show exactly the amount called for by the way-bill. Notations, such as "short," "over," etc., should be made on the freight received book, but never on the expense bill.

Cash Book.

The cash book should show in detail, the total receipts and disbursements at each station. It must be balanced daily, and the balance due the company remitted by express to the Local Treasurer. By footing and closing the cash book every day, agents know their accounts are exactly right.

All entries on the cash book should be made at the time of the transaction, and show clearly, the character of the entry, and why made.

On the last day of each month, agents should take a trial balance,

In order that errors and omissions may be discovered, and rectified before the last remittance for the month is sent in.   If the amount of cash to be remitted, as shown by the cash book, does not balance the account as shown by the trial balance, the account should be checked as follows :

The footing of the prepaid ticket, and advanced charges column should be compared with the report of each.

The miscellaneous columns of the cash book should be carefully analyzed, and compared with the balance sheet, item by item.

The total amount of the remittance columns of the cash book, added to the amount of the remittances brought forward from the preceeding month, should be compared with the amount entered on the trial balance.   If they do not agree, check the remittance items on the cash book, item by item, with the items on the balance sheet, until the difference is found.   To ascertain which amount is correct, refer to the remittance slips, as credited by the Local Treasurer, and make the necessary correction.

Examine the overcharge book, to see if the entries have been properly made, see that no credit has been taken on the cash book for overcharges not yet refunded, and see that all overcharges that have been refunded are credited on the cash book.

To analyze the account in this way, will save considerable time, and will show at once what part of the account it is necessary to check in detail.

Should there still be a discrepancy, examine the items which make up the debit balance from the last month's account, to see if they are properly accounted for in the remittances or other credits of the current month, and that the errors of the preceeding month are properly adjusted on the overcharge, or cash book, as the case requires.

A petty disbursement made by the agent during the month, and carried as cash, awaiting the approval and payment of vouchers, may also affect the balance.

The cash book should be checked with the freight received book, to see that the unchecked items appearing on the cash book are to be found on the list of uncollected freight bills on hand.

It will be found advantageous to use different forms of check marks for the cash and freight received books in checking the list of uncollected bills.

The list of uncollected, additional uncollected from the previous month, and the freight received book account for the current month,.

should be carefully checked, to see that every item is accounted for, as either paid or uncollected.

Then examine the cash book carefully to see that nothing remains unchecked. If there are any unchecked items on the cash book, see if they are not duplicate entries, if they are, adjust them through the miscellaneous column.

As the various parts of the account in which errors are likely to occur have been proved, the account should be in balance. If the account does not balance, re-examine the cash book footings, the uncollected freight of the present month, the uncollected freight of last month, or the columns on the balance sheet.

The errors as shown on the correction sheet from the Department, should not be entered up in bulk, but the items of which it is made up should be carefully examined, and proper adjustment of each made on the overcharge or cash book, or elsewhere, as the case may require.

It must be understood that the monthly correction sheet from the department referred to above, is an official notice to the agent of the final result, (as it affects his balance sheet,) of the audit and examination of his accounts by the several departments.

This sheet gives the amount originally entered by the agent to his debit or credit, and the amount as corrected, also the balance to be carried forward to the succeeding month's account.

In examining or transferring a station, the accounts of such station must be written up from the close of the last month which has been regularly audited. That is, if the examination or transfer is made, say on the 20th of August, it must be necessary to examine the affairs of the station from July 1st, as June would be the last month regularly audited, the accounts for the month of July being still incomplete.

Before visiting a station for the purpose of transfer or examination, you should be provided with the following data, and such other as you might need, in order to make the examination as accurately and expeditiously as possible.

1st. A statement showing the commencing numbers of local tickets at the commencement of the current month; also the highest number on hand at the time of the examination or transfer.

2nd. If the station is to be transferred, take a statement from the general ticket office of the coupon tickets, if coupon tickets are on sale at the station to be transferred.

3rd. Take the amount of the balance brought forward on the

agent's account current from the "previous month," with the list of the items which go to make up such balance.

4th. Should any corrections have been made by department officers in previous month's account, you should obtain, if necessary, from the department interested, a full explanation so that proper entries may be made upon the station books.

5th. You should take an itemized statement of every remittance that has been credited to the agent during the period of time to be audited, or for which transfer is to be made.

6th. You should take a list of the uncollected freight on hand, as shown by the last balance sheet, so that you may personally see that the list was in every respect correct and truthful.

7th. The last balance sheet returned by the agent should be verified in every respect, as far as possible.

In auditing station accounts, you should first count the cash on hand, inquiring particularly for the exact amount of all cash belonging to the company. The balance called for by the cash book added to the receipts of the current day should agree exactly with the amount of cash found to be on hand, making due allowance for foreign collections, if any. Should the cash on hand exceed this amount, you should ascertain how the surplus occurs, and the reason for it.

The cash should be counted immediately upon your arrival at the station, so as not to give agents time to replace money.

The cash book when properly written up and containing only the current day's business, should agree exactly with the cash on hand, less the working fund, and the amount of cash on hand should, in turn, be the precise amount required to balance the agent's account. Any other result is inconsistent and invites careful examination.

You should then take off on your ticket blank the closing numbers from the tickets in the local ticket case; using these numbers in making up the amount of the ticket sales for the current day.

Take account of the uncollected bills on hand, and compare them with the freight receipt book to see that the bills are made for the same amount as called for by the way-bills. Then see that the freight receipt book does not show delivery of the freight.

The bills which are accounted for as uncollected, should be indicated on the freight receipt book, by some appropriate mark.

The last way-bill made for freight forwarded, should be noted to see if the check book indicates any prepaid or advanced charges for which way-bills have not yet been made.

Note on the cash book the last item entered which is taken into the account as cash.

Then note the last way-bill entered on the freight receipt book.

Then compare the uncollected freight bills with freight on hand, examining with great care all credit items claimed. In examining the uncollected freight charges for goods on hand, be particular to see that the address and marks on the freight compare with those shown on the bill, you should strive to accurately identify the freight, in all other ways possible. Should the freight have been delivered, and charges claimed to be outstanding uncollected, you should have the bills presented for collection in your own presence; and observe closely if they are acccepted and paid without question by consignee.

You should then make up the account of tickets sold during the period for which the examination is being made, and compare the amount with that shown by the footing of the ticket column on cash book added to the amount of cash credited on account of tickets sold in current day's business.

An account of prepaid freight and advanced charges on freight forwarded should be made and compared with the cash book. This comparison with the footings of the cash book should always be made, as a check against any errors in your own work or in that of the agent. Any differences that might be found should be located and adjusted at once.

You should make an abstract of the way-bills on hand for freight received to see that the amount of way-bills as abstracted agrees with the footing of the freight received book. This is done as a proof that all corrections made on the freight received book have also been made on the way-bills, and, also, as a check against errors in abstracting or in writing up the freight receipt book.

To the list of remittances obtained from the Treasurer's cash book, add those made by the agent since the last item which appears on the list. The remittances from the agent's cash book must be compared and checked with the express messenger's receipt book, as a proof that all have gone forward as claimed by the agent. A statement of them should be sent to the Local Treasurer for comparison with his cash book.

Ascertain from the overcharge book the amount of the unrefunded overcharges to be charged on the balance sheet, being assured that each overcharge is properly computed, and that no overcharges have been audited on the cash book which have not actually been refunded and receipted for on the overcharge book.

From the extra baggage book ascertain the amount of extra baggage collections to be charged, and see that the same have been entered on the cash book.

From the cash book ascertain if any storage or other miscellaneous charges have been collected; if so, charge the same on the balance sheet which you have made. On the balance sheet you should next enter the balance from last month's account, as shown on the monthly correction sheet from the Local Treasurer.

In an examination for the purpose of transferring the accounts of an agent, you should examine in detail every way-bill received, to ascertain the exact amount collected for loading, dockage, demurrage or other purposes incidental to the transportation of freight.

In way-billing freight with charges of the foregoing character attached, it is necessary to insert the amount of such charges in the body of the bill, otherwise, in dividing with other roads or leased lines, they would get a proportion of such charges.

You should also ascertain and trace the exact amount collected by the agent on account of Insurance Companies, Post Office Department, various persons, or for other purposes foreign to their accounts as agents.

Should the account now prove not to be in exact adjustment, or, in other words, if the balance due the company, as shown by the cash book, differs from the amount shown to be due by the balance sheet, check the uncollected bills and other items which make up the "balance brought forward from last month's business," on the monthly balance sheet, to see that the items and accounts are properly accounted for in the remittances or other credits of the current month. If there is yet a discrepancy not located, check the freight received book with the cash book, the other portion of the account having been previously examined.

All entries in the miscellaneous column of the cash book should be carefully examined and analyzed to see that they are right and proper.

You should be particular to see that the local ticket book and coupon register are properly and promptly written up and completed at the close of each month's business.

In your investigations you will ascertain if there are any tickets on hand, either in the case or elsewhere, that have been stamped, or otherwise bear evidence of having ever been sold. Every possible device should be exercised by you to enable you to discover any arrangement between agents and others in reference to the return and re-issue of tickets. See that the numbers run in consecutive order, also examine each ticket to see that tickets of a low rate of fare are not substituted for tickets of a higher rate.

To make your examination as complete as possible, you should demand of all agents receipts from the shippers, acknowledging the payment of charges advanced on freight for which they claim credit.

Way-bills for freight forwarded with advanced charges attached, made near the time of your examination, should be treated with especial attention.

In writing up prepaid freight forwarded, see that the way-bill numbers run consecutively. This will prevent any imposition being practiced upon you, by the tearing out of a leaf or leaves that would otherwise show prepaid freight forwarded.

While examining the freight received book, you should also examine the cash book carefully, to see that all overcharges credited on the cash book as having been paid, appear also on the overcharge book, and are properly receipted by payee. If they do not appear, charge the agent with same, on his cash book, and make proper entries on overcharge book.

If an agent also acts as express agent, it will be necessary, in order to prove the entire trustworthiness of the railway balances, that you should partly verify his express accounts. To do this, carefully check the express company's collection book. If the cash or collections are not on hand, agents should be able to show proper receipts for such collections from the express messenger.

Non-reporting offices pay their freight bills daily to the express messenger, therefore, the collection book is the only important book to be checked. If the agent is a reporting agent, call for a copy of his last statement; see that the cash then on hand is properly accounted for; charge him with amount of freight on hand, as shown by the statement; also for all way-bills received subsequently, and for all prepaid freight forwarded. Then credit him with uncollected charges for freight on hand, and for charges advanced by him on freight forwarded. The difference between these debits and credits must be represented by cash. Sometimes it is admissible to allow a credit on salary or commission due him by the express company.

In examining the collection accompaning freight, ascertain if all collections on goods delivered, billed "C. O. D.," have been accounted for and receipted for by the express messenger.

At stations where the telegraph receipts are required to be turned over to agents, or where the agent handles in any manner the receipts of the telegraph company, it is necessary that you should carefully check the telegraph accounts, to ascertain whether the receipts from that source have been fully and properly accounted for.

Transfer of Station Accounts from One Agent to Another.

To properly adjust and balance the accounts of an outgoing agent, without subsequent loss accruing to the company therefrom, is a duty of the utmost nicety, and requires that especial vigilance should be exercised in auditing the affairs of such agents.

In visiting a station for the purpose of installing a new agent, you should take with you the data referred to previously herein, as necessary whenever an examination or transfer of agent's accounts is to take place.

The incoming agent is usually inexperienced and·unskilled in the examination of station accounts, and is, therefore, largely dependent upon your skill to have the accounts adjusted, not only correctly, but in such a manner that he may be able to render a full and complete account of the whole month's business, without confusion, or loss to himself at the end of the month. All the checks to secure accuracy, which have already been mentioned herein, should be made use of to guard against any omissions of debits from the transfer balance sheet.

Transfer balance sheets are made up the same as monthly balance sheets, with the exception the debits and credits are entered on a transfer balance sheet for the whole time transferred, whether it be a whole month, or more, or less.

In computing the transfer balance, bear in mind that although the balance from the "previous month appears in its usual place," it must *not* be included in the debits transferred, neither must the remittances be included as a part of the credits transferred, neither should the final remittance due the company from the outgoing agent be determined exclusively by the balance sheet, but the result, as shown by the balance sheet, must be verified by the station cash book, they must agree.

The transfer balance sheet should be signed by both the outgoing and incoming agent.

Accounts at the Junctions with Other Roads.

Railway accounts as they are kept at the junctions with other roads are peculiar in many respects, and will, therefore, receive special attention.

When freight is billed through to, or from a point on some connecting line, the way-bills are *not* transcribed on the books at the junctions. It is only freight rebilled that is entered upon the books at junctions.

You should familiarize yourself with the system of accounts of the other railroad lines with which your company makes junction connection, at which a joint agency is established. You should do this so that, in case of examination or transfer of agency at such points, you may be able, in the absence of the traveling auditor of such connecting line, to adjust the accounts of both companies properly, so as to protect the companies against loss.

At junction stations, the transfer account is kept in the usual form of freight received book, except that an additional column is inserted in the book, into which is carried the total amount of charges on freight to be transferred. The local business at the junction must be kept distinct, and this result is accomplished by carrying the amount of charges into the local columns provided for such purpose. All way-bills received are entered in this book, the pages of which are posted and balanced daily.

The total of the two consignment columns agrees in amount with the total of way-bill columns.

The entries in the transfer column of your company's freight received book, check with the charges billed out as advanced on the connecting line's way-bills, and the entries in the local consignment column, with the debit entries on the cash book of your company.

The footings of pages of each freight received book are recapitulated at the end of the week in freight received book, and the recapitulation is footed and balanced.

The way-bills received are abstracted at the close of the week, and the total of way-bills, as abstracted, is compared with the footing of freight received book.

The total of transfer column in your company's freight received book, added to the charges advanced on local business as shown by connecting road's cash book, equals the total of advanced charges as shown by that road's report of freight forwarded. The same check is applied to freight received by the connecting line and billed out on your road. Should the result of this checking by footings be satisfactory, no itemized checking of this portion of the account is required.

Settlement of the transfer account is made as often as once a week, and is made upon the footing of the transfer columns of freight received books. At the end of the week when settlement is made, the total amount of charges due your company on freight, turned over to the connecting line, as shown by the transfer column of your company's freight received book, is in one amount in the freight column on the debit side of your company's cash book, as amount collected of connecting line.

The same amount is entered in the advanced charge column, credit side, of the connecting road's cash book, as amount of charges advanced your company.

The amount owing to the connecting road for charges on freight received from that road, and billed out over your company's line, is entered in advanced charge column, credit side of your company's cash book, and in freight column, debit side of the connecting road's cash book. This amount is the footing of the transfer column of the connecting company's freight received book.

If the amount received from the connecting road is greater than that delivered that road, a draft is drawn on the Local Treasurer of your company for the difference in favor of the connecting company. This draft is entered on the debit side of your company's cash book in the miscellaneous column.

The transfer charges entered in the freight column, with draft added, balance the amount entered to credit in advanced charge column of cash book. On the connecting company's cash book this draft must be entered as a remittance to balance cash book, for the reason that the amount charged in freight column as "amount of freight charges collected of your company," is that much greater than the amount entered to the credit in advanced charges column as charges advanced.

If the amount delivered to the connecting road is greater than that received from that line, the draft is drawn on the financial Officer of the connecting company, and is remitted as cash to the financial officer of your company. This draft is charged on the connecting company's cash book in the miscellaneous column, and entered as a remittance on your company's cash book.

The advantages secured by this system of keeping transfer accounts are numerous, and will commend themselves to those interested.

CHAPTER THIRTY-TWO.

Building Association Auditing.

There are in the United States more than 7000 building associations, with a membership of over 2,000,000, whose annual savings amount to $75,000,000. This vast amount of money represents the hard-earned savings of a thrifty and frugal class of people, whom circumstances compel to save in small amounts. The savings thus accumulated they are compelled to earn by hard labor. It is not interest on capital, nor rent from investments, but small savings from their daily earnings. If there is a class of people who cannot afford any risk or loss, or if there is money anywhere that might be considered sacred, it certainly is the members of building associations, and the money in their treasuries.

Purpose of an Audit.

The business risks of an individual, firm or corporation are carried by themselves or their managers, as it is their own money that is invested. They are naturally watchful, prudent and painstaking. They devote their time and attention to the business, and if they find that they are not prospering, they may proceed to wind it up, without consulting anyone, but in the management of a building association, the conditions are different, while the directors and officers are financially interested, this interest is of little importance compared with their outside individual interests, consequently their individual interests will receive the greater attention.

Although the officers of an association be ever so conscientious, ever so much interested, nevertheless the opportunities for error are greater in an association than in a private enterprise.

The business of a building association is open to many more risks of mis-use on the part of managers, than is the case where proprietory interests are involved. These facts give rise to a special necessity for a systematic and regular audit of the accounts of every association.

Auditing is supervision practically applied. It not only tests the accuracy of the accounts, and the efficiency and integrity of officers, but it secures practical economy, and adopts labor-saving and practical methods.

There are six principal reasons why every building association should be audited regularly by a disinterested Auditor, viz:

1st. For the protection of the affairs of the association as a corporate body.

2nd. For the protection of the individual members, both creditors and borrowers.

3rd. To determine whether or not, the buiness is conducted according to statutory requirements, and the constitutional provisions of the association.

4th. To determine whether or not the business of the association is conducted economically, and with the best labor-saving systems.

5th. For the purpose of being able at all times to produce a reliable and verified statement of the association's affairs.

6th. For the purpose of elevating and maintaining a high financial standing, and to furnish evidence of its safety and prosperity.

The Auditor the Representative of the Members.

Every Auditor for a building association should be appointed by the members and not by the officers. He should be appointed for the purpose of ascertaining, on behalf of the stockholders, that the affairs of the association have been properly managed, that their money has been carefully handled and properly acounted for, and that such other funds as have been expended have been applied as intended and as indicated in the accounts.

To certify that the transactions of the officers and directors in the management of the business of the association have been wise, discrete and according to the rules of the association, and that the statement and balance sheet rendered by them, represent correctly and accurately the actual transactions and the true financial condition of the association, and that the receipts and expenditures, costs, gains, assets, liabilities, etc., are exactly as represented, will require, on the part of the Auditor, a most careful and searching examination of all the accounts and records.

Qualifications of Auditors.

An Auditor is an investigator, an inquisitor, a dissector and a detective in the highest acceptation of that term. It is his business to verify that which is right and to detect and expose that which is wrong ; to discover and state facts as they are, regardless of whom it might affect. "He is the champion of honesty and the foe of deceit."

It is needless to say that an Auditor must be honest and incorruptible. He must be firm and courageous. He must know his duty and do it without fear or favor. He will find weakness where he expected strength. He will find himself antagonized and opposed. There are times when he will be placed under such a variety of circumstances, that he will find it difficult to prosecute his work faithfully. To surmount all the difficulties an Auditor must meet, he must first be an Expert Accountant, he must understand the philosophy and the principles of the line of business with which he is dealing. The principles of accounting are the same always and everywhere; but in each line of business the application of the principles must vary.

In every line of business, labor-saving systems have been intro duced, which not only make economy in time and expense possible, but also greatly simplify the plans and make the results more readily attainable and comprehensible. An Auditor should be able to devise and systematize. He should be up with the times and have a full knowledge of modern methods and improvements, and all labor and time-saving devices.

An Auditor should have an established character and a will of iron. He should be a man of tact and courtesy, having the faculty of finding out what he wants to know. He should be a discrete man, one capable of keeping his own counsel. He should go his own way, mind his own business, and reach his own conclusions. He should have the faculty of winning the confidence and esteem of those with whom he is brought into contact, and of commanding the respect of even those whose faults and shortcomings he may be called upon to expose. He should be a man of forebearance and moderation, he should not reach conclusions hastily, nor be disposed to take any improper advantage of his position or knowledge.

It is not the duty of the auditor to take the books and accounts of an association and put them into proper shape, if he does not find

them so. He is the representative of the shareholders and membership at large, and not an assistant to the secretary and other officers.
He is to take things as he finds them, and to report upon them as they
are, unless he is employed to supervise, correct and audit.

Disqualification of Auditors.

While an Auditor must be an expert bookkeeper, it must be understood that auditing is not book-keeping, therefore, stockholders
should bear in mind that it lies in their power to increase the advantages of auditing by selecting a competent Auditor, and the adoption of
the best methods as to the time, manner, etc., of making the audits.

An Auditor should have a thorough understanding of the meaning
of all figures and items, and should understand their philosophical
as well as their mathematical relations.

If an Auditor is not familiar with the work to be done, it would
be an easy matter for a dishonest official to keep him in a good humor
and prevent him from discovering fraud, by having him check this
book or that, adding here and checking there, and finally lead him to
believe that he was making a thorough audit. By such assistance in
making a fine array of figures, he could be effectually thrown off the
track of a fraudulent entry. In fact, he might in this way handle the
very item which covers or omits fraudulent transactions.

Assistance from Officials.

An Auditor who must be assisted is one to be avoided. If the
Auditor understands his business, he will call for all books and records;
when they are placed in his hands he should take full charge of them
until his audit is completed. He should first examine the system, and
if there is anything he does not thoroughly understand, he should call
upon the officials for explanations. If there is anything about the system of accounts that he does not understand, he can easily get the desired information without exposing his ignorance.

Having everything in his possession, and a clear understanding of
the system and methods, he is then ready to proceed to do his own
work in his own way. When information is desired, he should sum-
mon the secretary to answer questions and to make necessary explanations.

Economical, Labor-Saving and Simple Methods.

People do not want an unnecessary expenditure of money, nor a
cumbersome system which they do not understand. They desire econ-

omy and simplicity in the management of their business. The greater part of the stockholders in building associations do not possess any knowledge of accounts, but they always favor economical and labor-saving methods. Many associations have failed because their system of accounts was too intricate and complicated, requiring much unnecessary work, without showing the true condition of the associa ion.

An Auditor who is able to devise and systematize, can, with very little expense, place the association's accounts in thoroughly scientific shape, requiring the least amount of work and showing at all times its true financial condition.

Care of Books and Records.

One of the first duties of an Auditor should be to examine the books and records of the association, to ascertain if they are kept in a safe place, how they are handled, what condition they are in, and if they are clean. Books that are neat and clean, with entries nicely arranged, and accounts properly ruled off, etc,, will as a rule, be found to be correctly kept, while those that are carelessly handled, unclean, finger-marked and scratched, an Auditor may well expect to find carelessness in the accounts themselves, for carelessness in one thing, carelessness in all things may be expected.

Special Hints.

It is important that an Auditor should adopt a system of check mark peculiarly his own. Check marks should be made with ink, using different colors for different purposes. By putting an individual check on each item as he passes upon it, each item will then tell its own story at a glance, and not fall into confusion. To check in this way, an Auditor can readily tell when his work is completed, and his check marks will remain for information and guidance in making future audits.

Fictitious Accounts.

It is not an uncommon thing for officers and book-keepers to intentionally prepare and submit false statements, for the purpose of concealing their wrongdoing, and when such is the case the auditor will have a very unpleasant and difficult task before him.

We all are liable to make mistakes through inefficiency or carelessness but misrepresentations are made with the intention to deceive. Therefore, the Auditor may rectify mistakes, but misrepresentations must be exposed.

If an Auditor is competent, he will soon be able to detect all errors and misrepresentations. Should any such be discovered, he must tax his skill to the utmost, to discover and detect every possibility to deceive. He should not only be prepared to point out the errors in the accounts, but should be able to expose the method and purpose of the commission or omission. Under such circumstances, an Auditor must be cool, deliberate, level-headed and close-mouthed. He should conceal his suspicions, and should let nothing in his manner, spirit or actions indicate that anything out of the ordinary has been discovered, until the proper time comes for him to take decisive action. Then he should possess all the evidence available, so that his position may be unconquerable, and that when exposure is made, it may be complete and the guilty ones brought to justice or restitution as the case may require.

Errors of Omission.

It is impossible to lay down specific rules by which errors of omission can be detected with absolute certainty. It is comparatively an easy matter to make a thorough and correct audit, so far as direct cash transactions are concerned, but to detect errors of omission and render a complete statement of assets, liabilities, losses, gains, etc., will depend upon the intelligence, training and determination of the Auditor.

To guard against errors of omission in any part of the accounts, each item should be checked from its original entry to its final account, to ascertain if the association has been charged with all cash received, and liabilities incurred. All cash expenditures and credits must be treated in the same manner.

The financial affairs of many associations have become complicated and the interests of stockholders seriously endangered, simply because officials have been careless in their accounts, or through the incompetency and carelessness of the Auditor.

General Outline.

The books used in building Association accounting are: Member's Pass Books, Contribution Book for entering Receipts, Withdrawal Book or Order Book, Stockholder's Individual Ledger, Cash Book, General Ledger, Treasurer's Receipt and Treasurer's Cash Book.

To make your audit complete in every detail, you should.

1st. Verify all extentions and footings in the books of original entry.

2nd.   Check each item in the Member's Pass Books with the Contribution Book and Stockholder's Ledger.

3rd.   Check each entry in the Contribution Book with the Stockholder's Ledger.

4th.   Check each entry in the Withdrawal Book with the Stockholder's Ledger.

5th.   Check each entry in the Contribution Book and Withdrawal Book with the Cash Book.

6th.   Check the Treasurer's Receipt Book with the Contibution Book.

7th.   Check the Treasurer's Cash Book with the Withdrawal Book.

8th.   Check the totals of the Cash Book with the totals in the General Ledger.

Checking Payment of Dues.

The methods by which dues are received and recorded are so numerous that it would be difficult to make specific rules to cover all cases, however, a few suggestions may be made to put an intelligent Auditor upon the right track.

1st.   Examine each member's pass-book to see if he has paid all necessary fees, and that each book has been issued only after the member has complied with all the requirements of the association.

2nd.   Check the dates and amounts of all entries of dues, fines, etc., in each pass book.

3rd.   Check each entry in the Pass-books with the accounts in the Stockholder's Ledger to see if all items have been properly posted.

4th.   Each deposit account in the Contribution Book should be added across, and the totals compared with the corresponding entries in the Cash Book.

Proving the Cash Balance.

To verify the Cash Balance, as shown by the Cash Book, the cash must be produced and counted.

If the books are not audited until after the end of the term, the cash on hand must be counted, and a statement prepared, showing the receipts and expenditures since the close of the term. The Auditor should be engaged, and go to work before the close of the term; when this is done, it removes an element of uncertainty, and if any fraud were being planned, it would be impossible to practice it without being detected.

Secretary's Cash Book.

The General Cash Book is sometimes called the Secretary's Cash Book. It is immaterial what name is given this book as long as it will enable you to bring all the accounts together, so that they may be properly summarized and balanced.

The following accounts are usually kept in special columns in the Cash Book, viz., Dues, Interest, Fines, Premiums, Admission, Transfer, Books, Paid on Mortgages, Paid on Pass Books, Paid Up Stock, Overs and Sundries on the debit side, on the credit side, Loans on Mortgages, Withdrawals, Loans on Pass Book, Interest, Dividends, Salary, Stationery, Expense, Paid Up Stock withdrawn and Sundries.

When the Cash Book is arranged with special columns for the above accounts, it saves a great deal of posting, as only the totals are posted at the end of the month.

Treasurer's Cash Book.

The Treasurer should keep a Cash Book in which to enter the gross receipts of each meeting and all disbursements. It should be kept posted up at all times and show the exact amount of cash on hand.

The Auditor should check this book with the Treasurer's Receipt Book, the Warrant Book and the Bank Book, using an appropriate check mark.

Stockholder's Individual Ledger.

In auditing the accounts in this book, the following points should be considered:

1st. Check each stockholder's account in the Ledger with the entries in the Pass Book, using a special check mark to indicate that this has been done. This is necessary as the same accounts are checked from other sources.

2nd. Check each stockholder's account in the Ledger with the entries in the Contribution Book, using a special check mark.

3rd. Check the Withdrawal items with the Member's Pass Book, Contribution Book, and Warrant Book.

4th. Check the Dividend Account to ascertain if each member has been properly credited. If the Dividend has been drawn, the items must be checked with the Warrant Book.

5th. If there are any miscellaneous items, such as assessments, rebates, and others of a similar nature, they must be checked with the original entries.

Withdrawal.

Withdrawals should be. paid by voucher, showing the date, the exact amount which has been paid, and the shares affected thereby. The Auditor should compare the signatures on the voucher with those in the Constitution Signature Book, or otherwise satisfy himself that it is correct.

In checking the withdrawals, the Auditor should ascertain:

1st.   If the applications for money have been entered in the Withdrawal Book in regular chronological order, and if they have been acted upon in this order by the Directors.

2nd.   Check all warrants for the payment of withdrawals with the dates and amounts in the Cash Book.

3rd.   Check all partial withdrawals with the Member's Pass Book. If the withdrawal is in full, see that the Pass Book has been surrendered, and the withdrawal correctly entered therein.

4th.   Check all the amounts paid out on withdrawals, with the stockholder's account in the Individual Ledger.

General Ledger.

This is one of the most important books of the association, as all the accounts except the member's individual accounts are kept therein. From it the balance sheet and Financial Statement are made.

The general accounts usually kept are: Pass Books, Dues, Fines, Premiums, Interest, Admissions, Transfers, Shorts, Overs, Rents, Dividends, Salaries, Insurance and Surplus.

Assets and Liabilities.

The Assets and Liabilities which are also kept in the General Ledger, may be classified as follows, although the State Department furnishes the blanks upon which Annual Statements must be rendered.

ASSETS.	LIABILITIES.
Cash,	Paid up Stock and Dividends,
Loans on Mortgage Security,	Running Stock and Dividends,
Loans on Stock Security,	Contingent Fund,
Real Estate,	Bills Payable,
Furniture and Fixtures,	Deposit and Interest,
Other Assets, in detail,	Undivided Profits,

Other Liabilities, in detail.

Auditor's Certificate.

When the Auditor has completed his work and finds everything correct, he should hand the officers' statements and reports to the stockholders, with the following certificate:

To the Stockholders of the Blank Building and Loan Association.

I have carefully examined the books, vouchers, cash and accounts of your Association, and find the same to correspond with the Balance Sheet, Statements and Reports presented by your officers, under date of ....   I also find the present condition of the Association to be exactly as represented.

Respectfully,

......................................Auditor.

If everything is found correct, the above certificate is all the Auditor need give; however, there may be some matters to which he desires to call the attention of the stockholders, when such is the case, he must do so with great care and accuracy.

If the Auditor should differ with the Secretary or the Directors, upon some matter which may be of importance to the interests of the Association, he should state the matter plainly, so as not to be mis-understood.

If the Auditor finds that the officers do not have ample facilities for transacting the Association's business, he should recommend improvements.

If the Auditor finds that the mortgages, insurance policies, notes and other valuable documents are not systematically or safely kept, he should suggest improved methods for filing and absolute safety.

An Auditor in rendering reports on miscellaneous matters, must act deliberately, being careful not to do anything which might be used to the disadvantage of the Association, by some dissatisfied member or meddlesome outsider.

If an Auditor finds that the Accounts and Records are inaccurate, and incomplete from any cause, he must withhold his certificate, but must report facts as he finds them.

The instructions herein given will be found sufficient to put a careful Auditor on his guard.

CHAPTER THIRTY-THREE.

Expert Examinations of Street Railway and Other Corporation Property and Accounts for Banks, Syndicates, Trust Companies and Investors.

Money makers are the same the world over. They have not changed for three thousand years. Their practice conforms within the law to their desires. Persistent, aggressive effort to achieve fortune is commendable.

What one possesses others strive to obtain. This is called enterprise. Acquisitiveness is the animating cause of commercial activity; possession of wealth, the goal of mankind. If these truths were more generally kept in mind, men would be more wary in making investments; more painstaking in looking after investments already made.

Those who have money to invest in corporation securities should not buy without investigating, nor hold without guarding. Investors in corporations will be wise if they exercise equal foresight. It will be only common business prudence.

As long as men will buy securities without intelligent investigation, so long will they be disappointed in their investments. I do not say that securities selling below par, or at merely nominal rates may not be valuable; they may be more desirable than those selling at a premium. But wise men will not touch a security without careful investigation. Those who do are the most reckless of gamblers and unworthy of sympathy if their ventures turn out unfortunately.

While men should not buy securities without investigation, they should not sell without reason. Mere rumor should not disturb them. Stocks and Bonds are ever the subjects of manipulation. The effort to induce the public to sell when the market is going up, and to buy when it is going down, never for a moment ceases. Representations conform to these ends and markets are manipulated accordingly. Speculative classes are kept alive by the dupes who believe their misrepresentations.

Millions of dollars are lost every year, simply because investors neglect to make a proper investigation. Millions upon millions of dollars have been lost by investors, because Trust Companies act as Trustees, without investigating the corporate property, to ascertain if it is worth the bonds to be issued, or if the companies will be able to pay interest.

Every corporation proposing to issue bonds, increase the Capital stock, or ask accommodations of banks, should have its accounts, property and financial affairs examined, by a competent, disinterested Public Accountant, whose report should show the true financial condition, and be exhibited to all parties interested. If banks would require such statements, their losses would be considerably less. Trust Companies, before accepting the trusteeship of the bonds of any corporation, should have a thorough examination made by their own representatives, for the protection of investors.

To make an efficient examination as above referred to, you must not only be an expert accountant, but must have a thorough knowledge of property values of every description.

To make an expert examination of the accounts, property and franchises of a Street Railway company, I would make the following suggestions:

You should be clothed with your authority to enter the company's offices and property, with free access to everything necessary to make your examination complete.

The Articles of Incorporation should be examined with the greatest care and accuracy, and be compared with the charter received from the State Department, noting particularly the sections of the Statutes under which the company is incorporated.

In a recent examination made by the writer, it was found that the Articles of Incorporation were drawn under one section of the Statutes and the Charter granted by the Secretary of State under another section. It was an easy matter, however, to show the pure intent of the Incorporators, while the error was principally on the part of the Secretary of State. Otherwise it would have given rise to a very serious complication.

In your report you should give the Articles of Incorporation and the Certificate of the Secretary of State, to show that the company has been legally incorporated.

You should then give your attention to the Minute Book, Subscription, Stock Ledger, Certificate of Stock Book, etc., to see what resolutions have been adopted by the company, by whom the stock was subscribed, to whom issued, etc.; while it is not your duty to audit the books, you must compare the Balance Sheet for different periods with the books to ascertain if they are correct. In your report you should exhibit the Trial Balance for the last month previous to your examination.

The Operating Receipts should be examined for a period of two or three years, likewise the Expenses for Operating, Maintaining and Fixed charges, Tabulating the monthly totals, as will be shown in the Report.

Following the statement of Earnings and Expenses, should be given the Assets and Liabilities in detail. Although they are represented in the Trial Balance, they should be given separately.

The Trial Balance, statements of Assets and Liabilities, Operating Receipts and Expenses, having been prepared after a careful examination of the books and records, you should then examine the records in the County Clerk's and Recorder's office, to ascertain if there are any unsatisfied Mortgages, Liens or Judgments on file or record against the company, not shown on their books. You should report the findings of this investigation, and obtain a certificate of each officer to verify the same.

The real estate owned by the company should be examined, not only from the deeds, etc , but the property itself. Examine carefully the value of the same on the books, and compare vacant or unimproved property with the considerations mentioned in the deeds. Sometimes it might be well to get the price of the property from one having a knowledge of its true value. This information must be obtained, however, without creating any suspicion.

After the property has been examined, each piece should be described separately, the same as it appears upon the records. You should also make a plat of it, showing dimensions, location, boundaries, etc.

You should next examine the company's franchises; usually all companies have a copy of each, but if they are not certified to by the city, township or county clerk, as the case may be, you should not make use of them. A copy of each franchise can be obtained of the city, township or county clerk, with their certificate that they are correct. This will incur some expense, but they must be had.

After procuring copies of the franchises, study them carefully, and compare them with the road to see if all conditions have been complied with. The franchises and certificates may be inserted in your report just as they are received from the clerk. Although they are usually numerous and lengthy, I prefer to copy them for the sake of uniformity.

In order that the franchises may be more easily followed, I prepare a map upon tracing cloth, of the whole road, showing all streets, avenues, and highways, in which the company's tracks are laid, whether single or double, weight of rail, etc., also show the location of real estate. In large cities these maps can be purchased, but in smaller places they cannot be had, unless the company has had one prepared by their engineer, in which case, all you will need to do is to copy it.

Now you are ready to examine the construction and equipment, which will require close inspection and good judgment. You should have the Superintendent go with you over every foot of the company's road for the purpose of giving information ; you should ask questions upon every important point and make notes. The Superintendent can tell you the size and weight of the rail used, the kind and size of ties, their distance, etc.

You should give particular attention to the ballast condition of the track and pavement. This is one of the most important points to be considered, because the franchises may require the company to keep the pavement in repair, and if the road is rough and rail badly worn, it may require a vast amount of money to put the same in good condition.

The overhead construction should receive your attention at the same time, noting whether wood or iron poles are used, and give the size, height, depth and condition. Give the size and make of trolley, feed and guy wires and appurtenances. The condition of switches, crossings, turnouts and sidetracks, should be examined carefully, as it is very expensive to replace them.

The road having been carefully examined, you should then go through the power house, barns, etc., here the Superintendent can give you full information regarding their system of operation, electric and steam machinery, motors, cars, trucks, etc.

Now that you have been over the whole property with the Superintendent and have received full information upon every point, you are ready to examine the property for yourself, which should be done about as follows : First get a pass and go over as much of the road as you think proper, in order to learn the condition, you should converse with the conductors, motorneers and gripmen about the condition of the cars and track, and the feeling between the company and the men.

These men know more about the condition of track and cars than the officers, and if they are handled properly, you can get all the information you desire.

You should then press the Line and Track Foremen into service, with them you can examine the overhead construction and track. In conversation with them, you can learn what is needed and where the defects are.

When you examine the steam and electrical machinery, you can get all the information you desire by conversing with the engineers and firemen; if there is any defective or worthless machinery you can get the details from them without any trouble. You should make a complete record of all of the machinery, giving the style, size, number and make of each. This is necessary, because it may be required by the attorney to insert in the mortgage.

The power, engine and boiler houses, shops and car barns should then be examined, noting the condition, material, fire protection, etc. Your description of this property should be complete, and shown upon a plat as has been stated.

Your attention should then be given to the motors and cars, noting in detail the number, style and condition of each motor, car and truck. The number and make of Motor cars, number of Trailers and Open cars.

Having examined the company's incorporation papers, accounts, earnings, assets, liabilities, real estate, overhead and surface construction, machinery and equipment, then you are ready to prepare your report, which should be plain and to the point; you should give all descriptions and explanations as shown by the records, so that the mortgage can be drawn without further examination. A report based upon the following sketch will be found to meet most requirements.

Articles of Incorporation.

Make a complete copy of the Articles of Incorporation.

Charter or Certificate of Incorporation.

Under this head, make a complete copy of the Charter or Certificate of Incorporation. This will show that the company has been legally incorporated.

List of Stockholders.

A list of the stockholders should be given, showing the number of shares owned by each, and the amount paid in.

Capital Stock.

Give the authorized Capital, number of shares, par value, and the amount paid up. Examine the books carefully to ascertain if the stock has been paid in cash or property, or whether it has been donated or watered.

Trial Balance.

The Trial Balance for the last month, previous to the examination, should be given in detail, excepting accounts receivable and payable, may be given in bulk.

Operating Receipts, Expenses and Fixed Charges

Make a statement of the receipts and expenses for a term of two or three years, arranged as given below. This will be the most interesting part of your report.

Date.	Operating Receipts.	Operating and Maintaining.	Fixed Charges.	Net Receipts.
Jan., 1895.	$——.——	$——.——	$——.——	$——.——
Feb., "	"	"	"	"
Mar., "	"	"	"	"
Apr., "	"	"	"	"
May, "	"	"	"	"
Etc., etc.	"	"	"	"

Classified Statement of Assets and Liabilities.

The statement of assets should show the value of the whole property and the liabilities, the funded and floating debt. Under this heading you should state the condition of the books and explain the system of accounting, whether good, bad or indifferent.

Certificates of the County Clerk and Recorder.

If there are any mortgages, liens or judgments on record for or against the company, they should be included in the statement of Assets and Liabilities. Then have the Clerk or Recorder give you a certificate to verify your statements. If the records are clear, you should also use their Certificates. ·

Real Estate.

Under this title you should give a complete description and plat of each and every piece of real estate owned by the company, as it is given on the records. This is absolutely necessary, as a mortgage cannot be executed without it.

Franchises.

The company's Franchises should be carefully reviewed. These can be secured from the city, township or county clerk, and should be given in detail, as the right to operate upon the streets and highways, is given therein.

Map of the Road.

Make a large, plain tracing of the company's lines, designating each line with a separate color, and name the streets and highways through which they run. This will make it easy to follow the franchises.

Track Construction.

In giving a description of the track construction, you should take up each line separately, and state the condition from beginning to end, taking each street or highway separately. Give the size, weight and style of the rail, size and kind of ties and the distance from centre to centre; the kind and condition of the pavements, and by whom they are to be kept in repair.

If the track and rail are in good order, you should so state it, but if the track is rough, and the rail worn, you should state the probable cost for proper repairs, specifying the style and weight of rail that should be used, and such other information as will benefit a prospective investor.

Crossings, safety switches, Y's and curves are very expensive, and their condition should be specially noted. If this point be overlooked, the company might be required to pay many thousands of dollars for improvements that were not expected.

Overhead Construction.

The condition of the overhead construction should be carefully considered. Specify the size and kind of poles used, their height, depth and how planted. Give the size of the trolley and feed wires, and state particularly the material used as guys.

Power and Boiler Houses, Shops and Car Barns.

The description of the power and boiler houses, shops and car barns, should be complete and clear. It is important to know how they are erected. the material used, location, dimensions and fire protection.

It is also well to state the amount of insurance carried, the rate, the name of the companies, and the amount carried by each. State also to what extent the company repairs its own cars, motors, etc.

Power Equipment,—(Steam, Cable or Electric Apparatus.)

This is an important part of the road, and your explanations should be carefully made. State first, the number, style, capacity and condition of the boilers, likewise the pumps, engines, generators, cables, etc.

Electric Motors.

Under this heading you should give the number of motors owned by the company, giving the make, style, H. P. condition, and the cost to keep in repair.

Motor, Grip, Freight and Express Cars, and Trailers.

You should give a complete list of the number of motor, grip, freight, express and trail cars, specifying the make of the car bodies, and trucks, and their condition. It is also well to give the number of each make and the car number, that is to say, 75, 25ft. Brill Car Bodies and Trucks, Nos. 1, 2, 3, 4, etc.; 19, 16ft. Pullman Car Bodies with McGuire Trucks, Nos. 76, 77, 78, etc., etc.

Bonds.

If the company proposes to issue bonds, you should give the amount to be issued, and state for what purpose they will be issued. If improvements are to be made, you should get an estimate of the probable cost and give the general items. In some instances it may be necessary to require a bond from the company, specifying that the proceeds of the bonds shall be used for improvements only.

Legalizing the Issue.

Before the Directors can mortgage the property of the company, they must be so instructed by the stockholders, therefore, it will be necessary for you to have the President or other proper officer call a special meeting of the stockholders in the general way, for the purpose of voting an issue of bonds and to so instruct the Directors to call a meeting for the same purpose.

If the stockholders and directors at their meetings vote to mortgage the property and issue bonds, then it will be legal to do so, otherwise it will not.

The minutes and resolutions of both meetings should be copied in your report, and when it is possible to do so, you should have them signed by the President and Secretary, with the corporate seal.

Ordinarily, this would conclude your report, but, if there are to be extensions built into new territory, or if the road is to change from animal to electric power you should give a general review of

The Locality and Its Possibilities.

If the improvements are to be extensive and the issue of bonds a large one, it might be well to give a general history of the city, its advantages and disadvantages, its growth, population, public institutions, government, schools, manufactories, railroads and any other information that would be of value to those not familiar with the facts. If the city is growing, and has places for public pleasure, with its citizens well employed, the probabilities are that the improvements will pay, otherwise they may not. However, in concluding your report you should state plainly whether or not you think the property in good condition, and if it is worth the mortgage to be placed upon it.

Report of Another Expert Examination of Street Railway Properties.

The examination and report given above are intended more particularly for a company proposing to issue bonds, while the report given below, is made from an examination of the financial and physical condition of three separate Street Railway properties which are operated under lease.

The examination was ordered by the court, at the instigation of a dissatisfied stockholder.

Hon. H. C. W .... Judge .... court.

Dear Sir:—I beg to submit herewith, the report of my examination of the financial and physical condition of the .... Street R'y Co., the .... Street R'y Co., and the .... Street R'y Co.

Capital Stock.

The capital stock account of each company has been carefully examined, and found to be fully paid up, there being no unpaid subscriptions or installments.

Accounting Methods.

The method of accounts and the bookkeeping of the .... Street Railway Co,, are admirably adapted to its purposes, as lessee of the other roads.   The statement of its receipts are in such form, and are protected by checking devices and detailed reports as to set forth the total income of the company for each day, in a complete and correct manner, and also as to place before the President on the succeeding morning, an exhibit of the gross earnings upon each line operated, together with the number of cars in operation, the number of trips, the mileage of cars, the wages of employees, and the net earnings after deducting wages.   The expenditures of the corporation are controlled by requisitions, orders, audits and certifications, by the various officers and employees through whose hands these accounts pass.   By the auditing system in use, each entry upon the books of the corporation is certified to, first, by the auditing committeee of the Board of Directors, then by the President, Secretary and Treasurer, and by each employee through whose hand the voucher passes.   This elaborate and comprehensive system of accounting was devised by the secretary and treasurer of the company, and is so complete as to deserve notice and commendation.

The .... Street Railway Company's books are the same as those used at the time of the organization of the road in 1865, the same form of ledger being still in service.   No fault can be found with their accuracy, but more elaborate methods should have been adopted when the change of motive power was made, from horses to electricity, in order that there could have been a more intelligent division of the items of expense.   The present secretary of the company appreciates the necessity for a change in system to more nearly conform to the system of the lessee road, and a new set of books will be opened forthwith.

Receipts.

A careful examination of the manner in which the receipts of the road are collected, taken from the time the fare is received by the conductor, its deposit in the receiving depot, its receipt in the office of the company, and its final deposit in the bank, each day's receipts from such source being deposited in their entirety, and of the bank book showing the daily deposits proves conclusively that the actual receipts are as stated.

Operating Expenses.

The net total of operating expenses, as reported by the company is $2,673,391.73, and I have no hesitation in saying, as a result of the examination, that no item is charged against this account which does not properly belong there. In detail, the items that have been made the subject of criticism are, viz.:

Repairs of roadbed and track $141,570.53. The examination of this account shows that none of the cost of changing the road from horses to electricity was charged to the account, but that it was all for repairs of roadbed and track. The labor and material used in the re-paving of the streets, amounted in round numbers to $70,000, and for the repairs of the track $71,570.53. The repairs to the pavement were caused by the settling of the paving done in the previous year, and because of the strict requirements of the department of city works, which ordered most of the repaving. The amount thus charged to repairs of track and special work, $71,570.53, is not excessive. The statement that no repairs would be required upon the roadbed and track of a properly constructed electric railway in five years, is not in accordance with the facts. With the very best construction, constant renewals of special work, repairs of joints and repairs of paving are necesssry.

Loans and Construction.

When the money of the.........Street Railway Company available for construction, had all been expended, it became necessary under the terms of the agreement, for the.........Street Railway Company to go on and complete the construction and make desired extensions. For the purpose of obtaining money to do this work, the.........Street Railway Company entered into an agreement with the.........Guarantee and Indemnity Co., whereby it was agreed that necessary funds to the extent of three million dollars should be loaned them for this purpose, upon notes made by the.........Street Railway Company, and endorsed by the.........Street Railway Company. Under the terms of the lease, the money so expended was to become in effect a lien upon the property of the.........Street Railway Company to this extent: the.........Street Railway Company agreeing in the lease to reimburse the.........Street Railway Company, either at the expiration of the lease, or at such time and in such manner as might be agreed upon by the contracting parties, for all moneys expended in extending or bettering.

Construction and Equipment Account.

The only portion of the criticism not considered is that relating to the construction and equipment account of the.........Street Railway Company. The force of this criticism depends upon the determination of the question, what proportion of the expense of changing a road from horse to electric power, is a charge to betterment. If horse power had been continued, the cost of replacing worn out tracks and equipment should have been charged to operating expenses, as the maintenance of the electric road must now be charged. But the tracks and equipment of the horse roads that have been changed to electric power are not worn out. A new condition of things came into existence. Improved service was demanded. Increased revenues were certain to result. Stockholders subscribed their money to make a radical and complete change in the system of operation and expected that their roads would earn enough to take care of the new stock and bond issues, the proceeds of which were to be expended for construction and equipment, as well as of the stocks and bonds then outstanding representing the stock of the road up to the time of the change. In many cases it has actually cost more to take up the old construction and put down new, then if there had been no old roadbed. Conversion of one method to the other was not the maintenance of the horse power in any respect. The latter was to pass out of existence. Its place was to be taken by new rules, new equipment, and a new method of transit. The earnings of the improved method have in all cases justified the charge of the entire cost of conversion as a betterment to the property. Wherever the horse car tracks were found to be suitable for use, under the new system, they were used, the cost of wiring, etc., being charged to construction as a betterment, and property sold. Wherever the old tracks were not suitable they were replaced by construction much better in every way than that required for horse-cars, and the whole cost charged to construction, less the amount received from the sale of useless material. It might be said that as the horsecar tracks would have to be kept up by charging to operating expense, a portion of the new construction should be charged to operating expenses. The reply is, that the track as it was would have answered for a long time to come for horse tracking; the new condition required the substitution of the new method. forcing practically the throwing away of the old construction.

The secretary affirms the propriety of charging interest and discount on moneys borrowed for construction to the construction account. The secretary also states that as far as can be ascertained, the work of construction was carried through with reasonable economy, and that no extravagance was shown in expenditure.

Summary.

The accounts of the.........Street Railway Company are correct, and properly set forth the transactions of that company. The terms of the agreements with the other companies have been fully and faithfully complied with, and at the time of this examination all accounts due the.........Street Railway Company had been paid.

The money obtained by the.........Street Railway Company from the sale of its stocks and bonds, for the purpose of changing the motive power of its road from horses to electricity, has been properly expended and charged to the proper accounts. These accounts have received full credit for the sale of useless material, and the relations of the two companies with the lessee company have been controlled in all respects by the terms of the lease.

Power Station.

The power stations were then examined. There are three in active operation as follows : The Eastern, which is the largest and is located at the corner of.........Street, and.........Street ; the Southern, at the foot of.........Street, and the Central on.........Avenue. An unused station at the corner of.........Avenue and.........Street is now for sale. Your inspector, in the inspection of these stations, found everything modern, material and workmanship of the best, and the machinery all in perfect running order, stable and permanent. The method of handing coal is very economical. The appliances all appear of modern construction and well cared for. The structures were also found well and durably made. The E. P. Ellis Company of Milwaukee had furnished the engines and these were found working smoothly, without the vibration usual in many instances. Great care has been taken in the foundation construction, concrete and granite being used in large quantities with Portland Cement. Stability is apparent everywhere, even in minor parts. Room was noted in each station for additional power for needs in the future. The boiler batteries were found in excellent condition, and ample room for additions were noted.

It is somewhat difficult to compare the cost of power generated in power stations in different parts of the country. The variation in the size of the cars, difference in grades over which cars are propelled, and the different percentages of loss in the transmission of power from the power stations to the cars are some of the hardest factors to overcome and equalize. The unit of comparison which is used generally, is the cost of power per car per mile. If the ampere hour unit at the station were used, many of the difficulties would disappear, as the unit does not vary. The cost per car mile, for the last six months, upon this system, reach as low as $1\frac{1}{10}$ cents and has not been above $1\frac{25}{100}$ cents. The nominal horse power of the three stations reaches close to 17,000. The maximum capacity would considerably exceed this easily.

Overhead and Track Construction.

The overhead construction was carefully examined upon all the lines, and was found as desirable as could be expected. The wires were taut, of ample size, well and securely connected and carefully attended to. Guard wires were found up in all instances where there was a possibility of other wires falling upon the trolley wires. The poles were found of extra material, well and securely set in the ground, and all strongly maintained. The trolley wires are of hard drawn copper, number "o," B. & S. guage. The span wires, supporting the trolley wires are of galvanized iron, and are insulated from the trolley wires and from the poles. The copper "bonds," which connect the rails, are bonded to supplementary wire running parallel to the rails, the entire length of the line. The arrangement of the return current cables and feed system were found complete, and in extra condition, and very well cared for. The matter of electrolysis has been also very well cared for, and the near future will no doubt see this troublesome feature entirely eliminated. Repair gangs were noted upon days of inspection, and appearances indicated close attention upon every line. This system, the second largest in the world, has some 200 miles of single track. Most of the lines have double tracks, which greatly facilitates the traffic. In addition to the main trackage, over 109 cross overs, averaging sixty feet each, making a total of 6,540 feet. A careful inspection of the tracks upon each of the lines, shows excellent state of maintenance. The different kinds of rail in use are as follows : Lewis and Fowler box girder, 5 inches high, and weighing 65 pounds per yard ; 9 inch girder, 12 bolts per joint, center bearing or horse car rails ; side bearing rail, steam rail, T form, and Johnson's 6 inch.

girder rail. The surface and adjustment of tracks are very good, showing constant attention and care. The pavements adjacent to the tracks and between them are, as a rule in good condition upon each of the lines. The lines extending to the suburbs are paved, and exceptionally cared for. The new 9 inch girder rail, recently laid upon .... Street, became necessary owing to increased traffic. Several of the lines will, the coming season, be laid with this heavy "section."

Real Estate—Car Shops and Cars.

The car repair shop upon .... Street, was found in permanent condition, and the outfit there is quite complete. Nearly all repairs are made there, and all cars equipped, some 1,600 in number. The change from horse power to electricity, upon the 24 lines, was made from May, 1891, to September, 1894.

The company owns 42 parcels of real estate, upon each are located, with few exceptions, car houses, stables, shops, transfer stations, etc. Each of the buildings was examined and found well cared for, and of good construction, a number being of stone and brick. The areas of the above parcels range from 1,895 square feet to 2,961 square feet. This class of property is generally closely watched and maintained, as its great value deserves. In round numbers, this company has 800 closed and 800 open cars. The general condition of the cars was found very good. The motors' running parts and cars proper, receive daily inspection, and repairs are made whenever needed, without delay.

Dummy Lines.

The dummy lines were inspected and found in good condition as regards track, roadbed and the like. Your inspector was informed, that these lines will, in the near future, be modified to electric power. Calculations show that the power stations are together capable of operating 425 miles of single track, with all the cars required, which will not be less than about 1,650 per day, without laying another brick or any other work, excepting perhaps, the addition of 4 engines, 8 batteries of boilers and 6 generators, the foundations for which are already erected and provided for.

In conclusion, your inspector would say that the whole system, in its financial and physical conditions, shows economical management, intelligent maintenance, modern construction and proper safety of the various track surfaces.

Corporation Stocks—Common and Preferred.

Usually the par value of a share of capital stock in a railroad and other corporations, is one hundred dollars. Sometimes the shares are fifty dollars each, and in some cases less. Frequently two kinds of shares are issued. Their printed form is substantially alike, but they have different rights and privileges. The higher grade is called preferred stock or preferred shares, the subordinate grade, common or ordinary stock. The rights these shares severally enjoy, and the maximum amount of each that may be issued, are set forth in the articles of incorporation, and this limit cannot subsequently be exceeded without formal consent of the parties in interest.

The only difference in the form of a certificate of common and preferred stock is that one is marked Common and the other Preferred.

Many railroad companies have more than two classes of stock. The relation they sustain to each other and to the property is determined by the peculiar circumstances that necessitated the diversity of interest.

The Grand Trunk Railway of Canada has five classes of stock, viz.: Ordinary Stock; Ordinary Stock, new issue of 1873; First Preference, Second Preference, and Third Preference. It has, besides, various kinds and grades of bonds.

The Chicago, Milwaukee and St. Paul Company's preferred shareholders are entitled to an annual dividend of seven per cent. before a dividend can be paid on the common stock.

The preferred shares of the Lake Shore and Michigan Southern Railway are entitled to an annual dividend of ten per cent. on their par value before the ordinary shares can receive any return. No dividend can be paid on the common shares of the Northwestern road during any year, out of the receipts of such year, until the seven per cent. has been divided among the holders of preferred shares.

When a company in poor credit is compelled to raise money, the best terms attainable are accepted. Sometimes mortgage bonds are created; sometimes new shares are issued (at a large discount, perhaps,) which shares, by consent of the holders of existing securities, frequently take precedence. It is in ways such as these that different classes of shares and bonds are brought into existence. The rights enjoyed by holders of preference and common shares, on different roads, are rarely the same.

When there are two classes of stock, preferred rights usually extend no further than a division of net earnings. Or, in other words, while the holders of a preferred stock may be entitled to a certain return before inferior shares can receive anything, still, in the event the property is foreclosed or sold, the surplus, after satisfying the mortgage and other debts, is divided equally among all classes of shareholders. In some cases, however, the rights of the preferred shareholders extend to a division of the property.

Mortgage Bonds.

The amount of the bonds issued in the United States with which to build and equip railroads is called Funded Debt. A mortgage is an absolute lien and, in the event the interest or principal is not paid as agreed, may be foreclosed and the property sold to the highest bidder. Bonds representing the funded debt are commonly signed by the president and secretary and countersigned by the trustee. The latter is a contingent agent of the bondholders.

Bonds vary in amount from one hundred to one hundred thousand dollars.

When there is more than one mortgage upon a property, the relation of the mortgages to each other is indicated by their designation, as first, second, third, and so on. It frequently occurs that a mortgage will be a first lien upon one piece of road and occupy a secondary place elsewhere. Each bond recites upon its face the property it covers and the rights its holders possess.

Owners are called bondholders. Sometimes a company sells its bonds directly to investors, but frequently through brokers. In the latter case a commission is usually paid. Bonds run for various periods, from one year upwards.

To enable bondholders the better to protect their interests they are sometimes allowed to vote at annual and special meetings the same as stockholders. Such a course naturally insures a very conservative management, as it is the interest of bondholders to divide as little of the surplus as possible among stockholders, and expend as much as possible in improving and building up the property, every dollar thus expended adding, of course, so much to the security of the bondholder.

The necessities of a company are sometimes such as to compel it to mortgage its surplus income—i. e., the balance left after meeting existing obligations. The securities thus issued are called Income Bonds. Specific articles of property, such as a building, bridge, engine, car or piece of machinery, are also sometimes separately mortgaged. Mortgages of this character, as well as those based on income, generally run for a short period only.

The extent to which a road may be properly encumbered depends, of course, upon its net receipts. Great conservatism is usually exercised. The multitude of properties that have passed into the hands of receivers represent, generally, risks well understood from the start.

There are sometimes as many as five distinct mortgages upon a piece of property. A fifth mortgage does not seem to be a very valuable security ; yet it may be preferable in every way to a first mortgage in another case. Its obligations may be promptly met and it may command a premium in the market, while a first mortgage in another case is discredited. The various mortgages on a property represent its different stages of progress and are usually evidences of prosperity. The objection to a mortgage on a railway is its lack of flexibility. It makes no distinction between a property destitute of value in itself and one requiring only time to build it up. Many of the mortgages that have been foreclosed and the properties sold at a deplorable sacrifice, would ultimately have been paid in full with interest if the owners had been compelled to wait. For this reason a mortgage is too rigid, too exacting, to meet the exigencies of the situation. Instead of protecting its holders it may be made the means, under false representations, of frightening them into sacrificing their investment.

Every mortgage provides for one or more trustees, whose duty it is, if the interest and principal are not paid when due, or within a specified time thereafter, to advertise and sell the property, if called upon by the holders of the bonds. The manner and form of action are prescribed. The minimum amount of bonds required to compel action upon the part of the trustee is also indicated. This amount is commonly made so small as to protect all the holders. In the event of default the trustee may, of his own volition in many cases, go ahead and foreclose without being called upon by holders. He is supposed to act always in their interests.

Mortgages take precedence according to their dates. Thus, the foreclosure of a third mortgage does not affect those of a prior date. But the foreclosure of a first mortgage invalidates all others; but if there remain any surplus over and above the amount required to satisfy such mortgage, it must be divided among the holders of the next succeeding mortgage, and so on until it is exhausted. In the event of the foreclosure of a first mortgage, or of any mortgage, the holders of the next succeeding mortgage usually redeem the property if its worth justifies.

Debenture stock is a favorite form of security in Great Britain. It has a fixed rate of interest and is a positive lien upon the property, but there is no trustee, no definite form of procedure involving the whole issue in case of default. A holder can, if his interest is not paid, levy upon the company's property wherever found and place his name upon it and hold it until his claim is satisfied. Co-operation with other holders is not obligatory and the sale of the property proceeds no farther than is necessary to reimburse the disaffected holder.

In some portions of the United States, mortgages must be recorded upon the books of the recorder of deed or other designated officer for each county in which the property is located. In other cases it is only necessary to record the mortgages at the state capital. An unrecorded mortgage has no value as against a recorded mortgage or the judgment of a court.

Attached to every mortgage bond issued by railroad companies are diminutive notes of hand called coupons. Each installment of interest covered by a bond, whether annual, semi-annual or quarterly, is represented by one of these coupons. The number of coupons attached to a bond is sometimes very great. A coupon when due is in the nature of a sight draft on the company issuing it.

Every bond specifies on its face where the interest and principal are payable; also in many cases the form of payment.

Registered bonds are somewhat different from coupon bonds; both principal and interest are payable to order. A registered bond can only be collected by the person in whose name it is registered upon the books of the corporation; this name is inserted in the body of the instrument. No coupons are attached to registered bonds. When interest matures it is forwarded to the address of the person in whose name the bond is registered. The expense and annoyance of transferring registered bonds when they change hands detract somewhat from their marketable value. They are, therefore, never issued except upon request.

The bonds of railroad companies and those of the government are much alike in form. The manner of paying interest is also much the same. The interest on different issues of bonds does not all fall due at the same time; no rule save the convenience of the company or of the proposed purchasers of bonds is followed in fixing the date and place for paying interest. In some cases interest is paid only once a year; in some cases quarterly, the general rule, however, is to pay it semi-annually.

Interest on bonds constitutes a separate item in the income or profit and loss account. It is called with rentals and guaranteed dividends, a fixed charge.

Such are some of the details connected with mortgage bonds. Where properties are leased, the amount paid as rental takes the place of interest on bonds in the accounts and returns of the lessee. In some cases, however, the interest on the funded debt of the property leased is assumed by the lessee, in which case it may thus appear in the returns in lieu of rental or as part payment of rental.

Railway bonds are classified as follows:

1. Mortgage Bonds.
2. Equipment Bonds.
3. Land Grant Bonds.
4. Collateral Trust Bonds.
5. Prior Lien Bonds.
6. Debentures.
7. Income Bonds.

A bond generally acknowledges that the railway issuing it owes a certain sum, to bearer, payable on a fixed date and at a certain place; it stipulates the rate of interest and the intervals at which such interest is payable; it states the amount of bonds belonging to its class issued, and the property pledged as security for the payment of principal and interest (usually inclusive of the earnings of such property), and further gives such stipulations as to redemption by drawings and sinking funds, conversion into other bonds or shares, etc., as may be necessary in its individual case. Bonds are usually signed by the President and the Treasurer of the railroad company and by the Trustees to whom most of them are made out, and who must defend the rights of bondholders should the company fail to meet any of the obligations it undertook in the mortgage deed.

The value of a bond depends of course upon that of the mortgaged property and upon the extent to which it is mortgaged. In some instances division bonds are issued which, as their name implies, are covered by divisions and not by the entire railroad. If a company requires funds for extensions it often issues extension bonds, which are secured by the additional lines built with their proceeds, and frequently in addition by rights upon the other property of the company, these rights, of course, ranking after those of prior mortgages placed thereon.

Frequently various descriptions of bonds are consolidated, and thus consolidated or general mortgage bonds are created. The issue of a general or "blanket" mortgage is usually resorted to with the double aim of obtaining new capital for extensions and of unifying various older descriptions, such unification being as a rule coupled with a reduction of interest, if possible under the stipulation of mortgages previously issued or permitted by their holders. It is superfluous to remark that such reduction is never voluntarily acceded to by bondholders unless a company gets into straits and is reorganized; and hence parts of general mortgage bond issues are kept in hand until existing descriptions fall due, when they replace them. If a general mortgage is issued the amount in excess of the portion destined to retire older descriptions is used for extensions or betterments; when the first is the case they have prior rights upon such new parts of the system as are completed with their proceeds; in the latter event it is obvious that their rights must yield precedence to older mortgages resting on the property. In consequence of the respective rights of these bonds first, second and third mortgages, etc., are spoken of. Equipment bonds are issued to acquire rolling stock, and are secured by a mortgage thereon. Akin to them are Car Trust Certificates, not met with in this country or quoted in New York, by the aid of which rolling stock can be bought on the "easy payment" system. These certificates are due at frequent intervals—usually semi-annually— and are secured by a lien upon the rolling stock in payment of which they are given.

Land Grant Bonds pledge lands granted by the Government as a guarantee for regular payment of dividends. The land being gradually sold, and the proceeds applied to the retirement of land grant bonds, the majority of these securities have been redeemed by this time. Owing to the low prices realized for land (usually less than $2.00 per acre) and considering the rapid rise in the value of real estate, it would probably have been more advantageous to railways to have retained their lands for some time to come, but need of funds and the advisability of reducing fixed charges induced them to accelerate these sales.

Collateral trust bonds are issued against no other security than funds of other railways. Many of the greater companies own vast amounts of stock or bonds of subsidiary concerns which securities give them control, the Pennsylvania R. R. Co., for instance, possesses upwards of $150,000,000 (nominal) of similar securities. When new funds are required they are often obtained upon the security of bonds of subsidiary concerns which are given in trust to trustees. The value of trust bonds, like that of all mortgages, depends upon the value of the security upon which the advance is made, but usually the securities

given in trust yield more than is required for the service of the collateral bonds, in which case the surplus as a rule goes towards a sinking fund out of which the trust bonds are redeemed.

Debentures are not frequently met with. They are bonds without
any special collateral security ranking after specified mortgage bonds,
and their value depends entirely upon the financial status of the company by which they are issued. Thus in 1889, the Wabash issued
$30,000,000. Debentures which have thus far yielded no returns and
which are practically issued upon faith, it being doubtful whether the
Wabash if sold to-day would yield $30,000,000 more than the amount
of its other funded debt, $48,000,000.

Prior lien bonds likewise are not frequently met with. They were
usually issued to pay debts enjoying precedence over mortgage bonds,
and in consequence they rank before all other mortgages.

Income bonds more resemble preferred shares than bonds, no
dividend being paid unless earned. At the same time they are akin to
debentures inasmuch as they are not issued upon any special security.
They differ from preferred stock because no voting rights attach to
them, and from debentures inasmuch as interest upon them in the majority of cases is non-cumulative.

In many cases bonds are redeemed by sinking funds. A sinking
fund is created by payment of an annual sum (usually $\frac{1}{2}$ to 1 per
cent., plus interest upon returned bonds) to the amount of which
bonds are cancelled, such bonds being singled out by means of drawings which take place at stated intervals. Drawn bonds are repayable
at any time, and cease to bear interest from the date on which they
fall due.

Gold bonds are so called because they are payable in gold, while
their interest must also be paid in that metal or its full equivalent.
Gold bonds are issued chiefly because of fears concerning a depreciation of the United States currency, a fear which was inspired by the
policy of the government which, it was thought, might cause a gold
premium in the Republic.

The issue of shares and bonds, as has been pointed out, is not
regulated or checked by legislatures, and this has led to various
abuses. Shares were usually given away and bonds frequently issued
at a discount, and sometimes both were appropriated by unscrupulous
managers sans autre forme de proces.

Interest and Dividends. The net revenue on railways, after
deduction of taxes and rentals (which are usually classed among fixed
charges) is available for returns upon capital. Whatever these returns

may be, the several mortgages have the first claim upon them according to their degree of priority, and if we omit Collateral Trust and Land Grant Bonds, which as it were secure themselves and pay their own interest.

Receiver's Certificates are issued by Receivers to maintain the road, or in cases of grave emergencies only; and for this reason the Courts have granted them first rights upon the property and placed them above prior lien and first mortgage bonds.

The various descriptions of bonds will generally be found to rank as follows:

1. Receivers' Certificates.
2. Prior Lien Bonds.
3. First Mortgage Bonds.
4. Second Mortgage Bonds.
5. Third Mortgage Bonds.
6. Debentures.
7. Income Bonds.

Income Bonds.

While income bonds have some advantages, they are also subject to serious drawbacks. The contest over the affairs of the Philadelphia & Reading calls attention to some of the dangers attendant upon present methods of railroad finance.

The advantages are best seen in a situation like that of the Atchison Company. In the Atchison reorganization it was necessary not merely to adjust the exchanges to the value of different securities, but also to their risk. Some investors wished a sure return, even though it were very moderate; others were willing to take more risk for the sake of increased chance of profit. The needs of the former class were met by an issue of mortgage bonds at low rates of interest. To prevent foreclosure, the company will need to earn only the comparatively small fixed charges on these bonds. Any excess up to five per cent., on the face value of the principal, or 10 per cent. on its original cost, will go to the income bondholders. They will receive their interest if it is earned; if it is not earned, the company will be protected from danger of foreclosure. At first sight, nothing could seem fairer or simpler.

Who is to determine how much is earned? This question at once introduces us to the difficulties and dangers of the subject. In any railroad, no matter how well managed its affairs, there is always a certain degree of doubt as to its actual condition. There is no fixed and automatic rule as to what may be charged to construction account, or what should be paid for out of current earnings. There are a few well-recognized general principles, but they are altogether too general to be made to fit each case as it arises.

One of the most difficult duties of the financial managers of a Railroad is to determine the actual amount of net earnings.

Sometimes the practical dangers connected with the decision of this problem are not so great as the theoretical difficulties. If the question simply is whether the stockholders shall receive a larger or smaller dividend, any slight misjudgment will correct itself in the long run. If dividends this year are made too large, the available surplus for subsequent years is diminished ; if they are made too small, the capital account is brought into so much better condition that there is a virtual accumulation of undivided profits. This is understood by the great body of intelligent investors. The public did not value New York Central Stock below par when that road was only dividing four per cent.; it does not value it any higher at present on account of its extra dividend. A comparatively small body of investors cares so much for having money to-day as to be unwilling to see it reserved for the future when a conservative policy seems to dictate such action. People who absolutely must have their two or three per cent. every six months ought to invest in bonds rather than stock ; and to a great extent they have actually done so. On the whole, a stock is valued by the condition and earning power of the property, rather than by the temporary rate of dividend.

But if the interest on an income bond is passed, there is no compensating benefit. If the management decides that the interest has been earned, the bondholder receives his money. If, on the other hand, the management chooses to spend that same money for new construction and to charge it to maintenance, he suffers an almost complete loss. The money is taken away from the bondholder ; the benefit of it goes to other interests in the property quite as much as to him. Instead of being a transfer of money from the present to the future, as is the case when stockholders fail to receive a dividend which has been probably earned, it becomes a transfer from one set of security holders to another.

Several causes combine to increase the danger from this source. In the first place the managers represent an interest wholly distinct from the income bonds. They are elected by the stockholders. When they act in a manner adverse to the immediate demands of the income bonds, their course at once gives rise to suspicion, and produces strained relations. Even if their decisions be made in good faith, the conflict of interests gives a partisan character to the whole affair. In this respect, preferred stock, even when non-cumulative, has a decided advantage over income bonds. The preferred stockholders have a direct voice, and sometimes a disproportionately large one, in the choice of directors. The question of income is determined by the representatives of different sides, and not in an ex-parte council.

So great are the possibilities of trouble of this kind that a voting trust like that of the Atchison is the almost necessary correlative of a large issue of income bonds, unless the security is to become a wholly speculative one. If the income bondholders are not to have any share in the determination of the affairs of the road, they must, at least, know who is to decide matters for them. To give stockholders control and leave the income bondholders none at all is to put the power out of the hands of those who are most affected by its exercise. The income bondholders are just on the margin, where a slight change of policy in making up accounts will give them full interest or nothing at all. In this view the value of their secureties is perhaps more affected by the action of the directors than that of the stock itself. To burden them with all this liability and give them no assurance as to the character of the management is contrary to the most fundamental principles of the public policy.

The more complicated the questions decided, the worse the case becomes. The combination of a coal business with that of a railroad company makes the position of the income bondholders more precarious because it increases the opportunity for variations of judgment on the part of both managers and outsiders. It is perfectly conceivable that in a system like the Reading, the authorities themselves should have had a somewhat mistaken impression of the actual state of affairs. But any such misjudgment was productive of such bad results, and furnished so many opportunities for speculative changes in value, that the sufferers can hardly be blamed if they put a worse construction on some matters then the facts themselves fully warrant. The system itself is at fault.

Accounting for Interest on Bonds—How Coupons Should be Treated When Paid—How Filed.

The method of accounting for interest payments on registered bonds is very simple compared with the methods devised for recording the payment of interest on coupon bonds.

In the former case the financial officer makes a certified statement of his disbursements for this purpose, and the accounting officer, after satisfying himself as to the authenticity of the same, allows the necessary credit.

While there are numerous methods of accounting for coupons redeemed, the following may safely be observed :

When a coupon is paid, the officer paying it should cancel it by punching it at least twice; this will prevent the possibility of its reappearance upon the street.

As a rule coupons reach a company through the various local banks and collecting agencies. All the coupons presented by each party or agent should, after cancellation, be enclosed in a separate envelope, and upon the face of this envelope should be written the name of the payee, the date of payment, the names of the mortgages from which the coupons have been detached, the number of coupons presented for each mortgage, the gross amount of such coupons, and, finally, the total amount paid. A history of each transaction will thus be preserved temporarily in its entirety for reference. This information, as may readily be supposed, will be invaluable afterwards in adjusting accounts, verifying payments and satisfying inquiries.

After payment is made, all the envelopes containing coupons, together with a detailed statement of the same, should be turned over to the accounting officer for examination and record. Upon their receipt the latter officer should proceed to verify the contents of the different packages and satisfy himself of the correctness of the accompanying statement in which the aggregate payment is given. The foregoing facts being determined, he should file away the various coupons received. A good plan for this is as follows : A record book is provided for the coupons of each class of bonds; the filing upon the back of the book specifies the name of the mortgage ; the first page corresponds to bond number one, and so on through the book. The amount of the bond is specified at the head of the page. Each page is divided into as many squares, or blanks, as there are coupons attached to the bond; the blanks also correspond in size to the coupons. Each blank space on the page is numbered, and if the bond has fifty years to run and the interest upon it is payable semi-annually, there are one hundred blanks provided —two for each year. The coupon maturing first is pasted in blank number one, the second in blank number two, and so on. The blanks in the book that are unoccupied, represent at a glance the coupons that are outstanding. The aggregate of the outstanding coupons is the amount of the company's liability for unpaid interest on its past due coupons. It is thus not only easy to ascertain precisely the aggregate liability, but it can also be determined readily for the different classes of coupons.

The plan is simple, economical and effective. The financial officer delivers up the cancelled coupons before receiving credit for their payment. After his accounts are verified, the cancelled coupons are pasted in the book by the accounting officer, in the manner described, and in such form and with such system that reference can be made in an instant to any particular coupon that has been paid.

Under this method of accounting any attempt to foist a spurious coupon upon a company could not possibly remain undetected, no matter how perfect the counterfeit might be, for the reason that when the time came for filing it away, the person performing this duty would find the place allotted to that particular coupon already filled; or, if the spurious coupon were paid before the genuine, then it would occupy the place of the latter in the file. In either case the counterfeit would be quickly detected.

The foregoing method of accounting for paid coupons affords, in the multitude of checks it enforces and suggests, the maximum amount of security attainable at the least possible cost.

There should be no connection between the person who pays the coupon and the person who audits the account of the payer and pastes the coupon in the record. The person who draws off the balance sheet of outstanding (overdue) coupons and balances it with the company's books, so incidentally verifies the accuracy of the statement, that every coupon claimed to have been paid, has actually been paid.

Sinking Fund Accounts.

In the first place, specific accounts should be opened on the general books of a company with each particular sinking fund, and to such accounts should be charged or credited, as circumstances require, each particular installment.

In order that the exhibits of a company may show a full and clear record of the sinking funds, the following rules are suggested:

When sinking fund installments are charged against revenue they should be embraced in income account in the month in which they accrue without reference to when they are paid, and such amounts should be carried on the credit side of the balance sheet under the head of "Accruing Sinking Fund Installments." This item will, of course, disappear when the installments are paid.

The amounts so paid should be shown on the balance sheet as an asset under the head of "Amount deposited with trustee of sinking fund," and on the opposite of the balance sheet an account should be opened with "Sinking fund installments paid;" the former account representing the amount of cash or bonds, as the case may be, in the hands of the trustee, and the latter the amount of income used for paying such sinking fund installments.

When sinking fund installments are not charged against revenue, the aggregate amount of the sinking fund will appear on the credit of the balance sheet under the head of "Past due sinking fund installments;" on the opposite side of the balance sheet an account should be opened to be known as "Unpaid sinking fund installments." Both of these items will disappear with the payment of the sinking fund, and the amount so paid will appear upon the debit side of the balance sheet as an asset under the head of "Amount deposited with trustee of sinking fund."

When bonds that are paid into a sinking fund, or bonds of a company owning the sinking fund which are purchased with cash payments to said fund, remain uncancelled, such bonds should appear upon the credit side of the books and in the accounts as "Live bonds in the hands of trustee of sinking fund;" these latter should, of course, be withdrawn on the books and in the exhibits from bonds outstanding.

When bonds paid into the sinking fund, or bonds of a company owning the sinking fund which were purchased by the trustee with cash payments to such fund, are cancelled, the outstanding bonds should be reduced upon the books and in the accounts by a corresponding amount, and no cancelled bond, whether in the sinking fund or elsewhere, should be embraced as an asset or liability upon the books or in the accounts.

When it is desired to recapitalize bonds that have been purchased for the sinking fund and cancelled, the progress, so far as the accounts are concerned, should be the same as when the securities were first issued, viz., the amount of the bonds or stocks issued should be credited as outstanding, cash being charged with the proceeds of same.

When bonds paid to satisfy sinking fund requirements, or bonds purchased with cash payments to said sinking fund, remain uncancelled and continue to draw interest, the trustee should be charged with all such interest received under the head of "Trustee of sinking fund account accretions from investment of installments;" and on the opposite side of the balance sheet an account should be opened to be known as "Accretions from investment of sinking fund installments."

When sinking funds are paid in cash or uncancelled bonds, the amount of such cash or bonds appears, as described above, as a debit until the obligation for which the sinking fund is credited is finally retired. When this event transpires, the accounts "Amount deposited with trustee of sinking fund," and "Trustee of sinking fund account accretions from investment of installments" should be credited, and "Live bonds in hands of trustee of sinking fund" charged with that portion of the sinking fund represented by bonds of the issue for the benefit of which the sinking fund was created which the trustee cancels and returns the company.

The balance of the sinking fund, if any, represented by bonds of other classes or cash, or both, as the case may be, being returned to the company by the trustee, should be added to its assets, the amount being credited in the same manner as stated above for cancelled bonds returned by the trustee, i. e., to the accounts "Amounts deposited with trustee of sinking fund" and "Trustee of sinking fund account accretions from investments on installments."

In the event the payments made to the sinking fund were charged to income, the amount of same, together with all accretions from their investment, should be transferred back to income account from "Sinking fund installments paid" and "Accretions from investment of sinking fund installments," respectively. These entries close the different accounts

By accounting for sinking funds as described the exhibits of a company will always show at a glance the amount of all funds in the hands of the trustee belonging to the sinking fund; how much of same represents respectively payments made to the fund and accretions to it from investment of such payments; and also what amount of payments, if any, were charged against income.

Voting Trusts—Corporations.

The voting trust of the Atchison Railway Company seems to be one of those rare cases where two wrongs make a right. A trust, in this sense of the word, is an arrangement by which the stockholders part with their voting power for a term of years, and during that time lose all control over the management. The object of such a scheme is to protect each individual investor from the effect of changes of policy which might arise if a majority interest in the stock should change hands. In an ordinary corporation this is an ever present possibility. But if the stock, or a majority of such stock, is placed in the hands of trustees, who give in return a set of trust receipts entitling the holder to all dividends on his stock, the investment and the management become separated. If the trust receipts change hands the dividends go to the new holder; the management remains where it was before, namely, under the control of the trustees.

Such is the recognized character and purpose of voting trusts. Their object is to secure permanence of management without sacrificing transferability of shares. The particular form of trust which arouses so much discussion to-day is simply an effort to apply this means to effect a virtual combination between different concerns by putting their stock in the hands of the same trustees. The legal objections to trusts in this sense do not apply to the plan proposed by the Atchison. Trusts in the modern form are a means to an end; it is the end rather than means to which the courts take chief exceptions.

Yet the law does not on the whole look with any great favor on the means itself. The courts do not like to make a man trustee in his own behalf even in an indirect fashion. The opposition to a proceeding of this kind is usually based on legal technicalities. But it really has wider and stronger economic ground. If a concern is owned and managed by its stockholders, the power and responsibility belong in the same hands. If some of the existing owners secure permanent tenure of management by means of a trust, and then sell their interest as investors to others, power and responsibility are at once separated. If a man wishes to make himself trustee in his own behalf, there is often a presumption that he wishes to retain the power and avoid the responsibility. and that his motives in so doing are questionable. Looked at from the standpoint of the community, the gain in stability of management is more than offset by the loss of safeguards against mismanagement. From this point of view a voting trust is wrong in principle.

But, as indicated at the outset, there are complications in a large system like the Atchison which may put a different face on the whole matter. If all the capital for a railroad had been furnished by the stockholders, there would be no sufficient excuse for asking them to resign their power of control. But where a large part of the money invested has been furnished by bondholders, the case is different. Management and investment have already become practically separated. To place the voting power in the hands of trustees may have the effect of giving more influence to the real investors rather than less.

Take the case of the Atchison as it stands. The nominal amount of the stock is $75,000,000. At present prices this amounts to about

$25,000,000 in value. The other interests in the system are worth, on the same basis of valuation, at least $150,000,000. The stock thus represents about one-seventh of the total valuation. A majority of the stock has power to control the operations of the whole. A property worth something like $175,000,000 is thus under the power of an interest commercially worth $13,000,000. This is very far from being management of the property by the investors. Of course it would cost a ring much more than $13,000,000 to secure control, but the case offers considerable chance for schemers who have other than legitimate ends in view, and affords most of the real investors comparatively little protection.

Under these circumstances the trust seems to afford the best and simplest means of giving the bondholders an assurance that the road will be run in their interest. Instead of offering chances for dishonest manipulation, it goes far to remove them. Instead of separating power and responsibility, it may really tend to unite them. If the result proves good it is not unlikely to furnish a precedent for subsequent reorganizations.

Had our railroads been built with stocks instead of bonds the question would not have come up in its present form. Had the stockholders furnished three-quarters of the capital, as is the case in England, it is doubtful whether a railroad trust of this kind could be justified on grounds of public policy. If investment and management were actually in the same hands, there would be no good excuse for separating them. But they are not in the same hands. They are already separated by the existence of the large investment in the form of bonds, whose owners have no direct voice in the management. This being the case, a necessary step in putting the control where it belongs may lie in taking it out of the hands of stockholders. This is what we mean by saying that two wrongs make a right. It is wrong, as a general principle, to build railroads with bonds instead of stock. It is also wrong, as a general principle, to deprive stockholders of the control of their property. But where the bondholders and not the stockholders are the real owners of most of what the property is worth, the second wrong may justify the first. It may result in putting the control where it belongs and securing legitimate rights, without the expense of foreclosure or the dangers of complete reorganization.

Needs in Railway Accounting.

The English system of accounting requires that experts shall certify to the correctness of a Railroad company's figures, and that a dividend has been earned, before any payment to the shareholders shall be made. Such an association of accountants was formed in America for examinations of Railroads here, but the English plan has been adopted by but few of our roads. The questions required to be answered by investors are not the same here as in England. English traffic conditions are comparatively simple. In America the stockholder asks not so much about the charging up of money spent, as to the need of spending it. Evidently a man may be an expert bookkeeper, and yet if he is not practically aquainted with railroad affairs in general, and with the conditions of transportation on the railroad in question in particular, his assertion that the railroad books balance will be of little practical use to his employers. Is the rolling stock running down or the maintenance of way scrimped, in order to make a showing of dividends? An association of mere accountants could hardly be expected to throw much light upon such questions.

There is all the more reason, then, for such a plain and simple report at the end of the year, that the real condition of the company can be ascertained by any one. Technical bookkeeping may hinder rather than help the investor, even where nothing is hidden. Take Reading corporations. The railroad company and the coal company are distinct, but as the former owns the latter, great care should be taken with their interlacing accounts. There is a question whether a coal carrier ought to go outside to buy coal lands, but there is none that the Reading paid in bonds extravagant sums for its coal estate, estimated at one-third the entire anthracite deposits in Pennsylvania.

Now, in its report for the year, ending Nov. 30, 1888, the Coal and Iron Company shows a profit from mining of only $28,650, and after deducting its bonded interest, a net loss of $806,221. One naturally asks how this loss was carried. No item of the kind appears in the railroad income account, (which is technically correct, of course.) In the railroad general balance sheet appears the enormous item of $72,615,374, representing the value of the railroad's investment in the coal company. In the report for the previous year, the bonds and indebtedness of the coal company to the railroad company were itemized. Adding these together, we find that the total was increased in 1888 by $12,000,000 of which the $800,000 loss was part. Thus the losses of the coal company become an asset upon the books of the railroad com-

pany (technically correct again.)   On the credit side of the railroad
balance sheet we find the "suspense account," which must mean floating debt, correspondingly increased.

Now it is a fair question, how is the ordinary investor to find all
this out?   The income account of the railroad company shows a paper
profit from transportation of $2,250,322, which was paid on the income
bonds as contingent interest fairly earned.   Besides the $800,000 loss
of the coal company mentioned, there was $500,000 more charged to
capital account for dead work in the collieries, which all mining
engineers are agreed is as much chargeable to operating expenses as
miners' wages.   Admitting the technical correctness of the bookkeeping, and that there was no intention to deceive (as undoubtedly is true,)
there remains the question, what simple check upon such complicated
accounts can there be, which will enable the average investor to see,
even if but faintly, the true results of the year's operation of his
property?   Such a check would be the publication in each railroad's
annual report of a condensed statement of the treasurer's cash transactions for the year.   This should show with sufficient fullness the
source of each cash receipt and the nature of each cash disbursment.

If we suppose such a treasurer's report in the Reading case mentioned, it would at once have shown that the year's expenses exceeded
the receipts, and that the treasurer had to borrow money or sell bonds
to pay for such deficit.   Then, afterwards the stockholder could find
out for himself where the deficiency was carried in the bookkeeping.
There are cases where the deception is willful, and there are others
where no technical fault with the accounts can be found.   But in
either case, the treasurer's cash account would do no harm if published.

Secretary.

The secretary of an incorporated company, is an officer of the
company, as much as the cashier of a bank is an officer of the bank,
and is not merely an officer of the managers or directors, by whom he
is appointed.

The secretary is the proper custodian of the corporate seal, and
when affixed by him, the presumption arises that he acted by the direction of proper authority, and it devolves upon those who dispute
the validity of his act to prove that he acted without authority.

The secretary of a company is the keeper of its records, and is,
therefore, the proper person to prove its books as a witness.   He is

the agent through whom the corporation ordinarily communicates to the public, knowledge of its acts, and hence, his official statement of such, when accepted and acted upon by third parties in good faith, is binding upon the corporation. But the power to communicate the acts and resolves of the corporation to the public is very different from the power to bind the corporation by original contracts made by and through himself. The law does not ordinarily imply, in the secretary of a business corporation, the power to bind the company by means of letters or documents signed officially.; though, of course, the corporation may become subsequently bound by ratification. He cannot in the absence of special authorization, give to a third person an acknowledgment that there is due him from the corporation a certain sum; nor bind the corporation by a "due bill" given a stockholder in consideration of his surrender of his stock; nor make an assignment of an account of the corporation against a customer, for goods manufactured and sold by it; nor release the makers of notes held by the corporation, from their liability thereon, although he may have received express authority to renew such notes; nor sign drafts drawn against his funds; nor, while performing the act of collecting a bill, settle or compromise a disputed claim with the debtor. But, of course, he may have larger powers by special appointment, from the directors, and evidence of such powers may be found in the circumstances of the particular cases.

When, as is often the case, the secretary of a corporation is also its general manager, he possesses powers much more extensive than those which the law ordinarily ascribes to a mere secretary.

The secretary is the custodian of the books of the corporation, which includes the Stock Ledger, Certificate of Stock Book, Transfer Book, Subscription Book, Minute Book, etc. The corporation is an agent or trustee of the shareholder, for the purpose of preserving theoretically his shares and preventing illegal transfers of them. This duty devolves upon the secretary, but, of course subject to the control of the President and the Directors, as are his other duties. Many corporations, however, employ a transfer clerk, whose sole duty is the transfer of shares. The officers of a corporation having charge of its books are bound to see that transfers of stock are properly made.

If upon the presentation of a certificate for transfer, they are at all doubtful of the identity of the party offering it, with its owner, or if not satisfied with the genuineness of the power of attorney produced, they can require the identity of the party in the one case, and the gentineness of the document in the other, to be satisfactorily established before allowing the transfer to be made.

The manner in which the secretary shall keep his books depends upon the nature and extent of the business.

He should adopt the very best system that can be devised, and should see that the work is promptly and properly done, and that the books should show at all times the true financial condition of the company.

Treasurer.

The treasurer of a corporation is the proper officer charged by law with the custody of its funds. The ordinary duties of the treasurer are to receive, safely keep and disburse, under the supervision of the directors, the funds of the company. Unless more extensive powers are conferred upon the treasurer by the charter or by-laws, he has no authority to assume the payment of debts without conferring with the directors. Nor can he set off debts due from against those due to the company. The power to transfer the negotiable securities of a business corporation, in the ordinary course of its business, rests upon a different footing from the power to create debts by emitting such securities or to emit without any liquidation of debts already created.

Authority to accept or indorse commercial paper in the business of a corporation obviously does not extend to accepting or indorsing for the accommodation of third parties, since corporations themselves have in general no such power.

The treasurer of a corporation cannot settle his own accounts; he has no authority, by virtue of his office, to pay to himself his own claim against the corporation until such claim has been approved by the proper officers; nor is the corporation estopped to deny the validity of such payment because it was entered by the treasurer on the corporation books of which he had charge.

When the duties of the treasurer are such that books are to be kept, they should be well systematized and conform with the other accounting systems.

If the treasurer's books are well devised, a true statement from them would oftentimes reveal the true financial condition of the company.

CHAPTER THIRTY-FOUR.

Expert Examinations of the Accounts and Financial Affairs of Executors, Administrators, Guardians, Trustees, Assignees and Receivers.

Before taking up this lesson you should carefully study Estate Accounting, in Lesson 28, as it bears directly upon this subject.

It is an easy matter to examine the accounts of Executors and others, but to be able to prepare statements for court, there are a great many legal requirements that must be understood, therefore, your attention is directed to a few of the points that must, and must not be incorporated in reports.

As stated before, the first duty of an administrator, is to file an inventory ; and it ought to be filed within thirty days.

This inventory should include only the personal assets of the decedent. A man, for instance, takes out a policy of life insurance, payable to his wife. That should not go into his estate. The proceeds of that policy belong to the wife, exclusive of creditors ; with that, therefore, the creditor has nothing to do. The wife has it as soon as the man dies. The executor or administrator is not entitled to a commission on it, and it is not necessary to put it in the account. They would very naturally like to include it for the purpose of swelling the account, and increasing their commission, but you should not allow it. I examined an administrator's account a few years ago, and found that he had reinvested the whole of the estate, and had charged himself again with the full amount of the securities sold. He had charged the commission of five per cent. on the double sum, making in reality, ten per cent., and quietly credited himself with it. All the parties interested signed a paper to the effect that they were satisfied with the amount, I was not satisfied with it, and undertook to cut it down one-half, and my action was sustained by the court.

Here is another instance that will serve to illustrate how far exceptions may come in. A man in his life time has had a piece of land taken from him, and damages awarded but not paid. They are paid after his death. Those damages are personal estate, although they have not been paid yet; inasmuch as the property has been converted during his life time, they should go into the personal estate. So you see what an easy matter it is to make a mistake, and how important to know the law.

The administrator of an estate has to deal exclusively with personal estate; his account is an account of personal estate.

There is, however, a single exception to this rule "every rule has its exception." As a rule, an administrator's account must deal only with personal estate; all the property of the decedent, however, is liable for his debts. His real estate, as well as his personal estate, is liable for his debts; but it is with the personal estate only that the administrator has to deal, until it is discovered that the personal estate is not sufficient to pay all the debts, and then recourse may be had to the real estate.

It is a very curious thing that the lawyers make many more mistakes in these matters than professional accountants. Lawyers very often make mistakes in their account, which show that they are either ignorant or else inconceivably negligent; for very often it happens that they bring in accounts in which rents are mingled with personal items.

Rents should not be entered with the accounts of an administrator. Although rents, when collected, are personal estate, yet if a man dies intestate and there are rents due him uncollected, they go to his heirs. If an administrator is directed to sell a portion of the real estate to raise money to pay debts, although he has a right to sell that estate, if he neglects to do so, within the limit of time, and goes on and collects rents in the meantime, those rents all go to the heirs. If the administrator charges those rents in the accounts, this result will follow. The administrator has given a bond for the faithful performance of his duties. He is responsible for the moneys that legitimately come into his possession. If he charges himself in his accounts with rents, the balance which he strikes is a mingled balance of realty and personalty. If there is a deficit and suit is brought against his sureties, they say: "Why, this balance is partly composed of the proceeds of real estate. This is no part of his duties." A great many losses have occurred in this way, and yet, we find every day that rents are included.

An executor differs from an administrator in that he derives his power from the will. The administrator has his authority from the law, which appoints him, the decedent having died intestate; the executor has his authority from the will, which has made him executor.

This makes some little difference in the duties of the two officers. In other respects their duties are very similar. An executor may charge himself with rents, because the law charges him with their collection.

An executor never has to give security, unless there is some doubt as to his fidelity. He is, by the confidence reposed in him by the testator, entitled to administer that estate without security; which is a very great difference between an administrator and an executor.

A guardian is required to file an account only in one of two cases —where he desires to be discharged from the trust, or where he is dismissed from the trust, the minor being of full age, or if the minor dies. These are the only cases in which he files a final account. But he is expected to file a triennial account, which serves as a guide to those who want to see how the estate is managed, and is an assistant to the man who makes up the final account; usually, these triennial accounts are never audited.

The function of the administrator is to collect and distribute, and this would apply also to an executor. The function of the trustee, on the contrary, is to hold. There is some little difference in their modes of action.

Distribution.

When it comes to the work of distribution, very frequently an administrator or executor places among other items in his account amounts of distribution. He has collected considerable money, and has paid some of the legatees in advance; he places these payments among the other items in his account. The Supreme Court has denounced that practice in unmeasured terms. The proper way is to make a separate table of distribution at the foot of the account. The object of the distribution account—the sole purpose of that account— is to find the balance which is due to the estate after the payment of all debts If you put in your account items of distribution, the balance that remains won't be the balance due the estate; it has been depleted by these amounts paid to legatees. Perhaps it would be well, just at this point, to refer to this question of paying legatees, before the audit of the account. The president of a bank in this city died about ten years ago, and left an estate of a quarter of a million dollars. He had been a prudent man, and his executors supposed they knew the amount of his debts. They were very few in number, and there was a very neat balance in securities and cash, over a quarter of a million. The executors concluded they would pay the legatees under the will, without waiting until the final settlement; they did this as an act of kindness and generosity. They did not take any refunding bonds from the legatees. When they filed this account nine months after that time, and a year after the death of the testator, they showed the balance which was due to the estate. The balance was about two hundred and seventy thousand dollars. Then they had a distribution account which footed up two hundred and seventy thousand dollars. Eight years passed and then was discovered what perhaps the creditors didn't even know. The decedent had gone upon a bond of a committee of the estate of a lunatic, and the man had defaulted, ran away with the money belonging to the lunatic's estate. Suit was brought and judgment recovered against the securities, of which this decedent was one. The executors went into court and asked for an opening of the account; they asked for permission to come down upon these legatees, paid eight years before, for a refunding of the account.

The Counsel said, "Oh no! You can't recover that amount paid eight years ago. You didn't take any refunding bonds. If you had done so, the executors would not have been liable." They said, "It is true that we did not take refunding bonds, but our account was confirmed by the court. That account showed the balance due the estate; and the distribution."

The answer was; "You chose to pay at the time when it was your duty to take refunding bonds. The court approved that distribution, believing that it had been made in conformity with the law. If it had been, it is to be presupposed that refunding bonds were taken by you. If you had waited and come in with the balance and received an order of distribution from the court, you would have been relieved of all responsibility." The result was that the executors were held liable. If they had waited for an order of the court, or if they had preferred to distribute before the order of the court and had taken refunding bonds, they would not have been liable. It is not a safe plan to distribute before the order of the court. If you do pay, you should see that you are secured by taking refunding bonds. When orders are received from the court, you should make it your business to see that such orders are entered in the Court's Journal.

Commission.

The question of commission is also very often misunderstood. The executor or administrator is entitled to be paid, just as any other professional man, in accordance with his services. A certain per cent has been adopted, merely as a matter of convenience; it only works approximate justice. It has been found, that for accounts that do not reach up into the thousands, five per cent. is a fair compensation.

When an estate reaches seventy-five or one hundred thousand dollars, courts hesitate a good deal, before they confirm this five per cent ; the compensation is then regulated by the amount of labor. Sometimes when there is a great amount of labor, as high as ten per cent. is allowed, and even ten per cent. is not enough. A man is never allowed any commission for re-investment. He is allowed commissions on excess over and above the appraised values of the securities. A trustee is not allowed commission until the expiration of the trust; there is no rate per cent.; his compensation depends entirely upon the responsibility and labor incurred. If the trust has lasted a good many years and involved a good deal of labor and a good many reinvestments, sometimes it is as high as five per cent. A man who is at the same time administrator and trustee is allowed commission on one of these functions.

There is another question which has rather agitated the courts. It is well known that an administrator is forced to give security. He now gets his security through a trust company in nearly every case; and this is more satisfactory for "a corporation never dies," while an individual may die or run away. The question is whether the administrator is entitled to charge to the estate the premium he pays to the trust company. This distinction is drawn: An administrator who pays a premium to a trust company is not entitled to demand that premium from the estate, because he knew, in accepting the appointment, that it was necessary to get that security, and he must be assumed to say: "I am satisfied with the commissions."

An executor does not have to enter security, except where real estate is sold; then the court forces him to enter security. He may charge the estate for that. There have been decisions on both sides of the question. But a case went to the Supreme Court, in which several thousand dollars had been paid for security, and the Supreme Court laid down the rule that the administrator would have to pay out of his own pocket; that settled that point.

Negligence in General.

There is another question very intimately connected with the duties of those who act in a fiduciary capacity; and that is negligence.

It may be laid down as a general rule, which all are safe in following (and this *is* a rule without an exception) that the degree of negligence which shall charge a trustee, an administrator, or executor to his harm, must be such a clear case of negligence that no man in the ordinary affairs of life would be guilty of. The ordinary diligence that a man exercises in regard to his own property is the care that is expected of a trustee. The law is pretty lenient in this respect with regard to trustees.

Under the head of negligence, it is important to see in what way the debts are paid. There are preferred debts, the first of which are for expenses incident to the last sickness and burial. Those debts must be paid in full. And then come wages of servants for a year, and rent for a year. The rent need not be for the last year; it may be for any year not barred by the statute of limitations; but the wages of servants must be within the last year. Great care must be exercised in the payment of debts. It is always advisable to pay them as soon as possible, but you must be very careful to see that the amount of the estate will be sufficient to pay all these debts in full. If a creditor is paid in full and the estate fails to produce enough to pay all in full, you are liable to the other creditors for the amount paid over and above his pro rata share.

Conversion of Property.

Another matter of vast importance especially to trustees. It is a matter, too, which has given rise to some of the most intricate questions in law—the subject of conversion of property, etc. A man, in his will, leaves certain directions in regard to the sale of his real estate; such as " I desire my trustee to sell my real estate." These words authorize or empower the trustee to sell, but it is a matter which is left to the discretion of the trustees. If these words be used: " I direct my executor or trustee to sell my real estate," that direction is absolute and becomes a part of the will. The result is, in the one case, where he leaves it to the discretion of the trustees, the real estate continues to be real estate. But where he directs by that last will, which takes effect at his death, that the property be sold, the real estate becomes personal property, and can only be treated as personal estate. Upon that question of the wording often depends the character of estate, and the people that shall take the property.

Again it often happens that a piece of real estate is required to be sold for the payment of the debts. A piece of real estate is sold and it produces $6,000. The debts that remain are only $4,000, leaving

$2,000 to distribute. That $2,000 becomes, by a fiction of law, $2,000 of real estate. It was only in so far as it was needed for the payment of debts, that it became personal estate ; the excess became real estate again. That makes a great difference, because the money, although it may be in the shape of money, gold or silver, is nevertheless impressed by the law with the character of real estate. It is liable to any judgments or liens there may be. For instance, John Doe, legatee, is to take $500 out of the estate which remains. He is entitled to that money, but you dare not pay it to him until you have made a search to see if there are any liens. If there are, the plaintiffs in those liens have a perfect right to come upon this $500, because it is real estate.

Capital and Income.

There is another question that often concerns the man that is drawing an account—the question as to what items are capital and what items are income. Sometimes you will be very much puzzled over this question. The lawyer is puzzled, the text writer is puzzled, and the judges are, or they would not have written so many conflicting opinions.

Sometime ago there was a unique company formed for the purchase and sale of real estate. It had a certain capital, and this capital was to be employed in the purchase of real estate, that was to be sold and the profits added to the capital, which was to be invested again. They were to continue the business of purchase and sale of real estate, just as a storekeeper carries on the purchase and sale of groceries. They sold to an English syndicate, through an agent who was supposed to know all about mining, a certain tract of land. They sold them that tract on the strength of a report by the agent, in which he declared that he was satisfied that the land contained silver ore, or something of that kind. They sold that land for an enormous sum of money ; it went up into the hundreds of thousands of dollars. The question in court was, whether that vast increase did not go to augment the capital of the company. The Supreme Court decided that it was profits.

A railroad forms a new company and it gives the owners of the stock of the original company an option to purchase stock in the new company. The question is, does that option impair the value of the capital? If it does, that is something to show that it belongs to the capital. Where a dividend is declared partly in stock and partly in cash, it is difficult to decide. The courts of Massachusetts have adopted a rule that is questionable, and has been utterly repudiated in

Pennsylvania. They say all dividends in cash are universally regarded as profits, and dividends payable in stock or script are capital. The question is, whether these dividends were actually earned during the life time of the decedent. If they were earned in his lifetime, they belong to capital. These questions are so many and so complicated, that they require the utmost circumspection.

Incidentally, I have noted legacies and how they should appear when they are placed in the account. An order of the court, ordering distribution, always protects the accountant. Where the legatees receive money under a mistake, they ought always to refund; but they cannot be compelled to do so if they have not given refunding bonds. A creditor who has been paid in advance of others does not have to refund if the estate proves insufficient to pay all the debts. A creditor who has been paid in full, without any fraud, is always protected. That is a distinction made between payment to a legatee and payment to a creditor.

Administrative and Pecuniary Legacies.

There is a difference between specific or administrative legacies and pecuniary legacies. A specific or administrative legacy is the last to abate for debts. If the personal estate is not sufficient for the payment of debts, the pecuniary legacies must remain undisturbed; the specific legacies must be paid in full. It is a very difficult matter sometimes to tell what is a specific legacy and what is not. If the testator says in his will "I give one hundred shares of railroad stock to my son James," and he has only one hundred shares, the inference is that those hundred shares go to the son. But if the estate is not sufficient to pay all the other legacies, it would be a very difficult matter to decide. There must be something to indicate that the identical stock was to go to his son; the mere fact that he happened to have only one hundred shares is not sufficient. If he had said, "I give my son, *my* hundred shares of stock," that would be specific.

Another important item, is the widow's exemption. That takes precedence of everything. The widow is entitled to her allowance in advance of other claims. The children are entitled to an exemption, in the absence of a widow, whether they are minors or not, if they are dependent. When there is only one dependent, that one is entitled to the exemption. It must be shown that they are dependent. They are entitled to it in case the widow is dead; or if the widow is alive, in case she has sundered the family relation; provided they are dependent. If they have means of their own, they do not get it.

If there are mortgages and a bond has been created by the testator himself, that mortgage is payable in the first place out of the estate. The general rule is, that if a man takes a property subject to a mortgage and then devises that property, the devisee takes subject to the mortgage ; if he devises a property and subsequently places a mortgage upon it, the mortgage is paid out of the estate.

When money has been advanced to legatees by the decedent during his lifetime, and he states in his will that the money which he has advanced is to come out of their shares, it is merely an advancement and does not bear interest. It would bear interest in this single case ; if the year has expired and the estate is not settled. The reason is that the legatees are supposed to receive their advancement at the time the distribution is supposed to have taken place.

When you are asked to prepare an account for an administrator, and the administrator is unwilling to give you the items, you should go into court at once, and ask that an order be issued compelling him to give the items. If he does not file the account in answer to the summons of the court, he has to go to prison. The court appoints a master and he states the account.

There are many other questions that might be considered. There is the question of how the contracts of decedents are to be complied with. There are the other questions as to the shares of intestate estates —what the widow takes—the husband's courtesy ; there are the liabilities of trustees for reinvestments. There are so many questions connected with this subject of uses of trusts that, before you act as trustee, executor or administrator, or examine their accounts, you should study thoroughly the entire law of your state on that subject.

As stated before, every executor or administrator must, within 18 months after his appointment, render an account of his administration upon oath, whether he then needs and obtains further time for the collection of assets, or not. If he obtains such further time, he must in like manner render such further accounts of his administration, and every 12 months thereafter, and also at such times as may be required by the court, until the estate is wholly settled.

Every executor or administrator, with the will annexed, or testamentary trustee, who does not make a final settlement of the decedent's estate within said 18 months, and who carries the administration of his trust from year to year thereafter, must, whenever he renders any such account above mentioned, make an oath to the Court, as a part of the account, a full itemized statement of all the funds of the decedent's estate under his control, the date and nature of other investments, and

the security thereof, and the rate of interest on income accruing therefrom. If the administrator or executor fail to render an account within
30 days after notice of expiration of time to do so, he risks the forfeiture
of all compensation.

If the estate be insolvent, the executor or administrator should
proceed as rapidly as possible to collect the assets and pay the preferred
claims against it, and after having done so, he should file an account of
his proceedings, and obtain an order from the Court declaring the
probable insolvency of the estate. But should the assets be sufficient
to pay the preferred claims only, the executor or administrator may,
upon payment of such claims, file a final account without representing
the estate to be insolvent, or obtaining an order declaring such insolvency.

Every executor or administrator is chargeable with the amount of
the sale bill, also with all goods, chattels, rights, and credits of the
deceased, which shall come to his hands, and which are by law to be
administered, although they should not be included in the inventory or
sale bill, also with all the proceeds of real estate sold for the payment
of debts or legacies, and with all the interest, profit and income that
shall in any way come to his hands, from the personal estate of the
deceased.

He must also charge himself with all moneys collected by him,
upon any claims due the estate whether such claims be mentioned in
the inventory or not, naming the dates when the several amounts were
received and entering principal and interest separately.

He must charge himself with any interest received upon the sale
of notes, and upon moneys of the estate, deposited in bank, or loaned,
or used by him in his own business.

He must charge himself with all moneys received by him from a
former administrator or from the executor or administrator of any other
estate in which the decedent had an interest as heir or legatee.

He must charge himself with any sums paid to him by a late partner of the decedent, as the avails of the partnership business, also with
any debt he owed the decedent when he died.

An executor or administrator who is indebted to the estate upon
a claim due the decedent in his lifetime, is bound to account for the
amount due from him, as for so much money received, and is liable to
an action upon his bond for neglecting to do so.

When any of the heirs or parties interested, furnish him with
funds or permit him to collect rents, rightfully belonging to them, for

the purpose of enabling him to pay debts, etc., and thus avoid the sale of real estate, he must account for such funds, rents, etc.

If any executor or administrator neglects to sell any portion of the personal property, which he is bound by law to sell, and retains, consumes or disposes of it for his own benefit, he will be charged therewith at double the value affixed thereto by the appraisers.

The statutes provide that no profits can be made by executors or administrators by the increase of any part of the estate, and it is a well settled rule in equity, that a trustee is not permitted so to manage the subject of his trust as to make or gain therefrom for himself. The beneficiaries in the trust have a right to expect and require the exercise of his best judgment, care and diligence on their behalf, and the gains resulting therefrom inure to their sole benefit. What such trustee may not do directly, he is not permitted to do through the intervention of an agent or an attorney.

The administrator cannot, therefore, be allowed, directly or through his attorney, to compromise with agents, and settle claims against the estate for which he is acting for less than their face value and put the difference in his own pocket.

Trustees cannot make a profit from trust funds by using them in any kind of trade or speculation, nor in their own business, nor can they put the funds into the trade or business of another and receive a bonus or other profit or advantage. In all such cases the trustees must account for every dollar received from the use of the trust money and they will be absolutely responsible for it if it is lost in any such transactions.

By this rule, trustees may be liable to very great losses, while they can receive no profit; and the rule is made thus stringent, that trustees may not be tempted from selfish motives to embark the trust funds upon the chances of trade and speculation. If a trustee stands by and sees his co-trustee employ funds in that manner, he will be equally liable.

Administrators and others having trust money to distribute must see that it reaches the person entitled to receive it, for if paid to the wrong person by mistake or otherwise, they are still liable to pay it to the rightful claimant, and are, therefore, not entitled to credit for such wrong payment.

If an executor or administrator deposits money (*in his own name*) in a bank and the money is lost by the bank's failure or otherwise, he will be personally responsible for such money, but if he *as executor or administrator* deposits it in a bank in good credit and repute till the time arrives to pay it to creditors, devisees, etc., and the bank fails, he will not be responsible, and he must render his account accordingly.

An executor or administrator is entitled to credit in his account for all payments on account of the decedent's last sickness and administration of his estate, also for all just debts and obligations as well as for other claims against the estate which are allowed by law.

The husband is primarily liable for the expenses of the burial of his deceased wife, and therefore such expenses if unpaid at his death are a claim against his estate. But her own estate is liable therefor under some circumstances.

It may be stated, as a general rule, that all costs and expenses including reasonable attorney fees, fairly incurred by the administrator or executor in suits for recovering, properly administering, and protecting the trust funds must be allowed to him by the court, and he should also be allowed those of suits decided against him, if he was honest and acting in good faith in such suits, and they were such as a reasonable and prudent man might reasonably have undertaken or exercised in the management of his own affairs.

It should be borne in mind that there might be claims of such uncertain validity both in favor of the trust estate and against it, that it might amount to a breach of trust to abandon them in the one case or put them in the other without decree of the court to direct the administrator or executor what he should do in relation to them. In such cases he should get the decision or order of the court, then his costs and proper expenses will be allowed.

A trustee will not be allowed to charge the estate with any part of the expenses of a controversy on the settlement of his accounts, when the controversy was occasioned by his own fault. The court has, however, full power to assess the costs in such cases against the trustee, the trust fund, or otherwise, as in its discretion seems just and right. But if suit is made necessary by the misconduct or failure of the trustee to do his duty, by his mere caprice or obstinacy, by his refusing to account, or by his careless manner of keeping correct accounts, etc., he must pay the costs.

It is apparent to any person of good judgment that the executor or administrator often needs the advice of a competent attorney, especially where suits in courts must be conducted for the sale of real estate, or in the defense or prosecution of the rights and property of the real estate, and reasonable fees for such services and advice are always allowed. It is the duty of every executor or administrator to take the advice of competent Counsel, learned in the law, on every question which affects his duty as such, of which he is in doubt.   Hence reasonable fees for such services paid in good faith, are proper items of credit in the administration account, and will be allowed.

The court, may on settlement, allow as a credit to the executor or administrator, a just and reasonable amount expended by him for a tombstone or monument, for the deceased, but it is not incumbent on any executor or administrator to procure a tombstone or monument. The court may also likewise allow him as such credit, a just and reasonable amount he may have paid to any cemetery association or corporation as a perpetual fund for caring for, and preserving the lot in which said deceased is buried.

An absolute bequest to a legatee of the interests and dividends from certain stocks and debts, is, after the death of the legatee, in an account with her estate by an administrator, to be settled on the following principles.

The income should be charged with the payment of all taxes on account of the principal during her lifetime.

The income should also be charged with the costs and expenses incurred on account thereof, and all other administrative expenses should be paid out of the residuum.

Commission due to the administrator should be charged against the principal and the income, in proportion to their respective amounts.

If the executor or administrator has been charged with the assets out of which the allowance for the year's support of the widow and minor children must be paid, he is, of course, to be credited with the payment thereof in his accounts.

The administrator and executor must remember that the decedent's debts and the cost of administration must be paid before any part of the estate can be distributed to the legatees or heirs, and that creditors are not even obliged to present their claims for one year after the notice of appointment of the administrator or executor, and that even after one year the owners of allowed claims only can be safely paid, not the heirs and legatees; that as against creditors the heirs and legatees can safely be paid only after four years, this being the limit of time given to creditors of the estate, in which to present their claims.

In some cases, the executor or administrator may be willing to pay before said four years expire, at least some part of the legacies and distribute shares, especially if secured in so doing by bond, securing the redelivery thereof, as he may deem it safer so to pay out money and be done with it, rather than to invest it and risk its loss.   The same rule applies to the delivery of property specifically bequeathed provided a refunding bond be given.

If he does then or later, pay any legacy or legacies in full, or in part, he is entitled to credit for such payments in his account, for this is in part executing the will. And the statute clearly contemplates this, as it requires vouchers for all debts and legacies paid. But he should not include any such accounts in payments made to the widow or widower, or heirs, on account of their distributive shares.

In rendering such account every executor or administrator must produce vouchers for all debts and legacies paid, and for all funeral charges, and just and necessary expenses.

These vouchers must be filed with the account, and they together with the account must be deposited and remain in the Probate Court.

On the settlement of an account of an administrator or executor, he may be allowed any item of expenditure not exceeding ten dollars, for which no voucher is produced, if such item be supported by his own oath, positively to the fact of payment, specifying when, and to whom such payment was made, and if such oath be uncontradicted. As such allowance is discretionary with the Probate Judge, an executor or administrator should be prepared to prove his payments with satisfactory vouchers, and thus guard against all contingencies.

As all accounts are recorded, and are open to examination by heirs and others interested, and as an executor or administrator cannot always be present to make such explanations as may be desired, relative to the various items composing his accounts, it is well to give at the foot of the account, explanations of all such matters, as are not entirely plain to persons not acquainted with the facts. Such memoranda may serve an excellent purpose in future years, when minors interested in the estate, arrive at full age, and the facts relative to many receipts or disbursements may have entirely escaped the memory of the Accountant.

When an account is filed within the time allowed by law or the court, the dates of the various receipts and payments need not be given, yet it is better as a rule to give them.

The form of the account may be such as will be most readily prepared and understood by persons having a limited knowledge of accounts.

The receipts should be entered upon one side and the expenditures upon the other, giving in all cases the items, to show the total receipts and total expenditures, and balance of cash and value of property on hand. The plainest form that can be devised will give the best satisfaction.

Having seen to the filing of his final account, showing the payment of all debts and legacies, and having been ordered by the court to distribute the remaining funds in his hands, and having ascertained to whom such distribution is to be made, the executor or administrator is ready to make the final distribution of the funds or estate remaining in his hands ; if he does not make this voluntarily, he may be compelled to do so.

An executor or administrator who has paid all the debts of an estate and has in his possession notes, bonds, stocks, claims, or other rights in action, belonging to the estate, may, with the approval of the Probate Court, enter on its journal, and with the assent and agreement of the persons entitled to the proceeds of such assets, as distributees, including executors, trustees and guardians, distribute and pay over the same in kind, to those of such distributees as will receive the same.

Such executors, trustees and guardians, as so accept such assets will be liable to return them, or the proceeds thereof, should the same be necessary to pay the claims or liabilities.

Each of the other distributees must give an indemnifying or refunding bond to the executor or administrator to the satisfaction of the court for the same purpose.

A distribution in kind in either case, will have the·same force and effect as the distribution of the proceeds of such assets. The executor should proceed to distribute the funds remaining in his hands, for that purpose, taking vouchers therefor.

Upon making payment to the widow, heirs, legatees, or other persons interested in the distribution of an estate, of the whole or any part of their several shares, the executor or administrator should take a receipt or voucher from each, specifying the amount and object of the payment.

Distribution cannot be made directly to a minor heir, as such heir cannot give a legal receipt therefor, but such heir's portion must be paid to his or her guardian. If any such heir has no legal guardian, one should be appointed at once.

When an executor or administrator has paid or delivered over to the persons entitled thereto, the money or other property in his hands, as required by the order of distribution, or otherwise, he must perpetuate the evidence of such payment by presenting to the court, within one year after such order was made, an account of such payments, or the delivery over of such property.

When such account or final distribution shall have been proved to the satisfaction of the court, and verified by the oath of the party, it must be allowed as his final discharge, and must be ordered by the court to be recorded. Such discharge will ever exonerate the party and his sureties from all liability under such order, unless his account shall be impeached for fraud or manifest error.

The following form is suggested for an account of final distribution.

In pursuance of the order of the Probate Court, the undersigned executor of the last will (or administrator of the estate) of John Doe, deceased, made distribution of the amount found in his hands upon final settlement as follows:

Date.	Distributions, Etc.	No. of Voucher.		
1896. Aug. 31	Amount found due estate as per said final settlement			
Sept. 5	Paid to A. B., widow of said decedent	1		
" 5	" " D. A., child " " "	2		
" "	" " L. M., " " " "	3		
" "	" " W.H., " " " "	4		
" 15	" " H. F., Atty., as to this account, etc.	5		
"	" ". Probate Court for filing this account	6		
	Total expended and disbursed			8,000 00

Assignees.

In its general sense, the term assignment means a transfer or the making over to another of the whole of any property, real or personal, in possession, or in action, or of any estate or right therein. It is particularly applied to transfers in writing, as distinguished by those by delivery.

An absolute sale of any property by a debtor to a creditor, or to several creditors in common, made in good faith, in the payment of a debt, might properly be termed an assignment, for the benefit of creditors in the sense defined above, and such a transaction would be legal; but this phrase is generally used as a shorter way of designating an assignment of a debtor's property in trust to an assignee or trustee for the benefit of creditors.

A voluntary assignment in trust for the benefit of creditors, may be defined as a transfer, without compulsion of law, by a debtor, of all his property to some person or persons in trust, to apply the proceeds thereof toward the pro rata payments of all the transferor's debts.

Generally the word assignor is used to designate by whom any of the transfers above mentioned are made, and the word assignee to designate to whom it is made, or in a more restricted sense, an assignor is a debtor who transfers his property to another person in trust, for the benefit of the creditors of such assignor, and an assignee is the person to whom the debtor makes such transfer.

A trustee is a person to whom property of some kind has been conveyed to hold or manage for the benefit of another. As generally used in relation to assignments in trust, for the benefit of creditors, a trustee means a person whom the court has appointed, or whom the creditors have elected to fill the place of an assignee who has declined to accept such trust, or who, after having accepted it, has been removed, has resigned, or died while acting as such assignee.

Assignments in trust for the benefit of creditors are also known as voluntary assignments, and these are divided for some purposes, into general assignments and partial assignments.

Voluntary assignments are so designated to distinguish them from those made by compulsion of law.

A voluntary assignment, which conveys all of a debtor's property in trust to his assignee, is a general assignment, even if property exempt by law from execution be retained. To constitute a general assignment, there must not only be a transfer of all property by the debtor, but it must be conveyed to a trustee in trust for creditors.

A voluntary assignment which conveys a part only, of a debtor's property in trust to his assignee, is a partial assignment. If any one should make a partial assignment, it would not prevent the assignor's creditors from seizing, by legal processes, for the satisfaction of their claims, all of his unassigned property not exempt by law.

There is a manifest, a well settled distinction, between an unconditional deed of assignment in trust for creditors, and a mortgage or deed of trust, in the nature of a mortgage. The former is an absolute and indefeasible conveyance of the subject-matter thereof, for the purpose expressed ; whereas the latter is conditional and defeasible.

The mortgage is the conveyance of an estate, or pledge of property as security for the payment of money, or the performance of some other act, and conditioned to become void upon such payment or performance. A deed of trust in the nature of a mortgage is a con-

-veyance in trust by way of security, subject to a defeasance, or re-
deemable at any time before the sale of the property. A deed
conveying land to a trustee is mere collateral security for the
payment of a debt, with the condition that it shall become
void on the payment of the debt when due, and with power
to the trustee to sell the land and pay the debt, in case of default on the part of the debtor, as a deed of trust in the nature of
a mortgage. By an absolute deed of trust the grantor parts absolutely
with the title, which rests in the guarantor, unconditionally, for the
purpose of the trust ; the latter is a conveyance to the trustee for the
purpose of raising a fund to pay debts, while the former is a conveyance in trust for the purpose of securing a debt, subject to a condition
of defeasance.

It is perfectly well settled that in a voluntary assignment by a
debtor, of his property to an assignee or trustee, for the benefit of his
creditors, the debts due to the creditors constitute a valuable consideration in the highest sense of the term, and that the assignee's obligation to perform the trust is such a valuable consideration as will be
binding upon him.

Among other things that result from this are that no consideration
need be expressed in the deed of assignment, and that no such assignment can be declared void, for want of consideration.

It is not necessary to the validity of an assignment in trust for the
benefit of creditors, that they should be parties thereto, or signify their
assent to it.

A debtor, who has made an assignment for the benefit of his creditors cannot, after it has been properly executed and delivered, revoke
it, or alter its terms.

The general rule applicable to general assignments in trust for
the benefit of creditors, and briefly stated is that all property whatever
owned by the assignor, at the time of making the assignment, and
not exempt by law from execution, passes to the assignee.

Among the things that have been held to be assignable, and that
therefore, pass to the assignee, by such assignment, are the following :
Every demand connected with a right of property, every estate and interest in land and tenements, and also every present and certain estate
or interest in incorporeal hereditaments, even though the interest be
future, including a term of years to commence at a subsequent period,
for such an interest is vested now, though it takes effect in the future,
the right, under written contract therefor, or otherwise, to have land
conveyed to the assignor ; the rights of a mortgager to redeem a ven-

dor's lien for purchase money, the interest of a tenant for life, growing crops, all contingent and executory interests and contingent estates of inheritance, as well as springing and executory uses and possibilities, coupled with an intent, mechanic's liens, insurance policies, money in bank, which the assignor had the right to withdraw by check, at the time the assignment was made, choses in action, including notes and bills, bonds, book accounts, decrees in equity, rights of action for damages, including actions for torts, which survive the death of the assignor: interests in pending actions, judgments and executions; the right to use a trade mark, unpaid subscriptions to corporation stock, claims against the United States, property outside the state, leasehold estates; interests of devisees, interests of heirs, and whatever rights the assignor may have acquired to his wife's separate property.

Another general rule, so nearly self-evident, that authorities to sustain it seem unnecessary is, that the assignor can assign his own property only, and nobody's else. Therefore, an assignment by a husband of all his effects and property of every kind, to a trustee, for the benefit of creditors, conveys none of his wife's separate property whatever. Her right to dowry in his real estate, and her right to select a homestead under certain circumstances, are among the wife's separate property rights not affected by his assignment.

Property assigned after its seizure in replevin, does not pass.

The general rule is, that the assignor can convey to his assignee only such rights in the property as possessed by the former at the time of the assignment, and the assignee receives it subject to all equities and to all valid liens existing thereon, against the assignor. It follows that the assignee takes real estate subject to all existing mortgages, mechanic's liens, equitable liens for purchase money, legacies and judgment liens thereon, and personal property subject to any executive liens of Carrier companies, banks, etc., that were in force upon it at the time of the assignment.

It is an undisputed rule, that trustees must at once take possession of the trust property, and preserve the estate from all detriment and loss.

No act should be omitted by the debtor, which can serve to express an absolute transfer of the possession and an entire renunciation of all control of the property, so as to give every quality or realty a good faith to the transaction. Among the acts most expressive for this purpose are the ordinary ones of delivery of the keys of the store or premises containing the goods assigned, together with all the assignor's books of account, and all evidences of debt or title to property.

But the necessary change of possession should not be left to the action of the assignor. The assignee must himself be active; he must take possession and not depend upon the assignor to give it. He should immediately enter upon the premises where the business has been transacted, assume the management of the business itself, take possession of the books of account, divest the assignor of all control of the property. An assignment of all his effects, for the benefit of all his creditors, by a person in embarrassed circumstances—the assignees never taking possession, and allowing the assignor to act as if no assignment had been made, will be set aside by the court, and if the assets have been misapplied, will hold the assignees accountable.

The assignee should notify the bank in which the assignor has money to his credit, of the assignment, to prevent the bank from paying the money on the assignor's check, or from parting from such funds, as they are no longer the assignor's property, but are assets in the hands of the assignee.

As soon as the assignee shall have given bond, the court must appoint three suitable, disinterested persons as appraisers of the property and assets of the assignor, and if the assignee fails to give bond, then such appraisers must be appointed for the same purpose, as soon as the trustee shall be appointed and shall have given bond.

As soon as the appraisal has been completed, the assignee or trustee should proceed at once to open the books upon the principles of double entry, charging all the assets as found in the appraisal. The liabilities should be ascertained at the earliest possible moment, and entered accordingly. If the business is to be continued. the books and accounts should be kept to show every source from which money is received, and for what it is expended. When the accounts have been kept in this manner, it would be very easy to render a complete account to the court, but if items are bulked, the report would be found very unsatisfactory.

The assignee or trustee having first filed the assignment in court and given bond, with the appraisal properly made and recorded, must proceed at once to convert all the assets received by him into money, and to sell the real and personal property assigned, including stocks and such bonds, notes and other claims as are not due, and which cannot probably be collected within a reasonable time at public auction, either for cash or upon such other terms as the court may order.

A report of all the sales of real estate and personal property made as provided by law, by assignees or trustees, must be returned to the court within the time prescribed, and must be confirmed before it will be complete and binding.

If an assignee or trustee deposits money in his own name, in a bank, and the money is lost by the bank's failure, or otherwise, he will be personally responsible for such money. But if he, as assignee or trustee, deposits it in a bank in good credit and repute, till the proper time for paying it to creditors, for use in paying the current expenses of administering the trust, etc., and the bank fails, he will not be liable. He must act in regard to this as a prudent man would in his own affairs, and must keep the account of such funds separate from the account of his own. His bank book and bank account for such funds should show that the account is with him as assignee or trustee of Mr. Blank.

No doubt the rule is, that where trustees, including assignees, act within the scope of their authority in good faith, and according to the best of their judgment, and exercise such prudence, care and diligence, as men of ordinary prudence manifest in like manner of their own, they will not be held accountable for losses happening from their management of the trust funds. But this rule will only protect the assignee as long as he manages the trust fund strictly as the law requires him to do.

Assignees and others having trust money to distribute, must see that it reaches the person entitled to receive it, for if paid to the wrong person, by mistake or otherwise, they are still liable to pay it to the rightful claimant.

At the expiration of eight months from the appointment and qualification of the assignee or trustee, and as often thereafter as the court may order, an account must be filed with said court, by such assignee or trustee, containing a full exhibit of all his doings as such, up to the time of the filing thereof, together with the amount of all claims remaining uncollected, and the amount thereof, which in his opinion may thereafter be collected.

Whenever any settlement shows a balance remaining in the hands of the assignee or trustee, subject to distribution among the general creditors, a dividend must be declared by the court, payable out of such balance, equally among all the creditors entitled, in proportion to the amount of their respective claims against the assignor, including those disallowed, as to which the claimant has begun proceedings to establish the same, and claims held under advisement.

There is no prescribed form of rendering an account to court. It should be made in as simple a manner as possible, and the simpler and plainer it is, the better, if it be accurate and complete. It is better that it should enable any creditor of ordinary intelligence to examine and understand it, without the aid of an expert.

The following form is suggested :

First, Second or Final Account of C. L. S., Assignee in Trust for the Benefit of the Creditors of D. J. C.

Accountant should charge himself as follows:

Receipts.	Amount.
Balance on hand from last account	$
Received from sale of R. E. (name it.)	
" " Sale Bill of Personal Property	
" " Personal Accounts	
" " Notes	
" " J. D. Book Account	
" " Etc., etc.	
Total amount received and not heretofore accounted for	$

Accountant claims Credit as follows :

Payments.	Voucher No.	Amounts.
Paid Probate Judge for Appraisement, etc	1	$
" Appraisers	2	
" Auctioneer	3	
" U. Nat. Bk. to satisfy M'at'g on R. E.	4	
" G. B. S., Att'y fee	5	
" self for services, 6 per cent. on $1000	6	
Etc., etc., etc		
Total Payments and Credits claimed		
Total amounts rec'd as above specified		$
" " paid " " "		
Amount in hands of Assignee for distribution		

Claims presented for allowance.	Amount.
Amount of Claims against said Assignor which have been presented to said Assignee and allowed	$
Amount presented to said Assignee, disallowed and sued	
" " " " under advisement	
Total amount of claims presented	$

Claims remaining uncollected.	Amount.
Amount of Claims due said Assignor, still remaining in the hands of the Assignee uncollected	$
Amount which, in the opinion of the Assignee may still be collected.	

Receivers.

Receivers are usually appointed when property is likely to be seriously injured, lost or consumed. The duties of receivers are about the same as those of assignees, except that they are under the direct control of the court. A receiver is appointed to preserve and keep together, while an assignee is appointed to distribute.

The receiver of an insolvent corporation represents both the creditors and stockholders, and may assert their rights when affected by the fraudulent or illegal acts of the institution.

A receiver is subject to all the rights and equities existing against the company. He takes the place of the company, and stands as its representative.

The receiver should allow every claim against the corporation which he is satisfied is justly due; but no claim which could not have been recovered against it, either at law or equity.

A receiver may be allowed to compromise disputed claims against the company, or to submit them to arbitration.

The receiver is the proper person to bring suit to enforce payment of a debt due the company.

A receiver, as such, is vested with all the rights of action which the company, of which he is receiver, had when he was appointed, and he can sue for torts committed before his appointment.

A common-law receiver cannot sue in his own name, but may sue in the name of the corporation, and may recover, against directors, penalties given by the charter to the corporation, and, in the event of its dissolution, to its creditors; but the declaration must aver that the suit is brought by the direction of the receiver.

A receiver cannot maintain a suit to collect assets of the corporation unless expressly authorized to " sue," authority " to collect " is not enough.

In a suit by the receiver against a stockholder, to recover unpaid subscription, the receiver must show a clear legal right to institute and carry on the same.

As often as required by law, a receiver of a corporation should present to and file with the court a full and definite account, verified by oath, itemizing with particularity the various claims made by him.

The duties of receivers regarding their accounts are given in lesson number 28, and need not be repeated here.

The following is a form of account suggested for receivers.

First account of J. H. Brown, Receiver The Brown Iron and Nail Co.

Accountant charges himself as follows:	Amount.
Mdse.　　　　　as per appraisal Jan'y 13th, 1894	
Material　　　　　"　　"　　　"　　"　　"	
Plant　　　　　　"　　"　　　"　　"　　"	
Real Estate　　　"　　"　　　"　　"　　"	
Personal Accounts　"　　"　　　"　　"　　"	
Cash　　　　　　"　　"　　　"　　"　　"	
Bills Receivable　　"　　"　　　"　　"　　"	
Other Assets　　　"　　"　　　"　　"　　"	
Total amounts of Assets received as appraised :	
Mdse. purchased by Receiver	
Material　　"　　"　　"	
Personal Accounts	
Bills Receivable	
Cash	
Other Assets	
Total amount of Assets Received	

Accountant Claims Credit as follows:	
Mdse. Sold	
Real Estate Sold	
Cash Paid	
Collected Accounts	
Total amount of Assets disposed of	
Value of Assets in hands of Receiver	

Accountant charges himself with Cash as follows:	
Cash received as per Appraisal	
"　　"　　from Sale of Goods	
"　　"　　"　Personal Accounts	
"　　"　　"　Sale of Real Estate	
"　　"　　"　other sources	
Total Cash Receipts	

Accountant asks Credit as follows:	Voucher Number.	
Cash paid Probate Judge		
"　　"　　Appraisers		
"　　"　　for Wages		
"　　"　　Jno. Doe		
"　　"　　John Jones		
"　　"　　Attorney J. B. Smith		
"　　"　　for other items all itemized		
Total amount of Cash paid		
Balance of Cash on hand		

Liabilities when appointed were as follows:		Amount.
Personal Accounts...		
Bills Payable..		
Mortgage Payable..		
(Other Items)...		
Total Liabilities when appointed............................		

Paid on Liabilities when appointed:

	Voucher Number.		
Paid Personal Accounts (itemized)			
" " " "			
" Notes..			
" other Liabilities....................................			
Paid on Liabilities when appointed...............			

Claims presented for allowance.

(Name Claimants)...		
" "		
" "		
Total amount of Claims presented......................		

Claims allowed.

(Names)		
"		
"		
"		
Total amount of Claims allowed...........................		

Claims disallowed and under advisement.

(Names)		
"		
"		
"		
"		
Total amount of Claims disallowed		

CHAPTER THIRTY-FIVE.

Handling Vouchers.

An ordinary voucher is a certificate of indebtedness, giving the name and residence of the payee, the particulars of the claim, and the amount thereof.

Every voucher should give a detailed statement of the purpose for which it is made and the date and amount. It should show upon its face, the account or accounts to which it is chargeable.

All papers and correspondence that belong thereto, or are in any way necessary to explain the authenticity of a voucher should be attached to it. All the facts in relation to it should be explained either upon its face or in the papers that accompany it.

Many concerns make a copy of the original voucher and use it in making payments; the original they file away with the papers attached. There are many things in favor of this plan, taking the voucher system as it is generally used.

A great many concerns use the ordinary voucher in making payments, but there are very few who use a complete voucher system. The voucher system when used complete, should consist of four vouchers and a voucher record. The voucher used for entering invoices in the voucher record is illustrated on pages 243 and 244. The Invoice Voucher Record is illustrated and explained in lessons 24, 26 and 27 and needs no further comment here.

The Journal Voucher is used to make all entries upon the Journal. These vouchers are made by the proper accounting officer. Not a single entry is allowed upon the Journal without a voucher properly made, signed, dated, numbered, etc.

They should be entered upon the Journal, checked, folioed, and filed away in numerical order. When a voucher of this kind is used, it is impossible for the bookkeeper to make any unauthorized entries.

A Cash Book Voucher is used for making entries upon the Cash Book. This refers to Cash Receipts only. The collections, cash sales, etc., are entered upon a Cash Book Voucher, from which it is entered into the Cash Book.

A Voucher Check is used for all Cash disbursements. The check and Voucher being combined, does away with the old-fashioned vouchers, which are often lost and sometimes never returned.

The Voucher Check is sure to be returned, if it is not, it will not be charged to your account at the bank. They are made up in regular check book form, and all particulars entered upon the stubs. The following is the form for voucher check, omitting the stub, size $3\frac{1}{2}'' \times 9''$.

The American Oil Company,

Voucher No.   CLEVELAND, O.,-------------------------

                    To---

This Voucher is payable in current funds, at

THE CLEVELAND NATIONAL BANK, OF CLEVELAND, OHIO.

When the receipt below is executed by proper authority.

Correct and approved for payment. | Received of THE AMERICAN OIL COMPANY,

_____ _____ Dollars, $_____
                        Secretary. | in full payment of above account.
Countersigned,
                                   | Date_____
_____
                        President. | Per____ _____

Do not detach this Receipt from Voucher.

Paying Vouchers—Branch Houses.

Many large corporations have a number of branch houses in different localities, some pay all accounts from the main office, through their local managers or agents, while others pay direct from the main and local offices. To make the instructions clear, and cover all systems of vouchers used, it will be necessary to refer to those sent through managers, as well as those paid direct by the ordinary form, while in other cases payment by voucher check will be referred to.

All vouchers should be made in favor of the person, firm or corporation to whom the company is indebted. In case of amounts due the national or state government, counties, cities, and the like, they should be made impersonally in favor of the official entitled to receive

the money, thus; Treasurer of the U. S., Treasurer or Collector of
...............County, etc.

Vouchers for material, should give the items in detail, and the
prices for each, the date of purchase being specified. Vouchers for
labor should contain a statement of the time worked, the place, rate,
date, etc. Vouchers for expenses, should give each item, date and
place, so far as possible.

When the voucher check is used it is not necessary to send
invoices or statements to be receipted. Vouchers should, so far as
possible, be embraced in the month in which the debt is incurred.
However, this does not refer to voucher checks.

Errors in name or initials of payee, place of residence, description
of claim or amount thereof, cause much inconvenience, and are the
occasion of expense and delay in the payment of the account. They
are also liable at any moment to involve a company in loss, if not discovered and corrected in time. Mistakes of this kind are frequently
the result of ignorance, or inadvertence upon the part of the maker of
the voucher, but more often the result of carelessness. It is highly
important, therefore, that especial care should be exercised in making
vouchers to see that the name of the payee as given, is technically
correct, and, if necessary, vouchers should be withheld by the maker
until satisfactory inquiries in this respect can be made.

Accounts against a company should receive immediate attention
from all through whose hands they pass. Vouchers should be made
promptly; should be entered soon as made, and should be approved
for payment without being held longer than necessary to verify their
accuracy. Finally, they should be paid soon as approved, unless
business reasons prevent.

The greatest promptness should characterize the making, and
auditing of vouchers and paying of bills; delay in such matters
evinces lack of attention or proper business methods; it inconveniences
and in many cases seriously embarrasses the parties interested.

Cases will sometimes arise of such urgency as to require money to
be paid in advance of the auditing of a voucher to cover the same.
When this is done the money thus advanced should be charged to the
official of a company who receives and disburses it, but no payment
should be made in advance of auditing, except under rules and regulations established by the proper officer.

Should any portion of the money advanced under the foregoing
rule be returned, it should be credited to the account originally
charged.

For such portion of it as may be disbursed, a voucher should be made by the official making the disbursement in favor of the person or persons to whom it is paid; the receipt of such person or persons should be attached to such voucher.

Vouchers made on account of money advanced, should be credited to the person charged with the advance. On the face of all such vouchers the person making the same should note in red ink, that it has been paid, giving the name of the person by whom paid, thus:

"Paid by R. S. Taggart, Mgr." A similar notation should be made on the back of the Voucher, underneath the filing. The notations should be plain and conspicuous, so as to prevent duplicate payment.

In entering on the "Record of Audited Vouchers," a bill that has already been paid, the fact of its having been paid should be noted on the record in every case, giving the name of the person by whom paid; this will enable the accounting officer to prevent duplicate payment in the event, the fact that the voucher has already been paid, should be overlooked by the treasurer.

Vouchers payable at or near a branch, are oftentimes sent to the manager to be paid. When the amount is large, or beyond the ability of the agent to pay out of the receipts, it is better to send check. If, however, a manager should be inadvertently asked to pay a voucher that the proceeds of his office do not render possible without waiting to accumulate cash, he should advise the treasurer of the facts in the case, and await his instruction. This is done where branches make daily remittances for their collections.

When more than one voucher is sent to a manager at one time, they should be paid as fast as the receipts of the branch will permit.

Vouchers should be remitted by the first mail after they are paid.

Should a voucher be sent to the wrong manager to pay, it should be returned forthwith by mail.

The signature to the receipt on a voucher should be exactly the same in every particular as the name of the person or persons to whom the voucher is payable; unless this is the case, credit should not be allowed the manager for paying the same.

Vouchers should be receipted by the person or persons to whom they are payable, or by some one known to be authorized to collect the amount and receipt therefor. In paying vouchers to persons holding orders, those paying them should see that they are receipted by the person or persons to whom the order is payable, attaching the order to the voucher in every case. Managers should be held strictly responsible for vouchers paid to unauthorized persons.

Sometimes it is necessary to pay money to an attorney or others, to satisfy some claim decreed by the courts, or otherwise. In such cases the disbursing officer should take the receipt of the attorney or agent for the money thus paid. This, however, is merely preliminary. When the money is finally paid, by the attorney or agent to the person or persons to whom it belongs, a receipt therefor should be taken. This receipt or voucher should be filed with the one already rendered to the disbursing officer by the attorney or agent. When a receipt from the person or persons to whom the money is finally paid cannot be secured, as sometimes occurs when money is paid to the officers of the courts, then all the facts connected with the payment should be recounted and placed on file in lieu of a receipt.

When the payee of a voucher cannot write, the person paying it should not act as witness.

If duplicate receipts are attached to a voucher, they should all be receipted, dated and returned with it.

Papers attached to vouchers should not be detached. Such papers are necessary to the completeness of the voucher and should not be disturbed. They are, moreover, as a rule, confidential in their nature, and should not be inspected, or read by the payee of a voucher, except when attached for his information. This is another great point in favor of the Voucher Check.

When a voucher is paid it should be stamped in a plain, legible manner directly under the filing on the back of it.

Should a voucher or check get lost, a company should require in every instance, a good and sufficient bond of indemnity to be filed by the payee before issuing a duplicate. This calls for the greatest care of vouchers and checks.

No unaudited voucher or account should be paid except upon the authority of the treasurer, and not then except in extreme cases, to meet the emergencies of business.

Great trouble and risk are sometimes experienced in the payment of vouchers in consequence of their not being made in favor of the right person or persons.

In some instances the initials of the payee are wrong; more frequently however, the name is given incorrectly; in case of corporations and firms, names are transposed, or the vouchers are made in the name of individuals. When an error of this kind is discovered, payment, should be stopped until the voucher can be corrected. Money should never be paid except to the person or persons named in the instrument.

When it is found that an error has been made in the amount or name of the payee of a voucher or check sent to a branch for payment, they should be returned at once, unpaid, with a statement of the facts in the case, so that the matter may be corrected.

Under no circumstances should a check or voucher be changed or defaced, new ones should be issued by the proper person.

If, for any reason, payment is not to be made to the person in whose name a voucher is made, the fact should be noted on the face of the bill, also on the back of the voucher, underneath the filing, giving the reason therefor, and the name of the person to whom the money is to be paid. This indorsement (except in the case of transfer orders attached) should be signed by the person or persons certifying the voucher and should be satisfactory in every respect to the treasurer, otherwise payment should be withheld awaiting satisfactory explanation.

In order that a company may avail itself of the advantage arising from discounting their bills on condition of prompt payment, the following expeditious method of providing for their settlement is suggested.

Bills that accrue at branches and department headquarters should be approved and paid by the proper officer. When paid, they should be stamped on the back, and forthwith remitted to the main office as cash.

No person should be authorized to pay any bill, voucher, certificate of discharge, or other evidence of debt against a company, except under established rules, on accounts duly audited and approved.

In the event, however, it should become necessary in the course of business, for a manager or agent to pay money in advance of the approval of the document, it may be done upon the written direction of the treasurer or chief accounting officer.

In such cases the manager should be directed to make the payment and take a receipt therefor, holding the latter, with the order directing the payment, until a voucher can be audited relieving him of the charge.

This voucher should be prepared without delay, and should be made in the name of the person to whom the money is paid.

This voucher should pass through the same channel as other vouchers, and be treated, so far as the methods of approving and auditing are concerned, as if unpaid. On the back of said voucher, however, under the proper filing, the maker should plainly note in red ink,

"Paid by —— Mgr. at No. 4 Branch," a similar notation being made on the face of the voucher.

When money is paid in this way the receipt taken by the manager should describe the purpose of the payment.

This receipt should be technically legal in form. When the approved voucher reaches the manager the receipt should be attached thereto by him, also the order.

The voucher should be remitted without delay as the rules describe. When such payments are made direct from branch or main office, the vouchers should be treated in the same way.

Cancellation of Vouchers.

When the books are closed and the statement of audited bills entered upon the general books, any error in the amount of a voucher may be corrected, or the voucher itself may be cancelled and withdrawn from the Voucher Record by simply cancelling the entry on such record. Afterward no correction is possible; if an error has been made in the amount, the instrument should be formally cancelled and a new voucher made.

When it is desired to cancel a voucher after the books are closed, it should be given to the chief accountant, so that the cancellation may be made on the books in due form.

Vouchers requiring to be cancelled after the books are closed should never be torn up or destroyed, as they are required for filing.

In case it is necessary to cancel a voucher, the request therefor should be noted on the back, giving the reason. This should be signed officially.

In cancelling vouchers, the amount should be credited to the account originally charged.

When it is desired to cancel or change a voucher before the books are closed, it should be referred back to the various persons upon whose books it appears, so that they may cancel or change the entry thereon.

Specific reference should be made in the voucher record to each voucher cancelled, and the reason for cancellation given.

Taking Receipts—How Endorsements Should Be Made and Receipts Signed.

Receipts to vouchers, acknowledgements for money, property, or other considerations, and all endorsements on the back of time tickets, orders, drafts and checks, etc., should correspond in every particular with the name of the person or persons in whose favor the instrument is made. For instance, if a document is made in favor of "Henry Schmidt," a receipt or endorsement should not be accepted signed by "Henry Smith." The practice of the United States Government in the case of vouchers, drafts, and checks is founded on correct methods, and should be observed in connection with all such documents. It is as follows:—"*The name of the payee, as endorsed, must correspond in spelling with that on the face of the warrant; no guarantee of an endorsement, imperfect in itself, can be accepted. If the name of a payee, as written on the face of the warrant, is spelled incorrectly, the warrant should be returned for correction.*"

Vouchers may be paid upon the presentation of an order properly drawn by the payee, or by the legal and binding representative of such payee. The authority should in every case be securely attached to the voucher.

Documents in favor of corporations should be signed by the duly authorized agent or officer of such corporation, the name and title of the person being given in full in every instance.

Signatures should be witnessed in all cases by some responsible person when the payee is not personally known.

Endorsements by mark should not be witnessed by a cashier or manager, if the acknowledgement is for money paid by him.

When a payee cannot write, he should make his mark in legal form in lieu of a signature. This mark should be witnessed by some responsible person personally known to the payee.

Checks, drafts, notes, bills of exchange and kindred documents should in all cases be endorsed by the payee. Orders should not be accepted in such cases.

Those who make payments should be held strictly responsible for the *bona fide* character of the receipt or acknowledgement and the payment of the money to the proper person or company.

When checks and drafts are received they should be stamped on the back, viz., "For deposit only," then should follow the name of the firm or company. Underneath this endorsement the name of the cashier, agent or others in authority should be signed.

If the draft or check is stamped immediately upon its receipt, its subsequent destruction or miscarriage can not involve a company in loss; stamping it in the manner described also prevents its misuse.

Signatures should never be inserted with a stamp. Some distinguishing mark or name should be written with pen and ink.

It should be remembered, that the signing by one person for another is not binding unless duly authorized, and whenever a person signs for another, the name of the person signing should be given.

If a person having a power of attorney signs, he should attach to his signature, "Attorney in fact;" if he signs as trustee, administrator, agent or otherwise, the fact should be duly stated beneath his signature.

It is the duty of the disbursing officer who accepts such signature, to satisfy himself at the time that the person signing is duly qualified.

It should be kept constantly in mind, by all who pay money, that while it is easy for them to assure themselves of the creditability of those to whom they pay before the transaction occurs, it is often difficult or impossible afterward. Men are ever willing to substantiate their right to receive money, if required to do so before the transaction. Afterward they are indifferent in many cases, and the burden of proof rests with the payor instead of the payee.

Collateral Security and Collateral.

By commercial usage, not only negotiable instruments, but also documents of title, quasi or non-negotiable in character, are available as collateral security for loans of money, or discounts of paper. The terms adopted, both in commercial circles and by jurists, describing such transactions—"collateral security" and "collateral," as distinguished from a mere pledge—illustrate the development of this special branch of the law, and emphasize the importance of the questions relative to the rights, duties and liabilities incurred by parties to such contracts of loan, secured by collaterals.

"Collateral Security" is a separate obligation, as a negotiable bill of exchange or promissory note of a third person, or document of title, or other representation of value, endorsed where necessary, and delivered by a debtor to his creditor, to secure the payment of his own obligation, represented by an independent instrument. Such collateral security stands by the side of the principal promise as an additional or cumulative means for securing the payment of the debt.

"Collateral," in the commercial sense of the word, is a security given in addition to a principal obligation, and subsidiary thereto; and is generally descriptive of all choses in action, as distinguished from tangible personal property including the usual negotiable instruments of commerce; the quasi-negotiable securities, as certificates of stock, bills of lading, and warehouse or cotton receipts; and the diverse non-negotiable choses in action and equitable assignments available as collateral.

The regular course of banks and bankers in discounting commercial paper, to receive the promissory notes of third persons as collateral security for the payment of the principal note given by their customers, is a recognized form of collateral security. Upon asking for such discount, it is usual for the pledger in his principal note to recite therein the collateral securities deposited, and the terms and manner in which the same may be sold or made otherwise available, upon default. Such recital does not affect the negotiability of the principal note, as the amount to be paid, the time, and the person to whom, remain the same. Where a note, pledged as collateral security, recites on its face that it is " to be held as collateral security for the payment of certain notes," of third persons, it is non-negotiable, even in the hands of a bona fide endorsee, for value, lacking certainty in amount, and being a contingent promise.

Bonds and Coupons as Collateral.

Negotiable bonds, payable to bearer, or "holder," issued under statutory authority, by municipalities or corporations, are negotiable instruments, the title to which passes by delivery. The delivery of such bonds by the pledgor to the pledgee, as collateral security, before maturity, for a valuable consideration, vests the full legal and equitable title in the latter. The same rule applies to dissevered coupon notes or warrants issued with bonds payable to bearer. When separated from the bond, such coupons cease to be mere incidents of the bonds, and become independent negotiable instruments, the title to which passes by delivery.

Delivery of negotiable instruments, to be held as collateral securities, is an essential condition of the validity of the act of pledge. In this respect there is no difference between a pledge of personal property and one of negotiable securities.

The holder of negotiable instruments as collateral security, receiving the same so as to become a party thereto, does not lose his right and title thereto, nor the proceeds thereof, by a redelivery of the same to the pledgor where such a delivery is made with the intention or upon the agreement that the pledgor shall proceed, for and on behalf of the pledgee, to make collection thereof, or do some other proper and necessary act in respect thereto.

When collection of collaterals is the object, the pledgor is regarded as the representative or agent of the pledgee. He acts in a fiduciary character, and the funds which he may collect upon such collaterals are the property of the pledgee, to be credited upon the principal debt.

The renewal of a negotiable bill or note representing the principal indebtedness, for the payment of which collateral securities have been deposited, does not affect the right of the creditor to restrain or enforce the collaterals. He is equally entitled to the benefit of the collateral securities as a means of obtaining payment of the note or bill given in renewal as in the case of the original evidence of indebtedness.

Bonds issued by a municipal or other corporation under statutory authority, and made payable to "bearer" or "holder," are valid commercial instruments, and a pledgee receiving the same before maturity, for a valuable consideration, without notice of equities in the usual course of business, is vested with the legal title thereto, free of prior equities between antecedent parties, as in the case of negotiable promissory notes and bills of exchange. The title of such pledgee so advancing a valuable consideration, upon the faith and credit of the representations of such negotiable collateral securities, in good faith, is good against the world.

In cases of the issue of negotiable bonds and coupons, by municipal or other corporations, where there is a total want of power on the part of such municipal or other corporation to issue the same, notice thereof is chargeable upon all persons dealing therewith, and no right, title, or interest can be acquired even by persons advancing money thereon, as against such municipal or other corporation upon any negotiation thereof. In the absence of statutory authority, municipal or other corporations are without power to issue negotiable bonds and coupons.

A different rule is applied to "registered" bonds for the payment of money by municipal or other corporations, which are but quasi-negotiable instruments, being made payable to a particular person, or "assigns" and not to "bearer" or "holder." Such bonds are like shares of stock, and usually books of registration and transfer are kept, and the transfer of such bonds is generally covered by statutory charter provisions, and are also by the terms thereof transferable only upon such books.

Negotiable bonds and coupons, when received after due as collateral security upon an advance, or as collateral security for an antecedent debt, are subject in the hands of the pledgee to the like equities and defenses as other instruments of commerce, bills of exchange and promissory notes. The pledgee, receiving such collaterals after maturity, obtains no better title or greater interest therein than the pledgor, and is subject to the defenses available against the holders, although for value, of dishonored paper.

When funds or securities are deposited with a banker as collateral security to cover a special advance or discount, the lien of the banker thereon is limited, and is discharged upon repayment of such special advance; and a claim of a banker of a general lien for balances or on account of other loans, upon such funds or securities, is not supported when a contract for the special appropriation thereof is established.

The pledgee of negotiable bills of exchange or notes acquires, when the same are transferred so as to make him a party thereto, the legal title in such negotiable collateral securities, and is entitled to receive the sum due upon the same from the parties liable thereon, and in the event of default, to proceed by action to collect the whole face value thereof, holding the proceeds to be applied in payment of the principal indebtedness. The pledgee, by such action, does not become a trustee of the pledgor, and is not bound to use more than due diligence in the prosecution thereof.

In cases where negotiable securities have been pledged for the payment of a particular debt or obligation, the pledgee is not permitted, in the absence of a special agreement, to retain the same, after payment or discharge of such debt or obligation, as collateral security for other special or general indebtedness of the debtors. When, however, the pledger, after depositing collateral security for a specific debt, less in amount than the value of such collateral, agrees that the surplus, if any, arising from the sale or collection thereof, shall be a pledge for other debts, such contract is enforced. In the application of the proceeds of such collaterals, the money is applied first to the debts of the oldest standing.

The pledgor is entitled to a re-delivery of the collateral securities deposited by him, upon payment of the principle debt, or a tender thereof. After such payment or tender, the pledgee has no authority to transfer such securities. The debt being discharged, his interest therein is at an end.

A convenient form of security for money loaned is found in the negotiable promissory note, secured by a mortgage of real estate. The note itself, being a negotiable instrument, has all the advantages of commercial paper in hands of a holder for value in good faith, and represents the personal liability of the borrower, which can be enforced at maturity, and upon default, as in the case of ordinary negotiable paper. Nor does it lose its negotiable character when secured by mortgage by an indorsement and delivery thereof apart from the mortgage.

Certificates of Stock as Collateral Security.

It has become a very common transaction in the commercial world to use certificates of stock, bills of lading, warehouse and cottonpress receipts, and other like symbols of property, as collateral security for the payment of loans and discounts of commercial paper. Such collateral securities are readily converted into funds, and the value thereof is easily determined by the quotations of the great exchanges.

A certificate of stock is a muniment of title; documentary evidence of the ownership of shares of the capital stock of the corporation issuing the same. By an indorsement in blank and delivery of the certificate, the shares of stock represented thereby become payable to bearer; the certificates may pass from one person to another like commercial paper so payable. The issue of such certificates, properly authenticated, is all that a corporation can do to show the interest of any person in its shares of stock. Such certificates are not shares of stock; and a title to shares may exist without a certificate. Such certificates are a solemn affirmation under seal of the company that a certain number of shares of the stock stand in the name of the individual mentioned in the certificate. A share of stock is a species of incorporeal, intangible property, in the nature of a chose in action, which can never be realized upon except by the dissolution and winding up of the corporation, and in the meantime entitles the holder to profits declared as dividends. A certificate of stock may be the subject of pledge, and the expression, loan or discount on a pledge of stock means that the stock of the persons obtaining the loan is expressly and specifically pledged at the time for its repayment.

A certificate of stock, when indorsed with an irrevocable power of attorney to transfer, signed in blank by the owner, has a species of negotiability which is rather quasi-negotiable than actually negotiable. Under the enforcement of the rules of estoppel, such indorsements in blank render certificates of stock almost negotiable. Certificates of stock bearing upon the face thereof the representation, under seal of the corporation issuing the same, that no transfer of the shares of stock represented thereby will be made except upon the surrender and cancellation of the certificate, is an intimation to all the world that such certificates are not intended for circulation.

The delivery of a certificate of stock, indorsed by the owner with an irrevocable power of attorney to transfer in blank, vests in the pledgee, upon a bona fide advance, the legal title to the shares of stock represented by the certificate, although no notice is given to the corporation issuing the certificate, nor transfer obtained upon its books. It is enough, as between the parties, that the certificate is delivered with authority to the holder, or any one he may name, to transfer it upon the books of the company, the consideration for the indorsement and delivery of the certificate being advanced in good faith.

The delivery of certificates of stock as collateral security with a power of attorney to transfer them to another person, confers a power coupled with an interest, and gives to any one claiming under an execution of the power a right to demand of the company new certificates of stock. The power thus given can be revoked only by payment of the debt, for which the stock has been transferred as collateral security. The pledgee of a certificate of stock in Massachusetts, while restricted by statute in his rights under a contract of pledge, so that he cannot sell, lend, or pledge the stock certificates held by him as collateral security, is still entitled to require a new certificate to be issued to himself or a third person. The title of the stock thus obtained is held subject to the agreement of pledge, but is permitted in order to render the collateral securities more available to the pledgee.

Upon the refusal of a corporation to make such transfer, upon demand and presentation of a certificate, with irrevocable power of attorney to transfer indorsed thereon, the holder for value may bring an action at law against the corporation for damages, recovering the actual value of the stock at the time of the refusal to transfer; or resort may be had to equity to require a transfer to be made, or to afford other suitable relief.

In cases where a pledgee for value of stock certificates has neglected to obtain, in compliance with statutory or charter provisions, a transfer of the shares upon the books of the company and the issue of new certificates, he receives an equitable title only and is subject to the equities of third parties.

Under such statutory or charter enactments, no person can acquire a legal title to the shares of stock, except upon a regular transfer thereof into his name upon the books of the company, and the issue of new certificates.

All that is necessary when the transfer is required by law to be made upon the books of a corporation, is that the fact itself should be appropriately recorded in some one or other of said books. An entry in a stock ledger, showing a debit and credit charge between the two parties, pledgor and pledgee, is a sufficient compliance with such statute, and vests the transferee with a complete and absolute title, and, so far as the corporation is concerned, the act is irrevocable. Or a notice at a meeting of the board of directors of the company is sufficient.

Statutory provisions, requiring transfer on the books of the company, are intended chiefly for the benefit of the company.

The use of certificates of stock as collateral security where made by a mere delivery of the certificates without any power of transfer properly signed, vests in the pledgee an equitable title only.

The pledgee is unable to enforce his security, upon default, by the ordinary processes of sale; but he may obtain relief in equity, where the performance of the necessary acts to render the security available may be decreed.

The holder of certificates of stock as collateral security, receiving the same indorsed with a power of attorney in blank, is entitled upon notice to the company, to collect the dividends accruing on such stock while such certificate remains in his possession. Nor is transfer on the books of the company material as to this right. Such collections are applied on the debt at maturity.

The title to such dividends is in the pledgee, the increase of pledged property going with the debt. The pledgee, indeed, is an owner; his special ownership imposes upon him the duties of a trustee. As such, he is bound to collect dividends, and may sue in his own name.

It is not necessary that he should become absolute owner by foreclosure before suing for dividends on the stock.

Equity will aid the pledgee of stock certificates, holding the same for value, with title, in cases where the pledgor is wasting the property and assets of the company, and destroying the value of the stock.

The pledgee of certificates of stock, indorsed with power of attorney to transfer, who has obtained transfer on the books of the company and received new certificates, becomes by his voluntary act, a stockholder in such company, with all the rights and liabilities of that position. By means of such transfer and the issue of such new certificates, the pledgee acquires a complete and absolute title to the shares of stock deposited as collateral security, and is enabled to render his security available by sale, upon default of the pledgor upon the principal debt, and notice of sale.

In the absence of statutory restriction, no stockholder can have greater rights, or be subject to other liabilities, than the pledgee thus transferring his stock collaterals upon the books of the company issuing the same, and receiving new certificates.

A person may by his acts or conduct, in respect to the stock of a corporation, render himself liable to the responsibilities of a stockholder, and will be estopped to deny such liabilities as against third persons, creditors, and others who have been deceived thereby to their loss.

In the absence of restricted statutes, the pledgee of certificates of stock, endorsed and 'iansferred on the books of the company, has a right to vote at its meetings. His name appearing as stockholder upon the records of the corporation, he becomes for all purposes a stockholder.

A pledgee holding certificates of stock as security, who, after transfer thereof and issue of new certificates, votes at meetings of the company is not liable to an action of trover for the conversion of such certificates.

The receipt of dividends on stock is sufficient to make a man a stockholder, as the responsibilities of the position go with the advantages.

Under general statutes giving authority to regulate the transfer of stock, it may be provided that no transfer shall be made upon the books of the company until after payment of all indebtedness to the company by the person who appears to be the owner, and in whose name the stock is credited on its books. Such lien extends to all the stock of the debtor, although it greatly exceeds the amount of the debt; nor will the lien be barred by the running of the statute limitations against the debt.

When a by-law required the special consent of the directors to a transfer of stock while the transferer was indebted to the company, a lien was given on the stock of one partner for a debt owing by the firm. The lien is not defeated by the taking of collateral security for the payment of any particular debt of the stockholder.

A pledge by a trustee of an estate of certificates of stock belonging thereto, the certificates showing a trust upon their face, or where the pledgee is, in any other way, informed or charged with notice that the stock is subject to a trust, as collateral security for money loaned for his individual use, is a breach of trust.

A pledge of stocks of the estate by a trustee is not within the ordinary course of business, as a trustee presumptively holds the property for administration; and although the consideration be a present loan, and the pledgee acts in good faith, he receives such certificates of stock as collateral security at his peril.

The pledgee holding certificates of stock indorsed with a power of attorney to transfer signed, as collateral security for a loan or discount of commercial paper, is entitled to sell such collaterals, at public sale, upon default of the pledgor, after due demand, and notice of the time and place. Having the legal title to the collateral securities, the pledgee is able to make them available, as the purchaser at such sale has a right to demand, as had the pledgee, transfer of the shares of stock to his own name on the books of the company, and to obtain new certificates.

Sub-pledgees of stock certificates, holding the same for value, are also entitled to sell such collateral securities, upon demand and notice. A private sale is not permitted to be made, even under contract, much below the current market quotation for the stock. Such a sale is open to inquiry and suspicion.

Bills of Lading as Collateral Security.

Bills of lading were among the earliest documents of title used in the commercial world for the purposes of collateral security. The discount by banks of bills of exchange, drawn upon consignees, for the purchase money of goods, the bill of lading being delivered as collateral security for its payment, or loans upon the deposit of bills of lading by the consignee, where they have been forwarded, in order to raise funds to pay the bills of exchange drawn for the purchase price, are common forms of loaning money.

The transfer of a bill of lading as collateral security to a pledgee, who has advanced money, or discounted commercial paper, in good faith on the credit of the representations contained therein, without notice, vests in him the legal title to the property and the right of possession, and his title is good against all the world.

Warehouse Receipts as Collateral Security.

Except in the rare cases where statutory enactments have made warehouse receipts negotiable as bills of exchange or promissory notes, a warehouse receipt is not a negotiable instrument, and its indorsement and delivery, or delivery merely when payable to "holder," carries none of the effects as to cutting off the defenses of the warehouseman against the original holder, nor is there any certain time at which it matures, nor is the title of the person loaning money upon it protected when lost or stolen, as in the case of commercial paper. Nor is the warehouseman a guarantor of the title of property held by him, and for which he has issued a receipt.

. The transfer for value as collateral security of warehouse receipts, by indorsement and delivery, or by delivery only, when such receipts are made payable to "holder" or "only upon return of this receipt," vests the legal title and possession of the property in the pledgee, and is equivalent to an actual delivery of the property. The warehouseman at once, without notice, becomes the bailee of the lender of money upon the receipt he has issued.

"KEY."

Ex. 1, p. 7—Bills Rec.......$1290.00
    Int. rec................... 13.33
    J. H. Brown 1256.67
        To Mdse............ $2560.00

Ex. 2, p. 7—Mdse............$1058.90
    Int. and Dis............ 11.25
        To Bills rec........ $450.00
        " Bills pay....... 411.25
        " H. J. Harris... 200.00
        " Cash............ 8.90

Ex. 3, p. 7—Loss & Gain or
    T. J. Smith............... $552.00
        To Cash............ 552.00

Ex. 4, p. 7—Mdse............$1920.00
    Int. and Dis............ 12.50
    Cash........................ 300.00
    A. R. Boyd............... 267.50
        To bills rec........ $2500.00

Ex. 5, p. 7—L. S. & M. S.
    Ry. Stock...............$20000.00
        To Cash............ $15000.00
        " Bills pay...... 5000.00

Ex. 6, p. 7—T. B. Wood.....$2000.00
    Exchange................. 5.00
        To Union Nat. Bk $2005.00

Ex. 7, p. 7—Cash $2980.00
    Discount.................. 20.00
        To Bills pay....... $3000.00

Ex. 8, p. 7—Cash.............. $995.00
    Discount.................. 5.00
        To A. K. Hudson $1000.00

Ex. 9, p. 7—Bills pay......... $500.00
    Cash........................ 304.38
        To Mdse............ $800.00
        " Dis............... 4.38

Ex. 10. p. 7—Cash $1575.50
        To L. & L. G. Ins
            Co. or
        To Insurance $1575.50

Ex. 11, p. 7—Cash............. $400.00
        To L. S. & M. S.
          Ry. Stock....... $400.00

Ex. 12, p. 8—Loss & Gain or
    Self...... .... $20.00
        To Cash............ $20.00

Ex. 13, p. 8—Expense or...
    Litigation $300.00
        To Cash............ $300.00

Ex. 14, p. 8—Supr. St. Blk.$450,000
    Euclid Ave. Res....... 80,000
    Cleve. Elec. Ry. St'k 10,000
    Cash...................... 5,000
        To Mortgage pay $20,000
        " Self or Stk. ac 525,000

Ex. 15, p. 8—Stern Bros.... $975.00
    Int. and Dis............ 12.19
        To Cash $987.19

Ex. 16, p. 8—Cash............ $487.25
    Loss and Gain 487.25
        To Bills rec....... $974.50

Ex. 17, p. 8—Mdse............ $170.00
    Expense.................. 5.00
        To H. N. Pratt... $170.00
        " Cash.. ... . 5.00

Ex. 18, p. 8—Bills pay.......$4500.00
    Dis. and Int 12 50
    Cash........ ... . 487.50
        To P. J. Jones..... $5000.00

Ex. 19, p. 8—S. Ewart & Co.$7000.00
        To Cash............ $6653.68
        " Com............. 245.00
        " Exchange..... 101.32

Ex. 20, p. 8—Powers......... $500.00
        To Cash............ $500.00

Ex. 21, p. 8—Cash............$1476.75
    Dis 23.25
        To Bills pay......... 1500.00
(No entry is made of the bonds.)

Ex. 22, p. 8—Mdse............$1000.00
        To Bills pay....... $400.00
        " C. B. Hildreth 300.00
        " John Ressler. 300.00

Ex. 23, p. 8—Cash............. $100.00
    Bills Rec................. 100.00
    E. R. Brewer............ 50.00
        To Theo. Hohl... $250.00

Ex. 24, p. 8—Thos. Davis... $500.00
        To Cash............ $500.00

Ex. 25, p. 9—Marshall & Co $300.00
        To Mdse............ $300.00

Ex. 26, p. 9—Roberts & Son $325.00
     To Keim & Harris $325.00

Ex. 27, p. 9—Cash $3000
    Real Estate...............10000
    Mdse........................ 7500
    Bills Rec.................. 1800
    Int. Rec.................... 17.70
    B. F. Miller. 125
    J. P. Keller............... 750
     To Bills pay $675
     " Int. " 15.75
     " Brown Bros...   5000
     " H.C.Patterson   125
     " Stock acc't.....   17376.95

Ex. 28, p. 9—Bills Rec $1000
    Bills Pay................. 1000
    Int..($9.72 and $12.50)   22.22
    D. K. & Co.............. 126.38
     To Mdse............ $2148.60

Ex. 29, p. 9—Cash............. $25
     To Com............ $25

Ex. 30, p. 9—Miller........... $120
     To Lewis.......... $120

Ex. 31, p. 9—My Books.
    Real Estate.............$5670
     To Cash............ $3500
     " Mortgage pay   1500
     " Int. pay.......   70
     " J. Young.......   600

    Taylor's Books—
    Cash......................$3500
    Mortgage Rec........... 1500
    Int. Rec.................... 70
    (J. Young)................ 600
     To Real Estate... $5670

Ex. 32, p. 9—Real Estate....$7800
    Farm Produce 200
    Personal Property..... 2000
     To R.E. Mt'g p'y $3500
     " Chat M'tg p'y   1000
     " Cash.............   5500

Ex. 33, p. 9—Cash............. $150
    F. M. Potter........... 100
     To H. H. Smith. $250

Ex. 34, p. 9—Cash. $27.45
     To Com............ $27.45

Ex. 35, p. 9–10—M.Nat B'k.$1921.51
    Dis. or Ex..............   3.59
     To Cash........... $1925.10
(No entry is made for papers left for collection until collected.)
    M. Nat. Bank..........$4321.51
    Exchange...............   3.59
     To Bills rec....... $1300
     " Cash............   1925.10
     " Int.............   100
     " W. H. Marker   1000
(If entry is made for whole amount.)

Ex. 36, p. 10—Bills pay...... $179.20
    Int. Pay.................. 4.09
    Cash............. .... 186.55
     To mdse........... $369.84

Ex. 37, p. 10—Bills Pay......$3000
    Interest................... 24.50
     To Bills Pay....... $2000
     " Cash............   1024.50

Ex. 38, p. 10—Cash............ $297
     To Loss and Gain $297

Ex. 39, p. 10—C. of C. B. R
     Bonds...$10750
     To Cash............ $10750

Ex. 40, p. 10—Bills Rec...... $279
    Int. Rec.................. 2
     To Mdse............ $250
     " Cash............   31

Ex. 41, p. 10—Cash..........$1064.41
    Loss and Gain......... 2128.83
     To T. B. Hood... $3193.24

Ex. 42, p. 10—Gould's Entry
    Vanderbilt........... ..$15000
     To Rockefeller.... $15000.00

    Vanderbilt's Entry
    Cash.....................$14966.66
    Dis. and Int............. 33.34
     To Gould.......... $15000.00

    Rockefeller's Entry
    Gould...............$15000
     To Cash $14966.66
     " Dis...............   33.34

Ex. 43, p. 10—Bills Pay......$1829.68
    Exchange............... 22.87
     To Cash........ ...... $1852.55

Ex. 44, p. 10—Mdse..........$3000
    Cash........ 4000
    Bills Rec............... 1570
    H. B. Wright.......... 950
    Win Wood............ 406
    Real Estate............ 2500
        To Bills Pay $3900
        " R. Thomas.... 1200
        " Wm. Edwards 640
        " Stock acc't ... 6686

Ex. 45, p. 10–11—Stock ac't$20000
        To Slade............ $12000
        " Potter.......... 8000

Ex. 46, p. 11—Expense...... $5.00
        To Cash $5.00

Ex. 47, p. 11—Cash $665
    Dis.................... 35
        To Carter & Co... $700

Ex. 48, p. 11—Smith......... $509
        To Cash............ $509

Ex. 49, p. 11—Bills Pay..... $500
    Int 15.25
        To Cash............ $515.25

Ex. 50, p. 11—Cash..........$3000
        To M., F. & Co... $2985
        " Com. or Col.. 15

Ex. 51, p. 12—[First Entry.]
    Nat. Ins. Co............$1300
        To Bills Pay $1300
        [Second Entry.]
    Sundry Shipments...$1175
        To Nat. Ins. Co.. $1175
        [Third Entry.]
    Bills Pay $1300
    Int. and Dis $36.54
        To Cash............ $1211.54
        " Nat. Ins. Co.. 125

Ex. 52, p. 12—Mdse.......... $565.32
    Int............ .... .79
        To Bills rec........ $375
        " Int............... 5.56
        " G. Cleveland. 185.55

Ex. 53, p. 12—Int and Dis .. $90.10
        To Cash $90.10
    Dis on C. D $100
    " " Ex 9.90
            $ 90.10

Ex. 54, p. 11—Bills Pay...... $590
    Cash...................... 489
        To Mdse............ $1079

Ex. 55, p. 12—James Hoke.

	Dr.		Cr.
Mdse..........	$50	6 mo Sal'y..	$360
Cash............	190		
Book	18		
Lost Time...	15.75		
Cash	86.25		
	$360.00		$360

Ex. 56, p. 12—Vanderbilt... $66.67
        To Gould $66.67

Ex. 57, p. 13—Bills Rec $150
    Gould.................... 100
    Astor..................... 50
        To Rockefeller... $300

Ex. 58, p. 13—Sommers' Entry.
    (Yourself)..............$1200
        To Bills Pay...... $1191.70
        " Int. and Dis... 8.30
    Dis on Inv $30.00
    " " Note. 21.70
            $8.30

Ex. 59, p. 13—Larimer..... $300
    Exchange .... .75
        To Cash $300.75

Ex. 60, p. 13—Cash..........$2500
    Mort. Rec.............. 3000
    1st Nat. Bank Stock.. 1300
    Horse and Wagon.... 500
        To Morgan... ..... $7300

Ex. 61, p. 13—Cash $654.75
    Disct 20.25
        To L.-T. H'd. Co $675

Ex. 62, p. 13—Cash $103.50
        To Mdse.:........... $103.50

Ex. 63, p. 13—Mdse........... $347.50
    Exchange .... .85
        To Cash............ $341.40
        " Disct............ 6.95
    or Mdse 340.55
    Exchange................ .85
        To Cash........... 341.40

Ex. 64, p. 13—Cash $6300
 Bills Rec.................$4224.65
 Freight.................... 795
  To Steel Rails.... $11250
  " Int. and Dis.. $69 65

Ex. 65, p. 13—Wilson......$15675.80
  To Cash $7837.90
  " Bills Pay...... 7837.90

Ex. 66, p. 13—Taylor & Co..$7218
  To Cash............. $7200
  " Com.............. 18

Ex. 67, p. 13—Bills Rec.....$2000
 Exchange................ 160
  To Bills Rec...... $500
  " Cash 1660

Ex. 68, p. 13—Cash............ $15.75
  To Interest........ $15.75

Ex. 69, p. 14—Bills pay......$8000
 Interest.................. 5.33
 Expense.................. 1.72
  To Real Estate... $4800
  " Cash............ 3207.05

Ex. 70, p. 14—Mdse.......... $30.00
  To N. E. Mfg. Co $30.00

Ex. 71, p. 14—C. H. Wood. $301.50
  To Cash............ $301.50

Ex. 72, p. 14—Real Est....$30000
  To Cash............ $25000
  " Mort Pay...... 5000

Ex. 73, p. 14—F.S Cramer.$11326.50
  To T.B.Pritchard $11326.50

Ex. 74, p. 14—Real Est......$9295
  To Mort. Pay..... $4665
  " Cash............ 4630

Ex. 75, p. 14—Tax or Ex.... $95.50
  To Cash $95.50

Ex. 76, p. 14—R. E. or Exp $215.75
  To Wm. Downie $215.75

Ex. 77, p. 14—Cash.... ....$5000
 Bills Rec................. 2500
 Mdse...................... 7500
 Wm. Johnston......... 1000
 Supr. St. Blk...........75000
  To Bills Pay...... $1500
  " Brooks & Co. 3200
  " W Bingham Co 300
  " Stock acc't.... 86000

Ex. 78, p. 14—Bills Rec.....$1000
  To Bills Pay $1000

Ex. 79, p. 14—Cash.......... $989.50
 Disc...................... 10.50
  To Bills Pay...... $1000

Ex. 80, p. 14—Bills Rec... $500
 Loss and Gain........ $500
  To Bills Rec...... $1000

Ex. 81, p. 14—Bills Pay.....$2000
 Cash.................... 355
 G. J. Warden........... 1000
  To Mdse............ $3355

Ex. 82, p. 15—E. S. Root... $500
  To Bills Rec...... $500

Ex. 83, p. 15—Cash.......... $20
  To Loss and Gain $20

Ex. 84, p. 15—Cash..........$3013.59
  To Bills Rec...... $3000
  " Interest..$? ?? 13.59

Ex. 85, p. 15—H. B. Claflin
  & Co...$2207.77
 Exchange.......... 11.09
 To J. Wanamaker $2218.86

Ex. 86, p. 15—E. A. Wright.$2096.24
  To Exchange..... $15.72
  " Int. and Dis.. 22.01
  " Cash..... ...... 2058.51

Ex. 87, p. 15—H. A. Miller.$2354.40
  To Bills Rec....... $2250
  " Interest........ 3.75
  " Cash............ 100.65

Ex. 88, p. 15—Insurance.... $202.50
  To Cash............ $202.50

Ex. 89, p. 15—A. T. Stewart
  & Co... $765.50
 Exchange................ 1.91
 Int. and Dis............. 11.86
  To Bills Pay....... $779.27

Ex. 90, p. 15—Hower.......$67500
  To Higbee......... $67500

Ex. 91, p. 15—Mdse.......... $675
 Disct............. .... .76
  To Bills Rec $350
  " Norris Bros. . 325.76

Ex. 92, p. 15—J. R. Zuck... $500
  To H. R. Freed.. $500

Ex. 93, p. 16—Mdse............ $350
        To J. S. McCaleb $175.32′
        " J. S. Braddock 174.68

Ex. 94, p. 16—Bills Pay...... $400
        To Cash............ $397.26
        " Disct........ ... 2.74

Ex. 95, p. 16—Bills Rec...... $200
      Cash..................... 100
        To A.H.Strickler $300

Ex. 96, p. 16—M.E.Johnson $485.10
      Exchange................ .61
        To State Nat. B'k $485.71

Ex. 97, p. 16—Bills Pay......$2000
      Exchange................ 15
        To Cash............ $2015

Ex. 98, p. 16—Self.............. $100
        To Cash............ $100

Ex. 99, p. 16—S. A. Boyd... $20
        To Cash............ $20

Ex. 100, p. 16—Loss & Gain $300
        To Mdse $100
        " Horse & Wgn 200

Ex. 150, Page 20-21.

Assets.		Liabilities.	
Mdse...................................	$7000.00	Bills Pay...........................	$3000.00
Bills Rec.............................	2000.00	P. D. Myer........................	431.11
Real Estate........................	15,000.00	Brown..............................	6709.20
Insurance...........................	25.00	Bingham..........	13,384.21
First National Bank Stock...	1476.00	Jones................................	13,209.21
Furniture and Fixtures.......	450.00		
Fuel...................................	36.00		
Cash............................	7659.63		
Mdse. Co. No. 1...................	450.00		
Adv. Co. No. 1.....................	875.00		
" " " 2.....................	200.00		
Carn's Consg't....................	57.10		
Q. Willson..........................	1505.00		
	$36,733.73		**$36,733.73**

Ex. 150, Pages 20-21.

Losses.		Gains.	
Sundries............................	$24.80	Sundries............................	$694.38
Salary Acc't......................	715.66	Commission	1225.00
Insurance..........................	100 00	Real Estate........................	1575.00
Furniture and Fixtures	125.00	Interest and Discount.........	120.00
Fuel...................................	391.30	Bank Stock........................	141.00
Rent.....	1575.00	Mdse.................................	1429.00
Adv. Co. No. 1....................	125.00		
Brown..............................	709.20		
Bingham	709.21		
Jones................................	709.21		
	$5184.38		**$5184.38**

Ex. 151, Page 21.

Net Gain................................ $3663

Day's Net Capital.................. $7221

Simon's Net Capital.............. 8232

Journal Entry.

Mdse $9241

Cash.. 850

Real Estate.......................... 3000

Accounts Rec...................... 6941

Furniture and Fixtures....... 571

Cash (J. D. W.)................... 3000

Mdse. "   2000

Bills Rec. "   1500

    To Bills Pay........................... $975

    Accounts Pay.................... 4175

    W. M. Day......................... 7221

    T. J. Simon...................... 8232

    J. D. Watterson................. 6500

Ex. 152, p. 35.

$9000 + $500 = $9500, Total Investment.

$5000 ÷ $9500 = 52$\frac{12}{19}$ per cent. Net Gain.

52$\frac{12}{19}$ per cent. gain $9000 = $4736.84 Brewer's share.

52$\frac{12}{19}$ "   "   "   500 = 263.16 Hohl's share.

Proof...............$5000.00

Ex. 154, Page 37.

J. B. Hoke.	W. H. Ramsey.	Investments.	Withdrawals.
$8000 X 4 = $32000	$8000 X 4 = $32000	$8000	$1600
1600	3200	8000	3200
			900
$6400 X 4 = $25600	$4800 X 4 = $19200	$16000	700
3500	3500		
		$16000—	$6400 = $9600
$2900 X 2 = $5800	$1300 X 2 = $2600		
900	700		
$2000 X 2 = $4000	$ 600 X 2 = $1200		

$9600 — 2600 = 7000 ÷ 2 = $3500 the amount each withdrew at expiration of 8 months.

$67400 - - plus - - $55000 = $122,400.

$122,400 : $67,400 : : $2600.00 = $1431.70 Hoke should receive.

$122,400 : $55,000 : : $2600.00 = $1168.30 Ramsay "   "

Ex. 156, Pages 40-41.

Webster.

Jan. 1.	Invested $8000.	Interest for 1 year at 9 per cent.....................	$720
Apr. 15.	" 6400.	" " 8 mos. 16 ds. at 9 per cent...........	409.60
May 20.	" 4000.	" " 7 " 11 " " 9 " "	221
June 24.	" 1600.	" " 6 " 7 " " 9 " "	74.80

Interest on investments............................$1425.40

May 5.	Withdrew $1200.	Int. for 7 mos. 26 days at 9 per cent...	$70.80
Aug. 13.	" 1800.	" " 4 " 18 " " "	62.10
Nov. 16.	" 2400.	" " 1 " 15 " " "	27.00

Interest on withdrawals............................... $159.90

Interest due on Webster's account...............$1265.50

Ex. 156, Pages 40-41.—*Continued.*

Clay.

Jan'y 1.	Invested $9000.	Interest for 1 year at 9 per cent........	$810.00	
July 24.	" 9000.	" " 5 mos. 7 ds. at 9 pr. ct......	353.25	
Oct. 12.	" 1600.	" " 2 " 19 " 9 "	31.60	

Interest on investment...................... $1194.85

Mch. 26.	Withdrew $3000.	Int. for 9 mos. 5 ds. at 9 per cent......	$206.25
May 5.	" 8000.	" " 7 " 26 " 9 "	472.00
June 14.	" 5500.	" " 6 " 17 " 9 "	270.87
Sept. 2.	" 4800.	" " 3 " 29 " 9 "	142.80

Interest on withdrawals.................... $1091.92

"   due on Clay's account........... $102.93

Calhoun.

Jan'y. 1.	Invested $7500.	Interest for 1 year at 9 per cent........	$675.00
" 25.	" 6000.	" " 11 mos. 6 ds. at 9 pr ct......	504.00
Feb. 14.	" 4000.	" " 10 " 17 " 9 "	317.00
May 25.	" 2800.	" " 7 " 6 " 9 "	151.20

Interest on investment...................... $1647.20

April 27.	Withdrew $2000.	Int. for 8 mos 4 ds. at 9 pr ct...........	$122.00
June 4.	" 3600.	" " 6 " 27 " 9 "	186.30
Aug. 2.	" 800.	" " 4 " 29 " 9 "	29.80

Interest on withdrawals.................... $338.10

Interest due on Calhoun's account..... $1309.10

Webster's.		Clay's.		Calhoun's.		Total.
$1265.50	+	$102.93	+	$1309.10	=	$2677.53 Net Interest.

$2677.53 ÷ 3 = $892.51, Average Interest.

$1265.50 — $892.51 = $372.99 Interest to Credit of Webster.

$1309.10 — $892.51 = $416.59 " " Calhoun.

$892.51 — $102.93 = $789.58 " Debit Clay.

Net Gain $6842.19 ÷ 3 = $2280.73 each partner's share.

Webster's credit balance $14,600 + ⅓ net gain, $2280.73 + his interest, $372.99 + his average interest $892.51, gives $18,146.23, balance due him.

Clay's ⅓ net gain to his credit and interest $789.58 to his debit shows his insolvency $208.85.

Calhoun's credit balance, $13,900 + ⅓ net gain, $2280.73 + his interest, $416 59 + his average interest $892.51, gives $17,489.83, balance due him.

Ex. 159, Page 42.

Assets at Closing.		Liabilities at Closing.	
Cash	$1875	Bills Pay	$3560
Real Estate	12500	Mortgages Pay	8000
Merchandise	4700	Interest Pay	72
Accounts Rec	2840	Accts Pay	4625
Bills Rec	2400		
Total Assets	$24315	Total Liabilities	$16257

Total assets $24,315 — $16,257 total liabilities = $8058, present worth.

Present worth $8058 + $4342 net loss = $12,400, net capital at commencing.

Three-fifths of $12,400 = $7440, Smith's investment.

Two-fifths of $12,400 = $4960, Randolph's Investment.

$12,400 Proof.

Ex. 161, Page 43.

Liabilities at Closing.		Assets at Closing.	
Johns & Co	$1614.77	Cash	$5160.00
W. A. Biddle	3164.37	J. P. Barr	2369.00
O. D. Myer	3765.14	O. P. Shupe	3140.00
J. L. Hudson	1211.62	J. D. Brown	435.00
Fox & Co	1240.72	Bills Receivable	4432.71
Bills Payable	8469.11	Interest Receivable	178.45
		Real Estate	2100.00
Total	$19,465.73	Total	$17,815.16

Total Liabilities $19,465.73 — $17,815.16 Total Assets=$1650.57 Present Insolv'cy.

Prest. Insolvency $1650.57 + $882.96 Net Gain = $2533.53 Insol'y at Com'c'g.

Knight.

$\frac{4}{11}$ of $2533.30 = Insolvency at Commencing ... $921.20

$\frac{1}{3}$ of 882.73 = Share of Gain ... 294.24

Present Insolvency ... $626.96

White.

$\frac{5}{11}$ of $2533.30 = Insolvency at Commencing ... $1151.50

$\frac{1}{3}$ of 882.73 = Share of Gain ... 294.24

Present Insolvency ... $857.26

Wright.

$\frac{2}{11}$ of $2533 30 = Insolvency at Commencing ... $460.60

$\frac{1}{3}$ of 882.73 = Share of Gain ... 294.25

Present Insolvency ... $166.35

$626.96 + $857.26 + $166.35 =$1650.57 Proof.

Ex. 162, Page 44.

Boyd Invested.........................$4720
"   Withdrew...... 250

Boyd Net Inv.........................$4470
"   ½ Net Gain..................... 980

Boyd's Present Worth..............$5400

Lyon Invested.......................$4200
" ½ Net Gain..................... 930

Lyon's Present Worth.............$5130
Boyd Pay Lyon....................... 5130

Ex. 163, Page 44.

Dodge.

Inv. $7000 4 mos. = $28,000 for 1 mo.
"   6000 8 "   = 48,000 " 1 "

$76,000

Hodge.

Inv. $3000 2 mos. = $6,000 for 1 mo.
"   9000 3 "   = 27,000 " 1 "
"   8000 5 "   = 40,000 " 1 "

$73,000

$73,000 + $76,000 = $149,000.

$149,000 : $73,000 : : $7,280 = $3,566.71, Hodge's Share of Gain.
$149,000 : $76,000 : : $7,280 = $3,713.29, Dodge's Share of Gain.

Ex. 164, Page 44.

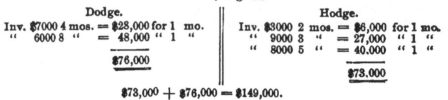

J. P. Keller.	F. A. Plotner.	Wm. Todd.
Invested $14000	Invested..... $14000	Invested.....$21000
Int. 1 yr 8 p.c 1120	Int. 1 yr 8 p.c 1120	Int. 1 yr 8 p c 1680
⅟ net gain... 4000	⅟ net gain... 4000	⅟ net gain ... 4000
———$19120	———$19120	———$26680
Withdrew ...$10000	Withdrew ... $8000	Withdrew ...$12000
Int 6 mo 8 pc 400	Int 6 mo 8 pc 320	Int 6 mo 8 pc 480
———$10400	———$ 8320	———$12480
N't cap at closing. $8720	N't cap at closing. $10800	N't cap at closing. $14200

Ex. 165, Page 44.

Doe's lost time 20 days.
Roe's " " 25 "
Coe's " " 30 "
    Total, 75 days ÷ 3 = 25 days average.

25—20 = 5 days net time gained by Doe.
30—25 = 5 "   "   " lost by Coe.
$4 X 5 = $20 Coe to pay Doe.

Ex. 166, Page 45.

Liabilities at Closing.		Assets at Closing.	
Bills Payable..	$2800	Merchandise	$7224
H. R. Freed...........................	8200	Cash	4324
B. F. Biller...........................	4500	Bills Rec...............................	1300
Capital Invested....................	12000	J. H. Brown...........................	8500
Total..................	$27,500	Total..................	$21,348

Total liabilities $27,500 — $21,348 total assets = $6152 net loss.

Ex. 167, Page 45.

Resources at Closing.

Cash...................$3125.25	
Mdse...................... 4222.84	
Bills Rec.................. 375.00	
Accounts Rec............ 1784.67	
Fur. and Fix............ 1596.00	
Real Estate.............. 4500.00	
Horse and Wagon..... 520.00	

Total Resources. $16,123.76

Liabilities at Closing.

Bills Pay $2575.00	
Interest Pay 172.49	
Acc'ts Pay................. 310.71	
Mortgage Pay.......... 2000.00	
Interest Pay 65.18	

Total Liabilities. $5123.38

Pres. worth of firm... $11000.38

M. T. H. total inv....	$13246	
" withdraw's.	7381	
" net invest..		$5865
S. M. total "	$12863	
" withdrawals....	5369	
" net investment		$7494

Firm's total net inv..		$13359.00
" pres't worth.		11000.38
Firm's net loss........		$2358 62
" total exp's ...		2148.94
Loss on mdse....		$ 209.68

Mdse. cost..............		$6128.07
" invt'y..........	$4222.84	
" loss..............	209.68	−4432.52
Correct amt. sales.		$1695.55

M. T. H. net inv......	$5865.00	
" ½ net loss...	1179.31	
		−$4685.69
S. M. net inv...........	$7494	
" ½ net loss.......	1179.31	
		−$6314 69
Proof........		$11000.38

Ex. 168, Page 45.

Assets at Closing.

Bills Rec................$1644	
Cash........ .... 2440.60	
Accounts Rec.......... 4234.73	

Total assets........ $8319.33

Liabilities at Closing.

Bills Pay.................$2149	
P. D. Myer........ ..... 3241.67	
W. E. Kneale.......... ... 1340.33	

Total liabilities... $6731.00

Present worth...		$1588.33
Expense paid by.....	$ 375.00	
Woodburn withdrew	260.00	−$115.00
		$1473.33

Gain $2136.72 — $1473.33 = $663.39 insolvency at commencing.

$663.39 ÷ 2 = $331.69½ each partner's insolvency.

Woodburn.

Insolvency at com.....	$ 331.70	
½ net gain................		$1068.36
Withdrawal..............	260.00	
Present worth..........	476.66	
	$1068.36	$1068.36

Rush.

Insolvency at com....	$331.69	
Investment...........		$375.00
Present Worth.........	1111.67	
½ net gain.............		1068.36
	$1443 36	$1443.36

Ex. 169, p. 45.

Total liabilities including investments....................$18794.16	
Net gain.......... 1240.60	

Total liabilities.including investment and gain.......$20034.76	
Resources given, except cash 12414.20	

Cash on hand... $7620.56

Ex. 170, Page 46.

According to the original conditions of the contract, the gains were to be divided: Brown ½, Black ⅓, Green ⅕, Gray ⅛, and the balance, 2⁄15, to go to the credit of Reserve Fund. Brown and Black failing to invest capital according to the proper conditions, cause a diminution in their respective shares of gain. Brown's shortage, $2000, makes his share ½—(⅓ of ½) or 3⁄15. Black's shortage,

Ex. 170, Page 46.— *Continued.*

$3000, makes his share $\frac{1}{4}$—($\frac{1}{4}$ of $\frac{1}{4}$) or $\frac{3}{16}$, $\frac{3}{18}$ + $\frac{1}{18}$ = $\frac{17}{144}$ or $2153.33, the share of gain lost by Brown and Black, which is to be divided according to the original terms. The total gain, $18,240, is therefore to be divided as follows:

Brown's $\frac{5}{18}$ or $\frac{200}{18}$ = $5066.67 $+$ $\frac{1}{3}$ of $2153.33 = $5784.45, Brown's share.
Black's $\frac{3}{18}$ or $\frac{135}{20}$ = 3420 " $\frac{1}{4}$ of " = 3958.33, Black's "
Green's $\frac{1}{5}$ or $\frac{144}{24}$ = 3648 " $\frac{1}{5}$ of " = 4078.67, Green's "
Gray's $\frac{1}{6}$ or $\frac{144}{24}$ = 3040 " $\frac{1}{6}$ of " = 3398.88, Gray's "
Reserve $\frac{1}{10}$ or $\frac{18}{10}$ = 912 " $\frac{1}{10}$ of " = 1019.67, Reserve Fund.

Total.........$16,086.67 $18,240.00

Gain $18,240 — $16,086.67 = $2153.33 to be divided according to original terms.

Ex. 171, Page 46.

Johnson invested......$2000			Resources at Closing.	
12 mo. int. on inv... 140			Mdse.................$6493.68	
Sal'y from Beidler. 600			Bills Rec............. 1921 60	
6 mo. av int. on sal 21			Int. Rec.............. 194.60	
			Cash................. 1096.40	
Total credit..... $2761.00			Accounts Rec......... 2184.50	
Withdrew............. $850			H. & W...... 370.00	
4½ mos. av int 22 32			Fur. and Fix.......... 294.00	
	$ 872.32		Total resources $12554.78	
			Liabilities at Closing.	
Net invest. or Cr... $1888.68			Bills pay.................$2834 60	
Beidler invested......$4000			Interest.................. 43.84	
12 mos. int. on inv 280			Accounts pay.......... 373.42	
Total credit.... $4280			Total liabilities.. $3251.86	
Withdrew............. $760				
5¾ mo. av int.......... 25.12			Pres. worth of firm... $9302.92	
Sal'y to Johnson... 600			Johnson' net credit...$1888.68	
6 mo. av int 21			Beidler's " " ... 2873.88	
	$1406.12		$4762.56	
Net invest. or Cr... $2873.88			Net gain.......... $4540.36	
M. E. Johnson.			$4540.36 ÷ 2=$2270.18 each partner's	
Net credit $1888.68			share.	
" gain.................. 2270.18			T. F. Beidler.	
			Net credit........$2873.88	
Present interest.. ..... $4158.86			" gain.......... 2270.18	
Original investment..$2000				
Withdrew .... 850— 1150			Present interest....... $5144.06	
			Less 66¾ discount on	
Net income............ $3008 86			his share of doub't ac. 72.81	
				$5071.25
			Am't loaned Johnson	3000.00
			Cash due f'm Johnson	$2071.25

Johnson to pay Beidler on withdrawal............. $5071.25
Beidler's original investment......................$4000
    "   withdrew....................$760
    "   salary to Johnson.............. 600   1360
                                                         2640
    Beidler's net income...$2431.25

Ex. 187, Page 68.

Interest on Kneale's credit, $8500, for 1 year...........................$ 510
    "   "   "   debit,   3500, " 261 days........................ 152.25

      Balance of interest to Kneale's credit..................... $357.75
Interest on Gibbon's credit, $10600, for 1 year...........................$ 636
    "   "   "   debit,   2000, " 165 days....................... 55

      Balance of interest to Gibbon's credit...... .... $581.00
Discount on the bills receivable for 140 days............................$ 175
    "   "   "   " payable   " 171 " 120.56
5 per cent. discount on the personal accounts......................... 290

Assets of the Firm.   Liabilities of the Firm.
Cash....................................$8000   Bills payable (prest. worth)...$4109.44
Bills rec. (pres. worth)......... 7325   Add capital invested.............19100.00
Personal account, 5 pr. ct. off 5510   Net Int. to K. & G............... 938.75

                  $20835 $24148.19
Add capital withdrawn.......... 5500

                 $26335 — $24148.19 — $2186.81 net gain.
Kneale's ⅔ net gain............. 1457.88
Gibbon's ⅓ "   " 728.93
                 —$2186.81 Proof.

Ex. 245, p. 82.
    Subscription........$106,300
    Bonus or good will 10,700
    Treasury stock..... 33,000
       To capital stock $150,000

Ex. 246, p. 83.
    Plant and Mach'y $40,000
    Pig Iron.............. 10,000
    Patterns 5,700
    Cash.................... 16,400
    Accounts Rec...... 32,941
    Bills Rec.............. 4,659
    Cash   (new subs) 5,000
    Pig Iron, "   "   5,000
    Bills Rec,"   "   1,000
    Real Est. "   "   1,000
       To Acct's Pay.. $10,400
       " Bills Pay.... 5,000
       " Subscript'n 106,300

Ex. 247, p. 83.
    U. S. bonds $10,000
       To Treas. Stock ;$10,000

Ex. 248, p. 83.
    Loss and Gain.......$17,500
       To Surplus..... $17,500

    Then Surplus..........$15,000
       To Dividend.... $15,000

Ex. 250, p. 83.
    Plant and Mch'y...$60,000 or
     "   "   " ... 40,000
    Franchise............... 20,000
       To Cap. Stock $60,000

Ex. 251, p. 83.
    Treasury Stock......$30,000
       To Work'g Cap $30,000

Ex. 252, p. 83.
    Cash.....................$10,000
       To Treas. Stk.. $10,000

Ex. 253, p. 83.
    Merchandise.......... $4,500
    Working Cap........ 500
       To Treas. Stk.. $5,000

Ex. 254, p. 83.
    Cash..................... $5,750
       To Treas. Stk.. $5,000
       "Working Cap 750

Ex. 255, 256, 257.
    Same as in Ex. 248.

Ex. 265, p. 99.
    Subscription.........$60,000
    Treasury Stock....... 20,000
       To Cap. Stock. $60,000
       "Working Cap 20,000

Ex. 266, p. 100.
    Real Estate...........$12,000
       To Cash......... $2,000
       " Treas.Stock 10,000

Ex. 267, 268, 269, p. 100.
    Same as in Ex. 248, 259.

Ex. 271, p. 100.
    Subscription $150,000
    Treasury Stock.... 50,000
        To Cap.Stock. $150,000
        "W'king Cap 50,000
Or   Subscription........$150,000
    Patent Right....... 50,000
        To Cap.Stock. $150,000
        " W'kingCap 50,000

Ex. 280, p. 116, 117.
    Treasury Stock.... $1,000
        ToSubscript'n $800
        " JohnHardy 200

Ex. 281, p. 117.
    Treasury Stock..... $1,000
        To L's & G'n.. $200
        " Subscript'n 800

Ex. 282, p. 117.
    Capital Stock....... $200
        To L's & G'n.. $200

Ex. 283, p. 117.
    Same as in Ex. 262, p. 91.

Ex. 284, p. 117.
    Same as in Ex. 259, p. 85.

Ex. 285, p. 134.
    Same as in Ex. 262, p. 91.

Ex. 286, 287, p. 134.
    Same as in Ex. 203, p. 77.

Ex. 288, p. 134.
    Mines and Plant..$500,000
        To Cap.Stock. $500,000

Ex. 289, p. 134.
    Capital Stock.......$250,000
        To L's & G'n.. $100,000
        " Mine & Pl't.. 150,000

Ex. 290, p. 134.
It goes to credit of Mine and Plant.

Ex. 291, p. 134.
They are surrendered and new ones
  issued for the remaining shares.

Ex. 292, p. 134.
Credit capital stock account and
  debit the stockholders for all
  shares surrendered or returned.

Ex. 293, p. 134.
    Capital Stock........
        To L's & G'n..
        " Cash ....

Ex. 294, p. 34.
    Capital Stock.......$250,000
        To Treas. Stk. $250,000

Ex. 295, p. 134.—If subscribed, entry
  would be—
    Subscription........$250,000
        To pfd.Cap.Stk. $250,000

Ex. 296, p. 134.—If paid in cash,
  entry would be—
    Cash...................$250,000
        To pfd.CapStk $250,000
If not subscribed or paid, entry
  would be—
    Franchise............$250,000
        To pfd.Cap.Stk. $250,000

Ex. 297, p. 134.—See page 94.

Ex. 298, p. 134.—Surplus.
        To pfd. Stk. Div. etc.
Ex. 299, p. 134.—Surplus.
        To pfd.Stk. Div. etc.
        " Div. No. 1, etc.

Ex. 306, p. 151.
    Gain................... $30,000

Ex. 307, p. 151.
    Mill and Furnace.. $75,000
    Pig Iron............. 20,000
    Bills Rec............ 17,450
    Acc'ts Rec.......... 77,550
    Mch'y & Patterns. 31,000
    Treasury Stock.... 10,000
        To Acc'ts Pay. $41,000
        " Bills Pay... 10,000
        " Cap. Stock.. 150,000
        " Loss & G'n.. 30,000

Ex. 308, p. 151.
    Loss and Gain...... $30,000
        To Div. No.— $10,000
        "Res've Fund 20,000

    Then, Div. No.—.. $10,000
        To Treas.Stk. $10,000

Ex. 310, p. 177.—Same principle as
  in Ex. 279.

Ex. 312, 313, 314, p. 199.—Same principle as in Ex. 273.

Ex. 315, 316, 317, p. 199 —Same as in
  Ex. 275.

325 Questions and Answers

Covering every important point on Signing, Accepting, Indorsing, Presenting and Protesting all kinds of Notes, Drafts and Checks, Under the New Negotiable Instruments Law.

1. What is a negotiable instrument?

A. By negotiable instrument is meant, paper that can be transferred from one person to another for valuable consideration, either by indorsement, assignment, or by delivery, so that the transferee or holder may sue the same in his own name as if it had been made to him originally.

2. How many kinds of negotiable paper are there?

A. There are several kinds of negotiable paper, the most important of which are promissory notes, bills of exchange (commonly called drafts), checks, bonds, bank notes, certificates of deposit, bills of lading, etc.

3. What is a promissory note?

A. A promissory note is an unconditional written promise, signed by the maker, to pay a specific sum of money at a certain time, either to the bearer or to a person therein designated, or his order.

4. How many kinds of promissory notes are there?

A. There are four kinds of promissory notes in general use, called individual, joint, joint and several, and bank notes.

5. What is an individual note?

A. An individual note is one in which but one person makes the promise to pay.

6. What is a joint note?

A. A joint note is one in which the promise is made jointly by two or more persons. It means that they will all join in paying it.

7. What is a joint and several note?

A. A joint and several note is one in which the promise is made jointly and severally by two or more persons. In a joint and several note, each signer assumes the whole responsibility. It means that if the payment is not made jointly it must be made severally.

8. What is an accommodation note?

A. An accommodation bill or note is one for which the acceptor or maker has received no consideration, but has loaned his name and credit to accommodate the drawer, payee or holder. He is not bound to the party whom he thus accommodates, but he is bound to all other parties, precisely as if there were a good consideration, otherwise it would not be an effectual loan of credit.

9. What is a bill of exchange or draft?

A. A bill of exchange or draft is an unconditional order in writing addressed by one person to another, signed by the person giving it, requiring the person to whom it is addressed to pay on demand or at a fixed or determinable future time, a certain sum of money to order, or to bearer.

10. What is a foreign bill of exchange?

A. A bill of exchange is foreign when it is drawn in one state and payable in another. The same is true between different countries.

11. What is an inland bill of exchange?

A. An inland bill of exchange is one which is both drawn and payable in the same state.

12. What are the original parties to a note called?

A. The maker is the party who makes the promise and signs the note; the payee is the party to whom the promise is made. In addition to the original parties to a bill or note, there are or may be an indorser who directs the amount of the bill or note to be paid to a person named in the instrument, or to his order, or to bearer; the indorsee is the person to whom the amount is ordered to be paid by the indorser; and the holder is the person having the legal possession of the instrument and who is entitled to recover the amount of the same.

13. What are the original parties to a bill of exchange or draft called?

A. The drawer is the party who makes the order; the drawee is the party to whom the order is directed; the acceptor, or the drawee, is the one who assents to the order and thus becomes principal debtor, and the payee is the party in whose favor it is drawn.

14. What are the essentials of a bill of exchange?

A. A bill or draft must contain an order, the order should appear to be the demand of a right, rather than a request for a favor.

15. What are the essentials of a promissory note?

A. A note must contain an unconditional promise. The promise must be absolute and for the payment of a certain sum of money, at a certain time. The note must be specific as to all the parties, and must be delivered.

16. Does a bill of exchange operate as an assignment of the funds in the hands of the drawee?

A. A bill of itself does not operate as an assignment of the funds in the hands of the drawee. The drawee is not liable until he accepts the bill.

17. When may a bill be treated as a promissory note?

A. If the drawer and drawee of a bill are the same person, or if the drawee be a fictitious person, or one without authority to contract, the holder may treat the instrument either as a bill of exchange or as a promissory note.

18. Can a bill of exchange be addressed to more than one drawee?

A. A bill of exchange may be addressed to two or more drawees jointly, but not otherwise, and they need not be partners.

19. What is meant by the rule that a bill must be addressed to some person?

A. It means that there must be a drawee named in the bill, or described in such a way that he may be identified; such person must be in being at the time the instrument is issued.

20. Upon what theory is a draft based?

A. The theory is, that the drawee has funds in his hands belonging to the drawer, or that he is otherwise indebted to the drawer for the amount for which the draft is drawn.

21. Is it necessary to use the words "Value Received" to make a bill or note valid?

A. It is an old custom to use these words; they do no harm, but they are not necessary. These words are used to show that the instrument is founded on sufficient consideration, but the note or bill itself imports a consideration.

22. When is a bill or note sufficiently signed?

A. It is sufficient if the name of the maker or drawer appears in any part of the instrument showing an intention to enter into a contract or obligation. The signature may be by mark or initials, either in ink, pencil or paint.

23. Are notes and drafts contracts?

A. Notes and drafts are contracts in the strictest sense of the term, and must have the elements of a contract. The rules of law on the subject of negotiable paper are more exact and technical than those of any other department of commercial law.

24. What is the legal status of a check?

A.   A check is simply a bill of exchange, payable on demand, and is drawn on a bank or banker.

25. Must the amount payable in a negotiable instrument be specific and certain?

A.   The sum must be stated definitely, and must not even be connected with any indefinite or uncertain sum.

26. Must a note be payable in money; or may it be payable in merchandise?

A.   It must be payable in money only.

27. If the word "dollars" be omitted, can it be supplied without altering the instrument?

A.   Yes.

28. If the written words and figures differ in a negotiable instrument, which is taken to be correct?

A.   The written words prevail over the figures.

29. If an unaddressed bill be accepted, what would be the effect?

A.   If an unaddressed bill be accepted it becomes the promissory note of the acceptor and is negotiable.

30. If an instrument is so ambiguous that there is doubt whether it is a bill or a note, what is the right of the holder?

A.   The holder may treat it either as bill or note.

31. If a signature is so placed upon an instrument that it is not clear in what capacity the person making it intended to sign, how will he be considered?

A.   He will be deemed an indorser.

32. What should be done if a name be incorrectly spelled?

A.   It should be indorsed as written, then indorsed correctly. The U. S. Government requires such instruments to be returned for correction.

33. What is accommodation paper?

A.   This question is fully answered in questions 8 and 197.

34. Is an accommodation note good in the hands of an innocent purchaser for value?

A.   Yes.

35. What is the effect of a forged signature?

A.   A forged signature will not bind the person whose signature has been forged, unless he is guilty of negligence. A depositor will not be permitted to dispute his account because some of his checks are forgeries, if he is negligent in examining the account and vouchers returned to him by his bank.

36. When is an instrument payable to order?

A. An instrument is payable to order when it is drawn payable to the order of a specified person or to him or his order. The payee must be named or indicated with certainty.

37. When is an instrument payable to bearer?

A. An instrument is payable to bearer when it is expressed to be payable to bearer; it may be payable to a person named therein or bearer; it is also payable to bearer when the only or last indorsement is an indorsement in blank.

38. When is an instrument payable on demand?

A. An instrument is payable on demand when it is expressed to be payable on demand, at sight or on presentation.

If an instrument is issued, accepted or indorsed when overdue, it is, as regards the person so issuing, accepting or indorsing it, payable on demand.

39. What are the rights of a holder?

A. The holder of a negotiable instrument has the right to sue thereon in his own name. Payment to him in due course will discharge the instrument.

40. What constitutes a holder in due course?

A. A holder in due course is a holder who has taken the instrument in good faith and for value, believing it to be complete and regular upon its face, that he became the holder before the instrument was overdue, and without notice of it having been dishonored, or containing any defect in the title of the person negotiating it.

41. When is a title to a negotiable instrument defective?

A. A title is defective when it has been obtained by fraud, force, duress, fear, illegal consideration, or other unlawful means or breach of faith.

42. What constitutes a notice of defect?

A. The person to whom an instrument is negotiated must have actual knowledge of its defects and infirmities, or such knowledge as would amount to bad faith.

43. Is a note written in pencil valid?

A. It is, but I would advise you to use ink.

44. When may blanks in a negotiable instrument be filled?

A. The holder of an incomplete instrument has authority to complete it by filling up the blanks, but he has no authority to insert any special agreement not essential to the completeness of the instrument.

45. Is a receipt for a partial payment of note or bill, good?

A. It might be if it can be proven, but it is very dangerous. See that all interests and part payments are indorsed on the instrument.

46. If a negotiable note is given in settlement of an account, does it extinguish the account?

A. Yes; but if the note should not be paid, suit would have to be brought on the note.

47. How is a negotiable instrument discharged?

A. An instrument is discharged when it is paid in due course by or on behalf of the principal debtor, by intentional cancellation by the holder, when the principal debtor becomes the holder at or after maturity in his own right, or by any other act which will discharge a simple contract for the payment of money.

48. Is a consideration necessary in a bill or note?

A. A valuable consideration is necessary between the immediate parties to a bill or note, just as much as in a simple contract. The immediate parties are, maker and payee, drawer and payee, acceptor and drawer, and an indorsee and his immediate indorser.

49. What constitutes a consideration?

A. Any value is consideration sufficient to support a simple contract.

50. What is meant by the rule that the "order" or "promise" must be unconditional?

A. It means that the payment of money must not depend upon any contingency.

51. Is a promise unconditional if it makes a statement of the transaction which gives rise to the instrument?

A. Yes.

52. Is a promise unconditional if it *indicates* a particular fund out of which reimbursement is to be made, or a particular account to be charged with the amount?

A. Yes.

53. Is a *promise* unconditional if it is made to pay out of a particular fund?

A. No.

54. When may a bill or note be dated?

A. If an instrument is issued undated, any holder may insert the true date of issue or acceptance, without voiding the instrument.

55. Is the validity and negotiable character of an instrument affected if it is not dated?

A. No.

56. Must the time of payment of a promissory note be specific and certain?

A. It must.

57. How may the time be expressed in a negotiable instrument?

A. Time may be expressed in a certain number of years, months or days, after a certain date, a fixed time after date or sight, on or before a fixed determinable future time, or at a fixed period after the occurrence of a specific event, which is certain to happen, even if the time of happening be uncertain.

58. How is the time in a negotiable paper computed?

A. If an instrument is payable at a fixed time after sight, after date, or after the occurrence of a specific event, the time of payment is determined by excluding the day from which the time is to begin to run, and by including the date of payment.

59. If a note on time is not dated, from when does time count?

A. The time must be counted from the delivery of the instrument.

60. If an instrument is ante-dated or post-dated, is it valid?

A. Yes, unless it is done for some illegal or fraudulent purpose.

61. Is the validity and negotiable character of an instrument affected if it does not specify the place where it is drawn or the place where it is payable?

A. No.

62. If a note is payable on demand, with interest after six months, when may demand be made and when does interest begin?

A. Demand may be immediate, but the interest will not begin until the note lies six months unpaid.

63. If a note is payable with interest twelve months after notice, when is it payable?

A. It is payable on demand any time after twelve months have elapsed from the notice.

64. When does negotiable paper mature?

A. It is payable at the time fixed in the instrument, without grace (excepting in a few states where grace still exists). If the due date falls upon a Sunday or a holiday the instrument is payable on the following business day.

65. How is negotiable paper to be known from non-negotiable paper?

A. Paper to be negotiable should be made payable to "bearer or order," but any other words in a bill or note from which it can be inferred that it is intended to be negotiable will make it transferable.

66. Would a note be negotiable if the promise was to pay A. or B.?

A. No, it would not, it is too indefinite. In this case neither party would have the full right to enforce the indorsement.

67. Is a note negotiable if payable to John Brown, deceased?

A. No, because the estate of "John Brown," deceased, is neither a person nor a body corporate or politic, nor do the terms point to any person with legal certainty.

68. Is a note payable to bearer or holder negotiable?

A. Yes, because the promise is made to any and every person who obtains possession of it and presents it for payment.

69. Is a note negotiable if payable to one as trustee?

A. No, because it would show upon its face that it was connected with a trust and was a part of a trust fund.

70. If commercial paper bears a seal, is it negotiable?

A. Yes.

71. If a note gives the holder an option between payment in money and some other thing, would it be negotiable?

A. If the option is with the maker, it would not be, but so long as the option rests with the holder it would be, for he has a right to demand money. The option is merely additional security.

72. Are share certificates negotiable?

A. No.

73. Is a certificate of deposit negotiable?

A. A certificate of deposit is negotiable because it is simply a promissory note.

74. Is a check payable through the clearing house negotiable?

A. No.

75. Is a check negotiable if it states on its face that the bank book must accompany it?

A. No, one who signs his name on the back of such check is not an indorser.

76. Are receivers' certificates negotiable instruments?

A. No.

77. If an installment of interest is unpaid, would it render a note non-negotiable even though the principal is not due?

A. According to the Supreme Court of Minnesota it would, but another authority says it would not affect the negotiability of corporate bonds.

78. Is a bond negotiable if it has a blank line for place of payment, but never filled in by anyone with authority?

A. No.

79. Is a railroad or municipal bond negotiable if it contains conditions?

A. No.

80. Is a note negotiable if it authorizes the sale of collateral securities in case the instrument should not be paid at maturity?

A. Yes.

81. Is a note negotiable if it authorizes a confession of judgment if the instrument should not be paid at maturity?

A. Yes.

82. Is a note negotiable if payable by stated installments?

A. Yes.

83. Is a note negotiable if payable by stated installments, with a provision that upon default in payment of any installment or of interest, the whole shall become due?

A. Yes.

84. Is a note negotiable if payable with interest?

A. Yes.

85. Is a note negotiable if payable in current funds?

A. No; but the kind of money may be stipulated without affecting its negotiability.

86. Is an instrument negotiable if payable upon some contingency?

A. No.

87. Is a note negotiable if payable with exchange, whether at a fixed rate or at the current rate?

A. Under the new negotiable instruments law, it would.

88. Is a note negotiable, with costs of collection or an attorney's fee, in case payment shall not be made at maturity?

'A. Under the new negotiable instruments law, it would.

89. What is the liability of a maker of a negotiable instrument?

A. The maker of a negotiable instrument is liable to pay it

according to its tenor; and admits the existence of the payee and his then capacity to indorse.

90. What is the liability of a drawer of a bill?

A. When drawing an instrument the drawer admits the existence of the payee and his then capacity to indorse; and engages that the instrument will be accepted and paid, or both, according to its tenor; provided due presentment has been made. He is liable to the holder, or to any subsequent indorser who may be compelled to pay it, provided it has been dishonored, and the necessary proceedings of dishonor have been duly taken.

91. What is the liability of an acceptor of a bill?

A. The acceptor of a bill is liable for the payment of it according to the tenor of his acceptance, which admits the existence of the drawer, the genuineness of his signature, and his capacity and his authority to draw the instrument, also the existence of the payee and his then capacity to indorse.

92. What is the liability of an accommodation indorser?

A. An accommodation indorser is liable on the instrument to a holder for value, notwithstanding such holder at the time of taking the instrument knew him to be only an accommodation party.

93. What is the liability of a person signing a negotiable instrument in a trade or assumed name?

A. He would be liable to the same extent as if he had signed in his own name.

94. What is the liability of a person signing a negotiable instrument as agent?

A. The agent will be personally liable for the payment of the instrument, unless he discloses his principal and signs as his agent.

95. How should an agent indorse commercial paper for a corporation?

A. The correct way for an agent to indorse commercial paper for a corporation is to write the name of the corporation, then add his own name as agent, thus: The Clear Ice Co., per John Brown, Agent, Secretary, Treasurer or Cashier as the case may be.

96. If a note is indorsed "without recourse," what is the liability of the indorser?

A. An indorsement "without recourse" passes the title to a negotiable instrument, but does not render the indorser liable to subsequent holders in case the acceptor or maker fails to pay the instrument when due. An "indorser" "without recourse" assumes more obligations than is generally understood; he guarantees the genuineness of the signatures; that the makers were competent to contract; that it was valid between the original parties; that there was no illegality in its conception, and that the amount expressed as due, is due. Indorsers without recourse have been held as guarantors.

97. Does an indorser of a non-negotiable note incur any liability?

A. The rule that one who writes his name on the back of a non-negotiable instrument is not an indorser, and incurs no liability, is sustained in many of the states.

98. If an instrument containing these words "I promise to pay," is signed by two or more persons, what is their liability?

A. They would be jointly and severally liable.

99. If a note is signed "Henry Brown, Assignee," would he be personally liable?

A. Yes.

100. What is the status of negotiable paper made by a minor? not be enforced, even in the hands of a bona fide holder; but if the party able at the option of the minor.

101. Is the negotiable paper of a person *non compos mentis* binding?

A. If the person has been adjudged imcompetent, his paper could not be enforced, even in the hands of a bona fide holder, but if the party has not been adjudged incompetent, his paper could be enforced in favor of a bona fide holder not knowing of his incompetency.

102. Is a secret partner liable on a partnership note?

A. A secret partner is not liable for the debts contracted after he leaves the partnership, although he gives no notice; previous to retirement, he is liable.

103. Is a nominal partner liable on a partnership note?

A. Yes.

104. Is an ostensible partner liable on a partnership note?

A. Yes.

105. Is a new partner liable on old notes of the firm?

A. Not unless he expressly assumes them, or agrees with the partners to be bound. If he owns the whole business of course he would be liable.

106. Can a partner bind the firm by making a joint and several note?

A. Not without express authority.

107. Is a firm liable to a bona fide holder, if a note appears to have been signed as surety?

A. Not unless the partners consent. Suretyship is not, in general, within the business of a partnership.

108. If a partner issues fraudulent commercial paper, will the partnership be liable?

A. The partnership would be liable to an innocent holder for value, without notice of the fraud, although the partners as between themselves had no right to issue the paper. They must settle that among themselves.

109. If a bill be drawn on a partnership, and accepted by one partner in his own name for partnership purposes, will it bind the firm?

A. Yes.

110. If the partnership does not require the giving of notes, would the firm be bound?

A. No; but it might be difficult to decide the requirements of the firm.

111. What is the authority of officers of corporations to issue commercial paper?

A. The directors sitting as a board have the power to issue commercial paper, but neither the treasurer, secretary nor the manager has, *prima facie*, such power. This authority must be granted.

112. What is the liability of a corporation as an indorser of commercial paper?

A. The same as an individual.

113. Has a corporation the right to make or indorse accommodation paper?

A. No.

114. What is the liability of a corporation as an accommodation indorser?

A. While a corporation has no right to make or indorse accommodation paper, it will be liable thereon, in the hands of an innocent holder for value.

115. How should promissory notes be executed so as to bind the corporation?

A. Omitting the date and form of words, the following words of a promissory note would bind the corporation and exonerate the agent, "The National Iron Co. promises to pay to the order of John Smith one thousand dollars ($1,000). Signed, The National Iron Co., per John Doe, Agent."

116. If a bill of exchange is drawn in a set and numbered, does each constitute a bill, or does the set constitute but one bill?

A. The whole set constitutes but one bill.

117. If the holder of a set of exchange indorses two or more parts to different persons, is he liable on each part?

A. He is liable on each and every part indorsed.

118. What is the proper way to accept a set of exchange?

A. The proper way to accept a bill drawn in sets, is to write your acceptance on *one part only*. If more than one part is accepted the acceptor will be liable on each part as though they were separate bills.

119. If the acceptor of a bill drawn in a set pays it without taking up the part bearing his acceptance, would he be liable to the holder thereon?

A. Yes.

120. If any one part of a bill drawn in a set is discharged, what is the effect upon the other parts?

A. If one part of a bill of exchange is paid or otherwise discharged, the whole bill is discharged, unless the outstanding parts have been accepted and not delivered up.

121. What constitutes a sufficient presentment for payment?

A. Negotiable paper must be presented for payment to the person primarily liable on the instrument by the holder, or one authorized to act for him. Presentment must be made at the payer's residence or place of business, at a reasonable hour.

122. Must an instrument be exhibited when presented for payment?

A. The instrument must be exhibited, and when paid must be delivered to the party paying it.

123. If an instrument is payable at a certain time, when must presentment be made?

A. Presentment must be made on the very day it falls due.

124. If an instrument is payable on demand, when must presentment be made?

A. If an instrument is payable on demand, presentment must be made within a reasonable time after its issue.

125. How should presentment for payment be made to persons liable as partners?

A. Presentment may be made to any one of them, even though there has been a dissolution of the firm.

126. When will a presentment for payment not be required to charge the indorsers?,

A. When the instrument was made or accepted for accommodation.

127. How should presentment for payment be made to joint debtors?

A. Presentment must be made to all, unless a place of payment is specified.

128. How should presentment be made when an instrument is payable at bank?

A. An instrument made payable at a bank is equivalent to an order to the bank to pay it. Presentment at the bank is sufficient.

129. When is an instrument dishonored by non-payment?

A. An instrument is dishonored by non-payment, if presentment is duly made and payment is refused or cannot be obtained.

130. When must notice of dishonor be given?

A. Notice should be given as soon as the instrument is dishonored.

131. To whom must notice of dishonor be given?

A. When a negotiable instrument has been dishonored by non-payment or non-acceptance, notice of dishonor must be given to the drawer and to each indorser. Any drawer or indorser not notified of dishonor is discharged of his liability.

132. Where must a notice of dishonor be sent?

A. If the address be given on the instrument, notice of dishonor must be sent to that address, otherwise, notice must be sent to the place of business, or residence, or to the post-office where he receives his letters, or to the post-office nearest to him.

133. By whom may notice of dishonor be given?

A. Notice may be given by or on behalf of the holder, or any other party to the instrument who might be obliged to pay it to the holder, and who, upon paying it would be entitled to reimbursement from the party to whom notice is given.

134. What form of notice of dishonor may be given?

A. Notice may be verbal or in writing, but must state specifically the details of the instrument, and give notice that it has been dishonored by non-acceptance or non-payment.

135. How should notice of dishonor be given?

A. Notice may be given personally or through the mail.

136. How should notice of dishonor be given to partners?

A. Notice to any one partner is notice to the firm.

137. How should notice of dishonor be sent to parties residing in the same place?

A. If notice is sent by mail, it must be deposited in the post-office in time to reach him in usual course on the day following. If given at place of business, it must be before the close of business hours on the day following; if given at residence, it must be before the usual hours of rest on the day following.

138. How should notice of dishonor be sent to parties residing at different places?

A. Notice may be sent by mail; if so, it must be deposited in the post-office in time to go the day following the day of dishonor.

139. May notice of dishonor be waived?

A. Yes.

140. May protest of negotiable instruments be waived?

A. Yes.

141. What parties will be affected by waiver of notice?

A. If the waiver is written above the signature of an indorser, it binds him only; but if it is embodied in the instrument itself, it binds all parties.

142. A. has allowed his note to go to protest, and has arranged with B. to pay two per cent interest per month until it is paid. Can B. collect more than the legal rate of interest on the agreement?

A. B. cannot collect upon the agreement at all. The promise is made upon a past default of A., which is no consideration at all. Consideration must be given for a promise.

143. A. holds a note of B.'s which he is unable to collect, owing to the statute of limitations. A. surrenders the note upon B.'s agreement to give a new note. A. sues upon the new note, and B. defends upon the ground that the surrender of a note which could not be collected was not good consideration. Was it a good consideration?

A. Yes. The surrender of a note would be good consideration whether or not it could be collected.

144. What are the duties of a pledgee of a negotiable paper?

A. The pledgee must present the paper when due, and in case of non-payment he must give due notice of such demand and non-payment in order to hold indorsers. If he fails to do this and loss occurs from such failure he must stand such loss.

145. Can notes be sold or transferred without incurring any liability?

A. If you hold a note that is payable to your order, it will be necessary for you to indorse it on the back; if you sell or transfer it, when you indorse it, you are responsible for the payment of the note, if the maker fails to pay it. But you can sell or transfer it with the distinct understanding that you are not to be responsible if you write over your signature "Without Recourse."

146. Is it safe to buy past due notes?

A. I would not advise you to make a practice of buying past due notes, especially if they are not secured, or if they have no indorsers. There are some that can be bought with safety, but a shrewd business man will generally let them alone.

147. If a person took a negotiable instrument after it was due, would he be a holder in due course, or a bona-fide holder?

A. He would not; the holder must have taken it before it was due. It must be taken in good faith and for value. It must be complete and regular upon its face.

148. Are negotiable instruments valid if written with pencil?

A. Yes; but it is a dangerous practice.

149. Is it necessary to state the place of issuance to make a negotiable instrument valid?

A. It is not necessary, but it always should be.

150. Must a negotiable instrument be dated to be valid?

A. If no date is given, the date of the delivery of the instrument to the person first entitled to receive it, is deemed to be the date.

151. Is a negotiable instrument valid if dated on Sunday?

A. If the instrument is dated on Sunday and delivered on Sunday, it is not valid; but if it is dated on Sunday and not delivered until some future week day, it is valid. If it be dated on a week day and is delivered on Sunday it is not valid, except in the hands of one who is ignorant of the Sunday part of the transaction.

152. When is a negotiable instrument complete?

A. It is not complete, nor does it become binding, until it is delivered and the consideration passed.

153. Is a negotiable instrument valid if dated on a holiday?

A. An instrument dated or delivered on a holiday (except Sunday) is not thereby prejudiced in any way.

154. If a negotiable instrument is signed by initials only, will it be binding?

A. Yes, if it can be proven.

155. If no time of payment is expressed in commercial paper, when is it payable?

A. It is payable on demand.

156. Can a negotiable instrument be payable in fixed installments?

A. Yes, if the time of payment of the installments is clearly expressed.

157. If an instrument is payable on demand, when must the demand be made?

A. The holder *must* demand payment within a reasonable time or the indorsers will be released, but he *can* demand payment at once.

158. If an instrument is payable at sight, is it payable on demand?

A. Yes, except in a few states which allow days of grace on paper payable "at sight." This is never the case, however, with paper payable "on demand."

159. If an instrument is payable at the death of the maker, is it negotiable?

A. Yes, because the event is sure to happen.

160. If the maker of an instrument draws it to the order of a fictitious person, what would be the effect?

A. If the maker knowingly made it payable to the order of a fictitious payee, in effect, it is payable to bearer, and is negotiable. The bona-fide holder may write the name of a fictitious person as indorser.

161. Is a note negotiable if it provides for the payment of attorney's fees, in case of suit being brought?

A. In many states it is not negotiable.

162. Do the laws of any of the states require that a negotiable note shall be payable at a bank?

A. Yes. The states of Alabama, Indiana, Kentucky, Virginia and West Virginia have passed laws which provide that negotiable notes must be payable at a bank in the state. In Kentucky such notes must also be indorsed to and discounted by a bank in the state.

163. What engagement does the maker or drawer of a promissory note undertake?

A. In signing and issuing it, he says that he will pay to the lawful holder the amount of money that is due and payable, when by its terms it is due and payable. If at the time he signs and issues the note he has no means with which to pay it, and does not see his way to meet the obligation when it becomes due, he commits no fraud or legal wrong. If he has property it can be seized, but the law punishes him in no other way.

164. What does the maker or drawer of a draft or bill of exchange represent to the holder?

A. He says, in legal effect, to the payee, that the drawee will accept the instrument, when presented to him, by writing his name across the face of it, and that the acceptor will pay the amount of the draft or bill when by its terms it is due and payable, and if the drawee or acceptor fails so to pay, that he, the drawer, will then pay. The drawer has committed no fraud or legal wrong in issuing the paper, if the drawee fails to accept or the acceptor to pay.

165. If a depositor makes a promissory note or accepts a bill payable at the bank, is the bank obliged to treat such note or bill, at its maturity, as it would the depositor's check?

A. Yes; the bank is required to pay it the same as his checks. The same rule applies to bills or drafts which he has accepted payable at the bank.

166. If the holder of a promissory note wishes to retain the liability of all parties, what must he do?

A. He must have it presented at the place of payment on the day of maturity. If payment be not made, he must have it protested for non-payment; if he fails to do so, the indorsers will be forever released.

167. What are the duties of the holder of a bill of exchange, if he wishes to hold all parties to their liability?

A. He must present it promptly for acceptance; if acceptance is refused, he must protest it for non-acceptance. When the bill matures it must be protested for non-payment. If the bill is not protested as stated all the parties thereto, except the maker and acceptor, will be released.

168. If a minor has had the full benefit of commercial paper which he has issued or indorsed, can it be enforced against him?

A. No, it cannot.

169. If several persons sign a note as makers, from which one of them can the holder collect?

A. The holder can collect from any one of them who is solvent.

170. If a note is presented to the bank at which it is payable and it is not paid, but is protested for non-payment, would the drawer be released if he was not duly notified?

A. The drawers or makers of a note would *not* be released, but the drawers or makers of a bill of exchange or draft would be.

171. When payments are made on a note, how should they be receipted?

A. When payments are made on a note, each payment should be indorsed on the back of the note with ink, as follows: "Received on within note fifty dollars ($50.00)," then signed by the holder. Some claim that an indorsement for a partial payment requires no signature; without it, such indorsement might easily be questioned. Do not make a partial payment unless you see the payment indorsed yourself, because an ordinary receipt is not good. Remember that a receipt for a partial payment of a note is not good; it must be indorsed with ink on the back of the note, and you should make it your business to see that it is done.

172. Is it a good policy to keep cancelled or paid notes?

A. I would advise you by all means to keep all your cancelled notes and drafts. They should be stamped "Paid" on the face. If your business is such that requires giving many notes, you should issue them the same as checks from a small book with stubs; when each note is paid stamp it "Paid," destroy a part of the signature, then attach it to the original stub. If kept in this way, it will prevent their being used. They are the best of receipts, and will facilitate an audit or investigation. Cancelled notes carelessly handled may cause your ruin.

173. What is a certified check?

A. A certified check is, in effect, merely an acceptance and creates no trust in favor of the holder of the check and gives no lien on any particular portion of the assets of the bank. It has a distinctive character as a species of commercial paper, the certification constituting a new contract between the holder and the certifying bank. The funds of the drawer are, in legal contemplation, withdrawn from his credit and appropriated to the payment of the check, and the bank becomes the debtor of the holder as for money had and received.

174. Who is liable in case a check has been fraudulently raised either before or after it has been certified?

A. A bank in certifying a check in the usual form, simply certifies to the genuineness of the signature of the drawer, and that he has funds on deposit sufficient to meet it, and engages that those funds will not be withdrawn from the bank by the drawer; it does not warrant the genuineness of the body of the check as to the payee or the amount named therein. If the signature be genuine, the drawer would lose.

175. Who is liable for the payment of an altered check?

A. If a bank pays a check which was cancelled, and the cancelling remain, or a check which has been torn to pieces and then pasted together, or one which is so long overdue as to be stale, or otherwise justifying suspicion and inquiry, it pays it at its own peril. And although it may have been rightfully drawn, the drawer, if he had actually cancelled or recalled it, may recover the funds from the bank. If it was the negligence of the drawer which led to the payment, or if he was the cause of the belief of the drawee that such a check, or even a forged or altered check, was valid and payable, and such a check is paid in good faith, the drawer loses it. A drawer of a check, who by fault of any kind, enables a third person to defraud a banker by means of the check, must lose the amount paid by the bank. If a bank pays a forged check, without some such excuse as above stated, of course it cannot charge the payment to the drawer. If the check be only altered by forgery, the drawer is still liable for the original amount, and no more.

176. If a bank pays a forged check, who is liable for the amount?

A. This is fully answered in the last question.

177. If a check has a forged indorsement, upon whom does the burden of proof rest?

A. If a check payable to order is paid by the bank on a forged indorsement of the payee's name, the bank is liable for the amount to the drawer, if the check had not passed into the hands of the payee, and is liable to the payee, if it was then his property. The burden of proving such indorsement genuine rests with the bank.

178. Should a bank pay a check after the death of the drawer?

A. A bank should not pay a check after notice that it was lost, nor before it is due, if on time, nor after notice of insolvency, nor after the death of the drawer; but if the bank pays the check after the death of the drawer, and before notice of the death, it is said to be a good payment.

179. If a check is drawn when the drawer has no funds in the bank, is it a fraud?

A. If a check be drawn when the drawer neither has funds in the bank nor has made any arrangements by which he has a right to draw the check, the drawing it is fraud, and the holder may bring action at once against the drawer, without presentment or notice.

180. What is the liability of a drawer of a check without funds?

A. As stated in the last question, a drawer of a check without funds may be sued at once, without presentment, demand or notice.

181. How should checks be drawn?

A. Checks should never be drawn without funds in the bank to meet them. In drawing checks, always fill out the stub first, no matter how much you may be in a hurry; to neglect to do so may cause a great deal of inconvenience and loss. I have seen many bank accounts overdrawn and many accounts paid twice, simply because mistakes and omissions were made by writing the checks and omitting to fill out the stubs.

If possible use safety paper and indelible ink; write plainly, always beginning at the extreme left to write the payee's name, and the amount in words and figures. If the amount be written and the figures be made so that other amounts could be placed before them, it would be your loss. To relieve the bank of a great deal of trouble and loss, also to relieve yourself of liability and loss by the raising of checks and forgeries, see that every check is drawn with the greatest care and accuracy in every detail.

182. If a check is drawn "in full of account," does it so hold?

A. If an account is disputed and a check is sent marked in full of account and the check is retained, it will operate as full payment even though it be for less than the amount of the account. If the account is not in dispute, it would not hold.

183. After a check has been issued, can payment be stopped by notifying the bank?

A. If a check has been lost or stolen, or you have other reasons to stop payment, you should give the bank notice in writing, giving the date, number of the check, to whom payable, the amount, and the indorsers if possible. An order from the drawer of a check not to pay it is as binding on the bank as one ordering the bank to pay it. At the best it is very inconvenient for a bank to stop payment of a check, therefore you should not stop any unless it is important.

184. Is a check dated ahead valid?

A. A check that is dated ahead is usually considered as a bill of exchange and not as a check. The bank will not cash it.

185. When must a check which is payable on demand be presented for payment?

A. Payment must be demanded not later than the next business day, if the holder and the bank upon which it is drawn are located in the same place. If they are not located in the same place, the holder must, in order to hold the indorsers, start it for payment not later than the next business day.

186. If a check is payable to "cash or order," to whom is it payable?

A. It is payable to bearer and is regular and valid.

187. What representation does the drawer of a check make by the mere act of drawing it?

A. He represents that he has an account at the bank upon which the check is drawn, and that he has as much money to his credit and not checked against as this check calls for. If such are not the facts the drawer in signing and issuing the check has committed a fraud, and may be punished criminally.

188. Can a bank make partial payment of a check?

. A. If the drawer's credit is not sufficient to pay the full amount the bank may, if it choose, make partial payment, but it is not obliged to do it.

189. Is a bank obliged to certify or accept in writing a depositor's check if it is good?

A. The bank may do so if it choose, but it is not under any obligation to do so.

190. When a bank certifies a check for the holder what is the order of liability of the parties?

A. If the holder has the check certified, the drawer and all of the indorsers are released. The bank is then the principal and only obligor.

191. If the drawer of a check has it certified, what is the order of liability?

A. Bank, drawer, indorsers in their order.

192. If the holder of a check desires to retain the liability of an indorser, what is his duty?

A. The holder of a check must have it promptly presented for payment and protested or the indorsers will be released.

193. Under what circumstances is the maker of a check released from liability?

A. If presentment for payment is not promptly made, the drawer will be released from liability if the bank should fail and the depositor lose the money against which the check was drawn; but if the depositor's money is not lost, delay in presentation to the bank will not release him.

194. What effect does the death of the drawer of a check have on its payment?

A. The death of the drawer usually revokes the authority of the bank to pay the check, and it has been held that bankruptcy or an assignment for the benefit of creditors has the same effect.

195. Will a verbal or telegraph acceptance or certification of a check bind the bank?

A. Yes, if the drawer has sufficient funds to pay it.

196. Who must stand the loss of a forged check?

A. If a bank pays or certifies a check for an innocent party, it must stand the loss, if the drawer's signature is forged.

197. What is Accommodation Paper?

A. Accommodation Paper is a device to supply credit. It is a bill or note for which the maker or acceptor has received no consideration, but has lent his name and credit to accommodate the drawer, payee or holder. He is not bound to the party he accommodates, but he is bound to all other parties, just as though there had been a good consideration, otherwise it would not be an effectual loan of credit. The party accommodated is bound to take up the paper, or to provide the accommodation acceptor, maker or indorser with funds to do so, or to indemnify him for taking it up.

198. Have corporations the power to make or indorse for accommodation?

A. A corporation has no power to make or indorse commercial paper for the mere accommodation of another person or corporation, unless the power is expressly conferred by its charter or governing statute, but no such charters are known to have been granted.

199. Is accommodation paper good in the hands of a bona-fide purchaser for value?

A. Accommodation paper is good in the hands of an innocent purchaser for value. If a corporate officer or agent has apparent authority to make or indorse such paper, it will be good as against the corporation in the hands of a bona-fide purchaser for value before maturity without notice that it is accommodation paper. There are circumstances under which such paper may be enforced against the corporation, although in the hands of persons chargeable with notice of the circumstances under which it is executed.

200. · Is an innocent purchaser of accommodation paper protected?

A. An innocent purchaser of accommodation paper is protected, if purchased for value without notice of its character.

201. Has a corporation power to lend its credit by issuing its bonds?

A. No.

202. What is evidence of notice that paper has been indorsed for accommodation?

A. It is difficult to detect upon the face of the instrument. Verbal or written notice should be obtained if possible.

203. Have the officers or agents of a corporation power to indorse for accommodation?

A. They have not.

204. If a managing agent accepts ior accommodation, will it bind the corporation?

A. It will not, without authority or ratification.

205. Is the acceptor or maker of an accommodation bill bound to the drawer, payee or holder?

A. No, he is not. See question 197.

206. Is accommodation paper within the scope of partnership business?

A. No, it is not. When such paper is issued, with the assent of all the partners, an innocent purchaser for value without notice will be protected.

207. What is the effect of a transfer of accommodation paper as collateral security?

A. It is universally conceded that the holder of an accommodation note, without restriction as to how it should be used, may transfer it, either in payment, or as collateral security, for an antecedent debt, and the maker will have no defence.

208. Will an insane person be liable as indorser on the renewal of an accommodation note?

A. An accommodation indorser on a note given in renewal of a note on which he was also accommodation indorser, at its maturity, is not relieved of liability because of his insanity at the time of signing it, if the bank taking it in renewal had no notice of his insanity and he having been sane when the prior note was executed.

209. Can a National Bank receiver recover upon notes made for the accommodation and sole benefit of the bank, without consideration?

A. No.

210. Are accommodation indorsements or acceptances by a National Bank void in the hands of holders with notice?

A. Yes.

INDORSEMENTS.

211. What is an indorsement?

A. The written transfer of negotiable paper is called an indorsement. because it is almost always written on the back of the instrument; but it has its full legal effect if written on its face.

212. What constitutes a negotiation of commercial paper?

A. An instrument is negotiated when it has been transferred from one person to another in such a manner as to make the transferee the holder. If the instrument is payable to bearer, it is negotiated by delivery. If it is payable to order, it is negotiated by indorsement and delivery.

213. For what purpose is an indorsement made?

A. Indorsements are made for the purpose of transferring the title to a negotiable instrument, or to strengthen the security of the holder by assuming a contingent liability for the future payment.

214. How many kinds of indorsement are there?

A. There are five kinds of indorsement, called: Blank, Full, Conditional, Restrictive, and Indorsement without Recourse.

215. What is a blank indorsement?

A. An indorsement in blank consists in writing only the name of the holder upon the back of the instrument; its effect is to make the instrument payable to bearer, thus, "John D. Sullivan."

216. What is a full indorsement?

A. An indorsement in full is one in which the indorser writes over his signature an order to pay to a certain person, thus:

"Pay to H. C. Hawkins or order,

"J. C. Grabbe."

The effect of a full indorsement is to transfer the title to the indorsee, who can transfer the title to another only by indorsement.

217. What is a conditional indorsement?

A. A conditional indorsement is one by which the possession of the instrument passes to the indorsee; but the title thereto either does not pass until the happening of some condition named in the indorsement, or passes subject to defeat upon the happening of some condition. For example, "Pay to John Harris if he arrives at 21 years of age," or

"Pay to Henry Wolf or order, unless before payment I give you notice to the contrary."

218. What is a restrictive indorsement?

A. A restrictive indorsement is one which does not pass to the indorsee any beneficial interest under the instrument. There are two classes: indorsements to an agent for collection or deposit, and indorsements for the benefit of a third person, as where the indorsee is trustee. In the first class the indorsee cannot further negotiate the instrument, but in the second he can. For example:

"Pay to George H. Howard, only,

"J. J. Sullivan."

219. What is an indorsement without recourse?

A. An indorsement without recourse is one which passes the title to the instrument, but does not render the indorser liable to subsequent holders in case the acceptor or maker fails to pay the instrument when due. This indorsement is made by the indorser writing over his signature the words, "Without Recourse," or any similar expression, thus,

"Without Recourse,

"J. S. White."

This is also called a qualified indorsement.

220. Must the indorsement be of the entire instrument?

A. The indorsement must be of the entire instrument; but if the instrument has been paid in part, it may be indorsed as to the balance.

221. When is a person deemed an indorser?

A. A person would be deemed an indorser if his signature has been placed upon an instrument other than as maker, drawer or acceptor, unless he use such words as would bind him in some other capacity.

222. What is the liability of a general indorser?

A. Every indorser who indorses without qualification warrants to all subsequent holders, that at the time of his indorsement the instrument was valid, and that on due presentment it shall be accepted or paid, or both, as the case may be, and that if it be dishonored, he will pay the amount to the holder, or to any subsequent indorser, who may be compelled to pay it, provided all necessary proceedings have been duly taken.

223. What is the liability of an irregular indorser?

A. If the instrument is payable to the order of a third person, any one not otherwise a party to the instrument, who places thereon his signature in blank, before delivery, is liable to the payee and all subsequent parties. If the instrument is payable to the order of maker or drawer, or is payable to bearer, he is liable to all parties subsequent to the maker or drawer. If he signs for the accommodation of the payee, he is liable to all parties subsequent to the payee.

224. What is the effect of a transfer without indorsement?

A. If the holder of an instrument payable to his order, transfers it for value without indorsing it, the transferee acquires such title as the transferrer had therein, and is entitled to have the indorsement of the transferrer.

225. If a person negotiates an instrument by delivery, or by a qualified indorsement, what does he warrant?

A. He warrants that the instrument is genuine; that he has a good title to it; that he has no knowledge of any fact that might impair the value or validity of it and that all prior parties had capacity to contract. If the negotiation is by delivery only, the warranty extends to the immediate transferee only.

226. What is the effect if an indorsement be stricken out?

A. The indorser whose indorsement is stricken out, and all indorsers subsequent to him, are thereby relieved from liability on the instrument.

227. What is the liability of an indorser where paper is negotiable by delivery?

A. One who places his indorsement on an instrument negotiable by delivery incurs all the liabilities of an indorser.

228. What is the liability of an agent or broker as indorser?

A. An agent or broker who negotiates an instrument will be personally liable, unless he discloses the name of his principal, and that he is acting as his agent only.

229. What is the effect of an indorsement of an instrument payable to bearer?

A. If an instrument payable to bearer is indorsed in full, the indorser is liable to only such holders as make title through his indorsement, although it may be further negotiated by delivery.

230. What is the effect of an instrument drawn or indorsed to a person as cashier?

A. Such indorsement is deemed to be payable to the corporation or bank of which he is such officer. An instrument so indorsed may be negotiated by either the indorsement of the bank, or that of the cashier.

231. In what order are indorsers liable?

A. In respect to themselves, indorsers are liable in the order in which they indorse.

232. What is the power of corporate officers to indorse and transfer negotiable paper?

A. A corporation may have the power to indorse and transfer negotiable paper, and yet it may not have empowered its officers or agents to exercise the power in its behalf. Corporate officers should be authorized by the by-laws. Bank cashiers and managers of most corporations have this power by implication of law.

233. What is the power of agents of corporations to indorse negotiable instruments?

A. An agent of a corporation may have authority to transfer negotiable paper by indorsement, without authority to bind the company as indorser; as stated before, such authority should be clearly defined.

234. Have corporations the power to indorse for accommodation?

A. Corporations have no power to indorse for the accommodation of others. However, such paper will be good as against the corporation in the hands of a bona-fide purchaser for value before maturity without notice that it is accommodation paper.

235. Has the president of a corporation power to indorse its negotiable paper for the purpose of transfer?

A. The transfer of negotiable paper is incident to the transactions of most every kind of business, and as the president is the usual officer to execute the company's written contracts, he has implied authority to indorse its negotiable paper for the purpose of transferring title to it in the ordinary course of its business.

236. Has the treasurer of a corporation power to transfer negotiable securities by indorsement?

A. The treasurer of a corporation, other than banking, should, on principle, be presumed to have the power to transfer its negotiable securities in the ordinary course of its business, although this power rests upon a different footing from the power to create debts by omitting such securities, or to omit them in liquidation of debts already created.

237. Has the treasurer of a corporation power to make, accept or indorse for accommodation under a general power to indorse?

A. Not by any means.

238. Is a bank liable for the fraudulent indorsements made by its cashier?

A. The cashier would be exceeding his authority and the bank would be liable.

239. When does the absence of indorsement upon bonds put intending buyers upon inquiry?

A. When bonds have been properly issued, they will be properly indorsed by the proper officers, designating place of payment, etc. The absence of such indorsements would be sufficient to put a purchaser on his guard. It would indicate fraud.

240. How should an agent indorse for his principal so as not to bind himself?

A. When an agent indorses for his principal, to avoid personal liability, he should first sign the principal's name, then add his own as agent, just the same as in signing a contract, thus, "The Natl. Rivet Co. by John Harrison, Agent," or "Secretary" or "Treasurer." The universal usage among bankers is that a cashier need only to sign his own name, with the addition of the word "Cashier."

241. Is an indorsement by an infant binding?

A. An infant may indorse a bill, and the indorsement will have the effect of transferring the papers so far that title may be made through the infant; but such indorsement will not hold him liable, nor will it pass the property in the note out of him, as against his interest.

242. Is an indorsement by a married woman binding?

A. Parsons, a leading authority on commercial paper, says that a married woman's indorsement would neither transfer the paper nor make her liable. See question 262.

243. When is an executor *personally* bound by his indorsement?

A. An executor or administrator, like any other trustee, would be held by his indorsement personally, although he add to his name the word, "Executor" or "Administrator," unless he say expressly that recourse is to be had, not to him, but only to the estate of the deceased.

244. If any one member of a partnership indorse in the partnership name, will it bind the firm?

A. Yes.

245. If a note is indorsed by a partnership before dissolution, but not negotiated until afterwards, is it valid?

A. It is doubted by good authority. I would advise against using it.

246. When should an indorsement be made?

A. Any time before maturity.

247. Is an indorser bound for any sum subsequently written?

A. Yes, if the indorsement was made first, and the amount to be written later.

248. Can a note be transferred without indorsement?

A. A negotiable note may be transferred by assignment instead of indorsement.

249. Is a person liable as indorser on a mere promise to indorse?

A. Not unless his name is written in some way on the instrument.

250. Does misspelling vitiate indorsement?

A. No.

251. If a note is covered with indorsements, and there is no more room, what is to be done?

A. When the instrument is covered with indorsements, a piece of blank paper may be attached to it, called "allonge."

252. What is the advantage of a blank indorsement?

A. A blank indorsement is effectual to pass the paper, and gives to the transferee unqualified power of disposing of the paper, and is therefore more convenient to him, while it lays no additional obligation on the indorser.

253. What is the advantage of an indorsement in full?

A. When an indorsement is in full, no one can acquire property in the paper without his indorsement.

254. Who is the owner of a note payable to bearer which has been lost by or stolen from the owner and transferred to a bona-fide holder?

A. It becomes the property of the bona-fide holder.

255. Is a banker obliged to pay his acceptance on a forged draft?

A. Bankers must always pay their acceptance on a forged draft, because they are bound to know the handwriting of their customers; consequently they must bear the loss, when the signature of a drawer is forged and they have accepted.

256. Is a note with indorsements in full and one in blank negotiable?

A. Yes.

257. For what purpose may accommodation paper be used?

A. The holder of an accommodation note, without restriction as to the mode of using it, may transfer it either in payment, or as collateral security for an antecedent debt.

258. What is the liability of an accommodation indorser?

A. A person making or indorsing a note, or drawing, accepting or indorsing a bill, or becoming liable in any way on negotiable paper, for the benefit of another person, is liable to a third person, even with notice of the want of consideration, but is not to the person accommodated.

259. Does the indorser of a non-negotiable instrument incur any liability?

A. He does not, except in a very few states.

260. If an indorser pays the note, can he collect from any of the other indorsers?

A. If an indorser has to pay the note, he can reimburse himself in full from the maker or any or all parties who indorsed above him, but he has no recourse from those who have indorsed below him.

261. If several persons have signed a note on its face, as makers, what would be their liability among themselves?

A. They agree among themselves each to pay one-third of the amount; but if one has been forced to pay all, he can make the others contribute their share, unless a different agreement can be shown. The holder can proceed against any or all of the parties for the whole amount regardless of these agreements.

262. Can women, generally, bind themselves as makers or indorsers of commercial paper?

A. They cannot, except in states where they are empowered to do so by special statutes. See question 242.

263. If one indorser is released, does it release all of them?

A. If one indorser is released, all who have indorsed below him will be released; but not those who indorse above him or those who have signed on the face of the paper.

264. Can the time of payment of a note be extended without releasing the indorsers?

A. If the extension is made without the consent of the indorsers, they will be released. If some consent and some do not, those who consent will be held, those who do not consent cannot be held.

265. If the maker of a note has given the holder collateral security and they agree to release the collateral, what effect would it have on the other parties?

A. If the holder releases the security to the principal obligor, all the other parties will be released.

266. Can the holder of a past-due indorsed note accept a partial payment of principal and interest, without releasing the indorsers?

A. The holder may accept partial payments of principal and accrued interest; but, if he take interest to a future date, the indorsers will be released.

267. If a member of a firm having the authority to sign and indorse notes for the firm should indorse the firm name on his own note for his own use, would the firm be bound by the indorsement?

A. Each partner of a firm has implied authority to sign and indorse commercial paper in the firm name, for partnership purposes; but this authority does not authorize such use of the firm name to accommodation paper.

268. Is an assignment or an indorsement on a detached paper equivalent to an indorsement?

A. No, it is not.

269. If the maker of a note subsequently gives security to one of his several surety, who has the benefit of the surety?

A. It would be for the benefit of all.

270. Is a guaranty, in itself, when written on the back of a negotiable instrument, always equivalent to an indorsement?

A. No, it is not, and certain guaranty will destroy the negotiability of a note.

271. If a note is payable to one as trustee, and he properly indorses it, is a bona-fide purchaser protected in taking it?

A. A note payable to a trustee or an executor is a non-negotiable instrument. Such note would represent a trust which should be thoroughly investigated. I would advise you not to handle such paper.

ALTERATIONS OF COMMERCIAL PAPER.

272. What is a material alteration of commercial paper?

A. A material alteration is one that will lessen or increase the burden of any of the parties to a negotiable instrument, such as changes in the date, time, place, amount, rate of interest, or change the liabilities or obligations of any or all of the parties, such as adding or removing the name of a maker, drawer, indorser, payee or co-surety, or adding words of negotiability, changing the form of an indorsement, or changing the liability from joint to several.

273. If the words "with interest" be added on a note, what is the effect of the alteration?

A. This would be a material alteration if added without consent, and would release the maker and indorser, because it is a different contract than originally entered into.

274. If the name of a second indorser as additional payee is inserted on a note, what is the effect of the alteration?

A. It releases them.

275. What would be the effect of the alteration if an additional name is added as maker to the face of a note?

A. It would release the other makers.

276. If it is an alteration to add place of payment on a note, what would be the effect?

A. To alter a note by adding a place of payment without the consent of an indorser, would release the indorser.

277. If a certain rate of interest is added to a certificate of deposit, what effect would the alteration have?

A. If added without consent, it would destroy the certificate and extinguish the debt it represented.

278. If the amount of a note is reduced, what effect would the alteration have?

A. If made without the consent of maker and indorser, they would be released.

279. To alter the date of a check, what would be the effect?

A. If a bank pays a check with the date altered, it would have to make good the amount.

280. If the date of a note is changed, even though it benefit the maker, what would be the effect?

A. It would release him.

281. What would be the effect if I procure an additional signer to the face of a note, after its inception?

A. It would release the signers.

282. What is the effect of an alteration of a surety bond?

A. Even though the alteration be for the benefit of the surety, it would release him, if made without his authority.

283. If the date of a note is altered, would it be void in the hands of an innocent purchaser?

A. Yes.

284. If a draft is drawn payable in a certain place, and it is permitted to be accepted payable elsewhere, what would be the effect?

A. The acceptance would release the drawer and indorsers and make the collecting bank absolutely liable for its payment.

285. If an extension of time of payment is indorsed on a note without consent of the maker, what would be the effect?

A. An indorsement so made, without the consent of the maker, is an alteration which would vitiate the note.

286. Can mistakes in a note or bill be corrected?

A. Mistakes in a note or bill may be corrected, and the alteration will not vitiate it; when possible have the maker make the corrections.

ACCEPTANCE OF DRAFTS AND BILLS OF EXCHANGE.

287. What is meant by "acceptance?"

A. Acceptance as it is used in connection with commercial paper is somewhat misleading. It is an agreement to comply with the request contained in a draft or bill of exchange. If Jones in Pittsburg owes Howard in New York and Howard draws a draft on him for a certain amount payable in a certain time at a certain place to a certain person, and Jones acknowledges the amount to be correct, and agrees to pay it when due, it would be his "acceptance" of the conditions, which may be expressed or implied, verbal or written, before or after maturity, or prior to drawing the bill.

288. What constitutes an acceptance?

A. There is no special form or manner or words of acceptance; the custom is, however, for the drawee to write across the face of the bill the word "Accepted." This is frequently done in red ink, but it is not necessary, the name is then signed and dated. When many acceptances are used, a rubber stamp is used instead of writing. If a bill is presented to a drawee for his acceptance, and he does anything to or with it which does not distinctly indicate that he will *not* accept it, he will be held as an acceptor, for it is his duty to put this question beyond all possibility of doubt. The words "Accepted" or "Honored" without a signature, or the signature alone, have been held equivalent to an acceptance. To avoid mistakes and misunderstanding, write "Accepted," date it, and sign your name.

289. To what class of commercial paper does acceptance apply?

A. Acceptance applies to bills and not to notes.

290. When is an acceptance complete?

A. An acceptance is complete when in exact conformity with the tenor of the bill.

291. What is a qualified acceptance?

A. An acceptance is qualified when it is an agreement to pay but at a different time, place, or in a different manner from the tenor of the bill..

292. What is a conditional acceptance?

A. An acceptance is conditional when the obligation of payment is to commence on the happening of some particular .event or circumstance.

293. Can the holder of a bill accept or refuse a qualified acceptance?

A. If a qualified acceptance be offered, the holder may receive · or refuse it. If he refuses it, he may treat the bill as dishonored; if he receives it, he should notify antecedent parties and obtain their consent,, without which they are not liable.

294. What is the proper way to refuse to accept a bill?

A. The proper and only safe way to refuse to accept a bill is to make a positive refusal in words, but without writing. It has been said that, "I will not accept this bill" being written upon it is, by the custom of merchants, a good acceptance. I do not think such a custom would hold in law; however, I would advise you to say *no*.

295. Is a promise to accept equivalent to acceptance?

A. There appears to be a conflict of authority as to whether a promise to accept a bill to be drawn is equivalent to acceptance. In England a promise to accept a non-existing bill is not valid as an acceptance; but it is equivalent to acceptance if the bill exists, and the promise positive, it may then be in the nature of a contract. I would advise you to be very careful in making such promises.

296. Is the acceptor liable for any amount inserted, if he accepts in blank?

A. If a bill is accepted in blank, the acceptor may be made liable for any amount which the person receiving it chooses to insert. It is not necessary that the bill be drawn by the same person to whom the blank acceptance is handed. Do not accept, indorse or sign any papers in blank, you may regret it.

297. Has the secretary of a corporation power to accept negotiable paper for the company?

A. The secretary of a corporation can accept negotiable paper for the company only when authorized by the by-laws of the corporation.

298. Has the treasurer of a business corporation the power to make and accept negotiable paper without special authority?

A. The treasurer of a corporation is presumed to have authority to make and accept negotiable paper without special authority. Such duties should be fully set forth in the by-laws.

299. Has the cashier of a bank the power to accept for accommodation?

A. The cashier has no authority to accept for accommodation.

300. Has the treasurer of a corporation the power to make, accept or endorse for accommodation under a general power to indorse?

A. Authority to accept or indorse commercial paper in the prosecution of the business of a corporation does *not* extend to accepting and indorsing for accommodation, as corporations themselves have no such power.

301. If an agent of a corporation accepts a draft in his own name, does it bind him personally, or the company?

A. The acceptance would bind the agent personally.

302. Will a draft drawn upon a special fund, bind the one on whom it is drawn if it is not accepted?

A. No.

303. Can an acceptance once made be withdrawn?

A. An acceptance once made cannot be withdrawn.

304. What does acceptance admit?

A. Every acceptance admits the signature of the drawer. The acceptor is liable to an innocent holder for value, although the signature be forged. If a bill be drawn by one as the agent of another, acceptance admits his authority to draw the bill, but not his authority to indorse it. If a bill be drawn in a fictitious name, the acceptor not only admits this to be good, but is said to be bound by any indorsement of the same name by the same hand.

305. Will a release before maturity discharge acceptor from liability to bona-fide holder?

A. No; the acceptor will not be discharged from liability to pay to a holder who took the bill in good faith, without notice of the release.

306. If a draft is drawn on Brown, agent, and is accepted by, Brown, agent, would Brown be liable personally?

A. Brown would be personally liable; there is nothing to indicate for whom he is acting as agent; the addition of the word agent to a name is not sufficient to exempt a party from liability on such a contract.

307. How much time is allowed a drawee to accept a bill?

A. The drawee of a bill is allowed twenty-four hours after presentment in which to decide whether or not he will accept the bill.

308. If a drawee retains or destroys a bill, what is his liability?

A. If a drawee has been presented with a bill for his acceptance, and he destroys or refuses to return the bill accepted or non-accepted to the holder within twenty-four hours after such presentment, or such other time as the holder may allow, he will be deemed to have accepted it.

309. When must presentment for acceptance of a bill be made?

A. A bill must be presented for acceptance when it is payable after sight, or in any other case where presentment for acceptance is necessary in order to fix its maturity, also where the bill is drawn payable elsewhere than at the residence or place of business of the drawee.

310. How should presentment for acceptance be made?

A. If a bill be addressed to two or more drawees, who are not partners, presentment must be made to them all, unless one has complete authority to act for all, then presentment may be made to him only. If the drawee is dead, presentment should be made to his personal representative. Presentment must be made by or on behalf of the holder at a reasonable hour on a business day and before the bill is over-due.

311. When is a bill dishonored by non-acceptance?

A. A bill is dishonored by non-acceptance, when it is duly presented for acceptance, and when such an acceptance is refused or cannot be obtained, also when presentment for acceptance is excused and the bill is not accepted.

312. What is the duty of the holder where a bill has not been accepted?

A. If a bill is duly presented for acceptance and is not accepted within the prescribed time, the person presenting it must treat the bill as dishonored by non-acceptance or he loses the right of recourse against the drawer and indorsers.

313. What is the right of a holder where a bill has not been accepted?

A. If a bill is dishonored by non-acceptance, an immediate right of recourse against the drawers and indorsers accrues to the holder, and no presentment for payment is necessary.

314. When is it necessary to protest a bill of exchange for non-acceptance?

A. If a foreign bill of exchange is dishonored by non-acceptance it must be duly protested for non-acceptance. If such a bill has not previously been dishonored by non-acceptance, but is dishonored by non-payment, it must be duly protested for non-payment. If it is not so protested, the drawer and indorsers are discharged.

315. When should protest of non-acceptance of a bill be made?

A. A bill must be protested on the day of its dishonor.

316. By whom should protest for non-acceptance of a bill be made?

A. Protest may be made by a notary public, or by any reputable resident of the place where the bill is dishonored, in the presence of two or more reliable witnesses.

317. How should protest for non-acceptance of a bill be made?

A. The protest or a copy thereof must be annexed to the bill, and must be made under the hand and seal of the notary making it, and must specify when, where and how presentment was made, why it is protested, etc.

318. Where must protest for non-acceptance of a bill be made?

A. A bill must be protested at the place where it is dishonored.

319. Before a drawee has accepted a bill, what implied obligation is he under to the holder?

A. He is not liable to the holder in any way until he accepts the draft or bill.

320. If the drawee of a bill of exchange is indebted to the drawer, is he under legal obligation to accept and pay the drawer's drafts payable to a third person?

A. No, he is not.

321. May the drawee accept a bill payable at his bank in a nearby city or town, but different from the one to which the bill was addressed to him?

A. He may specify place of payment, but only in the city, town or village in which the bill is addressed to him.

322. If the drawee is willing to accept on certain conditions or with certain qualifications, and will state them in the acceptance, should or must the holder allow him so to accept?

A. The holder of a bill must not allow the acceptor to qualify or make conditional his acceptance in any way, and if the drawee does so accept, the makers and indorsers will be released if the bill is not protested.

323. What is the order of liability among themselves to an accepted bill of exchange?

A. Acceptor, Drawer, First Indorser, Second Indorser, etc.

324. If a bill has been protested for non-acceptance, must it be protested for non-payment?

A. Protest for non-acceptance is sufficient.

325. If after acceptance of a bill of exchange by the drawee, he should ascertain that the drawer's signature was forged, would the drawee be obliged to pay?

A. The drawee has no recourse against an innocent party, because he is bound to know the drawer's signature.

INDEX

TO 325 QUESTIONS AND ANSWERS.

☞ Figures refer to number of Question ☜

D—Continued.

Drawer, liability of, 90, 170, 179, 180.
——engagement of, 163, 164.
——death of, 178, 194.
——of check, 187.
——has check certified, 191.

E

Executor, bound by indorsement, 243.
Extension of time of payment, 264.

F

Fees, attorney's, 161.
Figures, differing from written words, 28.
Firms, when liable, 106, 107, 109, 110.
——member of, indorses, 267.
Forgery, of signature on bill of exchange, 325.
Fraud, in raising check, 174.
——in altering check, 175.
——in forgery, 176.
——forged indorsement, 177.
——no funds in bank, 179.
Funds, particular, relating to payment, 52.
——none in bank, 179.
——draft upon special, 302.

G

Guaranty, not equal to indorsement, 270.

H

Holder, 40.
——rights of, 39, 313.
——has check certified, 190.
——can retain indorser's liability, 192.
——duty of, 312.
Holiday, 153.

I

Indorsement, forged, 177.
——for accommodation, 202, 203.
——nature of, 211; purpose, 213; kinds, 214; blank, 215; full, 216; conditional, 217; restrictive, 218; without recourse, 219.
——of entire instrument, 220.
——transfer without, 224, 248.
——stricken out, effect of, 226.
——of instrument payable to bearer, 229.
——to a cashier, 230.
——by corporate officers, 232.
——by corporation agent, 233.
——fraudulent, 238.
——absence of, upon bonds, 239.
——how made by agent, 240.
——by infant, 241.
——by married woman, 242.
——by executor, 243.
——by member of partnership, 244.
——when to be made, 246.
——promise of, 249.
——misspelling in, 250.
——paper covered with, 251.
——blank, 252; in full, 253.
——in full and blank, 256.
——binding on firm, 267.
Indorser, liability of, 96, 97, 126, 168, 227, 231.
——insane, 208.
——who is an, 221.
——liability of general, 222.
——liability of irregular, 223.
——bound for sum subsequently written, 247.
——liability as, on promise to indorse, 249.
——of non-negotiable paper, 259.
——power to collect, 260.

I—Continued.

——release of, 263, 266.
Infant, indorsement by, 241.
Initials of name, when binding, 154.
Ink, indelible, 181.
Insane, liability of, as indorser, 208.
Installments, 156.
Instruments, payable to order, 36.
——payable to bearer, 37.
——payable on demand, 38.
——ante-dated or post-dated, 60.
——place not specified, 61.
——non-negotiable, 86.
——payable at bank, 128.
——dishonored, 129.
——in favor of fictitious person, 160.
——drawn or indorsed to cashier, 230.
  See also Negotiable Instruments.
Interest, 62, 63, 142.
——unpaid, 77.

L

Laws, relative to negotiable paper, 162.
Liability, incurred, 145.
——of all parties, how retained, 166, 167.
——of a minor, 168.
——for payment of raised or altered check, 174-177.
——order of, on certified check, 190, 191.
——of indorser, how retained, 192.
——maker's release from, 193.
——of indorsers, 231.
——for fraudulent indorsements, 238.
——of indorser of non-negotiable paper, 259.
——of several makers, 261.
——of acceptor, 296.
——personal, 306.
——for bill destroyed or retained, 308.
——order of, on accepted bill of exchange, 323.
Loss, on forged check, whose, 196.

M

Maker, of promissory note, 163, 164, 169.
——of check, how released from liability, 193.
——of accommodation paper, 205.
Makers, several, 169.
Minor, 100.
——enjoying full benefit of paper indorsed by him, 168.
Misspelling in indorsement, 250.
Mistakes, can be corrected, 286.

N

Negotiable Instrument, 1, 2.
——specific amounts payable in, 25.
——blanks in, when to be filled, 44.
——discharge of, 47.
——time of, 57.
——maturity of, 64.
——how known, 65, 66.
——payable to deceased, 67.
——payable to bearer, 68.
——payable to trustee, 69.
——liability of maker, 89.
——liability of drawer, 90.
——liability of acceptor, 91.
——liability of accommodation indorser, 92.
——liability when signed in trade or assumed name, 93.
——liability when signed by one as agent, 94.
——past due, 147.
——written in pencil, 148.
——place of issuance, 149.
——date of, 150, 151, 153.
——when complete, 152.
——payable in installments, 156.

☞ *Figures refer to number of Question* ☜

N—Continued.

——payable on demand, 157.
——payable at sight, 158.
——payable at death of maker, 159.
See also Instrument.
Negotiation, 212.
——by delivery, 225, 227.
Non-acceptance, 294, 311, 312, 324.
Non compos mentis, paper signed by, 101.
Non-payment, 129.
Note, individual, 5.
——joint, 6.
——joint and several, 7; made by partner in firm, 106.
——sufficiently signed, 22.
——payable in money, 26.
——omission of word "Dollars," 27.
——written in pencil, 43.
——negotiable, in settlement of account, 46.
——undated, 54, 59.
——when negotiable, 80-85, 87, 88.
——indorsed "without recourse," 96.
——surrender of, 143.
——sold or transferred, 145.
——past-due, 146.
——providing for fees, 161.
——treated as check, 165.
——presented at bank and not paid, 170.
——cancelled or paid, to be kept, 172.
——payable to bearer, lost, stolen, etc., 254.
——with indorsements in full and one in blank, 256.
——indorsed, past-due, 266.
——payable to one as trustee, 271.
——acceptance not applied to, 289.
See also Bill, Draft, Instrument, Negotiable Instrument, Promissory Note.
Notice, waived, 141.

O

Omission, of word "Dollars," 27.
Order, unconditional, 50.

P

Parties, to a note, 12.
——to a draft, 13.
——liability of all, how retained, 166.
Partners, secret, when liable, 102.
——nominal, 103.
——ostensible, 104.
——when liable, 106-110.
——presentment for payment to, 125.
Partnership, scope of, 206.
——indorsement in name of, 244.
——indorsement, before dissolution of, 245.
Payment, option on method, 71.
——presentment for, when and where to be made, 121, 123, 124; how, 122, 125, 126.
——how to be receipted, 171.

P—Continued.

——how to be stopped, 183.
——when to be demanded, 185.
Partial Payment, receipt good for, 45.
——of check by bank, 188.
——of past-due indorsed note, 266.
Pledgee, duties of, 144.
Presentment, when to be made, 309; how, 310.
Promise, unconditional, 50-53.
——to accept, 295.
Promissory Note, 3, 15, 163.
——bill of exchange treated as, 17.
——time of payment specific, 56.
——signed by several persons, 98.
——when binding upon a corporation, 115.
——liability of all parties to, how retained, 166.
Protest, waived, 140.
——examples of, 142.
——when, by whom, how, and where to be made, 314-318.
Purchaser, innocent, of accommodation paper, 200.
——protected, 271.

R

Receipt, for partial payment, 45, 171.
Receiver, power to recover, 209.
Release, of indorser, 263.
——and extension of payment, 264.
——before maturity, 305.

S

Seal, on commercial paper, 70.
Security, given by maker of note, 269.
Share certificates, 72.
Signature, ambiguous, 31.
——misspelled, 32.
——forged, 35.
States, laws in, 162.
Sunday, 151.

T

Time, how expressed, 57.
——how computed, 58, 59.
——not expressed, 155. ⁴
Transfer, without indorsement, 224, 248.
——by corporate officers, 232.
——by agents of corporations, 233.

V

"Value Received," 21.

W

"Without Recourse," indorsement, 96, 145.
Woman, married, indorsement by, 242.
——not bound as maker, 262.
Words, written, prevail over figures, 28.

INDEX.

L

L—Continued.

M